THAT BODY OF BRAVE MEN

THAT BODY OF BRAVE MEN

THE U.S. REGULAR INFANTRY
AND THE CIVIL WAR IN THE WEST

Mark W. Johnson

DA CAPO PRESS
A Member of the Perseus Books Group

Designed by Scribe Publishing.

Cataloging-in-Publication data for this book is available from the Library of Congress.

First Da Capo Press edition 2003

ISBN 0-306-81246-0

Published by Da Capo Press
A Member of the Perseus Books Group
http://www.dacapopress.com

Da Capo press books are available at special discounts for bulk purchases in the U.S. by corporations, institutions, and other organizations. For more information, please contact the Special Markets Department at the Perseus Books Group, 11 Cambridge Center, Cambridge, MA 02142, or call (617) 252-5298.

1 2 3 4 5 6 7 8 9—05 04 03

TABLE OF CONTENTS

For

Thomas W. Johnson
Colonel, Infantry, United States Army

and

Karen Elizabeth
Watching from the High Ground

INTRODUCTION

The beauty of the United States Military Academy leaves a lasting impression on most visitors to West Point, New York. Trophy Point on the north side of West Point's parade ground usually attracts much attention, for it provides the best vantage point from which to view the panorama of granite buildings nestled into the highlands of the Hudson River. The most impressive structure among the collection of war trophies and monuments on Trophy Point is Battle Monument, a massive granite column surrounded by eight granite globes and sixteen cannons. Any West Point Plebe can tell you that Battle Monument is one of the "largest shafts of turned granite in the world," and that resting atop it is the statue "Lady Fame." Beyond these bits of West Point lore, however, few cadets will be able to tell you anything more. That was all I could have told you prior to my first close-up look at Battle Monument in 1982. The bronze lettering on the column provides some clues to Battle Monument's significance:

IN MEMORY
OF THE
OFFICERS AND MEN
OF THE
REGULAR ARMY OF THE UNITED STATES
WHO FELL IN BATTLE DURING THE
WAR OF REBELLION
THIS MONUMENT IS ERECTED BY THEIR
SURVIVING COMRADES

Battle Monument was dedicated in 1897 as a tribute to America's professional military men killed during the Civil War. The names of 2,230 soldiers are inscribed on the monument's granite shaft and globes, arranged by regiment. The designations of those regiments immediately caught my eye. They all contained the letters "U.S." instead of state abbreviations. These units were part of the Regular Army, America's permanent, professional military establishment— the nineteenth century version of the modern United States Army. I made a note to be on the lookout for these United States regiments when it came time to study the Civil War during my stay at the Academy.[1]

I was disappointed to learn that there was virtually no mention of the Regular Army during the Civil War in the Academy's basic military history course. The course text, *The West Point Military History Series*, stated only that the Regular Army was very small at the beginning of the war, that most of it was scattered in small garrisons across the continent, and that its size increased somewhat during 1861. Perhaps this dearth of information was necessary considering the amount of material the course had to cover, but I thought an opportunity had been missed to learn some of the history of the army I would soon join.[2]

Receiving an army commission in 1986, I was soon immersed in pursuits more pressing than the names on Battle Monument; I quickly put them on the back burner. They came to the forefront again three years later, when I was assigned to the 2nd Battalion, 15th Infantry Regiment. When I first saw the battalion's colors, I noticed some campaign streamers colored blue and gray. On them were inscribed words like "Shiloh," "Atlanta," and "Kentucky 1862." I thought of the names on Battle Monument, realizing that some of those soldiers had died while earning these battle honors. Out of curiosity, I resolved to learn as much as possible about the Civil War experiences of the 15th Infantry. I initially discovered only a few general facts: the regiment was formed on May 3, 1861, fought in most of the major battles of the Civil War's Western Theater, and belonged to something called the "Regular Brigade" during the last half of the war, as did the 16th, 18th, and 19th Regiments. Much to my surprise I discerned that the Civil War experiences of these four regiments had never been adequately investigated. It was hard for me to believe that such a void in the written history of the United States Army could have existed for more than a century. With the exception of some scattered accounts that tell only part of the story, and a few blue and gray battle streamers silently adorning modern regimental colors, the existence of these regiments during the Civil War is a fact scarcely known today.

It is understandable how the small regular establishment could be so easily overlooked, for very few regulars participated in the Civil War. Two separate components made up the bulk of the Union Army: state volunteer regiments and the Regular Army. The volunteers stood forefront in the mind of the American public during the war and in the decades since, for the vast majority of Northern soldiers served in volunteer units. Faced with the need to quickly raise a large army in 1861, the Lincoln Administration relied on a massive force of temporary volunteer regiments organized by the various states. The War Department utilized volunteer manpower throughout the war, although it also maintained a small force of regulars. More than 2.8 million Americans served in the Union Army during the war, but only about 75,000—less than 3 percent—served in the Regular Army. Calculated another way, less than 1.5 percent of the Union Army's regiments (30 of 2,047) were regular formations.[3] By early 1863, most of the Regular Army's infantry and cavalry regiments had been pooled together to form three larger units: the Army of the Cumberland's Regular Brigade, the Regular Division in the Army of the Potomac, and the Reserve Cavalry Brigade, which also fought in the East.[4]

Regulars differed little from volunteers in some respects. Soldiers in both components were recruited from the same cities and farms, wore the same uniforms (although there were a few differences in dress), and were fighting for the same cause. There were also significant differences. Bruce Catton, the dean of American Civil War historians, perhaps summed up these distinctions best in his final book, *Reflections on the Civil War*. In commenting on Pennsylvanian John B. Greyser's transfer from a state regiment to the Regular Army, Catton wrote:

> To go from a ninety-day militia unit into the regular army in the summer of 1861 was to cross a gap as wide as anything the American military system could show. The ninety-day lads had enthusiasm (at the start, anyway), and nothing else; the regulars quickly outlived what enthusiasm they ever had, but they had all of the other things the volunteers lacked: hard, impersonal discipline, the equipment a soldier had to have and rigorous schooling in the way to use it, the habit of moving and acting as professionals with professional tradition and leadership rather than as spirited but confused amateurs

guided by men of imperfect knowledge. Out of all of this the regular got something to substitute for the volunteer's enthusiasm—pride in being a soldier, a man who had mastered a hard trade and had become a respected journeyman. If the professional lacked the volunteer's capacity for now and then surpassing himself and doing the impossible...well, you can't have everything.[5]

There was a portion of the Regular Army that came closer to "having everything" than most units in the Union Army. There were actually two types of regular soldiers who served in the Civil War: members of the prewar regular establishment (the "Old Army") and those who joined newly-authorized regular regiments after the war began (the "New Army"). Catton's comments about lack of enthusiasm are applicable to some Old Army soldiers, for they joined the antebellum army for any number of reasons and then suddenly found themselves caught up in a war for which some of them may not have had much ardor. Members of the New Army were different from their Old Army brethren. Citizens who joined regular regiments during the war did so with the same enthusiasm for the Union's cause that volunteers possessed. The New Army regular regiments were stiffened by a leavening of officers transferred from existing regular regiments and other Old Army veterans. The New Army units therefore combined the best of both worlds. Their troops had enthusiasm for the war effort (although perhaps still not quite as much as some state regiments possessed) and also professional pride and discipline. The regular regiments featured herein were all part of the New Army, and their combat record shows that they were as fully capable of occasionally surpassing themselves and "doing the impossible" as were the best volunteer units.

While being a tiny drop of professionals in a very large bucket of volunteers explains most of the regulars' postwar anonymity, other reasons exist as well. Not all regulars took an active part in the war. Many served on the War Department staff and in other administrative roles. The entire 9th Infantry Regiment and a few batteries of artillery remained on the West Coast throughout the war, far removed from the active theaters. One study estimated that on average there were 22,000 regular troops present for duty at any given time during the war, of whom only 16,000 were serving in the field. Despite these paltry numbers, some Regular Army units were present on every major Civil War battlefield from Fort Sumter to Appomattox.[6]

Casualties took a toll on the regulars during that journey. In addition to the 2,230 combat deaths listed on Battle Monument, about 3,800 additional regulars died during the war from diseases, accidents, and other causes. A number of them survived the war only to perish in combat with Native Americans a short time later. With so few regulars actually serving in the field, and many of those meeting an untimely death, their story has been a difficult one to piece together. Scholarly narratives about the Regular Army in the Civil War are rare. Books about volunteer units, on the other hand, overflow the Civil War sections of most bookshops and libraries today. A small army of volunteer veterans wrote of their wartime experiences, producing a flood of published memoirs and unit histories that continue to find interested readers in their respective states. The availability of these sources has tended to focus Civil War military history on volunteer soldiers and state organizations. Lined up beside this plethora of volunteer unit histories are but few published works about the Civil War regulars—some short articles and a handful of book-length studies.[7]

The regulars have received such sparse literary attention mainly because they lack the volunteers' state affiliation, the local ties that bind together Civil War veterans, their posterity, and modern local historians. The regulars early in the war actually had some local flavor, for many regular recruits in 1861 came from communities clustered near the headquarters of their regiments. During late 1862, however, most of the Regular Army's regimental headquarters were moved to different cities, changes of venue that destroyed whatever regional character these units had managed to forge in the war's first eighteen months. Since throughout the war all regular regiments manned recruiting stations spread far and wide without regard for state boundaries, the Regular Army in the Civil War ended up being the same national force it has been throughout its existence. Citizens from every eastern and mid-western state in the Union, including a large number of foreign-born recruits, served in the four regiments of the Regular Brigade. Starting in the summer of 1864, most of the regulars who entered the service in 1861 came to the end of their three-year enlistments and were discharged. They made their way back to their scattered homes and discovered that there was generally no eager hometown audience interested in learning of the former regulars' wartime experiences. Those regulars who remained in uniform through the end of the war were soon enforcing

Reconstruction laws in the conquered South or were heading west to stabilize America's frontier regions. Most of the regulars who survived the war simply lacked the time or opportunity to publish information about the events of their recent past.

There have been only sporadic efforts to remedy this lack of literature about the Civil War-era Regular Army. George T. Ness's *The Regular Army on the Eve of the U.S. Civil War* and Durwood Ball's *Army Regulars on the Western Frontier, 1848-1861* provide absorbing snapshots of the nation's professional military forces as the war began.[8] Narratives such as these are useful references, for they are filled with information about the Regular Army's antebellum regiments and biographical data on officers who went on to prominence in the Civil War. Nineteen-ninety was a watershed year for Regular Army historiography, for that year saw the publication of Timothy J. Reese's *Sykes' Regular Infantry Division, 1861-1864: A History of Regular United States Infantry Operations in the Civil War's Eastern Theater*. Reese's work belongs on the bookshelf of anyone interested in this subject, for this study provides a wealth of information about the Regular Army in general and the campaigns of the Army of the Potomac's regulars in particular. A few books by and about regular soldiers have also appeared through the years, such as *Ten Years in the Ranks, U.S. Army*, the autobiographical account of August Meyers and his days in the 2nd U.S. Infantry, and Michael N. Ingrisano's *An Artilleryman's War: Gus Dey and the 2nd United States Artillery*, his examination of the eleven-year military career of a regular who served as an artilleryman in the Trans-Mississippi Theater. In 1993 the memoir of Sidney Morris Davis, a private in the 6th U.S. Cavalry, was published as *Common Soldier, Uncommon War: Life as a Cavalryman in the Civil War* (Davis himself had attempted to publish his memoir in 1879, but could not find a publisher interested in the subject).[9] While these works and a few others all provide much-needed information on America's army of the nineteenth century, none of them offer more than a tantalizing glimpse here and there of the regulars who campaigned in the Civil War's Western Theater. For the regulars who fought at Shiloh, Atlanta, and points in between, it is long overdue for their experiences to receive a thorough, scholarly examination.[10]

While this examination may be overdue, it dovetails nicely with the current popularity of the Western Theater in Civil War historiography. Long neglected as a secondary theater of the war, the campaigns west of the Appalachians are now receiving an unprecedented amount of attention. The battles of Shiloh, Perryville, Stones River, Chickamauga, Chattanooga, and the campaign for Atlanta have all been examined in detail during recent years, some of these events being thoroughly analyzed for the first time since the nineteenth century. Even relatively bloodless clashes such as the Battle of Mill Springs and the Tullahoma Campaign are subjects of fresh scholarship. New or re-released biographies of many central figures of the Western Theater on the Union side—Don Carlos Buell, George Thomas, Henry Halleck, William S. Rosecrans, and others—are now available. Regimental histories on units that fought in the West are also becoming more numerous.

Yet there is still much unexplored Western territory, particularly about the experiences of specific brigades. Union forces in the West were reorganized on a fairly regular basis throughout the conflict, with armies, corps, and divisions being molded and shaped to meet various circumstances and requirements. One of the few constants in that process of change was the brigade, the building block of Civil War field armies that controlled anywhere from three to about six regiments. The regiments comprising Federal brigades sometimes changed, particularly early in the war and also during 1864 as many volunteer units reached the end of their enlistments, but some brigades maintained a fairly stable regimental mix from mid-1862 onward. By 1865, troops in these units felt an attachment to their brigade that was almost as strong as the ties to a soldier's immediate military family, his regiment. The Regular Brigade had a firm composition throughout its existence, making it a sturdy platform from which to view how the Federal armies in the West were organized and maneuvered to achieve the North's military objectives.

Although the Regular Brigade was a cohesive organization in terms of its constituent units, the same cannot be said for its personnel, particularly its officer corps. Regular officers were constantly in demand for assignments that kept them away from their regiments in the field, ranging from staff positions to recruiting duty. Regular units experienced leadership changes at rates unknown among volunteers. Regular Army soldiers seemed to have a new commander every few months during the war, yet for the most part regular units still performed well in battle. If one keeps in mind that regular units rarely had the same commander from one battle to the

next, readers will discern that the combat performance of professional military formations often transcends assigned personnel.

But this volume is not a throwback to the "old" style of military
history, concentrating on commanders, battlefield events, and nothing more. While the smoke of gunfire is present on many of the following pages, the narrative also explains who the men were that
comprised these regular units, why and how they ended up in the
Regular Army, what kept them going, and what happened to them
after the war. Fortunately, a large amount of scattered material on
these western regulars has survived through the years. While no
published unit histories written by the veterans themselves exist for
the four regiments of the Regular Brigade, a number of soldiers who
served in them left behind letters, diaries, and other unpublished
manuscripts. Many of these written accounts are now located in
small repositories and private collections across the nation. By har-
nessing the power of the Internet, researchers have a newfound ability to quickly track down obscure primary sources that in previous
years would have taken much labor to unearth.

Officers who remained in the army after the Civil War wrote
many of these primary accounts. After participating in America's
wars of the late nineteenth and early twentieth centuries, a number
of these grizzled veterans left behind written accounts of their military careers. Some of the more insightful of these soldier-authors are
Edgar R. Kellogg (16th U.S.), William H. Bisbee and Anson Mills
(18th U.S.), and Alfred Lacey Hough (19th U.S.). Five members of
these regiments won the Medal of Honor during the Civil War. Two
of them, Henry B. Freeman and Frederick Phisterer, also penned
detailed accounts of their wartime experiences. The writings of
enlisted men such as Jacob Van Zwaluwenburg (16th U.S.), Robert
Kennedy (18th U.S.), Eli Tarbell (19th U.S.), and others provide soldier's-eye views for many of the regulars' actions. Among the most
valuable primary sources used in these pages is a large collection of
detailed letters written by Arthur B. Carpenter of the 19th Infantry,
who started the war as a sergeant, received a commission, and commanded a company in most of his regiment's battles. I let these soldiers tell their experiences in their own words as much as possible,
correcting spelling or grammar only when absolutely necessary.

Other sources provide additional insights. The War Department's
*War of the Rebellion: The Official Records of the Union and
Confederate Armies* contains numerous after-action reports of the

regular regiments. This source is by no means comprehensive. The reports of the regulars who participated in the Corinth and Kentucky Campaigns were lost, misfiled, or perhaps never written; they were not published in the *Official Records*. The reports that made it into print give a decent account of a unit's participation in a particular battle, but are often rather brief and lacking in detail. The contrast in styles between a typical regular report and that of a volunteer unit is striking. Volunteer officers sometimes wrote their reports in an attempt to glorify their unit's deeds in the eyes of their hometown followers, and perhaps to advance the writer's reputation. Regular commanders tended to state facts plainly and with little flair—not that the regulars' experiences were any less eventful, but because their professionalism required a certain level of restraint in official correspondence. "Regular soldiers performed as many deeds of daring-do as their more idealistic camp mates, the citizen-soldier volunteers, performed," James Ronan stated in a 1993 article, one of the few written about the Civil War regulars. "But their previous military experience gave their deeds a more matter-of-fact appearance, as though they were expected to lead the way in the hero business." Lewis M. Hosea, a Civil War veteran of the 16th U.S. Infantry, asserted that this restraint contributed to the regulars' postwar anonymity: "According to the traditional custom of the 'regulars' of that day, the official reports of the commanding officers, as the war progressed, are as colorless and exact, within narrow limits, as photographs. It is not surprising, therefore, that their record of splendid service to the country has largely escaped attention and remained unwritten."[11]

The National Archives in Washington is another rich source of information. Regular regiments submitted monthly reports to the War Department and kept copies of official letters, orders, and other records. Personal correspondence to the War Department was also preserved, although finding relevant information among the mounds of documents filed in the records of the Adjutant General's Office is a daunting task. Another resource is the records of the Judge Advocate General's Office, the War Department's legal branch, which contain thousands of court-martial trial transcripts of Union soldiers who ran afoul of military authority. This source, which sheds much light on Regular Army discipline in the Civil War, has never before been systematically examined in regard to regular soldiers. While the National Archives has much information on the regulars (including at least four battle reports that did not appear in either the *Official Records* or *Supplement to the Official Records*), these documents vary in usefulness. The colonel of the 18th Infantry was meticulous in his paperwork and a large volume of that regiment's records has survived through the years. Holdings pertaining to the 15th, 16th, and 19th Regiments are sparse in comparison. The hazards of campaigning caused additional gaps in the records. On two occasions, at the Battle of Stones River and during the Siege of Chattanooga, some unit records were captured or destroyed. The records of the Regular Brigade itself (as opposed to its subordinate regiments) are also missing. While that headquarters undoubtedly generated a large amount of paperwork, the current location of those records is unknown. A portion of the 16th U.S. Infantry's records were misfiled with those of the 16th Illinois Infantry after the war, an oversight that was not corrected until 1997. Perhaps the Regular Brigade's records suffered a similar fate and were just misfiled somewhere in the dark recesses of the National Archives, patiently awaiting discovery by some future researcher.

The 18th Infantry Regiment looms prominently in the following pages for a number of reasons. More than 4,700 men passed in and out of that regiment's ranks during the Civil War, making it perhaps the largest regiment in the Union Army. This regiment's large size was due to the efforts of its colonel, Henry B. Carrington. He was the adjutant general of Ohio prior to the war, with a forte in recruiting manpower and organizing units. Carrington was thus able to obtain an adequate number of recruits for the 18th while other regular regiments were having trouble filling their ranks. He was also well connected in Ohio's collegiate communities and attracted to the 18th Infantry many bright and literate men. Given this base, more letters, diaries, and other material exist today from the 18th Infantry than from the other three regiments combined. Carrington himself recorded many observations about the initial recruitment and training of his command. The officers in charge of the other regiments left behind nothing comparable.

I will not attempt to prove that these four regiments consisted of the best, most courageous, or hardest fighting soldiers in the Union Army. There were other organizations that were in the field longer, fought in more battles, and perhaps had a more decisive impact on the war's outcome. What I hope to underscore is that being a soldier in the Civil War was a difficult enough undertaking for anyone in uniform, but being a soldier in the Regular Army was even more so. A regular's lot in life was tough in part because many nineteenth-century Americans believed professional military forces were more of a liability than an asset to the nation. That this attitude managed to continue amidst the bloodiest conflict in American history is one of the great ironies of the Civil War. The roots of this attitude ran deep, dating back to the founding of the republic. Resenting the presence of the British Army in colonial America, many Americans considered professional armed forces to be tools of despots, threatening to both the process of democratic government and the liberty of common citizens. Although there had been no real evidence to confirm America's distrust of its army, Congress latched onto this notion as a way to keep the peacetime army as small and inexpensive as possible well into the nineteenth century. The Secession Crisis and Federal battlefield defeats during 1861-1862 reopened the debate and caused different but related suspicions to surface. Many Northern citizens believed that military professionals, if not being responsible for the war itself, were at least suitable scapegoats for setbacks such as the First Battle of Bull Run and the Peninsular Campaign. And it did not help the Regular Army's cause that about a quarter of the American officer corps rallied to the Southern cause or that the president of the Confederacy was a West Point-educated former regular officer. "The regular army is as rotten as corruption can make it," volunteer general and future president James A. Garfield wrote in July 1862. His attitude was not uncommon.[12]

While this popular lack of faith was directed mainly against regular officers, regular enlisted men endured similar biases. Differing notions about what it meant to be a soldier drove a wedge between the Civil War's volunteers and regulars. One of the reasons many thousands of young men so eagerly enlisted in the Union Army during 1861 was the belief that to be a soldier required only heavy doses of enthusiasm and determination. The majority of volunteers deemed such niceties as discipline, training, and knowledge of all things military—hallmarks of the regular soldier—to have little utility. While perhaps inwardly admiring the military skills of the regulars, volunteers oftentimes displayed an outward hostility toward them (a feeling the regulars reciprocated more often than not). Historian Archer Jones believes this attitude permeated the entire Northern war effort: "In fact, many [volunteers] had a prejudice against regulars, especially graduates of the U.S. Military Academy.

Critics often disparaged these trained men as an overeducated elite, filled with impractical theory and lacking in practical knowledge. Private soldiers...did not have a monopoly on this point of view and these biases; many of the important civilian and military leaders shared this feeling." Eventually, most Union soldiers came to the realization that winning the war required both grim determination and adequate training and discipline. This realization did not occur until after many seeds of discontent were sown between the Union Army's volunteers and regulars. Not since colonial times had America's disdain of military professionalism been more pronounced than it was during the Civil War. When one combines that popular attitude with the government's failure to define the regulars' role within the mushrooming Union Army of 1861, and also considering the difficulty Regular units experienced in recruiting manpower, it is remarkable to learn that regulars in the Civil War performed as well as they did.[13]

This narrative consists of two parts. The first five chapters cover the years 1861 and 1862, during which time the 15th, 16th, 18th, and 19th U.S. Infantry Regiments were assigned to two different brigades in the Army of the Ohio. Following initial recruitment and training in Ohio, Indiana, and Illinois, these four regiments deployed to Kentucky in late 1861. They fought at the Battle of Shiloh, and subsequently marched through Mississippi, Alabama, and back into Kentucky before ending up in Nashville toward the end of 1862. The Regular Brigade in the Army of the Cumberland is examined in the final six chapters. Formed in December 1862 through the assignment of the Army of the Ohio's four regular regiments to a single brigade, the unit's baptism of fire occurred at the Battle of Stones River, and it went on to see further action at Chickamauga, Chattanooga, and the campaign for Atlanta. The end of the war found the western regulars at Lookout Mountain, Tennessee. They spent the last seven months of the conflict in garrison there, having been withdrawn from the field in September 1864 to prepare for postwar assignments while recovering from the severe losses they had sustained during the previous three years. A prologue and epilogue flank the eleven chapters. The prologue briefly covers the evacuation of Regular Army troops from Texas in early 1861, for that story is tightly woven into the saga of the Civil War regulars. Many of the officers who would later serve with the western regulars were involved in the evacuation of Federal troops out of Texas after that state joined the Confederacy. One event that occurred during that operation, the capture of Captain Robert S. Granger, ended up having a profound impact on the Regular Brigade later in the war. The epilogue completes the narrative with an examination of the postwar fortunes of the regulars and their commanders.

The pages that follow chronicle the experiences of Regular Army infantrymen in the Armies of the Ohio and Cumberland, a few regiments in what for many years was considered the Civil War's secondary theater. The western regulars did not play the most prominent role in the war and certainly have not received as much attention over the years as have either volunteer units or the Army of the Potomac's Regular Division. Studying the history of these regiments reveals that they are not even among the Regular Army's more famous organizations. The 3rd Infantry Regiment, the "Old Guard," will always remain the army's oldest regiment, while the 7th Infantry's record number of battle and campaign streamers (seventy-three as of 1991) will surely never be exceeded. Setting the 15th, 16th, 18th, and 19th Infantry Regiments apart from the others is the fact that their Civil War experiences dwelled in history's shadows for more than 138 years.

ACKNOWLEDGMENTS

The genesis of this book was a thesis written in pursuit of a graduate degree at the University of Wyoming. Researching and writing such an academic requirement is by definition an individual task, and at first I assumed I would prepare this narrative for publication also largely on my own. I am thankful I was mistaken in that notion. Among the numerous people who assisted in this effort, Rick Baumgartner, Frank Fleagel, Al Gambone, Michael Hughes, Dennis Keesee, Karl Larew, George Pimentel, Linn Pittmann, Doug Roush, and Wiley Sword offered crucial advice and research assistance. First Lieutenant (Retired) George Gentry, president of the 18th Infantry Regiment Association, likewise provided valuable insights. I also owe a large debt of gratitude to the talented faculty and staff of the History Department at the University of Wyoming, in particular Dr. Herb Dieterich, whose patience, knowledge, and professionalism taught me the historian's craft.

My particular thanks go to James Ogden, historian of the Chickamauga-Chattanooga National Military Park, who provided steadfast encouragement for many years. Historian-at-large Major (Retired) James B. Ronan, whose interest in the regulars of yesteryear predates mine by a wide margin, made available his considerable research talents on a number of occasions. Doctor Thomas P. Lowry's ground-breaking work with the files of the Judge Advocate General's Office in the National Archives has introduced a new generation of historians to what this untapped resource has to offer, and he pointed me down research paths that yielded vital information about Regular Army discipline and Civil War military justice. I must also salute Theodore "Ted" Savas of the former Savas Publishing Company for his decision to publish material on a relatively unknown subject, first as an installment in his outstanding journal

Civil War Regiments[14] and later as this present volume. I hope readers of these pages will validate Ted's foresight.

I would be remiss not to mention two persons whose assistance was invaluable: Tom Crew of Long Beach, Mississippi, and Mark Slover of Indianapolis. I initially thought this pair would have just passing interests in the western regulars, but they turned out to be dedicated research associates and razor-sharp editors. They are both veterans of the Civil War Regular Army re-enactor circuit, and their knowledge of Civil War uniforms, weapons, equipment, and drill made up for any deficiencies I had in those areas. They also reviewed draft manuscripts on countless occasions and logged many hours on the Internet and elsewhere tracking down elusive subjects. The story of the western regulars could not have been fully told without Tom and Mark's input, although responsibility for any errors or omissions is mine alone. I am honored to rank these gentlemen near the top of the list of persons who made this book possible.

The person at the very top of that list is my lovely wife Elyse. She "signed on" relatively late in this campaign, but her understanding, patience, and faith were crucial. While she deftly balanced her own career, my writing, and the needs of our children, she provided the encouragement no one else could as I concluded my long tour of duty with the regulars. It is indeed a fortunate historian who marries an archeologist.

Prologue

Texas, 1861

Captain Richard W. Johnson, 2nd U.S. Cavalry Regiment, shook some dust from his faded blue uniform and tried to ward off the chill of a dark Texas morning. Although it was only a few hours after midnight, he located Private Larkin, his bugler, and told him to sound reveille. The West Pointer, Class of 1849, wanted his command up and moving well before sunrise. Johnson and his 143 cavalrymen, two companies of the 2nd Cavalry plus the regimental band, had left their post at Fort Mason in central Texas on March 29, bound for the town of Green Lake on the Texas coast. In nearby Matagorda Bay a steamship was supposed to be waiting for them. There they would join other soldiers for evacuation out of the Southern Confederacy. As Larkin played his notes and the captain woke up the troops, they did not realize they were then in a nation changing irrevocably before their eyes. It was the morning of April 12, 1861.[1]

The captain's movements on that cold morning resulted from a long series of events. As states seceded from the Union in 1860 and 1861, troops manning Federal installations in those states suddenly found themselves deep in hostile territory. While no shots had yet been fired, the Texas regulars were cut off from reinforcements, provisions, and transportation. Paralyzed by indecision and not wanting to make a bad situation worse by provoking hostilities, the lame-duck Buchanan Administration issued no guidance to commanders in the field beyond vague instructions to keep garrisons in place and avoid clashes with state authorities. Nothing more would be done until the Lincoln Administration took over on March 4 and determined America's policy toward the seceded states.

At places such as Pensacola and Key West in Florida, Charleston, South Carolina, and Hampton Roads in Virginia, the regulars manning seacoast fortifications waited for the incoming president to determine their fate. The garrisons of these strong bastions could hold out for a while, for everyone knew that the South could take possession of the forts only by force of arms. The situation in Texas was vastly different. Of all the slave states, only Texas and Arkansas still had sizable Native American populations in the early 1860s. This plus an explosion of white immigration into the Lone Star State during the 1850s necessitated a strong Federal military presence. There were roughly 2,600 Regular Army troops in Texas at the beginning of 1861, the entire 2nd Cavalry and 3rd Infantry Regiments along with five batteries of artillery and substantial portions of the 1st and 8th Infantry Regiments. Representing about 15 percent of total army strength, thirty-six companies of regulars were scattered about the state in twenty-one forts and camps. Unlike coastal fortifications, military posts on the Texas frontier served only as shelter for soldiers and equipment. Few were laid out to withstand a formal assault, and defending them against anything more formidable than a determined horse thief was out of the question.[2]

The commander of the Department of Texas, Brevet Major General David E. Twiggs, complicated this difficult situation. He had no intention of defending anything. A Georgian by birth, Twiggs did not hide his secessionist sympathies and realized the secession of Texas was just a matter of time. "If an old woman with a broomstick in hand came to me, and having authority from the State of Texas demanded my surrender," Twiggs stated in February 1861, "I would yield without a word of protest." Apparently the old woman arrived on the 18th of that month. Although the ordinance of succession passed by the Texas legislature on February 1 had not yet been ratified by the state's citizens, General Twiggs surrendered his command to the State of Texas. He authorized the Texas government to take control of all posts, stores, and equipment, and ordered the regulars to march to the coast for evacuation by sea. Presented with a *fait accompli,* the War Department chartered a small flotilla of steamships to bring the troops out. The soldiers in Twiggs's department immediately branded him a traitor but there was not much more they could do. Scattered about in remote locations, resistance would have been futile. Representatives of the Texas government arrived at each of the garrisons during February and March. Large numbers of state militia troops backed them up as the officials negotiated surrender and evacuation.[3]

On the morning of March 29 Captain Johnson marched his small command out of Fort Mason. After they had gone about a mile, Johnson noticed a fire raging throughout the fort. "As it then belonged to the Confederate States, I had no particular interest in it, and never inquired how the fire originated," he recalled, "although I shrewdly suspected that it was fired by some of the men of my command." After marching past San Antonio, the 2nd Cavalry column was joined by Companies G and K of the 1st U.S. Infantry, commanded by Captain Robert S. Granger. The infantrymen had departed Ft. Lancaster on March 19, and were also bound for Green Lake. The two commands marched together. After the treachery of Twiggs and the resignation of many southern-born officers, suspicion was rampant among the Regulars heading for the coast. Although Johnson and Granger were old friends (they had served together in the 1st Infantry for two years prior to Johnson's transfer to the 2nd Cavalry in 1855), for some reason Johnson now did not trust his fellow captain. As the column came to within a few days' march of Green Lake, Granger started encamping his infantrymen a mile or so in advance of Johnson's horsemen. It was an innocent enough act, probably the result of the foot soldiers knowing that sleeping a distance away from the sounds and smells of a cavalry camp resulted in a much more restful night. Johnson smelled trouble: "Supposing that [Granger] knew something that I did not know and that he had some object in pushing ahead, I resolved to beat him at his own game." Granger probably had more cause to be suspicious about Johnson. While Granger was an Ohio native, Johnson was from a slave-holding family of Kentuckians. For whatever reason, Johnson wasn't taking any chances. After waking up his tired troopers in the wee hours of April 12, at two in the morning the captain had Bugler Larkin sound "Boots and Saddles," the traditional cavalry call to mount up and prepare to move. Johnson's troopers quietly moved out a short while later, passing by Granger's still-sleeping infantrymen.[4]

The 2nd Cavalrymen arrived at Green Lake at ten o'clock in the morning. Johnson learned that his command would complete the manifest for the steamship *Empire City*. The cavalrymen continued on to the Indianola Quartermaster Depot and turned over their horses to Texas authorities. They then boarded the lighters *Fasion*

and *United States* for transportation outside the bar of Matagorda
Bay to the ocean steamer. On board the *Empire City*, Johnson found
two other companies of the 2nd Cavalry, 130 men under the command of Captain Charles J. Whiting. Whiting's men had completed
treks from Camp Wood and Fort Inge two weeks ahead of Johnson.
Also on board were five companies of the famed 3rd Infantry, the
oldest infantry regiment in the Regular Army.[5]

* * *

Brevet Major Oliver L. Shepherd, 3rd U.S. Infantry, shielded his
eyes as he gazed out at the Gulf of Mexico's shimmering waters from
the deck of the *Empire City*. The transfer of Johnson's troops from
the lighters to the steamship was a slow process, and Shepherd was
growing impatient. The major and 300 troops of his regiment had
been at Matagorda Bay for more than two weeks, waiting for additional troops to arrive and fill the steamer. Dark-haired, stocky, and
somewhat short, Shepherd had never been a very patient person.
With the nation drifting toward war he desperately wanted to leave
Texas and get into the action.

Not that war was anything new to Oliver Shepherd. Born in 1815
at Clifton Park in upstate New York, he grew up on an uncle's farm
after the death of his father in 1825. After completing his secondary
education in Saratoga County, Oliver spent a few years teaching,
clerking in a drug store, and studying medicine. He had always
wanted to be a soldier and in 1836 secured an appointment to the
Military Academy. "Shepherd we never much cared for," William T.
Sherman once wrote of the New Yorker, a fellow member of the
Academy's Class of 1840, "but I heard he has made a good soldier."
Sherman's comments touch upon two notable aspects of Shepherd's
personality. Oliver Shepherd was not a very personable fellow and
had few friends. He was never really concerned about what others
thought of him, except when the issue was his professional reputation. But in the military realm Shepherd was in his element. He could
rattle off the Articles of War without a second thought and developed into a demanding commander, setting high standards for both
himself and his troops. He cared little for those who fell short of his
expectations. Shepherd ranked thirty-third in an academy class of
forty-two graduates, far behind Sherman, who ranked sixth.[6]

Shepherd displayed his military abilities on numerous occasions
during his twenty-one years of service prior to the Civil War.
Following graduation from West Point, he was assigned to the 3rd

Infantry and participated in the difficult guerrilla campaigns of the 2nd Seminole War in Florida during 1841-1842. He remained in Florida until 1843 and was then posted to Jefferson Barracks, Missouri, and Ft. Jesup, Louisiana. He briefly served as a junior member of General Zachary Taylor's staff in 1845 and went on to see extensive service in the Mexican War. With the 3rd Infantry Shepherd fought in a number of that conflict's major engagements. His was the first company to cross the Rio Grande into Mexico. He fought at the Battles of Palo Alto and Resaca-de-la Palma in May 1846, and the next year participated in the Mexico City Campaign. Lieutenant Shepherd earned a brevet promotion[7] to captain for meritorious conduct during the Battles of Contreras and Churubusco on August 20, 1847, where his company was among the first to breach the Mexican fortifications. Another brevet for gallantry followed for his actions at the Battle of Chapultepec the next month, and he also participated in the final assault on Mexico City. As the Mexican War ended, Shepherd was one of only five members of the Class of 1840 to have earned two or more brevets.

He served in the American Southwest throughout the 1850s, during which time he became fluent in Spanish and married into a prominent Hispanic family (decidedly unusual activities for an eastern-bred West Pointer). During 1859 he commanded two of the first expeditions to explore and map remote sections of Navajo Lands in present-day Arizona. The next year he was at the center of one of the largest battles of all pre-Civil War western Indian campaigns. Shepherd, commanding little more than 200 troops of the 3rd Infantry, in April 1860 successfully defended Ft. Defiance in New Mexico Territory against a daring nighttime attack by about 1,000 Navajo warriors. The action impressed Brevet Lieutenant General Winfield Scott, the army's commanding general, who remarked in his 1860 annual report to Congress: "The Defense of Fort Defiance reflects great credit upon Major Shepherd, his officers, and the men of his command."[8]

The War Department transferred the 3rd Infantry from New Mexico to Texas in the summer of 1860 to assist in securing the Mexican border along the lower Rio Grande, an area that had been recently inflamed with tension from raids by Mexican bandits, Comanches on the warpath, and lawless Texans. The headquarters of the regiment and five companies (including Shepherd's own Company B) were stationed at Fort Clark, a post at the headwaters of the Las Moras River some 120 miles due west of department headquarters in San Antonio, while the balance of the regiment was strung out along the Rio Grande between Fort Clark and the Gulf Coast. As the secession crisis deepened during the first months of 1861 and many southern officers resigned their commissions, Shepherd took a dim view of the War Department's cordial treatment of men he considered traitors and recommended they all be arrested for treason. On February 21 he sent the War Department a list with the names of six currently serving officers whom he suspected of disloyalty. Five of the six eventually wore Confederate uniforms.[9]

Shepherd composed his words of warning from Fort Duncan, a post on the Rio Grande about twenty-five miles south of Fort Clark. He and his company had been ordered there on February 14. Anticipating Twiggs's surrender, the War Department had ordered the five artillery batteries in Texas to leave the state. Three of the batteries had been assigned to Fort Duncan. Shepherd's company occupied the post as the artillerymen departed for the Brazos Santiago Quartermaster Depot at the mouth of the Rio Grande.

Contingents of Texas militia arrived at the 3rd Infantry posts in late February and early March. Shepherd had to perform the distasteful duty of surrendering not one post but two. The 3rd Infantry's commander, Colonel Benjamin L.E. Bonneville, was on leave, resulting in Shepherd being the regiment's senior officer on duty in Texas. Shepherd surrendered the regiment's headquarters at Fort Clark on March 19. Just as Johnson's 2nd Cavalrymen had done when leaving Fort Mason, the Fort Clark regulars were determined not to hand over their post in perfect condition. To prevent the Texans from raising their state flag while Federal troops were still present, one of Shepherd's sergeants cut the halyards from the post's flagpole as the regulars formed up to leave.

Fort Clark's four companies and the regimental band headed for San Antonio, but Shepherd himself rode south to Fort Duncan. He surrendered that post the next day. While Company B marched for the coast, the hard-riding Shepherd hurried back north and caught up with the Fort Clark troops. He commanded the larger column during the march to Green Lake. The movement was generally uneventful until the regulars approached San Antonio. After receiving word that the local citizens would not appreciate a battalion of Yankee soldiers marching through their good city, Shepherd staged an impromptu full dress parade. With "every man and officer as fine as brass and bullion could make him," the regulars made their way through the heart of the city without incident. They arrived at Green Lake during the last week of March, where the *Empire City* was ready and waiting for them. Brevet Major Larkin Smith of the 8th Infantry, commander of the camp at Green Lake, instructed Shepherd to wait for the other six companies of the 3rd Infantry to arrive. The entire regiment would then ship out on the *Empire City*.

But time was rapidly running out. Events in Charleston Harbor, involving another isolated group of regulars, had brought the nation to the brink of war. Shepherd's patience fortunately ran out as March became April. Whiting's 2nd Cavalry companies had joined Shepherd's troops at the Green Lake rendezvous, as had Company B of the 3rd from Fort Duncan, but the remaining five companies of the 3rd Infantry were no where to be seen (Shepherd did not realize that two companies of the regiment had marched to Brazos Santiago and were already safely away; the remaining three companies were still on the road to Green Lake from their posts in the lower Rio Grande valley, but their exact whereabouts were anyone's guess). On April 11 Shepherd convinced Major Smith to allow the troops then present at Green Lake to depart the next day on the *Empire City*. The still-inbound companies of the 3rd Infantry would take the next available steamer. Larkin Smith agreed. He was happy enough to see the troops leave, for Smith was a Virginian and would exchange his blue uniform for a gray one little more than a month later.

Captain Johnson's timely arrival on the morning of April 12 with his two companies of the 2nd Cavalry filled the ship to capacity. Shepherd and Smith had unknowingly timed the *Empire City's* departure extremely well. At about the same moment Bugler Larkin had been sounding "Boots and Saddles," Confederate batteries were opening fire on Fort Sumter. Instead of conducting a peaceful evacuation, the Texas regulars found themselves at war.[10]

* * *

Captain Granger could not believe his bad luck. He had become one of the Confederacy's first prisoners, a result of his old friend Richard Johnson waking up early and stealing away in the night. Granger's 1st Infantrymen arrived at Green Lake during the afternoon of April 12 only to find Johnson's cavalrymen already there and the *Empire City* fully loaded. He had no choice but to wait for the next ship. The steamer *Star of the West* arrived at Matagorda Bay the next day, the same vessel that had unsuccessfully attempted to provision Fort Sumter the previous January. The ill-fated vessel's luck had not improved in the three months since the incident in Charleston harbor. With the beginning of hostilities, the Confederate government was determined to prevent any further departure of Federal troops from Texas. A contingent of Texas militia led by Earl Van Dorn, ex-major of the 2nd Cavalry and newly commissioned Confederate colonel, captured the unarmed ship on April 17. The seven companies of regulars who had expected to be evacuated via the steamer, Granger's 1st Infantrymen plus three companies of the 3rd U.S. and two more of the 8th Infantry, surrendered on April 25.

Robert S. Granger became a prisoner of war. "Granger was not exchanged for a year or so, thus losing rank and experience," Richard Johnson recalled years afterward as he looked back on the incident. "I have thought how lucky it was to conceive the idea that Granger was seeking an advantage over me. It may have been, and doubtless was, all imagination on my part, but it was a very happy conception, as it turned out." To most observers, Granger's capture was but a small footnote in the momentous events of the Civil War's beginning. But for Oliver Shepherd and five battalions of regular army infantrymen, the capture of Robert Granger began a series of events that two years later would impact them in a way they could never have imagined.[11]

The 15 officers and 580 troops on board the *Empire City* sailed the Gulf of Mexico unaware of the turmoil they left behind. The ship's first stop was in Havana, where it took on coal and provisions—and received the news about the attack on Fort Sumter—before proceeding to New York. It then sailed up the Atlantic seaboard and on April 25 picked up a pilot off Sandy Hook, New Jersey, for guidance into the harbor of New York City. The sight of a busy port of a country at war left a deep impression on men who were fresh from the desolation of the Texas frontier. "As we got closer to the city," one of Shepherd's lieutenants recalled, "boat after boat passed us loaded with troops and munitions of war, colors flying, bands filling the air with patriotic strains, soldiers rending the skies with their cheers as the boats passed or overtook each other."

Shepherd's regulars remained on board the *Empire City* the night of April 25 and disembarked the following morning. The 3rd Infantrymen marched to Fort Hamilton on Long Island. They remained there until May 3, when they headed south to join the forces gathering to defend Washington. The four companies of 2nd

Cavalrymen boarded a train on April 26, bound for the regiment's new headquarters at Carlisle Barracks, Pennsylvania. At Carlisle, Captains Johnson and Whiting reported to Major George H. Thomas. Although Thomas was a Virginian he had remained in Union blue, the only field-grade officer of the 2nd Cavalry to do so. Thomas's road to Carlisle was much less eventful than Johnson's, although it had a painful beginning.

While pursuing a band of Comanche raiders on August 28, 1860, a warrior shot an arrow that struck the major's chin and lodged in his chest. Thomas survived the painful wounding and departed Texas on medical leave shortly afterward. He spent some time recuperating at his family home in Southampton County, Virginia, before heading for New York City, where his wife lived. Thomas cut his leave short and reported for duty at Carlisle Barracks when the war began. By the time Johnson and Whiting's troops arrived in Pennsylvania, the balance of the 2nd Cavalry was already present there with Major Thomas. These troops had also escaped from Texas, arriving in New York City aboard the steamer *Coatzacoalcos* on April 11.[12]

When the *Empire City* arrived in New York, the presence of yet another troopship caused little excitement. In contrast with that ship's muted reception at the port, the *Coatzacoalcos* arrived prior to the firing on Fort Sumter and the whole city took note. The *New York Times* reported that excitement swept through Fort Columbus on Governor's Island in New York Harbor with the announcement that the steamer laden with regulars from Texas was entering the port: "Off-duty men rushed to the beach to cheer their returned comrades; even the day's guard forgot the dignified disregard of events going on off their post, which sentinels generally observe, and went as far from the guard-room towards the wharf as they dared." The post band, long tired of playing the melancholy tune "The Girl I Left Behind Me" for departing troops, eagerly struck up the lively "Paddy Carey" as the *Coatzacoalcos* churned by (the tune traditionally played for arriving troops, "See the Conquering Hero Comes," was deemed to "not exactly suit the case").

The *Coatzacoalcos* had left Texas on March 31. In addition to the 2nd Cavalrymen, on board were Companies A, H, and I of the 1st Infantry Regiment. The ship first landed at Key West. Two of the infantry companies, commanded by 1840 West Point classmates Stephen D. Carpenter and James N. Caldwell, put ashore on the island to reinforce the meager garrison of Fort Jefferson.

Waterborne operations in the Gulf of Mexico region were nothing new to Captain Carpenter, for in the early 1840s he had campaigned in the swamps of Florida during the 2nd Seminole war; in the war with Mexico he commanded the very first company of American troops to splash ashore at Veracruz in March 1847, the initial act of Scott's decisive Mexico City Campaign. Fourteen years later during the evacuation of Texas, Carpenter put up a show of defiance against Texas authorities that probably made General Scott proud. Carpenter was stationed at Camp Cooper, a post on the Clear Fork of the Brazos River in north central Texas, as the war clouds gathered. His command consisted of his own Company H of the 1st Infantry and two companies of the 2nd Cavalry. Word of General Twiggs's impending surrender had not yet reached Camp Cooper in early February as suspicious persons began to gather about the post. Carpenter let his garrison know that if attacked the regulars would defend their honor to the fullest measure: "Should their number be a thousand to one, their cause, when compared to ours, will be more than that odds against them. In a strife like this we have but one course to pursue, for each would rather lay his corpse to molder upon the plain he defends than to drag it hence to be the laugh and scorn of every honest lover of his country's glory."[13]

Colonel W.C. Dalrymiple and scores of Texas militiamen arrived at Camp Cooper on February 18, demanding surrender. Carpenter briefly considered abandoning the camp and marching his garrison overland to Fort Leavenworth in Kansas, but realized the impracticality of such a movement. The captain eventually yielded to Dalrymiple's demand, although Carpenter's written reply to the surrender ultimatum was still defiant:

> My reply to your demand...could be no other than an unqualified refusal; but in the present agitated political condition of our country I feel compelled to regard, in connection with this demand and its refusal, the perilous consequences that must result to the whole nation. The policy of the administration and the wisest statesman of the land is to avert, if possible, the shedding of blood, and while I have before me this fact exemplified at Forts Sumter and Pickens, and especially in the case of the Star of the West, and also the fact that the arsenals throughout the South have been yielded to State authorities without a struggle, I do not feel justified to act from the promptings of a soldier.[14]

Carpenter handed over Camp Cooper on February 26. The garrison struck out for San Antonio and eventually reached the Texas coast, where they rendezvoused with the *Coatzacoalcos*. After depositing the troops in Florida, the steamer made for Havana, obtained provisions, and sailed for New York. The 1st Infantrymen at Key West would see only limited action in the upcoming war's campaigns, but Captains Carpenter and Caldwell would see considerably more.[15]

Captain John H. King of Company I, 1st Infantry, commanded the regulars on board. King, forty-one, had already spent more than half his life in uniform. Originally from Sackets Harbor, New York, where his father was a militia officer and veteran of the War of 1812, he moved at a young age to Michigan. He was raised there by Hugh Brady, colonel of the 2nd U.S. Infantry Regiment and commander of Fort Wayne, a relative of King's who had seen service in the Regular Army during the Indian campaigns of the 1790s and as a regimental commander in Winfield Scott's crack brigade of regulars during the War of 1812. The military heritage of King's family inclined John toward an army career. As the army expanded in the late 1830s in response to warfare with the Seminoles and the Indian removal policies of the Jackson and Van Buren Administrations, the number of new lieutenants required each year was greater than the size of the classes graduating from West Point. A large number of men were commissioned directly from civil life, without any formal training. John King was one of them, at the tender age of seventeen receiving a commission in 1837 as a second lieutenant in the 1st Infantry Regiment.

The youth developed into a tall and robust officer during the 1840s and 1850s. He earned the nickname "Iron Bull" and was considered a hard working and highly competent leader. His pre-Civil War career in the 1st Infantry mirrored Oliver Shepherd's in the 3rd, with service in the Seminole and Mexican Wars. While commanding Company I of the 1st Infantry in 1860, King was assigned to San Antonio Barracks and for a time served on Twiggs's staff as adjutant general of the Department of Texas. After Twiggs's capitulation, King helped organize the camp at Green Lake and then sailed with his company on the *Coatzacoalcos*. Upon the steamer's arrival in New York, the regulars disembarked at the Warren Street wharf. Major Thomas was waiting for the cavalrymen and put them on the road for Carlisle Barracks. King's infantrymen marched to Fort Hamilton.

They were soon on their way to the nation's capital, where King and his men guarded the arsenal at Washington Barracks.[16]

* * *

The arrivals of *Coatzacoalcos* and *Empire City* in New York concluded the Texas evacuation. The Federal regulars who were not able to make it out, about 1,300 in number, were taken prisoner in Texas and New Mexico during April and May. Most of the officers were paroled, but the soldiers were forced to work as laborers at some of their former posts. Almost two years would pass before the last of the Texas regulars were exchanged and set free. It was but small consolation for them that President James Buchanan dismissed General Twiggs from the army on March 1, 1861, for "treachery to the flag of his country." Twiggs fled to New Orleans, where he received a hero's welcome and a major general's commission in the Confederate Army. He died in July 1862, playing no further significant role in the war.

Despite losing a sizable portion of the U.S. Army and the *Star of the West*, the Texas evacuation had some positive effects on the Union war effort. All five regular artillery batteries in Texas managed to escape onboard the steamers *Daniel Webster* and *General Rusk*; four were put ashore at Forts Jefferson and Taylor in the Florida Keys. These forces, along with the 1st Infantrymen from the *Coatzacoalcos*, ensured that those posts remained in Federal hands throughout the war. The 2nd Cavalry Regiment proved useful during early-war operations in the Shenandoah Valley. The companies of the 3rd Infantry from the *Empire City* played a crucial role at the First Battle of Bull Run in July 1861, where they covered the Federal army's retreat from the battlefield. Perhaps most significantly, the officers who escaped from Texas were available for immediate service in the rapidly expanding Army of the United States. Richard Johnson, Oliver Shepherd, John King, Stephen Carpenter, James Caldwell, and George Thomas would see extensive action together. All of them would be involved in the operations of Regular Army infantry battalions in the Civil War's Western Theater.[17]

PART ONE

The Regular Battalions in the Army of the Ohio

1861–1862

Chapter 1:

The New Regular Regiments

"The Regiment Will Make You Feel at Home"

T he Army of the United States went to war in the spring of 1861. It was a war unlike any other in the nation's history, and the Federal army that fought it was also unique. The number of men who served in the Union Army would eventually reach an unprecedented level for an American military force, the total of more than two million soldiers remaining unsurpassed until the twentieth century. While the state volunteer units comprising that army were organized, manned, and equipped after the war commenced, a small number of Northern regiments had lineages that spanned multiple decades and some had been in existence in one form or another since 1784: units of the Regular Army of the United States. America's military professionals were few in number at the time of the Ft. Sumter bombardment, numbering less than 16,000 officers and men. Making a bad situation worse was where the regulars were located. In April 1861 most of the regulars were either stationed west of the Mississippi River or marking time in Confederate prisons. Of the Old Army's nineteen regiments (ten infantry, four artillery, two dragoons, two cavalry, and a regiment of mounted riflemen), the only forces available for immediate service were a handful of artillery companies scattered along the East Coast and the troops who had escaped from Texas. Even if all the Old Army regulars had quickly united, such a small force would still have been inadequate for the defense of the nation's capitol, not to mention the military conquest of the Confederacy. The loyal states had to furnish the vast majority of the manpower for these tasks. Barely noticeable in this massive mobilization were eleven additional regiments of regulars that were also organized in 1861, starting a new chapter in the history of the United States Army.

* * *

Anson Mills scratched out the message in large letters on a scrap of paper: "No separation—Anson Mills." It was February 17, 1861, and this was his vote on the Texas secession ordinance. Although the young El Paso resident had been told his life would be in jeopardy if he voted against secession, there was never any doubt in his mind about what to do. Just to be safe, Mills carefully strapped on a pistol belt before heading for the El Paso polling place, a large saloon. He strode to the center of the gambling hall, held up the paper for all to see, and announced: "Gentlemen, some of you may be curious to know how I am to vote. This is my ballot." He left the saloon without incident. His vote was one of only two against secession in El Paso County.

Mills had resided in the Lone Star State for a couple of years but was still a Union man. A native of Indiana, he spent two years at West Point in the late 1850s before failing a math exam and resigning from the Military Academy. Mills headed west and ended up in Texas, where he worked as a teacher and surveyor. One of the more enduring legacies from his time there stems from his making the original survey of a small border town on the Rio Grande and naming it El Paso. The transplanted Hoosier also found employment through the War Department, working as a surveyor on a military commission that laid out boundary lines between Texas, New Mexico, and Indian Territory.[1]

Realizing his vote against succession would not change the inevitable, Mills left Texas in early March 1861. After a lengthy journey by stage and rail he arrived in Washington and early the next month was appointed as a sergeant in a District of Columbia militia unit known as the Cassius M. Clay Guards. Sergeant Mills applied for a Regular Army commission after the war began. To expedite the process he enlisted the aid of friends at West Point. Mills wrote to Cadet Charlie Hazlett, then a senior at the Academy, and asked for a recommendation. Hazlett called a meeting of the Class of 1861 and read Mills's request to them. Thirty-eight members of the class placed their signatures on a letter they sent to the War Department:

West Point Military Academy
West Point, N.Y., April 30, 1861.

Lorenzo Thomas,
Adjutant General
Washington, D.C.

Dear Sir:

We, the undersigned, members of the First Class at the United States Military Academy, respectfully recommend to your favorable consideration the claims of Mr. Anson Mills, an applicant for a commission as Second Lieutenant in the United States Army.

Mr. Mills was formerly a member, for nearly two years, of the class preceding ours, when he resigned. During that time his habits and character conformed to the strictest military propriety and discipline, and we feel assured that he would be an honor to the service and that its interests would be promoted by his appointment.[2]

Nearly two months would pass before the adjutant general acted on the recommendation. In June Sergeant Mills received additional help in his quest from Captain William R. Terrill, one of his former West Point instructors who was then in Washington assisting with the organization of the new 5th U.S. Artillery Regiment. Terrill also gave Mills a favorable recommendation, and on June 22, 1861, the multiple endorsements secured for the well-traveled Texan an appointment as a first lieutenant in the 18th U.S. Infantry. Mills's last task prior to leaving Washington was to physically secure his commission certificate. A stubborn War Department clerk insisted that regulations required such documents to be mailed to Mills's home of record in El Paso. Unlike the clerk Mills realized the certificate would be lost forever if it were mailed to an address in the Confederacy. The aspiring lieutenant had a friend in the Treasury Department explain the situation to Secretary of War Simon Cameron. The clerk acquiesced to the high level pressure. Lieutenant Mills and the precious document made their way to 18th Infantry Headquarters at Columbus, Ohio, arriving on June 25.[3]

That same day in Washington, a messenger from the War Department delivered to Brevet Major Oliver Shepherd a large piece of carefully folded, expensive paper. The missive was a commission appointing Shepherd as a Regular Army lieutenant colonel in the same regiment as Mills, with date of rank as of May 14. Shepherd was excited about wearing the grade's silver oak leaf insignia, something that had been an almost impossible dream in the peacetime army of the previous decade, but he probably did not realize just how close he had come to remaining a brevet major. In early June 1861 Secretary Cameron put together a slate of Regular Army promotions and Shepherd's name, among others, was not mentioned. The president noticed that a few prominent names were absent from Cameron's list, and also that a large proportion of the names present were men who hailed from Cameron's home state of Pennsylvania. While expressing concern that almost a quarter of the new regular officers hailed from a single state, the president decided to let Cameron's list stand. Lincoln did direct Cameron to add a few names, for the president wanted to reward some officers who had served in the field during the tense period immediately prior to the war. A note from Lincoln to his war secretary on June 17 ordered Cameron to promote the heroes of Fort Sumter, Robert Anderson and Abner Doubleday, and the defender of Fort Pickens, Adam Slemmer. The commander in chief also mentioned the officer who had led the largest contingent of regulars out of Texas: "I wish Oliver L. Shepherd, now Captain in the 3rd Infantry and Major by brevet, to be a Lieutenant Colonel, you to find the place for him." The place Cameron found for Shepherd was in the 18th U.S. Infantry.[4]

The promotion could not have come soon enough. Two weeks after disembarking from the *Empire City* in New York, Shepherd marched the Texas battalion of the 3rd Infantry by ship, road, and rail to Washington. In early June General Scott decided to reinforce Major General Robert Patterson's attempt to capture Harper's Ferry with "the best re-enforcements within my reach," and sent him Thomas's 2nd Cavalry from Carlisle Barracks, a battery of the 4th U.S. Artillery, and Shepherd's 3rd Infantrymen from Washington. Patterson occupied Harper's Ferry on June 17, after which Scott ordered him to return the regulars. Back Shepherd's battalion went, and upon arrival in Washington Shepherd relinquished command to Captain George Sykes, commander of the 3rd Infantry's Company K. Shepherd was assigned to court-martial duty, and while attending to that tedious assignment his promotion arrived.[5]

Shepherd was looking forward to assuming his new duties with the 18th Infantry. He already had an indication that the 18th Infantry was a good outfit. "I am delighted to hear of the good condition of your regiment," Shepherd wrote the unit's colonel, "and hope soon to be identified with it as I was my old regiment." Shepherd was still the nominal commander of the 3rd Infantry's Company B, and had to take care of some administrative tasks in New York City before he could report for duty with the 18th. On July 5 he received orders from the War Department "to proceed to his station (Columbus, Ohio) *via* Ft. Hamilton, New York, and to delay at the latter place a sufficient time to enable him to dispose of the public property appertaining to Company 'B,' 3d Infantry, for which he is now responsible." Much to Lieutenant Colonel Shepherd's dismay, the temporary stay in New York City turned into a lengthy one. Just as he was finishing his 3rd Infantry paperwork, Shepherd was placed on detached service from the 18th U.S. and assigned to the staff of the Department of the East, serving as the department's chief mustering officer. While Shepherd pushed papers in a drab office at 76 White Street in Manhattan, George Sykes had been promoted to major and then made some headlines while leading a battalion of regular infantry at the First Battle of Bull Run. As the long summer days slowly came and went, Shepherd began to think the war was passing him by.[6]

* * *

Throughout the war's first summer, Mills, Shepherd, and many other officers obtained commissions in new regular regiments like the 18th U.S. Infantry, one of eleven regiments added to the Regular Army's rolls after the start of the war. The expansion of the Regular Army in May 1861 was a great step forward in mobilizing the North's manpower, particularly when compared with the Union's first attempt at mobilization. With war a reality, the Lincoln Administration scrambled to assemble an army. The only troops immediately available in addition to the Old Army's regulars were state militia forces, but most citizen-soldier militias were poorly equipped, ineffectively led, and virtually untrained. Even worse, the Militia Act of 1792 stipulated that state militia troops could actively serve for no longer than three months at a time. Still, the militia was better than nothing at all. On April 15, 1861, President Lincoln issued a proclamation calling for the states to furnish 75,000 men to serve ninety days. He soon realized that ninety-day troops were not the right tools for a long-term job. Winfield Scott, general-in-chief of the United States Army, later that month recommended to the president the raising of an additional force of about 80,000 men, which would consist of both Regular Army troops and volunteers. Regiments of Federal volunteers, which did not have to conform to the Militia Act's restrictions, would provide the government with a large pool of long-service manpower. A sizable contingent of regulars would add a reliable corps of professionals, setting the standard for the entire army in discipline, training, and professionalism. Scott, America's preeminent soldier of the nineteenth century, had always preferred to employ well trained regular troops to the greatest extent possible, a formula that brought him success in the War of 1812 and the war with Mexico. As the Civil War began he assumed the same technique would be successful again.[7]

The first step was to organize this new force. Since the War Department was swamped with getting the initial 75,000 state troops equipped and deployed, the task of organizing the next contingent was turned over to the Treasury Department, where Treasury Secretary Salmon P. Chase possessed a loud voice in determining administration policy. Chase in turn gave the project to two army officers: Captain William B. Franklin, a topographical engineer who was the supervising architect of the Treasury Building, and Major Irvin McDowell, an officer assigned to the Adjutant General's Department who was also General Scott's military secretary.[8]

After studying the issues for a few days, Franklin and McDowell recommended an increase of about 23,000 men for the Regular Army. This force, collectively referred to as the "New Army," would consist of eight regiments of infantry (the 11th through 18th), one of artillery (the 5th), and one of cavalry (the 3rd).[9] The new infantry regiments would be organized quite differently than were the units of the Old Army. Old Army infantry regiments, as well as state volunteer units, were organized along British lines. Each regiment consisted of ten companies, with a company consisting of up to eighty-nine officers and men. The New Army regiments would have an organization patterned after the large regiments of the French Army. The new regiments would have an authorized strength of 2,444 officers and men, almost three times the size of the old regiments, in three battalions of eight companies each. Each company would contain one hundred troops of all ranks. Two of the battalions would serve in the field, while the third would remain at a regimental depot. The depot battalion would supervise recruiting and training, forwarding additional troops to the field battalions when needed. This system was ideally suited for long term campaigning, as it attempted to keep the units in the field at their authorized strength. Another advantage of the French system was that officers in the grade of major would command the battalions. Colonels too old for combat service commanded most Regular Army regiments. When the Civil War began the colonels of the Old Army's nineteen regiments averaged sixty-three years of age, with Colonel John Erving of the 1st U.S. Artillery topping the list at age eighty, a soldier since 1809. Nine of these men were veterans of the War of 1812. Under the new system, these ancient colonels could remain at their regimental headquarters and take care of their traditional duties of recruitment and paperwork while younger, more energetic officers commanded the regiment's field forces. With each regiment containing three battalions, promotions to command them would go to the army's young and fit officers.[10]

Finally, Franklin and McDowell recommended that the existing regular regiments and all volunteer units be re-tooled into the French system. They also recommended that volunteer soldiers serve a three-year enlistment, as opposed to the five-year term of the regulars. Secretary Chase accepted the French organization for the new regular regiments and the three-year term of service for Federal volunteers, but did not approve the reorganization of the rest of the Union Army's infantry regiments. Chase believed the old regulars and state units were already familiar with the British system; it would be too great a burden for them to reorganize.[11]

The plan was finalized in early May 1861. On May 3, the president issued a proclamation calling for 42,034 Federal volunteers and increasing the strength of the Regular Army by 22,714. The War Department endorsed the program and published it in General Orders on May 4, 1861. Congress subsequently gave its approval on July 29, but the final version passed by Congress contained a few significant changes. The legislators authorized an additional regiment, the 19th U.S. Infantry. No mention was made of the depot battalions; each regiment would consist of three field battalions, with no provision for a regimental recruiting and training apparatus. While the original plan had authorized an adjutant and quartermaster as staff officers for each battalion, Congress stipulated that the officers filling these positions would be taken from those assigned to the battalion's companies. This bit of congressional penny pinching meant that a regiment would be shorthanded officers even when all were present for duty.[12]

Another section of this law ensured that regular outfits would never have all their assigned officers on hand: officers were authorized to simultaneously hold commissions in both the Regular Army and in state forces. When given the choice between serving as a Regular Army captain or a volunteer colonel, most of the army's ambitious officers naturally choose the latter. Authorizing regular officers to serve in state units unquestionably increased the effectiveness of many volunteer regiments and was a great benefit to the Union war effort, but this practice made it a certainty that regular regiments would be chronically short of officers.

This lack of foresight in providing leadership for the regular regiments is a good indication that neither Congress nor the War Department had a clear notion of how to employ the Regular Army in the Civil War. Under Lincoln's May 3 proclamation, a 39,000-man Regular Army (the 16,000 already on the books plus the increase of 23,000) would be a significant portion of an 80,000-man force. But General Scott greatly underestimated the manpower needed to put down the rebellion. On July 1, 1861, there were 170,329 volunteer troops under arms; when the war ended they would number more than a million. For the duration of the war, however, the size of the Regular Army would not rise above the 39,273 soldiers Congress authorized in its July legislation.[13]

Some key leaders did not even realize this minuscule Regular Army increase had taken place. When Major General Henry W. Halleck arrived in Washington during July 1862 to become general-in-chief of the Union Army, he took a room at Willard's Hotel. In the hotel lobby the next morning he noticed a colonel walking toward him. The officer's uniform caught the general's eye, for the garb included the distinctive regulation-issue black felt Hardee hat. The front of the hat sported a gold-embroidered bugle, indicating that the wearer was an infantry officer. A silver-embroidered "18" was also on the hat but there was no state designation. The officer approached the general and was about to speak when an angry Halleck beat him to it.

"What 18th Regiment?"

"The 18th U.S. Infantry, General Halleck," the surprised colonel replied.

Halleck's next words became legendary among the 18th Regulars: "There is no such regiment, and when I reach the War Department you will lose those straps or go into arrest!"

Unbeknownst to the Union Army's latest general-in-chief, the officer standing before him was Henry B. Carrington, commanding officer of the new 18th Regular Infantry. Carrington was a friend of Treasury Secretary Chase and had been sent to Williard's to arrange a meeting between Halleck and President Lincoln. "General Halleck, my commission warrants my uniform," Carrington replied to the general's outburst. "I sought this introduction to give instructions from the Secretaries of State, the Treasury, and the Navy, to advise you that at 10 o'clock this morning they will come to this hotel with carriages to escort you to the Soldier's Home, there to meet President Lincoln. I have discharged my duty, sir, good morning sir." Carrington kept his shoulder straps, but he and Halleck that day developed a mutual hatred that would continue to the end of their lives, all due to Halleck's unfamiliarity with a key part of the diverse Union Army.[14]

By the time the Halleck-Carrington encounter took place, the War Department had been wrestling with the problem of assigning officers to the New Army regiments for more than a year. New officers were needed to lead the new regiments. A plan used successfully in 1855 (the last time regiments had been added to the Regular Army) was employed again: for first lieutenants and higher, half of the New Army officers would come from existing regiments, promoting the transferred officers one grade, while the balance would be men appointed directly from civil life, preferably citizens with some sort of previous military experience. Regimental commanders would create their own second lieutenants by commissioning selected soldiers, with the exception of two second lieutenant billets in each regiment, which were reserved for proven sergeants of the Old Army. In a July 1, 1861, message to the president, the secretary of war reported the results: "Of the civilians appointed as regimental commanders, all except one are either graduates of West Point or have served with distinction in the field, and of the lieutenant-colonels, majors, captains, and first lieutenants, a large proportion have been taken from the Regular Army and the volunteers now in service, while the second lieutenants have been mainly created by the promotion of meritorious sergeants from the regular service."[15] The

War Department's judgment was quite good in appointing officers to command the new infantry regiments:

Table 1: Colonels of the New Army Infantry Regiments, 1861

Colonel	Regiment
Erasmus D. Keyes	11th U.S. Infantry
William B. Franklin	12th U.S. Infantry
William T. Sherman	13th U.S. Infantry
Charles P. Stone	14th U.S. Infantry
Fitz-John Porter	15th U.S. Infantry
Andrew Porter	16th U.S. Infantry
Samuel P. Heintzelman	17th U.S. Infantry
Henry B. Carrington	18th U.S. Infantry
E.R.S. Canby	19th U.S. Infantry

Unfortunately for the Regular Army, the quality of these officers ensured they received high-ranking appointments in the volunteer service. All of them would eventually don general's stars. Six of the nine—Keyes, Franklin, Sherman, Fitz-John Porter, Heintzelman, and Canby—rose to the corps command level or higher. Only one of these officers spent a significant amount time serving as colonel of a regular regiment—Henry B. Carrington of the 18th Infantry. He was the exception Secretary Cameron mentioned, for Carrington had neither field experience nor a West Point diploma. But he had other qualities that made him an ideal choice to organize a regular regiment from scratch.

Born in Wallingford, Connecticut, in 1824, Carrington developed an interest in the military during his youth while observing local militiamen drill and parade. He later became a learned student of military history, in particular the American Revolution. Henry desired to attend West Point but chronic health problems turned him to Yale instead, from which he graduated in 1845. He then taught chemistry and Greek at the Irving Institute in Tarrytown, New York, prior to returning to Yale to study law in 1847. Because of continuing ill health (he would suffer from on-and-off respiratory problems most of his life), Carrington decided to move to a different climate upon completing his legal studies. In 1848 the young lawyer arrived in Columbus, Ohio, where a cousin had a thriving law practice. Carrington became one of the leading citizens of Columbus in the decade that followed. He was named to the board of trustees of a number of colleges and universities, became active in Whig (later Republican) politics, married into a prominent Ohio family, was a dedicated abolitionist, and served in the Ohio militia. Carrington campaigned vigorously for the successful reelection of former U.S. Senator Salmon P. Chase as Ohio governor in 1857. Chase had retained Carrington for legal counsel on a number of occasions, and in July 1857 Governor Chase appointed Carrington as the judge advocate general of the Ohio militia, responsible for the militia's legal and regulatory affairs. He later named Carrington the state's adjutant general, the administrative commander of Ohio's militia. Chase left the Ohio governorship to return to the U.S. Senate in 1859, and William Dennison, one of Carrington's law partners, won the election that year to replace Chase as governor. Dennison reappointed Carrington as adjutant general. Political connections thus provided Carrington with a backdoor to the military career he had always desired. Carrington made another important political connection less than two months prior to the Civil War. In February 1861 he accompanied the military escort of Abraham Lincoln as the president-elect journeyed across the Buckeye State, on his way to Washington for the presidential inauguration.[16]

Despite having no military experience prior to assuming the Ohio staff positions, Carrington performed his duties surprisingly well. An acquaintance described the thirty-three-year-old adjutant general as "below the medium size, slender, nervous and active...of a finely cultivated mind and good literary acquirements."[17] A dissertation on Carrington describes how, with Governor Chase's backing, Carrington set about improving Ohio's militia during the late 1850s:

Chase shared Carrington's enthusiasm for a revitalized citizen militia. He wanted to shape it into something more than military social clubs that entertained the public during parades and sham battles. In his inaugural message to the Ohio legislature, Chase urged the overhaul of the state militia to make it a more organized, disciplined, and reliable body of citizen soldiers. Carrington was asked to prepare a manual with new state regulations governing the militia. He produced a thorough delineation of military hierarchy, protocol, parade, and discipline for promulgation throughout the state. ...With a meager allowance from the legislature, Carrington managed to hold two annual encampments. The sham battles he had seen in Wallingford and his own study of Revolutionary battle formations now came in handy. He formed the companies into regiments and exercised them in battle maneuvers. It was hardly the level of drill and discipline which they would need should war come, but it was as much as the state legislature was willing to fund.[18]

Carrington's prewar efforts resulted in Ohio's militia being better prepared than that of most states when the war began. Just sixty hours after Lincoln's April 15 call for 75,000 men, two regiments of Ohio militiamen were on their way to Washington. With the call for Federal volunteers in May, Carrington proved adept at organizing manpower into units, getting the new soldiers equipped, and shipping them to the field. Rapid deployment of the Ohio militia played a key role in the May-June 1861 campaign for control of western Virginia.[19]

By late spring 1861 Adjutant General Carrington wanted to move on to different fields, although he feared his health problems would limit his opportunities. When Senator Salmon P. Chase was nominated to become secretary of the treasury in the Lincoln Administration, Carrington called upon him for a federal appointment, hoping for a diplomatic posting to France. Chase responded with offers of serving as a regimental sutler or perhaps as an army paymaster. Carrington thought these stations to be beneath him, but was pleased in early June when he was nominated to serve on the West Point Board of Visitors, an Academy oversight committee of presidential appointees and members of Congress. He was considering accepting the position when on June 17 Secretary Chase sent Carrington word of a new opportunity: "Dear Colonel: I give you the title actually conferred only today, though decided upon sometime since, [your name] having been on General Scott's original list."[20] During the next month, Chase sent more details on Carrington's impending appointment as colonel of one of the new regular regiments:

> I take great pleasure in enclosing herewith your Commission as a Colonel in the 18th Regiment of Infantry. ... I believe that you will organize a regiment that will do honor to yourself and the service. ...your headquarters will be, Columbus, Ohio, and I look with confidence to your success in recruiting one of the best Regiments in the Army. It is indeed a trial for your modesty that you out-rank officers of more experience, but the rule of appointing one-half the officers of the new Regiments from civil life, makes this unavoidable. I am sure no one who serves under you will find any cause of complaint.[21]

Colonel Henry Carrington resigned his position as adjutant general of Ohio on June 29, 1861. He then embarked on the challenging task of recruiting, organizing, and training a regiment of regular infantry.

* * *

Frederick Townsend knew what combat was like, for he was one of the "officers of more experience" assigned to the 18th Regulars. Townsend was Carrington's counterpart in New York prior to the war, the Empire State's adjutant general. A native of Albany and graduate of Union College in Schenectady, Townsend was also a lawyer, a member of the New York Bar since 1849. He became a captain in the New York militia during the mid-1850s and soon after became colonel of New York's 76th Regiment. Townsend's performance in that position caught the attention of New York Governor John A. King, who appointed him adjutant general in 1857. Governor Edwin D. Morgan reappointed him in 1859. Townsend, age thirty-six in 1861, had the ideal appearance of a nineteenth-century military officer, being "tall, well proportioned, of stately, soldierly bearing, active in his movements, courteous in his manners, and endowed with a high order of conversational powers." He was also an excellent choice for adjutant general, for he had traveled widely in Europe and had a sharp knowledge of military affairs.

Townsend had an early taste of Civil War combat prior to joining the 18th Infantry, although the experience was for the most part regrettable. He organized the 3rd New York Infantry Regiment shortly after the war began, was appointed its colonel, and commanded the green unit at the Battle of Big Bethel, Virginia. This clash on June 10, 1861, was more skirmish than battle, but occurring so early in the war it generated big headlines. The entire affair was poorly handled on the Union side and resulted in a Federal defeat. The enemy caused only a few casualties in the 3rd New York's ranks, but the regiment lost two killed and nineteen wounded to friendly fire from the 4th Massachusetts and 1st Vermont. Townsend's troops were clad in gray, the traditional uniform color of New York state troops, and the New Englanders mistook them for Confederates. "I would rather be a major in the Regular Army than a colonel of volunteers!" Townsend declared after the Big Bethel fiasco. He contacted Colonel Carrington, whom he had known while the two were serving as state adjutants general, and through the Ohio colonel secured a major's commission in the 18th U.S. Infantry.[22]

Townsend recruited his new regiment's band prior to leaving New York. The major obtained the services of Joseph Trigg for the 18th Infantry, a native German who had been serving as bandleader at the Brooklyn Navy Yard. The law organizing the New Army regiments authorized the pay of a second lieutenant to the leader of a regimental band. This was an increase in pay Trigg could not turn down. Trigg's connections in New York resulted in a full complement of skilled musicians enlisting for duty with the 18th. Carrington outfitted the musicians with high-quality instruments made of German silver, from Dadworth's of Astor Place in New York City. Trigg obtained a unique instrument from his own homeland contacts, an item the 18th Infantry Band would continue to use after the war: "Mr. Trigg secured from Germany a set of bell chimes set in circles around a staff which was topped with an eagle and various plumes and called the Shellebaum ['tree of bells']. Skill in its elevation and withdrawing gave a very effective effect in contrast with the cymbals. It was always retained with the Band, and even while on the Plains was an object of great envy on the part of all visiting Indian Chiefs, and almost fabulous quantities of skins, pelts and even ponies were offered for its acquisition."[23]

As Townsend and the band made their way from New York to Ohio, Carrington was busy organizing the regiment. Scores of Columbus citizens lined up at the downtown 18th Infantry recruiting rendezvous as soon as it opened in early July. The regiment's headquarters was in the Crittenden Hotel building on West Broadway in Columbus. Carrington's staff used the four-story structure as offices, storerooms, lodgings, and classrooms. A vacant building nearby on Broad Street served as a barracks. The first batch of recruits reported in on July 10.

Colonel Carrington's experience as Ohio adjutant general served him well in his new duties. His well-known name, long association with state military forces, and success while managing Ohio's volunteer recruitment resulted in a large number of men signing up for service with the 18th Regulars. One volunteer regiment in particular channeled a large number of men into the 18th Infantry. The 16th Ohio Volunteers, a three-month regiment recruited in the Columbus area shortly after the war began, had styled itself as the "Carrington Guards." Toward the end of the unit's ninety-day existence most of its soldiers were not willing to reenlist in another volunteer outfit, but upon learning that Carrington was organizing his own regular regiment they sent word that they were eager to join the 18th Infantry. Carrington arranged through the War Department to have these men discharged early from their three-month commitment and transferred directly onto the 18th Infantry's roles.[24] Other contacts with Ohio civic leaders yielded additional manpower. One of Carrington's recruiters, Captain Lyman M. Kellogg, enlisted the aid of a local militia officer:

> Columbus O July 25th 1861
> Head Quarters Recruiting Rendezvous
> 18th Infantry, U.S. Army
> Old Broadway House

To Capt. McLille
Columbus O

Dear Sir

We are now earnestly engaged in organizing the 18th Infantry U.S. Army, commanded by Col. H.B. Carrington late Adjutant General of this State. It is desired to effect this organization as rapidly as possible. Knowing your patriotic efforts, and acquainted with the deep interest you take, in the maintenance of our government, I confidently address you, hoping it may be in your power to give us effectual aid. This Regiment will be armed with the Springfield Rifle, a weapon superior to any other, either at long or short range. It is hoped we can organize this Regiment consisting of Twenty Four Hundred Men in four weeks. When organized *one third* of *the officers will be taken from the ranks.* The opportunity thus given for promotion from the grade of *Private* to that of commissioned officer in the Regular Army, ought to be a great inducement with patriotic young men in *our State to enlist.* It is no longer expected that this war will be a short one; indeed it may take much longer than *five years* to crush out this great rebellion in our land. I forward you herewith Rosters in English and German for use among your friend and acquaintances. For every recruit you send me I will pay you the sum of *two dollars.*

> I remain sir
> With great respect
> Your Obt Servant

L.M. KELLOGG
Captain 18th Infantry USA
Recruiting Officer[25]

The regiment was not filled as quickly as Captain Kellogg hoped, although four companies were organized in less than a month. The regulars would soon learn that the volunteer service held a number of advantages in attracting recruits, but Kellogg's letter mentions two distinct advantages the regulars possessed. One was the fact that regular units were equipped with the best arms and equipment available. The American arms industry was woefully inadequate as the war began. The armory at Springfield, Massachusetts could produce only about 3,000 rifles per month during the war's first summer. Many volunteers in 1861 were equipped with either antiquated firearms that had been gathering dust for years or with substandard imported weapons; oftentimes, the civilian purchasing agents responsible for arming state volunteers could obtain nothing better. The regulars had access to Federal arsenals, and the U.S. Ordnance Department equipped all regular infantrymen with the model 1861 .58-caliber Springfield rifle, then the state-of-the-art for mass produced, muzzle loading firearms. "We have just received our new muskets," one of the new regulars of 1861 excitedly wrote his parents. "They were made at Springfield and are perfect beauties, just the thing for '*seshess*,' and we have men who know how to use them." Even as late as November 1862, the four volunteer regiments with which the 18th Infantry was brigaded were all armed with a hodgepodge of weapons: 56 percent of the 9th Ohio's weapons were smoothbore muskets, the 2nd Minnesota carried four varieties of weapons including some smoothbore, the 35th Ohio's troops all carried either imported Enfields or .69-caliber rifles, and the 87th Indiana wielded Austrian rifles of three different calibers. Only the 18th Regulars in this brigade carried what is considered the standard infantry weapon of the Civil War. The rest of a regular's clothing, equipment, and accouterments matched the superiority of his firearm. While it was common for volunteer troops in 1861 to be clad in makeshift uniforms, regulars were decked out in nothing less than full regulation kit, to include dress uniforms of nine-button frock coats, wide-brimmed black felt Hardee hats, brass shoulder scales, and prewar style dark blue trousers.[26]

Another factor working in the Regular Army's favor, as Kellogg alluded to in the letter to McLille, was the War Department's authorization to fill the second lieutenant slots in New Army infantry regiments from the enlisted ranks. Carrington used these commissions (which totaled twenty-four per New Army infantry regiment) as very effective recruiting incentives: "Quite a number of students from Colleges with which I had been associated as Trustee, or through other intimate relations, who had sought commissions in the State Volunteer Service, expressed a preference to enlist in the 18th, if after enlistment they were assured of receiving an appointment [to second lieutenant] according to the excellence of their service, and military acquirements during the first year."[27]

In addition to Shepherd and Townsend, other officers assigned to the 18th Infantry had a great deal of experience. Six captains and four first lieutenants were regulars transferred from Old Army regiments. One of the former, Henry Douglass, was an 1852 West Pointer and the son and grandson of West Point faculty members. Douglass, a lieutenant in the 9th Infantry, was himself on the Academy's staff as the war started. He and a few other officers were dispatched from West Point to Washington in the late spring of 1861 to assist the War Department with the army expansion. Douglass was attached to Major Sykes's regular infantry battalion on July 5 and commanded Company K of the 3rd Infantry at the First Battle of Bull Run. Douglass received his captaincy in the 18th U.S. after the battle and reported to Columbus on October 28. Most of the 18th Infantry's other officers had served with militia or volunteer units, such as Captain Charles E. Denison, an 1845 graduate of Norwich (a military college in Vermont) who had commanded a company in the 8th Illinois Volunteers during the early months of the war. Lieutenant Robert Sutherland of New York had experience of a different sort, he having spent some time as a midshipman at the United States Naval Academy, a former member of the Class of 1856. The two Regular Army sergeants assigned to the 18th Infantry as new second lieutenants were particularly experienced. Lieutenant James Simons had served eleven years in the ranks and had been a first sergeant in the 4th U.S. Artillery prior to being assigned to Carrington's regiment. Lieutenant James Powell had spent even more time in uniform. He had served in the Mexican War as a private in the wartime-era 11th U.S. Infantry and then earned his first sergeant's chevrons on the frontier with the 1st U.S. Dragoons and 1st Cavalry. At the other end of the spectrum, a few of the 18th's officers were as green as the privates. One new recruit could only speculate on how the first 18th Infantry officer he met had received a commission: "The recruiting officer, Captain Jacob M. Eyster, had been appointed in the regular service from

Pennsylvania, by Simon Cameron, Secretary of War. The reasons were not apparent, but might have been surmised from his previous quasi-military life as commandant of a school of cadets somewhere in Pennsylvania, or possibly, to his having a large, fierce moustache, [which was] intensified by forming a large part of his small stature something like five feet."[28]

Carrington opened recruiting offices across Ohio, Indiana, and Pennsylvania. Major William A. Stokes, recently a judge in Greensburg, Pennsylvania, was appointed commander of the regiment's 3rd Battalion in September 1861. He managed the recruitment of his battalion in the Keystone State, while the 1st and 2nd Battalions were based out of Columbus. Officers not assigned as recruiters remained at the regiment's headquarters, learning the basics of officership and infantry tactics. Captain Kellogg, an 1852 West Pointer with experience in the prewar 10th Infantry and 3rd Artillery, conducted most of this initial instruction. Kellogg had been cashiered for misconduct in May 1860 (his drinking habits kept him in constant trouble), but upon the outbreak of the war had immediately signed up for service with the 24th Ohio. He performed well as a company commander in that regiment and in early July received a Regular Army captaincy in Carrington's unit.[29]

Colonel Carrington established a training camp four miles north of Columbus on the Delaware Road, naming it Camp Thomas in honor of Colonel Lorenzo Thomas, the army's adjutant general. Temporary structures, timber walls with canvas roofs, were constructed to house the camp's headquarters, hospital, and guard room. Streets for the battalions were staked out and soon lined with tents. The first residents arrived on August 11, marching from the Broad Street barracks under the command of 1st Sergeant Henry B. Freeman of Company B, 2nd Battalion, an Old Army veteran of the 10th U.S. Infantry. Camp Thomas rapidly filled with recruits during the coming weeks. Enough troops had gathered by the end of August to flesh out the 1st and 2nd Battalions. These battalions contained more than 1,200 soldiers the following November. The 1st Battalion, commanded by Captain Henry Douglass, consisted of Companies A, B, C, D, and F, 1st Battalion, plus Company D from the unformed 3rd Battalion. Major Townsend's 2nd Battalion also contained six companies: A, B, C, D, E, and F.

Townsend had arrived at Camp Thomas in early September. Since he was probably the only major in the Regular Army at that time who could claim to have led a regiment in combat, Townsend took over the training program of the 18th's officers. Captains and lieutenants gathered at camp headquarters for class each evening. Upon a large table were wooden blocks representing the companies of the regiment, with which the major illustrated intricate tactical maneuvers. His students would then take turns manipulating the blocks in response to Townsend's commands. Like the officers, the men of the 18th Infantry were learning the details of military life. A daily routine of guard, drill, and parade instructed them in the care and use of their uniforms, weapons, and equipment. As summer changed to autumn in 1861, Colonel Carrington recorded that the routine at Camp Thomas began to resemble that of any Regular Army post: "From the first installment of the Camp and the organ-ization of the Band as well as the drum corps, guard mounting was a strictly formal parade as was the sunset dress parade. On those occasions all officers appeared in full uniform as well as the men, and all details of soldiers to act as Orderlies depended upon the brightness of their brass soldier scales, their gloves, and their shoes. During evenings, weather permitting, the Band played before Headquarters for the entertainment of the garrison."[30]

In addition to drilling and garrison duties, maneuvers in the field schooled the men in other aspects of soldiering. Carrington requested permission to conduct rifle target practice with live ammu-nition during early November. Although marksmanship training would become more widespread in the Union Army during the last year of the war, practicing with live ammunition in 1861 was a key aspect of the regulars' training that set them apart from their volun-teer comrades.[31] An exercise that took place in downtown Columbus during early October made headlines in local newspapers:

> The street parade of the 18th U.S. Infantry, in full dress, and sup-plied with twenty rounds of blank-cartridge was really a wonderful exhibition of the possible use of troops against a riot, in force. Nearly 1200 men participated in the parade, marching in column, by sec-tions, as the streets were too narrow for a full platoon front. A few skirmishers scattered along the flanks occasionally fired a round as if picking off offenders at windows along the route. Upon reaching State Street, moving southward, firings were delivered in turn by sec-tions east, south, and west through the exposed streets. As soon as the first section fired it moved by the right flank at double time to the rear, and was instantly replaced by another until the whole advancing column had in turn delivered fire from the same standing

point, and the original first section, as well as the entire column was at its original halt.

Hardly twelve minutes had passed when the Order "Left, into line, wheel, march" was given. Then followed, first, "fire by Companies, beginning on the right;" second, "fire by battalions, beginning on the right;" third, "Attention, Brigade" each battalion commander repeating the appropriate order in accordance with previous notice. Three rounds were to be given for the "firing at will" which was done. When the bugle sounded, "cease firing" and upon the Order "Forward head of column to the left," the Band struck up "Yankee Doodle," and the whole column, after a brief street parade, moved back to Camp Thomas, and went without either officer or man having been allowed to turn his eyes to, or speak to any observer during the entire afternoon's drill.[32]

* * *

Unfortunately, most Regular Army regiments were not able to duplicate the 18th Infantry's successful recruitment and were having a much harder time filling their ranks. Regular officers proved to be their own worst enemy in this endeavor. With the colonels commanding the new regiments soon promoted to general officer positions and many other regular officers accepting commissions with volunteer units, command of regular regiments went to the ranking officer who reported for duty. This was usually a lieutenant colonel or major, sometimes a mere captain. None of the other regiments had a commander with the local prestige Henry Carrington.

The majority of the officers who remained with the regulars, regardless of rank, were inexperienced in recruiting. Prior to the war regular regiments occasionally enlisted troops directly, but the majority of new soldiers came from two specialized organizations: the General Recruiting Service, which recruited manpower for infantry and artillery regiments, and the Mounted Recruiting Service, which did the same for horse regiments. Infantry recruits were sent to Fort Columbus, New York, for initial training. They were then dispatched on an as-needed basis to the regiments in the field. This centralized recruiting system worked well in the antebellum era, particularly since the recruiting services concentrated their stations in the populous cities of the northern United States, where there was always a surplus of unemployed immigrants willing to enlist. The recruiting services were shutdown during the expansion of the Regular Army in 1861, for the Federal government did not want to interfere with the states' recruitment of volunteers. Instead of relying on the recruiting services, each regular regiment was to fend for itself and manage its own recruitment.

While the 18th Infantry's recruiting effort in 1861 was easily the best of any regular regiment, even that performance paled in comparison with how quickly most state regiments were filled with troops. Recruiting officers for volunteer and regular units often set up shop alongside each other in a community. It did not take long for regular recruiters to find out that it was difficult to compete for manpower with state regiments. Most regular officers were strangers to the locals, while volunteer officers were usually established leaders of the local populace. Recruits overwhelming preferred to enlist in a volunteer regiment, led by men they knew, than in a regular regiment officered by strangers. The Regular Army's reputation for high standards and tough discipline also discouraged recruiting. Most men rightly considered the volunteers to be a much smoother path to military service.

The rapid mobilization of volunteer regiments interfered with the Regular Army's recruiting effort in other ways as well. One of the most common intrusions on a regular officer's time in the early months of the war was being placed on mustering duty. After a state regiment completed its initial recruitment and assembled the requisite number of companies, the volunteers were sworn (or "mustered") into Federal service and officially became members of the Union Army. The signature of a Regular Army officer was necessary on the documents to make everything legal. The only regular officers available in many areas were the recruiters attempting to sign up men for the Regular Army. It is understandable why many regular recruiting officers spent more time assisting in the organization of full-strength, motivated volunteer regiments when their only competing activity was the frustrating work of trying to convince potential recruits to join the regulars. Mustering duty also afforded regular officers a chance to rub elbows with a community's political leaders, and many of these officers in due time were offered state commissions to command volunteer regiments.

If this did not make things bad enough for the Regular Army, citizens easily discerned that the deck was stacked decidedly in favor of joining a volunteer unit. A volunteer committed himself for only three years or the duration of the war, whichever was shorter. A regular had to sign up for five years in uniform regardless of how long the war might last. The Regular Army traditionally did not enlist married men, while the volunteers were under no such restriction. A third strike against the regulars was the large cash bounties that many local governments paid recruits for enlistment in state regiments. Depending on the time and place a volunteer joined up, he could look forward to a tidy sum from his city, county, and state. The Federal government threw in a national bounty as well. Regular recruits received Federal bonuses and nothing more. Perhaps worst of all was the deduction of $2.13 per month from a regular's pay. The accumulated monthly two dollars would be returned to him upon discharge. This was another leftover regulation of the Old Army, a method to cover excess clothing expenses and also a subtle way to discourage desertion. The thirteen cents went to support the Soldier's Home in Washington, a retirement home for disabled veterans. Since a private's pay was only thirteen dollars a month, these deductions meant regulars received 14.2 percent less "take home pay" than volunteers. The War Department eventually corrected some of the Regular Army's regulatory disadvantages, but their being in place during the initial rush to the colors in 1861 caused many potential Regular Army recruits to look elsewhere. Faced with choices like these, it is amazing that anyone signed up for service with the regulars.[33]

Only about 65,000 citizens joined the Regular Army during the Civil War, a slight number when compared with the many hundreds of thousands of soldiers who served in volunteer units. Some of those who signed a regular enlistment contract did so for the fine uniforms, equipment, and weapons. Although the Regular Army's professional reputation discouraged many, it also attracted a few men into the ranks; then as now, tough military service appealed to a small segment of the American population. William H. Bisbee was a Rhode Islander residing in Delaware County, Ohio, when the war broke out. He had served in the prewar Ohio militia, but decided to join the ranks of the 18th Infantry. "President Lincoln believed [the war] would soon be ended, but by summer this fallacy grew more apparent," Bisbee explained in his postwar memoirs. "More men were wanted, recruiting offices were opened and after carefully pondering over the question of what regiment to enter, I joined the regulars, believing they would be led by more experienced officers." A number of discharged Old Army veterans signed on again with new regular regiments, while the chance to earn a regular commission, a military credential identical to that bestowed upon graduates of West Point, brought in other enlistees.[34]

Men of all stripes ended up in regular uniforms. The Regular Army attracted its share of down-and-out persons and criminals, but not at rates much different from the volunteers (at least not for the first half of the war). Immigrants also joined in large numbers. Foreigners had made up a large portion of the prewar Regular Army, a majority in some units. This trend continued during the war itself. A recent analysis of Regular Army enlistment records reveals that 46 percent of regular soldiers in the Civil War were born overseas. Having recently arrived on American shores, many foreign-born recruits lacked the regional attachment that led their American-born neighbors to join state units. The majority of the immigrant regulars came from Germanic states or Ireland, although just about every company of regulars contained a sprinkling of troops from a number of European nations. An immigrant from the Netherlands who trained at Camp Thomas was impressed with the national makeup of his brother regulars: "The personnel of our company was of all nationalities, about as hard a lot of men as could be put together, Irish, German, Polish, French, English, Yankees, three of us Hollanders. Most of them came from railroad and canal work and were given to drinking as a duck is to water." Ethnic volunteer regiments were not uncommon in the Union Army, but a rather unique array of nationalities stood side-by-side in Regular Army ranks, the result of regular units recruiting their troops from many localities in a number of different states. These men were excellent soldiers more often than not, and America was fortunate to have their services. It is safe to say that neither before nor since has an army been so filled with foreigners who were more willing to fight for an adopted nation.[35]

Although the Regular Army's ethnic makeup was indeed varied, many of the new regulars were just average Americans, possessing the same motivations and hopes as their volunteer comrades. In the bewildering world of the Union Army in 1861, few recruits had a real notion of what they were getting themselves into. Many ended up in the Regular Army simply because a regular recruiting station was the first they happened to see. Such was the case of Virginian Robert Kennedy: "I...went to Parkersburg and enlisted under the first officer I met, who was Lieutenant Ogden of the regular army. As I was not yet twenty years of age, I had to get my father's consent to join the army. The lieutenant fixed up the papers for me. I took them away, forged my father's name to them, took them back to him and was sworn into service on the 27th day of August 1861, by a justice of the peace; and thus became a member of Company C, 2nd Battalion, 18th U.S. Infantry."[36]

* * *

Sergeant Major Frederick Phisterer enjoyed barking out commands to both immigrant and homegrown recruits on the Camp Thomas parade ground. His thick *Württemberger* accent caused some amusing incidents on parade as he put the 18th Infantry's recruits through their paces, but he knew that making regular soldiers out of raw manpower was never an easy task. Of all the men then gathering at Camp Thomas, Phisterer was the man for this job. Although he was only twenty-four years old and the three light blue chevrons and matching arches on his frock coat sleeve looked rather new, single half chevrons on Phisterer's lower sleeves belied his youth and the brightness of his insignia. The service stripe indicated that the sergeant major had already served five years as an Old Army regular. He was one of the many foreigners in Carrington's regiment, a German immigrant from Stuttgart who came to America in 1855 (one of the reasons he left his native land was to avoid conscription). Phisterer lived amidst the burgeoning German-American population in New York City and Pennsylvania for a few months, vainly attempting to earn a respectable living. Curiosity about the rest of America soon got the better of him. He had been enamored with the American West since his younger days, and also realized that to make his way in his new country he would have to improve his rudimentary English. He decided to leave the immigrant communities in which he had been residing and in December 1855 enlisted in the Regular Army. Being only nineteen at the time, he had to lie about his age. He was posted to California and spent the next five years exploring the lands he had dreamed about, but never quite losing his German accent. Prior to completing his term of service in December 1860, the young Phisterer had been promoted to sergeant in the 3rd U.S. Artillery, participated in the 1857–1858 operations against the Mormons, accompanied some mapping expeditions, and saw action in a number of short campaigns against native tribes of the Pacific Northwest.[37]

Phisterer was trying his hand at farming in Medina, Ohio, immediately prior to the rebellion. The ex-sergeant decided that "after the

first battle of Bull Run, I considered it my duty to re-enter the service" and he signed up with the 18th Infantry on July 31, 1861. Being
one of the few enlisted men in the regiment with service in the prewar regulars, Phisterer was immediately promoted to sergeant major
of the 1st Battalion. "Of course, I had my hands full," Phisterer
recalled about the early days at Camp Thomas, "drilled recruits,
instructed non commissioned officers, looked after the office work
of the companies as they were organized, made returns and reports,
and was a sort of advisor in everything and to everybody. As general
instructor and helper all around, I officiated at guard mountings as
adjutant and officer of the day, and at parades as adjutant."
Carrington recognized talent when he saw it. The short, dark-haired
German became the first 18th Infantry sergeant to receive a commission from the ranks. He began wearing the unadorned sky blue
shoulder straps of an infantry second lieutenant on October 30,
1861. "Excellent in all respects," the colonel wrote on the new officer's commission certificate. "Capable, prompt and faithful in every
line of duty." Phisterer was appointed adjutant of Major Townsend's
2nd Battalion.[38]

Lieutenant Colonel Shepherd could have greatly assisted
Phisterer in whipping the men into shape, but the regiment's number two officer was able to spend only a short time at Camp Thomas
that autumn before being recalled to New York for more mustering
duty. The extent of Carrington's reliance on Shepherd's advice and
comradeship is evident in a letter the colonel sent to Shepherd on
October 28, 1861: "I miss you very much indeed. I have twelve good
companies in camp. ...You would not know the 18th today. Of over
1000 men not a man was in hospital and the camp is as clean as a
floor. I risk nothing by saying *others* call it a model camp. Is there
no end to the N.Y. mustering, or must I loose your experience and
trust as is usual? Give me some hope that I may soon welcome you
back, where the Regiment will make you feel at home."[39]

The 18th Infantry began to forge a reputation for being an elite
regiment of regular troops as these battalions took shape during the
last half of 1861. Although the men who joined the regulars early in
the war were largely indistinguishable from those signing on with volunteer units, the presence of a few leaders transferred from the Old
Army provided a leavening of experience that made all the difference.
Officers and sergeants who knew their business, not enthusiastic
amateurs, trained regular outfits like the 18th Infantry. After a few

months of training, the men of the 18th began to think of themselves as a special breed of soldier, much different from the men in the Ohio volunteer regiments also training near Columbus. While being from the same town or county generated much *esprit de corps* in volunteer companies, the regulars took pride in their more thorough training, superior equipment, competent leadership, and professionalism. When Sergeant Amos Fleagle of C/2/18th U.S.[40] learned that his younger brother Uriah was thinking about joining the Union Army, the sergeant immediately wrote home to his family in Maryland: "if he wants to enlist, I will give him a piece of advice: let him enlist in the regular armey. ...if he has the makings of a soldier, by good conduct and attention to duty he can easy rise to the possision of a Non commisioned officer and from this class the law provides that meritorious men may be selected as the warrants of the service may require it for promotion to the ranks of commissoned officers. and if he's Bount to enlist by all means enlist in the 18th U.S. Inf'y which when full will be the largest and best equipt regiment in the service."[41]

* * *

General Winfield Scott was impressed. Carrington's training program at Camp Thomas was rapidly producing a first-rate unit. Scott was not as impressed with the other new regular regiments, most of whom were still lagging far behind the 18th in terms of readiness for field duty. The New Army's eleven regiments and the existing nineteen regiments of the Old Army all began to recruit in earnest during June and July 1861, but just a paltry 1,916 men joined the regulars during those two months. That was not nearly enough to fill the existing vacancies in the Old Army, much less service the 20,000 empty billets of the New Army. Recruiting received a boost in August when Congress reduced the enlistment term for regulars from five years to three, and 3,098 men became regulars that month. The August success was short-lived. Enlistments averaged only 1,590 each month for the remainder of the year. By the end of 1861 only 14,476 men had joined the Regular Army since the beginning of the war—and about 10 percent of those new troops were concentrated in just one regiment, the 18th Infantry.[42]

To remedy this situation, the general-in-chief designated Camp Thomas as a training depot for regular infantry regiments. Being located at Camp Thomas with Carrington's command hopefully would cause the efficient recruitment and training of the 18th

Infantry to rub off on other units. Scott laid out his plan in late October:

SPECIAL ORDERS   WAR DEPARTMENT,
No. 285   Adjutant General's Office,
                    Washington, October 23, 1861.

A camp of instruction will be established at Columbus, Ohio, for the 18th Infantry and other such regiments of the Regular Army as may from time be ordered to that place. Unless otherwise ordered by the Department, the senior regimental officer present will command the camp.

The 16th Regiment of Infantry, under the officers now at its depot, will immediately be put *en route* for Columbus, at which point the recruiting of the companies not yet organized will be superintended by the regimental commander.

By Order:

L. THOMAS,
Adjutant General.[43]

A similar order established another camp of instruction at Perryville, Maryland, for regular regiments in the East. These instructions represent Winfield Scott's final attempt to ensure that the Civil War regulars were properly organized and trained. The aging general retired one week later, and Major General George B. McClellan was appointed general-in-chief of the Union Army.[44]

A battalion of the 16th U.S. Infantry, a New Army regiment based out of Chicago, arrived at Camp Thomas on November 3. The growing pains this regiment experienced during 1861 exemplifies the Regular Army's early-war difficulties. The colonel of the regiment, Andrew Porter, was the grandson of a Revolutionary War general and a cousin of President Lincoln's mother-in-law. A brevetted Mexican War veteran, Porter was a captain in the Regiment of Mounted Riflemen when the Civil War broke out. Shortly after his appointment to colonel of his new regiment, Porter was promoted to brigadier general of volunteers and never served with the 16th Infantry. The second-in-command, Henry M. Naglee, was also unknown to the unit. An 1835 West Pointer from Pennsylvania, Naglee had resigned his commission before serving a single day in the army. His education and also limited service as a volunteer in the Mexican War was deemed enough to qualify him to be the lieutenant colonel of the 16th Regulars. He spent the first winter of the war in Washington, resigned his regular commission in January 1862, and became a volunteer general the following month.

With the colonel and lieutenant colonel absent, command of the regiment went to Major Adam J. Slemmer. This 1850 West Pointer's name had been a household word throughout America for a short time in early 1861. As a lieutenant in the 1st U.S. Artillery, Slemmer commanded the Federal installations at Pensacola, Florida, during the Fort Sumter crisis. His resolute actions in holding Fort Pickens in Pensacola Bay while surrounded by belligerent Floridians propelled the lieutenant into the national spotlight and caught President Lincoln's eye. His rewards included a gold medal from the city of New York and a promotion from lieutenant of artillery to major in the 16th U.S. Infantry. In command of the 16th Infantry by default, Major "Old Pickens" Slemmer set about organizing the regiment. He opened regimental headquarters in Chicago on July 7, 1861. On August 21 the major established a training camp sixteen miles outside the city near Desplaines Station on the Chicago & Northwestern Railroad. Slemmer dispatched officers on recruiting duty and began a training program at the camp, which the men christened Camp Slemmer.[45]

Just as the new major was getting things rolling, he was detached from the 16th Infantry. In late August the commanding general of the Department of the Cumberland in Cincinnati appointed Slemmer the department's inspector general. One of the most critical shortages in the rapidly expanding Union Army was experienced officers to serve in high-level staff positions. Commanders everywhere routinely stripped away talented subordinates from their units and assigned them to staff duty. Regulars were the officers of choice for these assignments, particularly field-grade officers (i.e., majors, lieutenant colonels, and colonels) possessing Old Army credentials, but anyone holding a regular commission was subject to such a levy, even a civilian appointee whose Regular Army experience was practically nothing. While inexperienced volunteer generals gained a significant asset by having regulars as staff officers, these assignments further ensured that regular units usually had very few officers available for troop duty. Major Slemmer would remain on the department staff for most of the following year.

The 16th Infantry's next ranking officer, Major Franklin Flint, proved to be of no use to the regiment. An 1837 graduate of West Point, he spent the first two years of the war commanding a depot

Recruiting Poster, 16th U.S. Infantry
Philadelphia, May 1862

In addition to "Good Pay, Good Food, Good Officers," this poster's fine print informs potential recruits that "The Col., Andrew Porter, and the Lieut. Col., Henry M. Naglee, have had long experience in military life, and are both distinguished sons of Pennslyvania." It fails to state that neither of these officers ever served with the 16th Infantry.

at Alton, Illinois, and was then promoted to lieutenant colonel of
the 7th U.S. Infantry in October 1863. Major Phillip Sidney
Coolidge was next in line and took command of the 16th Infantry
as Slemmer departed. Coolidge was technically a civilian appointee,
but the prewar resume of this Massachusetts native included a number of adventures that few professional soldiers could match. A
great-grandson of Thomas Jefferson, as a youth Coolidge was educated at a military school in France. After a somewhat wandering
early adulthood traveling throughout Europe and Asia, Coolidge
settled down at the age of twenty in 1853 and took a job as a
research associate at the Harvard Observatory, which was then
America's foremost center of astronomy. Coolidge developed into a
skilled astronomer, and was the first person to observe certain
aspects of the rings around the planet Saturn, discoveries that are
still being analyzed a century and a half later. In 1855 Harvard sent
Coolidge abroad to determine precise longitudes between Europe
and America. He and his accompanying forty to fifty chronometers
logged six trans-Atlantic voyages and more than 18,000 miles at
sea accomplishing the task. Coolidge apparently became bored with
the scientific world by the end of the 1850s. He returned to Europe
and fought against the French in the 1859–1860 battles for the uni-
fication of Italy, and then somehow found time in 1860 to stir up
anti-French agitation in Mexico before accompanying an American
expedition exploring distant reaches of the Pacific. Sidney Coolidge
arrived back on American shores the next year to find his homeland
at war with itself and a coveted field-grade Regular Army commission awaiting him.[46]

Major Coolidge reported for duty in Chicago during late August
1861. While the major possessed abundant energy and determination, it took him a few months to acquire the finer points of recruiting, organizing, and training a regiment of regulars. Coolidge
eventually got things running smoothly, but the troops at Camp
Slemmer keenly felt the disarray at headquarters during late summer and autumn. Lieutenant William J. Stewart, an officer with no
previous military experience, served as the regiment's commissary
officer and quartermaster. The requirements and paperwork of his
duties quickly overwhelmed him. The adjutant of Camp Slemmer,
Lieutenant Samuel B. Lawrence, sent a series of urgent requests to
Lieutenant Stewart during October 1861. On October 6, the issue
was potatoes: "The party with whom you made a contract for

potatoes, has failed to deliver them, and we have been without for two days past." Three days later, candles: "I beg to call your attention to the candles, last sent to us. They are inferior to the former ones and are made of tallow, made by a patent process to resemble the adamantine. The allowance for each tent does not burn over an hour, and there is much complaint in consequence." Also on October 9, beans: "The beans sent to us yesterday are very inferior and dirty and unfit for use, and we hold them subject to your order, and you will please furnish us as soon as possible with a like quantity of proper quality." In late September Major Coolidge sent word to the army's quartermaster general in Washington that clothing was also a problem: "I have the honor to state...that neither Drawers nor haversacks have been received. I respectfully beg that permission be granted me to have Drawers for four companies made here at once by contract, if they cannot be forwarded, as the men are beginning to suffer for want of them." With most of the leaders' efforts focused on procurement of basic necessities, training recruits became a secondary priority.[47]

The regiment's shabby condition also hindered its recruiting effort. "I have...the honor to state that recruiting for the regiment is very slow," Coolidge informed the War Department on September 20, "and that in the large towns and cities it is almost impossible to procure men." By the end of September, when 18th Infantry strength was approaching 1,000, only 274 men were present for duty in the 16th Infantry's ranks. Coolidge organized three skeletal companies that month, with D/1/16th U.S. being formed in October.[48] The 16th Infantry's anemic recruiting effort during the winter of 1861–1862 so alarmed the War Department that Adjutant General Lorenzo Thomas requested a written explanation from each of the regiment's recruiting officers. Lieutenant William Smyth's reply should have been required reading for all War Department staff officers:

Recruiting Station 16th Infantry
Milwaukee, Wis. Feb 10th 1862

Gen. L. Thomas
Adjutant General U.S.A.
Washington, D.C.

Sir-

In a letter from your office of the 29th ult. I am directed to report to the Adjutant General in regard to my failure in securing recruits. A duplicate there of to be furnished my Com'g Officer.

In justice to myself I beg leave to submit that I commenced recruiting only on the 10th day of December 1861, when I relieved 1st Lt. A.W. Allyn, since which time, thought left without any permanent party and having to commence entirely on my own, I have enlisted ten Recruits, an exhibit which I think can hardly be called a *failure*, at least compared with results obtained at other Recruiting stations of the Regular Army.

The reasons for want of *greater success*, may I think be easily & briefly stated, as follows, viz:

1st. The State of Wisconsin has already raised Twenty Three Regiments, which have taken up nearly all her available men.

2nd. Nearly all who wish to enlist, prefer the Volunteer to the Regular Service for two very obvious reasons: 1st- because the term of enlistment is in all probability shorter & therefore the bounty greater, the volunteer who serves one or two years, receiving an equal bounty with the regular who serves three; and 2nd- the State of Wisconsin pays the sum of Five Dollars per month to every volunteer who has a family dependent upon him, some counties & Cities also furnishing an additional gratuity amounting in some instances to nearly Thirty Dollars per month for the total pay of the Volunteer Soldier.

> Very Respectfully Sir
> Your Obedient Servant
>
> WM. SMYTH
> 1st Lt. 16th Infantry
> Recruiting Officer[49]

Private Jacob Van Zwaluwenburg of Michigan was one of the 16th Infantry recruits assigned to Company D. Unlike most American "Dutchmen" of the nineteenth century, Van Zwaluwenburg actually was Dutch and not German, born in Gelderland Province of the Netherlands in 1843. He and his family came to America in 1850 to avoid the conscription of Jacob's older brother Gerret, although Gerret immediately joined the 2nd Michigan Volunteers in April 1861 after Lincoln's call for 75,000 three-month troops. The youthful Jacob wanted to join also, but as he stood just a little over five feet two inches and was only 18 years old, his older sister told him that the army "wanted men, not boys." After further calls for troops later in the year, he could no longer resist. He walked down Burdick Street in Kalamazoo on October 10, 1861, and the first recruiting office he came across was Captain

Henry Tilden's of the 16th Regular Infantry. Tilden did what he could to discourage the young recruit:

> Captain Tilden, the officer in charge, sized me up and said, "My boy, you are too young and lack a half inch of the required height," and he advised me like a father to go home, saying the war would most likely last the whole term of service, three years, and depicted the dangers and hardships of war in such strong language that would discourage most anyone. I pleaded to be accepted, that if he refused I would try the Thirteenth Michigan office across the street. "Well, if you are bound to go," he said, "you will have to secure consent of your parents." I told him I had none. "Then consent of your guardian, or appoint one." So I appointed a stranger sawing wood in the back yard, who gave consent.[50]

It is not surprising that the 16th Infantry could scrape together only a few hundred troops when an officer like Captain Tilden was one of its recruiters, a man who could depict the "dangers and hardships of war" even though he was a civilian appointee who had never heard a shot fired in anger (he would end up being dropped from the Regular Army's rolls in February 1862). With recruitment proceeding so slowly, Major Coolidge became concerned about quartering his troops during a winter in northern Illinois. In early October he requested funds to transform Camp Slemmer into a more permanent post:

> Head Quarters 16th Inf.
> Chicago 2 October 1861
>
> General Montgomery C. Meigs
> Quartermaster General
>
> General
> I have the honor to inform you that the approved estimate of funds required for the service of the Quartermaster Department of the 16th Inf. for the last quarter of 1861 was forwarded today.
> In explanation of the estimates for materials for Buildings, Hire of mechanics, hire of teamsters, hire of ground for encampment, I beg respectfully to call your attention to the following facts:
> In one month the troops now in camp will begin to suffer from the severity of the weather. It will be impossible for them to remain in tents during the winter. The regiment is being recruited very slowly. At its present rate of increase it will require two years to raise it.

The said estimates are for funds to erect barracks for one battalion, of sufficient durability to last the necessary time to raise the three battalions forming the regiment without material repairs.

I respectfully request the approval of the estimates to be forwarded in time to have the troops moved into winter quarters by the 2nd week of November at the latest.

I also respectfully request that permission be granted me to use my own discretion in building them.

> Very Respectfully
> Your Obdt Svt,
>
> SIDNEY COOLIDGE
> Major 16th Inf.
> Commanding[51]

Instead of funds for upgrading Camp Slemmer, the War Department replied with Scott's General Orders 285. Camp Slemmer was shut down and the 16th Infantry sent to Camp Thomas. Although Coolidge's 16th Infantry consisted of only the regimental headquarters and four weak companies when it arrived in Ohio, the regiment included a number of experienced officers. Captain Edwin F. Townsend commanded 1/16th U.S., an 1854 graduate of West Point who served two years in the 3rd Artillery prior to resigning his commission in 1856. He had also briefly served with the New Army's 14th Infantry prior to joining the 16th. Lieutenant William H. Ingerton marched with Townsend, an eleven-year veteran of the Old Army and former sergeant major of the 1st U.S. Dragoons. Other officers with no prewar experience, such as Captain Robert Erskine Anderson (R.E.A.) Crofton, an Irish-born Delawarean commanding A/1/16th U.S., were quickly catching on to the Regular Army way of doing business. Carrington's 18th Infantry staff integrated Major Coolidge into the command structure at Camp Thomas and began to smooth out the rough edges on Captain Townsend's battalion. The 16th Infantry's drill and discipline were approaching Regular Army standards less than a month later. Simply being stationed at Camp Thomas greatly improved the regiment's enlistment numbers. Two hundred forty-eight men joined its ranks in November 1861 alone, more than double the regiment's monthly average. Major Coolidge organized two additional companies, E and F, out of the new manpower.[52]

One of the regiment's new members was nineteen-year-old Edgar R. Kellogg, younger brother of Captain Lyman Kellogg of the 18th Infantry. A native of Norwalk, Ohio, where he had been studying law before the war, Kellogg already had some field experience prior to signing on with the 16th regulars. He enlisted in an Ohio volunteer company on April 15, 1861, the day he found out Ft. Sumter had fallen. He was a good soldier and natural leader, becoming a corporal two days after enlistment and a sergeant the next week. Kellogg's company was formally mustered into Federal service as Company A, 24th Ohio Volunteers, in Columbus during June 1861, and the youthful Kellogg was appointed as the regiment's sergeant major. He met Henry Carrington that summer and the colonel urged him to join the 18th Infantry and apply for a regular commission, but the 24th Ohio was heading for the field in West Virginia and Kellogg declined Carrington's offer. The sergeant major became a lieutenant in the 24th Ohio on July 6 and during the next three months saw action at the Battles of Cheat Mountain and Green Brier. By the time the West Virginia Campaign was drawing to a close, he was reconsidering Carrington's offer to join the regulars. Kellogg had become "tired of politician soldiers and military cabals," and resigned his volunteer commission on October 31. He then "at once hunted for another musket." Arriving at Camp Thomas in November, Kellogg discovered that he now had two regular regiments from which to choose: "I went to Columbus, Ohio, and enlisted as a private soldier in the 16th U.S. Infantry—instead of the 18th U.S. Inf—in which I had previously been offered a commission—because one of my brothers—a graduate of West Point—was a captain in the 18th, and I wished to avoid the appearance of owing promotion in any degree to his influence. I determined to advance myself in the regular service from the grade of a private to that of an officer through my own exertions."[53]

The 18th Infantry's Major Edmund Underwood reported to Camp Thomas at about the same time that Kellogg signed on with B/1/16th. The major did not share the private's enthusiasm about serving there. Underwood had more than thirteen years of regular service to his credit when the Civil War began, having received a commission in the 4th U.S. Infantry at the end of the Mexican War. He spent the majority of his prewar career on the Pacific coast, where his most significant duty was being officer-in-charge of a remote commissary depot in California, commanding a grand total of twenty men. Even though Underwood was himself short of practical command experience, the new major was not quite prepared to serve in a regiment under a colonel who had not spent a day in a Regular Army uniform prior to 1861.

The journey from California to Ohio was a time consuming one and Underwood did not arrive in Columbus until late November. Upon arrival in Ohio, he ensconced himself in Columbus's American Hotel and sent word to Camp Thomas that he was not yet ready to report in person: "I have not decided whether to accept the commission of Major in a regiment whose Colonel is not a regular army officer," Underwood wrote to Carrington, adding "I have the personal permission of the Secretary of War, to delay acceptance." Underwood was a Pennsylvanian, and like virtually all officers from the Keystone State, he seemed to have a direct channel of communication with Simon Cameron. If Underwood thought he could use political connections to manipulate an assignment, he was a lightweight in this field when pitted against his new colonel. Outraged, Carrington sent his adjutant to the hotel. Lieutenant Charles L. Kneass relayed Carrington's order for Underwood to proceed to Camp Thomas without delay. If the good major continued to resist serving under a so-called non-regular, "the Secretary of War would be immediately telegraphed that Major Underwood gave such an excuse for disobedience of orders to report in person at Camp Thomas."

Underwood was at Camp Thomas's front gate the next morning. Carrington had a suitable welcome in store for him. An orderly saluted, silently handed the major the reigns of a horse, and presented a piece of paper. It was an order assigning Underwood as commander of the 18th Infantry's 1st Battalion, and also stated that brigade drill would commence in one hour. At the appointed time Carrington formed his battalions with Major Frederick Townsend's 2/18th on the right, the newly-assigned Underwood's 1/18th in the middle, and Captain Edwin Townsend's 1/16th on the left. The Townsends were prepared for what followed. Underwood was anything but. "Change front forward on the first battalion!" Carrington commanded, wanting to rotate the brigade's front ninety degrees to the right. Major Townsend could execute such an order in his sleep: "Change front forward on first company, by company, right half wheel, march!" His company commanders were likewise well drilled and in short order 2/18th U.S. was in position. Captain Townsend had meanwhile moved out his 16th Infantrymen in a double column. After marching a full battalion interval past Major

Townsend's new position, the captain brought his troops into line: "Right into line wheel, left companies on the right into line, battalion, guide right, march!"

The two battalions were on the new line with a precise battalion-sized gap in between. All eyes were on Major Underwood to fill it. Unfortunately, drilling a twenty-man commissary detachment had not fully prepared him for his present challenge. Underwood simply repeated Major Townsend's commands, resulting in 1/18th coming to rest directly behind 2/18th instead of plugging the gap between the other battalions. Colonel Carrington stepped forward to sort out the traffic jam and the drill then continued. "I never before witnessed such regulation tactics in all my military life!" Underwood exclaimed afterward. Major Townsend had a new student handling the wooden blocks during the officers' class that evening. Henry Carrington may indeed have been a Regular Army neophyte, but he was learning fast.[54]

An important administrative issue that even Colonel Carrington could not fix was the matter of flags for New Army regiments. Since the United States Army had never before officially employed multi-battalion regiments, no one was sure what to do in regard to battalion colors. All regiments of the Regular Army were authorized a regimental flag and the national colors. The Philadelphia Quartermaster Depot issued regimental colors to the New Army regiments during the winter of 1861–1862, but these flags remained at the regimental depots. Since New Army regiments were to operate in the field as three distinct battalions, one set of regimental colors would not be enough. The quartermaster general attempted to obtain battalion colors for some of the regiments. In early January 1862 the 16th Infantry received three sets of battalion colors, but the flags did not meet Regular Army standards. They were made of dark blue silk and displayed the national coat-of-arms, but the symbols had been cheaply painted on the cloth instead of being embroidered as regulations required. Even worse, the scroll beneath the coat-of-arms, which should have been inscribed "16th Regiment Infantry," instead proudly showed off the name of the manufacturer. Major Coolidge rightly considered carrying no flags to be better than displaying such ridiculous banners, and the 16th Regulars never used them. There is no evidence indicating that any other New Army regiment in the Western Theater ever received battalion colors. The 1st and 2nd Battalions of the 18th Infantry each obtained national colors, privately purchased with their own funds, the only flags those battalions ever carried during the Civil War. When shortly after the war the general-in-chief authorized the 18th Infantry to inscribe the names of certain battles on its colors, the commander of 2/18th U.S. replied: "This Batt is without colors of any description except a small National Color, the property of the officers of the Batt. There has never been any Batt. Colors issued to the command, and our Camp Colors have been worn out during the active field operations of the last four years." While virtually every volunteer regiment in the Civil War proudly carried elaborate flags supplied to them by their city, state, or even private organizations, many regular outfits had none at all. It was a distinction the regulars would have rather done without.[55]

* * *

For newcomers such as Major Underwood and Private Kellogg, the stay at Camp Thomas turned out to be a short one. Events in nearby Kentucky caused a premature abandonment of General Scott's plan to use Camp Thomas as a training depot for regular infantry regiments. Kentucky had tried to remain neutral as the war began. Both sides kept forces out of this border state during the first few months of hostilities, neither wanting to push Kentucky's divided population into the other's camp. The situation irrevocably changed on September 3 when the Confederate commander in the West, Major General Leonidas Polk, ordered troops under Brigadier General Gideon J. Pillow to move northward from Union City, Tennessee, and occupy Columbus, Kentucky, on the Mississippi River. Later that month, Confederate forces occupied Bowling Green, while further to the east, additional Southern troops took control of Cumberland Gap and moved into the mountainous southeastern portion of the Bluegrass State.[56]

Polk's sudden seizure of Columbus caught everyone by surprise—including the Confederate high command—and Federal leaders in the West struggled to organize forces and ship them south of the Ohio River. President Lincoln had authorized Federal recruiting camps to be established in Kentucky during August 1861 (after local elections on August 5 revealed that Kentucky Unionists were in firm control of the state's political scene), but while the Union's hands-off policy toward the Bluegrass State was in effect, most of the organized Federal troops in the West were assigned to more active fronts in Missouri and western Virginia. Sufficient Union forces were available in southeastern Missouri to enable Brigadier General Ulysses S. Grant to seize Paducah and Smithland in Kentucky, the points at which the Tennessee and Cumberland Rivers empty into the Ohio, the day after Pillow's Confederates marched into Columbus.

Federal operations in Kentucky east of the Cumberland River were the responsibility of Brigadier General Robert Anderson, commanding the Louisville-based Department of the Cumberland. In contrast to the manpower assigned to Grant's command, Anderson had few troops readily available as the Kentucky front heated up. Fearing that the Confederates at Bowling Green would move northward and threaten Louisville, on September 20 Anderson dispatched a small force southward along the Louisville & Nashville Railway. Led by Brigadier General William T. Sherman, the column of about 1,500 men represented most of the organized troops then available in Anderson's department. Sherman went as far as Rolling Fork, thirty miles south of Louisville, where a burned railroad bridge over the Salt River blocked further movement. While Sherman's operations provided Louisville with a little breathing room, Anderson searched for additional troops to counter Confederate threats. Most of the men available were soldiers in name only. Few regiments had received more than rudimentary training and most were without proper uniforms and weapons.[57]

What Anderson wanted above all else was a force of regular troops. As his department's boundaries included Camp Thomas, he ordered the 18th Regulars to report to the Department of the Cumberland's headquarters in Louisville. These deployment orders did not sit well with Colonel Carrington. He insisted that his troops were not yet ready for active operations, and convinced the War Department to negate the orders. The War Department told Carrington to keep his troops in Ohio and "push the recruiting and drilling service at Camp Thomas to its utmost limit." With Camp Thomas off-limits for the time being, Anderson searched elsewhere for regulars. From Louisville on September 21, Anderson's adjutant informed the War Department that General Anderson "considers it almost indispensable that he should have a company of regular infantry here—at present at least. He has no means of enforcing his order in the city." Anderson's staff need not have worried, for troops of the 15th Regulars were already on their way and a contingent from the 19th U.S. Infantry was not far behind.[58]

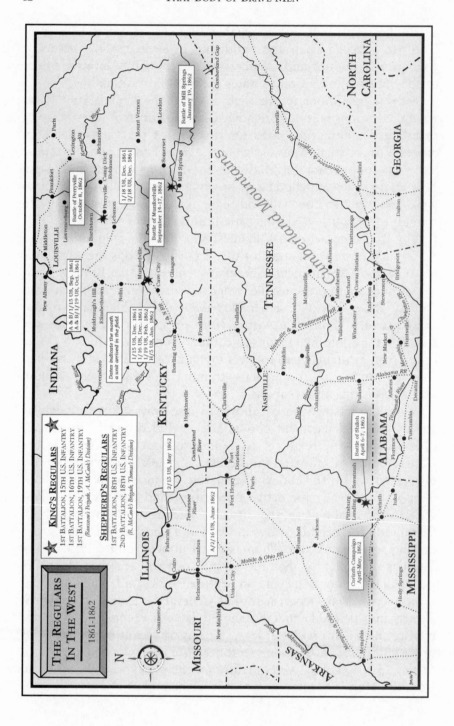

* * *

John King had been a busy man since making the journey from Texas to New York aboard the *Coatzacoalcos*, for he had almost single-handedly organized the 15th U.S. Infantry Regiment. While guarding the Washington Arsenal with his company of 1st Infantrymen, on July 1 Captain King was promoted to major and transferred to the new 15th Infantry. The War Department initially placed the regiment's headquarters at Wheeling, Virginia. King immediately set out for that point, and by mid-month reported that the regiment had present for duty a total of two majors, seven captains, and fifteen lieutenants. He also reported that finding men for the officers to lead was going to be problematical:

Wheeling, Va.
July 11th, 1861.

General L. Thomas
Adjutant General, U.S.A.
   Washington, D.C.

Sir,
    From what I can learn it will be almost impossible to recruit a large number of men in this place and within a reasonable distance of it. I therefore respectfully ask permission to remove the Head Quarters of the 15th Infantry to Cleveland, Ohio. I am satisfied that it will be greatly to the advantage of the Government if you allow me to do so. Wheeling is a very dull place and I am satisfied that I am out of position.
    I am waiting patiently for money to establish Recruiting Rendezvous.

I am, General
Very respectfully
Your Obt. Servt

JOHN H. KING
Major, 15th Inf.
Sup. Regtl. Rec. Service[59]

The War Department replied to King's request with $10,000 in recruiting funds and permission to relocate to Ohio, but instead of Cleveland, the regiment was sent to Cincinnati. Newport Barracks, Kentucky, an old Regular Army installation just south of Cincinnati, located on a bluff overlooking the confluence of the Ohio and Licking Rivers, was in need of a garrison. Major King reported there in late July and assumed command of the post, the 15th Infantry Regiment, and the regiment's 1st Battalion.[60]

King had to occupy three command billets because his regiment's more senior leaders spent little time serving in their regular commissions. The regiment's colonel was Fitz-John Porter, a captain in the Adjutant General's Department at the beginning of the war. He received a brigadier general's star on August 7, 1861, and never served with the 15th Regulars. John P. Sanderson was the regiment's second-in-command, a former Pennsylvania state senator, editor of the *Philadelphia Daily News*, and politician through-and-through. A friend of Simon Cameron, Sanderson's claim to fame occurred at Chicago during the 1860 Republican Convention.

As a delegate from the Keystone State, he brokered the deal that threw the support of the Pennsylvania delegation behind Abraham Lincoln's nomination in return for a high-ranking cabinet position for Cameron. Secretary of War Cameron appointed Sanderson as Chief Clerk of the War Department, making Sanderson the second-ranking man in the department and *de facto* assistant secretary of war. Sanderson desired to wear a uniform, and Cameron arranged a commission for his assistant as lieutenant colonel of the 15th Regulars. To his credit, Sanderson reported for duty at Newport Barracks on November 27 and assumed command of the regiment's headquarters. He did not put much effort into organizing the 15th Infantry. Sanderson spent most of his time investigating political conspiracies and dabbling with a bid to become an assistant editor of the *Louisville Journal*. He would serve briefly on the Army of the Cumberland's staff before dying from a month-long illness in October 1864.[61]

Two of the regiment's majors were also not of much help. William H. Sidell, an 1833 graduate of West Point, had resigned his commission immediately upon graduation from the Academy. He then began a career as a well-known explorer and surveyor of the American West. He reported to Wheeling in late June after that city was designated as the 15th Infantry's depot, but with the depot's shift to Ohio, Sidell's service with his new outfit ended. His famous name kept him on staff duty throughout the war. The 15th Infantry's third major, John R. Edie, had spent six months at West Point before resigning his cadetship in 1829. Edie hailed from Pennsylvania, which in 1861 was all that was necessary for fellow Pennsylvanian Simon Cameron to commission him in the regulars. Edie reported to

Newport Barracks in July with John King and was slotted to command the regiment's 2nd Battalion. He departed a few weeks later for Columbus, Ohio, on a three-month stint of mustering duty.[62]

Organizing the 15th Infantry was thus John King's responsibility. The regiment's captains and lieutenants consisted of the same mix of Old Army veterans and civilian appointees that characterized the initial slate of leaders in the 16th and 18th Regulars. In the 15th Infantry, nine company-grade officers had served in the prewar regulars. Of the twenty-eight civilian appointees, twelve had previously served in volunteer outfits. The War Department appointed additional officers to the New Army regulars during the latter half of 1861, volunteers who distinguished themselves during the war's early campaigns. One of these was Thomas H. Norton of Wheeling, Virginia. While serving as a lieutenant in the 1st Virginia Infantry (U.S.), he was commended for bravery at the Battle of Philippi, Virginia, on June 3, 1861. His reward was an appointment to captain in the 15th Regulars. Norton reported to Newport Barracks in September and was assigned to recruiting duty for the regiment's still-unorganized 2nd Battalion. Since he was only twenty-one years old at the time, Norton was thought to be the youngest man then holding the rank of captain in the Regular Army.[63]

Major King and his subordinates initiated the usual routine of recruiting and training. They encountered the same difficulty in obtaining recruits as had other regular regiments, as Captain Henry R. Brinkerhoff explained in an 1892 history of the 15th Infantry:

> Nearly all the officers assigned to the Fifteenth Infantry in 1861 were set to work recruiting for the regiment. Recruiting stations were established...and every possible means taken to hasten enlistments.
>
> Notwithstanding these efforts recruits were not obtained as rapidly as had been expected, and the companies filled up slowly. Volunteer regiments were frequently raised in a day, but it took months to fill up the ranks of the regular regiments. Men hastened in bodies to join the volunteer forces, but they came individually to join the regulars.
>
> The reasons were obvious. Social relations and the prospect for early preferment popularized the volunteer service, and thus enabled it to absorb the greater portion of available recruits.[64]

King's efforts showed some results after a few months. The 15th Regulars benefited significantly by being stationed at an existing Regular Army post. Established in 1803, Newport Barracks for many years served as headquarters of the Western Department of the army's General Recruiting Service, and had a complete staff as the war began. Two officers who just happened to be stationed at Newport Barracks ended up serving with the 15th Regulars. One was Clarence M. Bailey, a New Yorker who was appointed as a lieutenant in the 6th U.S. Infantry during August 1861. The headquarters of the 6th Regulars had been in California prior to the war. During the summer of 1861 its scattered companies were assigned to the defenses of Washington, D.C. For reasons unknown, Lieutenant Bailey found himself assigned to Newport Barracks. Major King unofficially attached the officer to A/1/15th U.S. and assigned him as the 1st Battalion's quartermaster.

The post adjutant of Newport Barracks for most of 1861 was Lieutenant Peter T. Swaine of the 10th Infantry, an 1852 West Pointer and another New York native. A veteran of frontier service in Minnesota, Texas, and Utah, Swaine became a captain in the 15th Infantry during the Regular Army expansion. Swaine was busy that summer organizing regular troops at Newport Barracks and volunteers in Cincinnati; for the latter he authored and distributed three training manuals on basic soldiering. A few score unassigned regular recruits were already present at Newport Barracks by the time the 15th set up shop there in late July, vestiges of the Old Army's recruiting service. These men mostly hailed from Cincinnati, the Regular Army being their only alternative for service at that time since nearly all the Ohio regiments north of the river were already filled to maximum strength. When Lincoln quietly authorized Federal recruiting in Kentucky during August, more men reported to Newport Barracks. By the beginning of September the 15th Infantry's strength approached 450 men in four organized companies. The 15th Infantry also obtained an excellent band after a number of musicians from Pike's Opera House in Cincinnati signed on with the regiment. Lorenzo Oberst, a talented musician and composer, took charge as the bandmaster. The 15th Infantry's band would later earn a well-deserved reputation as one of the Regular Army's best.[65]

After the movement of Confederate forces into Kentucky, Federal commanders south of the Ohio River needed every man in blue available. In contrast with Henry Carrington's delaying tactics, John King dispatched troops to the field immediately upon receiving orders to do so. The major sent two companies, A and B, 1st Battalion, by rail to Louisville on September 20 under the command of Captain Swaine. Although Anderson was still concerned about maintaining order in Louisville, he realized the regulars' services could be put to better use in the field. He assigned them to General

Bandmaster Lorenzo Oberst composed his "Fifteenth Infantry Quick Step" in 1865. The 15th Infantry Regiment Association adopted the piece as the regiment's official march 137 years later.

Sherman's command, which had just proceeded down the tracks of the Louisville & Nashville to prevent Confederate forces from closing on Louisville. The two 15th Infantry companies arrived at Rolling Fork on September 21.

The next day, Sherman moved his forces across the Salt River to Muldraugh's Hill, a good defensive position near Elizabethtown and the site of an old training camp of the Kentucky state militia. Lieutenant Clarence Bailey got the supply wagons ready that morning. Captain Swaine wanted rations issued prior to moving to Muldraugh's Hill, and as acting quartermaster for the two companies this was Bailey's responsibility. The men lined up and filed past, Bailey and his assistants handing out loaves of bread. Then, out of nowhere, General Sherman appeared. The general evidently thought Bailey's technique was too slow and took over from the lieutenant. "Here, catch this!" Sherman yelled as he grabbed loaves and tossed them to the troops filing by. After the one-star quartermaster finished, Swaine's regulars moved on to Muldraugh's Hill. They and the rest of Sherman's command established camp and continued training while deterring any Confederate forays toward Louisville. Captain Swaine's tiny force was the nucleus of what would eventually become the largest command of Regular Army troops in the Civil War's Western Theater.[66]

* * *

Two companies of the 19th Regulars joined Swaine's 15th Infantrymen in Kentucky the next month. Even after four months of recruiting, two small companies in the field were all the 19th Infantry could show for its efforts. Headquartered in Indianapolis, the 19th Infantry's colonel was Edward R.S. Canby, a major in the prewar 10th Infantry. Like most regular colonels, Canby spent the war elsewhere. He commanded the Department of New Mexico for the first year of the war, and became a general officer in May 1862. Edward A. King, a resident of Ohio who had previous experience in the Regular Army as an infantry captain during the Mexican War, filled the regiment's lieutenant colonel billet. He had also served as a colonel of Ohio volunteers in the spring of 1861. He took command of the 19th Infantry on July 10 and ran the headquarters until the following summer, when he was appointed colonel of the 68th Indiana Infantry. He would rise to brigade command prior to being killed at the Battle of Chickamauga on September 20, 1863.[67]

The 19th Infantry's company-grade officers were the familiar blend of Old Army veterans and civilian appointees. Among the more experienced of the former was Lieutenant Colin Bannatyne Ferguson, a native Scot with eleven years of Old Army service in the 2nd U.S. Artillery to his credit, the last three years of which had been as the regiment's sergeant major. One of the 19th's new officers, Alfred Lacey Hough, had to wade through War Department red tape to receive his commission that rivaled what Anson Mills had encountered. An ex-Quaker from Philadelphia, Hough was definitely not representative of the type of citizen joining the Union Army in 1861: he was thirty-five years old, had a wife and family, and ran a respectable business as a commission agent for paper manufacturers. He had served almost a decade in the Pennsylvania militia prior to the war and had been predicting for some time that the sectional conflict would boil over into open warfare (his associates labeled him "Crazy Hough" for his hawkish views). He was eager to serve in the war and on April 18 signed on as a sergeant with Colonel Frank E. Patterson's 1st Pennsylvania Volunteers.[68]

The first important duty for Patterson's men was a movement through Baltimore to Washington in early May, which was not a routine undertaking given that a secessionist mob had attacked the 6th Massachusetts when that regiment had moved through Baltimore two weeks earlier. The mayor of Baltimore had requested that United States regulars head the next contingent of Federal troops to pass through the city. General Scott gave the assignment to Oliver Shepherd's battalion of 3rd Infantrymen, then still in New York, along with a regular artillery battery and "any well-equipped companies of volunteers" that were available. Hough's regiment was in the right place at the right time and accompanied the regulars to Washington. They arrived on May 10, the movement taking place without incident. The Pennsylvania sergeant was impressed with Shepherd's Old Army troops, remembering them as "about the hardest looking party I ever saw having seen rough service on the frontier, they had but 5 officers left, the rest all having joined the Rebels."[69] The sight of a tough, well-trained body of soldiers lacking officers made Hough think that perhaps the Regular Army was in need of his services. He was well connected in both Pennsylvania and the nation's capitol; before the summer of 1861 had progressed very far, he was wearing the uniform of a regular officer:

I arrived in Washington on the 25th day of June and proceeded in accordance with the advice I had received to the Adjutant General of the Army, Col. Lorenzo Thomas, and reported myself to accept the position of Captain in the U.S. Army. I was in Sergeants uniform, somewhat shabby for wear; the Colonel was polite but rather austere in his manner, as he looked at me as though I was an imposter, and told me there was no appointment made. I was annoyed, of course, and hurried to my friend, the Hon. Wm. D. Kelley [a member of Congress] who advised me of my appointment. Upon finding him, he was as much astonished as myself, he said the Sect. of War Genl. Cameron had told him that I was appointed, and returned with me to the Adjutant General and asked him if he was not mistaken. The books were looked over and the same reply was made, "no such name on the books." My friend then arranged for me to meet the Sect. Of War personally that evening at Willards Hotel which I did. He expressed himself as much astonished that I was not appointed, as he distinctly recollected sending my name in for appointment. He closed the interview by handing me his card and telling me to present that the next morning at 10 o'clock at his private office.[70]

Sergeant Hough reported to the War Department at ten o'clock sharp the next day. The crowd waiting to see the secretary of war that morning consisted of about twenty officers, all resplendently decked out in glittering dress uniforms. They viewed the sergeant's rough sack coat and sky-blue trousers somewhat skeptically, as did the secretary's assistant, who hesitated to admit Hough to see Secretary Cameron. Hough presented Cameron's card and the assistant went into the secretary's office. He returned quickly and stated: "Captain, the Secretary says wait here and he will be out in a moment." "I shall never forget the looks of the surrounding officers," Hough recalled, "heretofore they had been inclined to look upon me as an intruder, now I was an object of curiosity." Cameron appeared and escorted Hough down the hall to the adjutant general's office. The secretary had Colonel Thomas draft up Hough's commission on the spot. Before the week was out Captain Hough reported to the 19th Infantry's headquarters at Indianapolis.[71]

The War Department initially assigned only two majors to the 19th Infantry instead of the authorized three. One of them, Augustus H. Seward, never served with the outfit. An 1847 West Pointer, Seward was detailed to the Army Pay Department throughout the war. The other major was Stephen D. Carpenter, an Old Army regular hailing from Bangor, Maine. The former 1st

Infantry captain had spent a few months in Key West after escaping from the Lone Star State with John King and James Caldwell onboard the *Coatzacoalcos*. Assigned to the 19th Infantry, Carpenter reported for duty at Indianapolis on August 7 and took over the regiment's training program. Similar to the task facing King, Slemmer, and Shepherd, it ultimately fell upon Carpenter's shoulders to instill in his new regiment the style and character of the Regular Army. Lieutenant Colonel Edward King was pleased to have an experienced officer of Carpenter's caliber present for duty, and spelled out the major's duties in detail:

Head Quarters 19th Regt. U.S. Infantry
Indianapolis, Ind. Augt. 10th 1861.

General Orders
No. 7.

I. Major S.D. Carpenter is assigned to the command of the recruits now at Reg. Head Quarters and who may hereafter join. He will make such rules and regulations for his command as may be necessary for its thorough discipline and instruction, and will daily report to the commanding officer its condition in all respects.

II. First Lieutenants Ely, Gilbert, Fogarty, and Snyder will report to Major Carpenter for duty with the recruits.

III. Major Carpenter will also take charge of the practical tactical instruction of all the company officers at Head Quarters and will keep the commanding officer advised as to their progress in tactical knowledge and their attention to their duties.

By Order of
Edw'd A. King
Lieut. Col. Comdg.[72]

In what was fast becoming the norm for regular field-grade officers, Carpenter was soon placed on detached service. The major was assigned as a mustering officer in Indianapolis during late October and would not rejoin his new regiment until February 1862. The regiment's final major's billet was not filled until February 1862, when Captain George L. Willard of the 8th U.S. Infantry received the promotion. A native New Yorker and Mexican War veteran who had been commissioned from the Regular Army's enlisted ranks during 1848, Willard served in the East on the staff of the Army of the Potomac and never served with the 19th Regulars. He received a volunteer commission as colonel of the 125th New York Infantry in late August 1862, and was killed at the Battle of Gettysburg on July 2, 1863.[73]

There were not many 19th Infantrymen for the majors to train anyway. During his tenure in command of the 19th Infantry's headquarters, Lieutenant Colonel Edward King probably set a record for Regular Army recruiting futility. He opened eleven recruiting stations across Indiana, Ohio, and Pennsylvania, but by the end of August a grand total of 128 men were present for duty. Captain Reuben D. Mussey, a civilian appointee from Ohio, was in charge of the regiment's recruiting effort in Jeffersonville, Indiana, a town on the Ohio River opposite Louisville. In a late July letter to a friend, Mussey attributes his recruiting difficulties to a number of factors, including Kentucky politics:

> I am in the dullest of dull towns, recruiting. Theoretically I am recruiting men for the United States Army. Practically, I am "recruiting" myself. I have been here a week and have got no one as yet. But I eat well, sleep well, and am generally in good condition.
>
> There interfere with my Recruiting several things. In the first place, Jeffersonville has been pretty well drained already. Secondly, the volunteer service is generally preferred by those who want to enlist. Thirdly, Rousseau [Col. Lovell H. Rousseau, 5th Kentucky Infantry] has a Camp but a mile and a half from here. Fourthly, in Louisville and Kentucky on which I am expected chiefly to operate, the Union men say any open work on my part would embarrass them until after the August election. I suppose you already know that the Union men of Kentucky are really with us heart and hand. And that the neutrality dodge is merely used by them as a means to get a Legislature and strengthen themselves so as to be able to impeach the Governor and depose him.[74]

The 19th Infantry slowly filled during the coming months as recruits trickled in. Captain Hough wrote to his wife on July 16 that at least the regiment's officer training was coming along well:

> I fear we shall have a hard time to get recruits from all accounts; the people will volunteer but not to join the regular army. ...I am getting along famously in a military way. We have examinations in tactics, and regulations, and practice in tactics for three hours every day; the latter has been conducted by Capt. [Lewis Wilson], the old Ohio Captain I spoke of. He went home on leave to-day and the Colonel appointed me instructor during his absence, and I have performed my duties to-day with satisfaction to myself. So I feel rather

proud to be drilling Captains and Lieutenants, most of whom have been officers before. The balance of the time I am occupied in preparing myself for such examinations as the Colonel gives us, I have no time for business except evenings.[75]

Arthur B. Carpenter (no relation to Major Carpenter) was one of the few 19th Infantrymen who joined the regiment during 1861. Originally from Monson, Massachusetts, Carpenter was a twenty-year-old cobbler's apprentice living in Indianapolis as the war began. He had wanted to enlist from the moment the first shots had been fired in Charleston harbor, but his young age meant he needed parental consent to join up. That was not forthcoming during the summer of 1861. During this time Indiana's initial quota of volunteer regiments were filled and shipped off to the war. Carpenter found an outlet for his military desires by joining a company of the Indiana Home Guard, the "Independent Zouaves," where he learned some drill and other rudimentary aspects of soldiering. Carpenter's desire to officially wear Union blue did not diminish as the months went by, but by September there were no volunteer units available near Indianapolis to join. The 19th U.S. Infantry was hiring, and Carpenter's quasi-military training would entitle him to a sergeant's warrant in the regulars.[76] He hoped the increased stature and possibility of a commission would soften his parents' resistance:

> My military ardor not having in the least abated, and my hope and ambition of living a military life still prevailing, I will again ask a favor of you and hope it will not be rejected. you would not permit me to enter the volunteer service and now an opportunity presents itself for my entering the regular Service U.S. Army. I am sure of entering the service as a sargent. the pay is from 25 to 35 dollars a month. 22 second Lieutenants are to be appointed from among the sargents, and the one who conducts himself straight, and has a good character stands the best chance of getting appointed second Lieutenant in the regular Army U.S.A. and has the privilege of continuing in the army for life or not as he pleases at $75 a month.
>
> I have always longed for the time to come when I could enter the army and be a military man, and when this war broke out I thought the time had come. but you would not permit me to enter the service. ...and now I make one more appeal to you, and hope you will not crush out the last spark of hope that I have left.[77]

The reply of Carpenter's parents to the appeal was lukewarm but not completely negative. The aspiring sergeant sent them another appeal on October 9:

> you ask why I cannot be contented to stay quietly at home; it is not in my temperament. I believe that a person has to go out in the world and engage in its conflicts. better against wrong, and every thing that tends to impede the progress of *liberty* and *equal rights*.
>
> Every body say go into the regular army by all means. it is a wrong idea that the volunteer service is the best. ...in the U.S. Army...everything is different. what an officer says is done. there is no deception. of course I have to run my chances in regard to promotion, but I can get a good start to commence with, that is as sargent. the second Lieutenants are appointed from the sargents. I can be a sargent in the regular army. ...Men who know, even officers, say that they had rather be a sargent in the Regular Army than a Lieutenant in the Volunteer Service.[78]

Consent was finally given and in mid-October Arthur B. Carpenter embarked on the greatest adventure of his life. He wrote his parents at the end of the month and informed them that he couldn't be happier:

> I have been a soldier about two weeks now, and like it first rate. I begin to think now that I have found my sphere. I am in Company C 1st Battalion 19th Infantry U.S.A. acting as sergeant. ...we expect to fill up in a month, and be ready for service. we are in good quarters occupying rooms on Washington Street. the government hires a man to furnish us in the eating line. we have course substantial food and no fine fixings, so we keep stout and healthy.
>
> The boys have to keep clean and neat. keep their boots blacked and are not allowed to spit on the floors so everything is clean and neat.
>
> Capt Wilson our capt. is a very pleasant man notwithstanding his power and strictness as a military commander, and all our officers our first rate.
>
> The 1st Sergeant or orderly of the company is Sergeant Johnson. he is a first rate fellow and a real soldier, he having been 3 years in the marine service. he never uses profane language, makes all mind him, and has considerable influence with the officers. ...the rooms are scrubbed out 3 or 4 times a week. this morning we all got up at 5 o'clock and commenced cleaning up for inspection of the officers at 8 o'clock. we have to get up at roll call (5 o'clock in morning, every morning), drill at 8–11–3 1/2 o'clocks 1 1/2 hours each time.

the rest of the time the privates have to themselves, but Sergeant Johnson and myself are kept busy most of the time, seeing that everything is straight.[79]

Private Eli M. Tarbell, a native Ohioan and Great Lakes mariner residing in Pennsylvania, was one of the soldiers in Company C that kept Sergeant Carpenter and ex-marine 1st Sergeant George Washington Johnson busy. The first entry Tarbell made in his wartime diary gives an indication of the thoroughness of the 19th Infantry's training program: "I Inlisted with Capt Thos C Williams in Co. C. 19 Reg U.S.I. for 3 years, or during the war, At Wilmore PA on the 10th dy of Oct 1861. At the End of one week the Co. was full & we wer Sent to Pittsburg. Remained in Pittsburg 2 days, was put in a big Building & a guard put over us. I thought it rather tough, couldnet get out without a pass, we wer then Sent to Indanapolis, Ind, arived there Oct. 17 & now our wok begins. we have good quarters here & 3 meals a day but Drill, Gad, it was tough, 3 drills a day, Co Drill, Battalion Drill, Skirmish Drill & all the drills Known in the Infentry Tacktic. With all our hard work we had some good times."[80]

While Sergeant Carpenter, Private Tarbell, and the rest of Company C drilled in Indianapolis during October 1861, Companies A and B of 1/19th U.S., led by Captains Mussey and Jeremiah H. Gilman, deployed to Kentucky and were assigned to General Sherman's command. Since the 15th's Captain Swaine ranked Gilman and Mussey, he took command of the four regular companies.

* * *

On October 8 Sherman turned over command of the troops at Muldraugh's Hill to Lovell Rousseau, colonel of the 5th Kentucky. Sherman headed back to Louisville and assumed department command from Robert Anderson, whose ill health had compelled the defender of Fort Sumter to retire. Sherman soon learned that the Confederates at Bowling Green did not appear to be moving any further toward Louisville. The day after Sherman departed, Rousseau advanced the Muldraugh's Hill troops to Nolin, a station on the Louisville & Nashville twenty-three miles south of Rolling Fork. They established Camp Nevin there, named for the secessionist owner of the plantation the Union troops occupied.

The change of department commanders caused a distinguished visitor to arrive at Camp Thomas in late October, Thomas Ewing.

He and Henry Carrington were old friends, having known each other in Ohio's legal and political realms before the war. Ewing, a former U.S. Senator from Ohio, had held cabinet-level positions in the administrations of Presidents William Henry Harrison and Zachary Taylor. He was also William T. Sherman's foster father and father-in-law. Carrington greeted the politician warmly, proudly showing off Camp Thomas and the 18th Regular Infantry. Ewing's visit to the camp was not strictly a social one, for he bore an urgent message from his son-in-law: General Sherman was desperate for troops. Ewing told the colonel that "the very safety of General Sherman's position might hinge upon the immediate support of the Camp Thomas regulars." In reply, Carrington politely explained that the men at Camp Thomas were under direct orders from the War Department to remain in place until thoroughly trained. The 16th and 18th Infantry Regiments were "subject to no orders from any other source." Although Carrington wore the uniform of a Regular Army colonel, he definitely remained a lawyer at heart.

William T. Sherman did not have much time to debate the issue, for he commanded the Department of the Cumberland only a few weeks. When Robert Anderson suddenly retired, Sherman was the department's ranking general officer and inherited the command more by circumstance than by design. Brigadier General Don Carlos Buell, a favorite of George McClellan who was then serving as a division commander in the Army of the Potomac, took over the department from Sherman on November 15, with Sherman in turn being reassigned to Halleck's Department of the Missouri in St. Louis. Buell's command became the Department of the Ohio and the new commander got down to business. Like his two predecessors, Buell wanted to have as many regulars in the field as possible. Little more than a week after assuming command, orders were again issued for the regulars at Camp Thomas to report to Louisville.[81]

Henry Carrington was not about to let the war effort upset his training program if he could help it. Just as he had in September, Carrington asked the War Department to cancel these latest deployment orders. Once described as a "pathological worrier about the minutiae of preparation,"[82] Carrington evidently thought his regiment's drilling had not yet reached the "utmost limit:"

> Headquarters 18th Infantry U.S.A.
> Camp Thomas, Ohio
> November 24, 1861

Brig Gen'l L. Thomas
Adjutant General
Washington

Dear General,

This Regiment and the 16th would be more effective if detained longer in camp. Our overcoats and tents are still behind, expected daily.

Five captains are on disbursing or mustering duty, so that I only average one officer to a company besides the staff.

While I can truly say, no better men were ever enlisted and I shall promptly take the field when the department directs, I must, in candor, say that I need more officers and some further preparation before taking the command to their best as soldiers of the Regular Army.

I remain, sir,
most respectfully,
Your obd't sev't,

H.B. CARRINGTON
Col., 18th Infty[83]

The War Department sympathized with Carrington's claim of unpreparedness and urged the colonel to complete the organization of his regiment as soon as possible. But Washington evidently thought the regulars at the Camp of Instruction had trained long enough. The troops then available at Camp Thomas were to join the Army of the Ohio in Kentucky immediately. With no court of appeal available, Carrington prepared the regulars for deployment. He also engineered a plausible reason for he himself to stay in Columbus. Major Stokes's 3/18th U.S. still consisted of just a few companies of untrained recruits in Pennsylvania. Carrington telegraphed the War Department on November 27: "Am I correct that I retain my headquarters in Columbus to complete the organization of the regiment?" The adjutant general's affirmative reply provided the colonel with his ticket out of the war. Carrington sent word to Stokes to shut down the regiment's recruiting operations in the Keystone State and report to Camp Thomas with all available recruits. In addition, four companies of the regiment's 1st and 2nd Battalions, along with F/1/16th U.S., all recently organized and largely untrained, remained at Camp Thomas. With so many recruits still training at the Camp of Instruction, Carrington reasoned that it would be best for all concerned if the colonel commanding the 18th Regulars remained in Ohio to supervise them.

On the positive side, Carrington arranged for a strong officer to command his troops in the field. Also on November 27, he sent a telegram to Lieutenant Colonel Shepherd in New York City: "Twelve companies take the field on Monday. When shall I expect you?" Shepherd finally convinced his superiors to release him for field duty and made preparations to leave New York, although he was not able to get away before the regular battalions departed Camp Thomas. Carrington, meanwhile, published movement orders for the troops. With his usual attention to detail, he gave exact instructions on everything from packing battalion equipment to ensuring that all canteens were filled with water or coffee.[84]

The regular battalions left Camp Thomas on December 2 with Carrington coming along for the time being. They marched to the Columbus rail depot, where a flag-waving crowd cheered as the regulars boarded a train for Cincinnati. Carrington's men spent the night in Cincinnati and the next morning shipped out for Louisville on board the steamers *Jacob Strader* and *Telegraph #3*, chartered from of the Louisville and Cincinnati Steam Boat Company. These craft were not large enough to accommodate all three battalions, so the *Jacob Strader* towed a barge. The 18th Infantry, along with the officers of the 16th, were billeted in relative comfort on the steamers while the men of the 16th were consigned to the barge. Edgar Kellogg of the 16th Infantry did not recall the trip down the Ohio River very fondly: "The weather was cold and damp...we were so crowded that exercise was almost impossible, and always as I look back to that day it seems to have been one of the most miserable of the many bad ones I have seen."

Private Kellogg's brief description of the trip is actually quite tame, for conditions on the barge were actually nothing short of chaotic. Some of the 16th Infantrymen secreted aboard large quantities of Kentucky whiskey and Cincinnati beer. With the unit's officers absent aboard the steamers, mayhem followed. Imbibing, gambling, and fistfights took place from stem to stern. At least one man fell overboard and perished. Jacob Van Zwaluwenburg was fast asleep when a fight broke out nearby. He barely had time to escape with his blanket and knapsack; one of the pugilists picked up the retreating Dutchman's rifle and threw if after him for good measure: "It went over my head, through a window, into the Ohio River where it is, I suppose, today." Officers of the 16th could only watch the madness from the nearby decks of the *Jacob Strader*. A few attempted to board the barge but quickly realized that nothing short of a battalion of Marines had a chance of success in a maritime operation against such inspired opposition. The drunken spree came to an end only after a red-hot stove was tipped over, which set the barge on fire. "A few of us sober ones quickly put the fire out," Van Zwaluwenburg recalled. "That seemed to sober up the crowd."[85]

Edgar Kellogg may have thought the journey miserable but it ended up being a definite boost to his career. The sergeant major of 1/16th U.S., an Old Army regular named Augustus Shearer, thought the trip was a bit too miserable and deserted shortly after the *Jacob Strader* reached Louisville on December 4. Officers in the 16th Regulars had noted Edgar Kellogg's abilities just as quickly as the leaders in the 24th Ohio had the previous summer. They wanted to push Kellogg up the ranks as fast as possible. On December 18 Kellogg made a remarkable jump, moving from private to sergeant major without a stop in between.[86] A week later, Major Coolidge sent word to the War Department that both Kellogg and another sergeant in 1/16th were ready for commissioning:

> Head Quarters 16th Inf. U.S.A.
> Columbus Ohio
> 25th December 1861

General L. Thomas
    Adjutant General

General

The 16th Regiment being short of officers and especially the 1st Battalion now in the field being in need of 2d lieutenants, I respectfully request that E Romayn Kellogg, Sergeant Major of 1st Battalion 16th Inf. and William G. Wedemeyer Sergeant Co F 1st Batt. 16th Inf be appointed 2nd lieutenants in the 16th Inf.

I respectfully beg to state that both these non commissioned officers are proposed for promotion...are in my opinion better qualified for promotion than any other non commissioned officers. ...I also respectfully beg to give the following reasons for proposing these non commissioned officers for promotion instead of others who have been in the regiment longer. It is seldom that apt subjects for promotion enlist, as the Volunteer service in greatly preferred, and these two are well qualified. They were both lieutenants in the Volunteers, they both resigned and enlisted in the 16th. When the officers of the first battalion 16th Inf were discussing which two non commissioned officers to propose for promotion they agreed upon these two.

Very Respectfully
Your Obdt Svt,
SIDNEY COOLIDGE
Major 16th Inf. Comm.[87]

While the War Department began the process of approving Coolidge's request, Colonel Carrington received orders for the three battalions in Louisville. General Buell parceled out the regulars between two commands in central Kentucky: the 16th Infantrymen were ordered to Munfordville for assignment to Brigadier General Alexander McCook's division, while the 18th Infantry battalions were assigned to Brigadier General George H. Thomas's division at Lebanon. The war's first eight months had come and gone with little participation from the new regulars, but their actions during the campaigns of the upcoming year would make up for the lost time. The peaceful conditions in which the regular battalions parted company in Louisville contrast greatly with the circumstances of their reunion, which would occur twelve months later in Nashville, Tennessee.

Chapter 2:

Mill Springs and Nashville

"The Wild Eye of the Colonel"

E ven though Kentucky's bid to remain neutral ended in September 1861, by December the war had still not yet reached the Bluegrass State. Federal regiments in Kentucky spent the last three months of 1861 training and being organized into brigades and divisions. Confederate forces conducted similar activities, although Southern raiders and scouting parties kept the Federal high command in a state of constant anxiety, particularly along the vulnerable Louisville & Nashville Railroad in central Kentucky. Substantial bodies of Confederates were present only at Columbus on the Mississippi, Bowling Green on the Louisville & Nashville, and at Mill Springs, a small town on the Cumberland River just north of the Tennessee state line in southeastern Kentucky, but it was not until the first two months of 1862 that Federal Forces were ready to begin active operations. While forces from Halleck's Department of the Missouri moved through Kentucky and into west Tennessee by way of the Cumberland and Tennessee Rivers, Buell's Army of the Ohio engaged Confederate forces at Mill Springs and advanced on Nashville. The four regiments of regular infantry in Buell's department saw little action in these maneuvers, but their experiences steeled them for the more difficult campaigns that were surely coming.[1]

* * *

The 18th Infantry remained in Louisville only a few days. While awaiting orders from General Thomas to move to Lebanon, Carrington's men had some opportunities to put their Camp Thomas training to good use. The 18th Infantry staged a full dress parade for General Buell and his staff, after which Buell commended the battalions on their fine appearance and discipline. As the regulars were marching back to their quarters, Buell's adjutant general, James B. Fry, gave Carrington an urgent message: there was some trouble at the Ohio River docks. Members of a Kentucky volunteer regiment had taken possession of the steamer *Texas* and were mutinying against their officers. The men were upset about not being granted a furlough that had been promised to many of them upon enlistment. The Army of the Ohio's pressing need for troops meant the regiment did not have a chance to give the troops their furlough, and in protest the angry Kentuckians locked up their officers on the *Texas* and refused to proceed to the field. A number of them also took possession of nearby Louisville saloons. The 18th Infantry's orders: proceed to the waterfront, restore order, and arrest all mutineers who do not immediately surrender. Deadly force was authorized against anyone who put up serious resistance.

Carrington sent word to his regiment's nearby barracks for quartermasters to bring forward live cartridges. Still wearing their frock coats and Hardee hats, the colonel marched his battalions to the Ohio River levee. Just as in the Columbus exercises, skirmishers preceded the formation through the streets. When the column reached the docks near the *Texas*, the regulars found the quartermasters waiting. A few cartridges were quickly issued to each man. In a voice loud enough for the mutineers to hear, Carrington commanded the regulars to load their rifles. Eager to show the mutineers exactly what trained soldiers were capable of, the men responded by executing the orders even more quickly than they had at Camp Thomas. After calling for the Kentuckians to surrender, Carrington opened up with shots across the *Texas's* bow: "The first battalion of the 18th advanced and at the word of command, the first division of two companies delivered volley fire in front of the steamer, broke to the right at quick time and in turn was succeeded by similar firing by the remaining divisions, all in less than two minutes; and all that appeared on the river surface was successive lines of white foam." The firepower demonstration had the desired. The affair ended peacefully as the mutineers surrendered, their officers took over, and the regiment proceeded to the field as ordered. This incident was the first time the 18th Regulars were used to enforce discipline among volunteer troops (it would not be the last) and it illustrates the differences between soldiers of the two services during the early months of the war. The regulars with their strict discipline and training stood in stark contrast with the more numerous and free-spirited volunteers. The Northern war effort would have been better served by having large numbers of both types of soldiers in the Union Army's ranks, although one would have had a hard time in 1861 convincing members of either service about this statement's validity.[2]

Henry B. Freeman, a lieutenant in D/2/18th U.S., was quite pleased with himself. The 18th Infantry's hasty departure from Camp Thomas meant that much equipment had been left behind, but by the time the regiment moved out from Louisville Freeman had more gear than he knew what to do with:

> I met some friends in Louisville who had made a campaign and as I was ignorant as a babe of what was required by myself for that purpose I asked them to go with me to an outfitting shop & help me to select what was necessary. The first purchase I made was an immense pair of revolvers. The next, was a rubber canteen, one of the old crescent shaped ones. The next was a haversack of the same material for carrying my bread & dinner. The next was a pair of woolen blankets and a rubber blanket, all of which I carried out to camp in high glee at being so well provided. When we were to march I put the pistols on my belt, buckled myself to them and my saber, strapped my blankets behind my saddle, my overcoat in front. Filled my rubber canteen with water, my haversack with bread and cheese and by a superhuman effort climbed into the saddle. Once there, safely ensconced between the huge rolls in front and rear, held down by the weight of my equipments, I felt sure that nothing less than a complete somersault on the part of my horse could throw me out of the saddle.[3]

Freeman, twenty-four, had never been on a campaign, even though he had once before worn a Regular Army uniform. Like Frederick Phisterer, Freeman lied about his age to enlist in the regulars back in 1855. Unlike the future 18th Infantry sergeant major, civil authorities caught up with Freeman and he was discharged for enlisting under false pretenses. He served only eight months as a private in the 10th U.S. Infantry, not long enough to acquire much experience. Freeman had been living in Kentucky and making a living as a printer immediately prior to the war. The events of April 1861 convinced him to return to his native state of Ohio and enlist. He arrived too late to sign up under Lincoln's call for volunteers in May but later met Henry Carrington in Columbus. Freeman enlisted in the 18th Infantry on July 8, the first person to join the new regiment. He became the first sergeant of B/2/18th U.S. in August 1861, and received a lieutenant's commission three months later. While Freeman's horse did not perform any gymnastics on the way to Lebanon, the lieutenant would have more than his fair share of excitement during the next few years.[4]

The 18th Regulars departed Louisville by train the morning of December 7, arriving in Lebanon early in the afternoon. They established Camp Sullivant that evening, named in honor of Carrington's wife, Margaret Sullivan Carrington. Carrington reported to General Thomas for orders and learned that the 18th Infantry's fine reputation had preceded the unit: "Upon first reporting in person to General Thomas, I found him at his headquarters in plain undress uniform, wearing heavy top boots, spurred for any immediate use, was received most cordially; and congratulated upon my 'splendid command,' of which he had heard through General Buel, as well as from his staff, whose Assistant Quartermaster General had assisted me in locating my Camp."[5]

George Thomas had been promoted a number of times since reorganizing the 2nd U.S. Cavalry at Carlisle Barracks the previous April. He became the 2nd Cavalry's lieutenant colonel on April 25 and then its colonel on May 3, positions that were vacant due to the promotion of Lieutenant Colonel Robert E. Lee to the colonelcy of the 1st Cavalry, and then the resignation of Colonel Albert Sidney Johnston. After commanding a brigade in the Shenandoah Valley during the summer of 1861, Thomas received a brigadier's star on August 17. On September 10, he assumed command of Union forces in central and eastern Kentucky. Five days prior to the 18th Infantry's arrival at Lebanon, his command was designated the 1st Division, Army of the Ohio. Thomas's three brigades were commanded by Brigadier General Albin Schoepf, Colonel Mahlon D. Manson, and Colonel Robert L. McCook.[6]

The 18th Infantry was not the only regular outfit on the move in Kentucky. Major John King arrived at Camp Nevin in early November with the regimental band and four companies of the 15th Infantry from Newport Barracks, forming the regiment's 1st battalion with Captain Swaine's two companies already present in the field. The 19th U.S. Infantry contingent in Kentucky still consisted of just two companies, and they remained temporarily attached to Major King's command. Enough Federal troops to constitute a division had arrived at Camp Nevin and nearby points by mid-October. On December 2 the forces there were officially designated the Army of the Ohio's 2nd Division. Its commander was Brigadier General Alexander McDowell McCook, an 1852 West Point graduate. The division's three brigades were led by Brigadiers Lovell Rousseau (4th Brigade), Thomas J. Wood (5th Brigade), and Richard W. Johnson (6th Brigade).[7] Johnson, the early-waking 2nd Cavalryman of Texas fame, had been promoted to brigadier general of volunteers in October 1861—not for any particularly distinguished act, but due to President Lincoln's tendency in 1861 to make generals of promising Kentuckians.[8]

* * *

As regular formations left their depots and headed for the field during late 1861, decisions had to be made on how best to employ them. Two theories emerged in the early days of the conflict on the proper role of the regulars in the Union war effort. One was the "Iron Column" (or "tactical nucleus," as described by historian Michael Huebner). All the regulars would be grouped together in a single corps and then tasked with making the North's main military effort against the Confederacy. Old Army professionals tended to favor this technique, for it was essentially the same course of action that had proven so successful in the war with Mexico. As early as the first week of May 1861, General Winfield Scott wrote that the Union Army's main column would consist of "our best regulars for the advance." William T. Sherman, who briefly served on Scott's staff the next month, recalled that the general-in-chief "spoke of organizing a grand army of invasion, of which the regulars were to constitute the 'iron column.'" Major General George B. McClellan favored the Iron Column throughout his tenure as an army commander. "I would...urgently recommend that the whole of the Regular Army, old and new, be at once ordered to report here," McClellan wrote the secretary of war from his army's headquarters in September 1861. "There should be no delay in carrying out this measure. Scattered as the regulars now are, they are nowhere strong enough to produce a marked effect. United in one body, they will insure the success of this army."[9]

The problem with having a single command of regulars was deciding where the Iron Column would operate. Department commanders throughout the North were desperate for regular troops and resisted attempts to have their few regulars assigned elsewhere. The Army of the Potomac came closest to fulfilling General Scott's dream. The War Department concentrated many of the Old Army's scattered units for the defense of Washington in the early months of the war, resulting in the bulk of the Old Army's regulars being assigned to the Army of the Potomac. Starting out with Oliver Shepherd's regular battalion during April 1861, the force of regular infantry in the Union's main eastern army eventually accounted for two brigades in the V Corps. But the Army of the Potomac did not have a monopoly on the regulars. Many New Army infantry regiments served in other commands.

The other theory on how to use the regulars can be called the "cadre plan," or "nucleus of professionalism." Under this arrangement, the Regular Army would cease to exist as a separate entity. Instead, every last regular officer, sergeant, and soldier would be scattered throughout volunteer regiments to serve as leaders and trainers. Championed by a number of politicians and journalists, the cadre plan was thought to be a quick way to raise the military expertise of the masses of civilians trying on U.S. Army blue for the first time. War Department resistance prevented such a drastic measure, mainly due to Secretary of War Cameron and General Scott's desire to form the Iron Column of regulars. They made it clear at the start of the war that regular officers were not to serve in volunteer regiments. Colonel Edwin D. Townsend of the Adjutant General's Department explained this policy to General Frank Patterson on April 30: "The General-in-Chief directs me to say that the Secretary of War has decided no officer of the Regular Army can be spared to serve in the quotas of volunteers from States."[10]

Support for the cadre plan became more widespread in the aftermath of the Union defeat at Bull Run in July 1861. Both military and government officials realized that the volunteers' primary shortcoming was leadership; if regular officers could hold commissions in volunteer regiments, that problem would be largely solved. "If I wished to-day to organize a heavy military force, such as we are calling into the field," Senator Henry Wilson of Massachusetts proclaimed during a July 1861 Capitol Hill debate, "I would abolish the [Regular] Army as the first act, and I then would take the officers from the

Army and place them where their talents fit them to go." Even at this point Scott and Cameron resisted allowing regular officers to serve in volunteer units. It was only after Congress sanctioned the practice as part of its July 29 legislation that regulars could simultaneously hold volunteer commissions "for the purpose of imparting to [the volunteers] military instruction and efficiency."[11] Congress was still debating the issue as late as early November, as reported by the Washington correspondent of the *New York Herald*:

> The members of Congress who are here are also discussing the propriety of wiping out the distinction between the regulars and volunteers, by declaring the volunteers to compose the army of the United States. Unless something is done to legally obliterate the distinction now maintained, and to do away with the tyrannical rule of the regular department, the volunteer system will be utterly destroyed. As it is now, no officer, however capable or meritorious, can obtain any position or consideration with the heads of the army bureaus, and nothing is conceded to the volunteers that can possibly be withheld. For their arms, clothing, equipments, transportation, &c., the volunteers must dance attendance, day after day, upon men who openly deride and malign them, and who never treat them with decency, and never speak of them except with contempt. It is astonishing the extent to which this feeling is carried.[12]

Congress's authorization of simultaneous commissions was the closest the cadre plan ever came to being realized. Much to the chagrin of cadre plan promoters, this legislation stopped well short of completely dismantling the Regular Army. A year after Congress took action, the Executive Committee of the U.S. Sanitary Commission wrote the president to express its disappointment that the cadre plan had never been fully adopted: "If we have learned anything, it has been that it was a mistake to keep the Regular Army and the Volunteer Army separate. Had the regulars been from the first intermingled with the volunteers they would have leavened the whole lump with their experience of camp police, discipline, subordination, and the sanitary conditions of military life. We should have no Bull Run panic to blush for. Our little Regular Army, diffused among the volunteers of last year, would within three months have brought them up to its own standard of discipline and efficiency."[13]

While motivated by the best of intentions, advocates of the cadre plan failed to consider a few harsh realities. While ending the

Regular Army's organizational existence may have seemed easy to do in theory, in practice it would have created a bureaucratic nightmare in the War Department. It was through the regimental system that the War Department regulated everything from promotions and pay to property accountability. Breaking up the Regular Army's regiments into hundreds of small cadres would have required the army's notoriously conservative staff departments to quickly change their entire mode of doing business, a paradigm shift of mammoth proportions. In addition, the Union Army's volunteers were quite democratic, suspicious of authority, anti-elitist, and invariably cliquish. While regular officers serving in volunteer regiments were often welcomed, many volunteer soldiers would have at least resented and at most ignored the presence in their ranks of a few enlisted regulars (most likely including a foreigner or two), sent to supposedly show the volunteers how to do their jobs. Besides, having all the skills necessary to be a truly effective trainer—technical knowledge, communication skills, patience, just to name a few—is a rare combination, even among military professionals. Only a minority of regulars had what it takes to efficiently transform civilians into soldiers. Among those few were the regular officers who aggressively sought out volunteer commands, the men Congress had in mind when it authorized simultaneous commissions. These officers proved to be a sufficient enough cadre for the Union Army. The Regular Army survived, although stripped of some of its best leaders.

There was no shortage of advice flooding into the War Department on how to raise and employ the wartime Regular Army. The head of the American Legation in Brussels went so far as to suggest that a "German Legion" of 20,000 European mercenaries be hired for the job, a curious twist on a similar British practice of the Revolutionary War. But after concentrating much of the Old Army in the East during the summer of 1861 and then permitting regular officers to hold volunteer rank, Washington seems to have forgotten that there was a professional presence tucked away in the Union Army's amateur folds. After General Scott's retirement there were no further attempts to issue definitive guidance on what would be the Regular Army's role in the war effort. Even the 1861 and 1863 editions of *Revised Regulations for the Army of the United States* failed to address the fact that nine of the Regular Army's nineteen infantry regiments were organized on completely different lines than were volunteers or the Old Army. By default, department commanders in the field were free to decide how to organize and employ their assigned regulars.[14]

The man who determined this for the regulars in the Department of the Ohio was Don Carlos Buell. Like many of his fellow generals in blue, Buell was an Old Army man. An 1841 West Pointer, he had seen extensive service in the Seminole and Mexican Wars. Although historians generally rank Buell toward the bottom of the list of effective Union combat leaders, he was an able administrator. This officer's sole modern biographer believes that "making soldiers out of civilians revealed perhaps Buell's greatest strength." The Army of the Ohio's commander had strong notions on the value of regulars and how to employ them. He wanted the regulars in his army to play a key role in the task of forming a coherent force out of the rabble of troops then in his department and devised a rather unique method of doing so. Buell would use his regulars as neither Iron Column nor cadre; the Army of the Ohio's regulars would not be doled out to the volunteers as trainers, but neither would they be grouped together in a single unit. Instead, he tried to combine the best elements of both theories. Buell wanted to organize each of his divisions with two brigades of volunteer troops and one of regulars. A brigade of regulars would provide each division commander with a force of trained and reliable troops, something the North desperately needed in Kentucky during late 1861. Simultaneously, the regulars' example of discipline and professionalism would hopefully inspire the division's volunteers.

Buell's ideas matched those of George Thomas. Since mid-October Thomas had been pressuring the War Department for the assignment of "some regular troops to steady the raw volunteers and afford rallying points in case of reverses." A similar plan was already being employed with great success in the Union Army's artillery. Wherever possible, one regular battery was assigned to a division along with a number of volunteer batteries, the commander of the regular outfit becoming the division's chief of artillery. By learning from the example of highly trained regulars, the efficiency of the division's volunteer artillerymen rapidly increased. Whether or not this technique could be successful in a non-technical branch like the infantry remained to be seen.[15]

When Buell assumed command of the Department of the Ohio, his army consisted of nothing more than diverse collections of regiments. On November 30, he organized these regiments into sixteen brigades (giving each brigade a sequential designation, 1st through 16th, a practice unique among Federal field armies), and two days later assigned the brigades to divisions. Buell's two most important concentrations of troops were those under George Thomas at Lebanon and Alexander McCook south of Louisville at Camp Nevin. These commands were designated the Army of the Ohio's 1st and 2nd Divisions, and as regulars reported for duty Buell assigned them to brigades in these two units. Buell organized three additional divisions simultaneously with the 1st and 2nd, led by generals Ormsby M. Mitchel, William "Bull" Nelson, and Thomas L. Crittenden, but Thomas's and McCook's commands were the only divisions in the Army of the Ohio that ended up containing any regular infantry. Looking about his department upon taking over in November 1861, Buell soon discovered that regulars were a rare sight west of the Appalachians. "I expected two regular batteries from Missouri," Buell lamented two years later. "About the 1st of January [1862] two companies of artillery, without batteries, making together about 70 men, with one officer, reported to me. The expectation of a regiment of regular cavalry resulted even worse than that. After my arrival at Nashville [in March 1862] two companies reported, with about 70 men." Few regulars were assigned to the Army of the Ohio because there were just not that many regulars to be had. The regular recruiting effort did not keep pace with losses from combat, disease, desertion, and other causes. On January 1, 1862, there were only 19,871 soldiers present for duty in the entire Regular Army, which was 51 percent of authorized strength.[16]

General Buell was heartened when Henry Carrington finally arrived in Louisville at the head of three well-trained battalions of regular infantry, but Carrington's men turned out to be the largest single infusion of regulars the Army of the Ohio ever received. With few exceptions, all of the Old Army's infantrymen were serving in the East. Of the nine New Army infantry regiments, four (the 11th, 12th, 14th, and 17th) were headquartered in eastern states and were also part of McClellan's army, while a fifth, (the 13th Infantry) was based out of Jefferson Barracks near St. Louis and was assigned to Halleck's Department of the Missouri. This left just four New Army regiments for the Army of the Ohio: the 15th, 16th, 18th, and 19th. Four small regimental field detachments were not enough to completely fill a single brigade in any of Buell's divisions. The most he could do with this force was to assign a few battalions of regular infantry and a regular artillery battery to a brigade and then flesh out the command with volunteer regiments, preferably ones led by experienced officers.

* * *

Upon the 18th Infantry's arrival in Lebanon, General Thomas assigned Carrington's men to his 3rd Brigade. The brigade's other regular formation was Battery I, 4th U.S. Artillery, one of the few Old Army outfits serving in the West. Led by 1856 West Point graduate Captain Richard Lodor, the battery had been stationed at Fort Randall, Nebraska, prior to the war. Three infantry regiments rounded out the brigade, all volunteer. One was the 9th Ohio, an all-German regiment from Cincinnati. Its colonel was the popular and free-spirited Robert L. McCook, younger brother of division commander Alexander McCook. McCook served as the 3rd Brigade commander, with Major Gustav Kämmerling, a veteran of the 1848 Revolution in Germany, in immediate command of McCook's regiment. Also assigned to the brigade was the 2nd Minnesota of Colonel Horatio P. Van Cleve, an 1831 West Pointer who had served just two years in the regulars before resigning from the army. Van Cleve's men at least looked like regulars, for he had somehow managed to have his Minnesotans issued regulation full dress uniforms. The brigade's final regiment, the 35th Ohio led by Mexican War veteran Colonel Ferdinand Van Derveer, was assigned a few days after the 18th's arrival at Lebanon.[17]

Carrington did not spend much time in Kentucky. Never enthusiastic about service away from the comfortable confines of Camp Thomas, he had thus far accompanied his battalions only because Lieutenant Colonel Shepherd was still in transit from New York. Carrington had his fill of field living after just three days. On December 10 he placed Major Frederick Townsend in command of the 18th Infantry's field detachment and headed north for Columbus. Carrington offered a weak excuse for his actions in his postwar memoirs: "I found that my absence from Camp Thomas, Ohio, was regarded at Washington as premature, until the 16th and 18th Regiments, then being organized, were filled to their maximum strength." Upon arrival back at Camp Thomas, Carrington proudly notified the War Department that the 18th Infantry was finally in Kentucky:

Headquarters Camp of Instruction
Camp Thomas, Ohio
December 11, 1861

L. Thomas
    Adjutant General

Sir,

I have the honor to report that I have just returned from Lebanon, Ky., having in accordance with orders of Genl Buell, conducted 12 companies of my regiment to that point.

I take pleasure in reporting that the Command en route, maintained order, sobriety and discipline, eliciting the commendation of the General of the Department and General Thomas to whose special command they are attached.

In the Brigade however to which they belong, they are commanded, (in my absence) by Col. R. McCook, 9th O.V.I. I hope before many weeks to complete my regiment and be in the field, at their head.

I remain
Most Respectfully,

HENRY B. CARRINGTON
Col., 18th U.S.
Commanding[18]

Carrington's letter to the Adjutant General was probably intended for public consumption, as was his postwar assertion that the War Department was concerned about his absence from Camp Thomas. His private correspondence during the deployment preparations at Camp Thomas reveals his intentions more accurately. Two days after asking Lieutenant Colonel Shepherd via telegraph "When shall I expect you?" the colonel sent Shepherd another message: "Take command of two battalions of the regiment at Louisville, Kentucky at earliest day possible." A cable Carrington sent the day before departure from Camp Thomas to Captain Henry Haymond, then on recruiting duty at Clarksburg, Virginia, is even more revealing: "Report to Camp Thomas Columbus to Major Stokes commanding 3rd Batt. I shall return to camp in a few days." Carrington's determination to stay in Ohio reveals much about his character. While he was a superb organizer and had great interest in the "spit and polish" side of the military, leading troops in the field was another matter entirely. For all his admirable efforts in recruiting and organizing the 18th Infantry, Carrington was in the end

more of a military administrator than a true field soldier. He successfully avoided field duty throughout the Civil War.[19]

Six days after Carrington's departure, the 18th Infantry began to
find out what Regular Army field operations were all about.
Lieutenant Colonel Oliver L. Shepherd completed his long journey
from New York on December 16 and assumed command of the regiment's 1st and 2nd Battalions. He could not have asked for a better command situation. He and George Thomas were West Point
classmates (Class of 1840) and had known each other for years; Don
Carlos Buell, Class of 1841, was an old 3rd Infantrymen and had
served with Shepherd during the Seminole and Mexican Wars.
Shepherd was not impressed by Colonel Robert McCook, but
thought it would not be long before he displaced McCook as commander of the 3rd Brigade. Given the rate at which field-grade officers of the Old Army were being promoted, Shepherd was confident
that he would soon be wearing the shoulder straps of a full colonel.
Since regular commissions took precedence over identical volunteer
rank regardless of promotion date, as soon as Shepherd was promoted to colonel in the regulars he would outrank all volunteer
colonels in the Union Army.

A test for any new commander is having the ability to take charge
of a good unit and make it even better. Shepherd passed this exam
with high marks. Having been schooled in the rigid discipline of the
prewar regulars, he applied that education to his new regiment,
starting with strict orders about camp guard, passes, and inspections. Lieutenant Henry Freeman vividly recalled the days following
Shepherd's arrival:

> Our commander had served in the Mexican War, and we young-
> sters looked with admiring and envious eyes on the gold leaf of the
> brevet rank which he had then won. On duty he was, as the boys
> would say, a holy terror; not the slightest delinquency escaped his
> watchful eyes. Perfectly familiar with every detail of the service, he
> was everywhere; now showing a teamster how to handle his mules,
> or a company cook how to utilize the rations; next, a soldier how
> and with what to pack his knapsack, superintending drills, making
> of returns, and all the thousand and one things necessary to the com-
> fort and efficiency of his inexperienced officers and men. At night, in
> front of his camp-fire, he would melt into the most genial mood, and
> with his stories and jokes led us to doubt whether the colonel of the
> day and of the evening were one and the same person.[20]

William Bisbee, who became sergeant major of 2/18th U.S. in September 1861, echoed Freeman's opinion of their new commander: "Colonel 'Black Jack' Shepherd, a West Point graduate of the vintage 1840, was to us youngsters a fearful martinet," Bisbee recalled of Shepherd's first few days in command. Even so, the sergeant major thought Shepherd's demanding standards were good things to have: "what we didn't know about campaigning would make several volumes and poor comradeship for the knowledge he possessed from experience in the Mexican War." Even the regiment's four-legged members did not escape Shepherd's gaze. An expert with pack animals from his explorations of New Mexico, he somehow found time to supervise a lame mule's return to the Quartermaster's Department. Determining that the mule had a slight case of distemper, which would probably cure itself in a matter of weeks, Shepherd urged the department quartermaster not to waste this government asset: "He is a good and valuable mule and ought to be taken care of, more care than we can do on a march." The lieutenant colonel also took special interest in the combat skills of the regiment. Three days after taking charge, Shepherd continued Carrington's marksmanship program and ordered his battalions to conduct rifle target practice on a daily basis. Everyone participated. Shepherd's tough discipline resulted in a number of 18th Infantrymen being in confinement at any given time, but he did not want these men to escape target practice. He made sure the regiment's sergeant of the guard escorted the prisoners from the guardhouse to the firing range each day. Shepherd also had a softer side, as noted in Freeman's recollection of his commander's after-hours congeniality. The lieutenant colonel ensured that all 18th Infantrymen had turkey for Christmas dinner.[21]

* * *

While Oliver Shepherd fine-tuned the 18th Infantry during the 1861–1862 winter, more senior officers hammered out the North's military strategy for the Western Theater. Two objectives—one geographic, the other political—dominated operations in this vast arena for most of the war. An advance down the Mississippi River, splitting the Confederacy in two and opening up the watery to northern commerce, was a geographic objective obvious to any Federal strategist. The necessity of the North's other western objective, an advance into east Tennessee, was subtler to military minds. This region contained a large Unionist population and the oppression

Confederate authorities inflicted on the loyal citizens there concerned President Lincoln to such an extent that he insisted Federal military forces occupy the area as soon as possible. There were militarily sound reasons for a campaign into east Tennessee as well. The rail line that most directly linked Virginia with the Confederate heartland ran through the region. Federal operations in east Tennessee would also bring pressure to bear on the far western flank of Confederate forces in northern Virginia and outflank the Southern garrisons at Bowling Green and Nashville.

Although the president in early October issued a directive for an advance into east Tennessee, the start of the campaign was repeatedly delayed. Southeastern Kentucky and east Tennessee were mountainous, desolate regions, served by few good roads and no rail lines along the potential route of Federal advance. To move through such a region required extensive logistical preparations and staff planning, something that stretched the abilities of the inexperienced Federal commanders and staff officers then in Kentucky. The command responsible for east Tennessee operations, the Department of the Cumberland/Ohio, went through three commanders (Anderson, Sherman, Buell) in little more than a month during October–November 1861, causing additional delays. Further complicating matters in the West was a divided Federal command structure. Kentucky east of the Cumberland River and the entire state of Tennessee were in Buell's Department of the Ohio, while Kentucky west of the Cumberland was the purview of Halleck's Department of the Missouri. Pushing Albert Sidney Johnston's Confederate forces out of Kentucky was a prerequisite for both advancing down the Mississippi and into east Tennessee. Doing so would require close coordination between Buell and Halleck, but the two department commanders did not coordinate their plans.[22]

While Halleck prepared to advance along the most promising route through Kentucky, up the Cumberland and Tennessee (or "Twin") Rivers, Buell concentrated on points east. General Buell considered the capture of Nashville to be the paramount Union objective in this region and was not enthusiastic about a wintertime offensive into east Tennessee's mountains. In late December, he eventually bowed to a combination of Washington pressure and urging from George Thomas, whose division was ideally situated to make a stab at east Tennessee. Cumberland Gap through the southern Appalachians provided the most practical route from central

Kentucky to Knoxville and east Tennessee, but before Union troops could approach the gap a 4,000-man Confederate force located at Mill Springs on the Cumberland River, forty miles from Lebanon, would have to be dealt with. Commanded by Brigadier General Felix Zollicofer, these Southerners crossed to the north bank of the Cumberland on December 5. Learning that Zollicofer occupied a threatening but perhaps vulnerable position on the north side of the river, Buell ordered Thomas to march from Lebanon and attack. One of Thomas's brigades, Schoeph's, had occupied an advanced position at Somerset, about nine miles northeast of Mill Springs, in early December to keep an eye on the nearby Southerners. Thomas ordered Schoeph to rendezvous with the balance of the division at a point north of Zollicofer's position. Once the division was consolidated, Thomas planned to strike. The Federal offensive got underway on New Year's Day 1862. Over the next two weeks, elements of Manson's and McCook's brigades slogged through freezing rain, occasional snow, and muddy roads while crawling over the broken terrain of southeastern Kentucky. Thomas's 5,000 cold and tired troops arrived at Logan's Crossroads, nine miles due north of the Confederate position, on January 17. Thomas ordered Schoeph to link up at that point.[23]

The 18th Infantry and a number of other recently assigned units were not part of Thomas's column. During the regiment's short stay at Camp Sullivant, Shepherd's men had not been able to acquire enough wagons and mule teams to haul their equipment. As the campaign commenced Shepherd's quartermasters frantically scraped together transportation. "These mules had never been broken to harness and you should have seen the fun," remembered Private Robert Kennedy of C/2/18th U.S. Infantry. "We hitched them to the wagons which we filled half-full of stones, took them out in a big field and there was fun and kicking. We drove them round that way for four or five days." With the mules sufficiently broken, the regulars departed Lebanon on January 13. Because most of the division had already moved over the same roads, the going was even slower for Shepherd's men. "This was our first, perhaps our hardest, march," Lieutenant Freeman recalled of the movement. "It rained almost incessantly, and the roads, cut up by the heavy trains in advance of us, were well-nigh impassable. ...Our daily marches were not made in very good order; each company, the men carrying their knapsacks, marched beside its wagon, ready to help it up the hills or pull it out of the mud as necessity might require. Frequently a wagon would sink to the axle in the tenacious yellow mud, when it would be necessary to unload it and carry the contents to solid ground; the wagon would then be lifted out and reloaded, probably to repeat the operation within a half a mile."[24]

Some of these difficulties were self-inflicted. Like most regiments at this point in the war, the 18th U.S. had not yet learned how to travel light while on campaign. Only after experiencing marches like the one to Logan's Crossroads did Civil War soldiers realize they could survive on a march with only a few bare necessities. During this movement Shepherd did what he could to educate Sergeant Major Bisbee: "Each Company had several wagons and the regimental train was a sight loaded with frozen tents that were too bulky to pack and all sorts of trash that soldiers unwisely felt inclined to take. Our [first] days march was essentially a halt, in the red Kentucky clay, as the distance gained was not over a mile after one of the hardest pulls of the war. Lord! How old 'Black Jack' Shepherd did go through the luggage after that. As Sergeant Major, I had charge of mail and for a letter box a small ammunition chest marked 'P.O.' which caught the wild eye of the Colonel, who took an axe and smashed it, adding a few choice remarks."[25]

The mobility the regiment gained through the destruction of Bisbee's letterbox did not fully compensate for the poor roads and bad weather. Two days later a local citizen arrived at the 18th Infantry's stalled column, bearing a message from General Thomas. The division commander was also trying to speed the regulars' advance:

> Hd Qrs. 1st Div. Dept of the Ohio
> Camp Near "Cains" Ky.
> Jan'y 16 1862.

Lt. Col. O.L. Shepperd.
  Com'g 18th U.S. Inft.

Colonel:

The bearer Mr. Fishback is a resident of this section of the country, and appears to be well acquainted with the most practicable rout leading to this camp. I have directed him to conduct you to this point by the practicable route.

If after consultation with Mr. F. you find that you will require additional rations, it will be advisable to go into camp and send your wagons back to Columbia for them, should you do so, you had better bring ten days rations (if possible) of hard bread, sugar, coffee, candles, etc, fresh beef can be procured here.

Should you require more transportation I think it can be obtained of citizens on the road, hire as much as will enable you to make this point, or Logans, with little delay as possible.

Respectfully,

GEO. H. THOMAS

Brig Genl U.S.V.[26]

Mister Fishback's help was still not enough and the regulars were mud bound while the balance of Thomas's division fought what came to be known as the Battle of Mill Springs (or Logan's Crossroads). The Confederates, now under the command of Brigadier General George B. Crittenden, were not content to wait for Thomas to attack. Crittenden marched his own troops northward in the pre-dawn darkness of January 19 and made contact with Thomas's command near Logan's Crossroads. As the fighting opened, Thomas sent word to Shepherd's column for the regulars to undertake a forced march and reach the battlefield. The 18th Infantrymen abandoned their wagon train and marched as fast as possible but arrived a few hours after the battle was over. The only member of the regiment to participate was Lieutenant Andrew S. Burt of B/2/18th Infantry. A native of Cincinnati who had enlisted in the 6th Ohio Infantry during the early days of the war prior to receiving a commission in the 18th Regulars, Burt was a friend of the McCook family. When the regular battalions were assigned to McCook's brigade, Burt was tapped to serve as an aide-de-camp on McCook's staff. During the height of the short engagement at Mill Springs, McCook had Burt take an important a message to General Thomas. The lieutenant was severely wounded during the ride but did not stop. "He carried the order and did not leave the battlefield," McCook wrote afterward, "or even stop to have the ball extracted from his side, until the battle was over and we had pursued the enemy to his works." In addition to a lengthy hospital stay, Burt received a brevet promotion to captain for his actions, the first member of the 18th to be so honored. While Burt did not come through the battle unscathed, Thomas and his command performed well. The Union brigadier routed his opposition and produced one of the first significant Federal victories in the West. The result of the small clash temporarily ended the Confederate presence in south-eastern Kentucky.

Thomas did not advance further after the victory. Buell had initi-ated the Mills Springs campaign more as a way to bring pressure to bear on the Confederate position at Nashville than as a serious attempt to advance into east Tennessee. The campaign's difficult march buttressed the general's belief that securing east Tennessee was impractical at this time. There were no railroad lines in the region, the poor weather and mountainous terrain made maneuver difficult, and the area provided little in the way of food and forage. Although Federal troops under Brigadier General Samuel P. Carter occupied Cumberland Gap in late January, that move proved to be the extent of the Army of the Ohio's advance toward east Tennessee for the time being. In the end, the Mill Springs campaign only tem-porarily diverted Buell's focus away from the endeavor he had always considered to be more worthwhile, the capture of Nashville.[27]

The 18th Infantry and the rest of Thomas's division encamped at Somerset after the battle, where Shepherd occupied the regular bat-talions with his usual routine of drill, target practice, and inspections. The brief campaign had been enough for Major Edmund Underwood, commander of 1/18th U.S., who had been in poor health for many years. He decided that field campaigning was not in his best interests and retired on February 27 (his health continued to decline and he would pass away in September 1863). Captain James N. Caldwell of the 1st U.S. Infantry was promoted to Underwood's vacated majority in the 18th, an assignment that would eventually lead to Caldwell being reunited with *Coatzacoalcos* shipmates John King and Stephen Carpenter. Caldwell and two companies of the 1st U.S. had sat idle in Key West until early 1862, when they shipped out for the war. After linking up with three other 1st Infantry companies in Missouri, they formed a small regular battalion in Brigadier General John Pope's Army of the Mississippi. Caldwell saw action at New Madrid and Island Number 10 during March and April 1862 as Pope's forces worked their way southward along the Mississippi. It would take until May for the newly promoted major to finally join up with the 18th Regulars. In the meantime, Captain Henry Douglass took Underwood's place in command of the 1st Battalion.[28]

Colonel Robert McCook put his brigade on the road back to Louisville on February 9. After a few days of travel by foot and rail, the brigade boarded a flotilla of river steamers for a leisurely journey down the Ohio and up the Cumberland to Nashville. The occupation of the Tennessee capital netted for Buell a promotion to major general of volunteers, but it was the operations of Brigadier General Ulysses S. Grant's Army of the Tennessee that caused the city's defenses to crumble without firing a shot. On January 29, Halleck launched a combined land-waterborne expedition under Grant and Flag Officer Andrew Foote of the U.S. Navy to capture Forts Henry and Donelson, the Confederate Twin River defenses in western Tennessee just south of the Kentucky border. Grant and Foote captured Fort Henry on February 6; Fort Donelson surrendered ten days later. The seizure of the two forts unhinged the entire Confederate defensive frontier in Kentucky and Tennessee. Little more than a week after the fall of Fort Donelson, Johnston withdrew the Confederate garrisons from Columbus and Bowling Green in Kentucky and evacuated Nashville. Nelson's division of Buell's army entered Nashville bloodlessly on February 25, two days after the Southerners evacuated. Robert McCook's brigade arrived there the evening of March 2. The 18th Infantry went into camp about three miles outside of town on the Charlottesville Pike. There, they waited for Halleck and Buell to determine how to follow up on their recent successes.[29]

Four additional 18th Infantry companies joined Shepherd's command in Nashville. This detachment consisted of G/1/18th U.S. and three companies from the regiment's 3rd Battalion. Major Stokes commanded the companies during the journey from Camp Thomas to Tennessee. Upon the detachment's arrival on March 6, Stokes assumed command of the 18th Infantry's four-company strong 3rd Battalion (one company of 3/18th had deployed with the 1st Battalion the previous November). This battalion did not remain a separate entity for long, for the Senate failed to approve Stokes's commission as a major in the Regular Army. He left Nashville later in March, returned home to Pennsylvania, and never again wore a uniform. Shepherd attached the 3rd Battalion's companies to the 1st and 2nd Battalions, assignments that would continue throughout the war.[30]

* * *

Five battalions of regular infantrymen were near Nashville by the first week of March. In addition to Shepherd's 18th Infantrymen, three battalions of regulars were encamped four miles south of the city on the Franklin Pike. These troops were part of Brigadier General Lovell H. Rousseau's brigade, part of the division which had been formed out of the original contingent of troops William T. Sherman led south out of Louisville during September 1861. The forty-three-year-old Rousseau was a self-educated lawyer who had served in the state legislatures of Indiana and Kentucky in the years leading up to the war. He also had some military experience, serving as a captain in the 2nd Indiana Infantry during the war with Mexico. When the Civil War began, he was a Kentucky state senator and one of Louisville's more prominent citizens. Like many Kentuckians, Rousseau was not in favor of waging a war against slavery, but was steadfast in his support of the Union. His uncompromising stance against secession in the spring and summer of 1861 helped foster Unionist sentiment in the Kentucky Senate. In addition to his political duties, Rousseau recruited the 5th Kentucky Infantry during the late summer of 1861 and became the regiment's colonel. In appreciation of the Kentuckian's exertions, President Lincoln made him a brigadier general of volunteers the following October. Rousseau was highly thought of and well respected. One of the regulars who served in Rousseau's brigade described the general as "a perfect gentleman, a Kentuckian, and careful of his men; always takes his quarters in a tent, though he might as well use a house. He is liked by everyone." Similar to Robert McCook's brigade in Thomas's division, Rousseau's brigade was a mixture of volunteer and regular units. The volunteers were Rousseau's 5th Kentucky, now commanded by Colonel Harvey M. Buckley, Colonel Thomas T. Crittenden's 6th Indiana, and the 1st Ohio of Colonel Benjamin Franklin Smith (an 1853 graduate of West Point). During the stay at Camp Nevin in October and November, the regulars included the two-company contingent of the 19th U.S. and Major King's 1st Battalion, 15th U.S. Infantry.[31]

McCook's command remained at Camp Nevin until early December, when Buell ordered it to move twenty miles south along the Louisville & Nashville. In preparation for the offensive against Nashville, Buell had to secure the massive railroad bridge at Munfordville, a small town of 400 inhabitants on the north bank of the swift-moving Green River. By December 11, the division was consolidated around the town. Each step southward had brought McCook's troops closer to the Confederates at Bowling Green, generating a few skirmishes and one small-scale battle, Rowlett's Station, on December 17.

Four days prior to that engagement, Captain Townsend's battalion of the 16th U.S. Infantry marched into camp. After parting with the 18th Infantry in Louisville, Townsend's command had boarded a southbound train and proceeded to Munfordville. Confederate cavalry had a sharp fight with Federal pickets the day 1/16th U.S. arrived. Federal casualties still lay beside the road near the Munfordville rail depot as the column of regulars marched by. "We saw here the first terrible effects of war," Private Jacob Van Zwaluwenburg recalled, "as ten of our boys had fallen in the skirmish and were laid out under a tree ready for burial." The effect of the 16th Infantry's stay at Camp Thomas was evident to William S. Dodge, one of General McCook's staff officers. "These troops, like those of the Fifteenth Infantry, were newly enlisted," Dodge commented, "but possessed the stamina of efficient soldiers." With the addition of the 16th Infantry, the thirteen companies of regulars in Rousseau's brigade had the manpower equivalent of a full-strength regiment. General Rousseau consolidated them under the command of the 15th's Major King. Captain Swaine took command of the combined battalion of companies from the 15th and 19th Infantry.[32]

The firepower of Rousseau's command increased significantly during January 1862 with the assignment to the brigade of Battery H, 5th U.S. Artillery Regiment. The 5th U.S. Artillery was another New Army regiment authorized under the May 1861 expansion plan. Commanding Battery H was Captain William R. Terrill, the officer who had assisted Anson Mills with receiving an 18th Infantry commission the previous June. Although Terrill was a Virginian—he was the son of a prominent Virginia legislator and had numerous relatives in the Confederate army—he had remained loyal. An 1853 graduate of the Military Academy, Terrill had served in the prewar 4th U.S. Artillery and as a mathematics instructor at West Point. He spent the summer of 1861 recruiting his command at Reading, Pennsylvania, a large contingent of Irishmen filling its ranks. On August 29, the War Department ordered Terrill to establish his headquarters at Newport Barracks and to "continue the recruiting and organization of his company as a battery of Light Artillery."[33]

The new artillerymen went through a relentless training program upon arrival in Kentucky. William Terrill, a tall, stern-faced officer with an exceptionally loud voice, was an Old Army regular and let his men know it. One of Terrill's gunners, James F. Mohr, described the discipline of the battery: "we have a good lot of Officers but if you dont mind you will be tied up there was two tied up already you must not miss roll call or they will put you on double duty the Captain is giveing some of them hell they are out drilling and they dont mind we cetch hell once in a while too I tell you rules are strict here and all we have to do to mind them there was a green horn on gaurd one night and the Captain of the day came around the gaurd ask him who was there and he said the Captain of the day and the gaurd said if the Captain of the night would meet him he would cetch hell."[34]

Instilling a sense of discipline was just part of Terrill's training. Battery H's commander was also a skilled artillerist. The unit was equipped with four 12-pound Napoleon brass smoothbores and two 10-pound Parrot rifles. Terrill was an expert with these weapons and painstakingly drilled his men in their use. Learning to employ and care for horses, guns, wagons, caissons, limber chests, and the plethora of small items necessary for the battery to function kept Terrill's men even more busy at Newport Barracks than John King's nearby 15th Infantrymen. Despite having so much to learn, Private Mohr noted that the gunners had mastered much of their craft by early November: "we are packing our Casons wagon every day with cartridges as far as we know we expect to leave before long, from here where to we do not know, very likely to battle. we was a target shooting yesterday we shot ten loads five out of our rifle cannon and five out of our brass cannon we shot a tree down with a twelve pound ball one foot thrue and the shells of our rifle cannon would burst at the target the pieces would stick all around the target to day we dont do any thing but clean our harness and our clothes for inspection."[35]

Terrill was fortunate to have two Old Army lieutenants assigned to the battery: Francis L. "Frank" Guenther, a New Yorker who had graduated from West Point in 1859, and Jacob H. Smyser, a Pennsylvanian who was among the youngest of the "old" regulars, being a member of the Class of 1861. The battery commander was particularly impressed with Guenther. As a second lieutenant with the 4th Regular Artillery, Guenther had a fine reputation in the Old

Army, and he had also campaigned extensively in West Virginia throughout the summer and autumn of 1861. Shortly after Guenther reported for duty with Battery H in early 1862, Captain Terrill sent word to General Buell that the lieutenant was suited for higher rank:

> Camp Wood, Ky
> Feb 8, 1862
>
> Capt. James B. Fry
> Asst Adjt General US Army
> Chief of Staff
> Head Qrs Dept of the Ohio
>
> Captain,
>   I have the honor to recommend that 1st Lieut. Francis L. Guenther 5th Regt US Artillery be made a Captain by Brevet to date from the 3d day of October 1861. He served on that day in Capt Howes Battery of the 4th US Artillery in the attack which was made upon the enemies Camp at Greenbrier in Western Virginia. Lieut Guenther acquitted himself with credit on that day. He is certainly a most deserving young officer; he has served continuously in the field since the 22d of June. We are deficient here [in McCook's division] in Artillery officers of experience. Lieut Guenther cannot now be placed in charge of batteries commanded by Volunteer Captains, but if he was a Capt his services could be rendered far more valuable to us.
>   Lieut Guenther was a stranger to me when he joined my battery. He has been a very faithful officer and one of considerable ability, and if the Genl Cmdg will make this recommendation I feel assured that it will be of service to the Artillery of this Department, and he will never have cause to regret such action.
>
> I am very respectfully
> Your Obedient Servant
>
> WM. R. TERRILL
> Capt 5th Artillery
> Chief of Artillery[36]

Brevet promotions were extremely hard to have approved this early in the war and Guenther remained a lieutenant for the time being. Battery H packed its caissons at Newport Barracks for the final time in mid-January 1862. The unit arrived at Munfordville on January 21 and General McCook assigned it to Rousseau's brigade. Additional regular troops also joined Rousseau's command on the banks of the Green River. Companies G and H of 1/15th U.S. arrived from Newport Barracks a few weeks into 1862, giving Swaine's battalion its full complement of eight companies. Captain R. Peabody Barry's F/1/16th U.S. and Captain William J. Sidell's G/1/16th U.S. joined Rousseau's brigade from Camp Thomas in February. Barry's first lieutenant, New Yorker Edward Mitchell, made some interesting observations of his company's movement to the Bluegrass State:

> We Left Camp Thomas on Monday, at 8 A.M., and reached Cincinnati at half-past seven, the whole city being splendidly illuminated in consequence of the news of the capture of Fort Donaldson. We were cheered by thousands; candles and lanterns and flags were waving continually, and we marched half a mile to the boat through mud, three, four, and five inches thick. We reached Louisville at half-past seven Tuesday morning; then we marched through the city, and before dark pitched our tents. Notwithstanding the mud, which is all about us, under the water, we are in a jolly, happy, and contended condition. We are enjoying what is probably as bad a time as we shall have while on campaign, unless we are all caught some night in a very wet ditch, without tents.[37]

The naive young lieutenant would soon realize that life during a campaign could be very much worse than his early experiences led him to believe.

Also in February, Major King detached the 19th Infantrymen from Captain Swaine's battalion of the 15th Infantry. Major Steven D. Carpenter reported to Munfordville that month with two additional companies of the 19th Infantry, establishing 1/19th U.S. as a distinct albeit small command. A fifth company, E/1/19th U.S., would later join the battalion at Nashville.[38] Carpenter was glad to finally be in the field at the head of his battalion after serving on mustering duty in Indianapolis since the previous October. While many regular officers took advantage of mustering assignments to arrange volunteer commands for themselves, Carpenter politicked only to ensure he served with his proper regiment:

Indianapolis, Indiana
January 25th, 1862.

Genl. L. Thomas
   Adjutant Genl, U.S. Army

Sir,

I would respectfully state to the Adjutant Genl that during the organization of the First Battalion of my Regiment it has been understood both by myself and by the Officers of my Regiment that in as far as the recommendation of the Lieut. Col. Commanding would avail, I should be placed in command of this battalion. I am now informed by Lieut. Col. King that two additional Companies are ready to take the field, and as many of the officers of the Companies now organized have been assigned to them at my request, and with a hope at least that they would be in my battalion, I would respectfully request that this favor may be granted to me if not inconsistent with the good of the Service. I am very anxious to command this battalion, and fear should it go to the field under any other Commander that it will not be permitted for me to join it. As I have always been on active duty my health, when confined to the office is poor tho I do not urge this as a consideration to be placed upon any other duty than what is considered the best for the Dept.

Should permission be given for me to take command of these four companies, it will be esteemed a great favor by Sir your most obedient,

S.D. CARPENTER
Major 19th Infy[39]

Lorenzo Thomas consented to Carpenter's request, a rare instance of the adjutant general believing that it would be best for a regular officer to be assigned to line rather than staff duty. If the green regulars of the 19th Infantry's new companies thought their training would be easier in the field than it had been in Indiana, they were disappointed. Lieutenant Louis M. Hosea, adjutant of Captain Townsend's 1/16th U.S., recalled that the regulars put their time that winter to good use:

Our volunteer neighbors used to make much sport of us during our stay at Green River, opposite Munfordville, Ky...because we were continually drilled, no matter how inclement the weather. Old Major Carpenter, commanding the Nineteenth Infantry, gave the cue when he said we would undoubtedly have to march and fight during bad weather, and therefore might as well prepare for it by drilling.

Officers were instructed in tactics and army regulations like school boys—and indeed many of us were so, and at that time knew scarcely the A B C's of warfare. Some, however, were men of many years' army experience, who were untiring and almost tyrannical in their efforts to make soldiers of us. Our enlisted men were about as good, and certainly no better, than the average volunteer; but here and there was one who had seen service in garrison or on the "plains" before the Civil War, and...their example was a most valuable factor...under whom the regular soldiers developed a sterner quality than their comrades of the volunteers.[40]

As Halleck's operations on the Twin Rivers got underway in early February, McCook's division was ordered to march back toward the Ohio River and prepare for a waterborne movement to join the expedition. The roads were in such poor shape that General Rousseau ordered his infantry to march along the bed of the Louisville & Nashville rails. That was not much easier. Captain Reuben D. Mussey of B/1/19th U.S. recalled that the rails were "ballasted with rough 'macadam' stones that cut into our feet as we went." Grant's unexpectedly swift capture of the Confederate Twin River defenses meant that McCook's division was not needed in western Tennessee. The unit halted its movement near Elizabethtown and then started on a return march to Munfordville.[41]

The regulars were back in their old camps only a few days before receiving orders to head for Nashville. The troops packed up their equipment as best they could amidst a blinding storm of sleet and freezing rain. Eli Tarbell, now a corporal, described the difficulty of the first day's march in a February 19 diary entry: "Struck tents & Marched two miles, & went into Camp, Raining hard, Road verry bad we are wet to the Skin...it is now we begin to find out what a solgers life is, but Every body makes the best of it."[42] Sergeant Arthur B. Carpenter had expected soldiering to be tough, but nothing had prepared him for this:

> We traveled by railroad to Mumfordsville Kentucky and marched the rest of the way and of all the rough times I never saw or heard of before, from Mumfordsville to within twenty miles of Bowling Green, the mud is about knee deep and it would rain every other day. One day in particular we struck tents in the morning about 8 o'clock the rain pouring down, and we had to push our wagons most of the way, the worn-out mules would get stuck every few minutes. We worked until 4 o'clock and had got only a mile from where we were encamped in the morning, just soaked in the rain we pitched our tents and had to lay on rails to keep us up out of the mud. Such is soldier's life, he must be exposed to every kind of danger and inconvenience.[43]

On February 23, the division camped amidst the abandoned Confederate fortifications at Bowling Green. It resumed the march three days later. South of Bowling Green, the turnpike was in excellent condition and the weather improved, so the column made rapid progress. The first recorded instance of a regular soldier in the Army of the Ohio encountering the enemy occurred during this movement, the honor going to Gunner Peter Fitzpatrick of Battery H, 5th Artillery. He lived to tell about it, thanks to a good horse. Fitzpatrick was an Irishman and typical of many Northern troops from the Emerald Isle. He was a good soldier and full of fight, so much so that Captain Terrill choose the burly Fitzpatrick to be his orderly and personal bodyguard.

Terrill commanded the advanced guard of McCook's column as it moved south from Bowling Green, the force consisting of Battery H along with a company each of volunteer infantry and cavalry. Toward dusk on the first day of the march, the advanced guard's cavalry noticed some enemy horsemen in an open field and gave chase. The Confederate troopers spurred their mounts to the rear, making a fast escape. About an hour later, as darkness closed in, Terrill's column came upon a dense wood. The captain could see lights emanating from a point about fifty rods into the trees. He deployed his infantry company as skirmishers and sent Fitzpatrick forward to poke around. The Irishman and his trusty mount Napoleon picked their way through the forest, passing close to a large mansion. He came upon the Federal skirmish line to the rear of the structure. The infantry's captain asked Fitzpatrick where he was going, and offered to come along upon learning that the gunner was going to find out where the lights were coming from. "You better believe I was glad of his company," Fitzpatrick later remarked. The infantryman walked beside Fitzpatrick's horse. A little deeper into the forest they finally saw some campfires and what appeared to be an enemy camp. Fitzpatrick wanted to get a closer look but the captain's curiosity seems to have been satisfied. He ordered Fitzpatrick to report back to Captain Terrill. The artilleryman replied that he wanted to move closer, at which time the captain grabbed Fitzpatrick's reigns, gave him a quick lecture on the proper relationship between officers and enlisted men, and ordered him to retire.[44]

Fitzpatrick rode back to the main road and reported what he had seen to Captain Terrill. The battery commander sent Fitzpatrick into the woods again with orders to do a proper reconnaissance instead of turning tail at the first sign of trouble. Back the Irishman went, determined to not let anyone get in his way. He moved through the skirmish line toward the enemy position. Alone this time, Fitzpatrick took a much closer look:

> I rode in through the thickest of the woods and took a good look at the camp. There were about a dozen fires and men were lying around them in a circle. I saw a solitary sentinel on the extreme right, sitting on a log, close to a large fire. I advanced towards him shaded by the trees from his view. I asked him who commanded the post. He told me that it was Captain Walker of the Texas Rangers. He drew his revolver and ordered me to dismount and consider myself his prisoner. I didn't believe in that logic, for I had my pistol ready primed. I aimed at his right shoulder, the shot told and I trusted to Napoleon to carry me safe back to the Battery. I think I must have been about a half mile off when I heard shots whizzing through the trees. I had two railfences to cross before I came to the road but Napoleon crossed them like a brick. Both me and my horse was received with a shout of joy, when we came up.[45]

Captain Walker's Texans, members of the 8th Texas Cavalry, could do little more than observe and report as the Army of the Ohio's powerful columns converged on Nashville. Alexander McCook's division crossed the Tennessee state line on February 27. Three days later, marching through a heavy downpour, the troops reached the Tennessee capital. That same day, steamers transporting George Thomas's division completed their ascent of the Cumberland River and discharged their passengers at the city's docks. The 18th Regulars of Robert McCook's brigade stretched their stiffened legs, glad to be off the crowded ships. Lieutenant Colonel Shepherd formed them up and moved them down the Charlottesville Pike to the camp of McCook's brigade. The legs of King's regulars in Rousseau's brigade were sore as opposed to stiff as they marched through Nashville to a camp on the Franklin Pike, the difficult march from Munfordville providing them the same hard lessons the 18th Infantry had learned during the Mill Springs Campaign.

While the Army of the Ohio assembled in middle Tennessee, forces from Halleck's Department of the Missouri moved further south along the Tennessee River. Halleck planned to break Confederate rail communications in northern Mississippi, isolate Memphis, and extend Federal control of the Mississippi River. Two

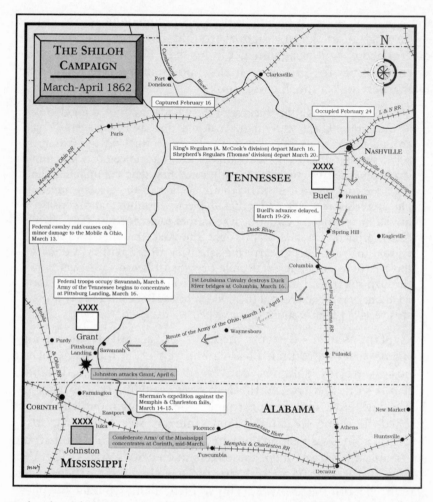

Federal raids against rail lines in the region got underway in mid-March, but the 5th Ohio Cavalry caused only minor damage to the Mobile & Ohio Railroad on March 13; a larger expedition commanded by William T. Sherman against the Memphis and Charleston Railroad the next day failed completely. Realizing that more than raids were necessary, Halleck ordered Grant up the Tennessee to assume command of Union forces in the area. The next move would be an overland advance to capture Corinth, Mississippi, a vital rail transportation hub and headquarters of Confederate General P.G.T. Beauregard's Army of the Mississippi. Grant, also wearing new two-star shoulder straps of a major general, on March

17 established headquarters of the Army of the Tennessee at Savannah, a small river town fifteen miles north of the Mississippi state line. Most of Grant's forces encamped at Pittsburg Landing, an obscure freight station on the Tennessee nine miles upriver from Savannah.

Halleck wanted Buell's army at Nashville to combine with Grant's for the assault on Corinth, but Buell, gripped by an unfounded fear of an enemy attempt to recapture Nashville, was reluctant to move out of middle Tennessee. Buell also thought that the best place to break Confederate rail communications was in Alabama, not Mississippi. These arguments become moot on March 11, when President Lincoln (after a considerable lobbying effort by Henry Halleck) reorganized the Union Army's command structure. Halleck assumed control of the new Department of the Mississippi, consisting of all territory between Knoxville and the Mississippi River. Now Buell's superior, Halleck ordered the Army of the Ohio to make for Savannah immediately.[46]

McCook's division led the Army of the Ohio on the march out of Nashville. King's regulars broke camp at six o'clock in the morning on March 16 and marched fourteen miles to Franklin. It was a pleasant movement for Lieutenant Edward Mitchell of the 16th Infantry, particularly as this was his first day as a company commander. Although Mitchell was still assigned to Captain Barry's F/1/16th U.S., the lieutenant had taken temporary command of G/1/16th U.S. because that unit's assigned commander, Lieutenant Arthur W. Allyn, was sick and had remained in Nashville. The new commander enjoyed marching through Franklin: "This is a very pretty town; and as we passed through, colors flying and bands playing, we evidently made an impression on the inhabitants. We passed beyond Franklin ten miles, and encamped. Having marched fifteen or sixteen miles, of course we felt disposed to take a comfortable sleep; but orders came for ten companies of regulars to go out on picket." After spending the night screening the army's front on a line of hills a few miles southwest of Franklin, the regulars barely had time the next morning to eat breakfast and pack up before they were on the move again. They marched another twenty-one miles that day to a point near Spring Hill and there established Camp Kirk, named after Colonel Edward N. Kirk, who had recently replaced General Wood in command of the 5th Brigade of McCook's division.[47]

The Army of the Ohio began to encounter resistance as it moved closer to Savannah—harassment delivered by the 1st Louisiana Cavalry. Terrill's battery again formed part of McCook's advance guard and had a number of brushes with the Louisianans. Captain Terrill's column found itself in a sharp skirmish one day. Peter Fitzpatrick was wounded in the left arm while defending his commander, but the private's marksmanship prevailed: "I suffice it to say that four dead lay at our feet." Fitzpatrick's Confederate opposition experienced greater success in destroying bridges on the region's numerous streams and rivers. Repairing the bridge over Rutherford Creek, four miles north of Columbia, delayed the advance three days. A more lengthy delay occurred at Columbia itself on March 25. The 1st Louisiana burned the two bridges there across the Duck River, which was running at flood stage due to wet weather that spring. While such an obstacle would have been quickly surmounted later in the war, in early 1862 Federal field engineering skills were not well developed. Rebuilding the destroyed bridge was a time-consuming task, and the Army of the Ohio's pontoon train was still in Nashville while Buell's divisions stacked up on the north side of the Duck. Buell's men were almost eighty miles from Savannah.

McCook's division settled into Camp Stanton near Columbia. Much to the amusement of the volunteers of the division, Major King used the time to continue training the regular battalions and held daily inspections and drill. Corporal Tarbell's diary entries during this time indicate that he did not particularly enjoy waiting for the Duck to be bridged. March 24: "Capt Williams Drilled the Co to day, Major Carpenter Jerked some of the Boys Endways for not Keeping in there place, our offenses are very strict." Two days later: "thare is not much fun about camp these days, the Boys are all drilled out." The river's level was low enough by March 29 to allow Nelson's division to ford the river and continue the march. Crittenden's division followed the next day as a pontoon bridge was completed and repairs to one of the permanent frame bridges were finished. Alexander McCook led his division across on March 31.

The Army of the Ohio's halt at the Duck gave the Confederates a great opportunity. By concentrating nearly all available Confederate forces at Corinth, the Army of the Mississippi (with Johnston now in immediate command) numbered more than 40,000 troops by the end of March. Learning that Buell was stalled near

Columbia, Johnston planned to strike Grant's isolated forces at Pittsburg Landing. While the Confederates at Corinth completed their preparations and moved toward Grant's unsuspecting troops during the first week of April, the Army of the Ohio was still strung out on the muddy road between Columbia and Savannah. Intermittent rains often slowed the Federal advance to less than a dozen miles a day. Nelson's division arrived in Savannah late in the day on April 5. Twenty-one miles away, McCook's division encamped for the night.[48]

* * *

George Sanderson listened intently, finally realizing what the dull booming sounds in the distance meant: a battle was going on somewhere up ahead. A lieutenant in E/1/15th U.S. and son of the 15th Infantry's lieutenant colonel, Sanderson and the rest of Rousseau's brigade led the march of McCook's division on Sunday morning, April 6. Moving out at seven o'clock, King's regulars marched only about two miles before they heard the distant cannonading. Private W.W. Worthington of C/1/15th U.S. also noticed the tell-tale sounds: "We had proceeded but a little way when the noise of battle...broke upon our ears. As we advanced the cannonading became each moment more distinct. It was plain that a desperate fight was going on somewhere: but not one of our number dreamed that Grant had been attacked. ...Indeed, the general belief was created by reports brought from the front that our gunboats were attacking some batteries at a place called Hamburg."[49]

Word soon reached the column that Grant's forces at Pittsburg Landing had been attacked earlier that morning. At noon the regulars halted in a cotton field, checked their weapons, had ammunition issued, and prepared rations. When they resumed the march they left behind their extra equipment and wagon train. The Army of the Ohio was closing on Savannah as fast as the muddy roads allowed. Buell's men did not yet realize that Grant's army was actually close to defeat on April 6. Indeed, Private Worthington recalled that the spirit in the ranks of King's regulars was quite high: "The cannon we continued to hear at intervals were said to be those hurried forward in pursuit of the enemy. You may be sure we were jubilant at this news. ...The men were in the best of spirits, rude witticisms, laughter and snatches of song ran along the whole line. Here and there some fellow boasted of the gallant deeds he would have performed had he been in the day's engagement. The officers, on the other hand, were more quiet than usual. They marched in silence or gathered in little knots and conversed in whispers."[50]

The fast pace was eventually too much for Private Jim Roach of D/1/16th Infantry. He fell out in mid-afternoon, too tired for the moment to go on. His company commander, Captain Patrick T. Keyes, would have none of that.

"I'll have you bucked and gagged!" Keyes threatened as he struck Roach across the back with the flat of his sword.

"You'll never get the chance," Roach sneered. "I'll shoot you first chance I get."

The captain moved on, like the rest of the officers exhorting his men to close up, perhaps not having heard Roach's retort.[51]

Rousseau's brigade marched into Savannah two hours before midnight. The hospital steamer *City of Memphis* by that time had brought in numerous loads of wounded from the fighting at Pittsburg Landing. For the men in the Army of the Ohio, most of whom had yet to experience battle, the town presented a macabre scene. Lieutenant Sanderson remembered Savannah as nothing but a vast, chaotic surgical ward: "Anything that could afford shelter was filled with the dead & wounded, the streets were filled with ambulances, men on litters, men hobbling, or carrying arms in slings, men and women rushing to & fro endeavoring to soften the sufferings of the wounded. ...the whole place was one hospital, & such confusion I never saw." Major King and the other leaders in Rousseau's brigade pushed their men through the confusion to the river docks. General Alexander McCook accompanied them and was shocked to find "no preparation made whatever to convey my division to [the] battle-field." He sent members of his staff aboard the boats at the landing, ordering the masters to get out of their bunks and prepare for a journey upriver. Eventually Rousseau's three volunteer regiments were away, followed by the regulars. McCook then started scraping together boats for his two remaining brigades and three batteries of artillery.

At about eleven o'clock that night the regular battalions boarded the steamer *Hiawatha* for the short journey upriver to Pittsburg Landing. Corporal Tarbell made a quick entry in his diary during the passage: "we hear Grants troops are whiped, onley wait untill we get thare." If the corporal had asked his comrades a day later if they would have preferred to wait to get "thare," many undoubtedly would have answered "yes."[52]

Chapter 3:

The Battle Of Shiloh

"You'll Catch Regular Hell Today!"

Private Worthington's spirits sank as the *Hiawatha* traveled upriver. During the nine-mile journey to Pittsburg Landing, the riverboat's crew gave the regulars their first semi-accurate reports of what had happened earlier that day inland from Pittsburg Landing. Johnston's Army of the Mississippi had assaulted the Army of the Tennessee at daybreak on April 6. After great initial success, the Confederate attack culminated at sundown. Although battered, as the fighting ended Grant's troops managed to hold a shallow perimeter around the landing. The news quickly spread among *Hiawatha's* passengers. In great contrast to their high spirits during the march to Savannah, a sense of impending doom began to settle over the regulars: "Regaled, as we were, during the entire passage from Savannah to Pittsburg Landing, with stories of defeat and forebodings of what would occur the next day, you may be certain that we were not as comfortable as if we were in the old barracks. It was plain to the dullest comprehension that McCook's, Nelson's, and Crittenden's divisions of Buell's army, then arrived at the scene of action, would have work enough to do early in the morning, and that too against an enemy flushed with recent victory. It seemed folly to hope for success."[1]

The regulars caught glimpses of the battle's aftermath from *Hiawatha's* decks as she neared Pittsburg Landing. Numerous steamers at the landing were laden with wounded, for there was neither enough room nor surgeons ashore to care for all the casualties. The *City of Memphis*, the only hospital steamer present on this stretch of the Tennessee, made the trip to and from Savannah throughout the night. Thousands of stragglers from Grant's army gathered at the landing. After the Confederates's rough handling of them the previous day, their only concerns that night were trying to stay warm, dry, and as far away from Southerners as possible. The vanguard of Rousseau's brigade, the 6th Indiana, arrived at Pittsburg a few hours ahead of the regular battalions. A member of that regiment recalled: "The groups of unorganized men stood around so thick that we could hardly find standing room on shore."[2]

Hiawatha pulled into the landing about one o'clock in the morning on April 7. After tying up, the boat's master insisted the regulars disembark at once. With all the unruly stragglers gathered on shore, he wanted his craft to spend as little time here as possible. Major King realized that the battalions would not be needed ashore until daylight. In reply to the master's pleadings, King reasoned that his troops would be in better condition to fight by resting onboard until daylight instead of joining the mob ashore at the landing. The master relented, granting the regulars a few more precious hours of rest.[3]

Although Pittsburg Landing was relatively calm throughout the night and the regulars were exhausted, few of King's troops were able to sleep. Those on the crowded steamer's outer decks had to endure a torrential rainstorm that had begun during *Hiawatha's* journey to Pittsburg and did not cease until 3:00 in the morning. The booming of cannons also disturbed their rest. Anchored a few hundred yards upriver were the Federal gunboats *Lexington* and *Tyler*, which spent the night intermittently lobbing shells from their huge guns toward the Confederate lines. The shelling did little damage to the enemy other than the noise making the night even more uncomfortable. The shelling had the same effect on the regulars. As this was the first time that most of them had been on a battlefield, the sound of outgoing artillery had not yet acquired the comforting sound it one day would. Jacob Van Zwaluwenburg well remembered the night's surrealistic images: "With our two gunboats firing shells every five minutes amid flashes of lightening and terrible claps of thunder, it seemed as if we were in the very infernal regions of Hades." Despite all this, King's regulars probably had a more comfortable night than many of the troops on either side. The 6th Indiana had disembarked immediately upon arriving at the landing.

The Hoosiers then stood on their arms in the mud and driving rain for the rest of the night. One 6th Indiana veteran considered that night the worst of his entire Civil War service.[4]

* * *

Bandmaster Lorenz Oberst of the 15th U.S. was a long way from Pike's Opera House in Cincinnati. Deep in *Hiawatha's* hold, Gustavus Taubner, the 15th Infantry's sergeant major, nudged Oberst out of his slumber around five o'clock in the morning. The bandsmen were to be first off the boat and were to take a position at the top of the bluff above the landing. Wiping the sleep from his eyes, Oberst looked around to see the rest of the dozing regulars coming to life. As the musicians assembled on deck, Oberst struck up the band and played selections from the popular opera *Il Trovatore*. Many Shiloh veterans recalled having their spirits lifted on that dreary morning by the 15th Infantry Band. "How inspiring the music was!" a young drummer boy from an Ohio regiment remembered. "Even the poor wounded men...seemed to be lifted up, and every soldier seemed to receive an impetus."[5]

The gray light of dawn was just beginning to stretch over the battlefield as Major King's 844 regulars disembarked. As they made their way up the bluff King's troops were greeted by the strains of "Benny Havens," an old Irish ballad that was (and remains) one of the most popular of all West Point songs. One of the regulars noted that the bandsmen of the 15th U.S. were playing "with all the spirit of a Newport Barracks afternoon concert." As 1/19th U.S. marched by, an excited officer from among the stragglers along the riverbank dashed up and yelled at Bandmaster Oberst: "Stop that damn noise, it will draw the fire of the enemy!" Major Carpenter was nearby and brushed the crazed officer aside with the grim remark "That's exactly what we're here for." The band played on.[6]

The regulars sorely needed the music's inspiration, for the sight that greeted them as they made their way off the *Hiawatha* was none too cheerful. A field hospital had been established around a small cabin near the landing and surgeons had been hard at work throughout the night. There were growing piles of amputated arms and legs stacked nearby. As G/1/16th U.S. came ashore, Lieutenant Edward Mitchell did what he could to cheer up the men in his company, reassuring them with his usual "pleasant words and sprightly air," which "had a most encouraging effect on the men." In nearby D/1/16th U.S., Jacob Van Zwaluwenburg could have used some of Lieutenant

Mitchell's encouragement. "Our boys had lost some of the jovial spirit of the day before," the private noticed as he surveyed the landing. Jests emanating from the crowd did not help. When one of the fugitives found out that regular troops were marching by, he called out: "There's a regular hornet's nest a little way beyond!" Another 16th Infantryman recalled: "As we pushed our way in the dim light of dawn through the crowd of demoralized fugitives cowering under the bank, we were treated to about all the dismal prognostication the human mind is capable of; but in silence our men marched up the bank and out upon the timbered levels beyond."[7]

The 15th Infantry disembarked last. They filed up the bluff, formed column, and dressed ranks.

"What regiment is that?" inquired another straggler nearby, noticing the unit's well-maintained arms and disciplined air.

"15th Regulars," one of King's men replied.

"Well go on," the skulker snapped, "you'll catch regular hell to-day!"

With that final bit of encouragement, the regulars moved inland on the Pittsburg-Corinth Road.[8]

General Rousseau glanced down the road and recognized the steady gait of the column marching toward him: the regular battalions. Rousseau and the brigade's three volunteer regiments had spent the night ashore, but now—about six o'clock—the brigade was assembled and its brigadier wanted to get moving. After Major King halted the regulars, Rousseau gave the ranks "a ringing speech, that cheered us up amazingly." "They had a little ball game yesterday and we'll have another today," Lovell Rousseau said in his best campaign-stumping voice, "but we'll fix 'em! Shoot low, don't hurt 'em much. Shoot 'em in the shins!" General McCook was with Rousseau, the division commander having arrived at Pittsburg with a portion of Colonel Kirk's brigade as the regulars were disembarking. General Buell soon joined them.[9]

Buell had spent the hours before daylight placing his forces in line of battle and attempting, with mixed results, to determine the lay of the land and position of Grant's army. Grant's last line of defense on April 6 was an "L" shaped position, with the end of the horizontal leg resting on Pittsburg Landing, the angle about three-quarters of a mile due east, and the end of the vertical leg extending northward toward Owl Creek. The closest the Confederates came to Pittsburg Landing on April 6 was during their twilight attacks across the

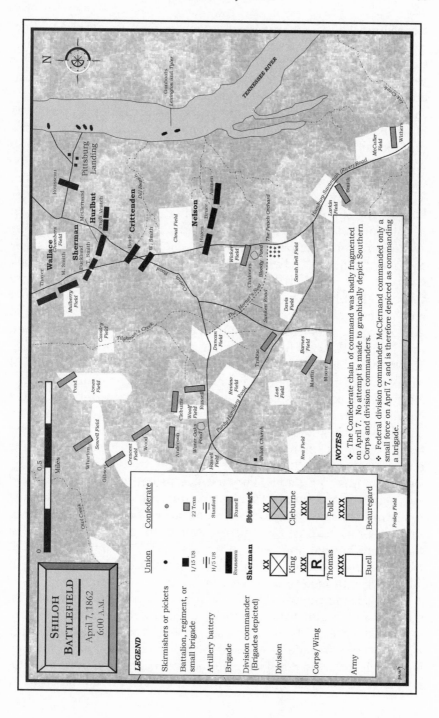

SHILOH
BATTLEFIELD
April 7, 1862
6:00 A.M.

LEGEND

	Union	Confederate
Skirmishers or pickets	•	•
Battalion, regiment, or small brigade	1/15 US	22 Tenn
Artillery battery	11/5 US	Stanford
Brigade	Rousseau	Russell
Division commander (Brigades depicted)	Sherman	Stewart
Division	King XX	Cleburne XX
Corps/Wing	Thomas R XXX	Polk XXX
Army	Buell XXXX	Beauregard XXXX

NOTES

❖ The Confederate chain of command was badly fragmented on April 7. No attempt is made to graphically depict Southern Corps and division commanders.

❖ Federal division commander McClernand commanded only a small force on April 7, and is therefore depicted as commanding a brigade.

Miles
0   0.5   1

treacherous Dill Creek ravine, approaching the base of the "L" line, barely a quarter mile from Pittsburg. Nelson and Crittenden's divisions had arrived at Pittsburg Landing during the night ahead of Rousseau's brigade. Buell fed their regiments in on Grant's left to counter the nearby enemy across Dill Creek, resulting in Buell's forces occupying the left/southern portion of the Union battle line as dawn broke on April 7. The task for the combined Union armies that morning was to push the Southerners back toward Corinth and ensure the security of Pittsburg Landing.[10]

The terrain inland from the landing dictated the flow of battle. The landing was located where it was on the Tennessee River because the Shiloh Plateau (named for a small church about two and a half miles inland) was the only firm ground in an otherwise swampy region. The plateau was bounded by water on three sides: the river to the east, Owl and Snake Creeks to the north, and Lick Creek to the south. Tributaries of these larger watercourses laced through the plateau itself, creating a number of steep ravines that compartmentalized the region. The only approach to the landing of military value was from the southwest and it was from that region that Johnston's army had emerged in the pre-dawn mists of April 6.

Pittsburg Landing was a center for local commerce. A number of roads crossed the plateau and converged there. The main road leading inland linked Pittsburg with the rail yards at Corinth. On the heavily forested Shiloh Plateau, the Pittsburg-Corinth Road ran past Shiloh Church and through a number of cultivated fields. These fields, variously sown with corn, cotton, and orchards, offered the only extended fields of fire in the area and attracted artillery batteries like moths to a flame. The first day of battle had been marked by a series of disjointed struggles for control of these fields, and the following day's actions promised to be more of the same. The campsites of Grant's army were also scattered about the area. Most of them were burned and tattered wrecks by the morning of April 7. Along with hundreds of mangled bodies, the ransacked camps added a grim touch to the scenes greeting the Army of the Ohio.

After spending a miserable night ashore, Nelson's division, nearest the river, had begun a slow, cautious advance about 4:30. It had been in contact since 5:20 with skirmishers from Brigadier General James R. Chalmers's Brigade of Mississippians. While Rousseau belted out his speech to his own brigade, Nelson was halted and awaiting support near Wicker Field. Crittenden's two-brigade division, then a few hundred yards up the Corinth Road from Rousseau, was moving forward to link up with Nelson's right flank. Buell told McCook to move up the road until he encountered Crittenden's line. Once there, McCook's troops would fall in on Crittenden's right and prevent any attempted Confederate advance to the landing along the Corinth Road. The Army of the Ohio would then continue its southwesterly advance. McCook's own right flank would be "in the air" for the moment, until either additional troops from Buell's army arrived or the Army of the Tennessee moved to fill the gap. Buell was not sure if any of Grant's forces would be available to support McCook's division. There had been some coordination during the night between the two Federal armies, but neither Buell nor Grant thought it proper to give the other an order.[11]

McCook relayed Buell's instructions to Rousseau and the brigade prepared to move. Rousseau deployed his regiments in a double battle line. The 6th Indiana, 1st Ohio, 1/19th U.S., and 1/16th U.S. were in front with the 5th Kentucky and 1/15th U.S. in reserve about 150 paces to the rear. Major King ordered his men to stack their knapsacks beside the road. After almost a year of recruiting and training, the new regiments of the Regular Army were entering battle.[12]

* * *

Rousseau's brigade cautiously moved along the Corinth Road, encountering evidence of the previous day's fighting. As the brigade passed Cloud Field it approached an area that would eventually be known as the "Hornet's Nest," a scene of some of the previous day's most intense combat. Dead bodies, most clad in Federal blue, still lay where they had fallen. The abandoned camps of Brigadier General Stephen A. Hulburt's division dotted the area, their tents shredded by bullet and shell. "As we march[ed] in line of battle to meet the enemy we met lots of wounded coming in" recalled Sergeant Arthur B. Carpenter of the 19th Infantry. "The ground was strewn with dead bodies and wounded, some with their legs shot off, some almost tore to pieces, groaning in the greatest agony. Some were shot through the brain...and yet were sensible. Some of them faintly waved their hands as we passed, while a smile appeared on their ghastly faces. But we had to leave them in their misery, to get along the best way they could."[13]

At a point just short of Tilghman's Creek, about one and a quarter miles from the landing, the 6th Indiana came on line with Brigadier General Jeremiah T. Boyle's brigade of Crittenden's division.

Rousseau's brigade halted in a small field near the abandoned camp of the 3rd Iowa. Rousseau's position was not ideal. A gap of about 200 yards existed between the 6th Indiana and Boyle's left regiment, the 19th Ohio. Rousseau's own right was unsupported. There was no sign of Grant's forces in that direction. The Corinth Road to Rousseau's rear was empty. Any enemy force advancing up the road could simply bounce off Rousseau's brigade, move around either of its exposed flanks, and march unopposed to the landing. These facts weighed heavily on the brigadier's mind throughout the morning.

As Rousseau and his staff dressed the brigade's line, a column of tired and dirty troops arrived to their rear. The unit was the 15th Michigan, or more properly what was left of it, 230 men led by Colonel John M. Oliver. The Michigan troops were survivors from Brigadier General Benjamin F. Prestiss's division of the Army of the Tennessee, a formation that had been shattered the day before in the Hornet's Nest. Having found McCook on the Corinth Road, Oliver told him that the small regiment still had some fight left and was looking for a place in the line. McCook took Oliver up on the offer and ordered the Michiganders to proceed up the Corinth Road to Rousseau's brigade. Gladly accepting the reinforcement and desiring to shore up one of his flanks, Rousseau posted Oliver's command on the brigade's left.[14]

Firing could be heard off to the southeast, where Nelson's division was hotly engaged near the Peach Orchard with Chalmers's Mississippians, Colonel Preston Smith's Brigade, and additional Confederates commanded by Brigadier General Jones M. Withers. To the unbloodied men in Rousseau's ranks, both regular and volunteer alike, the sound of approaching battle caused the lines to shudder and some faces to go pale. Sensing this, Major King shouted "Attention!" to his battalions as soon as they halted. King, a veteran of fighting with Seminoles, Mexicans, and Apaches, knew that the best way for troops to spend time before battle was to focus them on drill, directing their thoughts away from the coming storm. After the regulars snapped to in unison, King put them through the nine-step process to load their weapons. Lieutenant Louis Hosea, adjutant of 1/16th U.S., welcomed the commands: "That order...crystallized the wild turmoil of thoughts and focalized all upon the actual business of war. That first order to 'Load!' brought the panicky thoughts of men back with a sudden shock. I remember the 'thud' of the muskets as they came down upon the ground almost as one—for our men had been well drilled—and the confused rattle of drawing ramrods, and their ring in the gun barrels as they rebounded in ramming the charges home. Every movement and every sound was an encouragement."[15]

No support was yet available for the brigade's right flank so Rousseau extended his line to the north by moving Captain Swaine's 1/15th U.S. from the reserve line up to front. Simultaneously, the brigadier had King deploy a company as skirmishers to cover the brigade's position. King selected B/1/15th U.S. for the mission and Captain John Haughey's men were soon out in front. All was in readiness.

It was quiet along the Corinth Road, although battle sounds continued to emanate from Nelson and Crittenden's divisions to the southeast. General McCook galloped over to Rousseau's position, ordering the brigadier to advance the brigade about 300 yards forward to the low ridge on the far side of Tilghman's Creek. He also reminded Rousseau that the brigade's position was the center of the combined Federal armies and on the main road to Pittsburg Landing, a position that must be "held at every hazard." The division commander promised Rousseau support as soon as the rest of the division arrived and then rode off to bring up Kirk's brigade. Rousseau gave the order to move forward by the right company. Lieutenant Horace Jewitt, commanding A/1/15th U.S., echoed the command to his troops and the brigade's line lurched into motion. They waded into the bramble of springtime vegetation growing along the creek bed and crossed the shallow stream. Scrambling up the slope on the far side, Haughey's skirmishers continued to move a short distance to the front. There, they couched amidst the trees and waited for the battle to develop. They did not wait long.[16]

Buell had taken almost three hours of that April morning to deploy the Army of the Ohio. His opposition was grateful for the delay, for the Confederates were even more disorganized from the earlier fighting than were Grant's forces. The Army of the Mississippi's new commander, General P.G.T. Beauregard (Johnston had been killed the previous afternoon), had considered the battle won as night fell on April 6. He began having second thoughts the next morning. The presence of fresh brigades on the Federal left confirmed rumors of Buell's arrival. Frantic Confederate officers shook their weary troops out of their soggy slumber, aligned their ranks, and called forward supporting artillery batteries.[17]

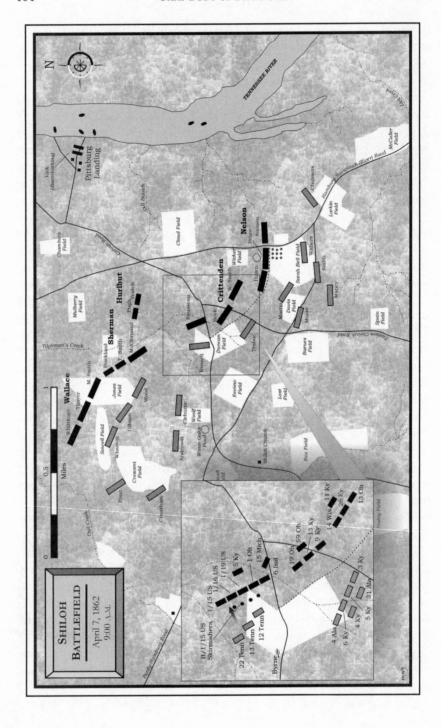

SHILOH
BATTLEFIELD
April 7, 1862
9:00 A.M.

Half an hour after moving west of Tilghman's Creek, the troops of Rousseau's brigade again heard firing off to the left. This time the tide of battle rolled toward their position. "The noise of musketry, deepening from the skirmish fire into the roll of the line of battle, crept nearer and nearer," Lieutenant Hosea recalled, "and was finally taken up by our own skirmishers in our front." The anticipation of waiting for what was about to happen almost overwhelmed Jacob Van Zwaluwenburg: "There were moments of intense nerve strain. we were not allowed to fire until the order was given. we knew they were slowly but surely coming right on us and the struggle must come any minute, the enemy flushed with victory of the day before were expecting an easy victory. Thots of home, and good and bad deeds passed rapidly along memory's gallery. that dread specter 'death' began to loom up in large proportions, when suddenly, the enemy emerged from the thicket in our front, a cloud of smoke, a hail of bullets, and our strange musings were over."[18]

Colonel Robert M. Russell's brigade, three Tennessee regiments, advanced across Duncan Field toward the 15th Infantry skirmishers. Captain Haughey's men opened fire, securing for the 15th Infantry the distinction of being the first new regular infantry regiment to engage in battle during the Civil War.[19] Russell's men returned the fire, inflicting the new regulars' first casualties. Having detected the enemy's advance, Haughey ordered his company back to the brigade's main line. The 15th Infantrymen retired in good order, firing as they went, carrying their handful of wounded. Tennesseans were right behind. The regulars in the battle line had their first view of the enemy. As the skirmishers came in, whispers of "There they are!" passed down the ranks. The woods prevented a clear view, but King's men caught glimpses of battle flags and a "surging line of butternut and gray moving rapidly across our front...perhaps fifty or seventy-five yards away." The undergrowth may have hid the Confederates but the lead that started to pelt the battalions' ranks confirmed the enemy's presence. The incoming fire was well aimed. The commander of C/1/16th U.S., Captain William H. Acker, took a bullet in the head and was instantly killed, while Captain John C. Peterson of F/1/15th U.S. also went down with a head wound. Although severely injured, Peterson would eventually recover.[20]

As the 19th and 16th Regulars opened fire, Captain Swaine noticed that the enemy was advancing obliquely from the brigade's left and had not yet arrived in front of the 15th Infantry's position.

He ordered his men to lay flat and hold their fire. When ordered to stand and engage, the discipline of the regulars was evident. Private Worthington recalled: "Our men, restrained by their officers, had not discharged a piece up to this time. But now each coolly marked his man; and when Captain Swaine, in a voice that could be heard along the whole line, gave the command to fire, our Springfield rifles dealt a destruction that was awful." Swaine reported that his men fired "with the regularity of a drill...well exemplifying their discipline."[21]

Black powder smoke, caught in the still air of the moist forest, soon enveloped the battle line. Most of the regulars could see little beyond the flashes emanating from their rifles. Only the constant zip of incoming bullets confirmed that the enemy was still near. Lieutenant Hosea recalled that casualties continued to mount: "As I passed up and down the line...a bullet struck a musket in the hands of a young Irishman of my own company, just as he was about to bring it to his shoulder, and the force of the impact shattered the stock and turned him partly about and almost threw him down. I saw blood spurt from his arm, for he had in the excitement rolled up his sleeves to handle his piece the better. I sprang forward to assist him; but with a cry of rage he stripped off his sleeve, and, with the assistance of a comrade, bound up his wound...and seized a dead comrade's musket beside him and went on with the fight."[22]

The firefight lasted about twenty minutes before the enemy fire slackened and finally ceased. Rousseau ordered skirmishers forward and moved the brigade about fifty yards westward from Tilghman's Creek. The skirmishers soon returned, reporting that the opposition had rallied and was again bearing down on the brigade. The crash of artillery was also heard as Captain Edward P. Byrne's Mississippi Battery wheeled into the far side of Duncan Field and opened fire. Rifle fire began to take its toll once again. The battalion commanders ordered their men to lie down, causing most of Byrne's shells to pass harmlessly overhead. "The attack [was conducted] more fiercely than before," General Rousseau recalled, "but was met by a very rapid and well-directed fire from the commands of Majors King and Carpenter and Colonel Smith [of the 1st Ohio], the 6th Indiana being out of range on the left. This attack was also, after a much severe contest, repulsed and the enemy driven off, our loss being much more than before." These attacks took place in the dense woods between the creek bed and the eastern edge of Duncan Field. On learning from the skirmishers that a large open field was a short distance to the brigade's front, Rousseau decided "to advance my lines after this last attack, and at once cautiously felt my way forward, but had gone far when I again encountered the enemy in heavy force."[23]

Russell's Tennesseans were largely spent after their two failed assaults on Rousseau's brigade, but General Braxton Bragg was nearby to divert reinforcements to this area. Colonel Robert S. Trabue's Brigade of Kentuckians (the soon-to-be-famous Orphan Brigade) opposed Crittenden's division on the southern portion of Duncan Field while Russell tangled with Rousseau to the north. Bragg detached the 4th Kentucky and 4th Alabama Battalion from Trabue, rallied Russell's troops, and had the combined force advance toward Rousseau. "The Fourth Kentucky Regiment and Fourth Alabama Battalion, having advanced to within 100 paces of the enemy's line, opened fire upon him," Colonel Trabue reported, "and received in turn a most destructive fire from both wings and the center." The regulars again took to ground and went to work. A back and forth struggle in Duncan Field and the woods to the north then took place; Trabue stated "The ground [was] crossed and recrossed four times." Sergeant Carpenter had been nervous before the battle, but he had calmed down by the time the fight had advanced into Duncan Field: "After once you get into the fight you don't care for nothing. We would load, and run up and give them a volley, and then lay down. Their bullets would whistle over us like hail...but some would be wounded or killed. A corporal in a company next to ours was shot in the head just as he was rising up. After we had been laying down and the bugle sounded the advance I thought that I was hit many a time the bullets came so close, but I escaped and lived to come off the field."[24]

Eventually the tide of battle turned in favor of the Federals at Duncan Field and elsewhere. Along the Army of the Ohio's line, Buell's fresh troops began to overpower the battle-weary Confederates. After a forty-minute struggle, by half past ten Rousseau's brigade had advanced across Duncan Field's 300 yards of open ground and gained the tree line on the far side. The Confederates who had defended Duncan Field fled westward. There was nothing to stop a further advance by Rousseau's brigade at this point—except the caution of its commanding general. Rousseau was still worried about his unsupported flanks. His left regiment, the 6th Indiana, had not accompanied the rest of the brigade during the advance across the field. The unit instead remained on the east side of Duncan Field assisting Crittenden's division in the struggle against the balance of Trabue's Brigade. Rousseau had also received several messages "announcing that the United States forces to our right...were giving way, leaving the center of the army exposed." Rousseau had already deployed his brigade reserve, the 5th Kentucky, to the right of the brigade's line. The rest of McCook's division was still nowhere in sight. The regulars and the 1st Ohio, the units which had born the brunt of the Duncan Field fighting, were riddled with casualties. Still foremost in Rousseau's mind was McCook's order that the brigade's position was "to be held at every hazard." These considerations caused Rousseau to dismiss any notions he may have held about pursuing the retiring enemy.[25]

The regulars sized up their situation as the firing died down. Company commanders dressed up the ranks while their sergeants checked on ammunition and casualties. They found the former running low and the latter in abundant supply. During the lull, Lieutenant Mitchell and Captain Barry of F/1/16th U.S. met behind the firing line, both thankful that they had made it through this far. In case that situation should later change, they exchanged scraps of paper with their family's name and address written on them. Mitchell then recalled that he still had in his pocket a letter to his parents he had finished writing five days previously. He took the letter out and made a note on the margin of the last page: "Monday, April 7. On the Battlefield. Loving you all dearly. If I die, my last wish will be that I could have kissed you first. GOD AND OUR COUNTRY."[26]

Rousseau's halt on the west side of Duncan Field lasted about thirty minutes. An hour before noon the brigadier noticed the field behind him filling up with Federal troops. Kirk's brigade had finally arrived. Colonel Kirk told Rousseau that the 5th Brigade was to support Rousseau's advance and that it was "ready for anything." Assured of support, Rousseau ordered his own brigade forward again. While no organized body of Confederates stood in their immediate way, small detachments of retreating Southerners put up a running fight.[27]

The 16th Infantry's line began to crowd toward its center as the movement resumed, a common problem of inexperienced troops in their first action. Finding it difficult to maintain Company F's alignment, Captain Barry reported the situation to his battalion commander. Captain Townsend told him to send word to Captain

R.E.A. Crofton, commanding Company A on the battalion's right, to make more room for the center companies. Lieutenant Mitchell of Company G heard Townsend's order, yelled "I'll go, sir!" and ran off in search of Crofton. Mitchell quickly found him and relayed the instructions. The conversation had just finished when a Confederate sharpshooter focused his sights on the lieutenant. A shot rang out and "a ball struck him on the right visor of his cap, passing again through the visor. He slightly raised his right hand, and fell without a groan—dead!" Realizing there was nothing he could do for the young officer, Captain Crofton left Mitchell where he fell and ran after the advancing battle line.[28]

A similar scene occurred at about that same time behind the 15th Infantry's line. While Captain Joseph S. York of G/1/15th U.S. was talking with Lieutenants Sanderson and Wikoff of Company E, another shot rang out and Wikoff went down with a bullet lodged in his left eye. As Sanderson stooped down to aid him, Wikoff weakly asked is he was seriously wounded. "No, cheer up," Sanderson replied, not wanting to make a bad situation worse. Wikoff thought otherwise: "It is not so—it is all up with me—get a surgeon." Sanderson detailed two soldiers to guide the blinded lieutenant to the rear. He then heard someone yell that Captain Henry Keteltas, Sanderson's own commander of E/1/15th U.S., had been shot. Sanderson left Wikoff in charge of the men, ran forward, and took command of the company. Both Keteltas and Wikoff survived their Shiloh wounds. Thirty-six years later, Colonel Charles A. Wikoff wore a patch over his left eye as he embarked on the Santiago campaign of the Spanish-American War.[29]

As Rousseau's brigade continued to march, firing was heard to its front. During the brigade's halt at Duncan Field, troops from Crittenden's division had continued advancing on the south side of the Corinth Road. As Crittenden's regiments approached Review Field, they ran into a new Confederate battle line. The Southerners opened fire and counterattacked. Crittenden's forces, disorganized and in need of regrouping, fell back in confusion. But when the victorious Confederates tried to advance eastward along the Corinth Road, they ran head-on into Rousseau. "They charged back upon us, giving us a volley which came like a blow," recalled Sergeant Major Kellogg of the 16th Infantry. "It astonished us but did not cause any disorder in our ranks. Kneeling or lying down our men sent a hail of bullets into the oncoming ranks that soon halted them.

The fighting was desperate for a few minutes, but we would not yield an inch of ground." The counterattack occurred at a bad time for Company D of Sergeant Major Kellogg's battalion. In the last moments before the Southerners appeared, D/1/16th U.S. had to maneuver around a huge fallen oak tree, a portion of the company going around each side. The split line was just beginning to come together when the shooting started. "Instead of two ranks we were driven into four," Private Van Zwaluwenburg remembered, "[which] made it dangerous for the front rank to raise to raise and fire. It was here Pvt. Brady was killed by one of our own men lying back of me who fired just as Brady rose to fire and sent a bullet thru the back of his head."[30]

A portion of the 5th Kentucky to the right of the regulars broke and ran under the onslaught. The regulars held firm, Captain Swaine refusing the 15th Infantry's right companies to cover the newly exposed flank. Swaine reported that his men "stood their ground, and poured such a deadly fire of rifle bullets into the ranks of the enemy that what bid fair at first to be a defeat was turned into a most glorious success." Lieutenant Sanderson recalled that his own troops did not display the same bravado during this attack as Sergeant Major Kellogg's 16th Infantrymen supposedly did. The 15th Infantry lieutenant observed that some of his men "collected in knots of 5 & 6, behind trees but the officers called upon them to return in line and in a minute we were again in line, and advancing." Fire from the regulars and 1st Ohio eventually halted the Southern advance, and the Confederates fell back to the west. One of the Southern victims of Rousseau's fire during this exchange was George W. Johnson, the Confederacy's provisional governor of Kentucky. Trying to do everything possible for "the Cause," he had picked up a rifle and joined the ranks of the 4th Kentucky in Trabue's Brigade. Between Governor Johnson's fatal wounding on April 7 and the loss of General Johnston the previous day, the Confederacy's leadership suffered heavily on the Shiloh battlefield.[31]

Shells again crashed among Rousseau's troops. The Southern counterattack may have been repulsed, but the Confederates managed to patch together a line in Review Field and the forest to the north. Captain Thomas J. Stanford's Mississippi guns had wheeled into battery near the northeast corner of Review Field and were spraying canister as fast as they could be served. "Large gaps were made by every gun at each discharge," the Mississippian reported.

"Three regimental flags being in full view, I gave orders to point at them, and soon had the satisfaction of seeing two of them fall to the ground, both being raised again." One of Stanford's shells exploded close to Lieutenant Hosea of the 16th Infantry. He was knocked down and bruised, shrapnel tearing through his left trouser leg and boot, but was otherwise miraculously unhurt. Stanford's fire caused the Federal advance along the Corinth Road to halt momentarily. McCook had no artillery available to counter the Southern guns. The division commander had been expecting the arrival of Captain Terrill's Battery H all morning, but his wait would prove to be in vain.[32]

* * *

Lieutenant W.T. Hoblitzell, aide to General McCook, searched through the crowd at Pittsburg Landing and recognized the tall, bearded artillery officer immediately. The captain he spotted was William Terrill, commander of Battery H. McCook had stationed Hoblitzell at the landing with orders to guide the regular battery forward as soon as possible. At 9:00 A.M., Terrill and his gunners finally arrived from Savannah via steamer and began to disembark, manhandling caissons, guns, and teams up the bluff. Once assembled, Hoblitzell guided the battery inland on the Corinth Road. The lieutenant took a wrong turn and the battery ended up near Bloody Pond on the Federal left. General Buell happened to be nearby and ordered Terrill to support Nelson's division. Nelson's advance had temporarily stalled near the Sarah Bell Field, but Battery H soon had the Federals moving. A private in the 6th Ohio of Nelson's division welcomed the battery's arrival: "Looking over my right shoulder, with what joy I saw artillery coming through the woods at a gallop! It was Captain Terrill's battery of regulars, just up from Savannah by boat, with Terrill himself—splendid officer and soul of knightliest honor—riding ahead of it. He dashed out to the edge of the wood, and, with a single sweep of the eye taking in the whole situation, waved his hand for the battery to wheel into position." Giving both friend and foe alike a demonstration in artillery drill, Terrill's six guns were in battery and firing less than two minutes later. The battery's second shot blew up an ammunition-packed limber chest of Captain Felix Robertson's Florida Battery. Robertson withdrew his guns and the Southern line began to waver. Nelson's division resumed its advance, Battery H along with it.[33]

Terrill dispatched Frank Guenther's section to the right of Nelson's division in support of Colonel William B. Hazen's brigade. The captain then advanced his other two sections past the Peach Orchard and into the Federal skirmish line, the well-aimed fire of Battery H's four guns systematically silencing any enemy artillery within reach. A heavy line of gray then emerged and charged upon the Federal skirmishers. Composed of perhaps half a dozen Tennessee and Mississippi regiments and commanded by General Chalmers and Colonels Preston Smith and George Maney, the Southerners were attempting to regain some of the ground lost to Nelson earlier in the morning. A "storm of musket balls, canister shot, and shell, which was truly awful," engulfed Battery H and the thin line of skirmishers around it. Peter Fitzpatrick found it hard to describe the intensity of the incoming fire: "I could compare the bullets that were flying around us to nothing but a handfull of sand thrown against a window." The Federal infantry near Battery H, elements of Colonel Jacob Ammen's brigade, gave way before the Confederate onslaught. Terrill's gunners were left unsupported. Again displaying the capabilities of well-trained regular artillerymen, Terrill orchestrated a textbook fighting withdrawal: "Lieutenant Ludlow's section was immediately sent to the rear to protect the retreat of Lieutenant Smyser's, which was well done. One of Lieutenant Ludlow's caissons was left here, all the horses having been killed or wounded, but we recovered it later in the day. I served one of Lieutenant Smyser's pieces (the fifth, a Napoleon) and he the other. We fixed prolonges and fired retiring. The enemy charged us, but were staggered by our discharges of canister. We checked their advance three times, retiring as they charged upon us."[34]

This portion of Terrill's official report, while accurate, was written in the typically subdued style of a Regular Army officer and does not convey the full extent of the captain's efforts. Fortunately, an officer of the 6th Ohio observed Battery H's performance during the counterattack. He prominently mentioned Terrill in an April 10 letter to the *Cincinnati Daily Commercial*:

I cannot refrain here from paying a tribute to this heroic officer—the bravest of the brave. Captain Terril's relatives are Secessionists. His father and three brothers hold high positions in the rebel army and he has been disinherited and disowned by them for his loyalty for the Union. The rebels will long remember the 'Napoleans' he handled so effectively on the 7th of April, 1862. At one time during the day they approached within fifty yards of a gun that he was commanding and killed or wounded every man but one, and yet he loaded and fired it with his own hands, until the foe fell back terror stricken. The piles of mangled bodies on this side of the field speak for the efficiency of his battery. I saw him with one shell kill five horses, dismount a gun, and scatter the rebel gunners in all directions. The brilliant results of the fight on the left wing was attributable mainly to his skill and heroism.[35]

While successful, the battery's withdrawal was costly. Most of its fourteen casualties occurred during the retreat, a total that outdistanced all the batteries in the Army of the Ohio and most of those in the Army of the Tennessee. For a while Lieutenant Smyser and Corporal Roberson served gun five alone, a job normally requiring seven gunners. Sergeant Metcalf, chief of gun six, took a bullet in the head but remained at his post despite the pain and loss of blood. He crawled his way to safety in the rear only after receiving another round in the leg. Gunner James Mohr was impressed with the conduct of his battery mates: "One gunner was left at one gun when he saw the last boy fall at his gun he commenced a crying and run for ammunition again and loaded and fought till they retreated," Mohr wrote in a letter to his brother three days later, adding "such boy's are worth having in the field."[36]

Battery H finally rejoined the main battle line of Ammen's brigade, Tennesseans close behind. Seeing the battery's battered condition and sensing the danger of the enemy advance, General Nelson rode up to the commander of the 6th Ohio, waiting in reserve nearby, and said: "Colonel Anderson, I have conferred upon your regiment the honor of defending this battery, the best in the service. It must not be taken!" Lieutenant Colonel Nicholas Anderson quickly moved his troops forward. Terrill welcomed the assistance, for his gunners had suffered so many casualties that they could no longer effectively man all the battery's weapons. The captain requested help and ten privates from Company A, 6th Ohio, ran forward to assist. When they did so, they saw a familiar face among the caissons. Lieutenant Israel Ludlow, an officer of "tall figure and ringing tones of command," commanded Terrill's section of ten-pound Parrott Rifles. He was a former member of this very company of Ohio volunteers now springing to the battery's assistance. Ludlow had accepted a commission in the regular artillery the previous summer, but the 6th Ohio still fondly remembered the tall lieutenant as the "little corporal" of Company A. Captain Terrill later reported that Ludlow, the only non-West Pointer among the battery's officers, "behaved with great gallantry, and for so young a man acquitted himself with great credit." With the assistance of the 6th Ohio, Battery H brought the Confederate counterattack to a standstill.[37]

Terrill's battery remained in support of Nelson's division throughout the day. Nelson was glad it did. "This battery was a host in itself," the division commander later reported. "Its fire was terrific. It was handled superbly. Wherever Captain Terrill turned his battery silence followed on the part of the enemy." Gunner Fitzpatrick learned from a captured Confederate after the battle what some of the opposition thought of Battery H: "Bureguard brought a brigade of Mississippians and offered every man $100, if they could take Turrells Battery," the artillerymen wrote to his wife. "But they found the Irishmen of our Battery to tough for them, for I must tell you that the Battery is composed of nearly all Irishmen."[38]

Private Mohr echoed Nelson and Fitzpatrick's opinions of Battery H performance: "we have won a name upon our Battery in the Battle at siloah that will be known for many years," Mohr wrote home the next month, "every General farely worships him—that is our captain." Historian Wiley Sword in *Shiloh: Bloody April* claims Terrill and Battery H "turned the tide" on this portion of the Shiloh battlefield. But Terrill's guns could not be in two places at once. While Battery H provided outstanding support for Nelson, McCook's division was without artillery. McCook's other two batteries waited for a steamer in Savannah most of the day and did not arrive at Pittsburg Landing until after the fighting ended.[39]

* * *

As the 6th Ohio helped man Terrill's guns near the Peach Orchard, Rousseau's brigade remained stalled near Review Field. Stanford's guns continued to pound away. Accurate rifle fire from Rousseau's brigade eventually caused the battery's infantry support to withdraw westward. Some Federal artillery then arrived. Captain John Mendenhall, an 1851 West Pointer who later in the war would emerge as one of the finest Union artillerists in the West, came galloping up the Corinth Road with his consolidated Batteries H & M, 4th U.S. Artillery, a regular battery assigned to Crittenden's division. Having thus far supported Nelson and Crittenden, Buell had ordered Mendenhall to support McCook upon learning of the check

"Battle of Shiloh.
Recapture of Artillery by a portion of Gen. Rousseau's Command"

Published in 1862 by Johnson, Fry, & Co. of New York, this lithograph bears little resemblance to actual events. The 19th Infantry's recapture of two guns belonging to the 14th Ohio Light Artillery on April 7 was a bloodless affair.

near Review Field. "The battery came up very cooly," recalled
Lieutenant Sanderson as Mendenhall's four guns arrived, "and as
deliberately unlimbered and commenced firing." From a position
along the Corinth Road, Mendenhall directed counterbattery fire
against Stanford. Lieutenant Samuel Canby, a section leader in the
battery, relayed Mendenhall's orders to a nearby artilleryman.

"Gunner, do you see that battery?"

"Yes sir!"

"Well I want you to silence it, and that damned quick too!"

The aim of Canby's gunner was true, and shells from the 4th
Artillery soon crashed among Stanford's pieces.[40]

The Mississippi battery was isolated and unsupported. As
Rousseau's brigade advanced southeastward to the north edge of
Review Field, Captain Swaine ordered his 15th Infantry battalion to
fix bayonets. While Mendenhall's fire diverted Stanford's attention,
the charge was sounded. Firing a volley as they came, the 15th

Regulars crossed the Corinth Road and ran toward the battery as fast as their weary legs could carry them. Casualties mounted as they neared the battery's position. Stanford fired his last rounds of canister when the regular battalion was just fifty yards away and then attempted to withdraw his six pieces. He was able to hitch up and escape with two of them before 1/15th U.S. was among the guns. "An opportunity [was] offered at this point to ascertain the havoc we had done," Private Worthington recalled, "Every horse in each piece and caisson lay dead in his harness, and the ground was covered with the killed and dying." An enemy artillery officer lay wounded near one of the captured cannon. Lieutenant Sanderson heard him exclaim: "You have killed all my men & horses, left only myself and a boy of 17, who are both wounded, now you can take the guns and be damned!"[41]

As this latest firing died down and the brigade resumed its westward movement, Rousseau received word that the 1st Ohio was out of ammunition. He withdrew it from the line, instructing Colonel Smith to move toward the Corinth Road and await resupply. The brigadier also sent an orderly to find the 6th Indiana and bring it forward. The remainder of the brigade continued moving west on the north side of the Corinth Road. After picking its way through the trees another two hundred yards, the brigade approached the eastern side of Woolf Field. As the 15th Infantry moved through the abandoned camp of McClernand's headquarters, the 19th Infantry recaptured two spiked guns of the 14th Ohio Light Artillery that the enemy had overrun the previous day. The arrival of Rousseau's brigade at Woolf Field could not have come at a better time for Grant's army. Northeast of Water Oaks Pond, a Southern counterattack was punishing Sherman and McClernand's divisions of the Army of the Tennessee. The fighting here was desperate. All of the Northern regiments involved were already worn out from heavy action on April 6. Many did not have much endurance left. McClernand felt that his situation "was most critical and a repulse seemed inevitable." Then, up the Corinth Road, Rousseau's brigade appeared. Rousseau's advance turned the right flank of the enemy counterattack, forcing the Confederates to break off their advance and pull back.[42]

McClernand needed help to steady his wavering troops and sent a staff officer to Rousseau asking for assistance. Rousseau sent the 5th Kentucky to McClernand's aid. McCook also dispatched Kirk's

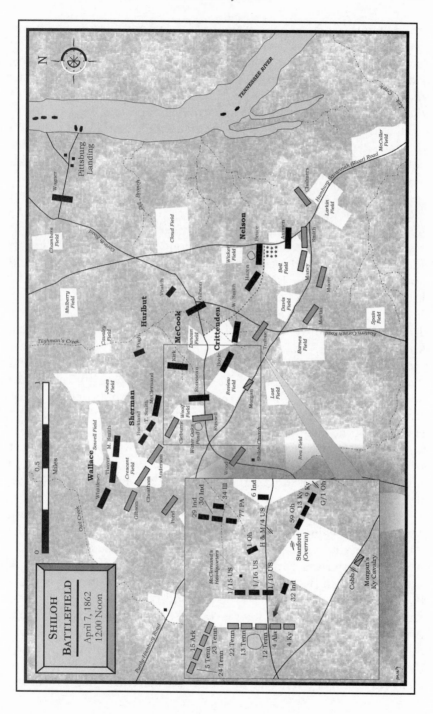

brigade to the right to help shore up McClernand's front. The front-line strength of Rousseau's brigade was then further reduced. Upon learning that elements of the Army of the Tennessee were nearby, Colonel Oliver moved the 15th Michigan off in their direction. They remained with Maj. General Lew Wallace's division for the rest of the battle. Rousseau now had only the regulars remaining in line.[43]

The regular battalions gained the eastern edge of Woolf Field, on the far side of which lay a new Confederate line. The battalions could go no further. Ammunition was all but exhausted and casualties had been heavy during the morning-long fight. King's troops fixed bayonets and laid down, but their leaders remained on their feet, "the traditional *esprit* of the service not permitting officers to hug the earth." While this practice may have inspired the troops, it also resulted in numerous casualties among the regular officer corps. Lieutenant Hosea had recovered from his shelling near Review Field and limped up to the 16th Infantry's new position. For support he leaned on Captain Patrick T. Keyes, commander of D/1/16th Infantry. The two officers had just seen Sergeant Brice Baker of the 16th U.S. receive a bullet in the forehead when they were both knocked down: "The sledge hammer struck one of us—for the moment I did not know which—and hurled us both to the ground backward. As I scrambled to a footing I saw Keyes's blanched face and the torn garment showing the passage of the bullet through the left shoulder joint, where a hasty examination showed that the bony structure of the vicinity had been shattered. He was taken to the rear and died the second day after." No one knew for sure whether friendly or enemy fire killed Captain Keyes. The straggler who had threatened to shoot Keyes the previous day, Private Jim Roach, deserted on April 8 and was never seen again.[44]

Rousseau's advance sputtered to a halt at Woolf Field. McCook sent another regiment into Woolf Field in an attempt to keep the advance moving westward along the Corinth Road. Kirk's brigade was still supporting McClernand on Rousseau's right, so McCook ordered forward the 32nd Indiana, a regiment of Johnson's brigade (Colonel William H. Gibson commanded Johnson's brigade at Shiloh, Richard Johnson having fallen ill during the march from Nashville). This regiment was an all-German outfit from Indianapolis and its colonel, August Willich, was a former officer of the Prussian Army. It was considered one of the crack Union regiments in the West. Willich's men had just marched inland from the landing and their commander was looking for a fight. The unit crossed the Corinth Road to the left of the regulars and entered Woolf Field, heading straight for a swampy thicket known as Water Oaks Pond. From his vantage point behind the 16th Infantry's line, Lieutenant Hosea observed Willich's advance: "The regiment was in a compact mass, closed by companies in the center, and with flags flying and drums beating, made a fine appearance." Willich's determination to close with the enemy carried the German Hoosiers into the Water Oaks before they could properly deploy into line of battle. "The absurdity of this formation seemed to strike even the rank and file," Hosea continued, "for it drew a direct and enfilading fire from the extended line of the enemy in front." Willich remained near the Water Oaks for about twenty minutes. The 32nd Indiana fought hard; Sherman reported that the regiment's struggle produced "the severest musketry fire I ever heard." The Confederates fought with equal determination and Willich's troops eventually broke for the rear.[45]

As Willich's regiment "scattered like cattle upon a thousand hills," the regular battalions expended their last rounds of ammunition. Kirk's brigade was in position to relieve them and Rousseau withdrew the regulars shortly after noon: "After we had exhausted our ammunition I called on Colonel Kirk, who was immediately in rear of my lines, and informed him of that fact. He at once gallantly and eagerly offered to take my position in front, and did so, a portion of my command on the right passing quietly through his lines and halting in his rear. All was done without the least confusion or even excitement. I told him that if needed before we received ammunition we would support him with the bayonet." Such a desperate measure would not be needed. Earlier in the morning, General McCook had dispatched to Pittsburg Landing his ordnance officer, Lieutenant J.A. Campbell, with orders to find some ammunition. Amidst all the confusion of the rear area, Campbell somehow found three wagons full of cartridges and brought them along the Corinth Road to the vicinity of McClernand's headquarters camp. Troops of the 1st Ohio were refilling their cartridge boxes as the regulars withdrew from Woolf Field. King's battalions did likewise.[46]

The battle continued to rage in Woolf and Review Fields as Rousseau's brigade regrouped and distributed ammunition. Kirk and Gibson's brigades of McCook's division were both in line and the battle became a crescendo of noise, smoke, and flame. At about two o'clock, Rousseau received word that Mendenhall's 4th U.S. Artillery battery needed infantry support. Still acting as Buell's personal fireman, the battery was positioned along the Corinth Road and firing at the Confederate line on the far side of Review Field. Rousseau ordered the 19th Infantry to the battery's support. Major Carpenter's battalion had just arrived at Mendenhall's gun line when Lieutenant Albert Andrews, commanding D/1/19th U.S., noticed some enemy battle flags and an advancing line of Confederates on the far side of Review Field. Andrews notified Carpenter and the major sent his adjutant, Lieutenant Louis T. Snyder, to find Rousseau and request reinforcements. The Confederate column Andrews had spotted was one of the Army of the Mississippi's final attempts to check the Federal advance south of the Corinth Road. Southern commanders had somehow rallied some scattered brigades for one more advance across Review Field.

As Lieutenant Snyder explained the situation to Rousseau, the 6th Indiana finally arrived from Duncan Field. Grateful for Colonel Crittenden's timely arrival, Rousseau dispatched the regiment as additional support for Mendenhall's guns. While the 4th U.S. Artillerymen poured canister into the approaching Confederates, the 6th Indiana took up positions on either side of the guns. "Here my regiment stood up and fired 20 rounds so rapidly as to make a steady storm of musketry," Crittenden reported. The combined fire of the 6th Indiana, 1/19th U.S., and Mendenhall halted the counter-attack within one hundred yards of the 4th Artillery's position. This, with the fire of the Kirk and Gibson's brigades, compelled the Southerners to fall back once again.[47]

By about half past two, Confederate resistance began to fall apart. The Army of the Mississippi was reaching the end of its endurance. Beauregard withdrew from Woolf and Review Fields, hoping to reform his line in the vicinity of Shiloh Church. While the Confederates pulled back, General Grant and his staff came riding up the Corinth Road. Sensing that the enemy was about to crack, Grant ordered what forces he could find nearby to charge. His orders went out to Colonel James Veach's brigade (from Hulburt's division of Grant's army) and Rousseau's brigade. Veach charged across Review Field, while Rousseau headed for Water Oaks Pond.

The regulars had finished their resupply. "An officer rapidly approached the battalions of the Fifteenth and Sixteenth Infantry from the rear," Captain Crofton later remarked, "and cried,

'Charge! Charge! by order of General Grant!'" The 1st Ohio and the two regular battalions formed up and moved forward. General Rousseau halted them as they neared the edge of Woolf Field. The brigadier had not ordered the movement, but upon learning of Grant's order Rousseau took charge of the brigade and led it forward. Moving around the right flank of Kirk's brigade, Rousseau's men approached Water Oaks Pond. General Sherman observed them: "A whole brigade of McCook's division advanced beautifully, deployed, and entered this dreaded woods. I ordered my Second Brigade...and my Fourth Brigade...all to advance abreast of this Kentucky Brigade before mentioned, which I afterwards found to be Rousseau's Brigade of McCook's Division."[48]

Most of the Federal line was advancing and by three o'clock engaged Beauregard's last line near Shiloh Church. The remaining Southerners began to leave the battlefield about half past three. "Rousseau's brigade moved in splendid order steadily to the front, sweeping everything before it," Sherman continued, "and at 4 P.M. we stood upon the ground of our original front line and the enemy was in full retreat." Resistance began to crumble by the time the regulars moved past Shiloh Church. Major King, on foot because his horse had been shot out from under him, noticed a group of retreating Confederates off to his right: "We pursued the Rebels through the former camps of Sherman's troops...completing the rout of all the enemy's forces in sight. They fled in disorder...and we were ordered to rejoin the brigade." As the regulars did so, General Rousseau "came riding up the line in a sweeping gallop, swinging his hat over his head," recalled a member of the 6th Indiana, "and in a voice that might have been heard for a quarter of a mile, 'The rebels are flying! The rebels are flying! The victory is ours!' and as the old hero, on his splendid sorrel charger went up the line, making the mud and water fly for rods in every direction, one spontaneous shout for joy rent the air, while the hats went many feet into the air; some laughed and some cried. Just at this time we got orders to stack arms...and then there was one universal handshaking."[49]

A determined pursuit of the retreating Confederates would have been a more useful action than stacking arms and shaking hands, but that was a decision to be made many echelons above the worn out soldiers of Rousseau's brigade. They were more than happy to call it a day. Among those shaking hands was General Sherman, who came over to congratulate Rousseau's troops. Speaking with

Major Carpenter, a West Point classmate, the general "compli-
mented most highly the work of the brigade and particularly of the
regular battalions." General Rousseau praised all the brigade's regiments in his official report on the battle, but singled out the regulars: "To Majs. J. H. King and S. D. Carpenter, of the Regular Army,
who commanded the regular troops in my brigade, I am especially
indebted for the valuable aid which their long experience as soldiers
enabled them to render. Capts. P. T. Swaine and E. F. Townsend,
commanding battalions under Major King...were likewise conspicuous for good conduct. I strongly recommend these officers to the
proper authorities as soldiers by profession, who have shown themselves amply fit for higher offices of usefulness."[50]

Sergeant Major Edgar Kellogg was not interested in official
reports or promotions as the fighting ended. He was tired and hungry, having lost his haversack full of rations sometime during the
battle. Like many of his fellow regulars, he simply dropped to the
ground, completely exhausted. Despite these hardships, Kellogg
actually recalled these moments fondly:

> Then came reaction from the strain on mind and body, and I real-
> ized how tired I was from the march of the previous day, the weary
> waiting in Savannah for a steamer, the sleepless night aboard it, and
> the many hours of stubborn fighting that followed. Stretching myself
> on the ground and pulling my cap over my face, I was about to for-
> get hunger in sleep when Kind Fate, in the guise of a friendly sergeant
> of my regiment proffered me one of the best meals I have ever eaten.
> There was neither "sow-belly" nor hardtack in it, but I forgot those
> staples of a soldier's diet when given a liberal supply of sardines,
> soda crackers, ginger snaps, chow-chow, cheese, perhaps one or two
> other things good for the stomach, and a box of good cigars.[51]

Incredibly, the Confederates had failed to discover a sutler's tent
near Sherman's camps. The 16th Infantry proved a bit more adept at
scrounging. Private Van Zwaluwenburg and a group of his comrades
came upon the tent and made short work of the sutler's delicacies,
the main prizes being a caddy of plug tobacco and a hogshead of
pig's feet. After finishing his impromptu meal and dividing the cigars
among some less fortunate comrades, Sergeant Major Kellogg
leaned his back against a log and "enjoyed a delicious smoke."[52]

Kellogg's relaxation proved to be short lived. Although the
springtime weather had been pleasant throughout the day, it turned
foul again that night. A steady, chilling rain soaked the battlefield.

The wagons loaded with the Army of the Ohio's camp equipment were still many miles away on the muddy road to Savannah. The regulars did not even have their personal gear. A detail went back down the Corinth Road to recover their knapsacks, but returned mostly empty-handed. Other troops had discovered the knapsack cache and picked it clean. Making due with what they had, Rousseau bivouacked his men for the night near the abandoned camp of the 57th Ohio. With no shelter available, Jacob Van Zwaluwenburg resigned himself to his fate: "I braced myself up against a tree and let the rain come, wet thru to the skin alnight." Adding to the private's misery was a severed arm in the mud at his feet and five dead Confederates sprawled nearby. He was too tired to care. Sergeant Carpenter's exhaustion almost got the better of him: "We had to hurry so to get to the fight that we left everything behind, and had no tents to sleep in, so we built fires and bivouacked. At dark it commenced to rain and rained all night. we had no overcoats or blankets, and were wet through, as a drowned rat, and were so sleepy. fought hard all day and had not much sleep the night before. I got asleep standing before the fire, and would have fallen in if someone had not caught hold of me. we suffered for sleep." At least Van Zwaluwenburg and Carpenter were alive. As the battalions gathered in their details and soldiers with minor wounds returned, an accurate headcount revealed the butcher's bill the regulars had paid. They had indeed caught "regular hell:" nearly a fifth of the regular infantrymen had been killed, wounded, or were missing, one of the highest casualty rates in the Army of the Ohio. Of the eleven officers in Rousseau's brigade who had been hit, nine were regulars.[53]

April 8 was a day of reckoning. Battle wreckage lay all around the victorious Union Army. Although such scenes would become all too common as the war progressed, the landscape of the regulars' baptism of fire left a deep impression on King's troops. "The dead were everywhere," recalled Private Worthington. "There never has been such carnage on this continent. I trust I may never again see anything of the kind. ...You may travel for a day around here and you will scarcely find a tree, sapling or twig, that had not been struck by a bullet. How any of us escaped is more than I can imagine." With more than 4,500 dead from both armies still laying where they fell, top priority was getting the bodies underground. Major King sent burial parties back to Duncan, Review, and Woolf Fields. Lieutenant Jacob Kline and a detail from G/1/16th U.S.

found Lieutenant Edward Mitchell's body in the forest west of Duncan Field. The 16th Infantry buried its fallen officer on a bluff overlooking the Tennessee River, Mitchell's sword in his crossed hands. Captain Barry performed the sad duty of writing Mitchell's next-of-kin, a task that was hard for the captain because his lieutenant was also a close friend: "Mr. Mitchell, every one in the battalion is profoundly grieved at your son's death, and none more so than the men of his company. To me the loss is severe; and I have often found my heart swelling at the thought of seeing him no more. Still, sir, you have the consolation of knowing that he died fighting gallantly in the defense of his country; and that, to the last, he did honor to his country, his position, and his name." Barry enclosed Mitchell's final letter home with the note. Kline had discovered the correspondence in the dead lieutenant's pocket.[54]

The Federal army remained near Pittsburg Landing until the end of April, licking its wounds and refitting under Major General Halleck, who took personal command of Grant and Buell's armies on April 12. Other than a few patrols and clashes among pickets, there was little contact with the enemy for the rest of April. Beauregard's troops dug in around Corinth, knowing the town was Halleck's next objective.

King's regulars had met their first test of combat and passed it with flying colors. George Mason, a lieutenant in the 12th Illinois of Grant's army, commented after the war that King's battalions during the second day at Shiloh were a sight to see: "It was my good-fortune to serve immediately on the left of the...United States Regulars, and their perfect discipline and regular movements lifted a load from our breasts, and filled us with a confidence we had well-nigh lost the day before." But the regulars had done more than prove to their brethren that they were skilled soldiers. By triumphing in their first battle they had also proven it to themselves. Sergeant Carpenter summed up this new attitude a few days later when he remarked: "One thing I know, that the rebels *cannot* whip us." This experience came at a price and the Battle of Shiloh set a dangerous precedent for the regulars: high casualties. The regulars fought hard at Shiloh and would continue to do so in future clashes. Since regular units were chronically short-handed to begin with, battle losses only compounded their manpower shortage. Buell's desire to use regular troops as the heart of two of the Army of the Ohio's divisions would work only if the few regular formations assigned to those divisions were kept up to strength. Whether or not the regulars' recruiting efforts could replace the lost manpower and continue to produce effective field units in the face of such losses remained an unanswered question.

The first real battle for the western regulars was over. If some fresh manpower could arrive to replenish their depleted ranks, the regulars would soon be ready for their next. It was no secret to Sergeant Carpenter where their next engagement would occur: "I have no desire to be in another battle. I have been in one and a tough battle, and I want to see no more. But I expect that we shall see one at Corinth, Miss." A further six weeks of campaigning would prove the young sergeant's expectations to be only partially correct.[55]

Chapter 4:

The Corinth Campaign

"Be Proud to Call Themselves Regulars"

While King's regulars marched to Pittsburg Landing and fought at Shiloh, other contingents of regulars were also moving toward southwest Tennessee. Oliver Shepherd's 18th Regulars were at the end of Buell's long column on the road to Savannah and thus arrived too late to participate in the battle on April 7. Their march was not without incident, and a battle of sorts between the regulars and volunteers in Robert McCook's brigade began to simmer in late spring 1862, a situation that would periodically threaten to boil over as the months went by. Regulars north of the Ohio River at the headquarters of the various regiments were also busy, training new troops and attempting to recruit additional manpower. Fresh companies from the 16th, 18th, and 19th Regiments were dispatched to the field in April and May, by which time the scene of action for the western regulars had moved further south, into Mississippi.

* * *

Captain Alfred Lacey Hough, 19th U.S. Infantry, strolled along the deck of the transport *B.Q. Adams*. His journey on the Ohio and Tennessee Rivers had been eventful, to include dealing with drunken troops and fishing from the water one soldier who had fallen overboard, but after a few days the excitement had calmed down sufficiently for the captain to relax. He had just finished scratching out a letter to his wife:

We are about 100 miles from Pittsburg Landing and all safe and in good condition. This is the first leisure moment I have had from active business, but am now all prepared to leave and march as soon as I report. We shall be there in the night and I shall report tomorrow. The regiment is some 10 miles from the landing and I expect to be with it on Monday night.

My men have behaved well and I have good assistance in Mr. [Lt. Howard E.] Stansbury; we hear no news and do not know what is going on in the world; we are not crowded and are very comfortable in the boat, she is very fast and we pass everything which makes some excitement. This is a beautiful river, and to-day is a beautiful day, and after finishing this I am going on deck to enjoy for the first time for 10 days a little leisure. Troops are coming here from all directions.[1]

Hough's company of the 19th Regulars, F/1/19th U.S., had left Indianapolis on April 22 by rail for Louisville. There they boarded the *B.Q. Adams* along with 200 soldiers and six officers of a volunteer regiment. Being the senior officer present, Hough assumed temporary command of all troops on board. The steamer arrived at Pittsburg Landing on the evening of April 26. The captain went ashore and spent the next twelve hours wading through mud and high water while trying to get directions to the 19th Infantry's location. Late in the morning the next day, he finally came upon the 19th Infantry's camp. Hough saluted Major Carpenter sharply and reported Company F at the landing and present for duty. Taking sympathy with the tired captain's mud-spattered appearance, Carpenter lent Hough a horse and instructed him to bring the men forward.[2]

Hough had spent that night and morning wading through both mud and the camps of a very large army. The Federal troops that he noted arriving "from all directions" were Halleck's concentration of three Union armies in southwestern Tennessee: Grant's Army of the Tennessee, Buell's Army of the Ohio, and the just-arrived Army of the Mississippi under Major General John Pope. The mission of this 100,000-man force was the capture of Corinth, Mississippi, a small town that was insignificant except that it was a vital transportation hub. Through it ran several important turnpikes, the Mobile & Ohio Railroad, and the Memphis & Charleston Railroad. With Corinth in Union possession, the Confederate garrison at Memphis would be cut off and outflanked. The capture of Memphis would in turn be a big step toward Northern conquest of the Mississippi

River. The huge Federal army at Pittsburg Landing would begin its move toward Corinth on April 27, the day after Hough's arrival.[3]

When the new company arrived in camp, Major Carpenter had Hough's soldiers pitch their tents along the battalion street. This was soon accomplished, but those members of Company F who entertained notions of napping away the rest of the afternoon were in for a shock. As soon as the tents were in order, Carpenter ordered the battalion to fall in for drill. A battle was expected in the near future and Carpenter was apprehensive about having a raw company in his command. He drilled them at every opportunity and kept pressure on Captain Hough to get Company F in shape. Hough studied the drill manuals, took pride in his work, and was determined to win the major's confidence. Two weeks after joining the battalion, Hough wrote his wife that Major Carpenter "told me yesterday that he saw a very great improvement in my company and was not at all afraid to trust me when necessary." Carpenter also made a good impression on Hough: "Major Carpenter has won laurels with everybody. What a gallant man he is. He is so sick that he can scarcely hold up his head but goes through with all his work, with conscientious industry; he is a lesson for anybody; I am proud to be serving under such a man."[4]

King's regular battalions had been busy during the three weeks between the Battle of Shiloh and the arrival of the Captain Hough's company. McCook's division had remained near the battlefield until April 15, awaiting arrival of the division supply trains. General McCook reported that his troops "suffered severely in this camp from sickness, occasioned by bad water and the stench arising from the unburied carcasses of horses." With the arrival of the baggage, morale and health improved. "We were paid off yesterday," Sergeant Carpenter wrote in an April 19 letter describing the new living conditions, "and the sutler came by so we could get some of the dainties of life, and it has made a new man of me. I am in excellent condition now. It is raining hard today, a real April rain, but we have our tents now and feel right at home."

McCook moved his command forward to a position one-half mile north of Lick Creek on April 29. The regulars immediately dubbed the swampy and inhospitable place "Camp Rattlesnake." They were soon hard at work building a causeway and bridge across Lick Creek and the adjacent bottomland, grateful for the timely arrival of fifty additional pairs of hands from the *B.Q. Adams*. They spent the next few weeks improving roads, constructing fortifications, performing occasional picket duty, and every now and then advancing a little closer to Corinth.[5]

* * *

Captain Hough's company was the second batch of regular infantrymen to reach Pittsburg Landing after the Battle of Shiloh. The first arrived early in the afternoon of April 9. One of the many transports at the landing that day was the *John Warner*. On board were sixteen companies of regulars, the 1st and 2nd Battalions, 18th U.S. Infantry, Lieutenant Colonel Oliver L. Shepherd commanding. George Thomas's division, last in the Army of the Ohio's order of march, did not leave Nashville until March 20, four days behind the Buell's lead units. Although Thomas's men conducted a forced march on April 7 in an attempt to reach Pittsburg Landing, the division made only at a point well short of Savannah by the time the Battle of Shiloh came to its end.[6]

Oliver Shepherd did not mind spending a few extra days in Nashville before moving out, for he was suffering from a severe bout with typhoid fever. Colonel McCook thought Shepherd was "endangering his life" by remaining on duty instead of taking sick leave, but the 18th Infantry's lieutenant colonel was not about to stay behind. "There are only a few officers of the regiment present with it," Shepherd said in reply to his brigade commander's concerns, "and there being a prospect for a fight ahead, I am determined to go at all hazzards." Shepherd had to be hauled in an ambulance during most of the march to Savannah.[7]

Since Shepherd was not able to spend much time in the saddle during March and April, he did not observe something that his troops quickly picked up on: discipline in the brigade's volunteer regiments was quite lax when compared with that of the 18th Infantry. While disciplinary problems such as drunkenness, straggling, and insubordination occurred in every Civil War regiment, how such problems were dealt with varied greatly between volunteer and regular units. Many volunteer officers, particularly those under Robert McCook's command, tolerated a certain amount of indiscipline in the ranks. Indiscipline in regular regiments was not tolerated at all. Courts-martial occurred in the Regular Army at rates many times higher than among state troops. A recent analysis of trial records reveals that Regular Army cases account for nearly 19 percent of all Federal courts-martial conducted during the Civil

War (15,398 of 82,744). Considering that regulars represented less than 3 percent of Union Army manpower, the standards of conduct regular soldiers were expected to maintain were extremely high. Writing about a certain "blockhead" soldier of the 26th Ohio, a volunteer regiment recruited in the Columbus area, a private in the 18th regulars once stated: "It is well for him that he is not in this regiment. He would have had his neck stretched before this time." Another 18th Infantryman, Isaac B. Jones, had previously served in a Pennsylvania unit and by July 1862 was regretting his decision to join the regulars: "I enlisted in a volunteer light artillery company the 10th of last October. On the 7th of march our company was discharged on account of the government not wanting any more volunteer artillery. I then re-enlisted the next day in the 18th U.S. Infantry. I don't like the regular service so well as the volunteers; we cant have half so many privileges. The regulars are exceedingly strict. The army regulations has to be carried out to the very letter. And you [know] the military law is the most t[y]ranical thing on earth."[8]

Private Jones, a member of C/3/18th U.S., experienced the strictness of army regulations to an even greater degree than regulars in many other companies. His commander, Captain John Henry Knight, was a demanding officer. A former captain in the 1st Delaware Infantry who accepted a captaincy in the 18th Regulars during April 1862, Knight was placed in command C/3/18th upon reporting to Camp Thomas. The captain composed a letter to his fiancé in June 1862 that includes one of the best descriptions ever written of Regular Army discipline in the Civil War. He started off by describing subjects typical of wartime correspondence: the routine of the previous day, his thrill of anticipation when mail call was announced, his dashed hopes when he realized no letters addressed to Captain Knight had arrived. He then put aside his pen for a moment to deal with some official business; when he resumed writing he went off on a different tack:

> I have just been interrupted right here by my orderly Sergeant who reported to me a man who "shirked" drill this morning. I ordered as follows: detail a corporal to make the man put his knapsack and accouterments on and drill him for two hours without interruption, the corporal to sit down under the shade, the man to stand out in the sun, his diet to be for all day: bread and water. I am very strict and exacting with my men. I always inflict punishment

bordering on severity and cruelty. I scarcely ever have to make a second application. Whilst I punish them for offences severely, I am very particular to acknowledge a good act and attention to duty. I also am constantly attentive to see that my men get all they are entitled to by law, and whatever else consistent with military discipline that will add to their comfort and enjoyment. They all know this and when injustice is done any one of them, they are sure I will see that they get a remedy. Whilst I believe every man in the company fears me, yet he is devoted to me and has the most unlimited confidence and respect for me. ...I rarely go in their street or in their quarters, but when I do every man bounds on his feet and takes the position of a soldier and salutes me. If they are in their tents, the first man that sees me rings out "Attention!" when every man in the tent rises and takes off his hat and stands in silence. I visit them about once in two days myself and I require the Lieut. to inspect their quarters every day. I inspect the kitchen every day myself. I give the cook fits if everything is not clean and in perfect order. Above all things I like to see the cooking apartment clean and sweet and the cooks themselves neat and clean.

The prisoners all dread when I come on officer of the day. ...Yesterday morning I found three prisoners in the guard house. Two of them I made stand on a barrel for two hours and then let them come off two hours. I made the guard keep this up all day until dark. The third one I made walk up and down with a sentinel all day with a stick of wood about five feet long and four inches in diameter. This morning I got them discharged [from confinement] and they appeared very glad to get away. These men will not be in arrest again soon, I don't think.

I wonder if you will think I am cruel. I think it justice and believe it a duty. I got the worst company in camp. It was said to be the worst company in the regiment. One of the officers remarked to me yesterday he believed I had the best company in the detachment. I believe, too, I have and I attribute the reformation to the rigid discipline which I have enforced. ...But I guess you are tired of this kind of talk. I had no idea of writing such a letter.[9]

At Camp Thomas and during the three-month stay in Kentucky, the 18th Infantry did not have much direct interaction with volunteer units. Most regulars of course realized there was a wide difference in standards between the two services, but chances to view those differences firsthand were few during the 1861–1862 winter. The 18th U.S. received a number of lessons on the road to Savannah. During one of the trek's marches, Shepherd's troops happened to be carrying their knapsacks while the brigade's volunteers were not. The light load was still too much for one of the state troops and he fell out to rest in a field beside the road. As the regulars marched by, the straggler yelled out: "No son of a bitch of an officer can make me carry my knapsack!" On another occasion, Major Townsend overheard a conversation among a few of his troops who were standing outside his tent. The men were amazed by the fact that some volunteers refused to salute officers—and got away with it. This laxity began rubbing off on Shepherd's troops, and the stay in Nashville and subsequent march to Savanna saw growing indiscipline in the 18th Infantry's ranks.[10] Ten days into the march, some of the regulars became bold enough to question whether they had to obey an officer's orders when that officer was assigned to a different company. Shepherd had to remind his troops about one of the basic aspects of soldiering:

> Hd Qrs Detachment 18th U.S. Inft.
> Camp near Columbia, Tenn.
> March 30th 1862

Orders
No 45

There is evidently a grave misunderstanding by the enlisted men of this Command regarding the responsibility to the orders of Officers and Non Commissioned officers of this Regiment, and the Army at large.

The orders of Commissioned Officers must be obeyed whether they belong to one company or another, the Officer being responsible by his Commission to the Government. All orders from Non Commissioned officers must in like manner [be obeyed] unless they are manifestly against Law and Army Regulations. Manifestly means at sight and without any process of reasoning. Error of judgement does not shield [soldiers] from responsibility.

Obedience is the first duty of Officers and Soldiers, and example their character. It is the rock upon which their reputations are based; without it they must ultimately become despised.

> By order of
> Lieut Col O.L. Shepherd
> Commanding Detcht.

ANSON MILLS
Adjt.[11]

Due to the debilitating effects of typhoid, Shepherd could do little more than write such messages in an attempt to maintain order. Some of his subordinate officers, meanwhile, cracked down hard on the regiment. One form of corporal punishment, reserved for extreme cases, was known as "tying up." The offender would have his wrists bound together, and the rope would be strung over a tree limb. He would then be hoisted up until his feet barely touched the ground. An hour of two of such treatment was usually enough to modify the behavior of more hardheaded soldiers. One 18th Infantrymen who seemed able to withstand even this punishment was a certain private with a fondness for alcohol and the eminently suitable name of Henry Tank. Today Private Tank's penchant for drinking would be diagnosed as a dangerous case of alcoholism. In 1862 he was simply labeled "a troublesome and insubordinate man." Tank's seemingly endless drinking binges were a constant thorn in the side of his company commander, which was unfortunate because Tank was a member of D/1/18th U.S. and his commander was Captain David L. Wood. Wood had been the quartermaster general of Ohio on Adjutant General Henry Carrington's staff before the war, and was one of the original 1861 appointees to the 18th Infantry. Despite his militia service, the captain seems to have learned little about leadership on the journey from Ohio to middle Tennessee. Unlike Captain Knight, who genuinely cared for his men and was as quick to praise as to punish, Captain Wood was just a sadistic bully. His troops, most notably Private Tank, were nothing but the objects of his scorn and the recipients of his inhuman notions of proper discipline. Wood had great latitude in handing out justice in the spring of 1862 due to Lieutenant Colonel Shepherd's incapacitation. Shepherd had delegated to his battalion commanders the authority to administer punishments to the men. Captain Douglass and Major Townsend had in turn unwisely authorized their company commanders to handle the specifics.

The 18th Infantry's disciplinary measures and the unit's relationship with the volunteer regiments in McCook's brigade created a tense situation as the Army of the Ohio halted in late March at the impassable Duck River. Thomas's division occupied a crowded camp near Spring Hill, Tennessee, and for the first time the regulars and volunteers of the brigade were encamped within eyesight of each other for an extended period of time. What the volunteers saw made them think the regulars, particularly the despised Captain

Wood, were going to extremes in disciplinary measures. This tense situation exploded on March 26. Two 18th Infantrymen were under arrest that day by order of Captain Wood. One was accused of being drunk on duty. This man's arms and legs were tied to four stakes in the ground, placing the victim in a "spread eagle" position. The other had been in charge of a work detail and was found lounging about with his charges instead of making them work. Captain Wood considered such behavior to be grossly negligent and ordered the lazy man tied up. The area where the regulars were being punished was on the edge of the 18th Infantry's camp, immediately next to the 9th Ohio's tents. This was too close for the volunteers, some of whom decided to take matters into their own hands. What happened next is minutely detailed in both the 18th Infantry's records and in a letter written by Corporal D.B. Griffin of the 2nd Minnesota: "There has been a good deal of excitement in camp this afternoon on account of the treatment the men in the 18th Regulars get. They had two men tied up to trees. They tie their hands and then raise them over their heads and tie them to a limb and make them stand on their toes for three or four hours at a time. So, today, the boys in the 9th Ohio went out and cut the ropes two or three times. When the officers tried to stop them, they knocked one or two of them down and hooted and groaned at them all afternoon. Our men are all down on the officers of the Regulars."[12]

Lieutenant Anson Mills, adjutant of the regular battalions, heard a commotion emanating from the area near the detachment's guard tent and sprinted there as fast as he could. He saw "one man in shirt sleeves running very fast from the vicinity of the guard tent to the camp of the 9th Ohio." There were plenty of volunteers nearby to replace this fleet-footed soul. Mills saw a mob of about 200 soldiers from the 2nd Minnesota and 9th Ohio gathering near the 18th Infantry's guard tent. They had been there for some time. After chasing away the regular sentinel posted near the prisoners, someone had placed a log beneath the feet of the man who had been tied up, relieving some of the strain on the prisoner's arms and shoulders. The mob became bolder after one of the shirking regular guards kicked the log away. The man in the shirtsleeves cut the overhead rope of the man who was tied up. Upon seeing the adjutant's approach, Mills recalled that the mob "began hooting and yelling and cursing me and the officers of the 18th Regiment in general and Colonel Shepherd in particular." The lieutenant rounded up some of the guards and had them re-tie the prisoner who had been cut down. Mills then ran to Shepherd's tent.

A riot threatening the discipline of his camp was enough to get the regulars' bed-ridden commander on his feet. He staggered out of his tent and walked with Mills to the guard area. Major Townsend and a number of other officers joined them along the way. Shepherd first tried to reason with the boisterous crowd, ordering them to desist as they were "disgracing themselves and the service." The mob replied with even louder insults ("tie the officer of the day up by his privates!"), and a hefty log was thrown at Shepherd's head. So much for reasoning. Dodging the incoming projectile, Shepherd ordered the nearby regulars to drive the mob away, yelled "Leave my camp you sons of bitches!" and swatted off the cap of the closest intruder. A general brawl ensued, with the outnumbered Regular officers and guards coming out on the losing end. Most of Shepherd's officers received a bruise or two, and Major Townsend was knocked unconscious. One of the regular officers was relieved of his sword and was forced to watch as a rioter broke it in two. Lieutenant Mills was a little more adept at the use of a blade, putting his West Point fencing classes to good use: "One man in front of me refused to go [back] saying he was a gentlemen. I gave him a thrust with the point of my sword in the rib and drove him back." Shepherd extricated himself from the fight and ordered the balance of the 18th U.S. to form up under arms. He also sent Lieutenant Mills to find Colonel McCook and request assistance in controlling the brigade's volunteers. The adjutant had to run a gauntlet:

> I started through the mob and many chips, sticks and clubs were thrown at me, three of which struck me. I tried to arrest some men but they only laughed at me and on inquiring their names would only give vulgar and obscene names. On inquiring for Col. McCook I found him absent and went to the next ranking officer. I don't know his name—a major now lieutenant colonel—and reported to him my orders. The major was lying down and got up very slowly saying "vell, vell!" acting as if he did not understand English. He refused to come with me. When I went to his tent I was followed by five or six men, who apparently made complaints to him in German which I could not understand.[13]

The regulars had managed to restore some semblance of order by the time Mills returned from his fruitless interview with the 9th Ohio's Major Kämmerling. After forming up the regiment and having his troops fix bayonets, Shepherd ordered a charge against the rioters that drove the mob back about one hundred yards. He then had his reinforced guards load their rifles. Shepherd at this point probably would have welcomed the mob's return, but the Ohio troops among the crowd had to depart the area and attend regimental drill. A few Minnesotans remained and kept up their verbal assault for a while, but stayed at a safe distance.[14]

Shepherd was very upset about the entire affair. He had never seen American soldiers exhibit such behavior during his entire twenty-two years of service. He sent a letter to Colonel McCook describing the lack of discipline among the brigade's volunteers, but the brigade commander brushed aside Shepherd's concerns. The 9th Ohio was after all McCook's own regiment, and the colonel's well-known free spirit had given the 9th Ohio its character.[15] With no redress forthcoming from McCook, Shepherd decided to address the Ohio troops directly. At the regulars' dress parade that evening, Shepherd had his two battalions form up facing the 9th Ohio's camp. Mustering as much strength as his feverish condition allowed, Shepherd and his adjutant rode out in front of the formation. With a gathering crowd of volunteers within earshot, Lieutenant Mills read aloud a general order:

> Hd Qrs Detachment 18th U.S. Inft.
> Camp "Charlotte," March 26th 1862

Orders
No 40

I. A crowd of men belonging to the 9th Regt of Ohio Volunteers and 2nd Minnesota Volunteers assembled this afternoon as a mob in front of the Guard Tent of this Command, one of them first cut the rope of a man who was under confinement and tied up, the Guard was neglectful of its duty in suffering such a mob like gang of rowdies to assemble so close to the camp of this Command.

II. The Non Commissioned Officers of the Guard and the Officers of the Regt were hooted hissed and groaned at by this crowd. All this was so great an insult to every soldier of the Regiment, who should be proud to call themselves Regulars, that every man should spurn such characters and deny all measure of association. The man himself who was undergoing the punishment which his officer had ordered, should feel pride and satisfaction that he does not belong to such a class of rowdies and contemptible wretches.

By order of
Lieut Col O.L. Shepherd
Commanding
ANSON MILLS
Adjt.[16]

Captain Wood, the man immediately responsible for this mess, was also upset. He feared that the attention focused on himself and his company might soon bring an end to his unbridled kangaroo court, and decided to inflict a few more punishments while he still had the chance. His usual whipping boy, Henry Tank, would be a convenient target. "I'm going to tie Tank up by his heels!" Wood proclaimed after the parade. His battalion commander heard the remark, but Captain Douglass had heard similar boasts from Wood before and paid it no heed.

Wood was serious this time. Sure enough, about noon the next day Private Tank was hung upside down from a tree limb with a rope around his ankles, charged with being drunk and absent from camp. Wood took the precaution of administering the punishment in the center of the 18th Infantry's camp and posted a strong guard around the area. The captain began having second thoughts about the punishment shortly after it began, an unusual display of clear thinking on Wood's part. He sent for Webster Lindsey, surgeon of the 18th Infantry, and asked for a medical opinion on how long it would be "proper" to keep Tank suspended upside down. "Captain!" the wide-eyed doctor exclaimed, "this is very harsh treatment for any man and he must be taken down immediately!" Tank was lowered to the ground. Lindsey gave him a quick examination and found "no evidence of his having suffered from suspension. ...I could not detect liquor in the prisoner's breath although Captain Wood charged him with drinking."[17]

While Tank came through the punishment in more-or-less satisfactory condition, damage of a more far-reaching nature had been done. As soon as the private had been tied up, word swept through the brigade's volunteer camps that the regulars were at it again. Colonel McCook sensed the discontent and sent his adjutant, Captain Andrew Burt, to find out what all the fuss was about. Burt made his way to Shepherd's tent and asked the lieutenant colonel if he knew what was going on. Shepherd did not, so Burt filled him in. The lieutenant colonel then decided to put an end to Wood's antics once and for all. He sent for his battalion commanders and was shocked to learn that Douglass and Townsend had given their company commanders exclusive jurisdiction over punishments. Turning to Captain Douglass, Shepherd asked: "Do you know that one of the men of your battalion was tied up by the heels?" Douglass did not. He thought Wood had been joking about tying up Tank the previous evening. Shepherd was incensed: "Such things should not occur again and any officer who would resort to such punishment should be deprived of the privilege of punishing his men." Shepherd ordered Douglass to "tell Captain Wood that hereafter when he wishes to punish a man he will report the case for punishment to his battalion commander. If he cannot punish discretely he will not punish at all."[18]

Shepherd should have hauled Wood before a court-martial, but evidently thought the non-judicial action against the captain was sufficient. Colonel McCook thought differently. The brigade commander had heard rumors dating from before the Mills Spring campaign of the 18th Infantry's supposedly brutal discipline. In addition to the Henry Tank affair, it had come to McCook's attention recently that one of Shepherd's officers had allegedly slashed a private with a sword. After Captain Burt briefed McCook on Shepherd's interview with Douglass and Townsend, the colonel penned a short note to the 18th Infantry's commander:

> Head Qrs 3rd Brigade
> March 28 1862
>
> Col. Shepherd
> Dear Sir:
>
> Duty requires of me that I should make the following inquires of you:
>
> I have been informed that an Officer in you command, struck a soldier over the face and head with his sword; cutting the man severely, and otherwise bruising him.
>
> Also that another officer in you command, had another soldier tied up by the heels for some time.
>
> If any such instances have happened in your command, I hope you will be pleased to give me in the form of an official statement, the names of the officers and soldiers connected with the matters and the circumstances under which the punishment was administered.
>
> I am yours truly
>
> ROBT L. McCOOK
> Col. 9th Ohio Regiment
> Com'd 3rd Brigade[19]

Oliver Shepherd read the letter and could not believe it. Typhoid fever, a riot, and now this. From Shepherd's point of view, McCook was meddling with the internal affairs of the 18th Regulars instead of doing something to control the brigade's volunteers and punishing the Ohio and Minnesota officers who had idly stood by while their troops went on a rampage. Shepherd replied to McCook's request immediately:

> Hd Qrs Detachmt 18th Inf
> Camp Charlotte
> March 28 1862

Col Robt L McCook
   9th Regt Ohio Vol
   Cmd'g 3d Brigade
   1st Div Army of the Ohio
   Camp Charlotte Tenn

Colonel

In answer to your letter of this date propounding enquires concerning "information" received by you relative to a man being struck over the head & face by an officer & another tied up by the heels I have the following to state.

Private Boyle of Co A. 3rd Battalion being attached to 1st Battalion doubled his fists & raised them to strike Lt. Freeman of the 2nd Battalion & officer of the Guard upon which he was very properly subdued by a blow from the hilt of the sword. Charges are preferred against Pvt. Boyle.

Capt. Wood of the 1st Battalion as I have found after enquiring tied up by the heels for a few moments leaving the shoulders to rest on the ground Private Tank of his company. The Capt. has been debarred henceforward from exercising corporal punishment which he has shown himself so improper a judge.

It is proper however, to say that Private Tank bears so bad a character, as to worry the life almost out of the Captain who wishes subordination in his company.

I must here respectfully mention that the information which the Col. Comd'g the Brigade has received, is irregular in its channel of communication, as it has never passed through these Head Quarters.

> Very Respectfully
>   Your Obt Servant
> O.L. SHEPHERD
> Lt. Col. 18th U.S. Inf
>   Comdg Detcht[20]

Shepherd did not stop there. In his mind, the 18th Infantry's current disciplinary problems were due entirely to the poor example set by the brigade's volunteers and their sloppy leaders. As soon as Shepherd finished his letter to McCook, he wrote another to division headquarters:

Hd Qrs Detachmt 18th Inf
Camp Charlotte
March 28 1862

Capt G.E. Flint
   Adj't Genl 1st Div
   Army of the Ohio
   Camp Charlotte

Captain

I respectfully enclose you two letters one from myself to Col. McCook comdg the Brigade and the 2d in reply to it.

Colonel McCook appears to assume a knowledge of the "facts of the case" which if true & he were present to know them would place him with other officers of his Regt under the 8th Article of War[21] which is a capitol offense.

A full naration of all the facts would swell a letter into many pages & I thought that none could be so short sighted as not to see that serious consequences would grow out of such conduct.

A more disgraceful scene and one more destructive to good order & military discipline, was never exhibited by a mass of men who are called soldiers and so mustered into the Service of the United States. On the day in question clubs, sticks, chips of wood, lumps of dirt were thrown from among the crowd at the officers of this command, and one of them, Major Townsend Comd'g 2nd Battalion, was severely struck & stunned on the head by one of these missiles, while all of my officers who were present were in the performance of their duties. I was myself among them on the ground, though scarcely able to stand on my feet owing to long sickness. I never exercised greater forbearance in my life.

Therefore, I respectfully request that my Regiment may be ordered immediately from under the control of Col McCook. Otherwise this Regiment will lose its character as disciplined troops. The officers of the Regt present are few in number and the bad consequences of such an example to a new Regt is already very apparent.

I should not be surprised at any moment or occasion to see life lost. An anonymous letter already threatens.

This Regiment has heretofore been submissive to orders and discipline; that is now disturbed. The speedy action of the Gen'l is respectfully requested.

> Very Respectfully
> Your Obt Servant
>
> O.L. SHEPHERD
> Lt. Col. 18th U.S. Inf
> Comdg Detcht[22]

Unfortunately for Shepherd, General Thomas was too busy leading his division on an active campaign to immediately deal with a discipline problem in Robert McCook's brigade. The Army of the Ohio was finally crossing the Duck River and resuming the movement to Savannah. While the events of late March could not be dealt with for the moment, word of the incidents would soon be printed in newspapers throughout the state of Ohio, and it eventually reached the Congress of the United States.

* * *

While the rift between the regulars and volunteers in McCook's brigade widened, the 18th Infantry arrived in Savannah on the evening of April 8. The following morning it boarded the *John Warner* and journeyed upriver. The crowded and confused conditions at Pittsburg Landing that King's regulars had noticed on April 7 still prevailed when Shepherd's men arrived. As the steamer tied up, Shepherd sent ashore Lieutenant Mills and the 1st Battalion quartermaster, Lieutenant Daniel W. Benham, to find out the position of McCook's brigade. Mills and Benham made their way up the bluffs from the landing, passing a small depression in which were piled corpses gathered from the battlefield. Looking at the grisly scene, Benham yelled: "My God, Mills, there's a man who's not dead! See, his face is red, and I can see his chest heave. What a cruel thing to turn him out for dead!" Raising the man's head and taking his pulse, Benham got a strong whiff of whiskey fumes. The soldier had become drunk the night before and then searched for a comfortable place to sleep it off. Seeing what he thought were soldiers sleeping, he decided to join them. The two lieutenants quickly lost interest in the "poor fellow" and proceeded up the bluff, where they eventually found Buell's headquarters and received instructions on where to place the 18th Regulars.[23]

Shepherd's troops disembarked from the *John Warner* and marched inland. The sight of the hospital at the top of the bluff was even worse than when King's men had passed it two mornings before. Henry B. Freeman of D/2/18th U.S. remembered many details of the scene when he wrote about it twenty-eight years later:

> There was a general field-hospital at the point where we landed, and the ground was simply bloody mud. The first sight that met our eyes as we reached the top of the bank was the ghastly pile of arms and legs bleached to a chalky whiteness by the rain, and which was being constantly increased in size by the surgeons, who, with blood-stained hands and clothes, were busy under canvas sheds close by, while frequently arriving wagons and ambulances were discharging their loads of wounded and suffering men, who were carefully laid down or hobbled to a convenient resting-place to await the attentions of the surgeons; and that no element of discomfort might be lacking, there poured from the lowering clouds a heavy, chilling rain. It was enough to weaken the stoutest heart, and we gladly hurried to the front, where we bivouacked in the mud and rain, and in our misery soon forgot the sufferers we had left behind.[24]

Moving inland, Brigadier General Alexander McCook greeted Shepherd's column. Receiving word that his younger brother Robert's brigade had arrived, the elder McCook was searching for him. While passing Shepherd's command, the general heard a familiar voice call out, that of Captain Henry Douglass. Douglass and McCook were old friends, having graduated together from West Point in 1852 and later both serving as instructors at the Academy from 1858 until the beginning of the war. Using their West Point nicknames, "Guts" McCook shouted hello to "Topog" Douglass, dismounted, and "with the usual McCook enthusiasm, shouted out many exciting incidents of the previous day's fighting, among others his immediate contact with Beauregard, whom he knew personally."[25]

While not sharing in the hardships of the Battle of Shiloh with the rest of the Army of the Ohio, the 18th Infantry did nonetheless suffer under the same miserable conditions for the next few weeks. "These days were among the filthiest of the War," recalled a member of Shepherd's command. "Baggage trains were all behind, leaving us without change of clothing, and the April showers soaking us daily, had in conjunction with natural exudations of the body and all absence of anything but mud holes to bathe in, left us in bad shape."

After their baggage train arrived on April 18 and the regiment was somewhat cleaned up, Shepherd put his regulars to work. Like King's men, they spent most of their time building roads, bridges, and fortifications while preparing to advance toward Corinth.[26]

The 18th Infantry received its first taste of combat the next week. A long, low piece of high ground south of Lick Creek known as Pea Ridge afforded good observation of the stream and marked the northernmost picket positions of the Corinth-based Confederates. Between the Federal positions north of Lick Creek and the Confederates on the ridge there was a three-mile-wide region of unoccupied land. Halleck sent Federal columns into the region each day to keep tabs on what the enemy was doing. On April 24, two regiments of McCook's brigade, the 18th U.S. and 35th Ohio, were part of the Union force scouting the region. The 8th Missouri, 11th Indiana, and 76th Ohio, all from Brigadier General Lew Wallace's division, Army of the Tennessee, rounded out the force. Brigadier General Andrew J. Smith, one of Halleck's staff officers, commanded the five regiments on the expedition, while Alexander McCook's entire division stood ready in support in case Smith's command ran into serious trouble. Smith's column moved out on the Monterey-Corinth Road at mid-morning. Near Lick Creek, it came upon an abandoned Confederate hospital site. A few Federal wounded who had been captured at Shiloh were still there, weak but grateful for their liberation. General Smith sent the casualties back to friendly lines and the column continued moving.

A mile south of Lick Creek, the column overran a force of Confederate pickets from Chalmers's Mississippi Brigade. Some shots were exchanged and Captain Douglass's 1/18th U.S. took a few prisoners before the Southerners beat a hasty retreat back to Pea Ridge. The Union force pursued and came upon the main body of Chalmers's command, three regiments drawn up in line of battle. General Smith deployed his command with the 8th Missouri, 18th U.S., and 76th Ohio to the front, with the 35th Ohio and 11th Illinois supporting. Smith's orders were to not to bring on a general engagement, so he did not advance against the enemy position. Chalmers probably had similar orders. Determining that the opposing Federal line outnumbered his own, Chalmers pulled back, abandoned his camp, and marched southward off the ridge.

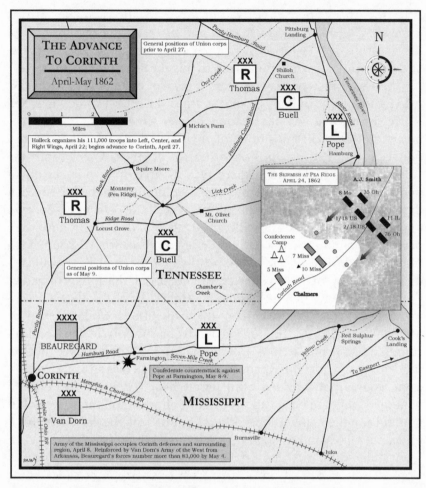

As the Confederates withdrew, Smith's flank regiments, the 8th Missouri and 76th Ohio, began to advance. Whether they did so on their own initiative or under Smith's orders is unknown. Shepherd had the regulars maintain their positions, for he had not received any order to advance. "When these regiments moved forward," recalled Captain Moses M. Granger of C/2/18th U.S., "there was much grumbling through the line at what we considered a slight in committing them before us." Sergeant Major Bisbee smelled a rat as he observed the volunteers moving out: "As we lay in line at Pea Ridge doing nothing, the 8th Missouri Volunteer Regiment came along looking for glory and formed line about twenty feet in front of us." Shepherd also did not like standing by as other units advanced. Orders or not, he gave the regulars the command to advance by the right flank, and the 18th U.S. was soon abreast of the other two Union regiments. The movement continued until the line reached Chalmers's deserted camp. "We surprised a Rebel camp while they were baking their cornbread and bisquits for breakfast," recalled Private Robert Kennedy. "They got up and left without ceremony and the breakfast they had prepared was very acceptable to us." While Kennedy and his mates downed their second breakfast of the day, other 18th Infantrymen rounded up fifty barrels of beef and twenty of flour. They burned any spoils that could not be removed. General Smith then led the column back to Federal lines north of Lick Creek.[27]

The April 24 skirmish soon came back to haunt the regulars. In mid-June, Major General Alexander McCook rode over to the camp of Colonel Robert McCook's brigade to pay a visit to his brother. The general almost leapt from his horse as he thrust into the colonel's hands a copy of the May 31, 1862, edition of *Harper's Weekly* and said: "How's the Dutch, Bob. Have you seen the news?" The paper ran an illustrated story based on a letter from a certain J.F. Gookins of the 8th Missouri:

THE SKIRMISH AT PEA RIDGE, TENNESSEE

We illustrate on page 348 a remarkable incident of the Battle of Pea Ridge, Tennessee, when the Eighth Missouri Regiment charged over the Eighteenth Regulars—the latter being composed of raw recruits, and showing an unwillingness to charge. The artist thus describes his picture:

PITTSBURG LANDING, TENNESSEE, *April 25, 1862*

To the Editor of Harper's Weekly:
Inclosed herewith please find sketches of a sharp little action which took place yesterday, some seven miles here. A reconnoitring force, consisting of two regiments from each division, was sent out yesterday morning to ascertain where the main body of the enemy lay. Some seven miles from camp the advance-guard of the Eight Missouri Volunteers discovered the videttes and pickets of the enemy directly in front and posted in the edge of the woods, and advancing drove them in. Our forces coming up discovered three regiments of rebels drawn up in line of battle in the edge of the woods on the

other side of a large open field, and protected by a strong fence. At this juncture the Eighteenth United States Regulars, having the advance, refused to go forward (this is a new regiment), the enemy having opened a heavy fire upon them. Colonel Morgan L. Smith, commanding the Eight Missouri, seeing this, gave his famous regiment the word, and off they went, double-quick time, *over* the regulars and after the rebels firing as they ran. ...Our forces then burned their camp—large amounts of clothing, stores, officers' trunks, etc.—besides capturing quantities of ammunition and arms. Nine prisoners were taken, and the estimate of the rebels killed, made by one of our artillery officers, is thirty. Not a man was lost by our forces.[28]

"The Eighth Missouri Volunteers Charging Over the Eighteenth Regulars at the Battle of Pea Ridge, Tennessee"

This illustration from *Harper's Weekly* depicts the 18th Infantry laying down at left, wearing the Regular Army's distinctive wide-brimmed Hardee black hats and dark blue trousers.

Harper's Weekly was one of the most widely read periodicals in America during the Civil War. The story resulted in Shepherd's men being the butt of many jokes emanating from the volunteer regiments of McCook's brigade, but, in the words of Sergeant Major Bisbee: "such was fame under an uncalled for feeling of Volunteers against Regulars." It did not help matters that Robert McCook's command started to be referred to as the "Pea Ridge Brigade," a handy reminder to Shepherd's regulars of their national notoriety. More than two months later, one of the 18th Infantry's company commanders was still upset enough to write home about the incident: "You perhaps have seen Genl. Smith's report of the reconisance at

Pea Ridge in which Harpers Weekly represents the 8th Missouri charging over the 18th Regulars. Genl. Smith pronounces it a malicious, unmitigated falsehood. The 8th Missouri never saw a rebel that day. This regt. [the 18th Regulars] charged on two rebel Regts. drove them from their camp and burnt everything in the camp, tents, offices, baggage and everything and withdrew in obedience to orders. Genl. Smith says 'no men ever acted cooler or braver.'"[29]

Colonel McCook was also displeased with the story. "Gen'l A.J. Smith, of Gen'l Halleck's staff, who conducted the reconnaissance, assures me that the [18th] regiment and officers acted with coolness and bravery," McCook wrote to his hometown *Cincinnati Gazette*, which had reprinted the piece, "they obeyed all...orders with alacrity and promptness...I am satisfied that the persons from whom you derived your information were mistaken."[30] Colonel Carrington went further, writing directly to the Harper Brothers of New York City:

> In your weekly of May 31st you publish a sketch purporting to represent the 18th Regular Infantry and their conduct in the reconnaissance, of Pea Ridge, near Corinth, April 24th 1862. It is simply a fancy piece, reflecting upon a large number of officers and men, but having no foundation in fact.
>
> Sixteen Companies of the 18th Infy under command of Lt. Col. O.L. Shepherd, an officer of large experience, are attached to the Brigade of Genl Robt L. McCook. The majors, of the two battalions, are Maj. F. Townsend, formerly the Col. of the 3d New York, Volunteers, an accomplished and brave officer, and Maj. James Caldwell, who for twenty two years, has been an officer of the regular army. Twelve companies of the detachment referred to have been in active service under Genl Buell, since November 1861, and include in their ranks a considerable number of old soldiers, wearing the badges of one, two, and even three, five-year enlistments.
>
> When it is remembered that in nearly every case during the war, when regiments have been accused of cowardice, the subsequent inquiry has shown that great injustice has been done to worthy and true men, by this indiscriminate and hasty criticism. The idea is suggested, that, it might be just and patriotic to have a little later intelligence, for the truth, and thereby save the honor of fair name of the deserving.[31]

At least one volunteer soldier present on the expedition came to the regulars' defense, although the charitable act did not occur until 1894. In his regimental history of the 35th Ohio, veteran Frederick

Kiel recalled that the 8th Missouri was "known for its peculiar capers" and gave his own version of the incident:

> Sometime later appeared in *Harper's Weekly* a full page illustration of this small affair; it represented the Eighth Missouri as charging over the Eighteenth Regulars, who, it was stated refused to advance, on the rebel camp. Some would be artist, wanted to give the Eight Missouri a send off, and make heroes of them, got up this illustration.
>
> The entire account was made of whole cloth. The Eighteenth was with us; and when the "brush" opened, was formed in line...while the Thirty-fifth formed a second line, immediately in rear of the Eighteenth. We moved forward in this order; and no Eighth Missouri was within a half mile of the Eighteenth Regulars when the affair opened, and no troops charged over that regiment that day. The entire was a libel on a good regiment.[32]

Other volunteers in the brigade did not share Keil's opinion of Shepherd's unit. The story in *Harper's Weekly* was just one of many damning newspaper articles featuring the 18th Regulars in the spring of 1862. In the aftermath of the Spring Hill riot, some volunteers in McCook's brigade (along with a few bold members of the 18th Infantry) had started a letter writing campaign to politicians and Ohio newspapers, describing the "brutality" of the 18th Infantry's disciplinary measures. The *Cincinnati Daily Commercial* broke the story on April 7:

A Chapter of Complaints—Abuses in the Army

> We frequently receive letters from soldiers making most bitter complaints against their officers. We do not question that these complaints are often just, but they can seldom be published with probable advantage, and we generally put them aside as belonging to a department of the history of the war, the time for the publicity of which has not arrived.
>
> Two letters of this character are before us, some portions of which we feel constrained to give. The first is concerning the 18th U.S. Infantry, COL. H.B. CARRINGTON'S regiment. It was principally recruited in this State, and a great many excellent young men joined it, thinking they could serve their country best as regulars. A good many of the privates were men of more brains, intelligence, and higher social positions than some of the officers, who were appointed under the dispensation of SIMON CAMERON. We quote from the letter:

* * * * *

"Lieut * * gets in a drunken fit, and with sword in hand, cuts their accouterments from them at half a dozen strokes, as he did young Michael Coons, at Lebanon—who, by the way, is there in hospital, with the point of the elbow cut off and the joint laid open, which the doctors say will disable him for life. This was done by the said Lieutenant for no offense whatever, and he had never been called to any account for the act."

[We learn from another source that Michael Coons' wounded arm was amputated at Lebanon—EDS. COM]

"Capt. * * he too, get drunk, knocks his men down, stamps them on the head, takes them by the throat and chokes them. And * * calls the men by the modest name of d—d sons of b—s; and that is not a light affair, for on a certain night, not long since, took a club and knocked down two sick men for standing by a fire, which priviledge had been granted them by their kind hearted company commander, Capt. Fetterman, Co. A., 2d Battalion. * * The question will naturally arise why do not the men seek redress through the commanding officer? The reason is that no one can approach or appeal to his majesty, Lieut.-Col. Shepperd, except through his company commander. * * Many of the men who have been induced to join this regiment with falsehood and flattery, now find themselves, instead of soldiers in the regular army, regularly enslaved. A general discontent reigns through the camp, every man feels his yoke of bondage, and every one hates * * and no one would rescue them from the enemy. Many of the men, thus brutally treated, are of excellent families, and have been educated in the best institutions in Ohio. They have kind friends at home who sent them here to serve their country, little dreaming that they were sending them to everlasting destruction, and with anxious hearts they are daily and hourly sending up prayers for their protection from the sword of the rebels, but we would fain hope that ere they close they would ask heaven in kindness and mercy to protect us from our heartless and drunken commanders."

We would not publish the above it we had not reason to believe it substantially correct. We omit the names of the officers charged with cowardly abuse of their men. In the letter from which we quote they are written out in full. The letter was signed, but we do not give the names attached to it, because the publication would draw upon the poor fellows the vengeance of their inferiors, who, by virtue of commissions, are their masters. COL. CARRINGTON has never been with his regiment in the field. It would be difficult to determine what a Colonel is for, if not to take charge of his regiment.[33]

The *Ohio State Journal*, the *Columbus Examiner*, and the German-language *Cincinnati Volkblatt* also printed letters and descriptions, for the most part inaccurate ones, of both the March riot and the later heel-hanging incident.[34] Back at Camp Thomas, Colonel Carrington was alarmed that the 18th Infantry's fine reputation was starting to tarnish. On April 9, two days after the stories hit the press, he wrote to Shepherd and related what the Ohio papers were printing. He wrote another letter of concern the next week:

> Headquarters 18th Inf U.S.A.
> Camp Thomas, O.
> April 14 1862
>
> Lt. Col. O.L. Shepherd
> Comd'g Field Detcht, 18th Inf
>
> Colonel,
> Since calling your attention to alleged violations of Regulations by officers of the Regiment I have been advised by gentlemen of the highest standing who claim to have personal Knowledge in the premises that several officers in command of companies have resorted to degrading punishments, are addicted to profane abuse of the men and have otherwise violated several regulations of the service.
> I pay no attention to newspaper correspondence in such matters, but, upon the basis of statements made to me, I deem it my duty to call for an investigation by you of the facts, and to make report forthwith as to the condition and especially whether illegal punishments and cruelty have been practiced by any.
> You will of course see the importance, to the regiment and the service, of prompt punishment through the proper methods of any officer so guilty. I shall be most happy to learn that I am misinformed.
>
> Most Respectfully
> H.B. CARRINGTON
> Colonel 18th Inf U.S.A.
> Commanding Regiment[35]

After reading Carrington's descriptions of the discontent on the home front, Shepherd told his colonel not to worry:

> Your letter of 9 April stated that the papers teamed with attacks upon two or three company officers for severe brutality.
> The regt was well pleased & disposed, till it came into contact with that infamous horde of Ruffians, mustered into the U.S. Service

as Soldiers, & called the 9th Ohio Volunteers. That Regt is a disgrace to our or any service.

Our Regt is in the main quite a good one, & we have got along
with less corporal punishment than I have seen in a single company
of the old regiments of Regulars.

The Officers of the Regt have striven to give character & tone to
their men, & would have succeeded admirably, but for the malign
influences of the 9th Regt of Germans, under Col McCook, who
looks to being elected Sheriff of Hamilton Co. Ohio upon German
votes.

I cannot but believe that men who generally behave themselves
with so much order & manifest so much disposition to be respectful
& obedient, will do well & achieve an honorable reputation as
Soldiers if they have not already done so. The recent skirmishing
with the rebels confirm me in this opinion.

There has been a few, but only a few, acts of indiscreet judgement
in punishments by a company officer. That has been corrected. But
for the association on all sides, with Volunteers, I believe the men
would be proud of the Officers of their Regiment, who have shown
themselves capable of commanding order & subordination among
them. The scurrilous newspaper paragraphs will ultimately enhance
the reputation of the Regt and the character of its officers.[36]

A regular officer who joined Shepherd's command later during
the campaign, Captain Henry Knight, also held a low opinion of the
volunteers with whom he had come into contact. The captain was in
a good position to judge the differences between the two services, he
having commanded a volunteer company of the 1st Delaware in
1861 prior to taking charge of a company of regulars in 1862:

> This army, or what I have seen of it, is a mob. ...Except the reg-
> ulars, the regiments I have seen are under no discipline whatever, and
> to me it is the greatest wonder that they can be managed in action at
> all. ...They scarcely understand any of the simplest principles of the
> profession and are under nobody's command. I have been surprised
> that these regiments should have fought at all. The regulars are of
> course kept under discipline. We are required to attend to every lit-
> tle thing as much so as if we were at peace with all mankind. I mean
> the little technicalities of detail—making out of papers and returns,
> etc, as well as attend to the drills and the discipline of soldiers—well
> drilled and disciplined. I never saw any set of men more subordinate
> [than the 18th Infantry].[37]

Although the regulars and volunteers in McCook's brigade wore similar uniforms, the Spring Hill riot illustrates that they were members of two different armies. Shepherd and Knight's comments that the 9th Ohio was a "disgrace to our service" and that volunteers in general were "under no discipline whatever" were right on the mark: by Regular Army standards, most volunteer units left much to be desired (although in fact the Prussian-drilled 9th Ohio was much better trained and led than most state regiments). But Regular Army norms are not the correct standards by which to judge volunteer regiments. The volunteers in McCook's brigade had not enlisted to become showpieces of military prowess. They simply wanted to get the war over with as soon as possible and return home. To most volunteers in 1862, the utility of Regular Army training and discipline was simply incomprehensible.

This preponderance of volunteer troops in an American army was unprecedented, even though there had always been a duality in the American military tradition of using both professional and part-time soldiers during wartime. In America's previous wars, which had much smaller troop requirements, manpower had been carefully divided between professional troops and temporary ones. The professionals (Washington's Continentals, and later the regulars in the War of 1812 and Mexican Wars) provided a long-term, reliable force upon which to build a wartime army, while the "short timers" (the minutemen of the Revolution and militia regiments of later wars) furnished a large pool of available troops. Leaders in those earlier conflicts used both forces to their best advantage, capitalizing on the strengths and minimizing the weaknesses of each. The huge number of soldiers needed in the Civil War made the Union Army much different from its predecessors. A massive expansion of the Regular Army was out of the question—few enough citizens bothered enlisting in the tiny Regular Army of 1861. With just a smattering of regulars present in the field, volunteers sometimes viewed isolated regular outfits like the 18th U.S. more as oddities than as something to emulate.

Competent leadership and a cooperative spirit solved this problem when Civil War regulars and volunteers served side-by-side, but cooperation was a word absent from the vocabulary of both Oliver Shepherd and Robert McCook. They had little respect for each other and in the aftermath of the riot refused to acknowledge that the other's style of leadership was the best way to lead their respective organizations. A brigade on the verge of war with itself was the result. Oliver Shepherd received a further indication of just how wide that war had spread on April 27, when he received an envelope addressed only to the commanding officer of the 18th U.S. Infantry at a "Camp Somerset, Tennessee." Shepherd read the enclosed letter and could not believe his eyes:

Washington, DC. April 14th 1862

Col. H.B. Carrington

Sir,

I am directed by the "Committee on the Conduct of the War" to ask that you would lay before that Committee the true statement of Brutality practised upon some men of your regiment, Captain Wood's company, said to have been perpetuated at camp near Somerset. The statement [is] that one man was hung up by the heels until he bled at the mouth and as a consequence died next day. Others of a similar import are printed and scattered through the country. Please let me hear from you at your earliest convenience.

Very truly yours,
B.F. WADE[38]

Benjamin Franklin Wade, the powerful Ohio senator and chairman of the Committee on the Conduct of the War, was only one of a number of legislators concerned with alleged brutality going on in the 18th Regulars. Another was Cyrus Aldrich, congressmen from Minnesota, who in early April received a letter from a soldier in the 2nd Minnesota describing the incidents that occurred in the 18th Infantry's camp on previous March: "The Officers of the 18th Regulars have made themselves quite obnoxious to the Volunteer Service on account of their severity to their men," Private George A. Wheaton explained to his congressional representative. "Men for slight misconduct are brutally flogged, hung up by their wrists suspended from a tree so that their feet cannot touch the ground. It's said that a man who was thus punished yesterday, or who was *hung up by the heels* has since died from the severity of his punishment." Aldrich did not know that Wheaton's account bore only slight relation to actual events; the congressman spread the word far and wide. He made a personal appeal on April 11 to the secretary of war to investigate the incidents, and the next day sent a letter to the War Department:

House of Representatives
Washington April 12th 1862

Genl Lorenzo Thomas
Adjutant General U.S.A.

Sir

Below I hand you an extract from the letter, which I exhibited to you and the Secretary of War yesterday, relative to the inhumane and barbarous treatment of the Privates of the 18th Infantry, Regular Army, by the Colonel of that Regiment, Col. Henry B. Carrington of Columbus, Ohio.

I trust the General Commanding will interfere in this cause of humanity, otherwise I would not portend to be answerable for what may follow. We are unused to witnessing such barbarity towards White Men, let alone slaves.

I suppose you are well aware that there is not much love lost between the Regular and Volunteer service.

I thought flogging in the Army and Navy was abolished. I consider such punishment as the Regular Army Officers inflict on their men, a disgrace to the U.S. Army.

Sir, it seems to me that such outrages and barbarous treatment and punishment, if you so choose to call it, demands your attention, and lovers of justice and humanity every where will rise up and call you blessed if you will interpose your authority. Put a stop to it at once, and cleanse from the Army any and all Officers, tyrants, monsters, who have or may cause such punishments on any one, created in the image of God. It is a disgrace to the age in which we live & ought to be stopped at once.

Most Respectfully
Your Obedt. Servant
CYRUS ALDRICH[39]

United States Congressman Sidney Edgerton, a representative from Ohio's 18th District (which included Columbus), and Mr. L.A. Markham, a Columbus citizen who had assisted in the recruitment of the 18th Infantry, were also concerned. "I have received letters from young men who are in the 18th U.S. Infantry telling me of the Brutish treatment they receive from their drunken officers," Markham wrote to Edgerton on April 21. "There are about 20 young men in that regiment whom I recruited. [Had] I known what I now know, they never should have gone where they are—but I should have put them in the Volunteer Service." Congressmen

Edgerton forwarded Markham's concerns to Secretary of War Edwin M. Stanton, adding some thoughts of his own:

> I do ask you in the name of all that is sacred, just & right to present this matter with all the bearing and power you have, and if possible get Hon. B.F. Wade to help you in the matter.
>
> If our young men cannot have humane treatment while they have given up all for their countries cause to maintain the honor of our glorious Government, why then the sooner the government falls the better. May God pitty this nation, if this government has got to [be] bolstered up by God forsaken, drunken tyrants & by riding down the very best young men of our land. But I suppose because they are Officers of the U.S. Regulars, they must be left alone to perpetuate their fiendish purpose upon good Christian men—just for sooth they never had a peep at West Point, and happen to be privates (who have no rights that drunken Officers are bound to respect) but not withstanding they are privates, many of them are far superior to their officers. Now I ask you for humanity's sake to present this matter with all bearing at your earliest opportunity, and as soon as possible report to me your success.[40]

While Shepherd could swallow his pride and ignore slanderous press reports about his regiment, Congressional concerns were official matters that had to be addressed. Shepherd forwarded Senator Wade's letter to Army of the Ohio headquarters and requested a court of inquiry to officially clear up the matter once and for all. The 18th Infantry's frustrated lieutenant colonel also addressed some rhetorical thoughts to the War Department when he learned that Minnesota Congressmen Aldrich was asking questions: "It seems somewhat surprising that the welfare of this Regiment [the 18th U.S.] should appear to be connected to the humane congressmen of the privates of the 2nd Rgt Minn. Volunteers. The question suggests itself: where is their Chaplain?" The request for the court of inquiry would not be addressed for many weeks, for General Buell had greater responsibilities at the moment. The day Shepherd sent Wade's letter to Buell, the same day Captain Hough's troops from the *B.Q. Adams* linked up with Major Carpenter's 1/19th U.S., was also the day the huge Federal army in southwestern Tennessee began to snake its way toward Corinth. Preparations for the movement during those last few hectic days precluded any formal investigation of the 18th Regulars.[41]

Shepherd sent his request for a hearing to General Buell, but as of April 30 the 18th U.S. was no longer part of the Army of the Ohio. Halleck organized the force at Pittsburgh Landing into corps-sized wings on April 22. The Right Wing consisted of Grant's Army of the Tennessee, the Center was Buell's Army of the Ohio, the Left Wing Pope's Army of the Mississippi. Another series of organizational changes, mainly involving Grant's army, took place on April 30. Halleck detached two divisions from the Right Wing and allotted them to a new Reserve Corps commanded by Major General McClernand. Thomas's division of Buell's army was assigned to the Right Wing and George Thomas replaced Grant as commander of the Right. Thomas had been promoted to major general of volunteers on April 25, a belated reward for Mill Springs, but was still junior in rank to Grant. Halleck made the switch due to a misguided lack of confidence in Grant's abilities. Grant became second-in-command of the combined armies, a meaningless position, and Grant's belief that Thomas had somehow conspired with Halleck to get the command (although Thomas had not) soured subsequent relations between Thomas and Grant.[42]

Thomas's old division went to Thomas W. "Old Tim" Sherman, a brigadier who had been recently assigned to the Army of the Ohio. Tom Sherman (a Rhode Islander and not related to the more famous William T. Sherman) was a hard-line regular artilleryman and member of West Point's Class of 1836. Known as a strict disciplinarian and unwavering in the enforcement of regulations, Sherman's fine prewar reputation landed him in a brigadier's billet in May 1861. Taking over Thomas's division on April 30, 1862, he soon began having problems with the commander of his 3rd Brigade. It would be hard to find two officers more opposite in character than Bob McCook and Tom Sherman (except of course McCook and Shepherd). The young Colonel McCook was an energetic volunteer officer who saw no need for most of the finer points of military regulations. He believed, quite correctly, that constantly subjecting volunteers to Regular Army discipline was not the best way to lead state troops. But McCook seemed to go out of his way to needle and irritate Sherman, never hesitating to disregard orders if he believed doing so was best for his men. When in early May Sherman wanted to reduce the large number of soldiers absent from camp without permission, the division commander required his brigades to have roll call three times a day. McCook considered this order to be yet another intrusive "Old Army" requirement. He ordered his troops to march out of camp just before each roll call, thus escaping Sherman's scrutiny. Gathering about him the 9th Ohio, McCook told them: "If there is anything to do, boys, we are always [out] there without having roll-call all day. Nonsense!" The 9th Ohio ignored the muster order and, in the words of a 9th Ohio veteran: "continued to do as we had done."[43]

Sherman's Regular Army command style bothered Robert McCook to such an extent that the colonel circulated a petition calling for Sherman's removal. McCook contacted his brother Alexander and told him: "the men were so angry with [Sherman] that he might meet with violence from their hands." While Colonel McCook's efforts to get Sherman relieved came to nothing, this general never did master the command of volunteer soldiers. One of the division's volunteers considered Sherman "a terrorizer of subordinates and an authentic martinet." Unlike other officers of the prewar regulars who successfully commanded volunteers in the Civil War, Tom Sherman never knew when to turn up the heat or when to lie back. Although competent and brave—he would lose a leg at Port Hudson in May 1863—Sherman did not advance beyond brigadier general in the Civil War.[44]

In contrast to Sherman's attitude about Bob McCook and his volunteers, the brigadier took great pleasure in having the 18th Infantry under his command. Sherman and Shepherd were cut from the same Old Army cloth. They had worked together as recently as May 1861, when Captain Thomas Sherman commanded the regular artillery battery that accompanied Major Oliver Shepherd's battalion of 3d Infantrymen during the movement through secession-inflamed Baltimore.[45] Sherman's admiration of Shepherd's regulars is evident in a letter the Rhode Islander wrote in 1867:

> During that siege [of Corinth] and the pursuit of the enemy, the 18th Infantry was the military life and soul of the brigade to which it belonged (McCook's). On it I relied for the basis of any readiness or promptness in the obedience to orders expected from that brigade. And if I had the power to do so by organizing that brigade for the great battle expected, I would have unhesitatingly placed Col. S[hepherd] in command of it, and thus relieved it of subjection to the over fatal effects of undisciplined and self-sufficient brigade and regimental commanders—ignorant almost of the alphabet of arms, and who by their too independent action frustrate the best laid

plans, and are destructive to the usefulness of the best army material in the world.[46]

* * *

Sherman and McCook's mutual hatred had plenty of time to simmer during the spring of 1862. Taking a lesson from Grant's near-defeat on the first day of Shiloh, Halleck had his troops fortify their positions throughout the advance to Corinth. Perhaps he learned this lesson too well, for the Federals spent more time digging than moving on the roads into Mississippi. Halleck's defensive mindset accounted for much of the slow pace, but poor roads, swampy terrain, and wet weather also hindered the Federal advance. Part of Halleck's caution was justified, for Beauregard's Army of the Mississippi received heavy reinforcements during April. Consisting mainly of Major General Earl Van Dorn's three-division Army of the West from Arkansas, the Confederates at Corinth numbered close to 84,000 by the first week of May, making it one of the largest armies the Confederacy ever fielded. Braxton Bragg assumed immediate command of the Army of the Mississippi (and retained a corps command) while General Beauregard directed the overall operations of the combined Confederate forces. Although Halleck's forces numbered more than 111,000 at that time, a number that would increase throughout May, the Federal manpower advantage was not great enough for Halleck to throw caution to the wind. These factors, combined with the Corinth Campaign being the first time Henry Halleck ever maneuvered an army in the field, meant the Union Army in southwestern Tennessee took more than a month to cover the twenty miles between Pittsburg Landing and Corinth.[47]

Pope's forces made the opening move of the Federal advance. On April 27, the Right Wing advanced five miles south on the road from Hamburg toward Farmington. Buell made a shorter advance two days later. From their camps southeast of Shiloh Church, Buell's men advanced two miles on the Pittsburg-Monterey-Corinth Road to the north bank of Lick Creek. McCook's men set about bridging the waterway, not resuming the advance until May 2. Thomas's Right Wing and the Reserve spent the first eight days of the advance largely motionless in their camps along Owl Creek west of Shiloh Church, sorting themselves out after Halleck's eleventh-hour reorganization.

The Confederates offered little resistance to the Federal columns as they advanced to the Mississippi-Tennessee border, but Beauregard saw an opportunity when Pope's Left Wing continued to push farther ahead than the Federal Center or Right during the first week of the advance. Pope was isolated from the balance of Halleck's forces, a situation that worsened on May 7 when Halleck ordered Pope to advance through Farmington and "Push forward a strong reconnaissance to-morrow toward Corinth...and drive in their outposts." As Pope's troops occupied Farmington on May 8, barely two miles from the Corinth defenses, Beauregard launched a spoiling attack against the overextended Federals. Brigadier General Daniel Ruggles's Division of Bragg's Corps advanced toward Farmington on the Hamburg Road from Corinth, while Van Dorn's Corps came up from the south. Heavy skirmishing took place near Farmington and Seven Mile Creek throughout the day on May 8, fighting that increased in intensity the next day. For a time it appeared the "great battle" Tom Sherman expected was about to happen. Facing a large enemy force, Halleck ordered Pope to pull back his forward units. Pope successfully extracted his forces from a precarious position, but Halleck expected Van Dorn to continue the counterattack the next day. The Union commander frantically shifted forces to support Pope throughout the night of May 9 and into the next morning. General Buell reported that his "whole force was on the 10th moved to the left some 3 miles" from its position north of Chambers Creek to close the gap between the Federal Center and Right Wing.[48]

Tom Sherman's division and the rest of Thomas's Right Wing on May 10 were near Locust Grove, Tennessee—more than eight miles from the scene of action near Farmington. Confusion reigned as orders went out from Thomas's headquarters for the wing's five divisions to take up the march as soon as possible. One 18th Infantrymen died during these maneuvers, but the bullet that killed Private Martin Wither was unfortunately fired by one of his own officers. Upon receiving word from Colonel McCook early on the morning of May 10 that the brigade would move out soon, Shepherd summoned the 18th Infantry's adjutant. Lieutenant Mills reported a few minutes later. "Release any prisoners who are not under general charges," the colonel instructed Mills, "as it is supposed we are going into battle." As the regular battalions formed up, the adjutant went to the rear of the column. Lieutenant Henry Freeman, officer of the guard, had the command's dozen or so prisoners assembled there. Mills relayed the instructions to Freeman and learned that most of the prisoners were in no condition to march, much less fight. Someone had slipped them some whiskey during the night. Mills "found them all drunk and most of them not under general charges refused to go to their companies." The adjutant left the recalcitrants in the charge of Freeman and Sergeant Jacob J. Wagmon, the sergeant of the guard.

Freeman had the prisoners gather up their arms and equipment for the march and ordered them into formation. The whiskey, impending combat, and being in hot water anyway combined to make at least two of the prisoners bold beyond reason. Privates Ferguson and McLaughlin, two Irishmen who were among the worst characters in the 18th Regulars, decided to attack Freeman and hopefully make a fast escape in the resulting confusion. They began to quarrel between themselves and staged a realistic fistfight. Lieutenant Freeman drew his sword and stepped forward to break it up. He grabbed Ferguson and threw him to the ground. The private got to his feet and threw a punch at the lieutenant while McLaughlin struck Freeman across the shoulder blades with his rifle. Sergeant Wagmon quickly pitched in, tackling and subduing McLaughlin. Freeman, stunned by the vicious attack, shifted his blade from his right hand to his left and drew his pistol. The weapon somehow fired in the process. Private Martin Wither, another prisoner standing nearby, was hit in the chest and died instantly. "I heard the report of a pistol," Anson Mills remembered, "and looking towards the guard saw a man fall from the ranks. I rode down where Lt. Freeman...reported to me that two of the prisoners had made an attack on him with their muskets and in drawing his pistol it accidentally went off and killed an innocent man. Lt. Freeman requested to be relieved. I reported these facts to Colonel Shepherd and he was relieved by Lt. McConnell."[49]

Joseph McConnell, a lieutenant who had been commissioned from the ranks and of Irish decent himself, took no chances with his boisterous countrymen. He had Sergeant Wagmon tie Ferguson and McLaughlin's hands behind their backs and then bound the two privates together with a short piece of rope. With the prisoners safely in tow, Shepherd moved his battalions forward. McCook's brigade marched about one and a half miles down the road toward Corinth before stopping for a moment at a wood line. As the formation halted, another of the 18th Infantry's drunken prisoners decided to head for the hills. He bolted out of ranks, a corporal of the guard in hot pursuit.

The prisoner ended up in the formation of the 35th Ohio, the regiment nearest the 18th U.S. in the brigade's column. He spread the word that regular officers were murdering innocent prisoners. The corporal of the guard arrived a few moments later, took charge of the escapee, and marched him back to the 18th Infantry's ranks. About 200 Ohioans followed the pair, intent on freeing the 18th's remaining prisoners before anymore of them could be shot in cold blood. The regular guards formed ranks to keep the mob at bay, and a great deal of pushing, shoving, and shouting followed. At least one Ohioan broke through the sentinels, but he was subdued before he could cause any further trouble. Some of the 35th Ohio's officers joined their men in the fray. One of them, Lieutenant Eckhart, tried to pass through the regular guards and received a rifle butt to the head for his efforts. Captain Lyman Kellogg of the regulars arrested both the semi-conscious Eckhart and the bold Ohio private.

It seemed to Adjutant Mills that the trouble with the prisoners would never end. Upon hearing the commotion he dismounted and headed for the rear of the column once again. Before he could get there, a rifle-wielding Ohio captain blocked his way. "You have arrested one of our men and one of our officers!" the excited captain yelled while pointing the weapon at Mills, "and I am going to have them or lose my life!" While Mills calmly listened to the irate captain and stared into the business end of what was hopefully an unloaded rifle, the 35th Ohio's lieutenant colonel carried on a heated conversation with Shepherd and Major Townsend. Before anything could be resolved, the 35th Ohio's colonel, Ferdinand Van Derveer, arrived on the scene. He demanded the release of the Ohio prisoners. "This is not the first regiment, Colonel Shepherd, that you have got into difficulty with," screamed Van Derveer, "and by god I'll show you that you can't ride on my regiment!"

The confrontation was about to explode when Colonel McCook rode up. "What is all this difficulty about?" the brigade commander asked. About a dozen voices started to explain things to him, but McCook was not listening. He took in the scene and immediately sided with his fellow Ohioans. "Colonel Shepherd, have your regiment stack their arms!" The regulars complied and Shepherd moved his guards away from the mob. McCook then had Shepherd release the two Ohioans. Lieutenant Eckhart and the private rejoined their comrades while Captain Kellogg turned over Eckhart's sword to Colonel Van Derveer, informing the colonel that the lieutenant was under arrest. The mob dispersed.[50]

Martin Wither was the brigade's only casualty on May 10, for Van Dorn and Beauregard decided to cancel the attack against Pope before it really started and withdrew the raiding Southerners back into the Corinth fortifications. This was fortunate for McCook's brigade. With the sowing of these latest seeds of discontent between the brigade's regulars and volunteers, it is likely that at least a few rifles in McCook's line would have been pointed in odd directions had a battle taken place that day. The fact that Lieutenant Eckhart was back on duty a few days later with sword in hand and no apparent punishment (except for his bandaged head) did nothing to salve the regulars' wounded pride. Lieutenant Freeman asked for a court of inquiry to probe the death of Private Wither, but the request was simply added to the growing pile of paperwork concerning suspicious events in the 18th U.S. Infantry. It would be dealt with after Corinth's fall.

* * *

If Halleck had been cautious in approaching Corinth before Pope's narrow escape at Farmington, the Union commander was even more so afterward. He spent the next few days ensuring that Buell and Pope were close enough to support each other. On May 13, Halleck ordered Thomas's Right Wing to advance two and a half miles south on the Purdy-Corinth Road. Thomas's wing was finally approaching the state line, but now a dangerous gap existed between Thomas and Buell. With most of the scattered Union columns approaching positions within three miles of Corinth, Halleck decided to finally unite his forces and present a solid front, from Russell's House in the north, through the Sarrat Plantation in the center, and on through to the Farmington area. Preliminary movements got underway with Thomas's May 13 advance. Halleck outlined his overall plan to his wing commanders during a staff meeting on May 16. All three Union corps would advance on May 17 to their designated positions. Once protected behind proper field works, Halleck's forces would emplace heavy siege artillery and then finally begin the formal reduction of the Corinth defenses.[51]

Lieutenant Henry Freeman was eager for any action that would help divert his thoughts from Private Wither's tragic death. The lieutenant observed that during the mid-May movements the 18th Infantry "found [the enemy] more inclined to resist our advance and had been every now and then exchanging shots with them." Some of those shots came uncomfortably close to Lieutenant Frederick Phisterer, adjutant of the 18th Infantry's 2nd Battalion. While riding amidst his battalion's advancing skirmishers on May 15, enemy sharpshooters opened fire: "One of [the sharpshooters] seemed to think I was a fair target and paid his respects to me repeatedly; one shot made my horse jump and I lost my hat." Suddenly realizing that skirmish duty is best performed by someone other than a mounted staff officer, Phisterer spurred his horse to safety behind the skirmish line. Being hatless was a serious blow to a Civil War officer's prestige, so the lieutenant dismounted, secured the aid of a nearby soldier, and "rescued the hat." Sergeant J. Nelson Pierce, a member of Company A in Phisterer's battalion, almost required much more than just having his hat rescued on May 15: "Our regt. was out skirmishing and our co. being in the advance when I got lost from the co. but it was no fault of mine and in trying to find the co. I ran upon the rebel pickets, there was ten or a dozen of them and they all fired at me and then ran. None of them hit me, I was alone and if the rebels would not have been such cowards they could have taken me prisoner as well as not, I began to think it was time for me to change my course so I started back to camp, the co. came in a few minutes after I got there having taken two prisoners."[52]

Two days later, the day of the general Union advance, the 18th Infantry led McCook's brigade as it advanced down the Monterey-Corinth Road. Shortly after noon the regulars approached the north side of the Widow Saratt Plantation, one of the few large-scale agricultural endeavors in the swampy countryside around Corinth. The brigade reached its designated position and Shepherd received orders to halt, which was most welcome news—his fever had abated somewhat, but he had not yet recovered all his stamina. While elements of the Colonel Mahlon D. Manson's brigade came up on the 18th's right, the regulars established a picket line and began to dig rifle pits. Major Townsend commanded the brigade's pickets, four companies of regulars and three from the 2nd Minnesota. One of the regular companies was D/2/18th U.S., under the command of Lieutenant Freeman. In mid-afternoon, Freeman advanced his company about 400 yards southwest along the Monterey-Corinth Road, posting his men along a fence in one of the Saratt Plantation's fields. To his right was the picket line of one of the Kentucky regiments of Manson's brigade. Looking over the half mile of open ground to his front, the lieutenant noticed some gray-clad troops disappearing into the woods on the opposite side of the plantation. "I had been in the service nearly ten months and this was my first glimpse at a genuine Confed with a rifle in his hand," Freeman recalled. "We were how-ever to have a much closer look at the individual before night closed in upon us."[53]

As Freeman mused about seeing his first armed Confederate, he heard a scattering of shots. The pickets of Manson's brigade in the forest to his right then opened up a "constant fusillade" of rifle fire. On the regulars' picket line, hands tightened on rifles and eyes anx-iously peered over sights, straining to identify targets. The fields to their front remained empty, but Manson's troops continued to pound away. Freeman dashed over to the right to see what had caused all the commotion. He only saw Federal troops firing blindly into a smoke-filled forest. Retracing his steps back to his company, Freeman had just returned when he heard "the report of rifles in our front and left. A line of Confederates deployed from the woods to the left of the road firing as they came on[,] whooping and yelling to drive us from our fence." Although the lieutenant was frustrated at not having a weapon to fire other than his short-range pistol, he reported that his troops "stood up manfully" to the enemy attack.[54]

Help was on the way. At the first sound of trouble, Shepherd had formed up the balance of the 18th Regulars. As the battalions formed line, Shepherd posted Captain Lodor's 4th U.S. Artillery battery to cover the road and then rode forward to the pickets. The firing had ceased by the time Shepherd arrived at the picket line. Townsend's men had turned back the attack, suffering one man slightly wounded, Private Anza Courtwright of A/2/18th Infantry. They also captured some prisoners. From them Shepherd learned that there were no significant Confederate forces between the Widow Saratt Plantation and the Corinth fortifications. The impor-tant ford where the Corinth Road crossed Bridge Creek, a mile beyond the 18th Infantry pickets on the far side of the plantation, was unguarded. Sensing the opportunity, Shepherd hastened the prisoners to the rear and brought the 18th Infantry forward. With darkness approaching, the regulars advanced across the plantation and cautiously crept up to the bank of Bridge Creek. The prisoners' information was correct; the crossing was unguarded. Capturing the ford, Shepherd posted a strong picket line along the creek and established his regiment's main line 200 hundred yards to the rear. Less than a mile down the road were the Confederate fortifications protecting Corinth; the 18th Regulars were among the first Union troops to venture this close to the Southern bastion. As far as they knew, the enemy had no inkling they were there.[55]

A strong attack on Corinth the next morning from Shepherd's position might have paid great dividends. Thomas Sherman thought so, stating that the 18th Infantry's capture of the prisoners on May 17 "led to the most important information from the enemy, which, had it been acted upon, would probably have led to the capture of the bulk of the hostile army." While Sherman was stretching the truth somewhat, it is doubtful that Halleck seriously considered such a proposal. Halleck's mind and his timetable were already set on how to capture Corinth, and the general was not interested in taking advantage of any fleeting opportunities his subordinates generated. Later that night, Shepherd received orders to withdraw the regulars from the advanced position along Bridge Creek. When a brigade from Nelson's division again advanced across the plantation toward Bridge Creek ford on May 21, it discovered that the Confederates had re-occupied the area in considerable force. Corinth would stand another fortnight.[56]

Sherman's division remained in the same general location north of the Saratt Plantation for the remainder of the campaign. Operations became more static, but the battlefield was still a dangerous place, with frequent artillery duels and clashes between skirmishers. That suited Shepherd just fine. He insisted his regulars snipe at the Confederates whenever possible: "This perfected the men in the use of their rifles, familiarized them with the presence of danger, and taught them self reliance by the habitual application of their skill and energy to the common work, which was to do all the possible harm to the enemy at the least possible expense to ourselves. Thus on our part of the line no one dared in daylight to put his head above the parapet of the rifle pit, while on the front of other regiments the men could move about freely and even stand up in full view without danger."[57]

The 18th Infantry's riflemen and their opposition made the swampy region between Bridge and Phillips Creeks a fertile killing ground. Just prior to dawn each day, sharpshooters infiltrated the region and kept a close watch for signs of enemy activity. Early one morning while on picket duty, one of Lieutenant Freeman's men took up a concealed position fifty yards in front of the rifle pits. Although of "mild and gentle manners," this private was one of the best shots in Freeman's company. The soldier's attention and the sights of his Springfield that morning were fixed on a small copse of bushes about 200 yards away, behind which he was sure was hiding his Confederate opposite number. In a rifle pit behind the regular marksman, his company mates had rigged up a dummy with a blue hat and coat to use as a decoy. When all was set, without moving a muscle the sniper whispered "Put it up." The dummy was raised, lowered, and then carried along the parapet. The ruse worked to perfection: "The bush stirred a little, a puff of smoke arose, a bullet whistled harmlessly over our heads, but the fish...had taken the bait, and exposed his body for a moment. Almost simultaneously with the other we heard the crack of our man's rifle, the rebel sprang into the air, ran a few steps, fell and was still. Our man ran back, jumped into the rifle pit in safety amid the crack of half a dozen rifles from the other side, crying triumphantly 'I got him, I got him!' 'Bully for you!' cry his comrades heartily, although a little jealous of his good luck."

Good luck was with General Halleck a few days later, while he and Thomas were riding just behind the lines on an inspection of the front. The two generals and some staff officers halted on the summit of a small hill to the rear of the 18th Infantry's position. The enemy, ever observant of this part of the line, noticed the group of general officers and brought to bear a section of artillery. Two shells were soon arching their way across Bridge Creek toward Halleck's party. The shells exploded halfway up the hill and caused no damage, although Lieutenant Freeman remembered that the shelling had a "very decided effect" on the length of time Halleck spent near the 18th Regulars for the balance of the campaign.[58]

Eventually even conditions along the 18th Infantry's line quieted down. This was not due to any lack of resolve on the regulars' part, but rather because the enemy had learned to stay a respectful distance away from Shepherd's troops. "Six days ago when our division took possession of this advanced Position, we had warm times for several days and nights," Sergeant Amos Fleagle wrote on May 26, "there pickets were only a thousand yards from our camps and a greate maney shots Fired at our Pickets, would finde there way to our camp; But we beate them at there own game and they have now drew there Pickets, Back out of reach of our camp."[59]

* * *

Shepherd had been concerned for some time about the number of troops present with his battalions in the field. Major James Caldwell was on duty, taking command of 1/18th U.S. on May 28. But the strength of the two 18th Infantry battalions had been greatly reduced during the past few months by disease, accidents, desertions, and a few combat losses. One of Shepherd's company commanders was shocked by how some of the regiment's companies had been so reduced in numbers:

> Disease has made sad havoc in [the regiment's] ranks—it is reduced full one half. There is one company right next to mine that went into the field last Dec. 84 strong, large fine looking men—now with the hardest effort not more than twenty of them can be mustered and it rarely has over 15 out. The Co. has been decimated by disease and others left behind in Ky. and Tenn. in hospitals. Many of them were discharged and sent home, others died. This is the sad history of the 16 Cos. that went out of Camp Thomas last Dec.—stout, Stalwart men, their superiors never went into a field. Their muster roles show more hard service than any regiment [in the] west. They were in the advance all the time in front of Corinth.[60]

A large number of Shepherd's troops had also been placed on detached service and fatigue duty. While this type of duty was common to all regiments, Shepherd believed Colonel Robert McCook was targeting the regulars for heavy details of troops. As the 18th Infantry constructed breastworks and settled into its position during the last week of May, Shepherd sent a complaint to brigade headquarters:

> Hd Qrs Detcht 18th U.S. Inf
> Camp near Corinth Miss
> May 25 1862

Capt A.S. Burt
    Asst Adj't Genl
    3d Brigade 7th Div
    Army of the Tenn

Sir

    I respectfully [send] you a list of the men detailed hitherto on Detach Service as Brigade Teamsters etc. and I desire to bring your attention to the fact such details are heavier than from any other

Regt of the same strength in the Brigade. And in as much as this morning there has been a further detail of *thirty* men for Capt. Lodor's Battery I respectfully request that all the men detailed as Teamsters etc. may be sent back to the Regt by being replaced by men from the other Regiments, who have not an equal number on detailed service.

The list of detached service does not include those on Recruiting service of which there is quite a number.

Very Respectfully
Your Obt Servant

O.L. SHEPHERD
Lt. Col. 18th U.S. Inf
Comdg Detcht[61]

A week later, Shepherd reported to General Thomas's headquarters that Colonel McCook had detached from the 18th Infantry 397 of its 1,039 troops, again requesting their return. Frustrating Shepherd even more was the fact that there were trained and ready regulars sitting at Camp Thomas. Carrington's recruiting program had not slowed down after the departure of the battalions from Camp Thomas the previous December. The officers remaining in Ohio and others more recently commissioned in the regiment expended a great amount of energy scraping up additional recruits while Shepherd's battalions marched through Tennessee and into Mississippi. Captain John A. Thompson was one of Carrington's new officers and took a leading role in the 18th Infantry's 1862 recruitment. A Chicagoan who, as a volunteer officer, had served in Missouri on the staff of Major General John C. Frémont during 1861, Thompson received a captaincy in the 18th Regulars on February 21, 1862. Carrington dispatched the new captain to the area Thompson knew best:

> Col. Carrington ordered him to return to Chicago and recruit a company of regulars, and he at once entered upon the work. At that time it was difficult to obtain men to enter the regular army, nearly all preferring the volunteer service, yet Capt. Thompson, by his energy and perseverance, speedily recruited one of the very best and most effective companies of troops that Illinois has sent to the war, which he drilled to a high standard of discipline. *"Captain Thompson's Regulars"* were the pride of Chicago while they were there. He was ordered back to Columbus with his company, and

placed in command of "Camp Thomas," a camp of instruction for the 16th and 18th U.S. Infantry.[62]

Edgar N. Wilcox was another of the 18th Infantry's newcomers. His experiences illustrate how the reputation of Carrington's regiment and the prospects of a regular commission were still attracting quality personnel into the 18th Infantry's ranks as late as ten months into the war. A University of Michigan graduate and civil engineer who had also logged a number of voyages sailing the Great Lakes and high seas, Wilcox served in the 7th Ohio for most of 1861. After campaigning in western Virginia most of the year, by the end of 1861 he was looking for a new challenge and perhaps a commission. He received a discharge from the 7th Ohio and his first inclination was to return to his home state and join the 1st Regiment of Michigan Engineers and Mechanics, one of the Union Army's few specialized engineering units, which was getting organized in December 1861. By the time Wilcox arrived in Michigan, the engineer regiment was already mustered in and about to head for Kentucky. He ended up in Kalamazoo, where the 13th Michigan Infantry was also getting ready for movement south. Just after Christmas, Wilcox determined that this outfit was not what he was looking for, for it already had all the officers it needed. "I have now been here some three days," Wilcox scribbled in his journal on December 29, "and have become thoroughly disgusted with the whole arrangement and think on the whole I made a mistake in coming [here]." Wilcox had a cousin serving at Camp Thomas, so he set his sights on Columbus: "I began to be dissatisfied with the way things were working out and wrote to Lu Brown who is in the United States Inf 18th Reg at Columbus O, asking about the prospects of promotion in said regiment. Today I came here from camp not having enlisted in the Engineering Corps and having received a rather encouraging letter from Lu...I shall go and join the 'regulars' as a private, promotion or no promotion."

He arrived at Camp Thomas on January 10, 1862, found his cousin Lu Brown, and was introduced to Colonel Carrington. A few days later, Wilcox witnessed the inauguration parade held for the Honorable David Tod, Ohio's new governor. Wilcox now had no doubt about what unit to join: "although it was a very cold day there was a grand review of all troops in the city. Col Carrington of the 18th acting Gen'l in Command. The Regulars made a fine appearance and I do not think I shall be at all sorry I came down here, especially with the chances which are offered for promotion." Wilcox joined the 18th Regulars the next day and spent the rest of 1862 moving up the enlisted ranks working as a clerk at Camp Thomas.[63]

While Halleck's forces slowly advanced to Corinth during May 1862, eight companies of 18th Infantrymen and two of the 16th Regulars were present for duty at Camp Thomas. Major Coolidge dispatched Captain Newton L. Dykeman's H/1/16th U.S. to Mississippi early in the month. The company arrived near Corinth on May 28, completing the organization of Captain Townsend's battalion. Lieutenant Colonel Shepherd wanted the other companies at Camp Thomas to head for the field as soon as possible, and a staff officer at Department of the Mississippi headquarters agreed with him. In early June, orders were sent for Carrington "to forward, without delay, to Corinth, Mississippi, six (6) Companies 18th U.S. Inf., to join their regiment." Carrington replied with his usual rhetoric: "I have the honor to report that before July shall close I expect to be able to march with the complement of my regiment, five (5) companies, maximum strength, and assure the General Commanding that they will be in condition to be a credit to the regiment and the service."[64]

Despite Carrington's promises, the 18th Infantry's field detachment would not receive these companies in the foreseeable future. The instructions to dispatch troops from Camp Thomas in June 1862 was the second such order Carrington had received in less than a month. He managed to avoid complying with both. The first deployment order, which arrived via telegram at Camp Thomas on May 27, was generated by events in the war's Eastern Theater. McClellan's Peninsular Campaign was in full swing at that time and fits of panic occasionally gripped the War Department and Congress while the Army of the Potomac was on the distant Virginia Peninsula. Concerned that elements of the Confederate Army of Northern Virginia were actually closer to the nation's capitol than were McClellan's forces, in late May the War Department reinforced the Washington defenses with whatever troops it could pull together. The telegram Colonel Carrington received on May 27 ordered all available troops at Camp Thomas to proceed to Washington as soon as possible.

A similar order had been sent a week earlier to the regiment of volunteers guarding Camp Chase. Located four miles west of Columbus, Camp Chase had been a training camp for Ohio volunteers during the war's first summer. In November 1861 it had been converted into a prisoner of war camp, and by the late spring of 1862, the Confederate population there was burgeoning. As the troops assigned to guard the camp departed for Virginia in late May, their guard duties were assigned to a contingent of Ohio Home Guards from Columbus—part-time soldiers who had virtually no training or discipline. The situation at the camp rapidly deteriorated. Conditions were so bad and sentries so lackadaisical that at times it was difficult to distinguish between guards and guarded. Rumors of a major breakout attempt at Camp Chase reached Granville Moody, colonel of the 74th Indiana and the camp's temporary commandant. Ohio Governor David Tod thought that conditions were getting out of hand. Not wanting a large force of renegade Confederates roaming around Ohio's heartland, on May 28 the governor sent a "pressing requisition" to Carrington for assistance in guarding the facility.[65]

Now this was the type of battle Henry Carrington did not mind: a clear-cut mission, an opportunity to show off his regulars, and a disarmed enemy. He disregarded for the moment the order to send his troops to Virginia and instead prepared them for more immediate duty. A little before seven in the evening on May 28, a column of one hundred regulars marched from Camp Thomas to Camp Chase. Their route took them through the heart of Columbus, where they unexpectedly had their first encounter with enemy prisoners. A small prison train with forty-one Confederates onboard had just pulled in at the Columbus rail station, a transfer of prisoners to Camp Chase from Johnson's Island (a prison camp on Lake Erie). Not present were most of the Union troops assigned to guard the captives. A company from the 61st Ohio was assigned that task, but upon arrival in Columbus, the guards had instead left the train, stacked arms, and proceeded to some nearby saloons. The regulars were marching nearby and heard the commotion. Carrington had them double time to the depot. When the regulars arrived, they could find only a single lieutenant from the 61st Ohio "resolutely determined to form a guard" and a certain Captain Young from a different regiment standing on the platform and announcing that no prisoner would get past him alive. Most of the prisoners remained on the train, but a few had already made their escape, and three more were confronting the captain on the platform. A least one private of the 61st was still nearby in the rail yard, drunk and firing his rifle into the air.

Carrington sent Lieutenant Thaddeous Kirtland and twenty men on to Camp Chase while the rest remained at the station and cleaned up the mess. A squad of regulars reinforced Captain Young on the platform and the Confederates there were informed that their next steps away from the train would be their last. Carrington dispatched a patrol to scour the blocks around the station for the escapees; it returned shortly afterward with fugitives in tow. Other regulars went through nearby drinking halls and roused out the guards, most of whom were in various stages of inebriation. Some told Carrington that their colonel had ordered them to desert their posts. Others claimed that their own captain had been so drunk on the journey to Columbus that some liquor for the men seemed quite proper. Carrington's sergeants browbeat the Ohio troops into some semblance of a formation while the prisoners dismounted the train. The regulars then escorted both prisoners and guards the rest of the way to Camp Chase. It was probably a toss up as to which group the regulars had more contempt for that evening.

The column arrived at Camp Chase just before midnight. Colonel Moody greeted Carrington at the front gate, wanting the regulars to "give nine cheers, and let the 'Rebs' know that reinforcements have come." Carrington declined the request, not wanting to warn the prisoners that additional troops were now present. The new prisoners were released into the enclosure, the 61st Ohio staggered off into the night, and the regulars prepared for action. Carrington made a circuit of the camp's ten sentry towers with Colonel Moody. Most of the prisoners were then asleep, but the camp commander informed Carrington that conditions were, if anything, worse than what the 18th Infantry's colonel had previously heard: "The prisoners had torn up floors and scantling for battering rams in breaking down the high fence enclosures. Occupants of the different barracks would pelt the sentries with junks of bread; jeer at them on the sentry platforms, step across the clearly indicated 'dead line' sing aloud and go from building to building during sleeping with undisguised contempt. ...there was a spirit of insubordination, that indicated a proposed outbreak, when sufficiently organized for that purpose."[66]

Just before daylight, Carrington's regulars relieved the camp's guards on the sentry towers. With the coming of dawn, Camp Chase's prisoners awoke to find a different type of soldier peering down at them. Instead of shabby Home Guards, the soldiers manning the perimeter now wore spotless frock coats, polished shoes, white gloves, brass shoulder scales, and wide-brimmed black felt hats complete with ostrich plumes. They also carried well-maintained arms and what appeared to be full cartridge boxes. Carrington instructed his sergeants and officers to inspect the guards often during the next few hours. The inspecting officer was to repeat the guard's special orders in as loud a voice as possible: "If any prisoner approaches the 'dead line' give the Order, 'Halt! fall back.' If not promptly obeyed, repeat the Order, 'Fall back,' and bring your piece to a ready. If still disobedient, Raise your piece, cock it, and repeat 'fall back, or I fire.'" The orders left unsaid what would happen next, but the stoic silence of the regular guards and the no-nonsense attitude of their leaders sent the prisoners a clear message that times had indeed changed at Camp Chase. A few Confederates tested their new keepers, but none dared to find out what would happen if he disregarded that third command to fall back.[67]

With order at least temporarily restored, Carrington went ahead with the next phase of his plan. He sent word to the senior ranking prisoners that "a detachment of Regular Troops had arrived to examine and inspect conditions at Camp Chase," and instructed the Confederate leaders to be at the camp's gate at noon. Just before the appointed hour, Carrington doubled the guards in the towers and formed up his remaining troops outside the camp's main entrance. At noon, the gate swung open. Colonels Moody and Carrington, three additional officers, and eight regular sergeants confronted the prisoners. Seventy more regulars were formed in two ranks behind the official party—rigid, silent, threatening. Carrington conducted a short and one-sided conversation:

> I treated the Confederate officers with the respect due their rank...and [said] that I should look to them, chiefly, for explaining to the Private Soldier, that open mutiny would be fatal to all concerned; that every sentry carried forty rounds in his box, and no blank-cartridges would be used under any conditions.
>
> At the same time, the officers were requested to make known in writing the names and regiments of any of their men, whom they

could not control, that they might be placed in separate quarters under special guard; and especially to furnish the Post Commander with the data for examination and redress of any complaints, whether of food or otherwise, that should receive relief at the hands of the governing authority.[68]

The regulars remained at Camp Chase for thirty days, after which time trained volunteers took their place. The 18th Infantry's presence prevented any serious violence from erupting this time, but they were periodically recalled to the prison whenever conditions took a turn for the worse. Governor Tod wanted a force of regulars to be available at a moment's notice and Colonel Carrington was more than happy to oblige. Meanwhile, down in Mississippi—where the Confederates could shoot back—Oliver Shepherd fought the 18th Infantry's real war. He made due with the 1,000 men of his two understrength battalions, minus Colonel McCook's details, anxiously awaiting the next dribble of replacements Carrington occasionally sent southward. In the aftermath of the Camp Chase episode, the War Department cancelled the order for all of Camp Thomas's regulars to report to Washington. Instead, five of Carrington's companies were to remain in Ohio for the time being, while three companies from the 18th Infantry and one from the 16th Regulars were sent to Mississippi. The campaign for Corinth was all but over as these regulars departed Camp Thomas.[69]

* * *

Major John King's regular battalions in Rousseau's brigade also participated in the advance on Corinth, although they did not see as much action as Shepherd's men. Buell designated Alexander McCook's division the Center Wing's reserve on May 10, which meant the division was out of the action during Halleck's mid-May advance. This arrangement was fine with King's regulars, who were happy to let someone else bear the brunt of the fighting this time around. Major King used the extra time to continue drilling his troops. The three battalions kept themselves in a high state of readiness for, as one regular put it: "We have a reputation, and are expected to keep it." Sergeant Carpenter wrote a short letter to his parents on May 18: "I have no news to send you as we have done very little but move our camp slowly nearer the enemy. We expect to move 3 or 4 miles nearer very soon. ...The only way in which we distinguish Sunday from any other day is that, we have no drill."[70]

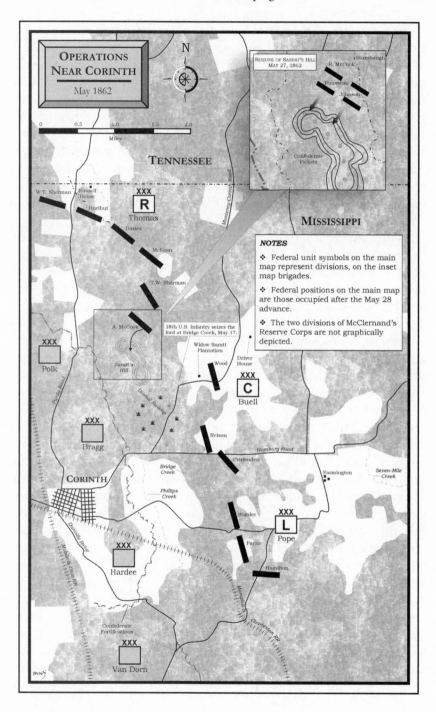

OPERATIONS
NEAR CORINTH

May 1862

N

0   0.5   1.0   1.5   2.0
Miles

TENNESSEE

SEIZURE OF SARRAT'S HILL
MAY 27, 1862

Stumbaugh
R. McCook
Rousseau
Johnson

Confederate
Pickets

W.T. Sherman   Russell
House
Hurlbut

XXX
R
Thomas

Davies

McKean

MISSISSIPPI

T.W. Sherman

NOTES

❖ Federal unit symbols on the main
map represent divisions, on the inset
map brigades.

❖ Federal positions on the main map
are those occupied after the May 28
advance.

❖ The two divisions of McClernand's
Reserve Corps are not graphically
depicted.

A. McCook

18th U.S. Infantry seizes the
ford at Bridge Creek, May 17.

XXX
Polk

Saratt's
Hill

Widow Saratt
Plantation

Wood

Driver
House

XXX
C
Buell

Dismal Swamp

Purdy Road

XXX
Bragg

Nelson

Hamburg Road

Crittenden

Farmington

Seven-Mile
Creek

CORINTH

Bridge
Creek

Phillips
Creek

Stanley

XXX
L
Pope

Danville Road

Mobile & Ohio RR

XXX
Hardee

Payne

Hamilton

Confederate
Fortifications

Memphis RR

Charleston RR

XXX
Van Dorn

mwj

Monterey-Corinth Road

By May 19, the Federal line was strong enough to resist any Confederate assault. Beauregard attempted a counterattack on May 21, again directed against Pope's wing in the Farmington area, by marching Van Dorn's and Hardee's Corps on a wide flanking maneuver around the Federal left. A combination of poor roads, Federal alertness, and too ambitious a plan resulted in Beauregard calling off the operation and recalling the Southern columns back to Corinth. These events, and worsening supply and manpower situations, caused the Southern commander to begin considering the necessity of abandoning the Corinth position entirely. At a meeting of Beauregard and his corps commanders on May 25, the decision was made to begin preparations for evacuation.[71]

While the Southerners put their evacuation plan in motion, on the other side of the lines Henry Halleck was perfecting the Federal plan. The position his army occupied after the May 17 advance was not close enough for his heavy guns to reach Corinth, so he ordered another series of short advances a few days later. On May 21, Thomas's wing occupied the northern reaches of Bridge and Phillips Creeks and brought forward the heavy guns. Pope's command advanced from Farmington to Bridge Creek on May 28. The day prior to Pope's advance, Buell's forces on the center of the Union line also pushed forward. Buell received instructions from Halleck on May 26 that stated "you will to-morrow establish your heavy batteries near Mrs. Serratt's house and drive the enemy's forces behind Bridge Creek." In addition to those tasks, Buell set his sights on a piece of high ground on the western edge of the Saratt Plantation known as Saratt's Hill, one of the key terrain features near Corinth. Located between Bridge and Phillips Creeks, this hill was the last significant natural obstacle northeast of Corinth between the Federal army and the Confederate entrenchments. Confederate pickets occupied the hill, but the main Corinth defenses were a half-mile to the east behind Phillips Creek. It was a serious oversight that the Confederate defenses did not include this high ground. From its summit, even light field batteries would be able to shell the town and also place enfilading fire along the northern segment of the Confederate breastworks. Beauregard later explained to Confederate President Jefferson Davis that Saratt's Hill was not included in the main defenses due to a lack of fresh water on the hill and the presence of heavy forest cover. Beauregard's arguments are not convincing, for good water sources were scarce throughout the Corinth region and some axes could have taken care of the trees.[72]

Buell gave the assignment of taking the hill to his reserve division. As darkness fell on May 26, General Alexander McCook moved his division to the front. Rousseau's brigade occupied the ground behind Thomas Sherman's division along Bridge Creek, the area the 18th Regulars had been fighting over for the past week. Brigadier General Richard W. Johnson, healthy again and back in command of his brigade, moved his troops adjacent to Rousseau's. For the attack the next morning, McCook planned to advance with Rousseau and Johnson in front. McCook's other brigade, now commanded by Colonel Frederick S. Stumbaugh (Colonel Kirk had been wounded at Shiloh), would be in reserve behind Johnson. Colonel Robert McCook's brigade from Sherman's division would support Rousseau. Alexander McCook's plan was to advance at first light on May 27 and seize the hill before the Confederates realized his division was out in front of the Union line. Sergeant Carpenter wrote of the movement of King's regulars that night: "We left our camp and marched to the front with 2 days rations in our haversacks, that night we slept behind our breastworks, the pickets were fighting about half a mile in advance. We had no tents but rolled ourselves in our blankets and slept as well as if we had been in the most magnificent mansion in the world."[73]

McCook's division prepared to advance on Saratt's Hill as the sun rose on May 27. Major King formed his three regular battalions into line, instructing their commanders to do so as quietly as possible. The division would cross Bridge Creek and hopefully reach the top of the hill without alerting the opposition. Captain Hough had woken up that morning a little worse for wear. He had been racked with diarrhea for the past few days and Major Carpenter recommended he stay in camp. Hough did not want to be suspected of cowardice and insisted on accompanying his troops forward. The exhilaration of entering combat for the first time picked up Captain Hough's spirits considerably. By 10:00 A.M., the regulars were at the foot of Saratt's Hill:

> At this time I felt as cool and collected as ever I did in my life and for the time was as strong. I felt a great work was in my hands and I must execute it. I had 50 men who looked to me for their every action, and almost for their every thought. I knew they had confidence in me, and if I did my duty they would do theirs. If we moved

another step farther [westward] we should go where none of our army had been before, so waited anxiously for the next order. A line of skirmishers were thrown in front of us, and then the order was heard very lowly given, "Forward March." Forward we went, quietly, solidly, and firmly. Not a sound was heard excepting the cracking of the bushes beneath our feet, we could just see our skirmishers occasionally, about 50 yards in front of us but no further. Onward and onward we went, and still no enemy, much to our surprise. We reached the top of the hill and accomplished what we went there to do, take possession of that hill at any sacrifice, as it commanded the town of Corinth.[74]

Sergeant Carpenter also observed little resistance: "We could see nothing in front, owing to the leaves on the trees and bushes, as soon as we were stationed we advanced skirmishing parties, and then the bullets came from the enemy's picket, but we laid low and they whizzed over our heads cutting the leaves as they went. We had two men wounded in the skirmish. A company in the 16th Regulars had 6 men wounded." McCook's plan had gone like clockwork. Johnson's troops encountered a heavy force of Confederate pickets, but drove them off after a thirty-minute skirmish. His and Rousseau's brigades then occupied Saratt's Hill. Rousseau's casualties totaled thirteen. The Federals dug hasty entrenchments while Stumbaugh's brigade occupied the area between Rousseau and Johnson. Battery H picked its way through the trees, occupied the center of Rousseau's line, and the artillerymen began hacking out fields of fire. Captain Terrill's battery was nearer to Corinth than any other Federal guns. The capture of Saratt's Hill and other short Federal advances on May 27 and 28 considerably tightened Halleck's grip on Corinth. The heaviest fighting of the campaign took place during this time as Federal gunners opened up on the Southern lines and Beauregard launched a few limited counterattacks, none of which succeeded in pushing back Halleck's men from their recently-won positions. Buell planned to advance the Federal Center further westward to Phillips Creek on May 30. General Halleck hoped that all Federal guns would then be in position to unleash a heavy bombardment on the Corinth defenses.[75]

The Federal plan never materialized, for the Confederates stole away during the night of May 29–30 after blowing up the supplies they could not move. The 16th Infantry's Captain Louis Hosea commanded his regiment's pickets that night, just 200 yards from the

Confederate lines. He remembered hearing "the drums and bugle calls of the enemy distinctly, as they assembled and marched away." Hosea wrote his remarks forty-one years after these events and his memory was colored by hindsight. Actually, Halleck and his army were almost completely unaware of the Confederate departure. One student of this campaign believes the Corinth evacuation "involved one of the most successful deceptions of the war." The noise Hosea and others heard during the night was thought to be Confederate reinforcements arriving, not troops leaving. It was well past daylight on May 30 before Halleck realized he was attacking an empty town. The regulars in Rousseau's brigade formed up for their advance that morning expecting the worst. As they advanced from Saratt's Hill and across Phillips Creek, they could discern a long line of artillery-studded breastworks looming before them. The going was slow as the regulars worked their way across the creek bottom and through the outer Confederate defenses, expecting with every step an eruption of bullets and canister. Much to their surprise, nothing happened. "When we finally reached the breastwork we found the enemy gone," recalled Private Van Zwaluwenburg. "They had slipped away during the night. They had rigged some logs on wheels to look like cannon. The terrific strain of expecting a volly as we slowly made our way in battle line thru the abatis was happily relieved and we breathed easier." Federal troops rushed into Corinth. Sergeant Carpenter was impressed with the mayhem that greeted them: "such a sight houses blown all to pieces barrells of flour sugar & molasses burning and every thing was destroyed."[76]

Once Halleck was sure Beauregard had indeed left, six Federal divisions started a halfhearted pursuit. Thomas Sherman's division and the 18th Infantry took part. After marching until nearly midnight the first night out, McCook's brigade bivouacked on ground previously occupied by Confederates under Sterling Price's command. The next morning, Private Kennedy discovered that his enemy could have used a lesson in personal hygiene: "We lay down and slept until morning and got more than we bargained for—lice. We started the next morning on the raid without a change of clothes, and that gave the descendants of General Price's 'leftovers' time to multiply by the millions on us. Whenever the brigade stopped, there was a stripping off of clothes and you should have heard the cracking, as we made an onslaught on this new enemy—not with guns, but with thumb nails."[77]

Shepherd's men marched through Farmington on May 30 and the next day were five miles south of Corinth. They moved deeper into Mississippi over the next ten days, reaching Booneville before Halleck called off the pursuit and brought the column back to Corinth. Beauregard, meanwhile, halted the Confederate retreat at Tupelo, a town fifty miles south of Corinth on the Mobile and Ohio.

* * *

"To sum up the whole," Captain Hough wrote to his wife on May 31, "we have been outgeneralled, and there is a feeling of intense disgust at everybody and everything that leads our Armies." Although the results of the campaign disappointed Hough and many others, Halleck's operations in April and May 1862 achieved the capture of Corinth. The loss of that crossroads caused the Confederates to abandon Fort Pillow on the Mississippi River, leaving Memphis all but defenseless. Union naval forces occupied that city on June 6. Halleck's securing of the Memphis-Corinth area provided the North a secure base from which to conduct further offensives deeper into the South. But there remained a dangerous Southern army in Mississippi, and it would be months before the Army of the Ohio again participated in a major battle. The Corinth Campaign was one of a series of maneuvers in the Western Theater during 1862 that involved more marching than fighting.[78]

The Army of the Ohio's regular battalions came through the advance from Pittsburg Landing to Corinth relatively unscathed, but the series of unfortunate incidents, accidents, and misunderstandings in Colonel Robert McCook's brigade had caused the relationship between its volunteers and regulars to be strained to the breaking point. In McCook's unit, the plan to assign regulars and volunteers to the same brigades in the Army of the Ohio was not working. With a temporary lull in operations following Corinth's fall, Oliver Shepherd was looking forward to the 18th Infantry's day in court.

Chapter 5:

The Kentucky Campaign

"March & March and Never Have a Winning Fight"

Major General George Thomas was in Corinth during the first week of June 1862, commanding the town's garrison. His troops included Alexander McCook's division and a division from the Army of the Tennessee commanded by Brigadier General John Blair Smith Todd. Thomas's own division, still commanded by Brigadier General Thomas Sherman, was near Rienzi, fifteen miles south of Corinth, part of the force watching the nearby Confederate army. Halleck ordered Sherman's division to Corinth on June 10 and restored Thomas as the division's commander. Sherman's command tenure had not been notably successful, although it was difficult for anyone to follow an officer like George Thomas in command of troops. Sherman was reassigned to the Department of the Gulf.[1]

General Halleck dispersed the large Federal army in northern Mississippi after the fall of Corinth. Pope's forces headed south toward Tupelo to keep an eye on the Confederates while the Army of the Tennessee, with Grant back in command, consolidated Federal control of western Tennessee and northern Mississippi in preparation for a further advance down the Mississippi River. Operations in Mississippi, culminating with the capture of Vicksburg, would occupy the attention of Grant's army for the next thirteen months. The Army of the Ohio's task, the capture of Chattanooga, would be the first step of the long-delayed Federal advance into east Tennessee and would take even longer to accomplish. Controlling Chattanooga was a vital task, for it was a railroad town whose importance rivaled that of Corinth. Taking it would disrupt Confederate rail movements throughout the southern Appalachians. With an eye toward the future, Chattanooga's position on the Tennessee River east of the Cumberland Plateau also meant its capture was a prerequisite for Federal penetrations of Georgia.[2]

The Army of the Ohio received its marching orders on June 9. Halleck stipulated that Buell's line of advance would be the Memphis & Charleston Railway, which ran from Memphis, across northern Mississippi and Alabama, and thence to the mountains west of Chattanooga. Maintenance and protection of this railroad would be a difficult task. Much of it was either damaged or had fallen into disrepair, and serviceable rolling stock was scarce. From Corinth to Decatur, Alabama, a distance of some ninety miles, the rails were south of the Tennessee River and provided Confederate cavalry and guerrillas with a host of vulnerable targets. Security was somewhat better east of Decatur, for the tracks there were on the north side of the river and a division of Federal troops was already in northeastern Alabama. Major General Ormsby M. Mitchel's division of the Army of the Ohio had advanced into Alabama and occupied Huntsville, while the balance of Buell's army marched to Savannah during March 1862. While Nelson's division set up a depot of supplies at Iuka during the second week of June, Buell set out from Corinth with three divisions (under Crittenden, Wood, and Alexander McCook), commencing a methodical advance eastward to link up with Mitchel's division at Huntsville. From there, the Army of the Ohio would be poised to strike at Chattanooga. Thomas's division remained near Corinth for the time being. The 18th Infantry had some legal matters that required attention.[3]

* * *

On June 15, General Halleck ordered a court of inquiry to "examine into certain charges of brutality or undue severity on the part of the Officers of the 18th U.S. Inf. towards their men." These were serious allegations, and Halleck wanted to be as fair as possible in selecting the court's members. He choose officers who could understand the issues from both the volunteer and regular points of view, men who held high-level volunteer commissions but who also had experience in the prewar regulars. The president of the court was Brigadier General Todd, one of Grant's division commanders who had graduated from West Point in 1837 and served nineteen years in the 6th U.S. Infantry prior to resigning his regular commission in 1856. Joining Todd on the court was Andrew Jackson Smith, Halleck's chief of cavalry, an 1838 Military Academy graduate and former colonel of the 2nd California Cavalry. Todd and Smith were both brigadier generals of volunteers. John Van Deusen DuBois, an 1855 West Pointer serving on Halleck's staff and colonel of the 1st Missouri Light Artillery Regiment, rounded out the court. The judge advocate and court recorder was also a regular, Lieutenant John T. Price of the 5th U.S. Infantry, one of Halleck's aides-de-camp.[4]

The hearing convened on June 17 at the 18th Infantry's camp one mile east of Corinth. General Todd summoned Lieutenant Colonel Shepherd, informed him of the nature of the allegations against the officers of the 18th Regulars, and said that an officer of the regiment could remain at the court to observe if Shepherd so desired. The lieutenant colonel exercised that privilege himself and Lieutenant Price opened the proceedings. There was no shortage of volunteers willing to testify against the regulars. The court choose eight to appear: four from the 2nd Minnesota, two from the 35th Ohio, one from the 9th Ohio, and Colonel McCook.

It is evident from the hearing's transcript that the two senior volunteer officers in the brigade, Colonels McCook and Van Derveer, did not want to leave behind any permanent legal record of whatever ill feelings they may have harbored against Shepherd and his troops. Robert McCook helped out the regulars' case immeasurably. First, he cleared up any confusion about the supposed death of Private Henry Tank. The court asked the brigade commander if Private Tank had in fact died as a result of being hung up by the heels, as had been reported in a number of newspapers. "I do not think he did," McCook responded. "I saw him a month after running around drunk at Pittsburg Landing with a canteen of whiskey in his hand trying to create another disturbance." McCook's answer to the court's final question came to the root of the brigade's command problems:

> QUESTION: What is the reputation of the 18th U.S. Infantry for order and discipline?
> ANSWER: Very good. Exceedingly good. Never heard anything against the discipline of the regiment except when the regiment was at Spring Hill. Before nor since. I believe that the most of the trouble has originated in a most rigid method of enforcing discipline, and principally from what I can learn in one company, Captain Wood's.

This condition of the regiment is owing to the officers having endeavored to conform more rigidly to the regulations than was or could be expected in the volunteers.[5]

The 35th Ohio's Colonel Ferdinand Van Derveer likewise had little to say against the regulars. His opening statement consisted of just two sentences: "I have no personal knowledge of the [18th Infantry's] discipline employed other than seeing their parades, drills, and guard mountings. So far as what I have seen...the discipline is good." The court did not even bother to ask this colonel any questions and moved on to other witnesses. None of the volunteer soldiers who testified mentioned anything about the Spring Hill riot. Doing so would have raised some eyebrows about their own soldierly qualities, perhaps generating some charges in return. They chose instead to bring up a series of trivial incidents that the court easily dismissed. The testimony of J.T. McCoy, a corporal in the 2nd Minnesota, was typical:

> I never saw anything except on one occasion I saw an officer strike a man with his sword. This was in the morning of the 27th day of March while I was on picket near Springhill, Tennessee. We were relieved on that morning by a company of the 18th, the name of the officer I do not recollect, and his company was falling in, when relieving us, from a road into the edge of a wood. He gave them the command to support arms, and just as one man brought his musket to the left shoulder the officer struck him on the left shoulder with his sword. That is all I have seen.
>
> QUESTION: When the sword was applied to the man was it such as to make him complain, or to admonish him of his duty?
>
> ANSWER: I should think to admonish him of his duty. I think it was because he didn't come to a support in time.[6]

If any of the volunteers could have been considered a star witness for the prosecution, it was Lieutenant Gustav Tafel of the 9th Ohio. He was the founder of Cincinnati's chapter of the Germanic Turner Society (*Turnverein*), a leftist, semi-military civic organization, and an important figure in the Cincinnati German community.[7] He had written a lengthy letter to the *Cincinnati Volkblatt* about that day's events and the riot of the preceding day. After Tafel was sworn in, Lieutenant Price handed him a copy of the newspaper article and asked Tafel if he was the author. Tafel replied that he was, probably regretting he wrote the passage that translates from the German as: "an unfortunate soldier was actually hung up by the heels until the blood spirted from his mouth and nose. ...Today the report becomes current that the abused man had died." With Oliver Shepherd's glare upon him, the lieutenant's testimony about the riot was somewhat less sensational than his writing:

> Some noise attracted my attention...and I went towards the line separating the 18th Infantry from my own regiment. ...I saw a man hung up by his wrists to a limb of a tree...there was another man staked out on the ground. ...The men of my regiment were much excited at this. I was present there merely as a spectator. ...I was a little back of the crowd, could see only the backs of the men. I heard Colonel Shepherd call the men sons of bitches and saw him knock the cap off one of the men from his head and order them to go away. The men did not go away. ...One officer of the 18th who was walking toward the headquarters of the 9th Ohio was treated with much disrespect. I do not of my own observation know what took place the following day.[8]

The court pressed the lieutenant for more specifics but Tafel finally had to admit he could honestly divulge nothing further. His barren testimony stood in such start contrast to his detailed letter to the *Volkblatt* that the court issued him a rebuke with its final question: "Do the duties of an officer or soldier require letter writing to newspapers?" Tafel's response was feeble at best: "I know of no such duty." The court sent him on his way.

After listening to volunteer testimony for the better part of two days, Brigadier General Todd and his peers must have been wondering who had thought a court of inquiry had been so necessary in the first place. The court then turned its attention to the regulars. Twelve members of the 18th Infantry offered testimony and unlike the volunteers they did not hesitate to discuss in detail the riot and its ancillary events. Surgeon Lindsey explained how the rumor of Private Tank's death probably started: "After I went to my tent I was sent for to see this man. He was pale and prostrated but I thought nothing serious was the matter. I went away after ordering some water to be poured on his head. I was told by some of the men that after I left he vomited up tobacco the effect of which would produce the appearance of prostration. He was well the next day."[9]

The 18th Infantry's adjutant, both battalion commanders, and three company commanders also testified.[10] In addition to the events of March 26 and 27, the regulars discussed other occasions when soldiers of the 18th had been tied up. The information each officer gave was similar: instances of tying up were few and far between and all occurred for valid disciplinary reasons, with the exception of some punishments handed out by Captain Wood. Major Frederick Townsend provided some of the most significant testimony. Here was a man all sides respected, for his credentials as a former state adjutant general, ex-colonel of a volunteer regiment, and commander of a regular battalion gave him an authoritative voice far beyond what would normally be the case for an officer wearing a major's gold oak leaf. He explained why the 18th Infantry's disciplinary problems had increased during the spring of 1862:

> QUESTION: Do you know of any events which have had a tendency to exasperate the men and officers of the regiment or have had the effect of creating discontent and insubordination?
>
> ANSWER: Yes sir! The discipline and subordination of the regiment were excellent until we came to Tennessee. I there observed that our men thence in contact with the volunteers of this brigade and associating with them had deteriorated and I felt that the officers had not the same control of their men as they had had formerly.
>
> QUESTION: Did the men ever appear to have discontent until they were on duty in a crowded camp with the volunteers comprising this brigade?
>
> ANSWER: No sir! I never heard any discontent until we joined this brigade. I have had some experience commanding bodies of men and our regiment gave every appearance of being a very superior regiment.[11]

The court then asked Townsend the decisive question: "Was this discontent owing to the severity of punishment for offenses or to the malign influence of the volunteers?" Townsend's answer was unequivocal. "I think it is entirely due to the influence of the volunteers of this brigade on the men," the major replied, "associating with the volunteers of our brigade whose discipline is different from that of Regulars."

The court also heard testimony relating to Lieutenant Freeman's shooting of Private Martin Wither, an act that General Todd ruled to have been accidental. After seven days of testimony and deliberation, the court rendered its opinion on discipline in the 18th Regulars:

> The court...after rereading all the testimony and mature deliberation finds the following facts:

That there were few if any cases of "tying up" which is the punishment complained of as brutal and unduly severe, until the 18th U.S. Infy was attached to Col. Robt. McCook's brigade.

That an insubordinate and undisciplined spirit was excited among the Enlisted men of the 18th U.S. Infy by men of other regiments of the brigade and by newspaper articles which required prompt and severe measures to suppress.

That Col Shepherd although in ill health and generally unable to mount his horse used every effort to prevent all undue severity of punishment in his regiment.

That the newspaper articles and letters charging the officers of the 18th Infy generally with brutality are either untrue or only founded on fact.

And the court does therefore recommend that no further action be taken in this matter except in the case of Capt. Wood.

The facts in the case of Capt. Wood...are as follows:

At Spring Hill Tenn during the month of March 1862 a private of the 18th U.S. Infy by the name of "Tank" was tied up by the heels for being absent from camp without permission, by order of Capt. Wood. That Capt. Wood sent for Surgeon Lindsey U.S.A. who directed the man to be cut down, determining of such punishment that the man was not injured as he was well the next day. The man Tank was of a notoriously bad character, but as the punishment was unusual & severe the court recommends that further action be had in this matter.[12]

Thus ended a rather unique episode in the legal landscape of the Civil War: the officer corps of a regiment being on trial for nothing more than attempting to soldier "by the book." The verdict settled things as far as the legality of the 18th Infantry's disciplinary system was concerned, but did nothing to change the attitude of anyone in McCook's brigade. The volunteers continued to view regular officers as tyrants, while Shepherd's low opinion of state troops just continued its downward spiral. Curiously, Shepherd somehow avoided complying with the court's recommendation that Captain Wood's actions be investigated further. Perhaps he knew that Wood's presence irritated the brigade's volunteers and so choose to do nothing. Wood continued on duty with his company through the end of the year. Shepherd must have kept a close eye on him, for there were no further complaints about the captain's disciplinary actions.

* * *

The day after General Todd published his findings, General Halleck ordered Thomas's division eastward to secure the Memphis & Charleston between Iuka, Mississippi, and Tuscumbia, Alabama. Nelson's division, which had been performing that role, had orders to move northeastward into middle Tennessee to secure the Central Alabama Railroad between Nashville and Decatur. Halleck ordered Thomas to establish his headquarters at Tuscumbia and concentrate his three brigades at that point, with detachments guarding the rails to the east between Tuscumbia and Decatur. The 1st Ohio Cavalry of Thomas's division would patrol the rails west of Tuscumbia as far as Iuka. Halleck also ordered Thomas to post a regiment at Iuka, to serve as provost guards at the burgeoning supply depot there. Iuka, a small town on the Memphis & Charleston line in the northeast corner of Mississippi twenty-three miles east of Corinth, was an important supply point for Buell's advance to Chattanooga. The Tennessee River's low water level during the drought-plagued summer of 1862 prevented steamers from safely ascending the waterway beyond Colbert's Shoals, a few miles upriver from the landing at Eastport. River craft had to unload at Eastport and the supplies were then hauled ten miles overland to the Iuka depot, where the items would be loaded on eastbound trains (at least as soon as an operable engine could be found). General Thomas assigned the important mission of guarding the Iuka region to the 18th Infantry. The recent legal proceedings had not diminished Thomas's confidence in Shepherd's troops.[13]

Shepherd's regulars departed Corinth on June 24, the day after the inquiry proceedings closed. One of Shepherd's companies remained near Corinth, guarding the Army of the Ohio's field hospital at Farmington. Three companies guarded the railroad bridge over Bear Creek, seven miles east of Iuka, while another company was at Eastport. The balance of the regulars guarded the Iuka depot and escorted supply trains traveling between there and the Tennessee River landings.[14] Shepherd published orders spelling out the duties for the Iuka-based men with his trademark attention to regulations. With the ink of the court's vindication scarcely dry, he ordered a little Regular Army discipline applied to anyone wandering about town without permission:

Hd Qrs Detcht 18th U.S. Inft
Camp Iuka, Miss June 28th 1862

Orders
No 76

I. There will be one Company on duty each day as Provost Guard in the town of Iuka, and will mount at 7 O'clock A.M.

II. The duties will be to guard the Depôt of Public Property, and the Railroad Depôt, and to preserve order in the town. Sentinels will be posted over the Depôts, and Patrols will be sent out every hour to different positions of the town, and every half hour if found necessary. This duty will not occur often to a company, and must be performed in the strictest and most rigid manner. All enlisted men found in town, without written authority, will be apprehended, and kept at work...till tattoo, when they will be sent to their Regiments under charge of Sentinels, and a Non Commissioned Officer. All men who may be apprehended as above, and refusing to work, will be tied up for the same period of time, and will not be let down for any purpose whatsoever. Rebel Spies, or suspicious persons whether denizens of the town, or otherwise, will of course be apprehended, and sent to these Head Quarters.

III. This Provost Guard will never be left without an officer.

> By order of
> Lieut. Col. O.L Shepherd
> Comd'g Detcht
>
> ANSON MILLS
> 1st Lieut 18th Inft. U.S.A.
> Adjt Detcht.15

Shepherd's troops took advantage of the break from active campaigning to relax. Iuka was famous for its mineral springs and had been a popular resort before the war. "I like this camp better than any we have been at yet," an excited 18th Regular wrote upon arriving in Iuka. "The Iuka Springs are close to camp, where there is three kinds of water running, each separately, vis sulphur, alum, and iron. And there is a number of springs of very good water besides." When not on guard duty or constructing fortifications, the 18th Infantry provosts enjoyed the town's billiard halls and tin pan alleys. As with many Civil War soldiers, some of the regulars found less temperate ways to pass their idle hours. Lieutenant Frederick Phisterer had fond memories of his stay in Mississippi: "In I-U-Ka we had a club, meeting in the sutler store, its sessions were continued as long as any one could say 'truly rural.'"[16] Anson Mills also had some memorable times in Iuka:

Shepherd selected a camp site in a dense forest, which added to our comfort in the heat. ...It was here I became known as the best shot in the regiment. One day, when we were all trying to rest and sleep, somebody called out, "See that squirrel!" pointing to where the little animal was eating buds in the top of an oak tree. He was perhaps one hundred fifty feet from me, but I was satisfied I could kill him. Many soldiers and officers looking on, I raised my pistol, fired, the squirrel fell to the ground, shot through the head; a better shot than I had intended. This, together with the fact that I was from Texas, gave me a better reputation as a crack shot than I deserved.[17]

It was not all fun and games for the 18th Infantrymen at Iuka, for guerilla activity in the surrounding countryside made this a dangerous place. On June 30, three of the regiment's soldiers were killed in an ambush. Private Isaac Jones recorded in a letter that another deadly incident occurred a few days later, but reported that this time the regulars were able to strike back: "The night of the 3rd of this month our men carried two soldiers in[to] camp a little after night. One was shot three times, and the other so badly wounded that he died in the morning. They were shot from a barn a short distance from camp. There was a few men sent out in my charge. We went and burnt his barn down, also his house and brought the gentlemen into camp."[18]

* * *

The regular companies that had departed Camp Thomas at the end of May arrived in Iuka on July 2. They almost never made it to Mississippi. Captain Henry R. Mizner of the 18th Infantry was in overall command during the movement, the troops consisting of his own F/3/18th and also C/3/18th (Captain John H. Knight), E/1/18th (Captain George Washington Smith), and A/2/16th (Captain Solomon S. Robinson). After a rail journey from Columbus to Cincinnati, Mizner's command boarded the steamer *Henry Clay* and sailed down the Ohio River. As the craft neared Paducah, Kentucky, Captain Knight wrote that the regulars were anxious for some action: "The Tennessee River into which we will turn tomorrow is invested with guerilla bands who attack vessels and transports on their way to Pittsburg Landing. We intend to be prepared for them and welcome them with conical balls from our long range rifles if they come within sight of us. We will issue in the morning 5 rounds of fixed ammunition to each man. We hope we will have some fun of that kind for it will give the men some experience."[19]

The cartridges went unused. The *Henry Clay* arrived in Paducah the evening of June 3, where the regulars learned that Brigadier General Kerley Strong, commander of the District of Cairo, had ordered all arriving troops to assemble at Cairo, Illinois. From there they would be shipped to Cape Girardeau, Missouri, where Confederate guerillas had lately been stirring up trouble. Mizner protested the order to General Strong when the transport arrived at Cairo the next day. The captain argued that the regulars had been ordered by the War Department to report to Corinth. Strong assured him that the change in orders was issued under General Halleck's authority, but Mizner refused to budge unless the regulars received the new order in writing. Night had fallen by the time General Strong signed the paperwork and the *Henry Clay* took on sufficient provisions for the trip upriver. The regulars would depart for Missouri the next day. Captain Mizner used the delay to telegraph Halleck's headquarters at Corinth, asking for help. Halleck "at once put his foot down on sending regular troops to fight guerillas" and instead ordered the regulars down the Mississippi to Columbus, Kentucky, were they were to remain for the time being. With the Tennessee River's low water becoming less navigable each day, after the fall of Corinth Halleck wanted to use the Mobile & Ohio Railway from Columbus to transport troops to northern Mississippi.[20]

The rail line between Columbus and Corinth was not yet in running order. Captain Knight fumed at the delay. "I am very anxious to join the regiment now below Corinth," the captain wrote after waiting in Kentucky a few days. "Lt. Col. Shepherd who is in command of it is an old, experienced officer and I want the benefit of his discipline." The stranded regulars waited for the Mobile & Ohio to be repaired, lending a hand in the work most days. "We are very impatient to get away from here," Knight complained on June 23:

> We do not like it at all here, in consequence of the mean duties we have to perform. It is fatigue work on the railroad. It is not right nor is it customary to put regular troops at that sort of duty. It is to them that all look for soldierly bearing, qualifications, and efficiency, for steadiness under all circumstances. How can it be expected of our soldiers if they are kept with axes, picks, and spades in the hands, doing the work of laborers. Many of the volunteers are fit for nothing else and they should do all the work. The professional soldier should never be put at such duty, it takes away from him that soldierly pride and feeling which he should possess. ...We are unfortunately under a

volunteer officer who cannot see the distinction. We hope soon Genl. Halleck will learn the state of affairs and will place us in our proper position.[21]

The commander of the Columbus district, Brigadier General Issac F. Quimby, wanted to retain Mizner's companies permanently, and the regulars began to feel they were destined never to leave Columbus. Lieutenant Robert Sutherland, the 18th Infantry's former Naval Academy midshipman, was so anxious to leave he seriously considered resigning his Regular Army commission and then heading south to Buenos Aries, where a recently tendered commission in the Argentine Navy awaited him. Private Frank Kelley, an Irishman in C/3/18th U.S., vented his frustrations in a more direct manor. According to Kelley's 1st sergeant, William M. Wallace, Kelley was "generally a very unruly character apt to get drunk at every opportunity." The private had spent most of his time at Camp Thomas in the guardhouse, and his behavior in Kentucky was more of the same. On June 20, he went on a drinking spree of legendary proportions, telling anyone who cared to hear "Kiss my arse, god damn ye!" and "I'll be damned if Kelly cannot whip any captain, sergeant or man in the camp!" After attempting to dismantle the tent of Captain Smith and being ordered to desist by Captain Knight, Kelly replied: "I'll be damned if I will let go this tent pole and you cannot make me do it!" Sergeant Wallace subdued the boisterous private after a short scuffle and clapped him in irons. Two months later, a court-martial convicted Kelly of conduct prejudicial to good order and military discipline, and also violating the 9th Article of War ("Any officer or soldier who strikes or threatens his superior with violence shall suffer death"). The court sentenced Kelly to be "shot to death at such time and place as the General Commanding directs." The Judge Advocate General of the army recommended mitigation of the sentence due to Kelly's drunken condition. President Lincoln, who personally reviewed all capital sentences, commuted the sanction to imprisonment for three months.[22]

General Quimby's effort to hold onto the four regular companies was partially successful. Captain Robinson's company of 16th Infantrymen remained behind as part of the Columbus garrison when the three companies of 18th Infantrymen boarded a southbound train on June 28. After experiencing a head-on train collision near Trenton, Tennessee, and further administrative delays at Corinth, four days later, Captain Mizner's command reported to

Lieutenant Colonel Shepherd in Iuka. As the column marched into camp, Captain John Knight was honored to receive a salute and handshake from Lieutenant Anson Mills. The two officers had gone to the same boarding school in their younger days and had not seen each other since 1852, the year Mills had received his appointment to West Point.[23]

Captain Knight may have felt indignant at having to perform rail repair work while in Columbus, but regulars throughout the Union Army were routinely employed on duties that kept them away from the frontline. Guarding prisoners and keeping a lid on civil disturbances were common rear-area tasks and most regular regiments in the Civil War occasionally performed these missions. An additional drain on manpower occurred when regular companies were assigned to field duties away from their regimental field detachments. Captain Robinson's A/2/16th U.S. ended up garrisoning Columbus for almost two years. The 15th Infantry also ended up with a sizable body of troops in western Kentucky. In early May 1862, 245 recruits at Newport Barracks were organized into Companies A, B, and C of the 15th Infantry's 2nd Battalion, with Captain E. Morgan Wood in command. The War Department must have thought there was a Confederate naval threat on the Ohio River that spring, for instead of joining John King's 15th Infantrymen in the field, 2/15th U.S. was shipped off to garrison duty at Paducah, Kentucky. A few months later, the battalion joined Captain Robinson's company of 16th Regulars in Columbus. It would be well into 1863 before the regular battalions then in Mississippi would have use of this manpower.[24]

A group of 19th Infantrymen experienced an extra-regimental odyssey that even the wandering companies of the 15th and 16th U.S. could not match. This regiment's poor recruiting effort of 1861 continued into the next year. It was not until May 1862 that Lieutenant Colonel Edward A. King organized the final two companies of 1/19th, G and H, at 19th Infantry Headquarters in Indianapolis. The commanders of the two companies, Captains Edmund L. Smith and Henry S. Welton, were both civilian appointees with little military experience. Some of their sergeants knew how to soldier, including Pennsylvanian James H. Gageby, the 1st sergeant of Captain Smith's company:

I entered the military service April 19, 1861, as a Sergeant, Co. K, 3rd Pa. Vols. "three months service," the company was known as the "Johnstown Zouaves" and as such was thoroughly drilled in Infantry tactics. I served with the 3rd Pa. Vols. in General Patterson's Column in Maryland and Virginia, was engaged in the battle of Falling Water, Va. July 2, 1861, was discharged July 30, 1861. I assisted to recruit a company for the 76th Pa. Vols. with a view of becoming a commissioned officer in that regiment, but prior to the organization of it I enlisted in the 19th U.S. Infantry, October 25, 1861, and was appointed a 1st Sergeant to date from enlistment; was on duty in Greensburg, Penn. several weeks drilling a detachment of the 19th Infantry, and at the Headquarters 19th Infantry, Indianapolis, Ind. was engaged as drill Sergeant until the organization of Co.'s G, and H, of the 1st Batt. 19th Infantry.[25]

First Sergeant Gageby probably had his mind on Mississippi as he trained the 19th Infantry's recruits, but events in Virginia soon eclipsed any chance of speedily joining Major Carpenter's battalion in the Deep South. The same orders that went to Camp Thomas in late May 1862 ordering all available men of Colonel Carrington's regiment to Virginia were also sent to Indianapolis. The two 19th Infantry companies boarded a train on May 27 and headed eastward. After arriving in Washington they spent the next month drilling and idly passing time. When Major Carpenter learned what had become of these men, he appealed to the War Department to have them transferred to the 19th Infantry contingent in Mississippi. If that was not possible, he requested "to have them assigned to duty with some regular battalion in the Army of the Potomac, where they might receive proper instruction and drill."[26]

George Sykes, the *Empire City* shipmate of Oliver Shepherd, was by this time a brigadier general of volunteers and commanding the Army of the Potomac's Regular Division. Regular manpower in the Eastern Theater was as scarce as in the Army of the Ohio, and Sykes had also been pressing the War Department for additional troops. As it was easier to ship the Washington-based 19th Infantrymen to the Virginia Peninsula than to Mississippi, on the first day of July the Indiana regulars marched to Alexandria and boarded a transport on the Potomac River. They disembarked four days later at Harrison's Landing on the James River, the place to which McClellan's army had retreated after its failed attempt to capture Richmond in the spring and early summer. The newly arrived companies were not the only 19th Infantrymen serving in Virginia, for the Army of the Potomac's provost marshal was the 19th Infantry's Major George L. Willard. He arranged for the two companies to join his provost guard. After McClellan's army turned back the Confederate assault on nearby Malvern Hill, the 19th Infantrymen had their hands full dealing with Southern prisoners. Sergeant Gageby wrote to his parents on August 6: "There was a nice little fight at Malvern Hill, yesterday. I heard the cannonading commence about 3 1/2 in the morning & they kept it up nearly all day. ...A great many prisoners came in last night, or rather, they were brought in by our men. Our hoosegow is full of gray jackets today. They are mighty fine looking men."27

The 19th Infantrymen's stay at Harrison's Landing turned out to be a short one, for the Army of the Potomac left the Peninsula during the latter half of August. The provosts were among the last to leave and thus did not see action in the ensuing Second Bull Run Campaign. The end of August found the 19th Infantrymen guarding supplies at Fairfax Station, Virginia. During the Maryland Campaign, Captain Smith's G/1/19th U.S. was attached to 1/17th U.S. in the Regular Division, while Captain Welton's H/1/19th U.S. served at Army of the Potomac Headquarters as McClellan's personal escort and bodyguard.

Both Lieutenant Colonel Edward King and Major Carpenter made numerous requests to have the two companies assigned to their proper battalion. With 1/19th U.S. consisting of just six depleted companies and rarely having more than 200 men present for duty, the battalion was less than half the size of a typical volunteer regiment. The War Department replied to King that the companies had been sent east by mistake and that "Gen'l McClellan (to whom the matter was referred) would have them ordered [west] as soon as other regulars could be obtained to supply their places as provost guard." Despite this assurance, the 19th Infantry orphans remained with the Army of the Potomac for the rest of year. They were present at the Battle of Antietam on September 17, but like the rest of the Regular Division and V Corps, they were held in reserve and did not engage. Captain Smith's company played a more active role at the Battle of Fredericksburg three months later. Three 19th Infantrymen were among the thousands of Federal casualties littering the frozen fields along Virginia's Rappahannock River in December 1862.28

The War Department shared the concerns of Sykes, Shepherd, and Carpenter about the Regular Army's lack of manpower. In June 1862, the headquarters of the various regiments were moved to established Regular Army posts in the more populous northern and eastern states.[29] The 15th Infantry was assigned to Fort Adams in Providence, Rhode Island, the 16th Infantry to Fort Ontario, near Oswego, New York, and the 19th moved north from Indianapolis to Fort Wayne, Michigan. The War Department handled the 18th Infantry with the usual kid gloves, and Carrington's headquarters remained at Camp Thomas. While the new locations were a step in the right direction, by the latter half of 1862, it was becoming obvious that the regulars would never recruit sufficient manpower when faced with volunteer competition. If the regulars' tough discipline did not turn a recruit away, the lack of a city, county, or state bounty usually did. With the exception of the 18th Infantry, the beneficiary of Colonel Carrington's Ohio prestige, none of the New Army regiments in the West were able to consistently field more than a single battalion. Those battalions often consisted of less than their eight authorized companies, and the companies present were always far below authorized strength. Since the regulars did not seem able to meet their recruiting needs through normal channels, in early October 1862 the War Department attempted a radical remedy: volunteers were authorized to transfer to the Regular Army if they so desired. The opportunity to earn a Regular Army commission, it was surmised, would be a strong incentive for career-minded volunteers to transfer and quickly fill up the regulars' ranks:

GENERAL ORDERS   WAR DEPARTMENT,
No. 154.   Adjutant General's Office,
                                          Washington, D.C., October 8, 1862

The commanding officer of each regiment, battalion, and battery of the Regular Army in the field, will appoint one or more recruiting officers, who are hereby authorized to enlist, with their own consent, the requisite number of efficient volunteers to fill the ranks of their command to the legal standard.

The enlistments will be made in the usual mode, and for three years, or for the remaining portion of three years which the volunteer has yet to serve, if he so prefer.

As an inducement to volunteers to enlist in the Regular Army, it will be remembered that promotion to commissions therein is open by law to its meritorious and distinguished non-commissioned officers; and that many have already been promoted.

BY ORDER:

L. THOMAS,
Adjutant General[30]

Frustrated regular recruiting officers were soon lurking near volunteer camps, recruiting depots, and even hospitals, using whatever means necessary to entice volunteers to join the regulars. Some of the recruiters unscrupulously promised a number of extra perks that volunteers would supposedly enjoy after transferring, from better rations to thirty-day furloughs. If this was not bad enough for volunteer commanders, their own troops sometimes used the transfer order as a bargaining chip: disgruntled volunteers would threaten to abandon their state regiments for the regulars if complaints were not heard, discipline not relaxed, etc. Lieutenant Colonel N.H. Walworth of the 42nd Illinois voiced some frustrations to his department commander after being ordered to transfer a few men to the 16th Regulars:

> I am in receipt of a communication of Capt Crofton's of the 16th U.S. Infty in regard to furnishing the Discharges and Final Statement for men who have enlisted in that Regt from the 42nd Ills together with your order requiring that the same be forwarded. ...three of the men whose names are on the list were at the time of thier enlistment on detached service, with the Pioneer Corps and the Company Commanders are unable to make out thier Final Statements being ignorant as to how thier accounts stand with the Government. The papers for the others are being made out, and will be forwarded at once. I would respectfully ask whether men of the Regt. are to be allowed to join the Regular Army at thier will?
>
> My experiences thus far has been that the privelege allowed men of joining the Regular Army has had a tendency to injure the military discipline in the Regt owing to the fact that where required to yield obedience, the men would assert thier independence and absenting themselves enlist in the Regular Army, thereby causing an evil tendency among those remaining. Since the tenth of November we have furnished twenty three men for the Pioneer Corps Eighteen as nurses; thirty eight to the Regular Army.[31]

State military and government officials across the nation were understandably incensed at the plan, like Walworth considering the order an unwelcome intrusion into their own affairs. "Complaints came pouring in from all the officers whose commands were endangered by these 'attacks from the regulars,'" the adjutant general of Indiana wrote in a postwar report, "and the Governor was earnestly entreated to use all his influence to cause the obnoxious order to be rescinded."[32] In an attempt to make the plan somewhat more palatable, the War Department modified it on October 21 by limiting the number of troops transferred to not more than ten from any single volunteer company. This measure was still not enough and the complaints continued. One man to whom the Indiana governor turned for assistance in this matter was none other than the 18th Infantry's colonel. In addition to commanding that regiment from Camp Thomas, as of August 1862 Henry Carrington had secured a position on Governor Oliver P. Morton's military staff as chief mustering officer for the state of Indiana. The whirlwind of misinformation, accusations, and counter-accusations swirling about the transfer plan compelled Carrington to distribute a circular throughout Indiana and attempt to set the record straight:

> Headquarters General Recruiting Service
> Indianapolis, Ind., November 25th, 1862.
>
> Being assured the improper representations have been made to induce enlisted volunteers to change to the regular service, and that much dissatisfaction prevails...the following statement will correct such misrepresentations as have been reported:
>
> 1st. The *bounties* are the *same*. The twenty-five dollar bounty and advance pay is only paid in the regular service to new recruits, or volunteers, who have not already drawn it. The premium is for enlisting new recruits only.
>
> 2d. The *pay* is the *same*, and the Government designs to pay each with equal promptness.
>
> 3d. The regular soldier need expect no *winter of ease* in northern cities, but to share the exposure of the field with the volunteer.
>
> 4th. The promise of "thirty day furloughs" is illegal, and could not have been made by any person with the approval of any army officer.
>
> Regulars and volunteers are in one common cause. The order of the War Department offers ambitious and efficient soldiers in the volunteer service the opportunity to strive for the promotions of the regular service, and was not designed to furnish insubordinate soldiers an outlet of escape from penalties incurred, or as a vent to ill-will against officers.

HENRY B. CARRINGTON
Colonel, 18th Infantry, U.S.A.
Chief Mustering Officer, Indiana[33]

Comments from regular recruiters indicate that they held out little real hope that the transfer plan would significantly increase the regulars' strength. Sergeant Edgar Wilcox of the 18th Infantry was sent from Camp Thomas to enlist volunteers who were stationed at Johnson's Island, but reported little headway: "Well we were gone a week but did not get any recruits for one of the very best reasons in the world—we couldn't."[34] Captain Alfred Hough of the 19th U.S. also encountered this resistance first hand. On recruiting duty since July 1862 and posted to Cleveland, Hough's efforts to enlist Ohio volunteers in early November ultimately came to naught:

> What may be done by transferring from the volunteers to us I cannot say, but that is the *only* way we can fill, and I think the Government will insist upon, but that will take some time to do. There is great opposition on the part of the State authorities and volunteer officers to our getting their men, and it is a very unpleasant duty on our part to try, but the men are willing if they will permit them. ...I was met by an order from Gov. Tod to prevent regular officers from enlisting in the camps until further orders from him. He has no doubt written to Washington to have the order suspended and I expect he will succeed. So it goes, everything is in the dark for the regular army.[35]

The transfer of volunteers into regular units did not make a lasting difference, for the plan was in effect only four months before escalating state resistance caused its cancellation on February 10, 1863. During those months, an estimated 7,500 volunteers transferred to the Regular Army, which represent 81 percent of all regular enlistments during that time period. Regular enlistments for all of 1862 totaled 15,901, comparable to the previous year's disappointing results. With disease, desertion, and combat starting to take an ever-increasing toll on the regulars, particularly in the infantry regiments, it was becoming increasingly doubtful that the New Army regiments would ever field all of their authorized battalions. The transfer plan helped somewhat, although it did not channel manpower where it was needed most. The overwhelming majority of transferees joined regular cavalry, artillery, and engineer outfits; only about 1,300 volunteers became members of the casualty-ridden

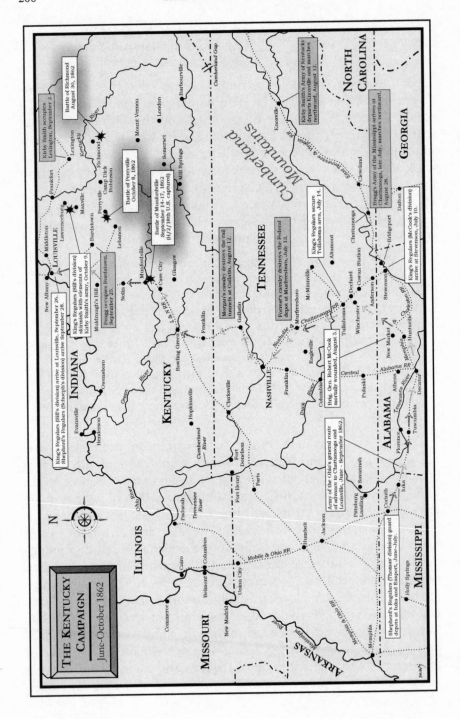

THE KENTUCKY CAMPAIGN
June–October 1862

infantry formations of the Regular Army. Regular infantry regiments thus had to finish out the campaigns of 1862 facing a manpower situation that worsened every day. On January 1, 1863, Regular Army present for duty strength stood at just 19,169, which was actually 702 fewer than on the same date in 1862.[36]

* * *

The summer of 1862 would see Major John H. King's regulars wearing out many a pair of brogans. Unlike the 18th U.S., which remained stationary for many weeks while performing its guard mission in and around Iuka, the regular battalions in Alexander McCook's division did not have the luxury of remaining in one place for long after the fall of Corinth. King's regulars spent only a week as part of the Corinth garrison before heading for Alabama on June 11.[37] Alexander McCook's division moved steadily eastward along the Memphis & Charleston Railway throughout June and July 1862. Sergeant Arthur B. Carpenter of the 19th Regulars wrote from Florence, Alabama, on June 18 that he was happy with the change in scenery:

> I am very healthy, and am glad to get out of the wilderness around Corinth. The country here in Alabama is better large plantation with their negroes at work gathering wheat and Barly.
>
> We are having nice times on the Tennessee river now go in bathing every day, but we expect to soon cross over and resume our march to Chattanooga Tenn.
>
> We march from 12 to 16 miles a day. Our baggage has been reduced and all extra clothing turned into the Quarter master. I enjoy myself finely and think that my prospects are good for the future. I have won the esteem of all my superior officers and they will all recommended me for promotion. The major has frequently taken me from my company while on Battalion drill, and had me take command of other companies whose Captains & Lieuts. were not able to command them. I can conduct a company through Battalion drill with as few mistakes as any officer in the Battalion.[38]

McCook's division completed the dusty trek from Corinth to Huntsville on June 30. Lovell Rousseau relinquished command of the 4th Brigade that same day, replacing General Ormsby Mitchel in commander of the division that had occupied Huntsville since March. Mitchel had recently alienated himself from both Buell and the men of his own division, the former due to disagreements with Buell on the management of the advance to Chattanooga, and the latter after failing to support one of his brigade commanders, the popular Russian Colonel John B. Turchin, after Turchin's brigade sacked the town of Athens, Alabama, on May 2. With Rousseau in command of Mitchel's old division, Colonel Harvey M. Buckley of the 5th Kentucky took command of the 4th Brigade's volunteer regiments and regular battalions.

While the generals debated how to supply the troops and tried to determine the best way to approach Chattanooga, Buckley's brigade spent Independence Day resting and enjoying what entertainment the troops could devise. "We had a speech from one of our Captains and a song from Lieutenant Millard with music by the 15th Infty band," recalled Sergeant Carpenter. "Our eatables consisted of a sheep some soft bread and a little whiskey. We managed to pass the day off pleasantly." Pleasantly enough, although Major King ordered up a dress parade for the regular battalions that evening. Over in Battery H, the end of Peter Fitzpatrick's day was not pleasant at all. When the artilleryman turned in for the night he found a copperhead snake curled up in his blanket.[39]

The frontline strength of King's regular battalions was further reduced at Huntsville, although not due to enemy action. General Buell had become dissatisfied with some of the volunteers comprising his headquarters guard and ordered them replaced with a picked force of regular troops. Jacob Van Zwaluwenburg of the 16th U.S. was one of the fifty regulars assigned to duty at Army of the Ohio headquarters. The assignment gave him an opportunity to rest his weary feet: "Our duty was to pitch, and strike headquarters tents, whenever the army moved, keep strangers away, one sentinal night and day in front of the generals tent. We had but little marching to do as we moved by train with the generals baggage."[40]

McCook's division departed Huntsville on July 5. During the next five days the column continued eastward, skirting the southern edge of the Cumberland Plateau and then advancing down the Tennessee River valley as far as Stevenson, Alabama, the point at which the Memphis & Charleston line merges with the Nashville & Chattanooga Railroad. Chattanooga was just thirty-two miles ahead, on the far side of Sand and Lookout Mountains. To advance beyond Stevenson, Buell had to stockpile supplies and cross his troops to the far side of the Tennessee River. Supplies were becoming a major concern. Low water on the Tennessee and damage to the Memphis & Charleston had combined to constrict the Army of the

Ohio's supply line. General Halleck barely had enough rolling stock to move supplies from Memphis to Corinth. Operable engines never seemed available to make the run from Iuka to Decatur. It was not until the third week of July that a provision train finally departed Iuka heading east—but the engine pulling the freight cars turned out to be too heavy to cross the bridge at Bear Creek.

As Buell advanced eastward from Corinth, he gradually divested his army from reliance on the vulnerable Memphis & Charleston, a route he had not wanted to use in the first place. The Central Alabama Railroad, running between Nashville and Decatur, was his next choice, but these rails were in dire need of maintenance and also ran through countryside teaming with enemy irregular forces. Confederate raiders in early June dealt a major blow to this route by destroying the rail bridge spanning the Elk River fourteen miles north of Athens near the Tennessee-Alabama border. The route remained closed until the end of the month. During the latter half of June, Buell ordered Nelson's division to Reynold's Station, about midway between Nashville and Decatur, to safeguard the region, but the tonnage the Central Alabama could reliably supply was well short of the Army of the Ohio's needs.[41]

Making matters worse was Buell's determination to protect private property of Southern citizens. The general was partly motivated by a desire to not inflame local sentiments against the Union Army, which he thought would only embolden the Confederate irregular cavalry and guerillas (known as "bushwhackers") infesting this region. According to Sergeant Carpenter, this enemy posed a real threat:

> there are no regular army C.S.A. around here. nothing but bush whackers. they dress like farmers, and if they see any body of our soldiers approaching they hide their arms in some bushes, or the fence corners, and stand with their hands in their pockets as unconcerned and independent as a hog on ice. they go round in pairs, no more than three together any way, and if they catch sight of one or two of our soldiers who have rambled away from their Regiment, they sneak up behind them and shoot them down. that is one style of guerilla warfare. another style is a party of cavalry of from 20 to 100 go together all about the country burning bridges and capturing baggage trains. These guerillas are all that we have to contend with now.[42]

Buell also believed the region through which his army was traveling, particularly around Huntsville, was already depleted of supplies.

His chief quartermaster would later state that "the country was entirely bare of resources along and near our lines of march, both of forage and subsistence." That may have been true, but many of Buell's troops thought otherwise. "This country is thoroughly secesh, as I believe the whole South is," Captain Alfred Hough complained in a letter dated June 29, written at a point a day's march west of Huntsville. "I feel disgusted as do all of us at the particular care taken that no one enters any dwellings by the way while we poor fellows are living on hard bread and pork these rascals have their cellars full of wholesome food." Marching through Alabama in a summer drought while subsisting on scarce rations was gradually wearing out the Army of the Ohio. "I have left behind in hospitals between Corinth and [Huntsville] 16 of my men," Hough continued. "I have now absent sick of my Company 21 men, have 4 sick with me two of whom I shall leave at Huntsville, the rest like myself have gained in strength...although some of them are very bare of clothes, they have been allowed to start with only the suit they had on. Some of them are barefooted and I myself am almost so having my last pair of shoes on and a large hole in one of them. If we don't get clothes at Huntsville we will be in a bad plight."[43]

Few supplies made it all the way to Huntsville. Mitchel's division alone had experienced difficulty in trying to subsist in this region. The situation deteriorated rapidly as thousands of additional Federal troops steadily marched into northeast Alabama. With the arrival of McCook's division at Stevenson on July 10, Buell hoped the Nashville & Chattanooga Railroad would solve the supply problem. These hopes were dashed three days later, when Nathan Bedford Forrest's Confederate cavalry destroyed the Federal supply depot at Murfreesboro, Tennessee. Buell's logistical situation remained precarious, and the Army of the Ohio's troops were put on half rations as of July 14. Things got worse early the next month, when Confederate raiders led by Colonel John Hunt Morgan destroyed a depot and sections of the Louisville and Nashville north of Nashville near Gallatin, Tennessee. In the aftermath of Forrest's middle Tennessee raid, Buell positioned additional forces along the railroads to keep his communications with Nashville secure. The regular battalions in Buckley's brigade were detached on July 14 and sent by rail to Tullahoma to secure the area.[44]

The regulars experienced a number of command changes at Tullahoma. The commander of 1/16th U.S., Captain Edwin

Townsend, was assigned to the Army of the Ohio's Ordnance Department in Nashville. Major Adam J. Slemmer was released from his inspector general duties on the department staff and replaced Townsend in command of the 16th Infantry's 1st Battalion. Another senior officer of the 16th, Lieutenant Colonel James V. Bomford, arrived while the regulars were in middle Tennessee. An 1832 West Point graduate who had served in the Mexican War, Bomford had been a major in the 6th Infantry prior to becoming the 16th Infantry's lieutenant colonel in January 1862. Arriving at Tullahoma on July 20, Bomford took command of the regular battalions and became popular with the men. Sergeant Major Kellogg remembered him as "a capable and efficient officer, and a gentleman in all that the word implies. As commanding officer he required prompt and implicit obedience, but he was always kind and courteous to every one." With Bomford on the scene, John King reverted to command of 1/15th U.S. and Captain Peter Swaine of the 15th became a company commander again. Although the regulars remained on half rations at Tullahoma, Sergeant Carpenter hoped their separate status would prove advantageous: "The 15th, 16th, and 19th Batts of Regulars are now separated from the division and brigade, we regulars seem to be a separate corps under command of Lt. Col. Bomford of the 16th, so we expect to see better times, more travelling by railroad. My company is doing duty now as Provost Guard. We have nice quarters in a house that has been deserted by its owner. We have to guard prisoners, protect private property, keep order in the streets, it is a sort of police duty."[45]

The regulars were the only Federal troops in this area, so they constructed fortifications at Tullahoma just in case Forrest's cavalry decided to pay the area a return visit. During the next month, detachments of regulars also guarded Manchester and Cowan, on the rails north and south of Tullahoma. The 19th Regulars surprised some Confederate quartermasters in Manchester on July 25 and captured more than 1,000 barrels of flour. Major Carpenter's men enjoyed flapjacks for breakfast the next morning. Enemy cavalry probed the area three days later and a sharp street fight ensued. Casualties were taken on both sides before the gray cavalry was driven off.[46]

Sergeant Major Edgar Kellogg had a more enjoyable experience in Manchester on July 31. He was walking toward the vacant house that served as headquarters of 1/16th U.S. when the battalion's quartermaster, Lieutenant William H. Ingerton, hailed Kellogg from across the street. The sergeant major ran over to the lieutenant and was about to salute when Ingerton extended his hand in greeting.

"Congratulations on your promotion, well earned!" Kellogg replied with silence and a confused look.

"Haven't you received your commission?" Ingerton asked.

"No," Kellogg replied, "I had not heard of it before."

"Well, it is in the adjutant's office. Go and get it."

Kellogg walked into headquarters and seated himself at his field desk. Neither Major Slemmer nor Lieutenant Louis Hosea, the adjutant, mentioned anything to the sergeant major about a commission, but about thirty minutes later Lieutenant Colonel Bomford strode in. He walked right up to the sergeant major, shook Kellogg's hand vigorously, and launched into a hearty congratulation. Kellogg and Major Slemmer did not care for each other to any great extent, so Kellogg relished the next few moments the rest of his life:

> The Battalion Commander, but a few feet away, saw and heard the colonel's greeting. He took up a large envelope containing something, looked at it, cleared his throat once or twice, and then said, "I think, Colonel, a mistake has been made. This commission is for a first lieutenant, and it ought to be for a second lieutenant. I will return it to Washington for correction."
>
> "Not at all, not at all, Sir," rejoined the colonel. "There is no mistake. No such mistake would be made in the Adjutant General's Office. Mr. Kellogg's commission as second lieutenant has been delayed somewhere enroute. This commission is a promotion from second to first lieutenant. Here it is, Mr. Kellogg, with my best wishes," and, taking the commission from the somewhat reluctant hand of the other officer, he handed it to me.[47]

Bomford was correct about Kellogg's commission as a second lieutenant being lost somwhere. Captain Edwin Townsend had recommended Sergeant Major Kellogg for a commission after the Battle of Shiloh, which, when added to Major Coolidge's December 1861 recommendation that Kellogg be commissioned, was enough to push the action through the Adjutant General's Office. There were a number of vacant lieutenancies in the regiment after Shiloh and Kellogg's date of rank as a second lieutenant was April 7, 1862. The War Department sent the commission certificate to the regiment's headquarters at Camp Thomas. Major Coolidge entrusted the paperwork to the regimental sutler, who was about to journey south to join the 1st Battalion. While traveling through Kentucky in early June, the sutler was captured by Confederate cavalry. The Southerners enjoyed ransacking the sutler's wagon and putting to the torch all the meaningless paperwork they found in the process. First Lieutenant Kellogg never served as a Regular Army second lieutenant.[48]

The regulars remained in middle Tennessee for more than a month. They soon became bored with guard duty, but Lieutenant Colonel Bomford kept them busy with drill as much as possible: "had drill in the Evening,, time drags hevey,, we would rather be on the march," Corporal Tarbell recorded in his diary on August 13. His routine had not changed six days later: "Policed Camp,, drill & Inspection to day,, Dress coats, White Gloves & clean Brasses,, & if they are not clean to the Guard House you go." The point of perhaps greatest strategic importance entrusted to the Regulars' care was the 2,228-foot Cumberland Tunnel on the Nashville & Chattanooga line near Cowan. Sergeant Arthur Carpenter was part of the guard force there on August 15: "Lt. Andrews...staid this side of the tunnel with 8 men, and gave me command of the other 8 men, and sent me through to the other side. We allowed no one to pass through except the workmen on the road, and had to prevent depredations from being committed by 'Bushwhackers.' If we had been attacked we would have retreated into the tunnel 50 or 100 yards, and could have engaged a much superior force, but during the three days we stayed there no one molested us."[49]

* * *

Much to Sergeant Amos Fleagle's disappointment, the 18th Infantry's guard and provost assignments in northern Mississippi came to an end during late July. "Our Reg't has been stationed at Iuka for [the] last month," the sergeant wrote to his family on July 20, "and our company with several others are guarding the Bridge on Bear Creek, Ala, and we had fine times. we had all the appels, Peaches, and yong corn we can devour. But alas these good times are not allways to last, for we are now under Marching orders to some Place in Ala, Some 90 or 100 miles distance." John Knight wished the move would be much farther than a hundred miles into Alabama. Receiving word of the fearful losses Sykes's Regular Division had sustained at the Battle of Gaines Mill during McCellan's campaign on the Virginia Peninsula, the 18th Infantry captain wrote: "I could not refrain my tears when I heard that... the Regulars [were] so badly cut up. The universal feeling here is 'Let us go to the rescue!!'

I think they ought to send McClellan all the regulars here anyhow. They will make a very effective brigade of infantry."[50]

General Buell was not about to let the 18th Infantry go anywhere except toward Chattanooga. General Thomas issued his division its marching orders on July 19. As soon as troops from Grant's army arrived and assumed the guard duties Thomas's men had been performing the past month, Thomas's brigades were to cross to the north side of the Tennessee River and then head east for Stevenson by way of Athens and Huntsville. Shepherd's scattered companies assembled at Iuka on July 22. Captain Knight's comments about preparations for the march illustrate how the 18th Infantry's campaigning skills had improved since the movement to Mill Springs:

> Each company was furnished with one wagon and six mules with which we carried our tents, consisting of five sibly tents, ten wall and one common or wedge tent, officers baggage and mess chest, ten days rations for the company and all the mess pans, cooking apparatus, etc and the soldiers knapsacks as well as ten days forage for the mules. It required close packing to get it all on and then it was a very heavy load. ...Each company, however, succeeded in getting all on and the mules to pull it, when the whole, with ambulances, commissary wagons, field and staff and hospital wagons moved off making in all about forty wagons and two hundred and forty mules.[51]

The regulars departed Iuka early on the morning of July 24. They marched to Eastport, joined Sergeant Fleagle and the other regulars stationed there, and spent the rest of that day and the next being ferried across the Tennessee River on a small steamboat. Some of the regulars used the opportunity to bathe in the river and Lieutenant Ansel B. Denton of C/2/18th nearly drowned in the process. On the 26th, they resumed the march. Shepherd's column encountered few of the enemy along the way, although Confederate bushwhackers roamed the countryside freely and ambushes were usually commonplace. With more than a decade of frontier experience to his credit, Oliver Shepherd knew how to deal with such a menace. He posted strong contingents of skirmishers to the front and rear of his wagon train and occasionally conducted multi-company sweeps of the surrounding countryside. The regulars found out why the opposition was giving them such a wide berth after marching past "one rather sharp looking negro" on the road one day. The man asked a group of Shepherd's troops who they were. When the bystander heard that these soldiers were 18th Regulars, he laughed heartily and said: "My laws Massa, dem bush men talk about you a good deal and dey fraid of you, dey fraid of you. I hears dem many times."[52]

The reluctance of bushwhackers to operate near the 18th Infantry notwithstanding, Shepherd was not going to provide the enemy with any easy targets if he could help it. After some 18th Infantrymen straggled on the march, Shepherd made sure his troops maintained the conduct expected of Regular Army soldiers. The lieutenant colonel's peculiar use of the word "volunteer" demonstrates the degree of contempt in which he now held anyone who was not a regular:

> Hd Qrs Detcht 18th U.S. Inft
> Camp en route to Athens, Ala.
> August 1st 1862

Orders
No 113

I. This command was disgraced yesterday by the misconduct of the men who straggled out of Ranks; therefore the Commanders of Companies will at starting on the march every morning count the number of men and thereby ascertain the number of stacks [of arms], and at each halt for a rest the stacks will be counted to see whether any men have left the ranks without proper permission.

II. Company Commanders must adopt some mode of punishment to put a stop to the disgraceful and Volunteer habit of their men leaving ranks and going to pillage property and disturb the inhabitants along the line of march.

> By order of
> Lieut Col. O.L. Shepherd
> Comd Detcht
>
> ANSON MILLS
> 1st Lieut 18th U.S. Inft
> Adjt Detcht[53]

The 18th Infantry passed through Florence, Alabama, on July 28 and there met General Thomas. The general joined Shepherd's column and together they continued marching to Athens, the place where the regulars were supposed to meet the balance of McCook's brigade. The regulars arrived there late in the day on August 1, ahead of schedule and two days' march in front McCook's other regiments—even though McCook's volunteers had been stationed at Tuscumbia and thus had thirty-two fewer miles to march. Traveling

alone was fine with the regulars. One of them remarked: "the balance of the brigade is volunteers and they did not march as fast as
we did. There not being much harmony between us and volunteers,
we preferred to march independent of them." On a personal level,
Oliver Shepherd wanted to stay as far away from Robert McCook
as possible. McCook had been promoted to brigadier general at the
end of June, and the sight of the brigade commander wearing star-
adorned black shoulder straps and a sash of buff satin irritated
Shepherd to no end.[54]

As the regulars filed into Athens, a messenger handed General
Thomas a note from General Buell that detailed a change in plans.
Thomas's division was no longer bound for Stevenson. The
Nashville & Chattanooga Railroad had been repaired and Buell
ordered Thomas's command northeastward into Tennessee, where
the division would assist in securing the Nashville-to-Stevenson sup-
ply line. Thomas was to establish his headquarters at Dechard
Station, a group of shacks a few miles up the tracks from Cowan
Tunnel. Thomas instructed Shepherd to march the 18th Regulars to
Winchester, a town on a railroad spur line two miles southeast of
Dechard. The regulars headed for Tennessee on August 2. They
marched fifty-five miles during the next four days, moving through
New Market, Alabama, and Salem, Tennessee, with the lofty heights
of the Cumberland Plateau on their immediate right. General
Thomas arrived in Dechard on August 4, while Shepherd's men set
up camp at Winchester the next day.[55]

Shepherd's feud with his brigade commander came to an abrupt
end while the volunteer regiments of Robert McCook's brigade
approached the Alabama-Tennessee state line. At about noon on
August 5 near New Market, General McCook and a small escort
were riding three miles ahead of the brigade's column, attempting to
locate a bivouac area for the coming night. While inquiring at a
house by the road, Confederate bushwhackers ambushed the
McCook entourage. The guerrillas shot McCook in the abdomen,
even though the general was ill and riding in an ambulance. The
18th Infantry's Captain Burt, still serving on McCook's staff, was the
first to reach the general, but there was nothing he could do. Robert
McCook died the next day. Troops from the 9th Ohio, outraged at
what they considered to be the "murder" of the their former colonel,
went on a rampage through the local area, burning houses and
hanging anyone who looked suspicious. It was only through "great

exertions" on the part of the 35th Ohio's Colonel Ferdinand Van Derveer that the Ohioans were reigned in and order restored. Captain John Knight thought Robert McCook had no one to blame but himself: "It is true that the volunteers are not vigilant enough. It has been their own fault every time they are surprised and taken. We had not left our posts two days near Iuka before they had 'gobbled' up the volunteers who relieved us ('gobbled' is an army terms and signifies to take by surprise). On the march...the rebels killed our brigade commander, who had with him three thousand soldiers. ...His command struggled along carelessly—never even sent out an advance guard."56

The Shepherd-McCook animosity did not completely transcend the 18th Infantry. Even Captain Knight, whose pride in being a regular matched Oliver Shepherd's, had to admit: "Altho none of this Regt. like him [McCook] yet the brutal murder and outrage has provoked the highest feeling throughout the entire body of troops camped here." It was fortunate for Amos Fleagle that Shepherd never learned of what the sergeant wrote in a letter home: "By the Death of McCook, our Brigade has sustained an irrepressable loss for a Braver and Better man never lived."57 As for Shepherd, he did not believe the brigade's command situation improved to any great extent as a result of Robert McCook's demise. Colonel Van Derveer had assumed temporary command of the brigade, and Shepherd did not want to serve under this officer any more than he had Van Derveer's predecessor. After the May 10 confrontation between the 18th U.S. and the 35th Ohio during the advance on Corinth, Shepherd and Van Derveer were barely on speaking terms. Three days after McCook's death, Shepherd sent a letter to Army of the Ohio Headquarters. The way a regimental commander addressed such a lofty level of command was to route the communication through the appropriate brigade and division commanders. The first person to see the letter was thus Colonel Van Derveer. He was not pleased with what he read:

> Hd Qrs Detcht 18th US Inf
> Camp at Dechard near Winchester Tenn
> August 8 1862

Col. J.B. Fry
Adj & Chief of Staff
Army Dist of Ohio
   Huntsville, Ala

Colonel,

I have the honor respectfully to renew my application of March 28 to have this Detcht of my Regt consisting of nineteen companies composing two Battalions, under my command, removed from the 3rd Brigade.

I am constrained again to repeat that its continuance in this Brigade is highly detrimental to the discipline of so new a regiment, to its character and ability to meet the duties which may be expected of it in any trying Emergency.

It is a disagreeable duty, to state that both officers & men are dissatisfied by the treatment which the Regiment has received while serving in this Army since December last.

The officers of the Regiment, possessing the highest education & intelligence and enthusiasm in their profession, have been interfered with and outraged by the malignant conduct of Volunteer Officers.

All these have exceeded the bounds which professional or philosophical indifference can bear.

It is altogether for the interest of the Regiment and of the service that the Regiment should be taken out of an Ohio Brigade.

The major portion, nine tenths of the men, have come from the same cities, towns, villages, & neighborhoods as the Ohio Volunteers who, under their peculiar modes do service widely different from what is required in this Regiment by the permanence of its organization in the Regular Army. The patience of the officers is exhausted, and they feel disgusted at the position of the Regt and this is keenly felt by the men likewise, who take an interest...in the standing of the Regiment.

The Regiment when by itself feels as strong and possessed of the ability to perform as much service alone against the enemy as any brigade in this Army. But associated as at the present and being maligned and traduced, and its ranks thinned by...large if not disproportionate details for teamsters, artillerymen, & other duties, it cannot in reason be expected to perform what its name as Regulars cause to be anticipated. I cannot but hope that the Commanding Gen'l will relieve the Regiment from duty in a Brigade which has proved so mischievous to its discipline.

Since his recent melancholy death, the Regt finds itself in the brigade under the command of Col. Van Derveer, 35th Ohio Vols. who was on one occasion directed by me, to leave the precincts of the Regt for disgraceful interference, seditious conduct & un-Officer like profanity threatening to the officers & designed to intimidate them in the discharge of their duties, till ordered away by Gen'l McCook himself.

Very Respectfully,
Your Obt Servant
O.L. SHEPHERD
Lieut. Col. 18th U.S. Inf
Comd'g Detcht[58]

These words eventually immersed Shepherd in very hot water. Van Derveer was insulted by Shepherd's comments about volunteers in general and himself in particular. After allowing the letter to gather dust for three days, the brigade commander took the unusual step of refusing to forward the communication to division head-quarters and instead returned it to Shepherd, stating that the letter "makes false & slanderous charges against the Volunteer Officers and soldiers of the Brigade." Shepherd fired back: "His [reply] is officially bold, but not at all surprising."

Brigadier General James B. Steedman, formerly the colonel of the 14th Ohio and a volunteer officer with whom Shepherd did not yet have any quarrels, took permanent command of the brigade two weeks after McCook was killed. With Van Derveer out of the way, Shepherd sent the written tirade forward once again. He apologized to General Steedman that "circumstances should have combined to necessitate my first communication through you, to be of the cast of the enclosed letter," but Shepherd also made some bold statements of his own in a cover letter accompanying the original:

> I am prepared to sustain all the allegations in the letter, and regarding their truthfulness I respectfully refer to the proceedings of the Court of Inquiry called by me on the part of the Regt., which convened in Camp near Corinth June 1862. [Colonel Van Derveer's] endorsement besides adds further proof.
>
> If however the officer in command of the brigade on the 11th inst, desires to provoke the issue, he can meet the charges, sustaining the remarks in the letter concerning himself.
>
> The base and slanderous paragraphs against the Regt, with which the newspapers in Ohio, have teemed cannot be ignored & but little credit can attach to any one who may endeavor to do so.[59]

Shepherd had complained about the brigade's volunteers once too often. The stubborn lieutenant colonel of the 18th Regulars had acquired a reputation for being a difficult subordinate; his chain-of-command would probably not hesitate to have him reassigned should the opportunity arise.

* * *

The Confederate army at Tupelo had not been idle while Buell's troops inched their way eastward along the Memphis & Charleston. Detaching Major General Sterling Price and 16,000 men to cover northern Mississippi, General Braxton Bragg (who replaced Beauregard in command on June 20) took the balance of the Army of the Mississippi on a circuitous rail journey through Mobile and Atlanta to Chattanooga, arriving there during the last week of July. From Chattanooga, Bragg at first planned to move his 30,000 men into middle Tennessee, force Buell to abandon the advance across Alabama, and then fight it out with the Army of the Ohio somewhere in Tennessee. But goaded on by Major General Edmund Kirby Smith, commander of the Knoxville-based Department of East Tennessee, Bragg eventually transformed the movement to Chattanooga into an invasion of Kentucky. Kirby Smith and other Southern leaders thought that strong Confederate forces in the Bluegrass State would induce Kentucky citizens to join the Confederate Army and then, just possibly, Kentucky secessionists might take their state out of the Union. Bragg reinforced Kirby Smith's weak force with a few brigades and the Knoxville column struck out for Kentucky on August 12. After waiting for his artillery and trains to complete an overland march from Tupelo, Bragg's movement north from Chattanooga began in earnest on August 27. Buell countered by canceling the sputtering Federal advance to Chattanooga and shifting forces back into Tennessee. He first attempted to concentrate his scattered forces at Altamonte, a remote spot on the Cumberland Plateau, but on August 29 ordered his men to Murfreesboro and then Nashville.

Lieutenant Colonel Bomford's regular battalions guarding the rails near Tullahoma prepared for the march northward. Late at night on August 23, Lieutenant Robert P. King, a Philadelphian serving in C/1/15th U.S., wrote his mother and told her the movement would be difficult: "I should be in bed, as we are under marching orders to move at an early hour to-morrow morning, I expect, at 3 o'clock, with forty rounds of cartridges in boxes, and forty extra rounds in wagons, with two days' full rations, and eight days' half rations, in all ten days rations. The Rebels having evacuated Chattanooga, are marching for the mountains, and we are to make a forced march to beat them up and occupy the mountains before them. We expect a fight, but then we have been fooled so often that it is impossible to tell anything about it." King's expected battle did not materialize, and once again the Army of the Ohio marched instead of fought. Sergeant Carpenter would be fairly worn out during the coming weeks: "We were at Cowan Station...and went to Tracy City and sent all out tents and baggage by Railroad to Nashville. From Tracy City we marched to Altamonte on top of the Cumberland Mountain, where our Division came together. Now all this time we were on half rations, and sometimes less than that, so by the time we arrived at Nashville we were pretty well worn down."[60] From a bivouac near Pelham, Tennessee, on August 28, Captain Knight of the 18th Infantry observed that troops in the Army of the Ohio were starting to ignore Buell's prohibition against foraging:

> When we broke camp (Sunday, Aug. 24) all our tents and baggage were sent to Decherd. Our men were by order put on half rations but it has been reduced to quarter rations in fact. That is in the issues by the government but every cow, pig, sheep, or goose that makes his appearance is sure to die. It is amusing to see two or three hundred soldiers get after one of these poor sharp long nosed pigs. They can run equal to race horses and I have laughed myself sore, seeing the soldiers run one of those lean long legged hogs down but when caught [on] a bayonet soon let out his life blood. We do not restrain our soldiers for they must subsist, must have enough to eat. I think they do better now than when they get only government rations. The cornfields are stripped—the soft corn is eaten by the soldiers and the fodder by the mules. ...I have no doubt but that we will meet the enemy and have a terrific battle, but it will not be where we now are. All are anxious to meet him and let the matter be settled. We feel that it is time something was done to reward us for our long fatiguing marches and privations.[61]

The 15th Infantry's Lieutenant King also noted the regulars growing skill at foraging, observing that although they had not been paid in more than three months, "we have been in this country long enough to know how to buy chickens, &c., without the money."[62]

Buell avoided contesting the Confederate advance into Kentucky, wrongly believing Bragg was heading for Nashville. Once Buell realized that Bragg's real target was one state to the north, the Army of the Ohio was on the move again. While Buell led the bulk of his army into the Bluegrass State, he ordered Thomas's division to remain in Nashville to safeguard the Tennessee capital. Shepherd's regulars arrived there on September 7. Thomas assigned them the task of guarding the vital railroad bridge that carried the Louisville

& Nashville's tracks over the Cumberland River into Nashville. The 18th Infantry remained in Nashville until September 15, when Buell ordered Thomas's division to rejoin the Army of the Ohio's main body. By mid-September Buell's army was positioned around Bowling Green, Kentucky. A company of 16th Infantrymen greeted Lieutenant Colonel Bomford's regulars as McCook's division marched into town.[63]

Similar to almost all new regular companies that had attempted to join their battalions in the field during 1862, the journey of B/2/16th U.S. turned out to be a long one. Captain James Biddle, a Michigan native who had spent the first year of the war recruiting in Detroit, reported to Camp Thomas in early May 1862 and was assigned to lead the new recruits of Company B. The unit was fully manned and organized by July. When Major Coolidge and the 16th Infantry's headquarters departed Camp Thomas for their new home at Ft. Ontario, New York, Biddle's company boarded a train in Columbus on July 14 with orders to report for duty with 1/16th U.S. in Tennessee. Two days later in Louisville, Biddle learned that Brigadier General Jeremiah Boyle, commander of the District of Kentucky, had ordered all troops passing through the city to stop and await further orders. Biddle produced his own orders from the War Department that required the company to proceed to the field and join its battalion, but to no avail. Biddle's regulars spent the next month participating in fruitless chases after Confederate raiders in central Kentucky, with the captain not enjoying having to serve under officers whom he considered barely competent. "Col. Lucas has guerillas on the brain," Biddle complained to his diary about one such leader on August 1, "and expects to find one under every bush." Biddle's regulars were at the small town of Ghent on the Ohio River on August 16 when the captain received a telegram from General Boyle ordering the company back to Louisville. Biddle's men boarded a steamer that night and arrived in Louisville the next day, although Biddle noted that their passage was initially in doubt: "Captain of boat said that my telegraphic orders were not good for transportation and that he would put me off at the first stop. Having 65 armed men at my back he changed his mind."

Having spent more than a month going nowhere, on August 24, Biddle's company was finally released and ordered to join its battalion. They made it as far as Bowling Green that day, beyond which point rail travel was not possible due to the wreckage of the tunnels and tracks north of Nashville. Biddle again found his company assigned to a local garrison, but he tried to make the most of the situation: "Reported to Col. Bruce, the commanding officer, and was directed to put my men in camp at a large spring, in a walnut grove 1 1/2 miles from the town. ...I found Col. Bruce was a real Kentucky-Colonel type and kept a barrel of whiskey on tap. I made it a point to enquire after his health twice a day." More weeks of tedium followed, which ended on September 14 as Biddle's men finally linked up with 1/16th U.S. as the Army of the Ohio moved northward into Kentucky.[64]

At least Biddle's company was able to finally reach its destination. Two other new regular companies were ordered to the field in September 1862, but neither of them made it to their battalions. Viewing the situation from Camp Thomas, Colonel Carrington considered the Confederate invasion of nearby Kentucky to be a serious enough threat to warrant the dispatch southward of two regular companies. On September 3, Carrington sent Captain Tenador Ten Eyck to Louisville via Cincinnati with H/2/18th U.S. and seventy-one additional troops for other companies in the 18th Infantry battalions. The colonel dispatched a similar force a few days later, built around Captain John A. Thompson's G/2/18th Infantry. Ten Eyck proceeded southward from Louisville in an attempt to reach the Army of the Ohio's position, but the fast pace of events in Kentucky prevented Thompson from venturing south of Cincinnati.

By August 18, Kirby Smith's Confederates had passed through Roger's Gap of the Cumberland Mountains and penetrated as far as Barboursville on the Cumberland River. He advanced deeper into Kentucky for the next eleven days, largely unopposed. On August 30, near Richmond, two veteran Southern divisions under Patrick Cleburne and Thomas J. Churchill routed a hastily assembled Union force of mostly untrained recruits led by General "Bull" Nelson, resulting in one of the most lopsided Southern victories of the war. Kirby Smith followed up the Battle of Richmond by continuing northward and seizing the fertile Bluegrass Region of central Kentucky, establishing his headquarters at Lexington on September 2. From there he dispatched an 8,000-man column under Brigadier General Henry Heth further to the north, toward Cincinnati. Heth's command was too small to actually capture and hold Cincinnati, but as the Southerners occupied Florence (a scant ten miles southeast of

Cincinnati) and made tentative probes northward during the first week of September, southern Ohio was thrown into a panic.[65]

Into the midst of this panic marched Captain John A. Thompson and the regulars of G/2/18th Infantry. Major General Horatio G. Wright, commander of the Cincinnati-based Department of the Ohio (a new administrative entity separate from Buell's army, responsible for Kentucky), snatched up the regulars as soon as they arrived and assigned them to the provost guard of Major General Lew Wallace, commander of the rapidly galvanizing Cincinnati defenses. General Wright later wrote to Carrington, hoping the colonel did not mind the highhandedness: "I have one of the Companies of your regiment here on provost duty, and am very desirous of retaining it. I know the objection made by regimental commanders to any portion of their regiment being detained; but this is the *only* reliable Company I have, and the *only* Regulars in the Department. Captain Thompson, the Commander of the Company, has become familiar with the City and its duties, and cannot be replaced by any officer in my command." Thompson was placed in command of Cincinnati's "City Guard," consisting of his own regulars and a few companies of volunteers. He also was in charge of Burbank Barracks in Cincinnati and the batteries covering the Kentucky approaches to Cincinnati across the Ohio River at Covington. Heth's Confederates, meanwhile, never made a substantial advance beyond the Florence area and by September 10 had rejoined Kirby Smith at Lexington.[66]

The crisis in Cincinnati passed. Many of Thompson's regulars then found that they had ample time to write letters, the daily routine of garrison duty not being very demanding following Heth's withdrawal. The 1st sergeant of G/2/18th U.S., Christopher Peterson, wrote to a friend at Camp Thomas on September 8 and said he was pleased with his duties:

> As we will in all probability stay here for a time, I take this opportunity to inform you of our whereabouts.
>
> We are encamped in a very nice park in Covington, assisting to guard the city.
>
> We man five or six batteries besides doing a considerable amount of other Duty. We are looked upon as something extra by both citizens and Volunteers and when you next hear from us it may be that we shall have distinguished ourselves and won laurels that will be an honor to the 18th U.S. Inf. I have a great deal to do for we have two

Companies of the 112th Regt. O. Volunteers attached to our command and as they are quite ignorant I have to assist them in almost every thing. The men as a general thing are quite healthy and seem to enjoy themselves highly, although they have not forgotten their friends at Camp Thomas.

The boys go on guard with one nights sleep. We are expecting an attack from General Smith every day with 40,000 men. As my time is limited I will close by asking you to give my respects to all the Officers and Non Com Officers and men remaining in Camp Thomas.

P.S. I go out about 8 o'clock every night visiting posts, forts and stations, returning about one and two. I have a splendid horse to ride also.[67]

According to another of the regulars in Cincinnati, Private Trine Swick, it was two months later before the Thompson's men were called into action. Their opponents were considerably less dangerous than Confederates:

We had one of the greatest times the other day I ever experienced. it was announced a day or to before hand that on the 4th [of November] they would give 5.00 in Postage Currency for 5.00 of Uncle Sams money, (It was to get the Postage Currency in Circulation) and long before the time came the Streets around the Custom house, was crowded so that it was almost impossible to get along, and they crowded around to the door so that they had to call on us for a guard. there were 50 men detailed for the purpose, and they could not do any thing with them. we had to take two companies and then we could hardly keep them back with the point of the bayonet. It came as near being a riot as could be. it came so near that they began to throw stones, one of them hit one of our boys on the chin and cut quite a gash. We arrested a good many for trying to hog in. Whenever we saw a man trying to fight, we just collared him and sent him off.[68]

Swick's nephew, Private Charles V. Bogart, was also a member of Thompson's company. Bogart let his mother know in late November that he and his uncle were having an enjoyable time in Cincinnati: "We are going to have a ball on the 4 day of Dec, the ladies of Cincinnati is going to give it. I expect that we will have a great time, we are going to take our guns up to the ball in the afternoon so to have a little drill in the evening when we get tired of dancing. I expect that there will be a good many of the Cincinnati big bugs there too, that is what we are going to take our guns for. I tell you that I do feel proud of the company that I am in. we are called the best that was ever in Camp Thomas, Columbus Ohio, or in Cincinnati." Even after almost one and a half years of war, regulars were oftentimes the only troops considered to be sufficiently trained and dependable to perform such rear-area tasks as riot control and escort for social events. First Sergeant Peterson and his "splendid" mount would have to wait much longer than expected before they ever saw a battlefield, for it would not be until the spring of 1863 that G/2/18th U.S. finished its journey and joined its battalion in the field.[69]

Like Thompson's men, Captain Ten Eyck's H/2/18th U.S. also ended up being of little immediate use to its battalion. By the second week of September, Bragg's army had crossed the border into southern Kentucky and was in a position to threaten Buell's lifeline, the Louisville & Nashville. While resting the travel-worn Army of the Mississippi near Glasgow on September 12, Bragg sent two brigades of Major General John M. Wither's Division further to the east to cut the Louisville & Nashville Railroad. One of Wither's brigades, commanded by Brigadier General James R. Chalmers, occupied Cave City late that evening. After receiving reports that nearby Munfordville, with its vital bridge over the Green River, was lightly held and ripe for capture, Chalmers determined to make a stab at this prize. His brigade unwisely attacked the Union position on the morning of September 14.[70]

Captain Tenador Ten Eyck's company of regulars happened to be part of the 2,122-man Munfordville garrison. The unit arrived at the Green River crossing the day prior to the attack, its movement south from Louisville halted due to the approach of Chalmers's Brigade. Ten Eyck's regulars and the rest of the garrison, under the overall command of Colonel John T. Wilder of the 17th Indiana, handily repulsed the Southerners, inflicting heavy losses on Chalmers's Mississippians. Wilder received reinforcements during the next twenty-four hours (including the 68th Indiana under Colonel Edward A. King, formerly the 19th Infantry's lieutenant colonel), which swelled Federal Ranks at Munfordville to more than 4,000 men. Additional Confederates also converged on the scene, the bulk of Bragg's army. Although Bragg had not planned to move on Munfordville in force during the campaign, he felt that he had to follow up Chalmers's rash attack. After being surrounded by vastly superior Confederate forces, Colonel Wilder had no choice but to surrender his small command. Captain Ten Eyck, Lieutenant

Thaddeous Kirtland, and 117 regular soldiers became paroled prisoners of war on the morning of September 17. They were sent back to Camp Thomas to await exchange.[71]

It was difficult for Bragg to maintain his army at Munfordville for long. He knew the Army of the Ohio was near, and wanted to avoid a confrontation before joining forces with Kirby Smith. Bragg also had no reliable method of obtaining supplies, except for gathering what was needed from nearby Kentucky farms, a tough proposition in a drought-plagued area. Bragg abandoned Munfordville on September 20 and moved northeastward toward Bardstown, a village closer to Kirby Smith's men at Lexington. Bragg hoped that the more fertile Bluegrass Region of Kentucky around Lexington would provide his army with what it needed to survive. By combining forces with Kirby Smith, Bragg also hoped the Confederates in Kentucky would be strong enough to confront Buell. Another factor in Bragg's calculations was the operations of Confederate forces in northern Mississippi under Earl Van Dorn and Sterling Price. Bragg had assumed from the start of the Kentucky invasion that the Confederates still in Mississippi would defeat Grant's forces there and then push northward into middle Tennessee. As Bragg abandoned Munfordville, he banked on Van Dorn and Price's ability to join in the Kentucky venture and keep up the pressure on Buell.[72]

Grant's Army of the Tennessee was more than capable enough to deal with Confederate forces in northern Mississippi, enabling Buell to keep his own sights focused on Bragg. Buell had briefly considered attacking Bragg while the latter was at Munfordville, but with Bragg heading northeast and the road to Louisville open for the time being, Buell hurried his troops to the Ohio River. Buell feared that the Confederates were trying to capture Louisville—although Bragg actually was not—and wanted the Army of the Ohio to reach that city as fast as possible. Left behind at Bowling Green was whatever baggage the troops had carried from Nashville. The summer's drought and parched landscape made for brutal conditions. "I have had [to] march over 200 miles and live on holy exertions," wrote David Smith, a private in Captain Biddle's B/2/16th U.S., "and the roads so dusty it was like going through an ash heap and the watter we had to drink out of mud holes." Smith's company commander also wrote of the dry conditions, noting that on one day in mid-September the only water to be had came from "a horse-pond in a barn yard." On a march later in the month, Biddle observed: "Dust so bad that we could not see the men in front of us." Sergeant Carpenter recalled the march to Louisville as his most difficult to date: "We had to push on and marched to Bowling green Ky and a hard march it was too. We marched nights when we were so sleepy that we could not stand up, which with our weakness from hunger rendered our suffering intense. I tell you the hardest thing I ever went through was to march at night when I was hungry and *so* sleepy. We had to push on and get to Louisville first if we could and we did it, but a more tired, foot-sore lame and hungry set of soldiers never was seen in the world. For nearly 2 months we had been travelling on nothing to eat hardly, and with only the clothes we had on our backs, no shelter at all."[73]

Steedman's brigade of Thomas's division traveled the last few miles to Louisville via steamer on the Ohio River. As the craft hurried upriver, Captain John Knight finally had time to write a letter home. Some of his thoughts were identical to those of Sergeant Arthur Carpenter:

> During this [march] we have been deprived of everything and marched until our feet were in many cases worn until they bled. I have had as many as a dozen blisters on my feet and would go into camp at night almost dying. Our men, many of them shoeless, went with their bare feet. ...I was so sick I had to go in the ambulance for the last two days. Only think how we have suffered. Officers and men have been on half rations and here we are now without a stitch of clean clothes to put on and perhaps our baggage all taken by Guerillas.
>
> We have marched over 400 miles since we left Decherd and all but about a week without tents. I am sick of everything and would gladly quit the service if I could do so honorably. I hope we will be sent to Virginia under McClellan. All are eager for it.[74]

Making morale even worse for Shepherd's regulars was the feeling that the 18th Infantry seemed destined to miss everything: mud-bound and immobilized during the Battle of Mill Springs, too late for Shiloh, not much happening at Corinth, guarding the Iuka supply depot during the advance on Chattanooga, guarding a bridge in Nashville while the rest of Buell's army pursued Bragg into Kentucky. Now Shepherd's men found themselves back in Louisville, the same place they had been during December 1861. And still no enemy in sight. When they heard there had been a "big fight" just a little more than a week ago at Iuka, the start point of their long march to Louisville, the 18th Regulars cursed their luck once again. Lieutenant Colonel Shepherd assured his men that their time would come. One of his officers confidently wrote home: "Col. Shepherd told me that he thought we might yet get a fight with Bragg and Shepherd is an old coon. He is not apt to say such things unless there is some reason for it. Shepherd, we all think, is one of the best officers of the old army."[75]

The citizens of Louisville were elated that the Army of the Ohio had made it through. They hailed Buell's dusty, sunburned troops as saviors, not realizing Bragg had never seriously planned to threaten their city. Alexander McCook's division arrived there on September 26. Corporal Eli Tarbell of the 19th Regulars must have thought he had entered another world: "the Citizens of Louisville gave every man a loaf of Bread. ...the Ladies, dear Creturs, Shook our hands with tears in there Eyes,, Oh my, it Sent the blood tingling through our vanes to Shake thoes lovely little hands."[76]

For a while it appeared that Don Carlos Buell would personally remain in Louisville but a short time. He had never been very popular with radical Republicans, and many officials in Washington were most dissatisfied that Buell had allowed Bragg's army to march unmolested from Mississippi almost to the Ohio River. President Lincoln relieved Buell of command during the last week of September and replaced him with George Thomas, although the officer bearing the implementing instructions was ordered not to deliver the paperwork if Buell was "preparing to fight a battle." Henry Halleck, Union Army general-in-chief as of July 23, learned through various sources that this was in fact the case and attempted to prevent the relief, but the orders were delivered on September 29 despite his efforts. At any rate, Thomas, making the greatest professional mistake of his career, refused to accept Buell's command. He argued that Buell's preparations to go on the offensive were nearly complete, and it would not be wise to change commanders in the midst of an active campaign, particularly since Thomas had to admit: "My position is very embarrassing, not being as well informed as I should be as the commander of this army and on the assumption of such a responsibility." Lincoln acquiesced for the time being, but Buell's future would continue to be in doubt unless that general quickly generated some positive results on a battlefield.[77]

The president was justified in his dissatisfaction with Buell's leadership. Many of the weary troops at Louisville felt likewise. The Army of the Ohio had been logging mile after mile for almost five months with nothing tangible to show for the effort. Buell's well-known conciliatory attitude toward Southern citizens and private property was not in step with the attitudes of many of his soldiers. Morale in Buell's army deteriorated with each passing day, to the point that Buell himself started to be the object of scorn. "I don't think there will be any fighting as long as Buell has command, for I don't think he means Fight," Sergeant Amos Fleagle of the 18th U.S. wrote after being in Louisville two days. Private David W. Smith of the 16th Infantry believed: "the Armey all think that old Buell is a Reebble and they say they will Shoot him the first time they get a chance." In the 19th U.S., recent events had disheartened Sergeant Arthur Carpenter: "for one year have we been enduring fatigue & hardship, and now we are just were we commenced. I think the sooner peace is declared the better." Captain R. Delavan Mussey of the 19th was also fed up: "I am too busy and too much desirous of rest to write out all the many acts of omission and commission which have brought even officers in Buell's army to the conclusion that he is either a Traitor or an Imbecile. The few Division Generals who 'patched him up' after the command had been assigned to Thomas may not agree with that opinion, but everyone else does. If the West is to be saved there must be a change."[78] Captain John Knight agreed with Mussey, although this 18th Infantry captain thought more than just a change at the top was necessary:

> The western army is filled with brainless, unmilitary egotists who have large commands and I feel confident will be outgeneraled, beaten, whenever they lead into action, the men under them. Old and experienced officers who were educated for the service and grown gray in it are found here with inferior rank and subject to the orders of these old broken down politicians. ...I have marched over three hundred miles since I came West and it looks as if I will have to march as many more miles before we reach a position of safety. But I hope that we will engage the enemy first, for we are all sadly tired of so much marching, without doing any fighting. I had rather fight a dozen battles than march so far. I believe if you hear of the 18th Infantry getting into action, you will hear a good report of its conduct. I believe it will sustain the deserving reputation won by the regulars whenever they have been in action. Not a stain has yet been

cast upon a regular regt. during this war and I do not believe there will be one.[79]

Buell had managed to keep his job thanks to Thomas, but other changes happened fast to the Army of the Ohio after it reached Louisville. A few brigades from Grant's Army of the Tennessee and numerous fresh regiments from Kentucky and points north joined the Army of the Ohio's tired ranks. Buell's forces soon numbered more than 75,000 troops, and he organized his expanded command into three corps. Alexander McCook took command of I Corps, Major General Thomas L. Crittenden led II Corps, and Major General Charles C. Gilbert commanded III Corps. George Thomas became Buell's deputy commander. McCook's corps consisted of McCook's old division (now commanded by Brigadier General Joshua Sill), Rousseau's division, and a new division commanded by Brigadier General James K. Jackson. Brigadier General Albin Schoeph took over Thomas's division, the unit being allotted to Gilbert's corps. Buell wisely assigned some of the raw regiments to his veteran brigades. The 87th Indiana, just mustered into Federal Service on August 31, joined Steedman's brigade, while the 93rd Ohio, another new regiment, would later march beside King's regulars in Buckley's brigade.[80]

Many regular officers also assumed new duties. Regulars were always in high demand for staff duty, but the rapid organization of additional Union brigades and divisions during the Kentucky campaign meant regulars were also sought for commands. General Horatio Wright, stretching his authority as Department of the Ohio commander to the limit, was the driving force behind the appointment of a number of regulars to command billets. He would later explain that while he was "fully supplied with troops," they were "all newly organized and without instruction or discipline, the officers as well as the men, almost without exception being wholly devoid of any military knowledge whatsoever. No officers of rank could, at that time, be furnished me for the command of brigades and divisions and therefore to have competent men for such positions I was compelled to take from the small regular force of the command the best officers I could select to fill these places." Wright's most suspect action was the appointment of Charles Gilbert, a captain of the 1st U.S. Infantry then serving on Nelson's staff, as an ersatz major general. Buell compounded this error by giving Gilbert command of III Corps, a position for which Gilbert would soon show himself to be totally unsuited. Fortunately, not all of Wright's selections were as dubious as this one. He appointed Captain William Terrill of H/5th Artillery to brigadier general of volunteers on September 1. This was a just reward for Terrill's performance at Shiloh, and would soon be fully sanctioned by both the president and the United States Senate. Brigadier General Terrill took charge of a brigade in Jackson's division. Captain Peter Swaine was stripped from his company in 1/15th U.S. through a Wright-authorized appointment to a volunteer colonelcy. General Wright placed him in command of a brigade in Cincinnati. Two weeks later, the governor of Ohio commissioned Swaine as colonel of the recently organized 99th Ohio Volunteer Infantry. During late September, Swaine took command of one of the Army of the Ohio's new brigades.

Horatio Wright was not the only general casting about for regulars. Alexander McCook selected the 16th Infantry's Lieutenant Colonel Bomford to be chief of staff of I Corps, which meant Bomford ended his short tenure in command of the three regular battalions in Buckley's brigade. Lieutenant Louis Hosea, adjutant of 1/16th, accompanied Bomford to the staff of McCook's corps, while Captain R.E.A. Crofton ended up on the staff of Gilbert's corps. Lieutenant Harrison Millard, 19th Infantry, was assigned to the staff of Rousseau's division. Lieutenant Jacob Smyser, a section leader in Battery H, joined the Army of the Ohio's Ordnance Department, where help was desperately needed in arming the thousands of new soldiers pouring into Louisville. "General" Gilbert tapped Lieutenant William Bisbee's D/2/18th to be the provost guards of III Corps.[81]

Brigadier General William Terrill faced a daunting task. His new brigade consisted of four volunteer regiments that had thus far received only rudimentary training, a consolidated detachment of companies from three other regiments, and an ad hoc artillery battery of eight guns manned by detailed infantrymen and commanded by Lieutenant Charles C. Parsons of the 4th U.S. Artillery. Terrill attempted to turn the recruits into soldiers using the same professional methods he had employed the previous year in training Battery H—although as historian Kenneth Noe recently documented, some of Terrill's volunteers responded with only mixed enthusiasm.[82] The general referred to his command by the sobriquet "Light Brigade" and attempted to instill in his men a desire to live up to the distinctive title. He also wrote the War Department and attempted once again to secure promotion for Lieutenant Frank Guenther, who had succeeded Terrill in command of Battery H:

Head Qrs Light Brigade
Louisville Sept 27th 1862

Brig Gen L. Thomas
Adjutant Gen USA
Washington, DC

General

I have the honor to request that 1st Lieut. Francis L. Guenther 5th Artillery be brevetted a Captain for gallant conduct in the reconnaissance at Greenbrier in Western Virginia on the 3d day of November 1861, and a Major by brevet for "distinguished gallantry and good conduct at the battle of Shiloh."

There can be no officer of the Army more deserving of a brevet than this modest and gallant man. He has served almost continuously in the field since he graduated at West Point. And by his cheerful discharge of duty, no less than by his gallantry in action, he has endeared himself to his commanders. From the beginning of the rebellion he has been constantly on duty. He is one of the best Artillery officers I have ever known. And his Services as Chief of Artillery of a Division would be more valuable to his country than in the position he now holds. My government has seen fit to honor me by appointing me a Brig Genl of Vols. for my conduct in the battle of Shiloh. And I would be wanting in principle did I fail in making this application, which I consider but an act of mere justice to a gallant Soldier who so much contributed to the success of my battery in that terrible conflict.

My promotion to a Brig Genl leaves my old Division of the Army of Ohio without a Chief of Artillery. That for the good of the Service I beg that Lieut. Guenther receive the brevets asked for, and be assigned to duty according to his brevet rank.

Wm R. TERRILL
Capt 5th Artillery
Brig Gen Vols[83]

An array of generals endorsed Terrill's request. Joshua Sill: "I know of but few officers of Mr. Guenther's age & experience who deserve so much of their country." Alexander McCook was likewise enthusiastic: "No regiment or corps can boast of a more gallant and worthy officer." It took another month, but Guenther would finally receive a brevet promotion to captain in November 1862 for Shiloh.

It would take much longer for Guenther to receive full promotion to captain, for the Union Army's artillery suffered under a defective personnel system, a byproduct of the belief that the battery was the only artillery organization necessary in the field. While capable officers in the infantry and cavalry often moved rapidly up the ranks, promotions in the artillery were hard to come by beyond the rank of captain. William Terrill still officially occupied the captain's slot in Battery H, which held up the promotion of a worthy lieutenant. It was not until later in the war that Union artillery was detached from infantry organizations and formed into separate artillery battalions and brigades, resulting in the need for higher-ranking artillerymen in the field. In the meantime, talented artillerists such as Frank Guenther toiled away in company-grade positions for most of the war.[84]

Steedman's brigade disembarked at the Louisville waterfront on September 28. In camp that evening, Oliver Shepherd decided it was time to move on. He had spent almost a year forging the 18th Regulars into a superb unit, but with so little progress in the war being made lately, he felt his talents could be put to better use somewhere else. His tainted reputation in the Army of the Ohio was a definite impediment to advancement, and rumors were flying that his good friend Don Carlos Buell would soon be relieved of command. On top of all that, his wife was ill. She had never been in the eastern United States until Shepherd brought her from Texas to New York City the previous year, and was finding it difficult to receive proper medical care due to her Hispanic origins.

Shepherd thought that recent events in the Army of the Potomac would afford him an opportunity to escape his predicament. Colonel Dixon S. Miles of the 2nd U.S. Infantry had been the post commander of Harper's Ferry, Virginia, when that point was surrounded by Major General Thomas J. "Stonewall" Jackson's Corps from the Army of Northern Virginia during the 1862 Confederate invasion of Maryland. Colonel Miles had surrendered the strategically vital point on September 15 after a shoddy defense, only to be mortally wounded in the final Confederate bombardment. Lieutenant Colonel Sidney Burbank of the 13th Infantry, then serving as commander of Newport Barracks, was the senior infantry officer of that grade in the Regular Army and thus first in line to inherit Miles's colonelcy, but the aging Burbank was in poor health and Shepherd had heard he was facing a mandatory medical retirement. The lieutenant colonel of the 18th Infantry ranked next behind Burbank, so according to Shepherd's calculations, it was just a matter of time before orders arrived promoting Shepherd to Miles's vacant position in command of the 2nd Infantry, a regiment serving in Army of the Potomac's Regular Division.[85] Shepherd was so anxious to head east that he decided to set the move in motion as soon as possible:

Camp near Louisville, Ky.
Sept 28, 1862

Col. J.B. Fry
   A.G. & Chief of Staff
   Army of the Ohios
   Louisville, Ky.

Colonel:

The assumed action of the retiring board and the recent death of Colonel Miles, render it quite certain that I am promoted; and desiring to be with my proper Regiment, in the exercise of my full rank, I respectfully request to be relieved from duty here and ordered to report to Washington.

I desire to state also that the two battalions of the 18th Inf now serving here, are respectively under the command of experienced & competent officers, Majors Townsend and Caldwell, chiefs of battalions, which obviates the necessity of my further stay here.

I am Sir very respectfully
Your obdt Servt

O.L. SHEPHERD
Lieut Col 18th Inf[86]

Shepherd's request was quickly granted. Given his reputation, the Army of the Ohio's leadership was glad to be rid of him. Shepherd was excited about his prospects, although somewhat melancholy about parting with the 18th Regulars. On September 30, he relinquished command:

Hd Qrs. Detcht 18th U.S. Inf
Camp near Louisville Ky
September 30 1862

Orders
No 153

Having been relieved from duty with this Detachment and ordered to Washington, the undersigned hereby relinquishes command to Major Townsend, the senior officer present. Serving with this Detcht of the Regiment almost from its organization & in arduous campaigns through the inclemencies of every season, in sickness as well as in health, [it] will ever find my highest wishes for the prosperity & welfare of the Regiment.

O.L. SHEPHERD
Lieut Col. 18th Inf[87]

The 18th Regulars were numbed by Shepherd's hasty departure. By candlelight at four o'clock in the morning on September 31, Captain John Knight wrote a quick letter home and tried to look on the bright side: "Just have been awakened and given orders to be ready to march at 6 1/2 this morning. How sleepy I feel! Lt. Col. O.L. Shepherd, who has commanded the Regt. all the time and has made it what it is leaves us this morning for Washington. ...We all think he will be made a Major Genl. for he is one of the best officers in the army. We are all cast down at his leaving." The officers of the 18th Infantry tried to make the most of the situation and sent a petition to President Lincoln requesting that the regiment follow its lieutenant colonel to the Army of the Potomac and urging that Oliver Shepherd be promoted to general.[88]

Everyone miscalculated. Sidney Burbank was not in fact medically retired and instead was the new colonel of the 2nd Infantry. Shepherd arrived in Washington full of anticipation and reported to the adjutant general's office, only to discover that he would continue to wear silver oak leaves for the foreseeable future. But since the 18th Infantry's lieutenant colonel had come to the War Department looking for a job, Adjutant General Lorenzo Thomas gave him one. Shepherd was placed on detached service from the 18th Infantry and assigned to an obscure court of inquiry at the Allegheny Arsenal in Pennsylvania.

* * *

The Army of the Ohio's footsore and threadbare troops spent a few day recuperating in Louisville, receiving full rations for the first time in weeks. Lieutenant Edgar Kellogg of the 16th Infantry thought his commanders made a number of errors while at Louisville: "First, the Regulars, and I do not know how many other commands, were crowded into a filthy place on the [Ohio River] levee with insufficient room for exercise, and with no regard for...privacy and decency. We were forbidden, both enlisted men and officers, to leave the bivouac without special permission from the Battalion Commander, and, so far as I know, he did not grant such permission to anyone but himself. These unnecessary hardships...produced their legitimate fruits—resentment and disobedience." The pay situation made things even worse. The Army of the Ohio had not been paid since the previous May at Corinth. Although Buell threatened to further withhold pay in an attempt to tighten up his army's deteriorating discipline, paymasters issued back pay to some units in Louisville, the regulars among them. It is easy to imagine the effect this had on the troops, being in a Union city for the first time in almost a year and having extra cash in their pockets to boot. Volunteers and regulars by the score left their commands to enjoy urban comforts. Some returned when their money ran out, others deserted permanently. When the 16th Regulars left Louisville a few days after payday, less than half its troops were present. Eight men were in the ranks of F/1/16th, while the strength of the battalion's Company D was exactly two soldiers: the commander and his 1st sergeant. The rest of the battalion's troops were absent and in various stages of inebriation, although most of them caught up with their leaders within a day.[89]

Buell was ready by the beginning of October. While the Army of the Ohio gathered its strength and shook out its new organization at Louisville, Bragg's Army of the Mississippi remained near Bardstown. Kirby Smith's Army of Kentucky was still in the Lexington-Mount Sterling region, sixty miles from Bragg. To keep the two Confederate forces separated and unsure about the Federal line of march, Buell sent a diversionary column toward Frankfort and Lexington to occupy Kirby Smith's attention. The column consisted of a division of untrained recruits under Brigadier General Ebenezer Dumont and Joshua Sill's veteran division with its three regular battalions. The balance of Buell's army went after Bragg, the Army of the Ohio's three corps each advancing toward Bardstown on separate routes. The offensive began on October 1.[90]

Sill's column moved out southeastward along the Frankfort Pike at eight in the morning. Colonel John S. Scott's cavalry brigade from Kirby Smith's army began harassing the Federals about five miles out from Louisville. Pushing through the resistance, Sill's men marched sixteen miles and stopped for the night near Middletown.[91] Lieutenant Kellogg recalled that some of the regulars that night were still feeling the effects of the recent Louisville binge:

A laughable incident of that bivouac on the first night out is still a vivid picture in my memory. I was awakened in the silent watches of the night, and raised myself on an elbow to ascertain what had disturbed my slumber. What I saw and heard more than repaid me for the loss of sleep. A laggard of my company who had come in after I had gone to rest and the first sergeant of D Company, both exhibiting the outward and visible signs of an inward and spirituous grace, were standing over a fire a few yards distant, and bombarding each other with quotations from Shakespeare. My man was firing chunks from Macbeth, and the sergeant was replying with missiles from Hamlet.

If the combat had been rigidly to the words of the immortal Bard of Avon it would have been funny beyond my powers of description, but the sergeant headed up the measure of my enjoyment by adding to each of his quotations this improvised peroration: "But, I have one glorious satisfaction—you are all going to hell."[92]

Sill's column neared the Kentucky capital of Frankfort on October 4. General Bragg and a large crowd of Kentucky secessionists were present in the city that day, attending the installation of Richard Hawes as Confederate governor of the Bluegrass State (a move designed to give a façade of legality to the conscription of Kentucky citizens into the Confederate army). The distant rumble of artillery at four in the afternoon, the product of a skirmish between Kirk's brigade and Confederate cavalry ten miles west of town, cut short the festivities and forced the Bragg entourage to flee. Sill's and Dumont's divisions remained in the Frankfort area for the next three days, little hindered by Kirby Smith's Army of Kentucky, then positioned southwest of Lexington. Early on the morning of October 8, Sill left Dumont in Frankfort and marched his own division south with orders to rejoin the main body of Buell's army.[93]

Kirby Smith attempted to intercept Sill's division as the Federals crossed the Salt River at Lawrenceburg on October 9, but Sill, driving his veterans on a thirty-hour forced march from Frankfort with barely a let up, escaped the trap. His division brushed aside a weak force of Southern cavalry at Lawrenceburg and passed through the town well before any additional Confederates converged on the scene. All Kirby Smith could do was send Jones Withers's Division in pursuit. Shortly after eight o'clock in the morning of October 9, Withers's troops made contact with Colonel Buckley's brigade, the rear element of Sill's column. A mixed force of Southern infantry and dismounted cavalry hit the front of the Buckley's strung-out command. Other Confederates headed for the division's wagon train at the rear of the column, which was guarded by Major Carpenter's battalion of the 19th Infantry. General Sill and Colonel Buckley began moving reinforcements to front and rear to confront the attackers.[94] Lieutenant Kellogg experienced the confusion of that day, and in the process reinforced his dislike of Major Slemmer:

> The combat was not marked by a large number of casualties, but I shall never forget the strain which it imposed on my breathing apparatus. It was a hot October day, there was no breeze, our division wagon train was jammed in between the front and rear of the division, and the road was narrow and dusty. First we were attacked in the rear, and the Sixteenth was hurried back to aid our friends there. Immediately we were assailed in front and the Sixteenth was rushed to that point. The disturbance there was quieted, at least for a time, but we found "no rest for the weary." Another assault on our rear comrades called us to their assistance, and back we went again, some of us, I am sure, swearing more than any soldier in Flanders ever did.
>
> The horse of our Battalion Commander was kept at a fox-trot nearly all of the time, and we poor doughboys who were not mounted had to run to keep up, winding through the wagon train from one side of the road to the other. I think nearly half of the Sixteenth officers and men fell by the wayside exhausted and we who finished, without a moment of rest, the return race to the rear of the division were reprimanded because there were so few of us!
>
> For sometime after this I was in no danger of being exploded by my esprit de corps, if that sentiment had to include the horse and his rider who seemed determined to do me to death.[95]

Kellogg must have been frustrated by the fact that the 16th Infantry was held in reserve upon reaching the rear of the column for the final time. At 8:00 A.M., a heavy force of skirmishers attacked the 19th Infantrymen guarded the division trains. The regular battalion held its ground long enough for Major King to arrive with 1/15th U.S., which fell in on the right of Major Carpenter's troops. The regulars checked the enemy advance momentarily, allowing enough time for the 1st Ohio to take up a supporting position to the rear of the regulars on the crest of a low ridge. The 1st Ohio's Colonel Edwin A. Parrott, being the senior officer present, took charge of the defense. He ordered King and Carpenter to fall back and form to the 1st Ohio's right. Lieutenant Guenther brought forward a section of Battery H, taking up a position on the Lawrenceburg Road while Gibson's brigade fell in on the flanks.

The Southerners continued pressing the improvised Union line, making their main effort against the 1st Ohio on the Federal left. Colonel Parrot ordered four companies of skirmishers forward to engage them, two from the 1st Ohio and one each from the 15th and 19th Regulars. The Federal skirmishers and two guns from Battery H kept up a brisk fire for a couple hours. "The section of Lieutenant Guenther's battery was handled with the usual vigor and skill of that accomplished officer," Colonel Parrot reported, "and was very effective in checking the advance of the enemy." The Confederates broke off the attack shortly after noon, leaving thirteen dead on the field, but capturing a train of sixteen wagons. Federal losses totaled four dead and eight wounded. Private John Baines of C/1/19th U.S. and Private Robert Putnam of A/1/15th Infantry were among those killed. Sill's division resumed its march during the afternoon, reaching Maxville by nightfall. Sill's skirmish with Withers south of Lawrenceburg was the division's only real action of the campaign. By the time that small affair took place, Buell and Bragg had already clashed at the Battle of Perryville (or Chaplin Hills) and the Confederates had decided to abandon their campaign for Kentucky.[96]

* * *

While Sill was advancing toward the Kentucky capital, the Army of the Ohio's main columns moved out on the roads leading to Bragg's position at Bardstown. Bragg knew that the first step in responding to the Federal offensive was to consolidate the two Confederate armies, but the question was where—in the north, to counter the column moving on Frankfort, or perhaps a more southerly point, for use against the Yankees heading for Bardstown? Since Bragg himself was in the Lexington area conferring with Kirby Smith when Buell's troops marched forth from Louisville, Major General Leonidas Polk was in immediate command of the Army of the Mississippi. Polk fell back to the southeast as Buell advanced, disregarding Bragg's orders to move toward Frankfort and take the Sill-Dumont column in flank. On October 4, as Sill's advance on Frankfort made a shambles out of the Confederate political ceremonies, Bragg ordered Polk to make for Harrodsburg, where Kirby Smith's Army of Kentucky would eventually join him.

Over the course of the next three days, the vacillating Bragg changed his mind again, mistakenly deducing that the Federals in the Frankfort area represented Buell's main effort. Bragg ordered the

Army of the Mississippi northward to Versailles for a rendezvous with Kirby Smith, although part of that army would stay behind to deal with the supposedly weak Federal force that had marched through Bragg's old position at Bardstown and was then approaching Perryville, a small town in the rolling hills of the Chaplin River valley. Major General William J. Hardee, in charge of the Confederate forces at Perryville, initially had only Simon Bolivar Buckner's Division available. Polk reinforced Hardee with two more divisions (commanded by Patton Anderson and Benjamin Franklin Cheatham) and additional cavalry, thinking this 16,000-man Confederate force would be sufficient to blunt the Federal advance. General Bragg ordered Polk and Hardee to attack and dispense with the Federals first thing in the morning on October 8, after which the Southerners at Perryville would take up the march northward to Versailles.

Polk had badly underestimated the strength of Buell's force. Gilbert's corps from the Army of the Ohio arrived in front of Perryville late in the day on the October 7. Desperate for water, two brigades from Brigadier General Phillip Sheridan's division crossed Doctor's Creek and occupied Peter's Hill that night, wresting control of the area away from a Confederate brigade from Anderson's Division. Buell, meanwhile, had ordered his two remaining corps to hurry to Perryville and fall in on Gilbert's flanks, hoping they would do so in time for an early morning attack on the Confederates the next day. It was not until late in the morning on October 8, however, that McCook finally arrived on Gilbert's left. It took a few hours longer for Crittenden to arrive on the Federal right. Buell postponed the Union attack until the next day.[97]

General Bragg had plans of his own. The Confederate commander arrived at Perryville mid-morning on October 8, drawn there because the expected Southern attack had failed to materialize. He learned that Polk had decided not to attack—the bishop-general had finally started to realize the growing strength of the opposing Federal army. Brushing aside Polk's concerns, Bragg decided to envelop and scatter the Federal left, after which the Confederates at Perryville would hurry northward for the long-sought after link up with Kirby Smith. The attack got underway at two in the afternoon. Bragg's attempt to maneuver around the Federal flank turned out to be too shallow; the assault instead ran head-on into McCook's corps. Five brigades of Rousseau's and Jackson's divisions had just

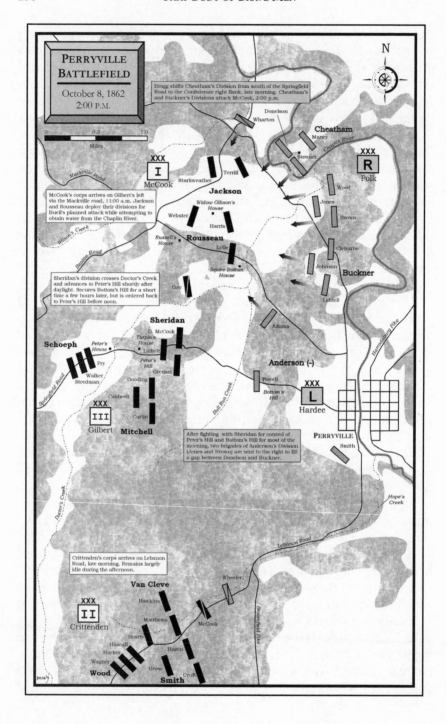

PERRYVILLE
BATTLEFIELD

October 8, 1862
2:00 P.M.

Bragg shifts Cheatham's Division from south of the Springfield Road to the Confederate right flank, late morning. Cheatham's and Buckner's Divisions attack McCook, 2:00 p.m.

McCook's corps arrives on Gilbert's left via the Mackville road, 11:00 a.m. Jackson and Rousseau deploy their divisions for Buell's planned attack while attempting to obtain water from the Chaplin River.

Sheridan's division crosses Doctor's Creek and advances to Peter's Hill shortly after daylight. Secures Bottom's Hill for a short time a few hours later, but is ordered back to Peter's Hill before noon.

After fighting with Sheridan for control of Peter's Hill and Bottom's Hill for most of the morning, two brigades of Anderson's Division (Jones and Brown) are sent to the right to fill a gap between Donelson and Buckner.

Crittenden's corps arrives on Lebanon Road, late morning. Remains largely idle during the afternoon.

taken up positions when the Southerners slammed into them. The contest raged from early afternoon until sundown, generating what some of the participants would remember as their most desperate moments of the war. Division commander James Jackson was killed during the first hour of the struggle. Brigadier General William Terrill, the next ranking officer in Jackson's division, was himself killed later in the afternoon amidst the wreckage of Lieutenant Parson's battery. McCook's corps were seriously battered and had to fall back westward nearly a mile to the far side of the Benton Road. The Union line held its ground there, but the only thing that saved the Federal left from complete disaster was the fact the Bragg had no substantial reserve with which to continue the assault.[98]

McCook fought this battle largely alone, even though the rest of Buell's army was within easy supporting distance. McCook did not bother to send word to Buell that a fight was taking place until almost two hours after the attack commenced. Gilbert, whose corps saw first hand what was going on, was also strangely unconcerned, while Crittenden's troops on the Lebanon Road—who could have walked into Perryville virtually unopposed—took almost no part in the afternoon's battle whatsoever. A combination of westerly winds and rolling terrain caused an acoustic anomaly that masked Buell from the sounds of the nearby fighting, and Buell himself could not mount up and inspect conditions personally due to injuries he had sustained the previous day when he fell from his horse. Only three of Gilbert's ten available brigades ended up coming to McCook's aid. One of these was a small brigade of cavalry commanded by Captain Ebenezer Gay of the 16th U.S. Infantry, a West Pointer and Old Army veteran of the 2nd Dragoons who was on detached service from his regiment, serving as Buell's chief of cavalry. Gilbert's corps contained three regiments of horse soldiers, and they were cobbled together to form a brigade with Captain Gay, "acting brigadier general," in command. Gay's brigade spent most of the day statically screening Gilbert's northern flank, but in the early evening Gay rode his regiments to the sound of the guns, ending up in the rear of McCook corps as the fighting concluded. At half past three, Gilbert dispatched a single infantry brigade from Brigadier General Robert D. Mitchell's division, Colonel Michael Gooding's, to McCook's aid. Gooding's presence on McCook's right flank proved to be crucial in finally blunting the Confederate assault.

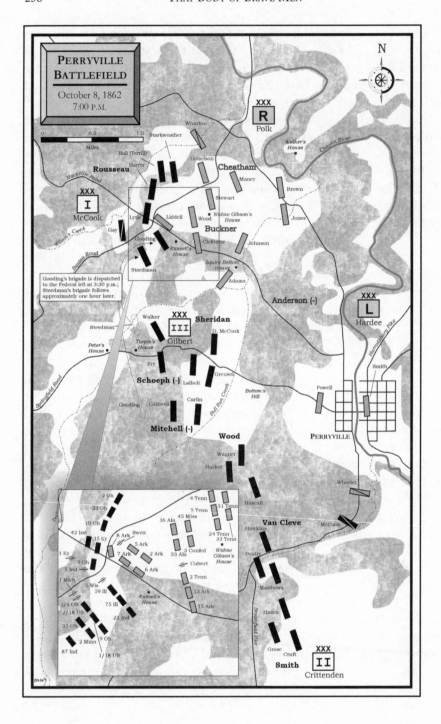

PERRYVILLE
BATTLEFIELD

October 8, 1862
7:00 P.M.

Gooding's brigade is dispatched to the Federal left at 3:30 p.m.; Steedman's brigade follows approximately one hour later.

Dusk would fall by the time the third and final brigade from Gilbert's corps arrived on the scene. During late afternoon General Buell, an accurate report from McCook finally rousing him out of the lethargy that had griped him most of the day, sent one of his aides, Major John M. Wright, to Gilbert with an order to send two brigades to McCook. Wright located Gilbert on the Springfield Road in the rear of II Corps and relayed the instructions. Gilbert's lead division, Sheridan's, was at that moment fighting with Colonel Samuel Powell's Brigade of Anderson's Division east of Peter's Hill. Not realizing his corps was facing only Powell's minuscule command, and since he had already sent Gooding's brigade to McCook, Gilbert felt it was safe to send only one additional brigade to McCook instead of the ordered pair. He told Wright to take any brigade he wished. Wright continued forward and came upon Schoeph's division. Schoeph agreed to release Steedman's brigade; Wright rode off to find General McCook as Steedman's troops began to march north. The major located the I Corps commander immediately to the rear of Rousseau's firing line. He told McCook another brigade was on the way and was composing a note to Buell when General Steedman appeared. "Here come the Pea Ridge Men!" McCook exclaimed, recalling the ribbing he had given his late brother the previous May about the story featuring the 18th Regulars in *Harper's Weekly*. Turning to Major Wright he added: "Tell the general I am all right now." As for Steedman, General McCook asked him the location of his brigade. Steedman answered that it was to the rear, nearby on the Benton Road. McCook then told Steedman to remain where he was for the moment, promising to return in a few minutes with orders.[99]

Steedman waited about twenty minutes, during which time there was no further sign of Alexander McCook. Frustrated, Steedman rode back to his brigade and was surprised to see the 18th Regulars marching toward the front. Major Townsend informed the brigade commander that General McCook had just ridden by and ordered the regulars to take up a position in support of Loomis's battery (the 1st Michigan Artillery, Rousseau's division). Steedman ordered Townsend to continue moving and brought up the rest of the brigade as well. By half past five that evening, all of Steedman's troops were in a supporting position on the forward slope of a small hill, near the intersection of the Benton and Mackville roads on Rousseau's right. The brigade's 18th Regulars and four volunteer regiments played no role in the action other than enduring incoming artillery fire for about three hours. The 18th Regulars were deployed on the left flank of Steedman's first line, immediately to the right of Lieutenant Frank G. Smith's Battery I/4th U.S. and Loomis's guns. Counter-battery fire from Southern guns against the Union artillery spilled into the 18th Infantry's position and wounded three regulars from Major Townsend's battalions (Corporal Bernard C. Connelly of D/3/18th U.S. later died from the wounding, the 18th Infantry's first combat fatality).[100] Private Isaac B. Jones of C/3/18th recorded a graphic description of the bloodshed:

> Night was growing fast upon us, and the combat grew every minute more ferocious. The flashes of the artillery was blinding, above, around, in front. Bombs, solid shot, canister and minie balls flew like hail whizzing & exploding in every direction. The shrieks and groans of the dying and wounded added to the horor & confusion of the moment, made up altogether a scene of consternation and dismay enough to appall the stoutest heart. I was over part of the battlefield the second day after the fight, & the ground was literaly strew with the dead & wounded. I seen one place where the surgeons were at work with the wounded. They then has a pile of legs and arms about four feet high. I seen one poor fellow with the whole of his lowerjaw shot off He was living yet, but never could [say] anything; and others equally as badly wounded. One man in our regt. had his leg taken off, another was shot through the lungs, & another had both of his arms blown off, & face & breast burned all into a crisp.[101]

The sight of his first real battlefield impressed Sergeant Amos Fleagle, just as the war-torn ground at Shiloh had left indelible impressions on the minds of King's regulars: "Our Division was now ordered forward to support the left wing; the Second Brigade soon drove the Rebels back. But they had by this time erected there batterys within 13 hundred yards of our lines, and our whole left was in danger of defeat. At this point our Brigade was ordered to its Support. Our Regt. now advanced followed by the 4th Regular Battery and the rest of the Brigade. We were soon in position and for 2 hours a continual storm of fire poured forth from both sides. Shot and shell flew through the air as thick as hail stones in a storm and I was thinking that Buell meant Fight. It was dark and a grander sight I never witnessed before." Down in the ranks of Sergeant Fleagle's company, Private Robert Kennedy was also moved by the panorama spread out before him: "Fireworks such as few can describe filled air as the musketry, firing along both lines, with shells flying in the air and bursting, scattering fire in all directions. The sight was magnificent but very dangerous."102

Although the fighting on October 8 near Perryville saw Southern arms largely triumphant, when the combat ended at nightfall, Bragg began to realize how outnumbered he was. Standing little chance of further battlefield success, Bragg decided to get out of Kentucky while he still had a chance. By now, the Army of the Mississippi's commander had lost whatever enthusiasm he may have once held for invading Kentucky. Confederate recruiting efforts had been a dismal failure, with few additional Kentuckians joining Southern ranks. In Mississippi, elements of Grant's army had defeated Van Dorn and Price at clashes near Iuka and Corinth. It was impossible for those Confederates to move into Tennessee, much less reinforce Bragg in Kentucky. Bragg withdrew his forces from the Perryville battlefield on October 9 and put them on the road back to eastern Tennessee. Kirby Smith's command also quit the state. Buell mounted a pursuit but only a few minor skirmishes took place as the invaders headed south. Buell abandoned the enterprise after only six days. The Army of the Ohio's commander seems to have developed an insurmountable reluctance to move into east Tennessee. Just as he had the previous January after the Battle of Mill Springs, he let a retreating foe escape and instead headed for Nashville. While the Army of the Ohio moved toward Bowling Green and the familiar tracks of the Louisville & Nashville Railroad, Bragg's troops filed southward through Cumberland Gap. The Army of the Mississippi was in Knoxville by the end of the month. The Confederate invasion of Kentucky was over.103

Operations in Kentucky during the autumn of 1862 produced frustration all around. For the South, Kentucky had not rallied to the Confederacy and hard-to-replace Southern manpower had been expended in an operation whose chances of success had never been very great. Braxton Bragg's job was in jeopardy after the Kentucky Campaign, but despite frequent and vocal calls for Bragg's removal, President Davis chose to stick with him for the time being and retained Bragg in command of the Army of the Mississippi. In November and early December, Bragg moved his forces out of Knoxville, through Chattanooga, and into middle Tennessee. He set up headquarters in Murfreesboro, a small community thirty miles southeast of Nashville. As it appeared that Bragg's army would not operate anywhere near its namesake river in the foreseeable future, its title was changed to the Army of Tennessee.[104]

From the Union's point of view, the Kentucky Campaign had thwarted the advance to Chattanooga and the Confederates had escaped back into Tennessee. Since the Confederacy ended up re-occupying northern Alabama and part of middle Tennessee, many in the North considered the campaign a Union defeat. Captain Mussey expressed his feelings in a letter dated October 16. Thousands of soldiers in the Army of the Ohio shared the sentiments of this regular officer:

> You have read the affair at Chaplin Hights the other day. In it Gens Buell and Gilbert showed themselves to be:
> 1. Cowards, or
> 2. Imbeciles, or
> 3. Traitors.
> Every officer in the Army knows that Bragg was in our grasp there if Gen B or Gen G had either of them done their duty. But so far were they from helping Gens McCook and Rousseau in their fight—3 hours of it harder, so says McCook, a good judge of fighting, than Shiloh—that Gilbert actually withdrew a Division which was on McCook's right and held it, *while the fight was going on*. If Gen Buell is not removed by the President—immediately—the Army will go to the Devil. In fact we all believe that Gen B is playing into Bragg's hands. Desertions are alarmingly frequent. The men are so disgusted at having to march & march and never have a winning fight under a Traitor.[105]

President Lincoln heeded the calls for Buell's removal on October 24. Buell would spend most of the next year and a half awaiting assignment orders that never came and answering questions at a court of inquiry probing his conduct as a department commander. He would resign his commission in June 1864. Bypassing George Thomas, Lincoln appointed Major General William Starke Rosecrans as the Army of the Ohio's new commander, an Ohio-born West Pointer who had been successful in subordinate roles in western Virginia and Mississippi. His army also received a new title: XIV Army Corps, Department of the Cumberland. Rosecrans began a major reorganization of this force shortly after assuming command. The Army of the Ohio's regular battalions would play a key role in this reorganization, for Rosecrans wanted them to be among the premier units of his new command. The status and role of the western regulars was about to change in a very significant fashion.[106]

PART TWO

The Regular Brigade in the Army of the Cumberland

1862–1865

Chapter 6:

The Battle of Stones River

"That Body of Brave Men"

Although Federal forces had met with defeat in many of the major battles of 1862, General-in-Chief Henry Halleck wanted to keep pressure on the Confederacy during the upcoming winter. December campaigns in Virginia, Mississippi, and Tennessee resulted. The Battle of Fredericksburg, Virginia, proved to be a thorough defeat of the Army of the Potomac at the hands of Robert E. Lee. In Mississippi, Grant's advance toward Vicksburg foundered at Chickasaw Bluffs and Holly Springs. With the Emancipation Proclamation due to take effect on the first day of 1863, the Lincoln Administration was desperate for a scrap of positive military news as 1862 neared its end. The president was grateful when operations in Tennessee finally provided the North with a victory, although the battle's outcome was more a matter of interpretation than calculable results. The regulars in the Army of the Cumberland played a key role at the Battle of Stones River, the culminating event of the winter campaign in the Volunteer State, and on December 31, 1862, performed one of the Regular Army's most significant feats of arms in the Civil War. With understandable self-centeredness, many of the regulars afterward believed that the battle would have been lost had it not been for their actions on that New Year's Eve.

* * *

President Lincoln made a good choice in appointing William Rosecrans to command the new Army of the Cumberland, for this

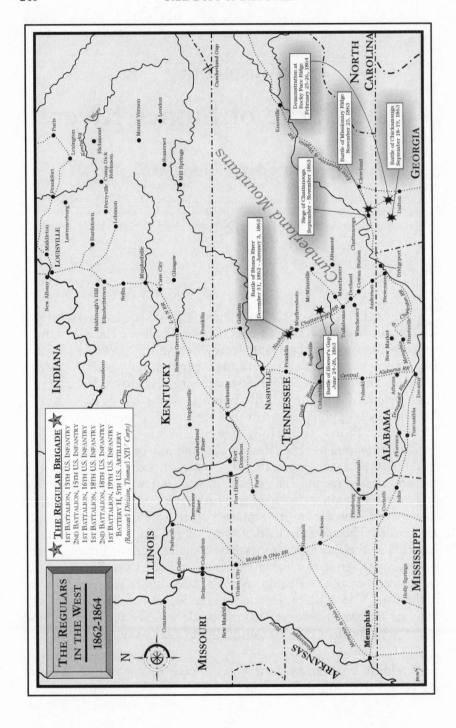

general was a superb organizer, strategist, and troop motivator—just the thing that army needed in the aftermath of the long and seemingly pointless Kentucky Campaign. Rosecrans had much in store for his army's regulars. Instead of dispersing the regulars in different units, Rosecrans planned to group them together in a single brigade. Having only four regular regiments in his command, this proposed brigade was a far cry from the true Iron Column of regulars envisioned by General Winfield Scott at the war's outbreak. But it was the best course of action possible at this point in the war. One brigade was not a large enough force upon which to base an army's operations, but it would provide Rosecrans with a sizable, well trained, and professional organization. Assigning the regulars to a single brigade would also allow them to preserve their unique identity and traditions free from intramural sparring with volunteer officers and state regiments.[1]

Before he formed his new brigade of regulars, Rosecrans tried to do something about the chronic manpower shortage in the regular battalions. One company of regulars, H/1/18th U.S., was ready and waiting at Camp Thomas, and Rosecrans ordered it to join the 18th Infantry detachment in the field. This company linked up with Major Townsend's battalions on November 25. Rosecrans also made sure his army knew about the volunteer-to-regular transfer plan and tried to make the process as reasonable as possible for his volunteer commanders: "The number of Regiments and Detachments of the Regular Army serving in this Department being limited, not more than three volunteers will be enlisted from any one Company." This effort helped the regular battalions somewhat, although much more would be needed if Rosecrans wanted the regulars to approach even half strength.[2] While Rosecrans could not materially affect the problems of Regular Army recruiting, he could influence how the regulars were treated within his department. As a clear signal to the rest of his command that the regulars now had a special status, the day after taking over the Army of the Cumberland, Rosecrans ordered John King's 1/15th U.S. to army headquarters to serve as the commanding general's personal escort and guard. Rosecrans also let it be known that no regulars were to be placed on detached service away from their battalions. Major Townsend sent word to General Steedman that the 18th Infantry was eager to end the detail of troops to the battery in Steedman's brigade, I/4th U.S. Artillery:

> Head Qrs. Detcht 18th U.S.Inf.
> Camp near Galatin Tenn
> November 15th 1862

Lt. Col. Arthur C. Ducat
    Ast. Insp. Genl & Chief of staff
    14th Army Corps Dept of the Cumberland
Colonel

Learning it to be the intention of the Major General Commanding the Dep't of the Cumberland to fill up the regulars in this Army to the maximum number, not excluding the regular Battery attached to this Brigade, I have the honor respectfully to request that the detail of some 40 men ordered to duty with such Battery...may be ordered to rejoin this Detachment as soon as their places are filled by Volunteers.

    I have the honor to remain

> Very Respectfully
>   Your Obt Servant
>
> FREDERICK TOWNSEND
> Major 18th U.S. Inf.
> Comd'g Detcht[3]

The artillery assignment quickly ended for Townsend's men and the forty regulars that had been detailed to Battery I/4th Artillery—almost the equivalent of an additional company—reported back to the 18th Infantry's ranks. The regulars welcomed these changes to the command climate, but they were not enough to prevent Major Steven Carpenter from becoming increasingly discouraged. Carpenter's 1/19th U.S. was still the smallest regular battalion in the Army of the Cumberland, and with the 19th Infantry's lieutenant colonel, Edward A. King, now serving as colonel of the 68th Indiana, the 19th Infantry's regimental depot was all but abandoned and its recruiting service shut down. Carpenter tried to make the War Department aware of what it was like to serve in the field under such conditions, making what the major hoped would be the final request to bring back west the two companies of the 19th that had been assigned to the Army of the Potomac:

> Head Quarters, 19th Regt. Infantry
> Camp near Nashville, Tenn.
> December 16th, 1862.

Genl. L. Thomas
    Adjt. Genl. U.S. Army
    Washington D.C.

Sir,

Although I have made several unsuccessful applications to the War Dept. for the two companies belonging to my battalion and sent East, I can but feel that under the circumstances it is my duty and my right to trouble yourself and through you the Dept. at Washington again upon this subject, for I still entertain hopes that this matter will be properly adjusted. Having served my government for nearly a quarter of a century, and having drilled this battalion, both officers and men from its organization to the present time without assistance from others save those first taught by myself (all officers of experience having been detached from the regiment) and having commanded this portion of my battalion at Shiloh and several skirmishes with scarce two hundred men present at any one of them, I feel that I have a right to ask that the few Companies legitimately belonging to my battalion be placed under my command.

While captains whose only military knowledge had been acquired under my tuition have been placed in command of regiments and Brigades, I have patiently, although not willingly, commanded from four to six small companies numbering for duty from one hundred and fifty to two hundred men.

Being willing and anxious to serve the government under which I live and have received a military education, I feel it to be my duty and my right to ask for the means of serving it (within my capacity) especially, in times like the present, when Brigades and Divisions are commanded by those not competent to drill a Company. I make this assertion not as a charge against any person, (for I presume the government tries to make the best appointments from those available) I simply state it as a fact and an argument in support of my request being granted.

True my *nominal* command is commensurate with my rank, being that of a battalion. But the law regulating the new organization contemplates a Major's command to be eight Companies with a maximum of 800 enlisted men and officers.

It is not unreasonable to suppose that my battalion may be ordered to support a Battery (as in fact it was at Shiloh). It may likely be met by a battalion or Regiment numbering 800 or 1000, and in spite of good conduct on the part of our officers and men both the battalion and battery captured. Now all know that numbers are not apt to be nicely stated in reports of battles, and both the result and report would in such a case disgrace the battalion captured their numbers be what they might.

I am so strongly influenced by the belief of what I have stated that unless the Department is willing to give me my proper command in the West, I herewith request that the Companies now under my Command may be ordered to the east for the purpose of joining those applied for.

The Companies in the East are, I understand, reduced to half their original numbers by desertions and other causes. This if true would render the cost of their transportation comparatively small. Should they be ordered to join I have reason to believe that under the order recently published in this department allowing enlistment from the Volunteer Service, they would soon be filled to the maximum numbers, and that few if any desertions would take place as all Soldiers are better satisfied as well as more efficient when serving together in respectable numbers than when reduced to insignificance.

Hoping that I shall not have to trouble the department again upon this subject I remain very respectfully

Your obedient Servant

S.D. CARPENTER
Major 19th Infy
Comdg Batt & Regiment[4]

Carpenter accompanied this letter with a request that his regimental colors be procured and forwarded to 1/19th U.S. at Nashville, Carpenter's battalion being the only functioning command of the regiment. The War Department never granted Carpenter's request for the flag, and it would be many months before all eight of 1/19th's companies were serving in one place. In the meantime, Carpenter's prediction that his small battalion would trade volleys with a numerically superior enemy turned out to be chillingly accurate.[5]

By the middle of November, the Army of the Cumberland had moved south from Bowling Green, reoccupied Nashville, and was consolidating its position in middle Tennessee. Much more was expected of Rosecrans than simply tightening the Federal grip there. General Halleck wanted the Army of the Cumberland to advance as soon as possible toward Chattanooga and east Tennessee. Rosecrans did not move as quickly as Halleck desired, taking time to reorganize his forces and stockpile supplies before going on the offensive. Restocking Nashville's warehouses would be a slow process. Just as Buell had discovered during the abortive advance on Chattanooga the previous summer, Rosecrans learned that maintaining supply lines and communication between Nashville and Louisville was difficult at best. Confederate cavalry roamed the countryside, tearing up track on the Louisville & Nashville Railroad. Since the Army of the Cumberland's own mounted arm was too ill equipped, poorly led, and weak in numbers to deal with the Confederate raiders, Rosecrans had to station brigades of infantry north of Nashville to repair and protect the rails.

Steedman's brigade drew railroad maintenance duty in early November. It was assigned to repair the South Gallatin Tunnel, on the Louisville & Nashville twenty miles northeast of Nashville. After their first look at the structure, the brigade's volunteers and 18th Regulars knew they had work to do. Colonel John Hunt Morgan's Confederate cavalry had completely wrecked the tunnel on August 12, just prior to Bragg's invasion of Kentucky. Morgan's troopers had set a train on fire and sent it with a full head of steam plowing into a barrier in the tunnel. The impact caused the locomotive's boiler to explode. Cars derailed, a vein of coal caught fire, and the roof of the tunnel collapsed. The destruction was so thorough that the structure was still obstructed three months later. Steedman's troops began clearing it on November 12. After two weeks of backbreaking work, General Thomas reported that the tunnel was partially cleared and trains were proceeding through at cautious speeds.

Although rail and river communications to Nashville were nominally secure by the end of November, the combination of Bragg's Army of Tennessee near Murfreesboro and persistent cavalry raids meant that the Army of the Cumberland's position was a Federal island in a Confederate sea. Southern cavalry forded the Cumberland River near Nashville frequently during the last three months of 1862, raiding depots and tearing up rail lines north of the city. In response, Rosecrans dispatched additional troops to defend the river crossings. During the last week of November, Steedman's brigade moved from the Gallatin Tunnels to the Cumberland River east of Nashville. Prudently keeping some distance between his regulars and volunteers, General Steedman posted Townsend's regulars at Belote's Ford, about twelve miles northeast of Gallatin, while the rest of the brigade encamped a few miles upriver at Cunningham's Ford. Adding guard duty to an already hectic schedule kept the regulars busy. "We have more than we ever had to do," Private Luke Lyman of A/2/18th U.S. wrote to his parents on December 10, "batt. drill twice a day and guard every third day. So we are put through to be sure." Sergeant Amos Fleagle of C/2/18th U.S. noticed a change in the behavior of the local opposition after the regulars arrived at the river: "Before [work on the rail tunnel] was completed, we were on the march for the cumberland river, and after several days march, over hills and valleys, we arrived at Billot Ford, on the river. This is the best & most important ford on the river, & the one by which the Rebels...crossed to commit depredations on the rail road north of the river. But they have kept a respectful distance since we are here, & I do not apprehend much trouble as long as we remain here for the Rebels have never showen any desire to court our acquaintanse, for the Rebels can never finde us napping like some of those raw Volunteers do."[6]

Belote's Ford and a nearby ferry were on the main road linking Gallatin with Lebanon; Major Townsend's battalions kept the crossings under close watch. The river bank on the south side was higher than the terrain on the regulars' side of the river, which afforded potential observers a clear view of the 18th Infantry's activities, so Townsend established his camp in a covered position 200 yards to the rear while keeping a strong picket force stationed at the ford itself. Captain Charles E. Denison of B/2/18th U.S., formerly a civil engineer, surveyed the crossing as soon as the regulars arrived on site. He informed Townsend that the ford was not able to handle wagons and it would take about two days of work to get the banks and riverbed in shape for vehicular traffic. Men on foot or horseback could cross with little difficulty. Townsend knew his position would not be threatened by any large enemy force, but had to stay alert for small patrols and individuals attempting to cross the river.

Although the Confederates usually "kept a respectful distance" from the regulars, suspicious activity abounded throughout the area. On the morning of November 26, Lieutenant John F. Hitchcock scanned the terrain on the opposite riverbank and noticed plumes of smoke ascending from a point a few miles away. General Steedman ordered the regulars to send a force across the river the next day to investigate. Townsend dispatched two companies, one to scour the riverbank to each flank and the other to patrol inland. Captain Ai B. Thompson's E/2/18th U.S. had the inland assignment. Thompson divided the company into two scouting parties, each taking a separate road. The party that Thompson personally led noticed smoke coming from the same general vicinity that Hitchcock had noted the previous day. The volume of smoke and tracks on the road indicated that a large mounted force was encamped nearby, certainly too large for half an infantry company to handle. Thompson's men retraced their steps back to the river. The company along the riverbank had meanwhile discovered two concealed ferryboats. After torching the craft all the regulars crossed back to friendly territory.[7]

Later in the day, an officer from the 2nd Indiana Cavalry informed Major Townsend that a Federal spy had just returned from a scout of the Cumberland's far shore and reported a sizable contingent of Confederate cavalry from Morgan's command encamped three miles away. Townsend sent Captain Thompson with a patrol back across in the early evening. The patrol made its way inland, but Thompson reported seeing no campfires or any other evidence of enemy activity. Suspicious campfires were seen along the riverbank later that night, including one that was set ablaze on the opposite side of Belote's Ford. Townsend alerted his battalions and formed them into line. The regulars captured two civilians who were attempting to cross the river, one carrying a Federal pass of questionable authenticity and the other dressed in a coat adorned with Confederate buttons. Townsend had the prisoners escorted to General Steedman's headquarters and the night quieted down again.

The major sent another patrol across the river the next day but employed a new technique. He rounded up a dozen officers' and quartermaster horses, and combed the battalions for troops who could ride. Townsend placed Lieutenant James Simons of F/2/18th U.S. in charge of the ad hoc cavalry, the lieutenant's eleven years of frontier experience with the Old Army making him a natural choice. Simons's patrol splashed across the Cumberland early in the afternoon of November 29. The regulars reconnoitered the shoreline for a mile and a half in each direction and also moved two miles inland on the Lebanon Pike. They did not encounter any hostile forces. Civilians in the area told them that Morgan's men had departed the previous day.[8]

During the next three weeks the 18th Regulars were called to arms a number of times, but rounding up suspicious persons was the extent of the regulars' active operations along the Cumberland. Lieutenant Anson Mills took advantage of one such alert to rid his company of a despised uniform accouterment. Late on a Saturday night during early December, Major Townsend woke his battalions a few minutes before midnight and told them to be ready to move in two hours with arms, field gear, and four days' rations. Each company was authorized to bring one wagon and mule team. Mills's company, A/3/18th U.S., one of the largest in the command, was not able to squeeze all of its gear onto a single vehicle, so the lieutenant starting going through his company baggage. He came upon a large

chest that was much too heavy to easily lift, and asked his first sergeant what it contained. "The scales, sir." Brass shoulder scales may
have been marginally useful early in the war for enticing recruits to
join the Regular Army, but regular enlisted men quickly discovered
that the accouterment was the one of the banes of their existence:
heavy, useless in the field, something else to account for, polish, and
wear only on parade. "While many intelligent men knew [the
scales'] uselessness," Mills recalled, "no one had the courage to
advocate [their] abandonment." Mills had sufficient courage that
dark December night in 1862. He ordered his first sergeant to throw
the chest into the nearest latrine.

The alert turned out to be a false alarm and the regulars went
back to their tents. It was a Sunday morning, so with the sun's rising, the battalions fell in for inspection. Frock coat and shoulder
scales were the enlisted uniform, and the unadorned shoulders of
A/3/18th were painfully noticeable. As Major Caldwell trooped the
line, he stopped in front of Lieutenant Mills.

"Lieutenant, where are your scales?" Caldwell demanded.

"I abandoned them for want of transportation, sir."

"Your company is out of uniform and I shall have to report you.
Have you made requisition for more?"

Mills replied that he had not and did not intend to. "Although he
ordered me peremptorily to do so, I never did. Whenever my company was inspected by others I was similarly reprimanded, and I
dare say the files of the War Department are today full of reports
condemning me." Mills's fears would prove unfounded, for he was
wearing a star on each shoulder when he retired in 1894.[9]

As of December 10, the 18th Infantry had a commanding officer
who would definitely not let the regulars nap while guarding the
river crossing. Oliver Shepherd returned from his self-imposed exile
on that date, his court of inquiry duties completed. "In rejoining the
Regiment after its recent service in the face of the enemy," Shepherd
wrote upon resuming command of the 18th Infantry battalions, "it
is gratifying to hear of its good conduct, and to observe its present
good condition." Major Townsend resumed command of the 2nd
Battalion.[10]

* * *

The Army of the Cumberland underwent a major reorganization
in November and December 1862. Rosecrans assigned his divisions
to three corps-sized organizations, the Right Wing, Center, and Left

Wing, with McCook, Thomas, and Crittenden as their respective commanders. King's regulars received a new division commander, as Brigadier General Richard Johnson replaced Joshua Sill. Johnson's division became part of McCook's Right Wing. Lovell Rousseau's division was assigned to Thomas's Center, and later in December Rosecrans allotted a special new unit to Rousseau's command. Having groomed his regulars for two months, Rosecrans decided it was time to consolidate the dispersed regular battalions:

SPECIAL	HDQRS. FOURTEENTH ARMY CORPS,
FIELD ORDERS	DEPARTMENT OF THE CUMBERLAND,
No. 23.	Nashville, Tenn., December 18, 1862

* * * * * * *

XV. The battalions of the Fifteenth, Sixteenth, Eighteenth, and Nineteenth Infantry, and Battery H, Fifth Artillery (Captain Guenther), are relieved from duty in the various divisions in which they are now serving, and are assigned to the Third Division, commanded by Maj. Gen. Lovell H. Rousseau. They will constitute a separate brigade, under the command of the senior officer on duty with them.

* * * * * * *

By command of Major-General Rosecrans:

C. GODDARD,
Major and Acting Assistant Adjutant-General.[11]

While it was not difficult for Rosecrans to form the new Regular Brigade, finding a qualified officer to command the unit turned out to be much more problematic. He did not have a spare brigadier on hand in Nashville and, at any rate, was hesitant to give the reigns of a regular unit to a volunteer general who did not also hold a Regular Army commission. When a general was not available to command a brigade, the brigade's senior colonel usually filled the position. That was not a good option for the Regular Brigade either, since most of the colonels of the brigade's regiments were gainfully employed elsewhere: Colonel Fitz-John Porter of the 15th Infantry was then a major general of volunteers commanding the Army of the Potomac's V Corps, while Colonel Andrew Porter of the 16th Infantry and the 19th Infantry's Colonel E.R.S. Canby were both volunteer brigadiers and firmly planted in the Eastern Theater.

There seemed to be only one regimental colonel who had both proper credentials and was theoretically available: Henry B.

Carrington of the 18th Infantry. During the Kentucky operations the previous autumn, Carrington had done well in hastily mustering thousands of new Indiana volunteers and shipping them south to Louisville. In the wake of President Lincoln's announcement of the Emancipation Proclamation in September 1862, Carrington's ardent abolitionist views were now an asset for potential advancement in rank. Rumor had it that the 18th Infantry's colonel would soon become a brigadier general of volunteers. Rosecrans had never met Carrington, but all indications pointed to Carrington being a suitable officer to command the regulars in the field. Rosecrans sent a telegram to Camp Thomas in mid-December, ordering Carrington to close the 18th Infantry's recruiting stations, dispatch all the regiment's officers and recruits to the Army of the Cumberland, and to prepare to assume command of the Regular Brigade in Nashville.[12]

The one man standing in the way of Rosecrans's designs was Henry Carrington. His enthusiasm for field service was just as weak in December 1862 as it had been in December 1861. The colonel's main pastime toward the end of 1862 was the suppression of political dissent and chasing down supposed conspiracies to topple the Federal government (to Carrington, these threats rivaled Confederate military forces in degree of danger to the Union's survival). Governor Morton of Indiana and Governor Tod of Ohio both sent word to Rosecrans that Carrington's services were still required in their states, but whether these were genuine concerns or the result of Carrington prompting is difficult to determine. Carrington's promotion came through in early 1863 and he was given command of the new District of Indiana. This district was carved out of the reorganized Department of the Ohio, whose commander at that time, Major General Horatio Wright, was an old Carrington chum. General Halleck wrote some comments to Wright's successor, Ambrose Burnside, upon hearing of Carrington's district command assignment. If Rosecrans had wanted a military man's opinion of Carrington's abilities, the general-in-chief could have given him an earful:

> It is reported in the newspapers that you have formed Indiana into a separate military district, placing General Carrington in command. The Secretary of War is of opinion that General Carrington is entirely unfitted for such a command. From my conversations with Governors Tod and Morton, I think the Secretary is right. I do not know General Carrington personally, but, from the best information I can get of him, he has not sufficient judgment and brains to qualify him for the

position. He has never been tried in the field. Perhaps he may do better there. I know that the War Department has very little confidence in him. He owes his promotion entirely to political influence.[13]

For whatever reason, Carrington never made a serious attempt to travel south of the Ohio River to take command of the regulars in the field. This was probably just as well, for he probably would have had great difficulty enduring the Army of the Cumberland's upcoming campaigns. With the first candidate for the job not available, Rosecrans looked elsewhere. On Christmas Eve 1862, he sent a message to Brigadier General Robert S. Granger, an 1838 Academy graduate, notifying that officer of an impending assignment to command the Regular Brigade. Granger was the 1st Infantry captain captured in Texas during April 1861 because there was not enough room for his troops on board the steamship *Empire City*. He had not been officially exchanged for active service in the field until August 1862, sidetracking his wartime career for more than a year. Granger had thus far served in obscure staff positions, although he had been promoted to major in the 5th U.S. Infantry during September 1861 and later became a brigadier general of volunteers. In December 1862, Granger was in charge of the post at Bowling Green, Kentucky. Marauding Confederate cavalry was keeping him so busy that he was not able to leave Kentucky and had to decline Rosecrans's offer to command the regulars. Rosecrans accepted the situation for the time being and thus command of the new brigade went to the senior officer on duty with it in Nashville, Lieutenant Colonel Oliver Shepherd. But Rosecrans, fearing that a senior volunteer officer with political connections might somehow force the issue and engineer a hostile takeover of the brigade, did not completely give up his quest to have the man of his choosing leading his regulars.[14]

Shepherd knew he was not Rosecrans's first choice for the command. Not wanting to serve if he did not enjoy his commanding general's confidence, he thought that perhaps it was time to look for another job again. From his field desk he dug out a thick sheaf of papers dated 1861. Colonel Sylvester Churchill had retired during the war's first summer while serving as the army's Inspector General. Oliver Shepherd, then still a brevet major in the 3rd Infantry, conducted an intensive lobbying campaign for the position. He personally wrote to Secretary of State William H. Seward, the ranking New Yorker in Lincoln's cabinet, and also had U.S.

Senator Preston King and Congressmen James B. McKean weigh in
with recommendations to the president and secretary of war. The
writing campaign went for naught, for Major Randolph B. Marcy
received the position and its promotion to full colonel.[15]

Although he no longer had a chance to be the Inspector General
of the army, Shepherd thought that perhaps he could secure a position as a staff officer in the Inspector General's Department. He sent
copies of the earlier paperwork forward again, stating that he would
gladly accept any inspector generalship if one were available. George
Thomas endorsed the December 1863 request with a glowing recommendation of his West Point classmate: "Having been personally
acquainted with Lt. Col. O.L. Shepherd 18th U.S. Infantry for more
than twenty years, and knowing his efficiency and zeal in the discharge of his duties[,] I can conscientiously recommend him as one
of the best and most suitable Officers that could be selected to fill
the vacancy now existing in the Inspector General's Department."
Alexander McCook also took up his pen, writing that Shepherd's
"abilities eminently fit him for this position. He has served with gallantry in the Old Army."

Rosecrans approved Shepherd's requested transfer to the War
Department staff, but these efforts were wasted. There were no
vacancies then available in the Inspector General's Department.
Shepherd remained a lieutenant colonel of infantry. At least there
was a bright side to his current assignment: his request to have the
18th Infantry separated from volunteer regiments had finally been
granted, and he was now in command of an exclusively regular force
of five infantry battalions and an artillery battery. If he could retain
command of the Regular Brigade, his Civil War career might finally
be on the right track. Shepherd set about organizing and training the
brigade using the same methods that had honed the 18th Regulars
the previous year—attention to detail, high standards, and tough
discipline.[16]

The Regular Brigade's official designation was the 4th Brigade,
3rd Division, Center.[17] The assignment of the regulars to Rousseau's
command gave that division the only four-brigade structure in the
Army of the Cumberland, for Rosecrans wanted the Regular Brigade
to serve as a special reserve force, a reliable and highly trained unit
that could handle difficult situations. There was no doubt in the
minds of the regulars about why the brigade had been formed.
Lieutenant Robert P. King of C/1/15th U.S. wrote to his parents on

Christmas Day that "Our battalion has been put into the Regular Brigade, or 'Forlorn Hope,'. ...We are attached to Genl. Rousseau's corps, and our duty is to do the hard fighting." In the Army of the Cumberland's return for December 1862, Rosecrans listed the Regular Brigade under a special category, "Reserve Forces."

Another Rosecrans innovation was his authorization on December 19 of distinctive flags for each corps, division, and brigade. The Right Wing flag was crimson, Center was light blue, and Left Wing was pink. Division flags were the same color as their corps flag, adding white stars corresponding to the division's numerical designation. Rosecrans assigned the Regular Brigade a flag like no other: "The headquarters flags of all brigades will be the flags of their divisions, with the number of the brigade in black, 8 inches long, in the center of each star. That of the brigade of regulars, however, will, instead of the white star and black number, have simply a golden star." With regimental flags for New Army regular outfits being such a rarity, Shepherd wasted little time procuring the Regular Brigade's distinctive light blue and gold banner. Lieutenant King mentioned it in his Christmas letter: "Our battle flag is of blue silk with a gold star in the centre." An enthused Arthur Carpenter also made note of the flag in his own late-December correspondence: "All the regulars have been put into one brigade. We are the brigade of the *'golden Star'*. ...it is the best brigade in the service."[18]

On December 23, a crowd gathered on the streets of Gallatin. The 18th Infantry had packed up its gear at Belote's Ford and was heading to Nashville to join the new brigade of regulars. George Thomas turned out his former division to bid Shepherd's troops farewell. Lieutenant Henry Freeman remembered the 18th Infantry's departure as an emotional moment: "The sidewalks were filled by officers and men of the old division, and as the column, with our fine band at the head, swept by in perfect alignment and cadence, we were greeted with a continuous round of applause. We had served a year with the old brigade, and although at first our relations were somewhat strained, we parted the best of friends. As we passed through their camp we halted for an hour to say good-by, and their hospitality was such that when we resumed our march there were a good many of us for whom the road was scarcely wide enough to travel in." Freeman's recollections, written long afterward, do not tell the whole story. It is safe to assume that respect did not generate all the applause he heard. Undoubtedly some of the noise was cheers of good riddance. Hard feelings about the 18th Infantry among the volunteers of Steedman's brigade were still present as late as 1877, when a veteran of the 9th Ohio wrote: "On December 23 the 18th Regular Infantry left our brigade. In this war...comradeship between regulars and volunteers never throve, especially among junior officers."[19]

The tense situation in Steedman's brigade contrasts greatly with life in Rousseau's old brigade of Johnson's division, where the regulars of the 15th, 16th, and 19th Infantry enjoyed a good relationship with their volunteer counterparts. Lovell Rousseau's command style made the difference. Instead of interfering with the regulars during his tenure as a brigade commander, Rousseau leaned on the regular officers for advice. He encouraged his volunteers to emulate the regulars' professionalism, much as General Scott had intended in the early days of the war when he recommended that the Union Army consist of both volunteers and regulars. Colonel Harvey M. Buckley, who commanded the brigade after Rousseau's promotion to division command in June 1862, followed the general's precedents. When these regular battalions received orders to leave their old brigade, there was genuine regret on both sides. The brigade's volunteer officers held a meeting to voice their displeasure at having the regulars ordered away. They made sure each of the regular units received a copy of the meeting's minutes:

At a meeting of the Officers of the 4th Brigade, Dec 20th 1862, to express their sentiments on parting with the Battalions of the 15th, 16th and 19th Regular Infantry, and Battery H, 5th Art, the following Regts. were represented: Louisville Legion [5th Kentucky], 1st Ohio, 6th Indiana, and 93d Ohio.

On motion Lt. Col. Strong of the 93d Ohio took the chair and Lt. A. Sidney Smith, Louisville Legion, was appointed Secretary.

Capt. A.H. Speed, Louisville Legion, in a neat and appropriate speech, stated the subject of the meeting, and moved a committee of eight be appointed to draw up resolutions, which was carried.

The chairman appointed the following Officers to said committee: Capts. Speed and Ferguson, Louisville Legion, Captain O'Connell and Lieut Leonard, 1st Ohio, Capts. Cavanough and Glasscock, 6th Indiana, and Capts. Martin and Smith, 93d Ohio.

The Committee retired and soon after reported the following resolutions, which were carried unanimously.

Whereas by the orders of the Gen'l Commanding we have been separated from the Battalions of the 15th, 16th and 19th Infantry, and Battery H, 5th Artillery, lately attached to this Brigade. Therefore *Resolved*, That while we submit to the orders of our superiors, we cannot help but feel that a connection of more than twelve months has united us in the closest bonds of friendship, and inspired us with a confidence only felt in those ever tried and found true, and that having fought side by side, on the horrible field of Shiloh, we felt that we had beside us friends staunch and true, whom we could on the bloody field of battle, rely on to the last.

Resolved That we have ever found the Officers of the Regular Army attached to our Brigade, to be gentlemen in every sense of the word, and while we regret their absence, we will never cease to hope they may find, wherever duty calls them, friends as true as those they left behind.

Resolved That we cordially wish in offering to Majors King, Slemmer, and Carpenter and Subordinates and to Capt Guenther and Lieut Ludlow of the Battery our best wishes that in future they may continue to merit the just praise so cheerfully given them by their grateful friends.[20]

A staff officer of Johnson's division agreed with the committee's sentiments. "What was General Rousseau's gain was the division's loss," William Dodge wrote on the transfer of the regulars from Johnson's division of the Right Wing to Rousseau's of the Center. "An attachment existed between the regulars and the volunteers which was lasting and of the most happy character."[21]

To genuine applause, the old 4th Brigade regulars marched out of Nashville and established a camp five miles south of town on the Franklin Turnpike. The 18th Infantry joined them on December 25. Also on Christmas Day, Rosecrans released the 15th Infantrymen from their duties at Army of the Cumberland headquarters and Major King's troops reported for duty with the Regular Brigade. Shepherd's command was the largest body of Regular Army troops thus far assembled in the Western Theater, five infantry battalions with forty-three companies between them. Adding in the artillerymen of Battery H, the brigade mustered more than 1,500 regulars. Although the Regular Brigade was the newest unit in Rosecrans's army, it contained some of the Army of the Cumberland's most experienced company- and field-grade officers. Shepherd came to the brigade with a ready-made staff, for he simply transformed his 18th Infantry Detachment staff into a brigade headquarters. A capable officer commanded each battalion and the battery. Shiloh veterans King and Carpenter led the 15th and 19th Infantry. Major Adam

Slemmer of the 16th had been on staff duty during the first half of 1862 and thus had not been present at Shiloh, but more than twelve years of soldiering had armed him with plenty of experience. Majors Townsend and Caldwell of the 18th had not yet led their battalions in a major engagement, but each had seen combat while serving elsewhere. Lieutenants Frank Guenther and Israel Ludlow were among the Union Army's most skilled artillerymen, although having only two officers assigned to Battery H instead of the authorized five kept them busy. Their workload eased somewhat in late December when Lieutenant Joshua A. Fessenden reported for duty with Guenther's battery. This was Fessenden's first assignment in the artillery, although during the previous year he had served seven months as a sergeant and lieutenant in the 1st Maine Cavalry and another four with the regulars as a lieutenant in the 1st U.S. Cavalry.[22]

It was fortuitous that the Regular Brigade had experienced leaders and well-trained troops, for Shepherd had little time to shake out the new unit. Corporal Eli Tarbell of the 19th U.S. had a feeling that a campaign was in the wind on December 23: "nothing much doing onley Camp duty,, it rained a little. We are under marching orders. the Rank & file neve Know what is going on, But from Presant Movments I think thare will be a fight Somewhare Soon. Every thing is So quiet,, it broods no Good." Christmas Day was a busy one as the regulars began to sort out their new camp, say hello to old friends, and meet new ones. Orders came down in mid-morning to pack up and prepare to march, only to be countermanded at noon. After the frenzied activity of packing and unpacking was dispensed with, most of the regulars tried to squeeze in some holiday festivities. The holiday fare for some was meager. "I have just eat my Christmas dinner," Private David Smith, 16th Infantry, wrote to his wife that evening, "a pint cup full of bean supe & Bread not vary expensive but we are glad to get as good a dinner." Sergeant Arthur Carpenter received a memorable gift from the War Department: "at last on christmas I received my appointment as 2d Lt. in the U.S. Army, a very nice christmas gift, the best one I have had for some time. ...we officers had a big dinner on christmas and enjoyed ourselves first rate." Arthur Carpenter had his battalion commander to thank for the commission. Major Steven Carpenter had sent no less than three requests to the War Department over the preceding months requesting commissions for Sergeant Carpenter and also for 1st Sergeants Douglass Edwards and George Johnson: "These men have all been well tried as Sergeants...are intelligent, of good habits, and of sufficient education to make good Infantry officers."[23]

Lieutenant King of the 15th U.S. did not particularly enjoy his holiday, but thought that something would happen soon: "my Christmas is very dull, very little like Christmas of old. I am in hopes my New Year will be livelier, as we expect a battle on or before the first of the year. ...You may expect shortly to hear of a terrible battle in this section, for it is bound to come, and when these two armies meet, it will be dreadful." According to Lieutenant Louis Hosea of the 16th Infantry, the regulars of Rousseau's old 4th Brigade "had barely time to give to our comrades of the Eighteenth a hearty welcome when our cherished hopes of brigade drills, inspections, etc., in true 'regular' style, were swept away by orders to move to the fateful battlefield of Stone River."[24]

* * *

Middle Tennessee was farm country. In contrast with the mountains of east Tennessee and the cotton fields along the Mississippi River to the west, the center section of the state was a nineteenth-century breadbasket. The region was blessed with fertile soil and a cooler climate than the subtropical Deep South, and it also had a well-developed transportation network—at least by Southern standards. A number of turnpikes and railroads converged on Nashville, where the Cumberland River provided the region with a seasonal outlet to America's interior waterways. Two thoroughfares linked Nashville with Murfreesboro. The Nashville-Murfreesboro Turnpike followed a fairly straight route between the two cities, with the tracks of the Nashville & Chattanooga Railroad just a stone's throw away in some spots, paralleling the turnpike for much of its distance. During normal times, passengers and commerce kept the two roads heavily traveled.

The times were, of course, anything but normal as William Rosecrans contemplated offensive operations in middle Tennessee during the winter of 1862–1863. The roads leading southeast out of Nashville were important not for commercial reasons but rather for where they led: toward east Tennessee. Moving an army from Nashville to Chattanooga involved crossing a series of rivers and rough terrain features, meaning that any Federal advance from middle to eastern Tennessee had to be carefully planned and supported by large supply stockpiles. Rosecrans appreciated the difficulties involved, and no amount of presidential or War Department prodding could get him to move toward Chattanooga before he was good and ready. The Army of the Cumberland may have spent the entire winter in Nashville had it not been for the actions of Braxton Bragg and Jefferson Davis.

From his Army of Tennessee headquarters at Murfreesboro, General Bragg planned for Rosecrans to encounter more than just geographic and logistical challenges on the road to east Tennessee. Bragg wanted to concentrate the entire Army of Tennessee at Murfreesboro, but supply considerations forced him to disperse his command. The shaky Confederate logistical system could not fully support Bragg's troops, so the Southerners had to rely on the local countryside for much of their subsistence. To facilitate this organized foraging, Bragg stationed Major General William J. Hardee's Corps between Triune and Eagleville, about fifteen miles west of the main body of Confederates at Murfreesboro, and one division of Polk's Corps at Readyville, twelve miles to the east. While this dispersal concerned Bragg somewhat, he did not think Rosecrans was going anywhere soon. To make the Army of the Cumberland's winter stay in Nashville as uncomfortable as possible, in mid-December Bragg sent about half his cavalry on raids into southern Kentucky and western Tennessee. Jefferson Davis was also certain Rosecrans was not a threat for the moment. The Confederate president detached Carter L. Stevenson's Division of 7,500 men from Bragg on December 18 and shipped the unit off to Mississippi, where U.S. Grant seemed to be a bit more energetic than Rosecrans.

Rosecrans observed these Confederate troop movements with great interest. Noting that Bragg's army was now stripped of many of its horsemen and reduced by the Mississippi-bound infantrymen, Rosecrans decided it was time to strike the Southerners at Murfreesboro. Having spent two months stockpiling supplies and preparing, the Army of the Cumberland was at last ready to take the field as 1862 came to an end. Rosecrans was not ready to start moving all the way to Chattanooga, but he deemed a short foray down the Nashville Turnpike to be well within his army's capabilities.[25]

* * *

The bounty of the surrounding countryside resulted in Nashville's sporting of many fine dining establishments, even during wartime. Bassett's Restaurant was one of the best and most popular. Lieutenant Henry Freeman and a few other officers of the 18th U.S. went to Bassett's on the morning of December 25, intent on having a proper Christmas breakfast. After the hustle and bustle of the previous few days, they were looking forward to a good meal. Unfortunately, Freeman ended up not enjoying anything close to Bassett's culinary delights that morning, nor would he for some time to come: "We had just seated ourselves...when an orderly appeared at the door saying that the regiment was about to march. We were in our best uniforms, and hurried out, hoping to find time to change, but we found the line formed and the wagons loaded." Freeman's orderly had managed to secure the lieutenant's sword, rubber blanket, and haversack with three days' rations. Freeman reluctantly donned his field gear, worrying that his frock coat and dress epaulets were about to suffer irreparable damage. To his immense relief, word came down shortly thereafter that the movement was a false alarm. The breakfast at Bassett's was canceled, but at least Freeman did not have to spend Chrstmas Day on the march in his formal attire.[26]

Genuine march orders were issued the next day, and the Army of the Cumberland fanned out southward from Nashville on three routes: Thomas by way of the Wilson Pike toward Franklin, McCook on the Nolensville Pike, and Crittenden on the main road to Murfreesboro. Rosecrans hoped Thomas's and McCook's movements would either isolate Hardee at Triune, or outflank him and force his withdrawal. Rosecrans believed that Bragg would contest the Federal advance from a position along Stewart's Creek, ten miles northwest of Murfreesboro. Should Bragg do so, Rosecrans's Center and Right Wing would be in position to outflank the main body of the Confederate army.

By the evening of December 26, while the Regular Brigade and Rousseau's division camped near Brentwood, advance Union units contacted the northernmost Confederate cavalry screens near Nolensville and La Vergne. As soon as Bragg learned of Rosecrans's movements, he ordered Hardee to close up with the rest of the Army of Tennessee. Most of Hardee's troops were actually nearer to Eagleville, well south of Triune, so they were easily able to escape the approaching Federal columns. Bragg did not sally forth to Stewart's Creek, further complicating Rosecrans's plan. The Confederate commander instead decided to defend a position just northwest of Murfreesboro. He also ordered the Southern cavalry remaining in middle Tennessee to make its presence felt and harass Rosecrans's columns, which forced the Northerners to proceed cautiously. The weather was also a factor. Chilling rains soaked middle

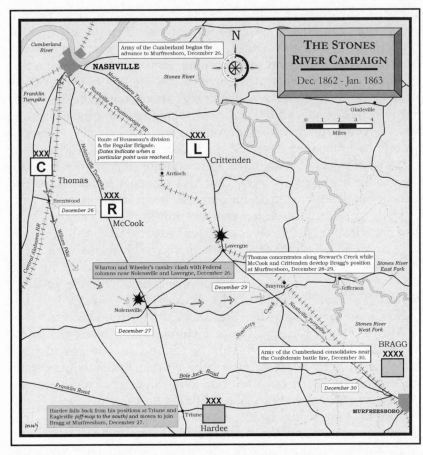

N

Cumberland
River

Army of the Cumberland begins the
advance to Murfreesboro, December 26.

NASHVILLE

Stones River

**THE STONES
RIVER CAMPAIGN**

Dec. 1862 - Jan. 1863

Franklin
Turnpike

Gladeville

0   1   2   3   4
Miles

Route of Rousseau's division
& the Regular Brigade.
*(Dates indicate when a
particular point was reached.)*

XXX
L
Crittenden

XXX
C

Thomas

Antioch

Brentwood

XXX
R

McCook

December 26

Lavergne

Thomas concentrates along Stewart's Creek while
McCook and Crittenden develop Bragg's position
at Murfreesboro, December 28-29.

Stones River
East Fork

Wharton and Wheeler's cavalry clash with Federal
columns near Nolensville and Lavergne, December 26.

December 29

Smyrna

Jefferson

Nolensville

December 27

Stones River
West Fork

BRAGG

Army of the Cumberland consolidates near
the Confederate battle line, December 30.

XXXX

Bole Jack Road

December 30

Franklin Road

Hardee falls back from his positions at Triune and
Eagleville *(off-map to the south)* and moves to join
Bragg at Murfreesboro, December 27.

XXX
Triune

Hardee

MURFREESBORO

jmwj

Tennessee four of the next five days. Dense fog blanketed the countryside each morning, usually not burning off until afternoon. For a
recently reorganized army under a new commander, the difficult
weather magnified command-and-control problems and slowed the
Federal advance even more.[27]

With the bulk of Confederate forces having fallen back from
Triune and Eagleville, on December 27 Thomas's column[28] moved
eastward from the Wilson Pike. Negley's division, which had
marched to Nolensville on the first day of the advance, proceeded to
Smyrna, while Rousseau's went to Nolensville. Little Federal move-
ment took place the next day, the devout Rosecrans having declared
Sunday, December 28 a day of rest. But he did allow a brigade from
McCook's corps to scout the region south of Triune to determine

Hardee's whereabouts. After it was determined that Hardee had moved to Murfreesboro and that the entire Southern army was now concentrated there, in the early evening of December 28, Rosecrans ordered the Army of the Cumberland's Left Wing and Center to concentrate along Stewart's Creek while McCook's Right Wing approached Murfreesboro from the west. Thomas ordered Rousseau to move immediately that night eastward from Nolensville. The column got underway as darkness fell, marching over unimproved roads toward the Nashville Pike. Lieutenant Freeman thought the march was as difficult as any he had experienced:

> It had been drizzling nearly all day, but toward sunset heavy masses of clouds began to gather near the horizon...and in a few moments the clouds broke upon us like a deluge. In a little time the dim road became a bog, and the darkness so intense that we could scarce see the man before us. The march through the sticky slug, from which we could scarcely draw our feet became fearfully tiresome. The road was occupied by what seemed to be an interminable train of wagons going in the opposite direction which mingled with our battery which seeking to pass the wagons, came into collision with them, and ended in all being stuck fast in the mud. The orders of the officers, the shouts of the teamsters, and the oaths of the cannoniers mingled with the reports of distant artillery and altogether produced a deafening tumult from which we could not escape without leaving behind us numerous stragglers, and the further we advanced the greater the number grew. Our hard...march had exhausted the men, and the shelter...of the wood through which we were marching offered to the tired men the opportunity of catching a few moments of rest. Many yielded to the temptations counting upon joining the Regiment at the first halt[.] The officers could do nothing. Companies and regiments mingled and in the obscurity we could no longer tell whether we were in our own column or not. The officers all kept in but nearly one third of the men were missing at the role call when we halted for the night at nearly one o'clock.[29]

The rain ended about midnight. The sky cleared, sending the temperature plummeting and adding to the misery of the soggy troops. The Regular Brigade passed through camps of Negley's division just prior to halting early on the morning of December 29. Some of Negley's regiments had reveille as the exhausted regulars dropped to the ground. Despite their fatigue, some of Shepherd's troops remained awake long enough to hear the fife and drums of a nearby regiment rousing out some slumbering soldiers. "The fifer was an artist," Lieutenant Freeman remembered years afterward when writing of that long night, "he played Bonaparte's march, and never shall I forget the piercing melody which filled the air of that frosty starlit night; it floated away above the drums, and seemed as if it would reach the ends of the earth. We all sat up to listen, and it lingered in our ears until, tired, cold, and hungry, we fell asleep."

December 29 dawned clear and cold. Lieutenant Colonel Shepherd, never fond of his soldiers straggling out of ranks, dispatched mounted officers to retrace the route of march. As the sun rose they herded forward the troops who had fallen out during the stormy night. By mid-morning, most of the stragglers were back with their companies. Rousseau's division remained in camp near Stewart's Creek that day, while the rest of the army continued to concentrate along the Nashville Pike northwest of Murfreesboro. On the morning of the 30th, the regulars crossed the creek and advanced four miles toward Murfreesboro. The Army of the Cumberland formed line of battle five miles northwest of Murfreesboro on the west side of Stones River. Bragg's army was arrayed less than a half mile from the Federal position. Wanting to cover both the northern and western approaches to Murfreesboro, four of Bragg's divisions were positioned west of the river, while a fifth was to the east.[30]

The terrain of the area would play a significant role in the upcoming fighting. By the 1860s, the best farmland near Murfreesboro had long before been cleared and planted. Much of the area in which the armies assembled was rolling pasture and crop land. The ground sloped gently upward from Stones River, a shallow but steeply banked waterway, dotting the landscape with a few small knolls. The elevation of these knolls was slight, and most travelers on the thoroughfares through the region probably never noticed them. Yet, to a trained eye looking from a military point of view, these knolls were crucial. Artillery positioned on them could dominate movement as far as the guns could shoot. Another significant terrain feature were dense groves of cedar trees. Like many species of pine, cedars grow well in soil that is loose, rocky, sandy, or otherwise well drained—the kind of ground farmers wouldn't look at twice. The locals had therefore ignored a strip of land between Stones River and Overall Creek, just northwest of where the Nashville & Chattanooga's tracks crossed the Nashville Turnpike. This was a belt of limestone outcropping that was definitely the kind of ground

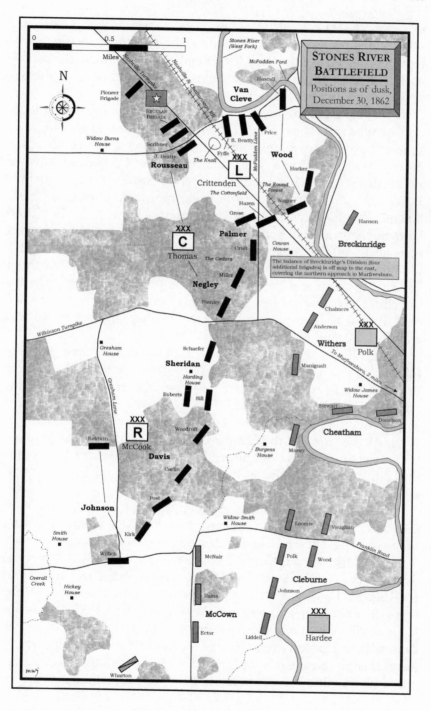

STONES RIVER
BATTLEFIELD

Positions as of dusk,
December 30, 1862

The balance of Breckinridge's Division (four
additional brigades) is off map to the east,
covering the northern approach to Murfreesboro.

Stones River
(West Fork)

McFadden Ford

Hascall

Van
Cleve

Price

S. Beatty

Wood

Harker

XXX
L

Crittenden

The Round
Forest

The Cottonfield

Hazen   Wagner

Grose

Palmer   Hanson

Cruft   Breckinridge

Cowan
House

XXX
C

Thomas   The Cedars

Miller

Negley

Stanley

Chalmers

Anderson

Withers   XXX
                 Polk

Wilkinson Turnpike   Maniguault

Gresham
House   Schaefer

Sheridan   Widow James
                  House
Harding
House   Stewart

Roberts   Sill   Donelson

XXX   Woodruff   Cheatham
R

McCook   Burgess   Maney
                House
Davis

Carlin

Post

Johnson   Loomis   Vaughan

Smith   Franklin Road
House
          Kirk   Widow Smith
                        House   Polk   Wood

Willich   McNair

Overall   Cleburne
Creek   Hickey   Johnson
          House   Rains

McCown
          Ector   Liddell   Hardee
                                          XXX

Wharton

Pioneer
Brigade

REGULAR
BRIGADE

Widow Burns
House

Scribner

J. Beatty

Rousseau   Fyffe

The Knoll

Nashville Turnpike

Nashville & Chattanooga RR

McFadden Lane

Gresham Lane

To Murfreesboro, 2 miles

Baldwin

Smith
House

mwj

N

0   0.5   1

Miles

in which cedars can thrive. They grew tightly packed among the rocks, interspersed with hardwoods and a few small clearings. The terrain provided ample cover for defending infantrymen, the combination of cedar and limestone forming a number of natural rifle pits that were almost bulletproof.

Few Federal troops gave the cedars[31] more than a passing glance on December 30. They marched right past them and kept going. The southern end of Rosecrans's line was more than a mile south of the groves. McCook's Right Wing confronted the Confederates, while Crittenden's Left Wing prepared to cross Stones River to deliver Rosecrans's main attack the following morning. Thomas's Center had only Negley's division in the line, inserted between McCook and Crittenden. Rousseau's division was the army's reserve, posted a mile north of the cedars on the Nashville Pike near Rosecrans's headquarters. The army commander had been anxious all day about having Rousseau and the regulars in the proper position. "On the march forward several dispatches from General Rosecrans reached me," Rousseau reported, "asking exactly where my command was and the hour and minute of the day."

To facilitate the movement of supply wagons and artillery through the dense forest, the Army of the Cumberland's Pioneer Brigade (a unit that was also a Rosecrans's innovation) cut roads through the cedars. After thirteen hours of labor under intermittent enemy fire, the pioneers managed to clear a number of crude pathways. As the Army of the Cumberland arrayed itself in battle order, the soldiers in its ranks did not realize that the cedars and the roads through them, positions well to their rear, would become focal points of the upcoming battle.[32]

Both Rosecrans and Bragg intended to strike on the morning of December 31. Their attack plans were virtually identical: amass forces on the left and throw them against the opponent's right. Rosecrans instructed General Crittenden to have two divisions of the Army of the Cumberland's Left Wing cross Stones River by way of McFadden's Ford at 8:00 A.M. and attack the Confederates on the east side of the river. During the night of December 30–31, Lieutenant Colonel Shepherd was field officer of the day at Army of the Cumberland Headquarters. He and Lieutenant Anson Mills, now a member of the Regular Brigade's staff, rode the lines that night transmitting Rosecrans's orders to division and brigade commanders.[33]

The regulars prepared for battle. Some kept their fears to themselves; others talked things over with comrades. "Everyone knew that in all likelihood an engagement would take place the next day," recalled Captain Henry Haymond, commander of E/3/18th Infantry. "Officers collected in groups and chatted silently over the events of the morrow, and gave each other the addresses of their friends and how to dispose of their effects in case they would be killed." There was much discussion in the camp of Captain William J. Fetterman's A/2/18th Infantry. This company had been heavily recruited from Delaware County, Ohio, and most of its members knew each others' families. Others were blood relatives, such as Luke, Oliver, and Phillip Lyman, brothers all. Luke did not have too much to worry about, for he had been detailed as a cook for Captain Fetterman and thus would remain in camp and not take part in the upcoming battle. As the private prepared the captain's dinner on the evening of December 30, a nervous sergeant, J. Nelson Pierce, walked up. Pierce, a close friend of the Lyman brothers, helped Oliver Lyman with his duties and asked the cook to march in ranks next to him should the regulars be committed on the morrow. The sergeant had been worried all day about his fate and was seen diving for cover whenever distant cannonading was occasionally heard. If he was killed, he wanted Luke Lyman to write his mother with the details. Cook Lyman agreed, although he was not enthused about marching in ranks. He tried to convince his friend that they would both make it through the day in fine shape.[34]

Many other regulars were also nervous. As the sun rose on December 31, members of C/2/18th searched through their largely empty haversacks for something to eat. Corporal Thomas Long walked over to one of his messmates, Private Robert Kennedy, and said: "Bob, this is the last time I shall see the sun rise." The corporal had dreamed during the night that he would die the next day. Kennedy did not have much time to reply, for the company was falling in. As the ranks formed, the private informed his company commander, Captain Ansel B. Denton, about Long's premonition. Denton walked down the ranks to the position of the worried noncommissioned officer.

"Long, do you think you will be shot today?"

"Yes, Captain, I'll never fire my gun."

Denton told him to fall out and report to the brigade surgeon, but Long had already resigned himself to his fate: "No, Captain, I'll die like a man, right with this company."[35]

As was his habit before battle, Lieutenant Colonel Shepherd released from custody any soldiers under charges so they could take their places in ranks. Captain Henry Belknap had a half dozen men from his company, B/3/18th, under guard. When the battalion adjutant, Lieutenant Phisterer, informed Belknap that prisoners were to march with their companies, the captain went to his company wagon to ensure his troublemakers collected their arms and equipment. Each one did except Private John A. Mallory, a soldier who was, according to Belknap, "not wanting in natural ability, but was not reliable." Belknap waited by the wagon as long as he could before joining Company B on the battalion line, leaving instructions with Corporal William Reed, the teamster in charge of the vehicle, to be on the lookout for the missing soldier.[36]

Rousseau put his division in motion a little after six o'clock in the morning. It marched a short distance southward on the Nashville Pike and halted in a large cotton field about a half-mile behind the Army of the Cumberland's main line. To the division's left was a small knoll, on either side of which ran the turnpike and railroad. To Rousseau's right was part of the limestone and cedar belt. Rousseau formed the division in a column of brigades, ready to react to any call for reinforcements during the upcoming fight. Colonel John Beatty's brigade was in front with Colonel Benjamin F. Scribner's brigade following. The Regular Brigade occupied the third line (Rousseau's other brigade, Brigadier General John C. Starkweather's, was then about eight miles to the northwest guarding Jefferson Ford on Stones River). With well over an hour remaining before the Federal attack was scheduled to begin, Rousseau's 5,000 troops stacked arms and waited.

While Brigadier General Horatio P. Van Cleve's division crossed Stones River in preparation for the Federal attack, Bragg's advance got underway. The right of Rosecrans's line, Richard W. Johnson's division of McCook's Right Wing, caught the brunt of the initial assault. Johnson's troops were almost completely unprepared for the attack, even though Confederate pickets during the previous night occupied positions as close as 300 yards from the Federal camps. Major General John P. McCown's Division slammed into Johnson's men at about half past six. Patrick Cleburne's Division advanced behind McCown's ranks. As McCown veered to the northwest while engaging Johnson's division, Cleburne's men closed with the next division in the Federal line, Brigadier General Jefferson C. Davis's. Johnson's entire division and Colonel P. Sidney Post's brigade of Davis's division quickly crumbled, but one of Davis's brigades, commanded by Colonel William P. Carlin, put up a respectable fight. Carlin's men doggedly held their ground for a short time against Cleburne, but mounting pressure eventually caused Carlin to fall back to the northeast, toward the position of Brigadier General Phillip Sheridan's division.[37]

About half an hour after McCown and Cleburne started to hammer the Union right, Major General Benjamin F. Cheatham's Division began the advance against the center of the Union line. Sheridan's division defended this area. Sheridan, one of the few senior officers of McCook's wing who had suspected that Bragg might attack on December 31, had his command ready. Along with Carlin's rallied brigade and Colonel William E. Woodruff's brigade (of Davis's division), Sheridan's command offered determined resistance and provided a much-needed check on the Southern advance. Cheatham failed to coordinate the attacks of his brigades, which allowed Sheridan to conduct a masterful fighting withdrawal. By nine o'clock, Sheridan, Woodruff, and Carlin had been forced back across the Wilkinson Pike and had entered the southern edge of the cedars. Negley's division secured Sheridan's left flank, but on Sheridan's right, Carlin and Woodruff's brigades, casualty ridden and disorganized, continued to fall back. Sheridan refused his right flank by positioning two of his own brigades on a line to the northwest, deeper into the cedars. This division commander had done all he could do to disrupt Bragg's attack, but he needed support on the right and ammunition for all to accomplish anything further. As Sheridan's tired men settled into their latest positions, McCown's and Cleburne's Divisions were preparing to maneuver around Sheridan's right and carry the fight into the rear of the Federal position.[38]

The men of Rousseau's division could only listen and speculate on what was happening as the sounds of battle reached them. Brigade commanders ordered their men to unstack weapons and lay down. They knew something had gone desperately wrong as the sounds grew steadily louder and stray Confederate fire began to reach the cotton field. One of the first incoming bullets went completely through an 18th Infantrymen's arm and then struck Corporal

Thomas Long above the left eye, killing him instantly. His disturbing prediction of seeing his last sunrise unfortunately came to pass.[39]

Rosecrans finally realized that his Right Wing was in dire straits. To halt Bragg's advance before it reached the Nashville Pike in the rear of the Federal army, Rosecrans committed Rousseau's division, the Army of the Cumberland's only reserve. Reuben Jones, a private in 1/19th U.S., remembered the moment the order came: "We were to act as a Reserve & we little expected the terrible battle that was close on to us. ...The woods were darkened with soldiers flying from the line of battle. some wounded—others without hats or guns— seemed scared to death perfectly crazy. Rousseau viewed the crisis with tears in his eyes and he rode before his veterans & spoke with tears rolling down his cheek & we were warned by him of what was left for us to do to rescue that portion (or division) of the army from a ruinous disaster. we must turn the tide of battle."[40]

At 9:00 A.M., General Thomas ordered Rousseau to take his division into the cedars to shore up Sheridan's right flank. "Old Rousseau is here and intends to stay!" the division commander bellowed out as he rode past his nervous command. The men got on their feet and formed column. The division quickly crossed the cotton field's 300 yards of open ground. Using one of the roads cut by the Pioneer Brigade the previous day, it entered the belt of dense cedar groves. "This ground was new and unknown to us all," Rousseau later reported. "The woods were almost impassable to infantry, and artillery was perfectly useless." After advancing about half a mile into the cedars on the Pioneer Road, Rousseau's troops came abreast of Sheridan's right. Rousseau ordered his lead brigade, Beatty's, to move left and adjacent to Sheridan, while the Regular Brigade was to fall in on Beatty's right. The general posted Scribner's brigade in reserve one hundred yards behind the forward units.[41]

Lieutenant Guenther brought his six guns across the cotton field with the Regular Brigade. As the brigade's column entered the cedars, Battery H's commander concluded that his guns were in the wrong place: "Finding it impossible to operate with the battery in so dense a wood, I reported to General Rousseau, who, after seeing the impossibility of taking up a proper position, ordered the battery into action in the open field, which it had previously left." Guenther moved his guns back across the cotton field, eventually placing them atop a small knoll between the Nashville Pike and the bed of the Nashville & Chattanooga Railroad. Battery H's position was on

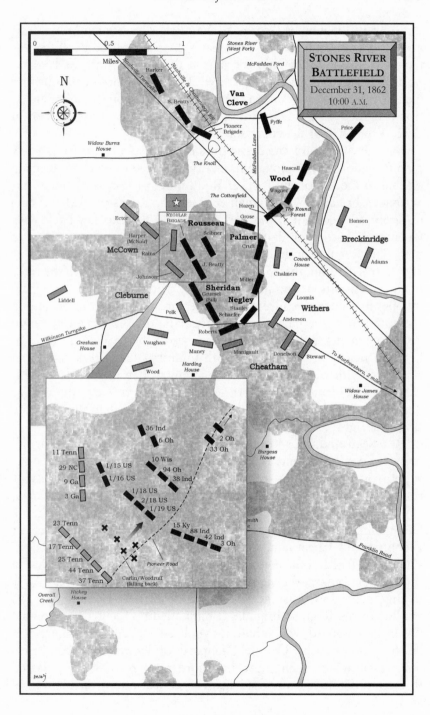

STONES RIVER
BATTLEFIELD
December 31, 1862
10:00 A.M.

the right of Lieutenant George W. Van Pelt's 1st Michigan Artillery, another battery assigned to Rousseau's division. Alfred Pirtle, a lieutenant from the 10th Ohio serving on Rousseau's staff, had earlier positioned the Michigan guns there. Pirtle had chosen the ground well, for the knoll was an excellent artillery position. Its slight elevation provided the gunners with a clear field of fire across the cotton field to the edge of the cedar forest.[42]

Back in the cedars, the dense trees made a shamble of Rousseau's plan for an orderly deployment. Beatty managed to place his brigade on line to the left of the Pioneer Road more or less as planned, but Scribner's brigade was fragmented. General Rousseau ordered two of Scribner's regiments, the 2nd and 33rd Ohio, to fall back with Guenther's battery and provide support should the guns require help. The Regular Brigade was also in pieces. The first two units of Shepherd's column, the 15th and 16th Infantry, deployed to the right of the road without too much difficulty. King's and Slemmer's battalions then advanced deeper into the forest. They were becoming separated from the balance of the regulars, for the three remaining battalions had a difficult time deploying off the road to fill the gap between Beatty's right and the 16th Infantry's left. While Shepherd struggled with deploying the 18th Infantry battalions and 1/19th U.S., he sent Lieutenant Robert Sutherland, the brigade adjutant, to King, ordering the major to take charge of the two battalions on the brigade's right.[43]

Rousseau and his subordinates could have straightened out the mess given enough time, but that was a Federal commodity in short supply on the last day of 1862. Retreating elements of Davis's routed division streamed past and through Rousseau's ranks. Colonel William P. Carlin was among the Federals falling back. He had just been through the fight of his life while standing fast against Cleburne and Cheatham, and had been wounded in the process. Carlin remarked in his memoirs that as he made his way northward through the cedars, the sight of the regulars was reassuring: "After falling back a short distance…perhaps a fourth of a mile, I came to the line of the Regular brigade, commanded by Lieutenant Colonel Oliver L. Sheppard, which had not yet been engaged, belonging as it did to another corps. Colonel Sheppard kindly opened a gap in his line to allow my men, now in disorder, to pass. I, too, passed through this gap. It was closed again as soon as all my men had gone through. The men in Sheppard's brigade seemed cool as if nothing particular was going on, but it soon became hot for them."[44]

Jubilant Confederates from McCown's Division were not far behind. From their isolated positions deep in the forest, King and Slemmer each threw forward skirmishers after the last of the friendly troops cleared their ranks. The 15th Infantry's skirmish company was E/1/15th U.S. under Captain Henry Keteltas. They had advanced about fifty yards in front of King's main line when Keteltas observed troops through the trees to their front. The cedars obscured Keteltas's vision somewhat; he thought these men were clad in blue and thus another group of retreating Federals. A volley from the drab figures dismissed this notion from the captain's thoughts, and he ordered the company to fall back to the battalion line. The skirmishers "fell back to the regiment fireing as they retreated," noted William J. Carson, Keteltas's bugler. "On came the enemy in overwhelming numbers on the right."[45]

Brigadier General James E. Rains's Brigade, more than 1,000 troops of the 11th Tennessee, 29th North Carolina, and the 3rd and 9th Georgia Battalions, was bearing down on the 629 regulars of the two isolated battalions. As soon as Captain Keteltas's men had reformed on the 15th Infantry's line, Major King ordered the battalion to open fire. Rains's men did likewise, inflicting heavy casualties among King's men. One of the first to go down was Captain J. Bowman Bell, a Pennsylvanian commanding D/1/15th U.S., who was hit in the left temple and instantly killed. As King's battalion delivered a few volleys at the Southerners to its front, additional Confederates began to filter through the trees around the 15th Infantry's exposed right flank. In danger of being surrounded, King ordered his men to cease firing and fall back. The sudden enemy threat on the right caused the 15th Infantry's cohesion to evaporate. The battalion's precipitous retreat unfortunately swept along with it two regiments from Brigadier General John M. Palmer's division, the 6th Ohio and 36th Indiana, which had been sent forward to support Rousseau's line. Some of the 15th Infantrymen kept up a brisk fire as they retreated. Keteltas had Bugler Carson sound the rally after the regulars had retreated about a hundred yards. Many of them did so, turning about and delivering some shots at their pursuers. One of the regulars pausing to fire was Private William B. McCall of Company A, a cousin of William Carson. After firing, he continued falling back while attempting to reload his Springfield. A bullet struck him in the shoulder, penetrating to his heart and killing him instantly.[46]

In the nearby 16th Infantry battalion, the thick cedars prevented Major Adam Slemmer from noticing what had happened to King's battalion. Slemmer's skirmishers, B/1/16th U.S. under Lieutenant William H. Bartholomew, had been out in front about five minutes when they fell back before the Confederate onslaught. Reforming Company B on the battalion's right flank, Slemmer opened fire. His troops occupied good defensive positions among the limestone and timber, and for a few minutes the battalion checked the enemy's advance. "Here the struggle of the day took place," reported a member of Slemmer's opposition, Colonel Robert B. Vance of the 29th North Carolina. "The enemy, sheltering themselves behind the trunks of the thickly standing trees and the large rocks, of which there were many, stubbornly contested the ground inch by inch. Our brave boys, cheered on and led by their field, staff, and company officers, advanced through a very tempest of leaden hail." Despite the tempest Slemmer's regulars were producing, it would not be long before some of Rains's troops slipped around the 16th Infantry's position.

Slemmer's battalion was becoming more isolated every minute, for General Rousseau had decided to withdraw from the cedars. Rousseau's division had arrived on Sheridan's right at the moment when Sheridan's three brigades started to fall back, his men being both exhausted and out of ammunition. Much of Rousseau's own division was still in disarray and trying to deploy properly. With no support on either flank, the Kentuckian decided to head back across the cotton field. He ordered the Regular Brigade to support Battery H by the turnpike. Shepherd relayed this order to the three battalions he still had contact with (1/18th, 2/18th, and 1/19th) but the message was somewhat garbled by the time it reached 2/18th; Major Townsend was told to support the battery, but was not told the artillery's location. The major had not seen Guenther's men since entering the cedars, which was the moment Guenther had taken the guns back across the cotton field. Townsend sent out two members of his battalion staff with orders to find the cannon: "The Battery had been directly in our rear when entering the Cedars, but now on my moving out of the timbers on the trail which the brigade had made on entering it, the Battery could nowhere to be seen. Thinking that it might possibly have pulled out from the timber before ourselves, and gone to the right of the brigade, Adjutant Phisterer at this juncture promptly offered to go to the right of the brigade to learn whether the Battery had passed us. I directed him to do so, and also sent my mounted orderly back to our original position, to learn whether the Battery had gotten there." [47]

Phisterer spurred his horse along a narrow forest track that he thought would take him to the brigade's right flank. The path unfortunately led him directly toward Rains's Brigade, the Confederates who were trying to work their way around the 16th Infantry's left. Troops of the 3rd and 9th Georgia Battalions fired on but missed the fleeting horseman. The lieutenant reigned his mount away from the danger and soon came upon the 16th Infantry's line, where Slemmer's men were still holding their ground against Rains's advance. Phisterer asked Slemmer if Battery H was nearby. "I have not seen anything of the battery nor of anything or anybody else except the enemy," the major testily replied. Phisterer explained that the 16th Infantry's left was being enveloped and that the division was falling back. Finally realizing that the 15th Infantry had already retreated, Slemmer decided it was time for his own battalion to do likewise. It did so in relatively good order given the difficult terrain and close proximity of the enemy. "The men performed this movement with the same order and regularity they would in an ordinary drill," Captain R.E.A. Crofton recalled. Lieutenant Edgar Kellogg dispensed with professional restraint in recording his own observations: "We were forced to fall back. But we did so in perfect order, and soon faced about, and again for several minutes we tamed the rebel yell. This we did several times, but each time we had to yield ground to the enemy to avoid being surrounded and overwhelmed by superior numbers."

Phisterer could have retreated in relative safety with Slemmer's troops, but instead chose to ride back to the 18th Infantry's position and tell Major Townsend what he had learned about Battery H's location. Back through the gauntlet of enemy fire he rode, arriving at the Pioneer Road a few moments later, amazingly unscathed. Phisterer reported that the battery was not in the cedars and must be to the rear. Townsend's orderly also made it back and confirmed the adjutant's report, stating that the battery had taken up a position near the turnpike. Armed with this knowledge, Townsend ordered his battalion to fall back to the turnpike. For saving the 16th Infantry from certain heavy losses while twice dodging a swarm of enemy bullets, Lieutenant Phisterer would later receive the Medal of Honor.[48]

Beginning shortly after ten o'clock, the regulars and Scribner's brigade debauched from the cedars and began a confused retreat across the cotton field toward the artillery by the turnpike. Two of McCown's brigades had bypassed the cedars to the northwest and were able to interdict the cotton field and also place fire on the Federal turnpike positions. Additional Southern units fired on the cotton field from positions east of the cedars. "On they came pouring voley after voley into our ranks," wrote Bugler Carson. "We then came to a corn field. As we were crossing that, I tell you, they packed it to us there." Captain William W. Wise of C/1/15th U.S. was hit three times during the retreat, the most serious injury being a neck wound. He was close to the railroad when hit and was carried the rest of the way to safety. The enemy fire might have been even worse. Beatty's brigade did not receive Rousseau's order to fall back and remained in the cedars while Shepherd and Scribner retreated. Beatty's men and Negley's division held up the Southern advance through the cedars and allowed the balance of Rousseau's division to make good its escape.[49]

Leaving behind a trail of dead and wounded, Scribner's brigade and the regulars moved back to the knoll between the turnpike and railroad. The 1st Michigan and H/5th U.S. Artillery then took over the fight as Rains's Confederates kept up the pursuit. Lieutenant Alfred Pirtle of the division staff recorded what happened as he gazed at the cedars: "As I looked on, an officer on foot, sword in hand, spring into view with a shout; in an instant the edge of the timber was alive with a mass of arms, heads, legs, guns, swords, gray coats, brown hats, shirt sleeves, and the enemy were upon us, yelling, leaping, running." With the cotton field full of Rains's men, Major Cyrus O. Loomis, Rousseau's chief of artillery, told battery commanders Van Pelt and Guenther to "give them double-shotted canister as hot as hell will let you!" Guenther turned to his battery and yelled "canister double shotted!" The gunners echoed the command and slipped down the muzzles of their twelve-pound Napoleons two tin cans, each containing forty-eight lead balls.[50]

Guenther held his fire for the time being, for he did not want to waste the carefully prepared volley before the enemy was in range. Van Pelt, taking his cue from the regulars, kept his Michigan battery silent for the moment also. Captain Henry Mizner of the 18th U.S.

remembered that during the tense wait a general rode up to Guenther and pointed out the advancing Confederates. Guenther coolly replied "I see them, sir," but still held back. The captain was again urged to open up, and again refused: "They are not near enough, sir."[51] Lieutenant Pirtle recorded what happened when Guenther determined that the time was right:

> By no order that I heard, the whole of the guns in the two bat-
> teries together fired, covering their front with a cloud of smoke, hid-
> ing all objects in it, and then as fast as they could load they fired into
> the cloud. I found myself at this moment between the batteries in
> company with Major Loomis and Major Carpenter, commander of
> the battalion of the Nineteenth Regular Infantry. Like me, they were
> fascinated by the rash bravery of our foes, who seemed determined
> to have those guns at any cost. I never saw guns served on trial drill
> as fast as those were now. Before the recoil was expended, the gun-
> ners grasped the spokes and threw the pieces into position; like
> lightning the sponge was run in, turned and withdrawn, the load
> sent home and the piece fired. Such a roar was deafening, making
> our little group use signs to each other.[52]

The ten-gun line poured fire onto the Confederates, but counter-battery fire from Southern guns sent some rounds in return. A solid shot instantly killed George F. White, the 1st sergeant of Captain Mizner's F/3/18th U.S., while another projectile severely mangled the leg of Captain Charles E. Denison, commanding Company B of Major Townsend's battalion. The Norwich graduate "refused to be carried to the rear, but lay where he was wounded, and continued to encourage his men." The 15th Infantry's Lieutenant Robert King had a narrow escape: "As one of the rebel batteries had the exact range of the railroad, at the point we were, it was anything but pleasant, round shot and shell falling all around us; and in one instance a round shot struck and killed a man, who was lying on the ground not two yards beyond me, and the ball ricocheted over my head. Whenever we heard a shell or saw a round shot coming, every one of us, either made a very low bow, or fell flat on the ground."[53]

"On they came like so many deamonds," remembered Bugler Carson as the Confederates made a determined attempt to dislodge Rousseau's men from the knoll. "They charged on our regular bat-tery and another one. They gave them grape and canister making gap after gap in their ranks. The fire was rather to hot to suit them and what fieu of them was left came to an about face and skedadled back to the ceeder woods for shelter." McCown pulled back his troops to the far side of the cedars, beyond the range of Rousseau's guns. A temporary lull came over this portion of the battlefield. In the Regular Brigade, battalions were regrouped and reorganized. The 15th Infantry suffered the worst during the short foray into the cedars. Fifty of Major King's 319 officers and men had been hit.[54]

While the fighting raged in the cedars and cotton field, Rosecrans and Thomas attempted to hammer together a new Federal line of resistance. Rosecrans had already thrown out his original plan of attack. At this point, his primary concern was preventing the enemy from gaining a position on the Nashville Turnpike. McCown's attack had come close to doing so, and it would not be long before Bragg tried again. Should the Southerners succeed in driving the Federals away from the turnpike, the Union Army would be cut off from Nashville and surrounded. Cleburne's Division was at this time flanking around the cedars to the west and north. Rosecrans pressed his Pioneer Brigade into infantry service and positioned it at the north end the turnpike position, reinforcing the pioneers with the Chicago Board of Trade Battery and two brigades from Van Cleve's division. Fighting on the north end of the line would continue intermittently through the early afternoon, but the forces Rosecrans dispatched to the area would prove sufficient to secure the Federal northern flank. The southern anchor of Rosecrans's new line was Major General John M. Palmer's division of Crittenden's Left Wing. The linchpin of Palmer's position was a small patch of timber called the Round Forest, in which was positioned Colonel William B. Hazen's brigade. One of Palmer's remaining brigades, commanded by Brigadier General Charles Cruft, was in the cedars plugging the gap between the Round Forest and Negley's left. Palmer's last brigade, Colonel William Grose's, held a support position in the southeast portion of the cotton field. From the Round Forest, the Federal line extended to the northwest, generally following the Nashville Turnpike.

Time was a major concern for Rosecrans. He had to get the new turnpike position organized before Bragg renewed his attacks, but the few Federal troops that had remained fighting in the woods to the front of the new line were beginning to fall back. While Major Slemmer's 16th Infantry had been trading volleys with Rains's Brigade in the cedars, elements of Major General John M. Whithers's and Cheatham's Divisions had renewed the assault on the Federal center. With Sheridan's stubborn division finally out of the way, Negley's division of two brigades and John Beatty's forgotten brigade of Rousseau's division bore the brunt. Beatty eventually ordered his brigade to fall back to the turnpike. His bullet-ridden regiments had fought hard, and it would be well into evening before they could be reformed. Further advances by two brigades of Cheatham's Division, led by Brigadier Generals Donald S. Donelson and Alexander P. Stewart, forced back Negley's division. Negley's withdrawal in turn left Cruft's brigade dangerously exposed and it likewise retreated. The regulars on the knoll watched as the last segment of Rosecrans's original line of battle began to collapse. "The enemy turned his attention to the troops upon our left, and in a few moments the face of the country was filled with fugitives from our overpowered army," noticed the 18th Infantry's Captain Haymond. "We were now completely flanked," Brigadier General Cruft wrote. "Our own troops impeded my retreat. Cannon, caissons, artillery wagons, and bodies of men in wild retreat filled the road and woods to my rear, precluding everything like proper and orderly retreat." The cedars had finally been swept clean of organized Federal resistance.[55]

Realizing the battle might be lost if the weak Union line along the turnpike was attacked again before it was ready, Rosecrans decided to send a force back into the cedars to delay Cheatham's advance, cover the withdrawal of Negley and Cruft, and allow Grose's brigade time to reposition nearer the Round Forest. This was precisely the type of situation for which Rosecrans had formed the Regular Brigade. Shortly before noon, the commanding general told George Thomas to order the regulars into the cedars. The corps commander galloped over to the Regular Brigade's position on the knoll and gave the order in a single, terse sentence: "Shepherd, take your brigade in there," Thomas calmly stated while pointing at the cedars just west of the Round Forest, "and stop the Rebels."[56]

The regulars were ready. Leaving Battery H on the knoll, Shepherd marched the battalions down the turnpike to a point just short of where it intersected McFadden Lane near the Round Forest. They moved into line-of-battle at the edge of the cotton field. As the troops formed up, Major Carpenter suggested to Shepherd that 1/19th U.S. be shifted from the brigade's left to its right, to help compensate for the reduced manpower of 1/15th and 1/16th. Shepherd concurred and inserted Carpenter's troops between the two right-flank units. Knowing that the upcoming mission in the dense cedars would be a hot and difficult one, Shepherd had his men drop their overcoats before moving further. Their nerves were wrapped tight as bowstrings while they stripped off their gear and prepared for battle. As Shepherd's men nervously glanced to the left and right, they could see no other troops accompanying the brigade into the cotton field. The regulars could still see Union troops retreating out of the cedars. Some sweating artillerymen, having lost all their horses, were dragging a cannon out of the forest by hand (the gun belonged to Battery B of the 1st Ohio Light Artillery, part of Cruft's brigade). It was perfectly clear to the regulars what was about to happen: they would take up an unsupported position in the teeth of the Confederate advance. Shepherd knew just the spot to head for. Another of the pathways cut by the Pioneer Brigade was nearby, leading through the cedars and pointing directly at the Round Forest. Surmising that the Confederates would orient their advance on the pathway, Shepherd intended to block it with the regulars. The 16th Infantry would straddle the road, with the 18th U.S. to the left and the 15th and 19th to the right. In a few minutes, the regulars' excess equipment was on the ground and the ranks dressed. With the brigade's blue-and-gold flag fluttering above the center of the line and the 18th Infantry's two sets of Stars & Stripes adorning the left-flank battalions, Shepherd gave the command to advance.[57]

"Shot and shell were whissing and exploding all about us," Jacob Van Zwaluwenburg recalled, quickly adding, "I had rather been in mother's back yard just then to tell the truth." One of the 16th Infantryman's comrades, Private Fuller, had boasted the previous day that there would not be a battle at all on December 31.

"What do you think now?" Van Zwaluwenburg asked Fuller as the brigade lurched into motion.

"I don't care," Fuller replied, "that bullet is not made that will hit me."[58]

Fuller was about to find out that the Confederates lurking ahead in the cedars had plenty of ammunition with which to try. The regulars advanced with the professional decorum that had become their trademark since the days of Camp Thomas and Newport Barracks. "During this movement the 2d Battalion of the 18th executed a change of front to the south, by companies on its left company, as if on ordinary battalion drill," Lieutenant Phisterer observed from his adjutant's station, "then marched by the right flank into the cedars; the other battalions moved up by their flanks and shortest routes, preserving proper intervals." For many of the regulars, these were the final drill commands they ever heard.[59]

* * *

Lieutenant William Bisbee of the 18th Infantry anxiously scanned the woods to his front. The regulars had penetrated into the cedars only about fifty yards before they saw retreating Federals, the last stragglers from Negley's division and Cruft's brigade. Bisbee was frustrated at having to hold his fire until the friendly troops cleared his front, knowing full well that the shadows deeper in the forest concealed a horde of enemy troops. The lieutenant's men settled into the best positions they could find among the trees and rocks while waiting for their comrades to get out of the way. The regulars laid down as Bisbee and others shouted for the stragglers to clear out. Negley's men scrambled over Shepherd's line to the rear. Shepherd's battalion commanders had not had time to deploy any skirmishers, but for now this tactical shortcoming actually worked in the regulars' favor. The stragglers gave Shepherd ample warning of the enemy's advance, while the absence of skirmishers meant the opposition had no idea that a Federal brigade was lying in wait.[60]

The stream of retreating Federals slowed to a trickle and finally ceased. The dark forest was still and silent for a few moments, save for the occasional scrape of a man's accouterments against limestone as he adjusted his position. The infantrymen breathed in the sweet, pungent scent of cedar while nervously peering into the forest. Hands slid along rifle barrels, checking primers and ensuring that sights were folded forward and set for the short-range work that was surely coming. Soon, the silence was broken as the regulars began to hear muffled voices, Southern officers directing their men. The sounds grew louder and shadows began to take shape—advancing infantry. To the 1,383 regulars in Shepherd's five battalions, it seemed as if every member of Bragg's army was emerging from the gloom. In actuality, only five Confederate brigades were then struggling through the forest toward the Regular Brigade's quarter-mile thin blue line, but numbering more than 4,000 strong, this force of Southerners was certainly powerful enough.

The advancing horde was about eighty yards away when Shepherd ordered the brigade to rise and open fire. The order echoed down the Federal line as battalion and company officers repeated the commands. The gray-clad troops were startled to see a

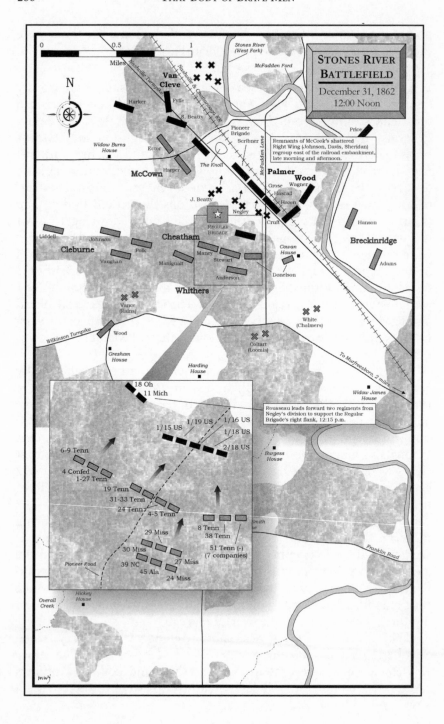

STONES RIVER
BATTLEFIELD
December 31, 1862
12:00 Noon

Remnants of McCook's shattered
Right Wing (Johnson, Davis, Sheridan)
regroup east of the railroad embankment,
late morning and afternoon.

Rousseau leads forward two regiments from
Negley's division to support the Regular
Brigade's right flank, 12:15 p.m.

solid line of blue uniforms suddenly appear in what had been an empty patch of woods. The Southerners were not able to study this new threat for long, for each of the Regular Brigade's forty-three company commanders immediately called out "Fire by file! Company, ready, commence firing!" The triggers of more than 1,300 Springfield rifles were systematically pulled, obscuring Shepherd's line in the white, acrid smoke of black powder. Eighteen months of training paid off as the regulars poured a sheet of flame onto the opposing ranks. Starting on the right flank of each company, each two-man file fired as soon as the file to its right let fly. The technique produced a methodical and continuous wave of rifle fire. Each man thought of little else as he fired, loaded, brought his piece to the ready, and fired again. Fragments of wood, vegetation, and limestone filled the air. "The first line of the enemy were scattered like chaff," a regular noted as heaps of torn bodies indicated the momentary limit of the Confederate advance. "The excellence of the firing by file by all the battalions of the brigade could not be excelled," Shepherd reported, "and was terrifying and destructive to the enemy." Frederick Phisterer, who saw much action in a long military career, later remembered these initial volleys as "the most deafening and terrible fire I had and have ever since heard." Phillip Lyman of A/2/18th remembered that "the rebels would charge on our men in ranks and the 18th would shoot them down like flies. I never heard such firing in my life. It was just one volley after another." In the 19th Infantry's line, Private Jones also noted the deadly effectiveness of the brigade's fire: "The butternuts came 6 deep double quick on us, but ah! 'The Regulars were there' the Regulars were there; we Poured such an unearing shower of bullets into their advancing columns. they returned the fire and now, I cant describe it. Language cant describe it—it begars description—we were only about 100 feet apart in the 'dark cedar woods.' they couldn't drive us it was to mutch for flesh & blood. In quick succession we poured volly after volly into the wasps. and if it was any satisfaction to our dying to see our enemy bite the dust they had it."[61]

Troops as far away as the knoll by the turnpike were startled by the sudden explosion of sound and smoke, including staff officer Alfred Pirtle: "Just then a tremendous fire of musketry broke out in the cedars, continuing for sometime, but I did not know until night that it was the desperate advance into the cedars made by the regular brigade." While the fire of the regulars was effective, there was not enough of it. Stewart's Brigade of Tennesseans, plus a portion of Donelson's Brigade confronted Shepherd's line directly. Additional Confederates, the balance of Donelson's Brigade and Brigadier General George Maney's Brigade from Cheatham's Division, plus two brigades of Whither's Division, were advancing beyond Shepherd's flanks. After recovering from the initial shock of the regulars' sudden appearance, the Southerners returned fire and began working their way around Shepherd's position. The regulars started receiving fire from the front and both sides. Luke Lyman, the cook marching in ranks beside his nervous friend Sergeant Pierce, recalled that "one column [of Confederates] would rise up and load, lay down and fire and the other column would walk over them and so on, That is the odds we fought against."[62] Captain Haymond remembered that some aspects of the terrain and visibility worked in the Confederates' favor:

> The enemy bore down upon us in three or four lines, their front rank would fire and fall down and load, the rear rank firing over their heads, by this means they poured an incessant fire into us. ...They had the advantage of position and in standing beneath the shadow of the pines enveloped in smoke, while we stood at the edge of the timber in bold relief against the light. They fired very low, and their shot told fearfully upon us. I was kept busy in urging my men to load rapidly and fire low, when suddenly I felt a sharp quick pain in my right knee and a momentary fainting came over me. I knew that I was hit, and immediately sat down to examine my wound. I soon found that I was not seriously hurt and at once got up and took my position. The shot of the enemy was fast thinning out my little company and the dead and wounded of other companies lay thick around me.[63]

The regulars' methodic fire-by-file quickly devolved into individual firing as Shepherd's troops sought cover. Many units would have broken under similar circumstances, but the regulars this day exhibited a sense of discipline that appears to be almost beyond reason. "All did their duty well," Maj Caldwell of 1/18th U.S. reported, "were cool, deliberate, and firm under the terrific fire that thinned our ranks, and not one gave way." Peter Fitzpatrick of Battery H made a similar comment in a letter dated a week after the battle: "The lads of our battery swore that they would never leave the field until every man should drop at their guns, and so did every man in the regular brigade for which reason they got so fearfully cut up." While the regulars stood fast and punished their opponents, incoming fire decimated Shepherd's ranks. Colonel Oscar F. Strahl, commanding the 4th Tennessee of Stewart's Brigade, later described the combat's intensity: "The slaughter of the enemy was very great just at the edge of the glade, as they were slow to leave the timber and our men were close upon them, and every shot did its work."[64]

Confusion and smoke made soldiers aware of little except what was happening to their immediate front. Lieutenant Edgar Kellogg's company, F/1/16th U.S., had an unusually clear field of fire:

> In front of the company which I commanded was a comparatively open space, extending to and somewhat beyond the enemy in front. Many of the Confederates in that open space tried to get into the cedars on one side or the other, although these saplings afforded no protection against bullets, but I suppose so slight a thing as a cornstalk might look good to a man who is trying to dodge Death.
>
> An officer on horseback, a most gallant man, forced these men back to their proper places and urged them to go forward. There was a man named Hicks in my company who was an exceptionally good shot. I shouted in his ear that I wanted him to knock that man out of his saddle, and I requested the same favor from some of Hick's comrades. Very soon afterwards the horse was riderless, but whose bullet emptied the saddle no one can tell.
>
> A torrent of lead came in our direction, and the number of our dead or wounded soon became so great that some of the men still unhurt had to change their positions slightly to avoid the contact and encumbrance of those who could no longer fight.[65]

Shepherd's men hammered away at the Confederates, but the regulars' own casualties mounted at an alarming rate. The fight in the cedars was Lieutenant Bisbee's first experience commanding a company, he having taken over B/2/18th U.S. after Captain Denison's earlier wounding on the knoll. The new commander well remembered the desperate fighting:

> Our muzzle loading muskets seemed slow as the gray fellows moved yelling towards us in overwhelming lines, their murderous fire mowing us down like pot hunters and we doing the same to them. In the midst of the deafening roar the murderous business is much clouded. ...As a lieutenant file closer in the rear rank, I had that much advantage though ranks are not well defined on such occasions, all officers and men being on the line. My sword not being of much use, I took a dead man's musket to help out. Sergeant Gates near me rolled up his sleeve displaying a flesh wound of which he seemed proud. Private Schouler, at my left, fell to the ground with

a deathlike groan and shriek and before I could tear his shirt open, he was dead. Men were dropping all along in great frequency, to lay as they fell dead or dying, until the battle ceased.[66]

The terrain in which Jacob Van Zwaluwenburg found himself was definitely poor for a defender. The 16th Infantryman had the misfortune of being in the very center of the Regular Brigade's line, positioned squarely in the middle of the Pioneer Road. He had only scant cover and, as Shepherd had surmised, the pathway was a natural route of enemy advance. The Dutchman's position became the focal point of a great deal of unwanted Confederate attention:

> that was the most nerve racking twenty minutes I ever passed. shells were screaming through the trees a perfect hail of bullets they went zip zip all around. I loaded my gun on my back turned on my right side and fired. a rebel flag was in my immediate front. about five minutes after lying down my right hand man Fuller raised to fire when I saw him drop his gun clasp both hands to his side and said "my God" and fell over backwards dead. a few minutes later my left hand man, Mr. Mesmer, was struck in the right cheek. the bullet came out at the back of his neck. he fell apparently lifeless against me. while aiming to fire a bullet struck the stalk of my gun glanced off on the barrel went over my right shoulder. a limb before me served me as a rest for my gun. it was hit a number of times as the bark flew in my face. I could see the enemy trying to surround us as I saw their forces on the double quick trying to get in our rear and cut us off. It was getting just then too interesting to be safe.[67]

Major Townsend's 2/18th U.S. came close to losing more than just men. The battalion's national colors were also in jeopardy for a while. Color Sergeant Samuel Dobbins was dead and the flag had fallen to the forest floor. Lieutenant Phisterer saw Dobbins go down and ordered Paul Fisher, a corporal on the battalion's color guard, to raise the banner. Fisher dropped his rifle and picked up the staff, raising the flag so high that it became entangled in some branches overhead. Sensing that the battalion could not remain in its position much longer and not wanting the colors captured, Phisterer rode forward to assist in untangling them. As the adjutant did so, a bullet struck Phisterer's right boot, cut his saddle strap, and passed completely through his horse's body. Phisterer jumped to the ground to inspect the damage and called out to Lieutenant Bisbee. Bisbee went to Fisher's assistance and assisted the corporal in untangling the banner. The lieutenant carried it for the remainder of the fight in the cedars. An enemy flag was one of the ultimate prizes on a Civil War battlefield. To the credit of the Civil War regulars, the Confederates had not captured a set of Regular Army colors prior to Stones River. The actions of Phisterer, Bisbee, and Fisher on December 31, 1862, ensured that the record continued.[68]

General Rousseau sensed that the Regular Brigade was in over its head and tried to deal with the unit's plight. He rounded up two regiments from Negley's division, the 18th Ohio and 11th Michigan, and led them across the cotton field toward the Regular Brigade's right. This diminished some of the pressure on that flank, but it was still just a matter of time before the regulars would be overwhelmed. "A regiment came up in line in the open field on the extreme right of the brigade," Shepherd later remarked, "but its fire, though brisk, came too late, and was unavailing against so large a force as filled the forest, three lines being discernible."[69]

Shepherd's brigade had stood its ground for about twenty minutes. General Thomas began to think the regulars had done enough. Rosecrans' new line along the turnpike had been shorn up and further sacrifice of the regulars was no longer necessary. Thomas dispatched one of his aides, Captain Oscar A. Mack, to tell Shepherd to pull out. Mack, a regular officer on detached service from the 13th U.S. Infantry, never made it to Shepherd's position. He was severely wounded while crossing the cotton field. Mack could have saved himself both the journey and the wound, for Shepherd had reached the same conclusion as Thomas: pull out before it was too late. Shepherd later wrote of his decision in undramatic Regular Army style: "I thought it proper to order a retreat, which was probably long enough deferred." Lovell Rousseau, his short-lived counterattack having failed to turn back the Confederate advance, also ordered the regulars to fall back. Lieutenant Harrison Millard of the 19th Infantry, Rousseau's inspector general on the division staff, delivered the message. Unlike Mack, Millard made it to the regulars' position. He first came upon Major Carpenter's battalion.

"The General directs the brigade to fall back to the railroad and support the battery," Millard told his old battalion commander.

"Tell the General we can not fall back until we have repulsed this attack!"

Carpenter was focused only on the narrow situation to his front and did not realize the brigade's precarious position. Millard informed Carpenter that the order was imperative, then rode down the line to notify the other battalion commanders. Carpenter gave the command to cease-fire, faced his battalion about, and marched the 19th Infantry out of the cedars.[70]

* * *

In a way, the worst part of the regulars' ordeal was just beginning. The cotton field to the brigade's rear was by this time a killing field swept by enemy fire. Captain Henry Douglass of 1/18th U.S. gave perhaps the best description of the bullets, shot, and shell crisscrossing the open ground: "A blacksmith shop full of rotten iron was being thrown at the command." The movement through the rotten iron was about as disciplined as could be expected. A few companies maintained a semblance of formation as they sprinted for safety, but most broke apart completely. "Our retreat commenced in good order," recalled Captain James Biddle of B/2/16th U.S., "but on reaching the open ground the men could not stand the heavy fire to which they were exposed but broke and ran to the shelter of our batteries nearly a quarter mile distant. How any of us got across that field alive I can not imagine." Always sensitive to acts of indiscipline among his regulars, Shepherd described the movement as charitably as he could: "The retreat of the brigade across the open field was done handsomely, and with as much order as was desirable, having in view to prevent further loss of life." Captain Ansel Denton did not mince words as he ordered his company to retreat: "For God's sake men, get back to the railroad or we'll all be killed!" As Captain Henry Haymond headed for safety, he noticed that "the enemy rushed to the edge of the timber, and poured showers of musketry into us, while their artillery tore through our ranks with fearful effect. One of my men was tore to pieces by a shell while crossing the field."[71]

Captain William J. Fetterman had to order his own company to cease-fire and fall back no less than three times, the noise, confusion, and his troops' mechanical loading-firing-loading routine being difficult to overcome. As Private Luke Lyman and Sergeant Pierce lowered their rifles and turned to leave, they caught each other's eye. "I'm alright!" Pierce exclaimed, amazed that he had lived this long. The two regulars laughed out loud and headed for safety. Just as they did so, Lyman saw a companion go down:

> I turned and looked to the left and saw Amos Sherman, another particular friend of mine who lives in Morrow County and whose mother is a widow, he was mortally wounded being shot through the

neck and he wanted to be taken from the field so bad that I stopped with him until the rebels were within forty or fifty yards of me, nor did I leave him till he was about dead, he could speak no more when I left and I was the last of our regiment to leave the field when I left I should judge that there were five hundred rebels fired at me at once from the shower of lead that came around me, knocked my gun off and cutting the blood on my lips, but rest assured it was the hardest shower I was ever in. While on the retreat a number of our regiment was killed and wounded.[72]

While Lyman was assisting Private Sherman, Sergeant J. Nelson Pierce was hit in the cotton field. He was shot in the chest and lived another thirty hours in extreme pain before mercifully passing away. Luke Lyman wrote to Pierce's widowed mother with the news, regretting that in the cotton field he could be next to only one wounded comrade at a time.

When Jacob Van Zwaluwenburg heard the order to retreat, he stood up immediately and headed for the rear. There were so many dead and wounded regulars around the private that he saw precious few of his fellow 16th Infantrymen doing likewise. Two that did were a few steps ahead, but they ran only a short distance before both were shot and fell in a heap. Van Zwaluwenburg could not avoid tripping over them. Confederates were near, so close that Van Zwaluwenburg heard one of them yell "Halt you Yankee sons of bitches or we will shoot!" Van Zwaluwenburg thought he had already been shot as he tripped over his two unfortunate comrades, but as he sprawled on the ground, he discovered that he was still in one piece. The private again jumped to his feet, dodging rifle fire as he picked his way through the last few yards of the forest. He then began the final phase of his journey, across the cotton field.[73]

As the 19th Infantry emerged from the woods a short distance to Van Zwaluwenburg's left, men were hit up and down the line. "Scatter and run, boys!" Major Carpenter yelled, wanting to give the enemy a less inviting target. He remained mounted and moved at a canter, not wanting to outdistance his men, an action that cost Carpenter dearly. The battalion had not gone far before a withering volley plowed into the 19th Infantry's fleeing mass. Private Joseph R. Prentice of E/1/19th U.S. had been in the battalion's front rank during the fight in the cedars. After the battalion faced about and marched out of the woods, he was in the rear. Shortly after receiving the order to scatter, Prentice heard a horse bearing down upon him:

As I ran, I looked around, and saw that it was Major Carpenter's horse dashing after us, frenzied by several slight bullet wounds. By yelling at him I managed to turn him and head him along our lines. Then I rushed after the boys to tell them the fate of the major, but did not manage to see any of the commanding officers until we had retreated about a quarter of a mile. Then I gained permission to return and look for him. Back I went at the top of my speed, and as I entered the clearing the enemy's sharpshooters opened a brisk fire on me. Still I was bound to find the major if possible, and, knowing about where he fell, rushed to the spot. Bullets ploughed up little puffs of dust at my feet and whistled around my head. A short spurt more and I was at the place. Glancing around I saw him lying face downward upon the dust, and rushed to his assistance. ...I picked him up and carried him to the rear, my ears filled with the mournful dirge of the bullets that threatened me at every step.[74]

Prentice carried Major Carpenter the length of the cotton field. Arriving at the knoll on the far side, he gently laid Carpenter down. Hit six times (twice in the head and four times in the body), the beloved major of the 19th Infantry, the heart and soul of his regiment, was dead. Shepherd later remarked that the major's death would be "regretted by all who knew him." Lovell Rousseau considered the loss "irreparable." Arthur Carpenter had known the major as well as anyone in the 19th Infantry, and his comments are even more poignant: "We all feel grieved at his loss for he was as a father to us." Joseph Prentice would be the second regular to receive the Medal of Honor for his actions at Stones River.[75]

Prentice's valor, while heroic to the extreme, was not uncommon as the Regular Brigade retreated across the cotton field. Bugler Carson of the 15th Infantry was about halfway across when a company mate went down: "I saw John Argo trying to get out of [the enemy's] way. He was wounded in both thighs. I ran to his assistence. He took me around the neck. I supported him the best in my power and succeeded in getting him out of harme." Lieutenant Kellogg had a similar experience during the exodus from the cedars, but his actions ended up more humorous than deadly: "One incident of our second falling back from the cedars added to, and then very much relieved my mental strain. Lieutenant [Samuel E.] St. Onge, a French Canadian, a most gallant, capable, and efficient officer, and one of my dearest friends, fell not far from me. I saw him fall, ran to him, and took hold of his coat-collar to help him to his feet, asking him at the same time if he was hurt. 'No,' he replied, 'only a bullet through my coat tails,' and he resumed his leg exercise while I quickly rejoined my company."[76]

Captain Henry Douglass went down shortly after 1/18th U.S. began crossing the cotton field, a shell fragment gouging an arm. Shock from the wound temporarily immobilized him with advancing Confederates nearby. Lieutenant Freeman in 2/18th U.S. heard Douglass's cry for help and noticed that the captain was about to be captured. Freeman left his battalion, ran through a storm of bullets, and picked Douglass up. He carried him to safety, and after the war received the Medal of Honor for his efforts. Other regulars were not as lucky as Douglass. Confederate Joseph Thompson, a sergeant in the 19th Tennessee of Stewart's Brigade, ran into the cotton field after the regulars, determined to capture a prisoner. He laid his hands on a straggler and was escorting the captured regular back to the cedars when the blue-coated soldier was shot dead. Not to be deterred, the intrepid Tennessean collared another member of the Regular Brigade and eventually managed to bring his prize safely into Confederate lines.

Major Carpenter was not the only battalion commander shot in the cotton field. Mounted officers were tempting targets throughout the battle, and a number were hit. The 15th Infantry's John King was rapidly struck three times in the left arm as soon as his battalion left the cedars. He fell from his horse, dislocating a shoulder in the process. Nearby in the 16th Infantry, Adam Slemmer received a severe wound in the left leg during the height of the combat in the forest. Both King and Slemmer survived the retreat, but for them the battle was over. Commanders in the 18th U.S. fared somewhat better. Caldwell and Townsend both had their horses shot out from under them, but they themselves emerged unscathed. Captain James B. Mulligan took over 1/19th U.S. after the death of Major Carpenter. Captain Jesse Fulmer took command of 1/15th U.S., and Captain Crofton replaced Slemmer at the head of the 16th Infantry. While commanding 1/16th in the cedars and during the retreat, three different horses Crofton rode were shot dead.[77]

Singly and in small groups, the regulars streamed rearward across the Nashville Pike. Major Townsend grabbed his battalion's national colors from Lieutenant Bisbee upon reaching the knoll. He stood on the crest of the low hill, waving the banner and providing 2/18th U.S. with a rallying point. Frederick Phisterer's horse, wounded in the cedars, finally gave out near the knoll after bearing its rider out of harm's way. The lieutenant was lucky to be alive, for his equipment had likewise been damaged: "My rubber blanket looked like a sieve from the bullets that had passed through it." Lieutenant Robert King was also fortunate to have made it through: "I escaped without a wound, but had my pants torn almost off of me and a bullet struck the tip of my sword scabbard off, and another passed across the front of my boot top, slightly tearing the leather. ...Almost every officer had a bullet pass through some part of his clothing." Private David Smith of B/2/16th U.S. recorded a similar experience: "it is a grat mistry to me how I got out alive the balls flew around me like hail I was struck by one ball it went through my coat cape and the Sleeve but did not go through the Skin it made a bruse the size of a Cent." Shepherd had the regulars continue a short distance eastward to the far side of the Nashville & Chattanooga tracks. The brigade regrouped, the knoll and railroad embankment providing shelter from enemy fire.[78]

Jacob Van Zwaluwenburg was one of the final regulars to make it back. The last of his strength gave out about halfway across the field. He could see the Federal artillery line ahead on the knoll. The pieces were in battery, gunners grasping lanyards and waiting for the command to fire. The private fell to the ground just as the guns opened up. The air above him was filled with yet more rotten iron, this batch heading for the cedars to discourage Confederate pursuit. With the cannons' report ringing in his ears, Van Zwaluwenburg scrambled to his feet one last time and staggered into the Federal position. At the Federal gun line, he spotted a member of his company nearby, Private James Mead. "Mead, this is rather tough," Van Zwaluwenburg blurted out between gulps of air. Mead was about to reply when a piece of shell struck him in the forehead and he fell to the ground at Van Zwaluwenburg's feet. To the Dutchman it seemed "as if his whole face was carried away and [I] left him for dead." Mead was fortunate. His wound was bloody but superficial, and he was back on duty in a few weeks.[79]

Robert Kennedy had a promise to keep. The private had retreated across the cotton field without a scratch, but one of his sergeants, Amos Fleagle, was not as lucky and had been hit during the movement. Before the battle, Kennedy had agreed to secure Fleagle's gold watch and silver-plated revolver should the sergeant fall in action. Kennedy had seen Fleagle go down but in the confusion of the retreat forgot about the two valuable items. After resting behind the knoll for a few moments, he worked up enough courage to go back into the cotton field and make good on the agreement. Kennedy found Captain Denton and told him what he wanted to do. The company commander sensibly told Kennedy not to try, certain that the chances of surviving such a hazardous venture were slim. Kennedy was persistent and repeated his request a number of times. Denton's resolve finally wavered.

"If you go out there you will never get back."

"Let me try it, captain."

Denton gave in: "Go!"

Kennedy dropped his rifle, threw down his equipment, and took off at a sprint into the cotton field. Retracing his steps back toward the cedars, he found his sergeant still alive but with a wound that would turn out to be mortal.

"Oh! Kennedy! What did you come here for?" Fleagle gasped as Kennedy knelt beside him.

The private was focused on his mission at this point: "For your watch and revolver. Where are they, Sergeant?"

Kennedy located the items, put them in his pocket, and then looked after the sergeant's comfort. He found a stray blanket nearby and covered Fleagle with it, using an abandoned knapsack as a pillow. He also placed a canteen near the wounded man's head. Kennedy then began to realize his own situation:

> While doing this, I had to fall at his side two or three times to save myself from being hit...as the cannon balls were flying in all directions. He begged me to leave him and to go back to a place of safety, saying if I did not, I would be killed. I started to run back to the railroad, and then I realized the danger I was in. I thought the whole rebel army was shooting at me. The balls were plowing into the earth on all sides of me. If ever a man ran for his life, I did then. This I consider the most foolhardy act of my soldier life, as it was going into the very jaws of death to go to Sgt. Fleagle where he lay between the two lines of battle. All I thought of on starting to him was to fulfil the promise I had made him, and nothing but the protecting care of kind Providence enabled me to carry out my purpose.[80]

Kennedy made it back to the knoll and turned over the watch and pistol to Captain Denton for safekeeping. Robert Kennedy had probably spent more time in the cotton field than any man then still on his feet. Although three members of the Regular Brigade would one day receive Medals of Honor for their actions on December 31, 1862, certainly more than three deserved some sort of recognition for what they went through on the first day of the Battle of Stones River.

* * *

Corporal William Reed, the teamster of Captain Belknap's B/3/18th in charge of the company's wagon, was happy enough not to have experienced the day's bloody events. He and the rest of the brigade's rear echelon had remained in camp near Rosecrans's head-quarters, assisting quartermasters in bringing cartridges to the front and surgeons in caring for the wounded. About one o'clock in the afternoon, Belknap's missing soldier, Private John Mallory, suddenly appeared at the wagon and requested his equipment. Corporal Reed asked the private where he had been all morning. Mallory replied only that he had been sick. Reed secured Mallory's rifle and car-tridge box from the wagon and with a few choice words thrust them at the private. While Reed was rummaging through the wagon for Mallory's waist belt and bayonet, he noticed that the private's trousers were muddy and torn. Knowing that Mallory was in trou-ble enough already and that a regular taking his place in ranks wearing disreputable clothing would only make things worse, Reed instructed Mallory to "get some clean clothes from your knapsack and make yourself neat." Mallory proceeded to the company's knapsack pile, but instead of his own trousers he secured a pair from a knapsack belonging to Private Green Shields. Another team-ster saw what Mallory was doing.

"Shields will be mad," the teamster warned.

"That is my business."

Mallory did not think his business included doing his duty that afternoon, for after he secured his equipment and the pilfered cloth-ing he again disappeared, not to be seen again for the rest of the battle.[81]

While Private Mallory headed for the hills, his braver comrades regrouped by the railroad embankment. The regulars knew they had taken a pounding in the cedars, but many of the brigade's survivors later stated they had no idea just how extreme their casualties were until after it was all over. When Shepherd took his brigade into the cedars at noon, nearly 1,400 officers and men were in ranks. When the regulars formed up by the railroad tracks about forty-five min-utes later, 806 remained unscathed, yielding a casualty rate of close to 44 percent. The 16th U.S. had the dubious honor of enduring the brigade's heaviest losses, suffering greatly in its position on the Pioneer Road. Of Major Slemmer's 309 officers and men, 186—an eye opening 60 percent—were killed, wounded, or captured. In all the battalions, the vast majority of these losses occurred during the short fight in the cedars and the quick retreat back to the turnpike. While such casualty rates were not unique in the Civil War, having the punishment inflicted in less than half an hour made the losses seem all the more shocking to those who survived.[82] Luke Lyman wrote a rather disturbing letter to his parents a few days after the battle, describing the casualties in his company of the 18th Infantry:

> The first man shot of our co. was S.A. Rose, wounded in the side severe. Dave Redman shot dead, Amos Sherman shot through the neck breaking it, Henderson Maxwell right arm broke twice above and twice below the elbow, John Sheppard through the breast died, Sgt. Dunken foot shot off, Sgt. Matthew a cannon ball glanced on his belly and a musket ball through his arm, Preston Brown wounded in the groin and taken prisoner, Nelson Peirce wounded but afternoon died, I want you to tell his folks about it and that he died a true hearted patriot and a christian as I never heard him swear an oath and always correcting those who he heard using profanity. He is missed more than any other of the co. I mourn him as a brother. ...Pat McDonnell leg shattered above the knee, Ira G. Brown through the thigh, Gordon Beard through the bowels died, Jo Dodds through the foot, The above is of Co. "A" 2nd, and the regiment suffered in proportion. I had my gun shot off and a bullet passed near enough to draw blood on my upper lip. Gen. Thomas gave us the praise of standing the hottest fire for the longest time of any other regiment.[83]

Other regular units matched this casualty rate. In F/1/16th U.S., just twelve of thirty-three enlisted men survived the battle intact. In C/2/18th U.S., only Captain Denton, Private Kennedy, and nine others made it back from the cedars in one piece. The Regular Brigade's losses had not been in vain, however. The enemy also paid dearly during the twenty minutes of fighting in the cedars. Peter Cozzens, in his battle study of Stones River, *No Better Place To Die,* points out that the 8th Tennessee of Donelson's Brigade suffered 68 percent casualties while attacking through the cedars to the Round Forest. Cozzens claims that this was the highest single battle casualty rate of any Confederate regiment during the war. While that claim is debatable, the 8th Tennessee's severe losses highlight the ferocity of the fighting in the cedars that day. Stewart's Brigade was likewise decimated. The Confederate brigadier halted his advance after Shepherd pulled the Regular Brigade out of the cedars, content with having his men fire on Shepherd's fleeing troops from the edge of the cotton field. With Stewart's Brigade going nowhere, the other four Confederate brigades in the area also ceased movement. The entire Confederate attack through the cedars, for the moment at least, ground to a halt. Troops from Negley's, Cruft's, and Grose's commands used the respite to take their places in Rosecrans's line along the turnpike. When the Southerners resumed their attacks later in the day, a solid line of Federal troops confronted them.[84]

Cheatham and other Southern commanders rallied their troops in the early afternoon, sending them across the cotton field toward the Union positions along the turnpike and in the Round Forest. The regulars unknowingly continued to delay the Confederate advance at this point. Shepherd's men had not been able to recover their overcoats during the retreat from the cedars, and the enemy mistook the regulars' pile of clothing at the far edge of the cotton field for a line of prone soldiers. Some of the Confederates halted in the field to engage the sky-blue coats, while Southern artillery also fired at the equipment occasionally.[85] Lieutenant Phisterer remembered that shells would make the gear "fly in all directions, but doing no other harm." Similar to the previous Confederate assault on the turnpike position, Union artillery fire had a telling effect. Shepherd had what was left of his battalions reformed and positioned as support for the batteries on the knoll. "We had them slightly below us in an open cotton field," Lieutenant Bisbee remembered of the engagement, the finale of a long day for the Regular Brigade, "and as they came bravely on with flags all flying, Guenther sang out 'Canister double shotted'... Raking holes were being made in their line plainly visible to us all. When within 500 yards...we opened with the infantry fire. Wavering, they finally broke and retired to the cedars. Many of them afraid to retire or advance, lay down, hiding in the cotton bushes to be captured all through the afternoon."[86]

"In a few minutes all was still, the smoke cleared away," wrote Lieutenant Freeman, "and we saw the field before us bare of life, as if swept by a hurricane." Bragg concentrated the balance of his attacks on the Round Forest, but Hazen's brigade and other units grimly hung on to the key position. The Confederate assaults ended at dusk. The Army of Tennessee had won the day, except that it had failed to drive the Army of the Cumberland completely off the battlefield. Bragg informed the Confederate nation of the victory that night, fully expecting Rosecrans to head back to Nashville the next day. Bragg would be surprised and then discouraged when he discovered that Rosecrans was staying put. The Army of the Cumberland had grimly hung on throughout the day in the aftermath of the collapse of McCook's Right Wing. Although some of Rosecrans's top subordinates advocated retreat after sundown, the Federal commander decided that his army was strong enough to continue the struggle. The Federals adjusted and strengthened their positions during the darkness. After digging entrenchments most of the night, at four o'clock in the morning on New Year's Day, the battered regulars were withdrawn from the front line. Shepherd moved his men to a small patch of woods near Rosecrans's headquarters. Here, they caught a little rest while again serving as the Army of the Cumberland's reserve. Even after the regulars' heavy losses in the cedars, Rosecrans still relied on Shepherd's command to be ready to go where the fighting was heaviest.[87]

One place the regulars wanted to go that night was back into the cedars to recover their wounded. Each sides' pickets were within speaking distance during the darkness and some arranged informal truces so parties could search for fallen comrades. A number of regulars ventured into the cotton field, recovering many of their brethren who had been hit during the retreat after the noontime foray into the cedars. The cedars themselves were too close to Confederate lines for safety. At least one party of regulars was captured that evening. Another group was also taken, but these regulars were able to convince their captors that they were under a flag of truce to recover the wounded and were permitted to head back to Federal lines. The scores of wounded regulars in the cedars suffered through the freezing, wet night without succor. Many died as a result, including one regular encountered by Confederate William J. McMurray of the 20th Tennessee:

> We were ordered...to furnish a detail of forty men...to go on picket. I was detailed as the officer of the pickets. ...A staff officer...led us through the thick cedars where Cheatham and his Tennesseeans had fought over during the day, and the ground strewn with the dead and wounded. ...No one was in front of us but the Yankees and they were about one hundred yards away.

> While I was making my rounds, about one o'clock A.M., I heard quite a halloahing and moaning some fifty yards in the rear. ...I crept back up a rocky ravine...and discovered, as I had expected a wounded soldier. I asked, "To what command do you belong?"
>
> He said Eighteenth Regulars and that he was badly wounded and nearly frozen to death. He asked me to make him a fire at his feet. I told him that I was a Confederate and on picket just in front of him, and by making a fire would draw the picket fire from the Yankee's post.
>
> He begged me so pitifully and as he was down in a ravine, I took the chances, and searched among the rocks and got some cedar limbs and made him a fire and gave him some water, placed his head on a knapsack and made him as comfortable as possible. ...The poor fellow had bled and laid on the ground until life was nearly gone.
>
> I went back in about two hours, but he had crossed over and was sleeping the soldier's sleep...and I could do no more for him.[88]

McMurray went back to the dead regular's position early the next day and "counted seventeen minie balls in one cedar tree that was not over twelve inches in diameter at the height of six feet, and twenty-two dead Federals lying within fifty feet of the tree."[89]

Lieutenant Alfred Pirtle had been busy. As Rousseau's ordnance officer, it was his responsibility to keep the division supplied with ammunition. After spending the day pushing forward rifle cartridges and artillery munitions, Pirtle returned to division headquarters at dusk and was shocked to learn of the Regular Brigade's heavy losses. Years after the war, he penned Shepherd's men a fine tribute:

> I had made the acquaintance of Major John H. King and several officers of the Fifteenth Infantry when it was recruiting at Newport Barracks, Kentucky, in the summer of 1861, becoming thus personally interested in the career of the battalion, having followed its history up to the time of the battle. I was also somewhat acquainted with officers of the other battalions, with whom I had been in business contact frequently. These facts of comradeship made me anxious, when I reached our headquarters at dark, and learned of the loss of Major Carpenter and other friends, to hear all I could about the gallant demonstration the brigade had made in the cedars.
>
> So high an estimate have I always had of this movement that I hold too little has been printed on the topic, nor do I think enough can be said in praise of the behavior of this command all during the fighting.

I do not mean to in the slightest disparage the deeds of the volunteers, because I belong to them, but here was a shining example of the value of the thorough training of officers and men, also of the esprit de corps which kept them at their post of duty though they realized they were being sacrificed.[90]

Enemy commanders also wrote of their encounter with the Regular Brigade. Perhaps trying to find a mitigating circumstance for his unit's high losses and failure to promptly attack across the cotton field after clearing the cedars, General Stewart wrote in his official report that "The force we engaged in this famous cedar brake was composed, at least in part, of regulars." Colonel Francis M. Walker, commanding the 19th Tennessee of Stewart's Brigade, also went out of his way to mention Shepherd's men: "The marks on the arms and equipments picked up on the field from which we drove the enemy, as well as statements of prisoners captured, show conclusively that the brigade or division which we fought was regular troops."[91]

* * *

By the time Shepherd's brigade moved back to Rosecrans's headquarters in the early morning darkness of January 1, fatigue among the regulars was almost overwhelming. An exhausted Captain James Biddle remained awake long enough to record the previous day's events in his diary, closing out the entry with: "We were all glad to see the sun go down that night for we had been under constant fire for more than 10 hours." It was almost sunrise before Lieutenant Anson Mills was able to get some rest. He had been busier than most of his fellow officers, for in addition to commanding A/3/18th U.S. of Major Caldwell's battalion he was also the Regular Brigade's subsistence officer. After seeing to his men, Mills tried to find a place to sleep. It rained intermittently during the night, and by the time the lieutenant was able to bed down he was soaked to the skin. A staff officer's duties never seem to be done, and Mills's rest was short-lived: "When I lay down, I rolled up in my saddle blanket. ...But I was not asleep yet. Colonel Shepherd sent me several miles to the rear with orders to seize some unguarded wagons which were filled with hard bread and bacon for the daylight breakfast. I folded my blanket, laid it on the ground and carried out the instructions, bringing the wagons back with me. When I returned, my blanket was missing. The loss was discouraging, and I was cold." Mills was not alone in his discomfort, for many of the regulars' overcoats had been shot to pieces while piled in the cotton field the previous afternoon.[92]

The rations Mills obtained turned out to be feed corn instead of bacon and hard tack. It was the only additional food the regulars were issued between December 26 and January 3. It did not amount to much and each soldier received but a single ear of corn. Rations were hard to come by because Rosecrans was not able to contain marauding Confederate cavalry during the battle. Although many of Bragg's horse soldiers were then far away in west Tennessee and Kentucky, Colonel Joseph Wheeler and three mounted brigades were near enough to wreak havoc with Federal supply trains in middle Tennessee. The Federal troops on the battle lines had to eat whatever could be scrounged from the local area. "We had not anything to eat for 3 days but parched corn and horse flesh, but little corn," wrote Bugler Carson. During the night of January 2 some famished 15th Infantrymen noticed a wounded horse just outside the lines. They finished off the animal with a pistol, quickly hacked off some steaks, and roasted the meat on sticks over a fire. Lieutenant King was one of the lucky partakers in the meal, recalling: "I never relished anything so much in all my life."[93]

The regulars did not have time to rest on January 1, even though the battlefield was relatively quiet as each side recovered from the intense combat of the previous day. When not constructing fortifications along the line, the Regular Brigade continued to serve as Rosecrans's personal reserve. He dispatched Shepherd's troops to threatened points throughout the day. The regulars were ordered to the front early in the morning, at which time Surgeon Webster Lindsey decided to move the brigade's wounded further to the rear. Troops of the 15th U.S. were encouraged to see Captain Wise riding upright on the front bench of an ambulance, hoping this was a sign he would recover from his neck wound. When the bandage was removed the next day, blood gushed down his throat and choked him to death.

Some regulars saw enemy cavalry firsthand. During the engagement's early stages, Rosecrans had ordered much of his army's equipment and baggage back to Nashville, fearing capture of these supplies if they remained near the battlefield. Confederate horsemen roaming the countryside between Murfreesboro and Nashville easily snapped up many of these lightly guarded wagon trains. The Regular Brigade's train of supply wagons started northward on the evening of January 1. On the Nashville Pike near La Vergne, enemy cavalry captured the convoy lock, stock, and barrel. Included in the booty were many of the wounded from the fight in the cedars (Major Slemmer among them) and also the 15th Infantry Band, complete with instruments:

> When the officer in command of the Confederate troops became aware of the character of his capture he at once set the men at liberty after exacting the usual parole. The transportation, however, and the instruments of the band, together with the personal effects of the men, were appropriated by the captors and carried away. The Confederate officer kindly addressed Major King by letter, entrusting his communication for delivery to a member of the band, announcing that he had paroled the men, and offering to return the instruments if their value in money was sent to his command under flag of truce. The result is not known, but it is believed that the instruments were never recovered.[94]

Captain Jesse Fulmer, commanding the 15th Infantry after King's wounding, was too busy to give more than passing notice to the enemy officer's request. At three o'clock in the afternoon, Rosecrans ordered the regulars northward on the Nashville Turnpike to protect a provision train that was being threatened by enemy cavalry. The movement turned out to be another exhausting exercise. "When about 6 miles out," wrote Captain Biddle of the 16th U.S., "we were overtaken by a staff-officer with an order to face about and return as quickly as possible as the enemy was again advancing and Genl. Rosencrans had need of every man to hold his position. We got back in an hour and a half, most of the way on the run, to find the enemy repulsed." With the January sun setting early, Shepherd again bivouacked his tired and hungry troops near Rosecrans's headquarters. They were allowed to build fires that night to ward off the chill.[95]

On January 2, the weather was unchanged: cold, rainy, and wet. Rosecrans ordered the regulars to the front before breakfast. As Shepherd brought the battalions forward to take their places in the line, Henry Douglass caught up with the column, his uniform spattered with blood and an arm in a sling. The 18th Infantry captain had spent the last two days recovering from his wounding in the cotton field. He was by no means healthy yet, but could not stand to be away from his unit any longer. As the regulars occupied their rifle pits, Douglass reported to Shepherd that he was ready to resume duty with the 18th Infantry's 1st Battalion. Shepherd needed every officer he could get (twenty-four of the brigade's seventy-three line infantry officers had been killed or wounded on December 31), but he took one look at Douglass and told the captain to go back to the hospital. The captain respectfully refused, and Shepherd allowed him to rejoin his company. Douglass's presence turned out to be unnecessary at any rate, for once again no attack materialized on the lines along the Nashville Pike. Having found Rosecrans's positions on the west side of Stones River too strong, Bragg decided on a desperate assault east of the river. Confederates led by Major General John C. Breckinridge launched the attack in the late afternoon. They managed to push back Van Cleve's division (then commanded by Colonel Samuel Beatty) before massed Federal artillery fire halted Breckinridge's advance. The regulars were held in readiness to join the battle but Rosecrans did not commit them.[96]

The next day the weather was worse, with temperatures hovering just above freezing and sleet slashing across the battlefield. Both armies were too exhausted to attack. Rousseau's division was then occupying the left of the line on the west side of the river, the Round Forest position that had been one of the keys to the battlefield during the fighting on New Year's Eve. During the night of January 2–3, a pioneer detachment hastily constructed a new line of earthworks about twenty yards in front of the Regular Brigade's position. Shepherd's brigade moved forward at daylight to complete the works. Lieutenant King recalled that fire from nearby Southern positions was a constant menace: "On the morning of the 3d, Saturday, our battalion finished the entrenchments, which was rather a dangerous piece of business, as the rebels had sharp-shooters, in a woods about 500 yards in advance of us, and the balls whistled past our ears and over our heads in fine style, but nobody was hurt, as they could not aim very well on account of the dirt." The exhausted condition of the regulars made some of them oblivious to both enemy fire and bad weather. Captain Biddle recalled: "The men were so tired that many of them lay [asleep] in the trenches until the water ran in to their mouths."[97]

The weary regulars finally had a decent meal that night, for a supply train had made it through from Nashville. While Shepherd's men feasted on salt pork, bean soup, and hardtack, General Thomas decided to do something about the nearby enemy sharpshooters. He sent a brigade each from Rousseau's and Negley's divisions into the cedars to attack the offending enemy in a daring night assault, a rarity in the Civil War. Thomas held the regulars in reserve, Shepherd's orders being to lay low if the attacking brigades should have to retreat, at which time the regulars would counterattack. Being in reserve meant the regulars were spectators to the sights and sounds of nocturnal combat. "We remained in the trenches all night, with bayonets fixed," recalled Lieutenant King, "ready at a moments notice to jump the bank and at the rebels, but none appeared." Lieutenant Carpenter also wrote of the night's events:

> The fight commenced about dark and lasted until about 9 o'clock. we had not much to do but stand and see it go on. The brigade that made the attack drove the rebels some ways, when their ammunition gave out and they had to come back behind our works. that was a splendid sight. we could see the flashes of fire from the muskets and as the 5th Battery [Battery H] opened upon the woods twas magnificent. we could watch the stream of fire follow the shells over into the woods and as the shells exploded we could hear some cry of pain, or exultant shout as some poor fellow had been hit or escaped unharmed. well we laid in and around these trenches all night. about 2 o'clock in the morning I laid down on the Railroad as it was the dryest place I could find, and went to sleep. I slept sound in the rain until very near daylight. then it was that we could appreciate feather beds. in the morning the rebels were gone.[98]

Thomas's nighttime foray was one of the battle's final engagements. Bragg, having convinced himself that Rosecrans was being heavily reinforced, decided on the afternoon of January 3 to withdraw the Army of Tennessee to a position south of Murfreesboro. Bragg extricated his army from the blood-soaked battlefield the next night, abandoning Murfreesboro and taking up positions along the Duck River north of Tullahoma. The Army of the Cumberland was itself too battered from the fighting to pursue and let the Confederates withdraw unmolested. The Regular Brigade was in poor shape, and Shepherd's men spent much of January 4 resting. At four o'clock that afternoon they started collecting and identifying the brigade's dead. Each battalion sent details into the cedars, the eerie sites in the shattered timber making the men wonder how they had ever survived the twenty-minute stand of four days before. They began the sad task of retrieving those that had not, an activity that took most of the evening. A group of 15th Infantrymen found the body of Captain Bell where he had fallen during the first fight in the cedars. He looked "very natural" despite having died four days earlier. Confederates had stripped the body of everything useful, taking even the buttons from his vest. Two other officers of the 18th Infantry were found in a similar condition: "The enemy stripped everything of value from our dead. Every pocket is turned wrong side out, shoes and in some instances stockings taken off. Captain Kneass and Lieut. Hitchcock of our Regt. who were left dead upon the field had everything off of them but pants and shirt."[99]

The sun had long since dipped below the western horizon by the time all the dead had been collected and the burial site prepared. The regulars recovered the bodies of five officers and eighty-nine enlisted men and wrapped them in blankets. A detail from each regiment dug a long burial trench on the Battery H knoll between the turnpike and railroad. With the Regular Brigade assembled and rendering military honors, a winter's moon and flickering torches illuminated the first internment in what would one day become the Stones River National Cemetery. The enlisted dead were lowered into the burial trenches and the bodies of the five officers were placed in separate graves to the right of their respective regimental dead. Additional regulars were laid to rest in the coming weeks as men died of wounds, while family members disinterred others for shipment home. In early January, a regular posted a sign on the path leading to the graves: "This patch of ground contains the bodies of ninety-three soldiers, of the 15th, 16th, 18th, and 19th U.S. Infantry. Do not disturb these graves by additions or otherwise." A reporter looking over the battlefield a few weeks later noted that while a number of hasty burial sites receiving little if any care were scattered about the area, the regulars' plot was "quite a cemetery— ninety-three prettily constructed graves, with an inscribed slab at the head of each."

"A battlefield is a hard place," Lieutenant Arthur Carpenter wrote on January 8 while reflecting on his recent experiences, "the dead and wounded lying around everything showing that the iron heel of war had made its print. I hope that we will have no more 5 days battle, 2 days are enough."[100]

* * *

Each side punished the other at Stones River, both suffering about 33 percent casualties. The battle was one of the bloodiest of the war, but tactically a draw. Because the Army of Tennessee retreated and left the field in Rosecrans's possession, the nation considered the clash a Northern victory. The Federal triumph at Stones River may have been excruciatingly narrow, but occurring as it did so soon after Union defeats in Mississippi and Virginia, it was welcomed indeed. Some of the first news the nation received about the battle came from the pen of Pont Mercy, a correspondent for the *New York Tribune*. "There is a record which shall be more amply made," the reporter wrote in a dispatch he filed from the battlefield, "when the Biography of the gallant Regular Brigade is ready for history. ...Almost one-half of [Rousseau's] casualties were regulars, while they numbered less than one-fourth of the entire division. The missing indicates discipline and skill of officers with unmistakable emphasis." A writer for the *Philadelphia Press* crafted a similar line: "Probably the most severe fighting which has been done by any body of men since the war commenced was that done by the Brigade of Regulars in Rousseau's division." While journalists later in the war would write similar stories about different units in other battles, the press coverage of the regulars at Stones River was for the most part accurate in the context of the war in the Western Theater as of January 1863.[101]

The Army of the Cumberland occupied Murfreesboro on January 5. Lieutenant Robert King recalled that, by then, men on both sides were speaking admirably about the Regular Brigade: "On Monday, we advanced into Murfreesboro'. Everything looks deserted, nothing there but wounded confeds, and our men. The rebels left over three thousand wounded men, in our hands. We are now encamped about one mile south of the town; I cannot say how long we will remain here. Since the battle, we have talked with officers who were in the cedar bush opposite to us, and they say that they had three divisions opposed to us, and that we cut them up terribly, it being the hardest fight of any. Every one of our Generals speak in the highest terms of our behaviour."[102]

"In the tangled cedar thickets bordering Stones River [the] regular brigade discharged the awful responsibility of saving the entire army." So claims Francis McKinney in his biography of George Thomas *Education in Violence*. Thomas B. Buell more recently made similar assertions in *The Warrior Generals*, his study of combat leadership in the Civil War. It is too much to definitively claim that the Regular Brigade's stand in the cedars on December 31 won the battle for the Army of the Cumberland. But New Year's Eve 1862 turned out to be the best day William Rosecrans ever had in managing events on a fast-paced battlefield, and one of his most crucial actions that day was his noon-time decision to send Shepherd's brigade into the cedars. The battle may indeed have turned out differently had the regulars not bought Rosecrans enough time to solidify the line along the Nashville Pike. When asked why he sent the unsupported regulars back into the cedars, Rosecrans allegedly replied: "I was compelled to sacrifice my regulars to save the rest of the army." Whether or not the general actually uttered that statement is not important. More significant is the fact that these words accurately reflect many of the surviving regulars' sentiments. Those twenty minutes in the cedars were the defining moments of the Regular Brigade's short existence. Frederick Phisterer believed the battle left an "indelible stamp of honor" on every regular there—certainly those killed or wounded, but also the men who made it through without a scratch. Many Regular Brigade veterans took every opportunity they could during the coming decades to inform both the army and nation at large about the brigade's role at Stones River. This effort began as soon as the battle ended. "The fate of the day being upon the balance," Captain Henry Haymond mentioned in a January 7, 1863, letter to his mother, "the regular brigade as a last resort was then ordered forward to check the enemy's advance until the army could be reorganized." Henry B. Freeman was still hammering home this point as late as 1890, when he told a gathering of veterans in Ohio that "the truthful historian of the battle will write that it was saved to the national arms by the Regular Brigade." It appears that Phisterer, Haymond, Freeman, and their comrades have convinced at least a few historians.[103]

Perhaps the highest praise for Shepherd's regulars at Stones River came from one of their staunchest supporters, Lovell Rousseau. By early 1863, Rousseau had emerged as one of the best division commanders in the Union Army. He knew his business and knew what it took to get the most from his men. On January 7, Rousseau hosted the Regular Brigade's officer corps at his headquarters in Murfreesboro, expressing his gratitude and congratulating the new brigade on its performance. "He shook hands with us all," Lieutenant Carpenter wrote the next day, "and chatted as familiar as could be. He is a splendid man."[104]

Oliver Shepherd was also pleased with the performance of the regulars. Although the brigade had been formed little more than a week prior to the battle, it had measured up to even Shepherd's high standards. With an eye looking toward his future job security, he closed out his report on the brigade's operations with a reminder that its role at Stones River ought not be forgotten up the chain of command: "It is hoped that the bearing and whole career of this brigade of regular troops during the five days' conflict were of a character to meet the approbation of the major-general commanding the division."[105] Shepherd must have been satisfied when he read Rousseau's post-battle report. Just as the general had done after the Battle of Shiloh, he singled out the regulars for praise:

> The brigade of United States infantry, Lieut. Col. O.L. Shepherd commanding, was on the extreme right. On that body of brave men the shock of battle fell heaviest, and its loss was most severe. Over one third of the command fell, killed or wounded; but it stood up to the work and bravely breasted the storm, and, though Major King, commanding the Fifteenth, and Major Slemmer ("Old Pickens"), commanding the Sixteenth, fell, severely wounded, and Major Carpenter, commanding the Nineteenth, fell dead in the last charge, together with many other brave officers and men, the brigade did not falter for a moment. These three battalions were a part of my old (Fourth) brigade at the battle of Shiloh.
>
> The Eighteenth Infantry, Majors Townsend and Caldwell commanding, were new troops to me, but I am now proud to say we know each other.
>
> If I could, I would promote every officer and several noncommissioned officers and privates of this brigade of regulars, for gallantry and good service in this terrific battle. I make no distinction between these troops and my brave volunteer regiments, for, in my judgment, there never were better troops than those regiments, in the world. But the troops of the line are soldiers by profession, and, with a view to the future, I feel it my duty to say what I have of them. The brigade was admirably and gallantly handled by Lieutenant-Colonel Shepherd.[106]

The end of the fighting brought the usual chores of policing the battlefield. Oliver Shepherd had an additional task: rebuild and retrain the Regular Brigade. Its ranks had been thinned considerably at Stones River, but many of those who remained felt a surge of pride about being part of a unique unit. Arthur Carpenter's feelings are evident in a letter he wrote to his brother on January 18: "Our brigade suffered more in this fight than any other Brigade in the army. we are all regulars, the only regular Brigade in the army."[107]

Chapter 7:

The Middle Tennessee Campaign

"No Regular Soldier Ever Forgets"

The Army of the Cumberland remained in the Murfreesboro area for six months after the battle of Stones River, during which time the Regular Brigade was reconstituted. By resorting to every feasible means, including the disbandment of decimated companies, the dispatch of new companies to the field, and—in at least one regiment—a renewed emphasis on recruiting, the Regular Brigade more than made up for its Stones River losses. There was also great turbulence among the leaders of the brigade as old officers left for other duties, untried officers arrived in the field, and experienced sergeants were promoted from the ranks. In a curious turn of events, John King and Oliver Shepherd ended up switching positions as the former took charge of the Regular Brigade and the latter became the new commander of the 15th Infantry Regiment. The Regular Brigade by the summer of 1863 was different in many ways from its pre-Stones River predecessor, but its reputation for being a highly trained and professional organization remained unchanged as it campaigned through Tennessee and approached the Georgia border.

* * *

Federal hospitals dotted the fields around Murfreesboro, the casualties from Stones River lying in tents and abandoned farm buildings. Wanting to see the wounded of his regiment one last time before they were moved to more distant facilities, Lieutenant Bisbee of the 18th Infantry visited the hospital of Rousseau's division as soon as his duties permitted. He later wrote of those officers who ended up not making the trip north:

> The dignified Captain Denison, with one leg amputated, remarked as I sat by his bedside, "Well, lieutenant, I shall have the satisfaction of selecting a new leg and foot to suit me, the old ones never did." In a few days this brave man was dead. Lieutenant "Jimmie" Simons lay desperately wounded in the thigh and side, a fatal case. We could not find Lieutenant McConnell in any of the beds but at last found him sitting in a chair by the fire-place, smoking and cheerful, as he told us that on Thursday he was going North to see his girl. He had been shot through the breast and the next day was upon a cot near a window, gasping for air; that night he died, after his father reached him from Ohio. Sad scenes all of them, to which we became too callous under the rough influence of field service.[1]

McConnell and Simons succumbed to their wounds on January 14; Denison passed away the next day. McConnell's father took his son's body back home to Michigan (Bisbee was mistaken in stating that the family hailed from Ohio), while Denison and Simons were buried beside the other regulars interned on the Battery H knoll. Relatives of some of the brigade's enlisted dead eventually made the trek to Murfreesboro to retrieve the remains of their loved ones for re-internment in the North. War Department regulations stipulated that the remains of all regular officers were to be returned to their home of record. The body of Lieutenant James Simons is one of the few that remains at Stones River to this day. This veteran of the Old Army's non-commissioned officer corps left specific instructions before he died that he wanted to remain buried on the battlefield, near the regular soldiers who had fallen alongside him.[2]

The body of Major Stephen D. Carpenter was removed from the Battery H knoll in late January and taken to his hometown of Bangor, Maine. Carpenter's wife was deceased and his only surviving child, a daughter, had left Maine to live with relatives. The citizens of Bangor found themselves with a dead hero and no family to claim the remains. After much discussion, on February 11, 1863, an elaborate funeral was conducted under the auspices of the Bangor city government. The event included as much military fanfare as could be locally assembled. A band, militia units, and color guard of returned and wounded soldiers escorted the casket from City Hall to Mt. Hope Cemetery. An Episcopal burial service followed, which included an address summarizing the major's career. It was an emotional speech, intended to stir even the faintest patriotic embers: "We honor ourselves in honoring him who honored his country, and while mingling our sympathies here...we may take pride in claiming him as a citizen, and in rendering this tribute to his glorious memory. He fell not too soon for his own fame, but too early for our country's need, which mourns to-day her many, like him, gallant but fallen defenders."[3]

The loss of Captain Denison was particularly hard on Major Townsend. The captain had been appointed to the 18th U.S. in the summer of 1861 after serving as an officer in an Illinois regiment. This experience plus his Norwich training resulted in Denison being one of the 18th Infantry's more capable company commanders. The captain and major had become quite close during the ensuing eighteen months. When it initially appeared that Denison was recovering from his amputation, Townsend wrote to Denison's wife with the good news. He had to post another letter a few days later:

> I did not think, when I addressed you a few days since, giving so favorable an account of your husband's condition, that I should so soon be called upon to break to you the melancholy intelligence of his death. He passed away calmly and with perfect consciousness, though for some time speechless, at half past eleven o'clock last night. He received every Kindness, that could be proffered by his brother officers and the care and attention of able surgeons and kind attendants, who were struck by the fortitude and nobleness of his bearing, even while lying prostrate on his bed, though still the gallant soldier.
>
> My dear Madam, your husband was my friend and throughout the many trials and exposures, incident to the various campaigns, which we have endured together, that friendship was unerring and I cherish it now as the only solace left in connection with his memory.
>
> Your husband will be buried tomorrow and with military honors in the cemetary, we have constructed, where lie the slain of our regiment, on a Knoll in front of the intrenchments, which the Regiment so gallantly defended.[4]

Captain Ansel Denton of C/2/18th U.S. also had to write a sad letter after the battle. Sergeant Amos Fleagle, wounded in the cotton field on December 31, had been located that stormy night by a search party. He was loaded into an ambulance and whisked away to a hospital, but that was the last the sergeant's comrades ever saw of him. As the weeks went by with no word of Fleagle's condition or whereabouts, Captain Denton wrote the sergeant's brother-in-law, David Bailey Flegeal, with the news:

> So long a time has passed since the battle, during which we have not heard one word concerning the whereabouts or welfare of your brother Sergt. Amos Fleagle, that we have all settled down in the belief that he is dead. We have heard in one way or another from every other wounded man in the regiment, and I think if he were alive we would have heard from him ere this. With this belief I send you his effects viz: 1 gold watch, 1 small revolver, 1 Bible, 1 Sergts warrant, 1 pocket book containing $9.05 in money, and some other small things of little money value.
>
> If you ever here anything further concerning your brother I would wish you to let me know.[5]

Nothing further was ever heard about Fleagle's fate, either by his family or comrades in the Regular Brigade. He was listed as missing in action as of January 3. About a month after Denton sent home the sergeant's affects, Fleagle's mother replied with a letter of thanks. The captain was so moved by the grieving mother's words that he sent for Robert Kennedy, the man responsible for retrieving the sergeant's watch and pistol. Kennedy, a corporal now, reported to Denton's tent. "Come in and sit down," the captain beckoned, "I have a letter to read to you." As Denton read the letter both his and Kennedy's eyes welled up. "The Captain and I were both young men about twenty-one years of age," remembered Kennedy, "and the tears flowed from our eyes as he read that letter of gratitude from that dear old mother who lost her darling boy at Stone River."[6]

With the loss of Sergeant Fleagle and so many other regulars at Stones River, most of the brigade's companies contained just a handful of troops. Shepherd requested permission from the War Department to disband thirteen of these units and distribute their men among other companies in the battalions. Eight companies of the 18th U.S. were broken up in January and February; the 15th and 16th lost two each and one company of 1/19th U.S. was discontinued. Even after this consolidation, the remaining thirty companies in the five battalions were woefully short of personnel. The Army of the Cumberland underwent organizational changes as well during the winter at Murfreesboro. The Center, Right, and Left Wings were re-designated the XIV, XX, and XXI Army Corps, retaining their old commanders. Rosecrans would later add a small Reserve Corps under Major General Gordon Granger. The ranks of all the army's divisions had been thinned at Stones River, so Rosecrans could no longer afford to assign four brigades to Rousseau's division of the XIV Corps. Colonel John Beatty's brigade was transferred to Negley's division, and Rousseau's command thereafter had the standard three-brigade structure common throughout the Union Army.[7]

Rail communications with Nashville were reestablished after the battle and trains were soon pouring into Murfreesboro. While supplies were stockpiled, the Army of the Cumberland built fortifications and winter quarters. The 16th Infantry's Captain James Biddle recalled that the weather presented numerous challenges in January 1863: "the ground being very wet & muddy from the constant rain we made several changes of location to try & better ourselves, but without much success, as could be seen from our large sick roll. ...Although we are supposed to be resting in camp we have much hard work to do being constantly out on picket duty & acting as guard to forage trains. A detail for the picket line is for 24 hours. The ground is always muddy & some times covered with snow & no fires are allowed. If we are not fortunate enough to find a log or a rail fence to sit on we have to stand up or take to the mud." Other than picket duty, the cold, wet weather curtailed activities for the moment and the troops welcomed the respite. Conditions improved somewhat the next month. "I am living the [life of a] gentleman," Lt. Arthur Carpenter wrote home on February 10, "eating and sleeping constitutes the principle part of my present employment for which 'Uncle Sam' pays me $105.00 per month. but I suppose I shall see enough of hard work in the course of two or three months to make up for my present idleness. such is military life."[8]

Less than fifty regulars had been captured or were missing during the Stones River fighting. A few of the latter straggled back to their companies during the week following the battle. Private John Mallory of B/3/18th suddenly showed up in camp on January 7, not having been seen since the afternoon of December 31, when he had secured his equipment at his company wagon and then pillaged another soldier's knapsack for a clean pair of trousers. Mallory explained his seven-day absence by claiming he had been "part of the time on the field and part of the time with the wagon train." Captain Belknap did not believe either part of the story and placed

Mallory under arrest, charging him with violating the 52nd Article of War ("Any officer or soldier who runs away or shamefully abandons his post in the face of the enemy shall suffer death") and also conduct prejudicial to good order and discipline for stealing the clothing. Mallory was arraigned before a court-martial three weeks later and quickly found guilty. His sentence was a six-month prison confinement with ball and chain, after which he would have his head shaved and be drummed out of the service. Given that the ten officers comprising the court were all regulars who had seen their men cut down by the score in the cedars, Mallory was lucky to have escaped a death sentence.[9]

A number of skirmishes took place during the winter months. Bragg had to send foraging parties far and wide to keep his army supplied, some venturing as far as southwestern Tennessee and southern Kentucky. Rosecrans responded by sending out raiding columns of his own to gather the stockpiled foodstuffs bound for Southern soldiers and to destroy the economic infrastructure that continued to supply goods to the Confederacy. An area with particularly strong Confederate sentiments was the countryside around Eagleville, a small settlement about sixteen miles southwest of Murfreesboro. A Federal column sweeping through the area in mid-January burned a large gristmill that was producing a prodigious quantity of meal for Bragg's troops.

Other mills near Eagleville were still at work a month and a half later. Major Townsend led a column of regulars into the region on March 2. They discovered so much milled corn stockpiled in a couple of barns that the wagons accompanying the column were soon filled to capacity. Townsend gave the owner of the corn a government receipt. If the farmer could prove Unionist loyalty, he would be paid for his goods. Given the sentiments of the Eagleville area, Townsend knew these supplies would be free of charge. While the wagons were being loaded, Townsend posted a picket line around the area. The rest of the regulars stacked arms and waited. A few troops struck up a game of cards to pass the time, others fell asleep. They had just made themselves comfortable when they heard the sharp report of rifle fire and the sound of charging horses. Captain James Biddle was among the 16th Infantrymen present: "the skirmishers in our front opened a heavy fire & five minutes afterwards about 200 cavalry came dashing down on our left, which was not covered by skirmishers. The Confederates evidently thought they had an easy thing of it, probably they imagined that the skirmishers were all the troops we had in that part of the field. We let them come on to within 100 yards when the old 16th, which was lying behind a fence out of sight, poured in a volley which sent them about face at a double quick. Two or three were seen to fall and others were supposed to be wounded. As they left us the 18th opened on them killing an other man."[10]

The Southern commander determined that there were too many alert infantrymen in the area and therefore broke up the cavalry squadron into small squads to harass the regulars. Townsend ordered the regulars and the train of wagons to make haste back to Murfreesboro, their flanks covered by thick forces of skirmishers. A running battle took place for a few miles; a few more enemy horsemen were shot and two captured. The regulars returned to camp late that night with their load of corn and one man slightly wounded ("a carbine slug pealed his scalp nothing serious").[11]

* * *

William Rosecrans's formation of the Regular Brigade illustrates his fondness for distinctive military formations. His efforts along this line did not end with Shepherd's troops. Shortly after Stones River, Rosecrans tried to form a separate corps of veteran infantrymen within the Army of the Cumberland. He directed each of his regiments to place their most distinguished soldiers on a "Roll of Honor," intending to form these veterans into elite "light battalions." Furthermore, Rosecrans intended to provide the light battalions with horses and carbines, a move that would finally provide the Army of the Cumberland with a sizable and effective cavalry force. But the plan miscarried because the War Department would not approve it: the scheme violated state authority to organize volunteer units. Rosecrans had to be satisfied with making renewed requests to have additional cavalry assigned to the Army of the Cumberland. He also began to toy with the idea of converting Rousseau's entire division, to include its regulars, into mounted infantry.[12]

Be it on foot or horse, Rosecrans wanted the regulars to perform in the next campaign as well as they had at Stones River. That would require a heavy infusion of new troops, and Oliver Shepherd knew where some were to be found:

Head Quarters Brigade U.S. Regular Troops
1st Division, "Centre" 14th Army Corps
Camp at Murfreesboro, Tenn
January 13th 1863

Major Goddard
    A.A.A.G. 14th Army Corps
    Dept of the Cumberland

Sir

On account of the heavy losses in the recent battles, it is very essential that every available company and Recruit should join their Regiments. I therefore respectfully request that Major Caldwell 18th Inf.. may be ordered to proceed to Camp Thomas, Ohio, with orders to bring on with all possible dispatch, the three companies of the Regiment already organized at that place, together with three hundred Recruits reported to be there also the company which has been on duty in Cincinnati for several months past.

Were these companies ordered on by themselves with inexperienced officers, dreading the service and discipline expected in this brigade, they would be long delayed along the way on various pretexts, as was done in every previous instance.

I have the honor to be
Very Respectfully
Your Obt. Servant

O.L. SHEPHERD
Lieut. Col. 18th Inf..
Comd'g Brigade[13]

Major Caldwell was duly ordered back to Ohio to empty Camp Thomas of recruits and then return. Caldwell had other plans, for his health had been faltering in recent months. He took a medical leave of absence upon arrival in Columbus. After a month-long rest, he convinced Henry Carrington to name him post commander at Camp Thomas. Carrington was sympathetic to Caldwell's reasoning, particularly since the order requiring all available 18th Infantrymen to head for Tennessee might well be followed up by a requirement for the regiment's colonel to follow suit. With a major superintending the regimental recruiting effort and keeping Camp Thomas running, Carrington's pretext for remaining on the sidelines retained a modicum of credibility.[14]

The plan for Major Caldwell to escort the latest batch of Camp Thomas regulars may have miscarried, but Shepherd and Rosecrans

were of one mind on reconstituting the Regular Brigade. "The regular brigade is so reduced in numbers since the battle," Rosecrans
wrote on February 12, "that it is very desirable all detached companies should rejoin their regiments." Some of the regulars that had
been scattered throughout the country the previous year headed for
middle Tennessee during the late winter and early spring of 1863.
The 19th Infantrymen in Virginia finally ended their theater-span-
ning travels and reported to 1/19th U.S. in March, giving the two
companies the distinction of being the only units to serve in both
the Army of the Potomac's Regular Division and in the Army of the
Cumberland's Regular Brigade. The Cincinnati garrison had to
make due with a new force of provosts, for Captain John A.
Thompson, 1st Sergeant Chris Peterson, and G/2/18th U.S. reported
for duty in Murfreesboro on March 12. Private Charles Bogart of
Thompson's company visited the Stones River battlefield shortly
after arrival in middle Tennessee: "We are now in Camp in a very
nice place, about half a mile from Murfreesboro, and about two
miles from the battlefield. I have seen the battlefield of
Murfreesboro. I tell you it looks hard to see horses and broken cannon wheels laying all over the ground. I only went across the field
and if I saw one horse I believe I seen 50, laying scattered here and
there all over the ground, and I did not see the worst of it either. I
also seen where the 18th was buried. they was buried by them
selves, and the rest that was killed was buried all over here and
there."[15]

Unlike Captain Thompson's company from Cincinnati and the
Army of the Potomac veterans of the 19th Infantry, the regulars sta-
tioned in Grant's Department of the Tennessee were still not able to
transfer to the Department of the Cumberland. Company A/2/16th
U.S. remained in Columbus, Kentucky, throughout 1863. The 15th
Infantry's small 2nd Battalion also continued its drab garrison exis-
tence. Three companies of 2/15th had been garrisoning Columbus
since the autumn of 1862, being joined by D/2/15th U.S. from Fort
Adams in December of that year. That same month Major John R.
Edie of the 15th Infantry was released from staff duty and assumed
command of the battalion. Edie and his men did not remain in
Kentucky long thereafter. In preparation for another advance
toward Vicksburg, on January 22, 1863, General Grant ordered to
Memphis some of the few regular infantrymen in his department,
Edie's battalion and a small contingent of the 1st U.S. Infantry then

near Corinth. Edie's 15th regulars arrived in Memphis on February 2, where they served for a time as artillerymen while manning the heavy guns covering the Mississippi River from Fort Pickering. Edie's troops performed their artillery mission well. In early April, Grant wanted the regular battalion to continue down river and join the Army of the Tennessee near Vicksburg, but the commander of the Memphis garrison wrote Grant that "I regret to lose the Fifteenth Regulars from the fort, but must supply their place as best I can." Grant canceled the movement and Edie's battalion remained in Memphis. Although 2/15th U.S. would see no action while assigned to Grant's department other than occasionally chasing guerrillas through the backwoods of west Tennessee, the unit earned a reputation for being an "efficient battalion."[16]

In addition to the companies that had been on detached service, new regular companies left their regimental depots and also headed for middle Tennessee to join the Regular Brigade. Sergeant Edgar N. Wilcox, still serving as a clerk at 18th Infantry Headquarters, wrote his sister on January 22 describing the preparations of troops at Camp Thomas to move south: "The Adjutant came back from a consultation with the Col. at Indianapolis last night and brought with him a huge lot of papers which I had to examine and file away, taking me until about 12 o'clock. I learn from the Adj't (though I wouldn't dare tell it in Camp) that Co. 'H' 2nd Battalion who have just been exchanged together with two companies of unassigned Recruits are to march to the field immediately and that the rest of us will follow with the Col in about 30 days. So I reckon we shall get into the field yet, before the winter is over."[17]

Henry Carrington was spending more time in Indianapolis than at Camp Thomas by this point in the war, but the regulars in Ohio still felt their colonel's influence. Daily inspections and guard mounting continued much as in 1861, with Major Caldwell presiding over the camp after assuming command during late February. Carrington refused to release new troops for duty with the Regular Brigade in the field until he felt the recruits' training and drill met Regular Army standards. He also wanted regulars to be available for occasional guard duty at Camp Chase. The peaceful routine of Camp Thomas aggravated some of the local denizens of Columbus, many of whom had relatives serving in more active parts of the war effort. In early 1863, the *Ohio State Journal* editorialized that it would be best for the troops at Camp Thomas if the government "put up brick or stone structures that will last a long time, and lay out a cemetery for the soldiers who will doubtless die of old age before they are ordered to the field." The editor also recommended that Camp Thomas be incorporated as its own town with Carrington as the mayor.[18]

The need to replenish the Regular Brigade's depleted ranks after Stones River shattered Camp Thomas's tranquility. Although the first contingent did not get underway as fast as Sergeant Wilcox predicted or Oliver Shepherd desired (and of course Henry Carrington remained on the governor's staff in Indianapolis, and Major Caldwell did not return to the Regular Brigade), Companies G/2, H/2, G/3, and H/3 of the 18th Infantry began the journey southward on March 14. These were the 18th Infantry's final companies, making Carrington's command the only New Army infantry regiment to deploy all twenty-four of its companies to the field during the Civil War. A few additional recruits signed on at Camp Thomas during the coming spring. Like many of their predecessors, these troops also seemed destined to become a permanent feature of the Ohio landscape. This time it was not Carrington's fault. Administrative commanders of Northern districts usually resisted losing troops of any kind, and Brigadier General John S. Mason, whose jurisdiction included Camp Thomas, had a habit of using the regulars there as his personal police force. Despite General Rosecrans desire that all regulars should report to Murfreesboro, Edgar Wilcox (whose desire to be commissioned was finally fulfilled in late March) wrote to a friend on April 30 that he was still in Ohio:

> Lt. Neill returned from Indianapolis yesterday with orders for us all to go to the field, but Gen. Mason, who has just assumed command here objects to it & says Gen Carrington has no right to order troops from his Dept. so here I am in the dark as much as ever as to my "Destiny." Night before last I was ordered to hold myself in readiness to take the troops in Camp Thomas to Wheeling in an hour & a half, in support of Capt. Hill's Battery, but Genl Mason finally sent Lieut. Ostrander and an hour from the notice they were on the train. The excitement, however, having died away somewhat down there I presume they will be back tomorrow or next day. ...We have nearly a Co. of men here belonging to the Detach in the field and as soon as the troops return from Wheeling Lieut. Truman will take com'd of them, and I of the men belonging to the Companies in the field, & the Band, and presto chango away we go. That is the idea, now, whether it will be carried out or not is another thing.[19]

While Wilcox and the others remained behind, the four-company contingent that departed in March made its way to Murfreesboro. Lieutenant Lucius F. Brown, Wilcox's cousin, was among these troops. An architect who had enlisted in the 18th Infantry during October 1861, Brown had spent the entire war thus far at Camp Thomas and was eager to get to middle Tennessee. A day's journey brought the command to Cincinnati, where Brown described in a letter his experiences thus far: "We have secured a boat, and one of the best, the 'Sultana' and hope to get off tomorrow—down the River. The General [Carrington] came in last night and will be here for Dress Parade this P.M. We had one last night and one regular Sunday morning inspection. We found miserable dirty quarters but now they are well cleaned up. Our boys *hate* dirt and are giving a lesson to the two regiments in camp here. We are observed and admired by all observers. The Commandant here says he never saw such a body of men." Boarding the *Sultana* the next day, the regulars settled in for the journey down the Ohio and up the Cumberland to Nashville. Having read the previous year's newspaper accounts of alleged brutal discipline on the part of regular officers in the field, Brown was eager to give his family a more accurate view. "It would astonish some growlers at the Reg. Army discipline to have seen our officers last night," Brown remarked about billeting the detachment aboard the vessel. "Not an officer relieved himself of his belt, sword & pistol, haversack & canteen or sought his own quarters until our men were fixed." After completing the waterborne portion of the journey, the detachment spent two days in Nashville wrestling with unbroken mules before the troops and their baggage train moved out on the Murfreesboro Pike. They made only four and a half miles the first day before a messenger from Nashville told the 18th Regulars to stand fast until a contingent of the 16th Regulars caught up.[20]

Based out of the 16th Infantry's new headquarters at Fort Ontario, New York, Major Sidney Coolidge had made some progress toward filling up his regiment's ranks during late 1862. In March 1863, the War Department ordered the 16th Infantry band, the recently organized Companies C and D of 2/16th, and all available recruits to proceed immediately to Murfreesboro, leaving only a skeleton crew at Fort Ontario. Numbering more than 270 strong, the 16th Infantrymen moved out on March 11 under the command of Major Coolidge. At Nashville, the 16th Infantrymen were charged with bringing to Murfreesboro 150 wagons and a herd of

800 mules. Linking up with the 18th Infantrymen just outside of town, Coolidge took command of the combined force. The column passed by the Stones River battlefield on March 26. The sights along the banks of Stones River were undoubtedly disturbing to the raw recruits from Ohio and New York. Arms and legs poked out from shallow graves, while tattered hospital flags still hung from the trees under which surgeons had performed their grisly tasks. The column hurried past the shattered wasteland and arrived at the Regular Brigade's bivouac near Murfreesboro later that evening. Major Coolidge assumed command of 1/16th U.S. from Captain R.E.A. Crofton, the battalion now including a total of three companies from the regiment's 2nd Battalion.[21]

Shepherd welcomed the additional companies, but precious few troops arrived to replenish the companies decimated at Stones River. The new companies assigned to the Regular Brigade in early 1863 consisted almost exclusively of men who enlisted during 1862. When Congress reduced the prewar, five-year regular enlistment to the volunteer standard of three years in August 1861, in that same legislation the lawmakers stipulated a return to five year terms for regulars as of January 1, 1863, wanting the Regular Army to be prepared for an eventual transition back to a peacetime footing. It should come as no surprise that regular recruiting hit a brick wall on that date. A total of just 6,368 men joined the Regular Army during 1863, a 60 percent reduction from the previous year (and 1,198 of the 1863 enlistments were volunteers who transferred during January and February). The nadir of regular recruiting for the war occurred in May 1863, when there were only 257 enlistments nationwide. Some regiments were hit particularly hard. One hundred eighty-two men had joined the 15th Infantry during the last five months of 1862. In the first five months of 1863, a grand total of just six hardy souls showed up at Fort Adams.

A return to three-year terms could only be affected through an act of Congress. While lobbying efforts began toward that end, the War Department took other measures to somehow channel manpower into the regulars. On June 25, 1863, the bounty for a recruit enlisting for a five-year regular hitch was raised to $402. The following August, the prewar General Recruiting Service was re-established and charged with coordinating the recruiting efforts of all regular regiments. The Federal Enrollment (or Draft) Act of 1863, which went into effect that summer, also aided the regulars' cause. The draft's main effect was to stimulate men to voluntarily join the Union Army, and regular recruiters saw a slight increase in business toward the end of the year as a result ("Let me know who all of my friends enlist and go to war as men," wrote the 15th Infantry's Lieutenant Robert King to his mother, "and also those who wait to be drafted, as I want to know amongst my acquaintances who are men and who are cowards, that I may treat them accordingly"). But none of these efforts materially altered the advantages the volunteer service held over the regulars when it came to attracting men into the ranks. Relatively few men joined the regulars during 1863, the year when some of the war's most important campaigns were waged.[22]

Although the future bode ill tidings, during the first few months of 1863 a steady stream of regulars headed for Murfreesboro. The new companies and a few replacement troops for the old swelled the Regular Brigade's ranks to more than 2,000 soldiers, a strength surpassing what it had taken into battle at Stones River. Incorporating the new soldiers into the battalions was a demanding task. Some of them were fairly well trained when they arrived, particularly those of the 18th Infantry. Others were little more than warm bodies in uniform. One of the companies composed of troops in the latter category was A/2/19th U.S., which completed its trek from the 19th Infantry's depot on March 23. It fell upon Lieutenant Carpenter's shoulders to mold these raw soldiers into proper regulars. His lazy days of living like a gentleman were over:

> I have been assigned permanently to Company "A" 2nd Batt. and it is a new company just come into the field and has a great deal to learn which must be taught by the officers. it had a Capt. and 1st Lt. but now the Capt is on a leave of absence, the 1st Lieut is appointed Battalion Quarter Master and I am the only officer now with the company and I will have a great deal to do to start it on the right track. there is a great deal more responsibility with such a company than with one that had been in the field a year, and have learnt to take care of themselves to a certain degree. the company is large, its ranks not having been decimated by a years service of fatigue and hardship.[23]

As winter turned into spring, Shepherd had his troops out in the field drilling whenever the weather permitted. "We drilled company drill, battalion drill and brigade drill untill we were sick and tired of drilling," recalled Corporal Robert Kennedy of his days in Murfreesboro.[24] A newly assigned lieutenant in 2/18th recorded a detailed description of the regulars' daily routine:

If you think we have nothing to do, listen—Reveille at 10 minutes before daylight when the Batt. turns our *under arms* and forms *line* of *battle* on the color line in front of Camp, where arms are stacked and Batt. remains under arms until breakfast call at 7. This is to be ready for a possible attack at daylight, our precautions and advance pickets rendering any surprise utterly impossible. Sick call at 7 1/2. School of non commissioned officers (sergts & corpls) from that to 8 1/2 for instruction by company officers. Guard mount at 9. Battalion drill from 10 to 11 1/2 on Monday, W., & F. Skirmish drill Tues., T. & S. Dinner call at 12 when com. officers attend Co. Roll Calls and read all orders to Co. Brigade Drill 2 1/2 to 5 1/2 P.M. When the 6 battalions of this Regular Brigade and the Artillery drill together under Lt. Col. Shepherd, act'g Brig. Gen., I tell you it looks grand to see about 3000 men drilling together under one command but it does not feel quite so grand by the time we come in tired with double quicking and covered and *filled* with dust. Our two battalions are *far* very far ahead of the rest in drill as well as discipline. Well then comes Retreat at 6. When the Co. turns out under arms and are inspected by company officers as to dress, arms and ammunition of which they must have a constant full supply. The officers report the roll call to the adjt. Tattoo at 7 1/2 when the company again falls out with arms, roll call and report to adjt. Then at 8 to 9 or sometimes 11 School of officers for examination and instruction by the Major. We *may* then go to bed and sometimes we *do*. That's a day's work—regular—then comes extras—guard—Grand Guard or Picket and Fatigue or foraging.[25]

Sunday parades and dress inspections, a time-honored tradition in the Regular Army, commenced on February 15. Captain Thomas C. Williams, commanding C/1/19th U.S., told his troops that he intended to have the sharpest company in the 19th Infantry, which was a tall order given the high standards most regulars maintained. Sergeant Tarbell and his comrades grumbled about the extra work, but they also took pride in their unit. "We are all in our tents cleaning & fixing for inspection in the morning," the sergeant recorded in his diary on February 21. "Capt. Williams is very particular with his Co. We must be just so clean or up you go to the Guard House. Well we have the name of being the best looking Co. in the Regt." The effort paid off in April, when General Rousseau selected C/1/19th to be the provost guard at division headquarters.[26]

As the brigade's manpower situation slowly improved, Shepherd simultaneously tried to find additional regular officers. He laid out the situation in a late-January letter to the War Department:

> Head Quarters 4th Brigade (Regular Troops)
> 1st Division, Centre, 14th Army Corps
> Camp at Murfreesboro, Tenn Jany 26 1863

Genl L. Thomas
Adjt Genl US Army
Washington City DC

Sir

I respectfully request that either Major Sidell or Major Edie 15th Inf. may be ordered forthwith to take command of the 1st Batt of the 15th Inf. now here, its major (King) being wounded and in consequence will be unable to join for a long time. If it be true that Major Edie as reported has four Companies of his Regiment under his command at Columbus, Ky, I request also that they may be required to join the brigade of Regulars.

I have also to request the same of either Majors Flint or Coolidge of the 16th Inf., Major Slemmer lately commanding the 1st Batt being wounded so severely as to prohibit his joining for a very long time, if ever.

It is absolutely required for the well being and efficiency of the Battalions present of the 15th 16th 18th & 19th Inf. that those officers should join without delay. The interest of the service requires that these battalions be placed in as efficient a condition as possible, having suffered so seriously in their organization by the losses in the recent battle of Stone River. I ask that there should be no time wasted in this matter.

The battalion of the 15th has 8 Companies present with but 2 Captains, 6 1st Lieuts, and 2 2nd Lieuts. There should be 24 Company Officers, showing a deficiency at present of 6 Captains, 2 1st Lieuts, and 6 2nd Lieuts–total deficiency 14 Company Officers.

The battalion of the 16th has 9 Companies present with but 3 Captains, 4 1st Lieuts, and 2 2nd Lieuts. There should be 27 Company Officers, showing a deficiency at present of 6 Captains, 5 1st Lieuts, and 7 2nd Lieuts–total deficiency 18 Company Officers.

The two battalions of the 18th Inf. have 16 Companies present with but 10 Captains, 6 1st Lieuts, and 5 2nd Lieuts. There should be 48 Company Officers, showing a deficiency of 6 Captains, 10 1st Lieuts, and 11 2nd Lieuts–total deficiency 17 Company Officers.

The battalion of the 19th Inf. has 6 Companies present with but 1 Captain, 3 1st Lieuts, and 6 2nd Lieuts. There should be 18 Company Officers, showing a deficiency of 5 Captains and 3 1st Lieuts–total deficiency 8 Company Officers.

I therefore respectfully request that enough officers of each grade form their respective Regiments should be ordered forthwith to join their Battalions whether the officers belong to the particular companies and battalions or not.

From the great number of absent officers in these Regiments, it would seem that there may be many hangers-on who care more for drawing pay than for rendering service in their proper places and spheres.

I beg leave respectfully to suggest that all the Officers of each Regiment wounded in the recent battle of Stone River & whose constitutions are exhausted or impaired by there patient and sever service during the past eighteen months in the field against the enemy, may be ordered as soon as recovered from their wounds, to relieve those now on other duty away from the enemy enjoying the advantages of all the casualties [i.e., promotion opportunities] without enduring any of the hardships, sickness, and dangers of the war.

It is of the last importance that there should be a full complement of officers in these battalions no matter whether they belong to them or not.

Very Respectfully
Your Obt. Servant

O.L. SHEPHERD
Lieut Col 18th Inf..
Comdg Brigade[27]

Regimental depots and recruiting stations were duly combed for available officers. Captain George Washington Smith of the 18th Infantry was one of the leaders who reported for duty at Murfreesboro. Originally from Virginia, but a prewar resident of Kansas, where his father was a prominent legislator, Smith had served as a lieutenant in the 13th Pennsylvania Infantry during the summer of 1861. He had always wanted to be a cavalryman, and when he heard in May 1861 that a new regiment of regular horsemen was forming, he applied for a regular commission. In early August of that year, he read in a Philadelphia newspaper that he had been appointed as a captain in the new 19th U.S. Infantry, which, while not the desired cavalry slot, was certainly good enough. Without even waiting for official notification, Smith resigned his volunteer commission and headed for Indianapolis. He reported to Lieutenant Colonel Edward A. King and soon learned that the newspaper had not been quite correct: Smith was actually an officer of the 18th Infantry, not the 19th. Another hurried journey brought him to Camp Thomas. Captain Smith spent the rest of the year recruiting and training his company, E/1/18th U.S., and departed for Mississippi as part of Captain Henry Mizner's contingent in May 1862. Following the Kentucky Campaign, Smith learned that the governor of Kansas wanted him to recruit the 14th Kansas Volunteer Cavalry and then serve as the regiment's colonel. Smith was excited about the prospect of finally serving as a horse soldier and even went out of his way to show ex-cavalryman George Thomas the appointment letter. Smith went on detached service from the 18th Regulars in November and returned to his adopted home state. Four months of recruiting efforts failed to raise enough men for the 14th Kansas and a frustrated George Smith was ordered back to the 18th Infantry's field detachment in March 1863.[28]

Unlike Captain Smith, most of the Regular Brigade's new officers had little in the way of field experience. Company D of 1/16th U.S. had no officers survive Stones River unscathed. The unit's new captain was Alexander H. Stanton, a nephew of the secretary of war whose staff duties up to this point had kept him far away from troops of any type, Federal or Confederate. Just prior to Stanton's first dress parade, he stepped forward to take charge of his company of tough-as-nails veterans. The captain was "arrayed in a new uniform, all spic and span," and in a "light feminine voice," attempted to march the company to the battalion formation. Company D's soldiers had fallen in with their rifles at the correct position of order arms. Before they could move anywhere, their arms would have to be shouldered. This was a fine point of which Stanton was not aware, his first command being "Right, face." Not a soul moved. He repeated the command; again nothing happened. Flustered now, he turned to his 1st sergeant.

"Sergeant, what is the matter with the company?"

"The company does not obey a wrong command," the 1st sergeant replied with a look of tired disdain. "You should have given the order 'shoulder arms' first."

"Oh yes, I forgot," Stanton timidly replied.

He gave the order and was almost knocked over backward as the company's rifles were raised with a crash and snapped into position before the good captain had even finished speaking. Regaining his composure, Stanton faced the company to the right and marched it to the parade ground. He was quickly in trouble again, forgetting to give the commands necessary to place his company in the battalion line alongside Company C. Major Coolidge noticed the mess and galloped over to Company D's red-faced commander. "Captain Stanton!" Coolidge barked out, "put up your sword, go to your tent and study your tactics!"[29]

It was not long before greenhorns like Stanton learned the ropes of conducting business to Regular Army standards. Another newcomer, Lieutenant Lucius Brown, wrote that in early April, while detailed to command a picket reserve force, he was "highly complemented" by the volunteer major serving as field officer of the guard and also by field officer of the day, a full colonel. Brown noted that regular officers were often considered a cut above their peers: "The orders are that the reserve shall be commanded by a Capt. but *they* (volunteers) themselves told me that it was generally considered that a Lieut. of Regulars was equal to a Capt. of Vols—I tell you there's no discount on the 18th Regulars *here!*"[30]

A number of observers noted the regulars' camp discipline and training as the weeks at Murfreesboro went by. Most were favorably impressed. Sergeant Tarbell wrote: "we have a nice camp. The volunteers are gelous & guy us about our camp."[31] Private Luke Lyman of A/2/18th U.S. wrote a more detailed description of the regulars' camp in a letter to his mother:

> We have our camps decorated with evergreens which look beautiful. I made an arch over the head of our street and Phil made an "A 2nd" of all cedar. And we swung them up with a little flag between the "A" and the 2. Most all of our camps have been decorated with cedars, even large trees by the hundreds being cut down and hauled into camps so that you may stroll into what appears a beautiful cedar grove and in it's midst you would find the accomadations...tents in abundance with there inhabitants persuing there evocations of profit or pleasure, in one tent sits a man in the highest enjoyment of single blesedness stripped to the hide sitting on the bunk mending his unmentionables. In the next is a game of old sledge or ewere is in progress. In the third a letter to there loved ones or the old folks at home is being composed on a reversed tin, but reading novels is the mania in camp and sitting in groups are men, some listening while others are reading there latest romance. We

have tracts distributed among us by the American Bible Tract Society. Reading those and the Bible is no uncommon thing.[32]

On March 19, Rousseau's division conducted a review for General Rosecrans and his corps commanders. Sergeant Tarbell recalled, that the commanding general was impressed with Shepherd's troops: "He spoke hiley of our neat aperance & our good drilling, comended us on our clean & well regulated camp. He said a grate many other things that touch us under the vest." Lieutenant Carpenter had similar recollections of this event: "I do wish you all could have witnessed it. it was a splendid sight. every thing moved like clock work. it is the best drilled and disciplined Division in the Army and our brigade takes the shine off of everything. I am not boasting, but speaking the truth. Gen. McCook said that it was the finest review that he ever saw. and that is a great deal for him to say of us."[33]

Carpenter and his fellow veterans did their best to bring the new companies up to standard, but the loss of many veteran leaders complicated the task. Captain Henry Douglass took command of 1/18th in early January when Major Caldwell departed, but the captain's wounded arm still gave him problems and he departed the field on April 6, bound for recruiting duty. Captain George Smith inherited the battalion at that point. Majors Adam Slemmer and John King, both severely wounded on New Year's Eve, spent months recuperating. Slemmer was promoted to brigadier general of volunteers on April 4 for his good service from Fort Pickens to Stones River. He had been immediately paroled after his capture with the brigade baggage train on January 1, but his leg wound was so severe that his days of field duty were over. Brigadier General Slemmer remained on detached service in Columbus and Cincinnati for the duration of the war, serving as the president of a board that evaluated the fitness of wounded officers.[34]

Staff requirements made their usual inroads into the Regular Brigade's officer strength. After a few new officers reported for duty and the thirteen regular companies were disbanded in January and February, Rosecrans felt he could afford to make another levy against the Regular Brigade for additional staff officers. Lieutenant Colonel Calvin Goddard, a member of the Army of the Cumberland's adjutant general's staff, sent the orders to the chief of staff of Thomas's corps:

HEAD-QUARTERS, DEPARTMENT OF THE CUMBERLAND
Murfreesboro April 14th 1863

Lt. Col Flynt
    AAG & Chf of Staff

14th Army Corps

Colonel,

As there are sufficient regular officers in your command unassigned to companies, it is deemed expedient to assign regular officers as Asst. Commissaries of Muster for the divisions of your Corps. General Rousseau has already selected an officer for his division, who had been detailed. Please select regular officers to serve in this capacity for the other four divisions of your command. This assignment will relieve the Commissary of Muster of the Corps from the necessity of countersigned all musters made by the Asst. Commissaries of Muster, as is the case of volunteer officers assigned to that duty, he would be obliged to do. Capt Howard 18th Infy & Lieut. Lowe 19th Infy have applied for this duty and would make efficient officers if they can be spared.

Very Respectfully
Your Obt. Servt.
C. GODDARD
Lt. Col. & AAG[35]

Rosecrans attempted to compensate for the staff assignments by requesting promotions and brevets for a number of the brigade's officers. He sent the first of a series of requests to the army Adjutant General in mid-February:

HEAD-QUARTERS DEPARTMENT OF THE CUMBERLAND
Murfreesboro Tenn February 15th 1863

Brig. Genl. L. Thomas
    Adjutant General
    Washington D.C.

General,

The following officers of the Regular Army, viz:

Lt. Col. Sheppard	Com'dg Reg.	Brig.Capt. Fulmer	15th Inft
Major Caldwell	18th Inft	Capt. Mulligan	19th Inft
Major Slemer	15th Inft	Capt. Crofton	16th Inft
Major Townsend	15th Inft	1st Lt. Guenther	Batty "H" 5th Arty
Major King	15th Inft	1st Lt. Parsons	Batty "M" 4th Arty

having specially distinguished themselves and having no such opportunity for promotion as in the Volunteer service, this being particularly the case with the battery commanders, I most earnestly hope that they will be rewarded with brevets.

Very Respectfully,

W.S. ROSECRANS
Maj Genl Com'dg[36]

Rosecrans followed up this request with another sent to General Halleck two weeks later, requesting brevets for twenty-two regular officers, including ten members of the Regular Brigade, who had been "specially mentioned" in Rosecrans's official report on the Stones River Campaign. Oliver Shepherd composed a more extensive list of thirty-seven regular officers who deserved brevets, and sent the request to Washington the next month. Rosecrans, meanwhile, composed individual brevet requests for a number of regulars. Among others, he noted that Captain Crofton of the 16th U.S., "a brave and efficient officer," deserved promotion. Rosecrans thought a promotion for Major John King was long overdue. On February 15, the commanding general sent a "Special Mention" of King to the War Department: "Maj. King 15th U.S. Infantry has commanded a Battalion of Regulars for more than a year in active service, and always praised by his superior officers for order and efficiency. Was in the Battle of Shiloh where he had a horse shot under him. Was second in command in the Battle of Stone River where he fought bravely. He is Respectfully recommended for a Brevet." King was making a slow recovery from his wounding. The two hits in his left arm proved to be superficial, but the injury to his hand was serious. "My left hand is almost useless," King reported from the Galt House Hotel in Louisville on February 11. By early April he felt strong enough for limited duties and requested the command of Newport Barracks, stating: "I would prefer the command of troops to mustering or staff duties." By the time he was cleared for field duty in early May, John King learned he had received much more than a brevet promotion. He was appointed a brigadier general of volunteers in April 1863, with a date of rank as of November 29, 1862. [37]

Shepherd thought Major Frederick Townsend was also deserving of recognition, particularly in light of James Caldwell's recent antics. When in early February Shepherd read a story in a Cincinnati newspaper that mentioned Caldwell and omitted Townsend, the 18th Infantry's lieutenant colonel felt compelled to set the record straight:

> Head Quarters 4th Brigade (Regular Troops)
> 1st Division, 14th Army Corps
> Camp at Murfreesboro, Tenn
> February 13th 1863

Colonel Goddard
Adjt General & Chief of Staff
Dept of the Cumberland

Sir:

My attention was brought last evening to a communication in the Cincinnati Commercial...which purports to be a copy of the Official List of distinguished officers in the late battle of Stone River, and which represents Major Caldwell, Commander of the 1st Battalion, 18th Infantry, as the commanding officer of the Regiment, and omits altogether his senior, the commander of the 2nd Battalion, Major Townsend.

If the communication alluded to be correct, a serious mistake and omission have been made, because Major Townsend was, beyond all question, equally distinguished with the lamented Major Carpenter and if any officer living was distinguished, Major Townsend is the one.

Majors King and Slemmer having been disabled and Major Carpenter killed, left Major Townsend next in rank to myself.

No officer excelled him, in intrepid courage, activity, and zeal animating to officers and men all around him.

An officer so distinguished in battle, and so deserving at all times and on all occasions, should have justice done him by the proper authorities and I hope it may be done by the Commanding General.

> I have the honor to be
> Very Respectfully
> Your obedient servant,
>
> O.L. SHEPHERD
> Lieut. Col. 18th Inf.
> Comd'g Brigade[38]

William Rosecrans was equally impressed with Townsend, and gave the major the honor of conveying to Washington the Army of the Cumberland's official reports on Stones River, along with enemy flags captured during the battle. Rosecrans perhaps reserved his highest written praise for Brevet Captain Frank Guenther of Battery H:

> Too much cannot be said in praise of this brave and accomplished officer. His services in Western Va, especially in the Battle at Greenbrier, deserve the most honorable mention. At Shiloh his heroic conduct and skill in managing his guns won universal admiration and Capt Wm Terrill his superior officer was made a Brig Genl for like brilliant services. At the engagement at Dog Walk he behaved with coolness and intrepidity. For his magnificent conduct at Stones River he fairly earned the Brevet of Major. This battery almost annihilated the 30th Arkansas Rebel Regiment, cut down and captured its colors. His splendid Napoleons double shotted with grape, defended themselves, frequently unaided by infantry, and gained for them the thanks and admiration of the army.[39]

Guenther finally received full promotion to captain in July 1863. Much to his dismay, he was slotted to command Battery I of the 5th U.S. Artillery, a unit assigned to the Washington defenses, and had to say farewell to the artillerymen he and William Terrill had molded since 1861. There was not a captaincy available in Battery H because Captain George A. Kensel had assumed command of the unit during the spring of 1863. An 1857 West Pointer who had seen action at the First Battle of Bull Run and along the Gulf coast, Kensel had lately been serving as chief of artillery in Major General Benjamin Butler's Department of the Gulf. Lieutenant Howard M. Burnham was also assigned to the battery that spring, joining Lieutenants Joshua Fessenden and Israel Ludlow as the battery's section leaders.

Burnham had been looking forward to a field assignment for sometime. A strapping six footer of nineteen years when the war broke out, Burnham was a native of Longmeadow, Massachusetts and had attended a military school in Connecticut for his secondary education. He applied for admission to West Point in 1860 and was crushed when he learned there was not a vacancy from his district available that year. The Civil War put Burnham's Academy yearnings on hold for the moment, and the status of his well-to-do family netted him a lieutenancy in the 5th U.S. Artillery. He was assigned to the regiment's Battery B and placed on recruiting duty in New York City, Albany, and even as far away as Dubuque, Iowa. These were assignments the young lieutenant did not enjoy, particularly since Battery B turned out to be the last of the 5th Artillery's batteries to be fully manned and organized. When the war started to get more active in the spring of 1862, Burnham wrote his parents that he was "as angry as possible at the thought of being kept at the *glorious* work of recruiting, while there is a prospect of a fight so near at hand. I would give three months' pay if my Battery was full and in the advance." He toiled away at his work through the late summer of 1862, when he went to Washington for an assignment as aide-de-camp to his uncle Major General Joseph K.F. Mansfield, commander of the XII Corps in the Army of the Potomac. Before the lieutenant had a chance to join his uncle's staff, Mansfield was killed at the Battle of Antietam on September 17, 1862. Burnham was instead detailed for duty at 5th Artillery Headquarters at Ft. Hamilton, New York, and spent another winter in garrison. Battery B was finally organized in November 1862, but Howard Burnham was not destined for field duty with it. In April 1863 Lieutenant Jacob Smyser of Battery H, on detached service in Louisville since the previous September, was transferred from the regular artillery to the ordnance corps. Burnham was assigned to Battery H as Smyser's replacement and reported for duty at Murfreesboro on June 1. He was quickly labeled a "young man of promise."[40]

The Regular Brigade's most significant personnel change involved its ranking officer. Oliver Shepherd's tenure as the brigade's commander was rapidly approaching an inglorious end, although all seemed calm until the second week of April. Shepherd worked hard during the first three months of 1863 in molding the old and new elements of the Regular Brigade into a cohesive force. Some of his Old Army sternness faded and he began to endear himself to his troops, realizing that his best chance for retaining command of the brigade (barring promotion) was to make himself as valuable as possible in his current role. William Rosecrans had been impressed with Shepherd's performance at Stones River. On February 15 the commanding general sent a Special Mention of the colonel to the War Department: "Lt. Col. O.L. Shepherd Comdg. Regular Brigade, commanded the brigade with bravery and skill at the battle of 'Stone River' and is specially mentioned in the report of Major Genl. Rousseau and of Major Genl. Thomas his Division and Corps Commander. The fearful loss in the Brigade being upwards of 35 per. ct. attests the obstinacy of the fighting. He is respectfully recommended for a brevet."[41]

Despite Rosecrans's desires, Shepherd did not receive a coveted brevet for Stones River during the war. In fact, no member of the Regular Brigade was so honored. Considering the barrage of the brevet requests landing in Washington during the weeks following the battle, the regulars took it for granted that they would soon receive official recognition for their actions. But as the months went by, the War Department was strangely silent. Shepherd was sure that someone in the War Department had seen the recommendations, for in March he learned that he would soon receive the brevets of colonel and brigadier general, an officer on the adjutant general's staff having informally sent Shepherd word of the impending action. The brevets never came. Shepherd later speculated that the War Department was already swamped with the Army of the Potomac's brevet requests for the Battle of Fredericksburg by the time the Regular Brigade's arrived for Stones River. Somehow, the requests for the Army of the Cumberland's regulars were never officially acted upon.[42]

There was no doubt among Shepherd's regulars that some sort of recognition was warranted for Stones River. The gravesite on the Battery H knoll was all the proof they needed. Oliver Shepherd decided that if the War Department would not honor those fallen comrades, the men of the brigade would do it themselves. He proposed placing a monument in the cemetery to commemorate the brigade's role in the battle and honor its dead. He laid the idea before the battalion commanders, who were unanimous in their enthusiasm for the project. A suitable memorial would require a tidy sum of cash, so Shepherd mobilized the entire brigade in support of the project. An order was sent to a local printer to have a circular engraved on expensive, heavy white paper. Shepherd had it distributed throughout the brigade:

> Camp of the Regular Brigade,
> (Near Murfreesboro, Tenn.,)

April 6, 1863.

Soldiers of the Regular Brigade;

It has been suggested that the officers and men of this Brigade, erect a lasting monument to the patriotism and virtues of those of our Brigade who were killed at the battle of Stone River or died in consequence of wounds there received. A committee convened by a Circular from Colonel Shepherd commanding the Brigade, has decided upon the following plan:

1st. To build a burial mound covering the entire ground where our comrades are buried, say 18 yards square and 7 feet high.

2nd. To erect thereupon at some future day a handsome marble monument with appropriate and national emblems sculptured upon it, and also the names of the dead, of the Brigade, killed in the Battle or dying of wounds received.

The committee have ascertained by reference to the rolls that there are 2135 enlisted men in this Brigade present. If each man contributes $1.00, over $2,000, will be raised towards this monument.

The committee further proposes that the officers of the Regiments and Battery "H," 5th Artillery in this Brigade contribute $5.00, each to this sum.

The money thus raised, the committee propose to have safely invested under the control of a Board of Trustees, one from each Regiment in the Brigade, to be appointed at once, these trustees to receive the money as paid.

The interest upon the money thus invested will defray the incidental expenses of erecting the monument, while the principal will be wholly devoted to the monument itself. In case anything should prevent the money being expended as proposed, both principal and interest will be equitably distributed to the several regiments contributing, for the benefit of the families of the sufferers at Stone River.

Soldiers! The committee asks you to contribute to this monument. Will you not show by your contributions, that no Regular soldier ever forgets to honor his brother Regulars who have died in the defence of our Country and our Flag?

(Signed)

R. Delavan Mussey,
Capt. 19th Infantry

Wm. J. Fetterman,
Capt. 18th Infantry

F.L. Guenther,
Capt. Battery "H," 5th Artillery

Horace Jewett,
Capt. 15th Infantry

Joseph L. Proctor
Capt. 18th Infantry

E.R. Kellogg,
1 Lt. 16th Infantry

Approved:
O.L. Shepherd
Lt. Col. 18th Infantry
Commanding Brigade.[43]

The next time a paymaster came to the Regular Brigade's camp, representatives of the monument committee stood beside the pay table and collected whatever contributions the men cared to give. Most gave something, even though the requested dollar represented almost 8 percent of a private's monthly paycheck. Contributions totaled $1,791 by the end of the day. The committee signed the funds over to army Paymaster William M. Fleming, who was instructed to place the sum at Shepherd's disposal. Subsequent donations totaled an additional $112, which were likewise forwarded to Shepherd.[44]

Shepherd was not present to collect the funds personally because on that payday he was no longer commanding the Regular Brigade. Despite the progress Shepherd had made in reorganizing and training the brigade during the first three months of 1863, by April, Rosecrans no longer considered Shepherd to be the best man for these important tasks. With the lull in operations during the winter, Rosecrans had again turned his attention to the question of who should command his brigade of regulars. From the moment Rosecrans had formed the Regular Brigade, he had wanted to have a general officer commanding the unit. Oliver Shepherd held brigade command at Stones River only because Rosecrans's first two choices, Henry Carrington and Robert Granger, were not then available. As it appeared that the War Department was not going to award Shepherd a brevet for his performance in battle, the lieutenant colonel commanding the Regular Brigade was still outranked by most of Rosecrans's regimental commanders. Many officers throughout the Army of the Cumberland thought that someone with heavier shoulder straps should command the regulars, but it would be difficult for Rosecrans to replace a brigade commander who had been performing so well. Rosecrans thought he found an easy way to deal with the situation in early April. He heard a rumor that Shepherd was to become colonel of the 13th U.S. Infantry, the regular regiment assigned to Grant's Army of the Tennessee. If true, Shepherd would be transferred. On April 9, Rosecrans hurriedly fired off a telegram to the adjutant general in Washington: "Has Lt Col O.L. Shepperd been promoted to Colonelcy of 13th Infty? The information is wanted because I wish to assign Brigade Commanders."[45]

The War Department answered the next day. Rosecrans had the right man, but the wrong regiment. Shepherd was to be promoted to colonel, but of the 15th Infantry, not the 13th. Major General Fitz-John Porter, commanding the Army of the Potomac's V Corps and still the nominal colonel of the 15th Regulars, had been cashiered in January 1863 after a court-martial found him guilty of disobeying orders the previous August at the Second Battle of Bull Run. It took until April for the proceedings to be closed and the sentence approved. The War Department wanted the Porter case to be over and done with, desiring the vacancy at the top of the 15th Infantry to be filled as soon as possible. The Regular Army 's senior lieutenant colonel of infantry in early 1863 was Oliver Shepherd, so the colonelcy was his. So instead of ending up with a convenient way to change out command of the Regular Brigade, Rosecrans was facing a dilemma. As the colonel commanding one of the Regular Brigade's subordinate regiments, Shepherd would outrank all volunteer colonels and could continue to command the Regular Brigade. Rosecrans's only alternative was to officially relieve Shepherd of command. Doing so would remove the problem entirely, allowing Rosecrans to appoint whomever he chose as commander of the Regular Brigade. Such a course of action might have been distasteful to Rosecrans, but he decided to go ahead with it. There was an unemployed general in the Army of the Cumberland who was badly in need of a field command, Robert Granger. Rosecrans had been keeping his eye on Granger for some time now. The brigadier had arrived in Murfreesboro during mid-January to serve as acting commander of Rousseau's division, General Rousseau taking a leave of absence. Rousseau returned to duty on March 29, resulting in Granger being a general without a job. Having already offered Granger command of the Regular Brigade the previous December, a position Granger could not then accept, Rosecrans put the offer back on the table in April. Granger accepted this time and Shepherd was relieved of command.[46]

Oliver Shepherd was furious. The relief was particularly galling because Granger was still only a major in the Regular Army, even though he wore a volunteer general's star. From Shepherd's point of view, someone junior in rank was replacing him as the commander of a regular unit. He demanded an explanation from Rosecrans but barely received one. Rosecrans had a habit of being abrupt with subordinates, and this characteristic is evident in his answer to the chagrined ex-commander of the Regular Brigade. His words were short and to the point: "You do not have sufficient rank to command so important a body of troops as the brigade has become and a general must have command of it."[47]

The affair ended. Shepherd became colonel of the 15th Infantry, with date of rank from January 21, the date General Porter had been dismissed. Shepherd refused to serve in the Army of the Cumberland any longer:

> Camp at Murfreesboro, Tenn.
> April 11, 1866
>
> Colonel C. Goddard
>   Adjt Genl, Dept Cumberland
> Sir:
>
> I have the honor respectfully, to request to be relieved from duty in this Department, and to be ordered to report at the Head Quarters of the Army.
>
> It is probably very well understood, that I have ample reasons for this application.
>
> I am very respectfully, etc.
>
> O.L. SHEPHERD
> Lieut. Col. 18th Inf.
> U.S. Army[48]

The endorsements of Shepherd's division, corps, and army commanders illustrate their varying attitudes toward him. Lovell Rousseau: "I regret deeply to lose the services of an officer whose bravery & efficiency have been so fully proven in the field." George Thomas took a dimmer view of the situation: "This application is respectfully forwarded and though not approved for the insinuated reasons set forth in the application, for the preservation of good order and efficiency in the 4th Brigade 1st Div of this Corps and for the good of the service generally, it is respectfully recommended that Lt. Col. O.L. Shepherd 18th U.S. Infantry be relieved from duty in this department." William Rosecrans had no further patience for Shepherd: "Respectfully forwarded to the Adjutant Genl of the Army & recommended. The only reasons I know of are that having put all the Regulars into one brigade for their benefit while yet Col Shepherd was a Lt. Colonel, to prevent their falling

under the command of a Volunteer Colonel I detailed Brig. Gen.
R.S. Granger to command the Brigade, he being a graduate of the
Academy senior to Col. Shepperd, and an accomplished and able
officer. The whole incident was designed to benefit greatly the
Regulars and I regret to find in this letter of Col. Shepperd that he
seems to have taken exception to it."[49]

Shepherd's departure from Murfreesboro was quick and virtually
silent. Normally a prolific writer, he was so upset about leaving his
beloved regulars for the second time in less than seven months that
he scribbled only a short note formally transferring command of the
18th Infantry battalions: "The undersigned having received notice
of his promotion to the Colonelcy of the 15th Infantry, hereby relinquishes command of this Detach. of the Regt. to Major Townsend.
I feel deep regret in being severed from a regiment, which has
achieved so high a reputation for valor and discipline."[50] Major
Townsend published a regimental order on Shepherd's behalf after
the colonel left:

> Head Quarters Detcht 18th U.S. Infantry
> Camp at Murfreesboro Tenn
> April 16th 1863
>
> General Orders
>   No 1
>   Col. Oliver L. Shepherd of the 15th Inf.. lately commanding offi-
> cer of this Brigade, not having had an opportunity of relinquishing
> the command of this Brigade in orders, desires that it should be
> understood that he parts with it under conditions such as becomes a
> Soldier separating from troops which he had the honor of leading
> during the five days battle of Stone River, in which every one who
> participated with him received the indelible stamp of honor, due to
> true and brave soldiers parting [with] their lives in their countries
> cause. The Commanding officer desires to testify to the gratitude due
> to Col Shepherd for his great zeal, and industry in perfecting the dis-
> cipline of this command which so gloriously culminated at the recent
> battle of Stone River.
>
> > By Order of
> > Major Fred'k Townsend
> > Command'g
> > FRED'K PHISTERER
> > Adjt[51]

Shepherd boarded a train at Murfreesboro on April 16 and made
his way to Washington, where he was again informed that the War

Department staff was not in need of his services. With nowhere else to go, Shepherd headed for the 15th Infantry's headquarters in Rhode Island in early May and immersed himself in the traditional duties that came with being the colonel of a Regular Army regiment, administrative paperwork and recruiting. Shepherd would have much preferred command of the Regular Brigade, but if that were not possible he was going to prove to everyone that it was possible to fully man a New Army infantry regiment (although the colonel was not altogether enamored with his new desk-bound job, once referring it as "a kind of Boss Recruiting Sergeant's duty"). Having been on the receiving end of the Regular Army 's defective personnel system throughout his time in the field, Shepherd was full of ideas on how the regulars could obtain manpower and keep the field battalions up to strength. The day after arriving at Fort Adams, he requested permission of the adjutant general to personally discuss these issues with the War Department staff:

> Hd Qrs. 15th Inf.. U.S.A.
> Fort Adams, R.I.
> May 6, 1863

Genl L. Thomas
   Adjt Genl, U.S.
   Washington, D.C.

Sir:

Having been ordered to this Post...with a view to Superintend the Recruiting Service of the Regiment, I respectfully request orders to go to Washington on permission to visit it, for the purpose of consulting and devising means, by which to full up speedily the Regt.

Quite a number of Regiments of 2 years Volunteers are about to be mustered out of the Service, both in New York City and Harrisburg, Pa, and I believe, if proper steps be adopted, that many men may be obtained, at those places, if not enough to fill up the Regt, which is now scarcely half full.

Recent achievements of the Regular Regts, indicate sufficiently the importance of having them completed and no longer remain under the bane of neglect for failing to have a full organization.

A short time at Washington it is presumed, will aid me very much in every respect, regarding the recruiting of discharged Volunteers, the obtaining of conscripts, and remedying the defects of the previous mode of enlisting.

The 1st Battalion has already distinguished its Regt, and I hope to have the 2nd & 3rd battalions raised and enabled to emulate it. I therefore trust that it may be consistent with the public Service to order me as requested, as early as possible.

> I have the honor to
> remain very respectfully, etc.
> O.L. SHEPHERD
> Col 15th Inf.. U.S.A.
> Comdg[52]

Shepherd had shown up unannounced at the War Department twice in the previous eight months looking for a staff position, and Adjutant General Lorenzo Thomas was not about to let him try a third time. He sent a curt reply to Shepherd, suggesting that instead of bothering the War Department, the new colonel of the 15th Infantry should tend to his regiment and become familiar with his duties. Such instructions from the army's archetypical administrator made Shepherd's blood boil. "I left the Dept of the Cumberland to organize and complete my Regiment and I am mindful of every portion of it," Shepherd icily replied. "Therefore I respectfully request all the aid which your Dept. is able to give. I supposed that the enormous amount of business with which your Dept. is burdened, may have rendered the actual condition of the Regiment not sufficiently well understood, and that explanations would not be unacceptable. I believe that I am the only Colonel actually in command of his Regiment, at least of the new Regiments, and that fact alone deserves consideration. It would have been an easy mater for me to have shirked my place and station and have been employed with the Volunteers."

In the coming months Shepherd continued to pepper the War Department with additional requests for recruiting assistance, but received little help. He asked for flexibility in the payment of enlistment bounties (permission denied), authority to enlist drafted men and substitutes (permission denied), and that the 15th Infantry's band be returned to regimental headquarters (permission denied). Despite losing these administrative battles, Colonel Shepherd was optimistic that the increased bounty and draft would do the trick: "The bounty which is just now being offered for Enlistments into the Regular Service, and the near approach of the Drafting," he informed the War Department July 2, 1863, "justify a great increase of Enlistments, and I believe that the [15th]

Regiment may be completed this summer." Shepherd's prediction of success was overly optimistic. The new bounty had virtually no effect, causing a negligible increase in the number of enlistments. Only 1,075 recruits joined the regulars during July and August. The Regular Army's five-year enlistment term was proving to be an insurmountable obstacle.[53]

Shepherd made due with what he had. The Sandersons, Lieutenant Col John P. and Lieutenant George K., had been presiding over the inactivity at 15th Infantry Headquarters for more than a year. Shepherd let them know that their services and those of the recruits that were lounging about Fort Adams were no longer required. All of them left Fort Adams within days of Shepherd's arrival, the elder Sanderson and the recruits by way of Special Orders 207 from the War Department, issued on May 9: "Lieut. Col. John P. Sanderson, 15th U.S. Infantry, will turn over the public property and funds in his possession to Col. O.L. Shepherd...and proceed with the enlisted men of his regiment now at Fort Adams, R.I. to join that part of his regiment serving in the Department of the Cumberland." The younger Sanderson came down with a sudden illness and was placed on extended sick leave.[54]

As the Sandersons left, Colonel Shepherd brought on board Lieutenant Frederick D. Ogilby, an energetic Stones River veteran who had lately been the adjutant of 1/15th U.S. in Tennessee, to serve as regimental adjutant at Fort Adams. Shepherd and Ogilby reorganized the 15th Infantry's headquarters and invigorated the regiment's stalled recruiting program. They combed out the regiment's recruiting stations and formed E/2/15th U.S. out of eighty-seven fresh recruits. Shepherd placed his regimental quartermaster, Lieutenant Samuel Shock Holbrook, in command of the new company, a former enlisted man who had served in the ranks of both the 1st Pennsylvania Volunteers and the 15th Infantry. Instead of shipping Holbrook's company off to oblivion with Major Edie's 2/15th U.S. at Memphis, Shepherd sent the unit in late June to the regiment's 1st Battalion at Murfreesboro.[55]

Lost in the confusion of the Regular Brigade's hasty command switch was the plan to appoint a board of trustees to oversee the safe investment of the Stones River monument fund. This oversight would later come back to haunt many of the brigade's veterans, Oliver Shepherd in particular.

* * *

Recruiting Poster, 15th U.S. Infantry
Philadelphia, Summer 1863

Posters such as this appeared throughout the northeast during the latter half of 1863 after Col. Oliver Shepherd took command of the 15th Infantry Regiment. The broadsheet emphasized the opportunity for deserving soldiers to earn regular commissions, and also promised "Military instruction under competent officers at one of the finest Forts in the United States," incentives Shepherd felt his regiment could offer that volunteer units could not. Shepherd's mid-war recruiting drive resulted in the 15th U.S. being one of the largest regular regiments of the Civil War.

Brigadier General Robert S. Granger took command of the Regular Brigade on April 17, 1863. Although George Thomas had thought Shepherd's reassignment was necessary for the "good order and efficiency" of the Regular Brigade, the move actually had the opposite effect. Shepherd's relief generated widespread resentment in the Regular Brigade's officer corps. A wholesale exodus ensued as officers who had served with Shepherd sought recruiting or staff assignments away from the brigade. Captain Alfred Lacey Hough of the 19th Infantry, on recruiting duty at Indianapolis since the previous summer, arrived at the regulars' camp in late March. On April 12, he learned of Shepherd's impending relief: "I am not as happy here as I was under the old regime. ...We do not like...Granger and are in trouble to-day hearing that he is to take command of our Brigade, relieving Col. Sheppard who we all like. I regret it very much as Col. Sheppard had taken especial notice of me, and I am told was instrumental in getting me rank with the Battalion. Col. S. was very kind to me and I don't know Granger and don't like his looks." Many of Hough's fellow officers didn't like Granger's looks either. "The few good officers left feel their position deeply," Hough continued, "and would resign most of them if they could, and all [are] trying to get on other duty."[56]

Officers of the 18th Infantry, the ones who not surprisingly felt strongest about Shepherd's relief, left in droves. Captains Frederick Phisterer, William Fetterman, and Ansel B. Denton, along with Lieutenant William P. McLeary, all left Murfreesboro on April 28, bound for recruiting assignments. That same month Captain Ai B. Thompson, commander of E/2/18th U.S., was assigned to the state of Ohio's provost marshal general's department. Captain David Wood, the tormenter of Private Tank, knew that Shepherd was the only man standing between himself and a court-martial, so he wisely accepted a War Department staff job in early May. Captain John Henry Knight, one of Shepherd's most partisan supporters, had been on sick leave since Perryville. He was fit for duty by April 1863, but did not bother to rejoin his regiment in the field for many months. The last of the brigade's veteran field-grade officers, Major Frederick Townsend of 2/18th U.S., departed on April 23. He was posted to Albany to serve as the acting assistant provost marshal general for the state of New York and never again served with the 18th Infantry. Captain Henry Douglass likewise never returned to field duty with his regiment. After his wounded arm healed, he took a position as chief mustering and disbursing officer for the state of Ohio. A number of officers from the brigade's other regiments also received new assignments. Captain R. Delavan Mussey, an experienced veteran of the 19th Infantry, took a position on the staff of Crittenden's XXI Corps. Captain James Biddle, 16th Infantry, was posted to Pennsylvania for service as the quartermaster of a state draft rendezvous. Captain Charles Howard of the 18th Infantry and Lieutenant William Lowe of the 19th applied for XIV Corps mustering duty at precisely the time Shepherd was relieved. Some of these changes were routine rotations of officers between line and staff positions; others resulted from officers being available for detached service after their companies were disbanded. But none of the changes took place until after Granger was appointed to command, and the sheer volume of reassignments in the weeks following Shepherd's departure is a clear indication that all was not well in the Regular Brigade.[57]

Although there were plenty of regular officers assigned to the Army of the Cumberland and XIV Corps, the competing demands of staff duty and volunteer commands—not to mention the two dozen or so officers recovering from battle wounds—meant that having regular officers assigned on paper did not equal having them available for troop duty. Making up the brigade's officer deficit came at a high price. The Regular Army was no longer authorized to commission civilians off the street as it had been during the expansion of 1861. The Military Academy was the traditional source of new officers for the Regular Army, but the small number of officers who graduated from West Point during the war were quickly placed on detached service from their regiments. Regular regiments could obtain new lieutenants only by commissioning sergeants from the ranks. Most of the Regular Brigade's senior non-commissioned officers became lieutenants during the spring and summer of 1863, such as Sergeant James H. Gageby of G/1/19th. Sergeant John Williams of C/1/15th and Sergeant Major Reuben F. Little of 1/18th U.S., a pair of native Englishman in the regulars, were also commissioned, as were Sergeant Martin Mahon of D/2/16th, an Irish-born veteran of the prewar 1st Infantry, Sergeant John Lane of B/1/18th, who had been a cadet at West Point for almost three years immediately prior to the war, and John K. Schiffler, the 16th Infantry's sergeant major who hailed from Bavaria. Sergeant Walter Clifford, an Old Army veteran from New York, took Schiffler's place as sergeant major of

1/16th, but Clifford was himself commissioned shortly thereafter. A few promising regular sergeants serving elsewhere were assigned to regiments in the Regular Brigade, including Sergeant Theodore Kendall, a ten-year veteran of the U.S. Army Corps of Engineers who received a commission in the 15th Infantry on May 12, 1863, and Robert Ayres, also a veteran sergeant of the Regular Army's Engineer Battalion. While most of these "mustang" officers performed their duties well, commissioning them placed a severe strain on their regiments' corps of skilled non-commissioned officers—the men who are traditionally the bedrock of the Regular Army. Privates who had demonstrated some potential, such as the 18th Infantry's Robert Kennedy and Philip Lyman, moved up to NCO rank to replace the new officers. Twenty-two members of 2/18th U.S. received new chevrons during the encampment at Murfreesboro and the other battalions experienced a similar leadership turnover. When one adds to this equation the untried officers who reported for duty with the Regular Brigade that spring, the brigade's leaders were now a decidedly different lot than the experienced campaigners who had marched into the cedars at Stones River a few months before. During the regulars' next major battle, just two of the brigade's forty company commanders would be able to claim that they had commanded the same unit in December 1862.[58]

The Army of the Cumberland's efforts against Bragg's cavalry and Southern foraging continued while turmoil brewed among the regulars in the wake of Shepherd's relief. On April 20, Rosecrans dispatched elements of Thomas's corps on another large-scale sweep of the surrounding area. Major General John J. Reynolds's division, reinforced by Colonel Robert H.G. Minty's cavalry brigade and Starkweather's brigade from Rousseau's division, conducted an eleven-day expedition in the countryside between Liberty and McMinnville, about thirty-five miles east of Murfreesboro. The operation yielded good results, including the destruction of a large cotton factory and two mills that had been supplying goods to Bragg's army, and also the capture of 600 blankets, 2 hogsheads of sugar and 3 of rice, 200 bales of cotton, 8 barrels of whisky, and 30,000 pounds of bacon. Minty's cavalry captured about 200 Southern cavalrymen near McMinnville on April 21.[59]

The Regular Brigade played a small part in this affair. On April 23, General Granger led the regulars on a two-day march to Liberty, escorting a provision train bound for Reynolds's column.

The regulars moved out at eight o'clock in the morning, marching eighteen miles before nightfall. They happened to camp that evening near the bivouac site of a brigade from Brigadier General Horatio P. Van Cleve's division of Crittenden's corps, commanded temporarily by Colonel Peter T. Swaine of the 99th Ohio, the former adjutant of Newport Barracks and commander of 1/15th Infantry. Swaine stopped by Granger's camp for a chat around the campfires that night, with the Shiloh veterans in the regular battalions giving their old comrade a hearty welcome.[60]

Granger's brigade completed the march to Liberty the next day and linked up with Minty's cavalry, turning over the supply wagons and in return taking charge of Minty's 200 Confederate prisoners. The regulars and their charges began the return march to Murfreesboro on April 25. "[T]hat days march was hard," wrote Lieutenant Carpenter the following afternoon, "the sun poured down his melting rays without mercy, and we had to be very vigilant that no rebel cavalry made a dash upon us and rescued the prisoners. Saturday night we camped about 10 miles from Murfreesboro. rebel cavalry were seen hovering round all that afternoon, and twas expected they would come in upon us in the night, but they did not try it. if they had, they would have met with a very warm reception. today we arrived at our camp at Murfreesboro with our prisoners, and thus ended the expedition."[61]

Corporal Robert Kennedy was one of the regulars guarding the Confederates upon their arrival in Murfreesboro. While Kennedy was posting his guards, two of the prisoners walked up to the 18th Infantryman. "Is your name Kennedy?" When the corporal responded that it was, the prisoners extended their hands in greeting. They turned out to be Robert Henderson and John Shanklin, Southern cavalrymen from western Virginia with whom Kennedy had boated oil on the Kanawha River before the war. Captain Denton noticed the fraternization and asked Kennedy if he knew the two men. "I told him I did," remembered Kennedy. "He told me to take them to my quarters, give them their suppers and treat them the best I knew how." Kennedy did so, but Henderson and Shanklin's fine treatment did not last long. That same evening, the prisoners were turned over to the Army of the Cumberland's provost marshal. They were soon on their way to Camp Chase.[62]

The regulars came to know the name of another prisoner captured during Reynolds's expedition, although this person's treatment was far from cordial. David Blaser was a private in the 4th Indiana Light Artillery of Rousseau's division, and the battery had been sent with Starkweather's brigade to participate in the operation. Blaser deserted on the morning of April 24, but was apprehended by some of Reynolds's troops five days later. The private was wearing a tattered gray uniform when he was captured and at first claimed to be a deserter from Morgan's Confederate cavalry. Blaser's captors were suspicious and eventually the private's real identity was confirmed. Desertion was a problem that plagued all units in the Civil War. The act carried a death sentence under the Articles of War, but the Union Army rarely stuck to the letter of the law on this offense. More often than not, an apprehended deserter was disciplined by his regiment and then permitted to shoulder his rifle once again. Deserting to the enemy was altogether another matter. A court-martial convened on May 6, and Blaser was pronounced guilty of desertion two days later. The sentence was death. General Rousseau approved the court's findings on May 18; General Rosecrans reported on June 17 that the president had approved the sentence. Blaser was to be executed between 10:00 A.M. and 12:00 noon on June 20. Rousseau decided that regulars would perform the execution. Twelve non-commissioned officers from the Regular Brigade were selected for the task. Robert Kennedy wanted to be one of them, but the corporal had just come off picket duty when the detail was being formed and, much to his disappointment, his brogans were judged to be insufficiently blackened.[63]

In the late morning of June 20, Rousseau's division marched into a large open field a few miles northeast of Murfreesboro. The division's brigades formed three sides of an open-ended square, each brigade arrayed in a single line of two ranks. A dozen sergeants and corporals from the Regular Brigade stood rigidly at attention in the center of the square, facing the open end under the watchful eye of the division provost marshal, Captain Thomas C. Williams of the 19th Infantry. After the brigades were in position, their front ranks marched forward ten paces and faced about. The convicted and his escort then marched around the square, through the open ranks of the brigades. A platoon from the division's provost guard, C/1/19th U.S., led the procession carrying reversed arms. Then came Private Blaser, a chaplain, and a wagon bearing a coffin. An additional platoon of provosts followed the wagon, these regulars carrying their rifles with fixed bayonets at the charge position. As the procession

approached a regiment that had a band present, the musicians began
to play the somber "Dead March." The air was soon filled with the
music of the division's massed bands.

The procession slowly marched to the center of the square. The last
strains of the music faded away while the ranks of the division were
closed and faced forward. Silence reigned on the wind-swept field as
teamsters unloaded the coffin and led the wagon away. The chaplain
had Blaser kneel and said a hushed prayer over him. The minister
walked away and Captain Williams took over. He had Blaser sit on
the edge of the open coffin and blindfolded him. The captain faced
about and marched to his place beside the firing party. He read
aloud Blaser's crime and punishment. The regulars brought their
pieces to the ready and took aim as General Rousseau gave the firing commands. Rousseau's order to fire was drowned out as twelve
triggers were pulled in unison. Blaser's chest exploded a split-second
later, the force propelling him backward into the coffin.

Rousseau then paraded the division past the coffin and its grisly
contents, where each soldier received a close look at the penalty for
desertion to the enemy. They saw that the aim of the execution detail
had been true. Six of the rifles had been loaded with blank cartridges
to prevent the detail from knowing exactly who would fire the fatal
shots. Of the six weapons with live charges, five had struck home.
After it was all over, Lieutenant Lucius Brown wrote that the morning's events had the desired effect on his company of the 18th
Infantry: "Our men think they'll carry their rifles awile yet rather
then desert."[64]

The officer in command of the Regular Brigade that somber day
was Brigadier General John H. King. Rosecrans, belatedly realizing
that relieving Shepherd had been a mistake, fortunately did not
allow the bad situation to get worse for long. Just nineteen days
after giving the Regular Brigade to Granger, on May 6 Rosecrans
replaced him with General King. The regulars welcomed King's
appointment, and the dust eventually settled on the brigade's having
three different commanders in less than three weeks.

King's assumption of command occurred too late to prevent the
departure of many experienced officers. Captain Alfred Hough
arranged a transfer to the staff of Negley's division in early May, just
prior to Granger's departure, to serve as that division's mustering
officer. Hough's entire chain-of-command resisted the assignment,
not wanting to lose yet another experienced officer. Captain

Augustus H. Plummer, commanding 1/19th U.S., requested that Hough be reassigned back to the 19th Infantry: "Almost any other officer of the Batt. could be better spared than Capt. Hough. He is an excellent line officer and is well fitted to command a company or a regiment." General King's endorsement was likewise negative: "The services of Capt. A.L. Hough 19th U.S. Infty are necessary with his Company. If the best officers of my command are to be selected for staff duties, who are to take my men into action?" Lovell Rousseau concurred with King, but the transfer went through despite the objections. General Rosecrans believed that "Capt. Hough's services are indispensable in his present position" on Negley's staff. The notion persisted that regular officers were more useful on staff duty than they were when serving with their regiments. The XIV Corps is widely considered to have been the best corps in the Army of the Cumberland. George Thomas's leadership is the main reason for that distinction, although the corps' robust complement of regular officers compared with other commands was also a factor. But as regular staff officers increased the efficiency of the corps, the Regular Brigade paid the price.[65]

General King was shocked to learn of the undermanned status of the brigade's officer corps. Just as Shepherd had done, King appealed to the War Department to rectify the situation. He started by addressing the whereabouts of Major James Caldwell. He found a copy of a letter in the brigade order book written by Oliver Shepherd on April 9 that ordered Caldwell back to Tennessee. King sent a copy of the letter to Rosecrans's headquarters and informed everyone that this sort of behavior from Caldwell was actually nothing new: "I most urgently request that Major Caldwell be ordered to join this command. I take this occasion to state that of my own knowledge Maj. Caldwell was on recruiting service for over two years during the Mexican War and now I find him about in the same duty, but in justice to him I will state that his Co...was never in Mexico." George Thomas endorsed King's request with a few sentences that got to the heart of the Regular Brigade's manning difficulties: "The 4th Brigade composed entirely of Regulars, is sadly deficient in Field and Staff officers, having suffered sever losses at the Battle of Stones River, besides having a large number of officers detailed for Recruiting and other duties. I recommend that Maj. Caldwell be ordered to join his Battalion, believing it to be for the best interest of the service." Even these arguments were not enough to overcome the influence Henry Carrington still had with the War Department. James Caldwell remained at Camp Thomas for the balance of the war.[66]

King next sent a request through the War Department to the commanders of the brigade's four regimental depots, urging that officers on detached service and recruiting duty be sent to the Regular Brigade. The general then moved on to address the situation of the regiment with which he was most familiar, the 15th Infantry. King knew that responsibility for this regiment's headquarters now rested with Colonel Oliver Shepherd, so King felt it was time for the regiment's lieutenant colonel, John Sanderson, to make himself useful:

> Head Quarters 3d Brigade
> 1st Division, 14th Army Corps
> May 28th 1863
>
> Lieut. Col. C. Goddard
>   Asst Adjt General
>   Hd Qrs Dept of Cumberland
> Colonel:
>
> I have the honor herewith to enclose Special Order No 207, ordering Lieut. Col. James [John] P. Sanderson, 15th U.S. Infantry, with all enlisted men of this regiment to join this command. No doubt when this order was issued, it was intended that is should be obeyed. I now learn unofficially that it has been countermanded. In justice to Lieut. Col. Sanderson, I must say that he is a good proper man, but being a line officer he should be made to come down to *Dixie* and do duty in the field.
>
> A number of officers of the 15th Infantry are now absent on "recruiting service," the first Battalion of this regiment has been in the field for fifteen months past, and as yet had not received a single recruit. I have to request in justice to the regiment that these Officers be ordered in from recruiting service.
>
> In conclusion I desire to say that in the beginning of the Rebellion, a great many Officers were very enthusiastic in their desire to have it "put down" or crushed at once, but up to the present time a number of them have never been *under fire* or even within sound of the Enemy's guns.
>
> I am, Colonel,
>   Very Respectfully
>   Your most Obt Servt,
>
> JOHN H. KING
> Brig. General
> Commanding[67]

The contingent of 15th Infantry recruits that Oliver Shepherd had herded out the gate at Fort Adams eventually reported for duty with the Regular Brigade, but John Sanderson was nowhere to be seen. Sanderson's departure from Rhode Island marked the end of his service with the 15th Regulars. The former chief clerk of the War Department pulled some strings and had his movement orders canceled. When he reported for duty with the Army of the Cumberland during the late summer of 1863, he was wearing the shoulder straps of a full colonel. William T. Sherman, the original colonel of the 13th U.S. Infantry, was promoted to Regular Army brigadier general on July 4, 1863. Sanderson moved up to the colonelcy of the 13th Regulars, and in that capacity secured a position on the Army of the Cumberland's staff. Meanwhile Lieutenant George Sanderson, like his father, also never again served with the 15th Regulars in the field. He remained on sick leave for many months after Shepherd took command of the regiment. Late in 1863 he was assigned as a mustering officer in Negley's division of the XIV Corps.[68]

Colonel Oliver Shepherd must have been livid when he read Rosecrans's positive endorsement to King's request that more officers be sent to the field, for Shepherd had been clamoring for much the same thing since taking field command of the 18th Regulars in December 1861. Shepherd was also quick to point out that it was the appointment of General Granger to command the Regular Brigade that had accelerated the brigade's worsening officer shortfall, meaning Rosecrans had no one but himself to blame. Shepherd informed the War Department that there were actually quite a few officers of the 15th Regulars on duty with the Army of the Cumberland:

> Head Quarters 15th US Infy
> Fort Adams R.I.
> May 21st 1863

Brig. Gen. L. Thomas
   Adjt. Genl. U.S.A.
   Washington, D.C.

General,

   Understanding that the Comdg Officer of the Brigade of which the 1st Battalion of the 15th Inf.. forms part, has made application for additional Officers to be sent on duty with that Battalion...I desire respectfully to state that there are now nine Officers on duty with the six small companies comprising that Battalion, and that

Gen'l Rosecrans, Comdg the Dept., has on his staff the Captain of Co. F, John C. Peterson, and the Captain of Co. H, James Curtis, and on other Staff duties, in his army, the Captain of Co. B, Jesse Fulmer; also the following officers of the Regt. who do not belong to the 1st Batt, viz: Capts John H. Young and Isaac D. Sailor, the latter having been ordered on duty with that Battalion but a few days ago.

There are besides in the Dept under Genl Rosecrans Captain Peter T. Swaine belonging to the Batt. and Capt. Chas. A. Harker, both commanding Volunteer Regts. making a total on Staff duties of five Captains, and two on Line duty with Volunteers.

Omitting the latter two, there are fourteen Officers in that Dept. designed for duty with that Battalion of six companies.

In my semi-monthly Report on the 15th inst, it may be seen, that all the companies of the 1s Batt. now existing, have all their officers on duty in the Dept. under Genl. Rosecrans, excepting those on sick leave, and one 2d Lieut. (Sanderson) who is himself an invalid to some extent.

Nevertheless I recommend that the successor of Capt. Wm W. Wise of Co C, killed in battle, may be ordered to his Company (C). His successor is supposed to be 1st Lt. G.M. Brayton.

The recommendation of the Officers of the 1st Batt. [is] for the promotion to 2d Lieutenant of First Sgt. John Williams of Co. C. 1st Batt. I respectfully urge the immediate action of the Dept.

If these two promotions of Captain and 2d Lieut be made, and ordered to duty with their Companies, there would then be *sixteen* Officers available for duty with the 1st Batt. of this Regt.

Respectfully,

OLIVER L. SHEPHERD
Col. 15th Infy[69]

* * *

The Army of the Cumberland's lengthy stay at Murfreesboro finally came to an end a few days after Blaser's execution. "We are expecting some fun now every day," Private Trine Swick of G/2/18th U.S. wrote to his sister in early June. "[T]here is a force of Rebels out about twelve miles from us, and we are expecting every day to go out to see them a little." The president, Secretary Stanton, and General Halleck all thought Rosecrans should have been on the move many weeks before, for Federal armies in Virginia and Mississippi had started their campaigns in the springtime. The Army of the Cumberland's objective was still the capture of Chattanooga.

Rosecrans's army remained immobile for so long in 1863 because he wanted to be thoroughly prepared for a lengthy and hazardous campaign. Moving from Murfreesboro to Chattanooga involved traversing a landscape that was anything but conducive to nineteenth century military operations. Four substantial rivers, the Duck, Elk, Sequatchie, and Tennessee, would have to be crossed. In between the waterways were a series of long ridges, militarily traversable only through a handful of easily defended gaps. The high ground was all perpendicular to the Army of the Cumberland's route of advance. Between Murfreesboro and the Duck River was a ridge known as the Highland Rim. Nestled between the Duck and Elk Rivers was a low plateau known as the Oak Barrens. It was south of the Elk that the most serious obstacle lay. The Cumberland Plateau, looming in the distance some twenty-five miles southeast of Murfreesboro, sat squarely athwart the route to Chattanooga. This was a terrain feature to be reckoned with, standing 1,500 feet higher than the countryside around Murfreesboro. It continued unabated for nearly thirty miles before the twists and turns of the Sequatchie and Tennessee Rivers cut it into another series of lengthy ridges. It would not be until after Rosecrans had captured Chattanooga and advanced well into northern Georgia that the terrain would start to moderate somewhat.[70]

Making matters worse was the soil in this mountainous area. It was much different from the fertile fields along the Cumberland River near Nashville. The region could barely support small-yield subsistence farming, so an army advancing from Murfreesboro to Chattanooga would have to carry virtually every logistical item it would need. Manufacturing large quantities of equipment and producing foodstuffs was not a problem for the North's burgeoning industries by this point in the war. Getting those supplies across the rivers and ridges of southeastern Tennessee by way of the vulnerable single-track Nashville & Chattanooga Railway would be a feat much more difficult to accomplish. It was a problem Federal commanders in the West had avoided for more than year. Having attempted and failed northern and southern end runs around the Cumberland Plateau during 1862 (the Mills Springs Campaign in January, followed by Buell's advance along the Memphis & Charleston Railroad throughout the summer), the Union Army in middle Tennessee was finally coming to grips with the necessity of advancing along the direct route from Nashville to Chattanooga.

For a methodical, scientific planner such as William Rosecrans, advancing toward Chattanooga involved a series of problems that could be solved only through thorough preparation. An army spending half a year at Murfreesboro was the result.

And, of course, there was a Confederate army in middle Tennessee to worry about. A key part of the Union's 1863 strategy was for Rosecrans to prevent Bragg's Army of Tennessee from shifting forces to Mississippi and reinforcing Vicksburg. Rosecrans believed he could do this by simply threatening Bragg from Murfreesboro, but on this point the Army of the Cumberland's commander miscalculated. In early June, 10,000 of Bragg's troops were sent to Mississippi. Grant's Army of the Tennessee had finally succeeded in laying siege to Vicksburg and the Confederacy was trying to form a relief force led by General Joseph Johnston. Although Johnston's ad hoc army would end up playing little role in the struggle for Vicksburg, the inactivity on Rosecrans's portion of the front was causing the Federal plan to play itself out in reverse. Instead of aiding campaigns elsewhere, Rosecrans was being aided by them. As summer approached, Rosecrans's well of Stones River goodwill in Washington was starting to run dry.[71]

The Army of the Cumberland's preparations were finally complete by mid-June, Rosecrans and his staff having spent the months at Murfreesboro studying the terrain and obtaining a fairly accurate estimate of Bragg's dispositions. The headquarters of Bragg's diminished army of 44,000 remained at Tullahoma, the place to which it had retreated after Stones River. The Army of Tennessee was strongly entrenched north of the Duck River, with fortifications stretching from Shelbyville to Beech Grove. Lieutenant General Leonidas Polk's Corps covered Shelbyville, along the most direct route of a potential Federal advance, while Hardee's Corps manned positions to the east. The low, rugged Highland Rim, north of the Shelbyville-Beech Grove line, screened the main Confederate positions and was likewise fortified. Pushing the Southerners out of this area appeared to be a daunting task.

Wanting to avoid another Stones River-style slugfest, Rosecrans instead planned to maneuver Bragg out of middle Tennessee. The Federal plan was to quickly move through the Highland Rim and outflank the fortifications along the Duck. The plan would work only if the Federal columns moved through the Highland Rim before Bragg could react. Rosecrans intended to deceive Bragg into thinking

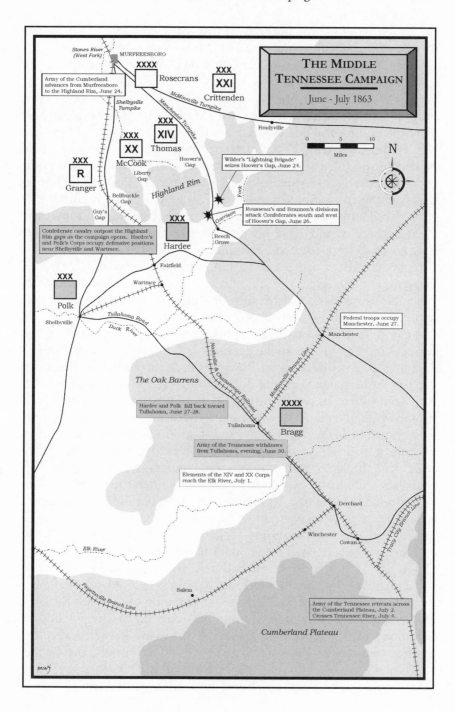

Stones River
(West Fork)   MURFREESBORO

XXXX

Army of the Cumberland
advances from Murfreesboro
to the Highland Rim, June 24.

Rosecrans

XXX
XXI
Crittenden

McMinnville Turnpike

Shelbyville Turnpike

Manchester Turnpike

Bradyville

**THE MIDDLE
TENNESSEE CAMPAIGN**

June - July 1863

0   5   10

Miles

N

XXX
XIV
Thomas

XXX
XX
McCook

Hoover's
Gap

Wilder's "Lightning Brigade"
seizes Hoover's Gap, June 24.

XXX
R
Granger

Liberty
Gap

Highland Rim

Bellbuckle
Gap

Fork

Garrison

Rousseau's and Brannon's divisions
attack Confederates south and west
of Hoover's Gap, June 26.

Guy's
Gap

XXX

Confederate cavalry outpost the Highland
Rim gaps as the campaign opens. Hardee's
and Polk's Corps occupy defensive positions
near Shelbyville and Wartrace.

Hardee

Beech
Grove

Fairfield

XXX

Wartrace

Polk

Shelbyville

Tullahoma Road

Duck River

Federal troops occupy
Manchester, June 27.

Manchester

Nashville & Chattanooga Railroad

McMinnville Branch Line

The Oak Barrens

Hardee and Polk fall back toward
Tullahoma, June 27-28.

Tullahoma

XXXX
Bragg

Army of the Tennessee withdraws
from Tullahoma, evening, June 30.

Elements of the XIV and XX Corps
reach the Elk River, July 1.

Derchard

Tracy City Branch Line

Winchester

Cowan

Elk River

Fayetteville Branch Line

Salem

Army of the Tennessee retreats across
the Cumberland Plateau, July 2.
Crosses Tennessee River, July 4.

Cumberland Plateau

mwj

the attack would come in the west toward Shelbyville, when in fact it would fall in the east toward Manchester. In the diversion, Gordon Granger's Reserve Corps would maneuver in front of Bellbuckle Gap, while McCook's XX Corps would attack Liberty Gap. On the eastern flank, Thomas's XIV Corps would seize Hoover's Gap and then push on to Manchester. Crittenden's XXI Corps would meanwhile conduct a wide flanking movement toward Bradyville, far beyond Bragg's eastern flank, where the corps would be in position to either continue turning Bragg's position or support other efforts. Once Manchester was captured, either by Thomas approaching from Hoover's Gap or Crittenden from the Bradyville area, Rosecrans would be astride Bragg's communications. The Confederates would have to either leave their fortifications and attack or fall back toward Chattanooga.[72]

For the XIV Corps, seizing Hoover's Gap was the first step. General Thomas gave the mission to Reynolds's division. One of Reynolds's brigades consisted of four regiments of mounted infantry-men, armed with new Spencer breech-loaders and commanded by Colonel John T. Wilder (the same officer who ten months before had surrendered the Munfordville garrison and H/2/18th U.S. to Bragg's invading army in Kentucky). Reynolds ordered Wilder to storm the gap while the balance of the division moved up to secure the area. Rousseau's division would support Reynolds, following immediately behind, while Negley's and Brannan's divisions brought up the rear. Rosecrans put his 65,000-man army in motion on June 24.[73]

Amidst a driving rainstorm, which would continue with scant relief for the next two weeks, the regulars formed up on the Manchester Pike at dawn. Many new faces dotted the ranks, particu-larly among the officers. Although most of the battalion commanders were veteran campaigners, all of them were relatively new to battal-ion command. Commanding 1/15th U.S. was Captain Henry Keteltas, an experienced leader who had commanded companies at Shiloh and Stones River. Captain R.E.A. Crofton, another long-serv-ice regular who had commanded the battalion since Major Slemmer's wounding on December 31, led the 1st Battalion of the 16th Infantry. Eighteenth Infantry Captain George W. Smith led that regiment's 1st Battalion, an officer who had experienced many marches but little combat thus far in the war. Captain John Thompson, the former Cincinnati provost marshal, commanded the 18th Infantry's 2nd Battalion. A subordinate described him as "a gentleman of refined intelligence, though unskilled in warfare, this being his first experience." Leading the troops of the 19th Infantry was Captain Augustus Plummer, an 1853 graduate of the Military Academy and veteran of the prewar 7th U.S. Infantry. Plummer had been promoted to captain in the 19th U.S. during the 1861 Regular Army expansion but his wartime duties thus far had been serving as mustering officer in Harrisburg, Pennsylvania. He reported for duty in Murfreesboro during late April and, being the ranking officer of the 19th Infantry present, took charge of the battalion.

General King officially commanded the Regular Brigade, but his left hand, mangled at Stones River, had still not completely healed and he was unfit for field service. Command temporarily devolved upon the only field-grade officer present for duty with the regulars, Major Sidney Coolidge of the 16th Infantry. Despite Rosecrans's best efforts to place a general in command of the Regular Brigade, a major took it into battle in June 1863. One can only imagine what Colonel Oliver Shepherd must have been thinking while he sat at his desk in Rhode Island as the Middle Tennessee Campaign got underway.[74]

* * *

The regulars began to plod their way down the wet Manchester Pike at ten o'clock. A few miles ahead, Wilder's mounted infantry captured Hoover's Gap in one of the outstanding small-unit actions of the war. Rosecrans's deception plan had worked to perfection. Bragg and Hardee shifted forces westward in response to Granger and McCook's demonstration on Polk's front, leaving only one small cavalry regiment, the 1st Kentucky, near Hoover's Gap. Wilder's hard-riding troopers brushed this force aside and occupied the gap's southern entrance near Jacob's Store. The Spencer-toting Federals then held off a counterattack of Brigadier General William B. Bate's Brigade from Major General A.P. Stewart's Division. Reynolds moved up his remaining two brigades in support of Wilder later in the day, but wanted additional forces to help hold the gap and requested a brigade from Rousseau's supporting division. Rousseau sent in the regulars. As night was falling on June 24 Major Coolidge moved forward at the head of four regular battalions and Battery H, Captain Keteltas's 1/15th U.S. having remained behind to guard the division baggage train. The regulars occupied the hills on the west side of Hoover's Gap next to Brigadier General George Crook's brigade of Reynolds's division. Captain Kensel's regular artillerymen proceeded through the gap, going into battery near the 21st Indiana Artillery in a position where the guns could command the road to Beech Grove.[75]

Rosecrans wanted to advance toward Manchester the next day, but continuing rains (not to mention Rosecrans's habit of not moving until all preparations were absolutely perfect) made that impossible. Crittenden's corps had become hopelessly mired on the poorly surfaced roads of the Bradyville area, so it was up to Thomas's corps to make the main effort toward Manchester. Thomas spent June 25 closing up additional troops at Hoover's Gap. Scribner's brigade of Rousseau's division relieved Wilder's exhausted troopers overlooking Jacob's Store, while Rousseau's other brigade, Starkweather's (temporarily commanded by Colonel H.A. Hambright), moved up in support. General Brannan's division also moved forward and was posted in reserve. The Regular Brigade remained in place. Battery H and the guns of Reynolds's division dueled throughout the day with Confederate batteries, while sharpshooters on each side took occasional shots.

More Confederate forces also arrived in the area, but the Federal maneuvers to the west caused Hardee to still be concerned about the Liberty Gap area. Only two additional brigades of Stewart's Division, those of Brigadiers Bushrod R. Johnson and Henry D. Clayton, reinforced Bate at Hoover's Gap. Stewart concentrated his troops south and west of Hoover's Gap, covering the approach to the main Confederate positions at Fairfield and Tullahoma. The road to Manchester was weakly held, secured by only the 9th Alabama of Bate's Brigade, a section of artillery, and a weak detachment of the 1st Kentucky Cavalry. General Thomas planned to push Reynolds's division down that road on the morning of June 26, but first he had to deal with Johnson's and Clayton's Brigades on the Federal right flank. He ordered Rousseau and Brannan to drive the enemy back.

Lovell Rousseau spent the night of June 25–26 shifting his brigades into their attack positions, a slow process in the ever-present rain. At daybreak, Rousseau and Brannan went forward to get a feel for the lay of the land. George Crook of the Reynolds's division served as their guide, he having a good grasp of the local topography after having been on this ground for two days. As Rousseau peered through the dripping foliage, he saw that the Confederates were drawn up on a line of low hills about a half-mile in front of the Federal positions. In between lay an uncut wheat field, its stalks heavy

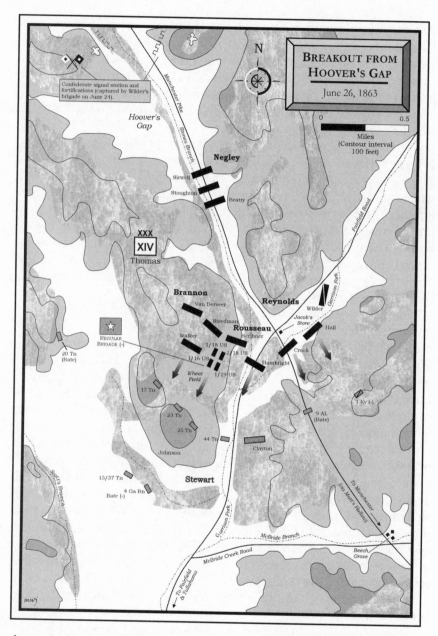

BREAKOUT FROM HOOVER'S GAP

June 26, 1863

from the recent downpours, and also a narrow skirt of light timber. The road to Fairfield, laid out beside Garrison Fork of the Duck River, bisected the Confederate position with Johnson to the west and Clayton to the east. The terrain left little room for maneuver, so Rousseau and Brannan decided to attack with a single brigade from each of their divisions, the Regular Brigade on the left and Colonel Moses B. Walker's brigade from Brannan's division on the right. The balance of the two divisions remained in support, although General Thomas ordered Hambright's brigade to advance down the Fairfield Road as soon as the way was clear.[76]

Everyone was in position by half past ten. In planning the Regular Brigade's attack, Major Coolidge put his French military education to good use. The major realized that moving through the soaked wheat field and wood line would be slow, while the concavity of the Southern line overlooking the area would expose the regulars to a murderous fire. Instead of slowly advancing in the standard line of battle formation, Coolidge instead decided to make the attack in column. He intended to use the regulars like a battering ram to quickly cross the open ground, move up the hills on the far side, and pierce the Confederate position.

The regulars formed up in two columns, the 16th and 19th leading, with a battalion of 18th Infantrymen behind each. "Column of divisions!" Coolidge called out, wanting each of the battalions to form a two-company wide column. Captain John Thompson, commanding 2/18th U.S., was unsure on how to execute the maneuver. Luckily his adjutant, battle-wise veteran William Bisbee, was close enough to whisper the orders to his commander: "Form divisions, left companies, left face, march." The four battalions formed up and fixed bayonets; the lead battalions deployed skirmishers. Coolidge ordered the command forward. Brigadier General Bushrod Johnson, his Confederate brigade about to receive the brunt of the Federal assault, observed the attack from his hilltop position on the south side of the wheat field: "The line of skirmishers was followed by two lines of infantry, about 200 yards apart, of which I especially noticed one regiment formed in column of divisions." More closely resembling an attack from the Napoleonic era than one from the American Civil War, the regulars charged. Bushrod Johnson's men replied with artillery and rifle fire. Lieutenant Carpenter of the 19th Infantry was in his usual place, the thick of the action: "As soon as we commenced moving across the field the enemy formed a line on the hill, and opened a battery giving us a severe fire. we started upon the run making for them as fast as we could giving cheer after cheer as we advanced. that was a nice little charge. we could see them plain and as the wreaths of smoke curled up from the muzzles of their guns we thought that we were sure to be hit, but nothing could stop us. we were going to have them off of the hill or die every man of us."[77]

"After moving rapidly forward for half a mile, the command entered a field of standing wheat, which, wet and matted, made the marching extremely laborious," Captain Smith of 1/18th U.S. reported. "The enemy's fire, from his commanding position on a range of steep hills immediately in front, began to take effect when the command had traversed the [first] half of the field." Most of the incoming fire overshot the 16th and 19th Regulars, landing amidst the 18th Infantry. A spent rifle ball struck newly promoted Lieutenant Reuben Little and knocked him senseless for a few moments. A more powerful projectile tore through Lieutenant Bisbee's overcoat: "A moment after the ball struck, I turned in my saddle to see Capt. Thompson being helped out of his. The ball that hit me passed in direct line to him, cutting through his hand, into his abdomen." Seeing the mounted officer unhorsed, Generals Rousseau and Brannan with their staffs rode forward to assist. The charitable effort did not help, for the large group of horseman only attracted more shellfire. The generals beat a hasty retreat after one shell in particular landed uncomfortably close. Thompson's first battle was his last. He wound proved fatal and he would be dead within a week.[78]

The regulars pressed home the attack despite the casualties. "This charge of the Regulars was one of the best illustrations I have ever seen of the demoralizing effect on an enemy of a swift and determined advance of disciplined infantry," recalled the 16th Infantry's Edgar Kellogg. From his position on General Negley's staff, Captain Alfred Lacey Hough also observed the regulars' advance: "The 1st Division and principally the Regular Brigade did the work. ...The Regular Brigade charged gallantly, and drove the enemy, suffering considerably, three men of my [old] Company were wounded and two killed." A correspondent for the *New York Herald* was near Hough's position and later wrote of Coolidge's regulars: "The Regular Brigade in the centre and holding the advance, had a more beautiful field than either Walker on the right or Hambright on the left, and the charge which it made across the valley was the feature of the advance—the men moved in most beautiful order, the line never wavering or becoming broken until the fence behind which the enemy rested was reached. Here a brisk engagement ensued—the rebels were driven back in great disorder, throwing away their blankets and canteens."[79]

Johnson began withdrawing his Confederates when the Union skirmishers were within about forty yards. His troops fled toward Fairfield, covered by the 15th & 37th Tennessee and the 4th Georgia Battalion of Bate's Brigade, which had taken up positions a mile away on the high ground overlooking Scott's Branch. An officer of the 16th U.S. believed the opposition fled so readily because the sight of the compact, steel-tipped mass of Federal infantry was enough to sap the strength of the most resolute defender: "The enemy saw that their guns were powerless to check us, for the ranks closed up the gaps and moved on without pause, and when, at close quarters, the double quick began and the glistening of bayonets could be seen, the artillerymen in consternation hauled off the guns in a gallop and the infantry lines fired their nervous volley and melted away."[80]

Coolidge halted the winded regulars at the base of the hills on the far side of the wheat field. Skirmishers continued forward in pursuit of the retreating Confederates. Federal batteries displaced forward to the deserted enemy positions and opened fire, artillery of the Confederate rear guard replying in kind. The regular skirmishers became uncomfortable bystanders in the middle of the artillery duel. Lieutenant Carpenter: "Twas splendid we being between the two lines. the shells whistled over us very musical indeed one shell fell about 10 ft. behind us and exploded hurting no one but making us dodge. we were soon relieved as skirmishers and returned to the brigade."

Hambright's brigade had meanwhile advanced about a half mile along the Fairfield Road, and Reynolds's division overcame feeble resistance and seized Matt's Hollow, a narrow, two mile-long defile on the Manchester Road south of Beech Grove. That night, Reynolds's troops camped within five miles of Manchester, the Army of the Cumberland's objective. Although rain had again slowed the advance, overall General Thomas was pleased with his corps' attack on June 26. Calling the assault of the regulars and Walker's brigade a "gallant charge," Thomas wrote: "the behavior of our troops was admirable—everything that could be desired." Major Coolidge had surprised many with his performance. One regular wrote that

Coolidge's "skill in handling his command, and his intrepid bearing under fire were both conspicuous and inspiring."[81]

Rosecrans ordered Thomas to continue advancing the next day on the roads to Manchester and Fairfield. Rousseau's division moved toward Fairfield, keeping pressure on the retreating Southerners. Reaching the town shortly before noon on the 27th, the Kentuckian reported the enemy retreating toward Tullahoma. Rousseau's column then headed for Manchester, which Reynolds had occupied that morning. Amidst yet another downpour, the Regular Brigade reached the town shortly after midnight. The countryside appeared quite familiar to some of the brigade's veterans, for this was the area the regular battalions of the old 4th Brigade had patrolled the previous summer. In Manchester, General Rousseau established his headquarters in the same house the 19th Infantry's Major Stephen Carpenter had occupied in August 1862.[82]

With Federal forces at Manchester and additional blue-clad troops pouring through Hoover's Gap, the Confederates along the Duck River had few options. Rosecrans's offensive had caught Bragg off guard and Bragg's subordinate commanders were slow to react to the initial Federal moves, even with the dismal weather slowing down the Federal advance. Bragg retreated on July 1. Rosecrans attempted to head off the fleeing Confederates at the Elk River, but Bragg's column managed to stay a few steps ahead of the victorious Northerners and made good its escape. On July 4, Bragg's demoralized force crossed the Tennessee River and arrived in Chattanooga.

At the cost of fewer than 600 casualties, in less than two weeks Rosecrans had advanced eighty miles and drove the Confederates out of middle Tennessee. The Regular Brigade suffered three dead and twenty wounded at Hoover's Gap, about half of the total losses in Rousseau's division for the campaign. Private Luke Lyman, who had remained behind sick in Murfreesboro while his two brothers marched with 2/18th U.S., described in a letter home what was perhaps the most interesting of the 18th Infantry's casualties: "I would like to be with the old 18th who are winning the rosiest laurels in the field, the 18th they say carries everything before it. I hear from Ole and Phil every day or so. I heard yesterday they were all right. there was a boy from the 18th who made a charge on a rebel capt and run him about a hundred yards and came so close the capt jumped into the Duck River, just as he jumped the boy run him through with his bayonett and held on to his gun so the weight of the capt pulled him into the river and they both went down and never came up."[83]

Regular officers at Hoover's Gap again attracted enemy bullets. Lieutenant John Shiffler of the 16th U.S. was wounded in addition to the 18th Infantry's Lieutenant Little and Captain Thompson, the only officer casualties in Rousseau's division. Lieutenant Lucius Brown of the 18th later mentioned a possible reason for the officer losses. He had been promoted to 1st lieutenant earlier in the year and in mid-August wrote his sister about how excited he was to wear his new shoulder straps: "I wear them always on my dress coat, though officers in front are permitted to wear only the bar, leaf, eagle or star without the rectangle of blue and the border. I hold however that a rebel sharpshooter can see my belt plate—bugle—hat cord and position as far as my shoulder straps of some kind...and much dislike to see officers running about without them. Some officers I know of (none of ours however) tore off their straps when under fire at Hoover's Gap. They may pick me off a dozen times before I'll do that."[84]

Captain Henry Haymond, a native Virginian who had served in all the 18th Infantry's campaigns up to this point as commander of E/3/18th, replaced Thompson in command of the 18th Infantry's 2nd Battalion. The 18th Regulars also lost the services of Lieutenant Bisbee. Although the bullet that killed Captain Thompson had only bruised Bisbee, the lieutenant came down with a severe case of rheumatism shortly after the battle. He took opium to kill the pain. Captain Haymond urged him to leave the field but the pride that came with being a veteran officer prevented Bisbee from following his commander's advice for a number of weeks. By the latter half of July the lieutenant's knees had swelled to such an extent that he could no longer walk. He headed for the rear on July 24:

> My first experience with an ambulance and hospital had come. No amount of disability had ever induced or compelled me to get into an ambulance, it having been a pride among the older marchers to avoid and discourage it. ...I was granted twenty days and started for Nashville. The trip of two miles over rough roads to the railroad was extremely painful. Once in the train, Private McNally, who had been sent along to help me, turned up the backs of two seats for a bed, upon which I reclined and suffered the jolts of a genuine military railroad until nearing Nashville. ...Here a conveyance took us to a hospital, which in its cleanly appearance gave promise of

improving my condition, despite the presence of hundreds of pallid faces in adjoining beds and the disquieting observation of the surgeon, that Captain Thompson of my regiment had died in my bed the week previous.[85]

* * *

While the Army of the Cumberland was proud of the outcome of the Middle Tennessee Campaign, much work remained: the capture of Chattanooga and destruction of Bragg's army. General Halleck and Secretary Stanton expected Rosecrans to continue the offensive immediately, but their extortions did little good. As William Rosecrans had shown ever since taking command, he never moved without thorough preparation. The Army of the Cumberland remained near Tullahoma for most of the next two months, improving roads in the Oak Barrens, putting the neglected tracks of the Nashville and Chattanooga line in running condition, positioning supplies in preparation for crossing the Cumberland Plateau, and waiting for what corn there was growing in the region to ripen. On July 13, the railroad bridge over Elk River was repaired. Trains were able to run all the way to Bridgeport on the Tennessee River by the end of the month. Captain Hough reassured his wife in an early July letter that the advance toward Chattanooga was not to be deterred this year: "One thing is certain you need not fear of another retreat on our part like Buell's of last year. No army could live in Tennessee this year, we bring our supplies after us, but what little there is in the country we are taking, but there aint much left, the people complain as much of the rebel army as they do of ours."[86]

Rosecrans was still not ready to move. The long Federal supply line in Tennessee was vulnerable to ever-present Confederate cavalry and Rosecrans wanted more horseman of his own to counter them. Rosecrans's efforts to obtain additional cavalry had a collateral effect of altering command assignments in the Regular Brigade. He dispatched General Rousseau and Colonel John P. Sanderson to Washington on July 26, seeking approval for Rosecrans's plan to convert Rousseau's command into a mounted infantry division. Nothing resulted of the effort, other than preventing Lovell Rousseau from participating in the upcoming campaign. Brigadier General John King, who had rejoined the Regular Brigade shortly after the fight at Hoover's Gap, moved up to temporary command of the division. Command of the Regular Brigade again trickled down to the ranking officer present, this time Major Samuel K. Dawson of the 19th Infantry. Although a Military Academy Graduate (Class of 1835) and Mexican War veteran, Dawson was perhaps past his prime by 1863. He did not have any Civil War combat experience prior to joining the Regular Brigade in the field during the waning moments of the Middle Tennessee Campaign. Major Dawson's date of rank was identical to that of Major Coolidge, but Dawson's prewar service made him senior to the 16th Infantry's major. Dawson's abilities did not impress some of the brigade's lower-ranking officers. "Maj. *Dawson*!! commands the Brigade," Lieutenant Lucius Brown wrote on August 15 to his brother in Ohio. "I think Gen'l Carrington'd better come down here. Just tell him we'd be very glad to see him." Captain Hough of the 19th Infantry was more direct in his comments about Dawson: "Of all the impracticables I have ever come in contact with, Maj. Dawson was pre-eminent. I can only excuse him from being thoroughly demonic by believing him to have been insane." Major Coolidge resumed command of 1/16th U.S. and Captain Crofton again took up his familiar duties in command of the battalion's Company A, the same unit he had led at Shiloh and Stones River.[87]

While Rousseau's fruitless mission to Washington transpired, back in Tennessee Rosecrans put the finishing touches on his plan to move across the Cumberland Plateau. The Regular Brigade crossed the Elk River on July 4 and moved down the rails to Cowan Station, arriving on July 14. The brigade remained there until the middle of August, Major Dawson keeping them busy with the usual Regular Army routine of drill and inspections. By early August, rumors circulated that the expected offensive would begin shortly. Lieutenant James Gageby of the 19th Infantry wrote to his sister on August 7: "We are under marching orders and expect to move soon, perhaps tomorrow. Look out for good news. ...I would like to be home for a few days but leaves of absence are out of the question. Maybe I will get wounded slightly in the next fight and then I can get a leave. I hope I will never get a leave in that way. At least I don't covet it." The Army of the Cumberland's immobility was starting to confuse people on the home front. Lieutenant Carpenter had to write his parents on August 9 and set them straight about the 19th Infantry's location in Tennessee: "It is a wonder to me how you all have the impression up north that we are in Georgia or Alabama. we have been in camp here nearly 4 weeks. tomorrow we expect to move from here, and go to Stevenson Ala. twill not be a long march, and if it is managed judiciously will be accomplished with very little hardship, that is for old soldiers."[88]

Rosecrans finally put the Army of the Cumberland in motion on August 16. It took most of the month for his columns to snake their way over the Cumberland Plateau to the banks of the Tennessee and Sequatchie Rivers. Arthur Carpenter had been correct about the timing of the advance, although his prediction of having an easy march was not quite as accurate: "The road that we traveled was very rough, our artillery and transportation had a hard time in getting along. Some places the road wound along the tops of hills, right on the brink of precipices several hundred feet down, and occassionaly a wagon would upset, sending its contents helter scelter down the hill. After exercising a great deal of patience, the things would be gathered up and we would be ready to start again."[89]

For the next four weeks, the Regular Brigade and a number of other units were spread out across southeastern Tennessee, repairing roads and guarding rail lines. His first sight of the mountain roads shocked Lieutenant Lucius Brown: "In about an hour we struck the mountain—*then such* a road *I* never saw. Steep, rough, rocky & full of deep holes, we went up about two miles & halted & sent back a heavy detail with axes, hammers, picks, shovels, etc. They *fixed* that part in about an hour." The battalions changed camp locations every few days as the roadwork progressed. Being perfectionists when it came to camp appearance and cleanliness, the regulars could clear out a patch of woods in no time at all. The comments of Lieutenant Brown again: "put up our shelter tents and put up our flies in proper position & set about policing and are now *about* cleaned up. Grass cut all off with the shovel, stumps & logs taken out, whole ground swept clean. Our camp now looks finely. [You] would be surprised to see the cleaning made by the Batt. in a few hours." An enlisted soldier in 2/18th U.S. was heard to grumble: "What nice places folks round here'll have for picnics when this cruel war is over."[90]

Although crossing the plateau was treacherous and exhausting, Rosecrans's army accomplished the movement without hindrance from Bragg. The Army of Tennessee, badly demoralized by its hasty ejection from middle Tennessee, remained near Chattanooga throughout July and August. Bragg had only skeletal forces screening his front and they were able to determine only that Rosecrans was on the move with ten Federal divisions crossing the Cumberland Plateau on an eighty-mile front. Adding to Bragg's troubles was another Federal force, the resurrected Army of the Ohio under Major General Ambrose Burnside, which was menacing East Tennessee. In late August, Burnside's column moved from central Kentucky, passed through Cumberland Gap, and advanced unopposed toward Knoxville. It marched into the city on September 2, to the cheers of the region's decidedly Unionist inhabitants.

Rosecrans halted after his columns closed up on the Tennessee and Sequatchie Rivers, preparing for what he hoped to be the decisive part of the campaign. This stop lasted only a few days, and the Army of the Cumberland was on the move again by early September. While Rosecrans can be faulted for not conducting his operations in complete accordance with the timetable of his political and military masters, it is difficult to deny that once the Army of the Cumberland had taken to the field in 1863, it had operated as anything but a well-oiled machine. Crossing the Tennessee River, capturing Chattanooga, and advancing into Georgia were the next steps. The movement across the river initiated the Chickamauga Campaign, a series of maneuvers that culminated in one of the bloodiest battles of the war. The regulars would play a prominent role in these events and shed a great quantity of blood in the process, for their casualties in September 1863 were even greater than those of Stones River. For the men of the Regular Brigade, the war's hardest fighting was about to begin.[91]

Chapter 8:

The Battle of Chickamauga

"Kill and Be Damned!"

Lieutenant Edgar N. Wilcox's birthday was a lonely one in 1863. All of his recent birthdays had found him far from home and hundreds, if not thousands, of miles from where he had spent the last, and this year was no exception. "Let me see," the 18th Infantryman wrote in his journal on August 11, "a year ago (1862) at Columbus, O. 1861 a private in the Vol Service (7th Ohio) & in camp in Western Virginia. 1860 a civil engineer in St. Joseph, Mo. 1859 a sailor & abreast the Sully Islands in the English Channel trying to see the world and at the same time to earn money enough to take me through my last year at college. 1858, going up Lake Huron bound for Chicago before the mast."[1]

"That's far enough back," he wrote as he closed out the day's entry. He had plenty of time to reflect on days gone by on this his twenty-fourth birthday, for he was camped in a deserted portion of middle Tennessee with but a corporal's guard of quartermasters for company. The Regular Brigade had left its camp near Cowan Station the previous day in preparation for crossing the Cumberland Plateau, but Wilcox remained behind in charge of the brigade's excess baggage and camp equipment. The lieutenant was an old hand at taking care of administrative tasks, for he had spent more than a year as a clerk at Camp Thomas before being commissioned the previous spring. He and Lieutenant James Ostrander had finally departed Ohio on June 6 with 84 recruits for the 18th Infantry battalions in the field, linking up with the Regular Brigade at Murfreesboro after a six-day journey by rail. Rosecrans's methodical advance over the Cumberland Plateau during the latter half of August meant that Wilcox spent many boring days at Cowan Station. "For the last week the heat & flies have been enough to drive me crazy," he wrote on August 16, "and it is fairly impossible to do anything from 9 o'clock A.M. till sunset but walk & cuss." The heat and forced inactivity drove the former mariner to ponder a career change that was anathema to any clear-headed infantryman of the Regular Army: "I'm sick of it & wish some kind friend would get me detailed on marine duty with the Steamer Michigan. Yes, I'd even be a Marine— that non descript whom neither soldiers nor sailors lay claim to—for the sake of getting out of this oven like country." He had to endure three more days of cussing and dreams of saltwater before Lieutenant Jacob Kline, quartermaster of the 16th Infantry, arrived at Cowan with orders to bring the baggage forward to the brigade's new camp near Anderson.

Wilcox lost no time. He borrowed two mule teams from the nearby camp of the 69th Ohio Volunteers and by sunset had all of the equipment at the Cowan rail depot. After securing an empty freight car, Wilcox kept his men at work late into the night until every last tent, trunk, and supply box was loaded on board. He then pitched his own tent right next to the rails at the siding, not wanting to miss the arrival of the next southbound train. A freight train arrived at Cowan early the next morning, bearing a pontoon bridge that Rosecrans's pioneers would soon lay across the Tennessee River at Bridgeport. Wilcox arranged to have the Regular Brigade's car hitched up, after which the quartermasters enjoyed a leisurely crossing of the Cumberland Plateau. They unhitched at Anderson Station, a group of shacks a mile north of the Tennessee-Alabama state line. The Regular Brigade's camp was a few miles away. While Wilcox and his men stretched their legs, Lieutenant Kline departed in search of some teams to haul the baggage.

Word came back to Wilcox that the brigade would soon be departing this area and to keep the baggage loaded up for now. The regulars were bound for Stevenson, Alabama, eighteen miles down the tracks from Anderson, so the baggage was to move on to that point. Wilcox spent most of the day on August 21 trying to get his car hitched up to another train. Three came and went without agreeing to take the regulars' baggage to Stevenson, but after some "expostulation and a little judicious cussing" Wilcox convinced a fourth engineer to take the brigade's car along. Arriving in Stevenson during the late afternoon, Wilcox searched for a spot to store the equipment. His choices were limited, since Stevenson at that time consisted of only about a dozen dilapidated buildings. All of the structures were already brimming with munitions and supplies, for the town was being transformed into one of Rosecrans's forward supply depots. Wilcox had no choice but to unload everything in the open near the station platform. The Regular Brigade marched into town a few days later. Lieutenant Wilcox directed the battalion quartermasters to their equipment, after which he finally linked up with his company, H/3/18th U.S., and received a few letters from home.[2]

Like many officers of the line, the 19th Infantry's Arthur Carpenter appreciated, but did not fully comprehend, the efforts of logisticians such as Edgar Wilcox. The sights in and around Stevenson impressed Carpenter, but his mention of them in a letter indicates that he thought Rosecrans's preparations for the advance across the Tennessee River were a bit more orderly than was actually the case: "The Chattanooga and Nashville Railroad...presents now a very busy scene. trains heavily loaded come puffing into town, and deposit their burden of provisions, forage, and munitions of war, and then hasten back for more. the roads are crowded with government wagons which haul the stuff off to the different commands, and places of storage. troops are moving here and there. One gazes on the scene with feelings of the highest veneration for the master mind who causes and controls the movements of all in this department. everything is like clock work, order and system prevails in everything."[3]

The Regular Brigade was able to see more of the activity at Stevenson than did most of their comrades. The Army of the Cumberland began crossing the Tennessee River on August 29, an operation that continued into the next week. The regulars remained on the west side, guarding rail lines between Anderson, Stevenson, and Bridgeport. Rosecrans was holding the regulars for possible shipment northward, for it was thought they might soon be on their way to New York City. Bloody riots against the draft had erupted earlier that summer in New York, and the War Department was sending regular troops to the city to maintain order. The Army of the Potomac's Regular Division had arrived there in mid-August; it was assumed the Regular Brigade would follow. New York was the last place Lieutenant Howard Burnham of Battery H wanted to go, for he was finally feeling that he was making a contribution to the war effort. In fact, he had jumped from section leader to division chief of artillery in just less than three months. Shortly after newly promoted Captain Francis Guenther has been posted to Washington, Captain George Kensel took a position as acting chief of ordnance on the staff of Alexander McCook's corps.[4] Burnham was the next ranking officer in Battery H, and with command of a regular battery came the additional duty of being the division's chief of artillery. The lieutenant wrote his father on September 3 that the regulars would be heading somewhere soon:

> You see by the date that we have again moved our camp, and are now lying close to the village of Stevenson. All the army are across the river excepting our brigade, who are doing guard duty in the town. Stevenson is at present the great depot of this army, and as we hear constantly the whistle of the engines, it seems a little more like civilized life. Yesterday I rode down to the river with our surgeon, and saw a brigade of cavalry cross on the pontoon bridge. The water looked so inviting that the doctor and I stripped and took a glorious swim, leaving my orderly with our horses. Our brigade will probably follow the army as soon as the reserve corps comes up, which will be in about a week. There has been no rain here for nearly a week, and I never saw such dust. Army wagons constantly moving keep up a cloud. Rumors are circulating through this brigade that we are to be ordered North to recruit, and join the Regulars in New York for a Southern trip by water, but they are not believed.[5]

Nothing came of the rumored New York move, and late in the afternoon on September 10, the Regular Brigade's 1,829 officers and men crossed the Tennessee via the pontoon bridge at Bridgeport. Brigadier General John King again led them, his command of Rousseau's division ending as a result of a personnel shuffle within the Army of the Cumberland. Brigadier General James B. Steedman had some "difficulty in his situation" while leading a brigade in Brannan's division and requested a transfer. Rosecrans moved Steedman to the Reserve Corps, where due to seniority he took command of Brigadier General Absalom Baird's division. Baird was assigned to Thomas's corps. Since Lovell Rousseau had still not returned from Washington, on August 23 Baird took temporary command of the XIV Corps's 1st Division. An 1849 Academy

Graduate who would later earn the Medal of Honor during the Atlanta Campaign, Baird had a good amount of combat experience and was a capable, respected officer. John King moved back down to the regulars.[6]

King's subordinate commanders had changed somewhat since the Middle Tennessee Campaign. Captains Smith and Haymond still led the 18th Infantry battalions, while Majors Coolidge and Dawson commanded the 16th U.S. and 19th U.S. respectively. The 15th Infantry had a new commander, Captain Albert. B. Dod, who joined 1/15th U.S. in early September at Stevenson. Since Dod outranked Henry Keteltas, Dod assumed command of the battalion and Keteltas resumed his command of the battalion's Company E. Albert Dod was one of the original 1861 appointees to the 15th Regulars, but this was his first tour of field duty. The 16th Infantry experienced a few other key officer changes prior to advancing into Georgia. Coolidge's battalion quartermaster, Jacob Kline, was placed on detached service as of August 28, Lieutenant Samuel E. St. Onge taking his place on the battalion staff. Lieutenant Edgar R. Kellogg, a fixture in the 16th U.S. since the battalion's short stay at Camp Thomas in 1861, contracted malaria at Stevenson and was hospitalized five days before the brigade moved out. Looking back on the events of September 1863, Kellogg and Kline would agree that their absence from the ranks of 1/16th U.S. was timely indeed.[7]

* * *

Rosecrans had been busy while the regulars marked time on the west bank of the Tennessee. Crittenden's XXI Corps had crossed the Sequatchie River and occupied the region north of Chattanooga. On August 22, Federal artillery on the north bank of the Tennessee began to shell the town. Crittenden's operations deceived Bragg into thinking the Federals would cross the Tennessee River north of Chattanooga, when in fact Rosecrans crossed upriver (to the west and south) at Bridgeport, Shellmound, and Caperton's Ferry near Stevenson. Columns from Thomas's and McCook's corps were soon climbing eastward over Sand and Lookout Mountains south of Chattanooga, threatening the Confederate supply line back to Atlanta. Bragg evacuated Chattanooga and retreated southward on September 8. Federal troops from Crittenden's corps occupied the town the next day.

As the Army of the Cumberland threaded its way through the high ground south of the Tennessee River, Rosecrans's three corps

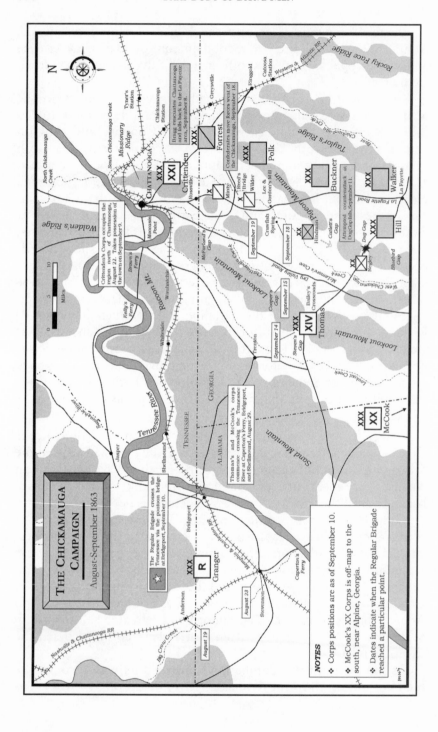

THE CHICKAMAUGA
CAMPAIGN
August–September 1863

The Regular Brigade crosses the
Tennessee via the pontoon bridge
at Bridgeport, September 10.

Crittenden's Corps occupies the
region north of Chattanooga,
August 22. Takes possession of
the town on September 9.

Bragg evacuates Chattanooga
and falls back to the La Fayette
area, September 8.

Confederates move forces west of
the Chickamauga, September 18.

Thomas's and McCook's corps
commence crossing the Tennessee
River at Caperton's Ferry, Bridgeport,
and Shellmound, August 29.

Attempted counterattack at
Dug Gap fails, September 11.

NOTES
❖ Corps positions are as of September 10.
❖ McCook's XX Corps is off-map to the
    south, near Alpine, Georgia.
❖ Dates indicate when the Regular Brigade
    reached a particular point.

were widely dispersed and could not support each other if attacked. This potentially dangerous situation did not worry Rosecrans, for he did not consider Bragg's army a serious threat. The Union commander thought the Confederates were heavily outnumbered and would not stop retreating short of Atlanta. This estimate of the Confederate situation was just partially correct. The Army of the Tennessee may have abandoned Chattanooga and retreated, but Bragg was simultaneously orchestrating a counterattack. In the aftermath of the Middle Tennessee Campaign, Confederate authorities in Richmond decided to send sizable reinforcements to Bragg in an attempt to stem Rosecrans's advance. They were able to do this because the fighting in Mississippi had quieted down with the fall of Vicksburg, while active operations in the East had slowed down considerably after the Battle of Gettysburg. Rosecrans's six months of inactivity at Murfreesboro were now coming back to haunt the Army of the Cumberland. Bragg received about 20,000 additional troops from Mississippi and east Tennessee during late August. Two divisions of Lieutenant General James Longstreet's Corps from the Army of Northern Virginia were also on their way. Burnside's occupation of Knoxville had severed the direct rail link between Tennessee and Virginia, resulting in Longstreet's command having to travel through the Carolinas and Georgia to reach the Chattanooga area. The Virginia-based troops were due to arrive in northern Georgia during the latter part of September. These additional forces gave Bragg a slight numerical advantage over Rosecrans, which the Army of the Cumberland's dispersal magnified. Bragg planned to strike the far-flung Federal columns as they emerged from the mountain passes, cut them off from Chattanooga, and then recapture the city.

Rosecrans received his first indication that Bragg was not cooperating with the Federal plan on September 11, the day after the Regular Brigade crossed the Tennessee. While General King pushed the regulars over Sand Mountain on the road to Trenton, the leading elements of Thomas's corps crossed Chickamauga Creek at McLemore's Cove and approached Dug Gap in Pigeon Mountain. The Federal column was isolated and not very strong. It consisted initially of only Negley's division, with Scribner's and Starkweather's brigades of Baird's division a short distance away. Bragg wanted to crush these Federals with overwhelming force. The Confederates had great difficulty coordinating their actions and, fortunately for Negley, the Southern attack sputtered to a halt without accomplishing much. The Federal column, nearly half of Thomas's corps, narrowly escaped a potentially dire situation. That evening, Rosecrans finally realized the Confederates had stopped their retreat and were looking for a fight. To prevent Bragg from getting between the Federal army and Chattanooga, Rosecrans ordered his scattered forces to move northward and close within supporting distance.[8]

On September 12, King's regulars had reveille at three o'clock and moved out an hour and a half later. They were still far behind the main body of Baird's division and struggled to make up the distance. The regulars buried their first casualty of the campaign the evening of the following day. Lieutenant James E. Mitchell, commanding G/2/18th U.S., had been bitten by something during the night—the consensus was a tarantula, although more likely it was a snake—and had died the morning of September 13. General King took time out at sunset to give the lieutenant a decent burial, complete with coffin, military escort, Episcopal service, and the Regular Brigade's officer corps standing by in full dress uniforms and side arms. The funeral was a harbinger of things to come for many of the bystanders. The ceremony marked the final time they would ever wear the brass and bullion of their Regular Army finery.[9]

Rosecrans's scattered forces hurried to assemble before Bragg struck again. The morning after Lieutenant Mitchell's burial, the Regular Brigade was marching by half past three. The brigade crossed Lookout Mountain at Steven's Gap on September 14. The experiences of 2/18th U.S. that day are a good indicator of just how difficult it was to maneuver in the mountains of northwest Georgia. The battalion's wagons were half emptied and dispersed among the companies before making the ascent. Captain Haymond's battalion took more than six hours to travel two miles to the top of the ridge, the unit's 400 troops heaving at its seven wagons the entire way on the road to the 2,400-feet summit. Lieutenant Lucius Brown of F/2/18th U.S. recalled that the journey down the far side was not any easier than the trip up: "The wagons here fell in our rear and we went on, the descent being if possible worse than the ascent, dust often knee deep (no exaggeration), road very steep, rough & winding and long before we reached the foot it was *dark as pitch*. At seven we got down and bivouacked at once on the hillside. I did not imagine they would attempt to bring the train down but it got down safe at 11 P.M. being too dark to see how bad the road was."[10]

The next day, King's brigade went northward on a narrow track along the eastern slope of Lookout Mountain and finally caught up with the main body of Baird's division at Cooper's Gap. Thomas's corps had occupied the Steven's-Cooper's Gap area ever since Negley's narrow escape from McLemore's Cove on September 11, waiting for McCook's corps to close up. McCook's column inadvertently took a circuitous route up from farther south, and Thomas's troops did not resume moving until September 17. Throughout that day and the next, Thomas's and McCook's corps moved toward Chattanooga. Their route roughly paralleled Chickamauga Creek, a narrow, meandering waterway that was militarily traversable only by way of the region's few fords and bridges. While McCook and Thomas moved north, Rosecrans ordered Crittenden to move the XXI Corps south from Chattanooga and take up positions along the Chickamauga near Lee & Gordon's Mill. North of the mill, Federal cavalry and mounted infantry screened the Chickamauga crossings. Between the cavalry screen and Chattanooga, a few brigades of Gordon Granger's Reserve Corps secured Rossville Gap in Missionary Ridge, the point at which the Army of the Cumberland would cross the ridge when the Federal columns finally closed on Chattanooga. Bragg, meanwhile, was pushing the Southern army toward and across the Chickamauga. His forces tangled with the Federal mounted troops for control of the Chickamauga crossings on September 18, secured Reed's and Alexander's Bridges, and by nightfall established bridgeheads on the west bank. Correctly discerning that Crittenden's position at Lee & Gordon's Mill was the Army of the Cumberland's left flank, Bragg that evening positioned his gathering forces to deliver Rosecrans a punishing blow come sunrise.[11]

The regulars were oblivious to these events as they arrived at Crawfish Spring late in the day on September 18 after yet another hot, dusty day of marching. Lieutenant Wilcox had a feeling that the campaign was about to reach its climax. "It is now nearly dark and we are still here and can occasionally hear musketry," Wilcox recorded in his diary by the light of a campfire. "We are in all probability on the eve of a great battle and I pray to God our forces may be victorious." His melancholy thoughts were dispersed by the arrival of a canteen of whiskey in the hands of Lieutenant Samuel J. Dick, an 18th Regular then serving on General Brannan's staff. Wilcox and Dick, joined by Lieutenant Ostrander and Captain Ten

Eyck, idled away a few moments with nips from the canteen and impromptu songs. It would be their last idle moments for some time to come. An officer from King's staff broke up the gathering with word that the regulars were to fall in and continue moving. With Confederates west of the Chickamauga, Rosecrans knew he had to immediately shift forces north or risk being cut off from Chattanooga. He ordered Thomas to leave Negley's division at Crawfish Spring and move northward with the balance of the XIV Corps—the divisions of Baird, Brannan, and Reynolds. They were to march past Crittenden's troops at Lee & Gordon's Mill and take up a position on the La Fayette Road that covered the routes to the bridges at which Confederates had reportedly crossed the Chickamauga. He also ordered two of Granger's brigades to probe from Rossville Gap to Reed's brigade.[12] Wilcox's diary provides a glimpse of the Regular Brigade's experiences that night:

> So about 8 P.M. we got started on the Chattanooga Road. Road lined with bivouac fires of troops. Passed through a great many. Bivouacked at 12 o'clock—very cold & I should suffer were it not for my heavy cavalry overcoat. Took up line of march, about 2 A.M. While halting on the road some cavalry horses run away through our Batt & created a perfect melé, in a moment every man rushed into the wood one over the other pell mell thinking the enemie's cavalry were on us. A few moments explained it but some lost guns, some Hats...about 1/2 my company went over me.
>
> Sat. Sept 19th On the field—We got into position here which is about 6 miles from Chattanooga just after sunrise.[13]

Historian Steven Woodworth persuasively argues that Rosecrans's orders for Thomas to conduct the night march on the evening of September 18–19 represent the Federal commander's "key decision of the battle," for the presence of Federal troops north of Lee & Gordon's Mill ended up completely unhinging Bragg's plan for the coming battle. Having forced passages across the Chickamauga during the afternoon of September 18, Bragg oriented his forces on the west bank for a strike against what he assumed was the Federal left flank at Lee & Gordon's Mill. While Bragg's troops bedded down for the night, Thomas's column slipped past them on the La Fayette Road. Reynold's column was snarled with some of Crittenden's troops and lagged hours behind, but Baird and Brannan managed to complete the night march more-or-less in good shape. Instead of assailing Rosecrans's flank Bragg would have to deal with

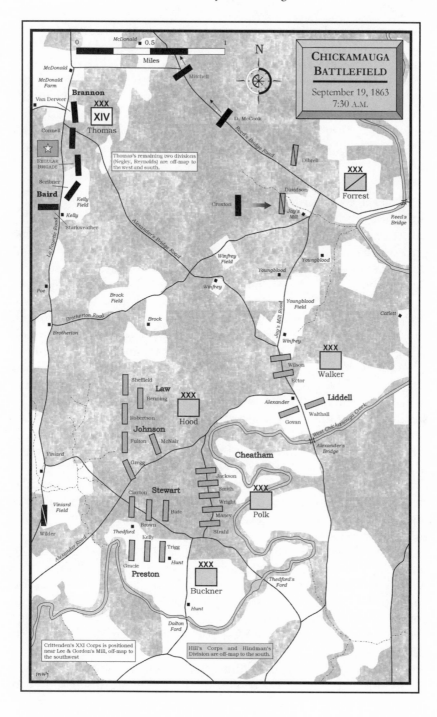

CHICKAMAUGA
BATTLEFIELD

September 19, 1863
7:30 A.M.

Thomas's remaining two divisions
(Negley, Reynolds) are off-map to
the west and south.

Crittenden's XXI Corps is positioned
near Lee & Gordon's Mill, off-map to
the southwest

Hill's Corps and Hindman's
Division are off-map to the south.

six enemy brigades where none should have been. Soldiers down in
the ranks of those Federal brigades had little idea of what was to
come. Most were so exhausted they could barely keep their eyes
open as they stumbled along. After marching five miles through the
night, it was a little after 6:00 A.M. on September 19 when the
groggy troops of the Regular Brigade, the van of Thomas's column,
reached an obscure clearing on the La Fayette Road called Kelly
Field. After experiencing the upcoming thirty-six hours, it was a
place the regulars would never forget.[14]

* * *

General King ordered his troops to stack arms and prepare
breakfast, knowing they would perform the day's work better with
full stomachs. Not having had time to eat anything substantial the
previous day, the famished regulars quickly gathered firewood and
sent details out for water. Water was scarce in the area and some of
the troops ranged more than a mile before finding any. By eight
o'clock, the regulars were gathered in small groups around campfires in the woods north of Kelly Field, waiting for coffee to boil.
Most of them did not finish the meal. They had heard occasional
firing off to the east since daybreak. Lieutenant Henry Freeman,
adjutant of 2/18th U.S., recalled that the sounds of battle started to
change around nine o'clock: "To our left and front the heavy report
of a single gun, followed by that of the bursting shell, then the
steady rattle of musketry, warned us that our breakfast, if indeed we
were to have breakfast at all, was to be a hurried one. For a moment
we stood listening to the noise of the battle on our left, while it grew
in intensity, coming nearer, the continuous roar of artillery almost
drowning the more deadly rain of musketry, until at last it reached
the division on our left and the shrill cheers or yells of the advancing Confederates piercing through the roar of battle told us that our
turn had come."[15]

Robert Ayres, adjutant of Major Dawson's 1/19th U.S., was one
of the better-known lieutenants in the Regular Army. Prior to the
war, Ayres had been assigned to the West Point garrison as an
enlisted soldier of the U.S. Army Corps of Engineers. There, he
courted and married the daughter of Benny Havens, a local tavern
keeper whom virtually every West Pointer of that era recalled fondly.
Perhaps some of his father-in-law's famous joviality had rubbed off
on Ayres. Upon hearing the telltale battle sounds, the adjutant cried
out to his battalion: "We're going to have a big discussun' wid

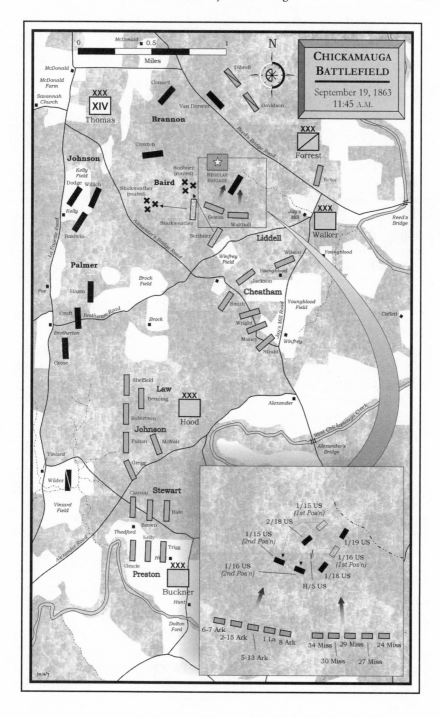

guns!" Battalion buglers sounded "To the Colors." The regulars fell in, some choking down hot coffee, others reluctantly abandoning the steaming pots.[16]

By the morning of September 19, elements of both armies were arrayed between Chickamauga Creek and Missionary Ridge. While the opposing forces were not far apart, the region's dense woods ensured that neither side was sure of the other's disposition. One of General Thomas's first actions that morning was to order Brannan's division into the woods east of Kelly Field in support of Colonel Daniel McCook's brigade. McCook's command and also Colonel John G. Mitchell's brigade, both from Granger's Reserve Corps, had arrived in the area the previous night in a belated attempt to support the Federal cavalry that had been defending Reed's Bridge. McCook captured a few Confederate stragglers from Bushrod R. Johnson's Division at dusk on September 18 as the latter's troops were hurrying southward after crossing the Chickamauga.

At sunrise the next day, McCook ordered a regiment forward to destroy Reed's Bridge while other units in his brigade sent details to scour the woods near Jay's Mill for water. After receiving orders to withdraw back to Rossville, McCook informed Thomas that he believed a lone Confederate brigade had crossed the Chickamauga and, since his men had just burned Reed's Bridge, it was ripe for capture. Thomas sent Colonel John Croxton's brigade of Brannan's division forward to investigate, while McCook and Mitchell prepared to march back to Rossville. Back at Jay's Mill, meanwhile, McCook's troops found Southern cavalry more plentiful than the prized water for their empty canteens. Bragg had ordered Brigadier General Nathan Bedford Forrest's cavalry forward from Reed's Bridge as a screen on the Confederate right. Dan McCook's brigade was soon embroiled in a heavy skirmish with a brigade of Confederate cavalry under Brigadier General H.B. Davidson.

McCook withdrew his brigade northward to Rossville and Croxton took up the fight. The fighting at Jay's Mill quickly became more than a skirmish: the Battle of Chickamauga was getting underway. Each side began to feed brigade after brigade into the fighting, the battle lines coming together "like a zipper closing from north to south." Another brigade of Confederate horseman arrived to aid the beleaguered Davidson; two brigades of Southern infantry from Major General William H.T. Walker's Reserve Corps soon followed.

Brannan pushed forward Colonel Ferdinand Van Derveer's brigade to Croxton's aid, and shortly thereafter sent in his final brigade, Colonel John Connell's. Thomas then ordered Baird's division into the fight. General Baird formed his division with the regulars on the left, Colonel Benjamin Scribner's brigade on the right, and Brigadier General John Starkweather's brigade in reserve. Although the rough terrain limited artillery effectiveness, Baird did not want his division's batteries left unsupported on the La Fayette Road and had them accompany their brigades. Shortly after nine o'clock, the division moved out from Kelly Field and marched to the sound of the guns.[17]

After moving through the woods about three-quarters of a mile, the regulars came upon Croxton's brigade, which was being hard pressed by Colonel Claudius Wilson's Brigade of Georgians and was almost out of ammunition. Passing through Croxton's line, the regulars took up the fight. After halting Wilson's Brigade and forcing the Southerners to withdraw, the regulars pushed forward another half mile. More Confederates then appeared to the regular's left along the Reed's Bridge Road, elements of Brigadier General Matthew Ector's Brigade falling back after a failed assault against Van Derveer. The 19th and 16th U.S. took this new enemy in the flank, "rolling them up like a curtain" and capturing "more prisoners than we had either time or means to care." The captured Southerners, 126 troops from the 9th Texas, were escorted to the rear. King's other front-rank unit, 1/18th U.S., had meanwhile continued forward after Wilson. Captain Smith's battalion at this point was taking on Wilson's entire brigade single-handedly, but the Southerners continued to withdraw, a movement hastened by the arrival on Scribner's brigade on Wilson's left flank. Finding his battalion alone, Smith withdrew back to the Regular Brigade's line.[18]

The forest west of Jay's Mill was quiet for the next half-hour, the regulars tending to casualties and hustling rearward their haul of prisoners. Jacob Van Zwaluwenburg found himself caring for a wounded officer wearing gray: "At one place where I lay for a moment a wounded rebel captain lay. He moved his lips to speak to me. I put my ear to his face when I heard him whisper 'water' I hesitated at first as I knew a great battle was on and would doubtless need all the water I had, but...[I] took off knapsack, haversack, and canteen and gave him all he wanted. I noticed a pink spot on his bosom...and his life was fast ebbing away. A grateful smile passed over his features, one of the few pleasant recollections of the horrid war."[19]

The Regular Brigade had thus far come through the battle relatively unscathed, but that was about to change. Van Zwaluwenburg barely had time to strap his equipment back on before he heard shots close by. The firing came from skirmishers of George Smith's 1/18th U.S., the first regulars to perceive a new danger. Smith's skirmishers on the brigade's right flank detected movement in the woods to the south and opened fire. Henry Freeman received a closer look at the approaching menace than he would have liked. He had been talking to Captain Anson Mills, commander of H/1/18th U.S., when the skirmishers opened up. Freeman attempted to mount his horse upon hearing the shots, but a stray bullet split the air by the steed as he did so: "I...had one foot in the stirrup, when...he jumped suddenly throwing me to the ground and ran off. My foot still hung and he was dragging me toward the enemy's advancing line but before he reached it he passed through the top of a fallen pine tree, where my foot becoming disengaged he ran off but I remained. The line came up but I lay perfectly still. They passed around the obstruction within ten feet of me." The Southern troops marching past Freeman belonged to Brigadier General St. John R. Liddell's Division. Sent north from its position near Alexander's Bridge to reinforce the Confederate right, Liddell's 3,000 men were in a perfect position to plow into the flank of Baird's division. Liddell's first victims were Scribner's and Starkweather's brigades. After offering slight resistance, the two brigades broke and scattered. Liddell's troops continued northward without missing a step. General Baird was at the Regular Brigade's position when the attack started. Warning King of the danger, he galloped off to see what could be salvaged from his other brigades.[20]

When Smith's skirmishers started firing, the regulars were facing southeast with Lieutenant Burnham's guns in battery between the brigade's two lines. John King knew he had to form the regulars facing southwest to meet Liddell's attack or they were doomed. He ordered Burnham to limber up and escape. The brigadier then started shifting his infantry. Major Coolidge's 1/16th U.S. moved first, taking up a position immediately south of Battery H to cover the artillery's withdrawal. "We hastily faced about and marched in the direction of the new danger," Private Van Zwaluwenburg recalled. "when half way down a hillside we met the enemy in large force. we layed down and began firing." Captain Dod's 1/15th U.S. closed up on the battery's right, while Haymond's 2/18th changed front to the rear and formed a hasty line. Burnham's artillerymen attempted to bring horses forward to haul off the guns, but alert Confederates shot the animals as soon as they came within sight. Seeing the enemy just a short distance away, Burnham realized he could not possibly escape in time and instead ordered his gunners to load their four 12-pound Napoleons with double-shotted canister (the battery also had two Parrott rifles, but those weapons could not fire canister and thus were not as effective at close range as the smoothbore Napoleons).

That was about all the regulars could do before the Southern swarm engulfed them. "We scarcely got into position before a division of Texas and Arkansas troops advanced upon us on the run," wrote Henry Haymond a week later. Battery H opened up as soon as the 18th Infantry skirmishers were clear, causing some of the enemy to take cover. The 16th Infantrymen in front of the guns occupied a slightly lower elevation and welcomed the sound of the shells flying over their heads. Private Van Zwaluwenburg noted that the battery's fire was all too brief: "our battery unlimbered back of us, but were enabled to do very little, as the men who manned the guns were shot down before they could load. I looked back once, whilst loading, to know why they were not firing and saw that the men were shot down as fast as they rallied to their guns." Battery H did not have much infantry support and Confederate fire dropped the gunners with alarming speed. Lieutenant Burnham was among the artillerymen to go down, shot through the right breast. A regular from the 16th U.S. was the first to reach the side of the fallen officer. "Lieutenant, are you hurt?" the soldier asked. "Not much," the fatally wounded Burnham gasped, "but save the guns!" Lieutenant Fessenden was wounded shortly thereafter, as was Lieutenant Ludlow. Noncoms and gunners were swept away. The 12-pounders managed to fire about four rounds each before falling silent.[21]

Colonel Daniel C. Govan's Arkansas Brigade surged toward the gun line. Major Coolidge's prone battalion could not stop them and was washed away in the Confederate tide. A Confederate officer called out for the regulars to surrender, but Coolidge raised his sword in defiance. The 16th Infantry's resistance held up a portion of Govan's line for a few moments, but Coolidge's men paid dearly.

Of the 307 officers and men in the ranks of 1/16th U.S. when the day began, all but thirty-five were killed, wounded, or missing by nightfall. Jacob Van Zwaluwenburg was one of the few 16th Infantrymen to escape. He ran rearward as fast as possible, doffing his knapsack to hasten the journey: "I made my way back between two of our guns and saw then not a man able to man the guns. most of our boys who tried to run back were shot down." Sidney Coolidge was among the killed. After overrunning Coolidge's battalion, a Confederate soldier picked up the dead major's sword and presented it to Colonel Govan.

A lone regular artilleryman still offered resistance as Govan's troops approached within a few yards of the Battery H's position. A wounded sergeant staggered to his feet and grasped the lanyard of a double-shotted and ready-to-fire Napoleon. The Confederates in front of the muzzle froze in their tracks, warning the gunner to surrender or die. "Kill and be damned!" bellowed the sergeant of artillery, pulling the lanyard and mowing a bloody swath through the enemy. The brave soldier was quickly dispatched, bayonets pinning him to the ground.[22]

The 15th Infantry let loose a few volleys before breaking for the rear. The story was much the same in the other battalions. Pockets of regulars here and there stood their ground and contested Govan's advance. Most of those who did were captured or killed. Govan reported bagging the guns of Battery H and more than 400 regular troops. Included in the haul were many members of H/2/18th U.S. Infantry. September 19, 1863, was exactly one year and two days since their previous capture at Munfordville, Kentucky. One of the U.S. infantrymen taken by the 2nd & 5th Arkansas, trying to salvage a bit of his wounded pride, exclaimed in despair that this was the only time the Regular Brigade's line had ever been broken.

The regulars fled. Private William J. Carson, a bugler in Captain Dod's 1/15th U.S., did what he could to bring order out of the chaos. With bugle in one hand and musician's sword in the other, Carson blew repeated bugle calls in an attempt to stem the tide. Attaching himself to the color guard of an 18th Infantry battalion, his rallied a portion of that regiment. The frantic bugle calls also confused and slowed down Govan's pursuit. Captain Dod reported that Carson's actions "attracted the notice and elicited the admiration of the whole brigade."[23]

The line of retreat was toward Van Derveer's brigade. This unit was Robert McCook's old brigade from the Army of the Ohio, the 18th Infantry's command the previous year. Some of the troops in the 9th Ohio and 2nd Minnesota, the regiments involved in the Spring Hill riot, probably broke into smug smiles as the disorganized regulars fell back through their ranks. Private Oscar P. Heath, a member of the battery attached to Van Derveer's brigade, I/4th U.S. Artillery, remembered the moment his fellow regulars came into sight: "The battle on our right was still reging with undiminished fury, but suddenly the fire slackened, a wild, exultant, Rebel yell arose above the din of conflict, and soon broken files of our troops belonging to the brigade occupying a position on our right came filtering through and to the rear of our lines. They were not panic-stricken but were sullenly falling back having been very roughly handled." Warned of Liddell's approach, Van Derveer's troops were formed and ready. An impromptu counterattack by the 9th and 17th Ohio broke the back of Liddell's advance, causing the enemy to fall back past Battery H's idle guns. The Ohioans, the 18th Infantry's nemesis the year before, then moved forward and recaptured the Regular Brigade's battery.[24]

General King reformed the remnants of his brigade on Van Derveer's left. Officers gathered in stragglers and sent walking wounded to the rear. Lieutenant Freeman had survived his wild ride at the beginning of the contest and was one of the troops wandering back through the forest. The battalion adjutant found his horse calmly standing in its usual place next to Captain Haymond's mount. As the stunned regulars recuperated, King received word that Battery H's guns were back in friendly hands. He looked for an officer of the battery and could find only one. Lieutenant Burnham was last seen prone and bleeding, while Lieutenant Ludlow by this time was in enemy hands. Lieutenant Fessenden had been painfully wounded in the side, but was present. King asked Fessenden if he was well enough to lead a recovery party to retrieve the pieces. Fessenden replied that he was and formed the detail from his remaining gunners and some soldiers from the 15th Infantry. They cautiously moved back to the regulars' old position and found the cannons where they had left them, with dead regulars, Confederates, and Ohio troops littering the ground at the battery's position. The surviving Ohioans had left the guns and returned to their own brigade upon learning that King had sent out a recovery party.

Fessenden located the prostrate body of the battery's commander. Burnham was still breathing. "Burnham, do you know me?" Fessenden asked. Burnham opened his eyes faintly and murmured only "On with the Eighteenth." Burnham was carried back to the regular's new position, but he lived only another hour. Fessenden's detail manhandled the battery's six pieces, rounded up a few stray horses, and hauled the cannons back to the regulars' line. General King dispatched the remnants of the battery back to the La Fayette Road. The rest of the brigade withdrew at two o'clock, General Thomas moving Baird's and Brannan's spent divisions to the army's left flank near the McDonald Farm. Richard W. Johnson's and John Palmer's Divisions, the next two Federal commands to arrive in the area, took up the fight in the forest west of Jay's Mill.[25]

* * *

When the Regular Brigade emerged from the forest that afternoon, it was just a shadow of the strong column that had gone into action a few hours before. Battery H was wrecked beyond immediate repair. Although the guns had been saved, Fessenden's gunners had no ammunition, for they had not had time or manpower to recover their limber chests and other battery equipment. Battery H would head back to Chattanooga early the next day for refitting. The 16th Infantry had ceased to exist; King attached its few shell-shocked survivors to 1/19th U.S. (now commanded by Army of the Potomac veteran Edmund L. Smith, Major Dawson having left the field with a wounded leg). The other regular battalions had less than half their men in ranks, numerous wounded among them. How could the Regular Brigade have been so quickly shattered? Many factors were at work that morning, the foremost being that King's regulars had found themselves in one of the most dreaded positions of nineteenth century linear warfare: facing the wrong way while attacked from the flank. Veteran Civil War infantry units could change fronts relatively quickly in response to new threats, but the restrictive terrain near Chickamauga Creek allowed Liddell's troops to approach almost undetected and whip through Baird's division like a whirlwind.

Next, some of the regulars had been in the field more than two years by the autumn of 1863, participating in two major battles and innumerable skirmishes. Even the bravest of infantrymen will eventually crack under constant exposure to danger and some of these old timers at Chickamauga were reaching the end of their endurance. Arthur Carpenter of the 19th U.S., who would end up seeing as much combat as just about anyone in the Civil War, gave an indication of this phenomenon in a letter he wrote from Murfreesboro back in February 1863:

> It is said that our division will remain here and garrison this town, which will be a second depot of supplies to the army. I hope we will have the good luck to remain here, as we all have had our share of running after the enemy and fighting them. I tell you what it is, ones bravery undergoes a great change after being in two or three fights. it is very nice to be brave at home, and imagine yourself to be leading a company of men *on to victory* in the face of 50 or 100 pieces of artillery and as many thousand muskets, but to do it is another thing. I am not fast for showing my bravery that way. you may excuse me, the whistling buzzing bullets, screaming shrieking shells, and the heavy humming of solid shot, makes one very little inclined to bravery. he don't hanker after it.[26]

For the regulars who survived Stones River, the morning of September 19, 1863, eerily resembled their experiences in that earlier battle. It was more than some of them could take. Finally, a large number of experienced officers had left the brigade the previous April and May in the wake of Colonel Shepherd's relief. The resulting turbulence in commissioning new officers and creating new corporals and sergeants had caused unit cohesion to suffer in proportion. A rather finite pool of leadership talent had been infused into the New Army regulars in 1861. By late 1863, that pool was just about drained. While man-for-man the regulars where as good as any troops, and probably better than most, as a whole the regular battalions at Chickamauga were not as well led and close-knit as they had been the previous year. Cracking under pressure was the result.

* * *

The Battle of Chickamauga still had plenty of pressure left. For a few hours on the afternoon of September 19, Baird's division rested while fighting continued elsewhere. The regulars ate their first decent meal in thirty-six hours, although many of them had to scrounge cookware and utensils to replace the gear they had abandoned earlier in the day during their unfinished breakfast. While the regulars gulped down coffee and hardtack, a great battle raged along a three-mile front, from the woods west of Jay's Mill in the north to Viniard Field in the south. Late in the afternoon, General

Thomas had to recommit Baird's and Brannan's divisions to the fight. He ordered Baird back into the woods east of Kelly Field to support Johnson's troops, while Brannan moved south on the La Fayette Road to reinforce the Union center. Thomas instructed Baird to hold the regulars on the Reed's Bridge Road near the McDonald farm. As such, the Regular Brigade was the left flank of the Union line, a position that Thomas ordered held to the "last extremity." If it were not, the Union Army would be cut off from Chattanooga, the battle's outcome in jeopardy. Luckily for King's diminished brigade, Bragg ignored the isolated regulars on the Federal left, and instead attacked Rosecrans's center and right throughout the afternoon. Fighting continued until sundown, neither side gaining a decisive advantage. The Confederates had one last card to play as dusk settled over the battlefield. Late in the day, Major General Patrick R. Cleburne's Division splashed across Chickamauga Creek and attacked the Federals in the much-fought-over woods west of Jay's Mill. The attack turned out to be unnecessary, for Thomas had already ordered Baird and Johnson to withdraw from the area come nightfall. [27]

One member of the Regular Brigade ended up experiencing Cleburne's foray firsthand. General Baird, receiving Thomas's order to withdraw, instructed the Regular Brigade to rejoin the division. As the regulars again moved into the thick woods east of the La Fayette Road, General King sent Lieutenant Freeman ahead to find the division line and guide the brigade into position. With the sun dropping behind Missionary Ridge, Freeman rode off. He located Baird, who reiterated his order to have the regulars close up. Freeman became disoriented as he retraced his path back to the Regular Brigade's column:

> By this time it was quite dark. The smoke of the day's battle began to settle upon the trees. I had gone but a short distance when a furious fire of musketry broke out some distance in front of me. Certain that I was now in the right track I pushed on and soon met stragglers and wounded men coming from the front. To my anxious inquires as to the whereabouts of the Regular Brigade, some answered "it is out there." Others that they "did not know." I very soon however found where it was not, for I had gone but a few rods further before I was surrounded by a party of men who turned out to belong to the famous Pat Cleburne's division of the rebel Army, into which in my anxiety to find my regiment I had ridden. [28]

Taken by the 154th Tennessee, Freeman was the last of many regulars captured on September 19. Cleburne's attack gained nothing significant beyond adding names to the casualty rolls.

The Army of the Cumberland held its position, but it had been a close call. All of Rosecrans's troops were already worn out from a week of hard marching before the battle and, with the exception of Sheridan's and Negley's divisions, had engaged in heavy fighting throughout the day. Bragg could count a total of eleven brigades, either on hand that night or due to arrive within hours, that had not extensively participated in the battle. The Southern commander planned to go on the offensive the next day and inflict on Rosecrans a crushing defeat.[29]

* * *

As it often does in north Georgia during autumn, the temperature dropped precipitously after sundown on September 19. During his few moments of rest that night, Jacob Van Zwaluwenburg regretted losing his equipment while running for his life near Jay's Mill: "I lost my knapsack during the retreat and found myself stif with cold before next morning as we were not allowed fires and the white frost was all over open ground." Nearby in the 19th Infantry, Arthur Carpenter's night was also uncomfortable: "at night we lay down on our arms and were just getting a little sleep when the rebels commenced shelling the woods we were in. we had to move back farther yet and lay on the cold ground with no blankets. the night was very cold." Captain Anson Mills's company was detailed to picket the brigade's front during the darkness. He recalled that his men were "compelled to listen to the shrieks and cries for water and help from the wounded and dying, who lay immediately in front, but whom we were unable to assist, although they were only a few hundred yards from us."[30] The most uncomfortable regulars that night were the scores who were in Confederate hands. Shortly after the war, Lieutenant Henry B. Freeman penned a detailed account of his first few days of captivity:

> I with a number of others was immediately sent to the rear and turned over to Gen'l Armstrong of the Rebel Army, and by him sent to General Wheeler, from there to General Hill. All of whom asked me many questions as to the strength and position of the Union forces, all of which I declined answering. Gen'l Wheeler took my horse, sword and spurs, one of his staff my gloves, and the rations out of my haversack. From General Hill I was sent under escort of a

squad of Forrest's Cavalry to the Prison Depot, 6 miles to the rear. The Sergeant in charge of the party said that Forrest had sworn to kill every negro he found in arms. We were 3 days on the route to Atlanta, during that time we were given nothing but a pint of raw meat and a pound of musty bacon.[31]

While Freeman and his unfortunate comrades marched into the night for points south, the battered Army of the Cumberland prepared to continue the fight that would resume at daybreak. Thomas expected the Confederate attacks of September 20 to hit the Federal left. At a council of war at Rosecrans's headquarters that night, attended by most of the Federal corps and division commanders, Rosecrans ordered Alexander McCook to hold the Federal right and cover the Dry Valley Road with Sheridan's, Negley's, and Davis's divisions; Thomas Crittenden's corps, reduced to just Wood's and Van Cleve's divisions, would occupy a reserve position on the eastern slope of Missionary Ridge. Both McCook and Crittenden were to be prepared to send forces northward to Thomas's aid. A few brigades of Gordon Granger's Reserve Corps were positioned near Rossville, holding the southern approach to Chattanooga.

Thomas's corps would anchor the northern end of the line at Kelly Field, with Brannan's division in reserve at Dyer Field. Shortly after midnight, Thomas's troops came into position: Baird and Reynolds of his own corps, along with Johnson's and Palmer's Divisions—a total of eleven brigades. To prevent the enemy from gaining a position on the La Fayette Road and moving behind the Army of the Cumberland's position, Thomas wanted his line to extend all the way to the McDonald Farm and block the Reed's Bridge Road. Unfortunately, the fighting on September 19 had so depleted some brigades that they each occupied a short frontage. Getting the tired troops into proper position during the darkness was also difficult. Johnson and Palmer's men, holding the center and southern portions of Kelly Field, were in particular tightly packed. Johnson had room for little more than one brigade in front and had to post his remaining two in reserve. Baird's division held the northern portion of the field and had more than enough room to place all three brigades in line. Baird's position ended in the woods north of Kelly Field, about a quarter mile short of the point at which the road to Alexander's Brigade intersects the La Fayette Road. Learning of this shortcoming at 2:00 A.M., Thomas requested from Rosecrans additional troops to extend the line northward to the McDonald

Farm and specifically asked for Negley's division, the only unit of the XIV Corps not then under Thomas's immediate control. Rosecrans replied within the hour, writing that Negley would be sent to Kelly field. Later, during early morning, Brannan's division, Thomas's reserve, moved forward and took up a position on Reynolds's left at Poe Field. It is unclear who ordered Brannan to do so; what evidence there is points to Reynolds. Thomas was thus unaware that Brannan was now the link between the XIV Corps and the rest of Rosecrans's army. It was only the first of what would turn out to be a long series of misunderstandings about just where exactly Brannan was located on September 20.[32]

The Regular Brigade held Baird's left, the north end of the Union line—at least until Negley arrived—and arguably the most important Federal position on the field that morning. Knowing he had to prevent the enemy from swinging around into Kelly Field, King placed his troops in a column of battalions. Captain George Smith's 1/18th held the front, while his sister battalion held the second line in support. Each of the 18th Infantry battalions numbered about 200 rifles. Behind 2/18th, 1/15th occupied the third line, Captain Dod having about 190 men in line. In the rear were 124 troops of the 19th Infantry. Attached to Captain Ed Smith's command was the minuscule remnant of 1/16th, five officers and thirty men. Robert E.A. Crofton now commanded this "battalion," the captain taking over from a wounded commander just as he had done at Stones River. King's orders for the two rear lines were to be ready to support the 18th Infantry in front or swing around to the left in case the line was outflanked. King deployed forward two companies of the 18th Infantry as skirmishers (Lieutenant Charles L. Truman's D/2/18th and Lieutenant James Powell's D/3/18th) and sent Lieutenant Alfred Curtis's H/1/19th U.S. into the woods on the brigade's left, a final guard on the open flank. The regulars constructed crude fortifications in front of their lines, as did the rest of Baird's division. Consisting of logs, rocks, and whatever else could be quickly gathered up, the barriers in most places were little more than two feet high, tall enough to lie behind and nothing more.[33]

George Thomas was worried about that left flank. Stopping by Baird's division at the start of a sunrise inspection, the corps commander gratefully accepted a cup of coffee from the division's provost guards, Captain Williams's company from the 19th Infantry. A heavy fog blanketed most of the battlefield that morning, but as

Thomas sipped his coffee, he could see clearly enough that the division he had requested hours ago to shore up the left had not arrived. As the sky brightened, General Rosecrans joined Thomas at Baird's line. Thomas pointed out the regulars' position to the commanding general, reiterating the need for additional forces on the left. Rosecrans promised once again to send up Negley's division (he had failed to do so as promised earlier) and had his staff issue an order for Negley to report to Thomas "at once" and for McCook to fill the resulting gap in the Army of the Cumberland's lines. The two generals then departed to have a look at the rest of Thomas's positions. The inspection apparently stopped short of Poe Field, for Thomas remained unaware that Brannan was there.

Moving Negley's division from its position at Brotherton Field would prove far more difficult than either Rosecrans or Thomas had thought (why Rosecrans agreed to Thomas's specific request for Negley's men, when any of the other divisions under Crittenden's or McCook's command would have accomplished the task much more easily, was never satisfactorily explained). After completing the inspection of Kelly Field, Rosecrans arrived at Negley's lines. Negley had his men on the road and ready to go even though his skirmishers had reported the woods east of Brotherton field to be teeming with Confederates. With his usual lack of tact, the commanding general upbraided Negley for pulling off the line before being properly relieved and ordered Negley's frontline brigades, commanded by Colonels Timothy R. Stanley and William Sirwell, back to Brotherton Field. Rosecrans then sent a dispatch to Crittenden, telling the corps commander to send Major General Thomas J. Wood's division forward to replace Negley in the line. It would take Wood until well after nine o'clock to get his division in position to relieve Negley's men. Rosecrans, in the meantime, told Negley to send northward his reserve brigade, Colonel John Beatty's, without waiting for Wood.

It was close to eight o'clock before Beatty's brigade arrived at Kelly Field. It took up a strong position on the Regular Brigade's left, but shortly thereafter orders came from Thomas to move northward to the McDonald Farm. Beatty and Baird were dismayed by the order, but assuming that the balance of Negley's division was not far behind, Beatty moved north again. Ominously, as his four regiments headed out on the La Fayette Road, their skirmishers became embroiled with Confederate pickets to the east. The brigade ended up being strung out along a half-mile front, from the McDonald

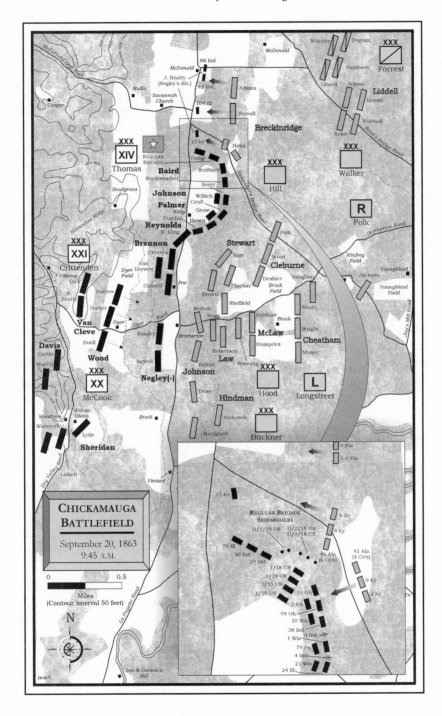

CHICKAMAUGA
BATTLEFIELD

September 20, 1863
9:45 A.M.

0   0.5

Miles
(Contour interval 50 feet)

house in the north to the Alexander's Bridge Road in the south. With Baird's left again in the air, Thomas ordered Colonel Joseph Dodge's brigade, one of Richard Johnson's units for which there was no room in the southern portion of the Kelly Field line, to take Beatty's place alongside the regulars. Dodge's three regiments had about 500 troops between them, but without time to construct fortifications, their ability to stand up to a determined assault was suspect.[34]

General King made some final adjustments at daylight. The ground in front of Captain Smith's front-rank 1/18th U.S. had sloped gently upward, restricting the battalion's field of fire. King moved the battalion about fifty paces forward across a small open space. Smith's regulars picked up their crude breastworks and took them forward, re-stacking the barriers at the new position. Haymond's 2/18th U.S. moved up to the 1st Battalion's original position. The sloping ground placed the Regular Brigade in a reverse-slope defense, partially sheltering the rear three lines from direct enemy fire. The defenders were about to need every bit of protection they could get. Lieutenant Arthur Carpenter, temporarily attached to Lieutenant Curtis's 19th Infantry skirmish company, dreaded the ominous noises he heard to his front: "we pretty soon heard the rebels coming up into line. we could hear their commands very plain. then we knew there was to be hot work." Much of the fog had burned off by half past eight. The Regular Brigade skirmishers had targets at which to shoot.[35]

* * *

General Bragg's plan for September 20 was exactly what Thomas feared: an attack on the Federal left. While good in concept, the Confederate attack was poorly executed. After a series of events involving botched orders, apathetic commanders, and missed opportunities, which Peter Cozzens aptly labels "one of the sorriest nights and mornings in the annals of the high command of the Army of Tennessee," the Confederate attack got off to a rough start. Bragg had ordered Polk's Right Wing to deliver a hammer blow against the Federal left at sunrise, but the attack boiled down to a wasted half-morning followed by just Major General John Breckinridge's Division approaching Thomas's position. While two of Breckinridge's Brigades advanced toward the McDonald Farm, a third, Brigadier General Ben Helm's Orphan Brigade of Kentuckians, moved against Baird's line at Kelly Field. Helm's Brigade inadvertently split in two as it approached Baird's breastworks. Half of

Helm's men moved westward on the Alexander's Bridge Road, while the rest advanced directly toward the regulars and Scribner's brigade. Truman and Powell's 18th Infantry skirmishers fell back to the main line, after which Captain George Smith's 1/18th U.S. pored a few volleys into the Confederates moving along the road. The regulars then turned their attention to the force assailing the lines. Two and a half Confederate regiments made three determined assaults during the next hour, but the enemy's numbers were too few and Baird's position too strong for the Southerners to make even a dent in the fortifications. Helm's assault was directed mainly at Scribner's brigade on the regulars' right; Smith characterized the action as "heavy skirmishing" rather than an attack and the regulars suffered few casualties. Lieutenant Edgar Wilcox, deployed forward with the 18th Infantry skirmishers, reported that his company lost only "6 or 7 men when the Rebs advanced" that morning.[36]

As Helm's attack ebbed, other Confederates to the south of the Orphan Brigade finally took up the fight. Cleburne sent his brigades forward against the Kelly Field lines, but the Federals of Johnson's, Palmer's, and Reynolds's divisions handily repulsed Cleburne's disjointed attack. Alexander P. Stewart's Confederates also joined in, going up against Brannan's division at Poe Field, an attack that likewise failed. George Thomas was probably unaware of the attack at Poe Field, or at least did not know the identity of the Federal troops receiving it. Being concerned about Baird's exposed left, at the height of Cleburne and Stewart's attack he sent a message to Brannan, whom he believed to be still lying in reserve, and ordered him to Kelly Field. After a hasty conference with General Reynolds, the senior officer in the vicinity, Brannan decided to ignore the order since Stewart's Confederates were at that moment still to his front. The most Brannan felt he could safely accomplish was to dispatch his reserve brigade, Colonel Ferdinand Van Derveer's, to Kelly Field.[37]

The first Confederate success of the day occurred north of Kelly Field, where Breckinridge's other two brigades, led by Brigadiers Daniel W. Adams and Marcellus A. Stovall, advanced toward the McDonald Farm. The only Federal unit standing in their way was John Beatty's scattered brigade, the unit that had briefly occupied the regulars' flank before moving north to extend the Federal left. Beatty's four regiments were quickly overwhelmed. Beatty managed to extract his two southern-most regiments, the 15th Kentucky and

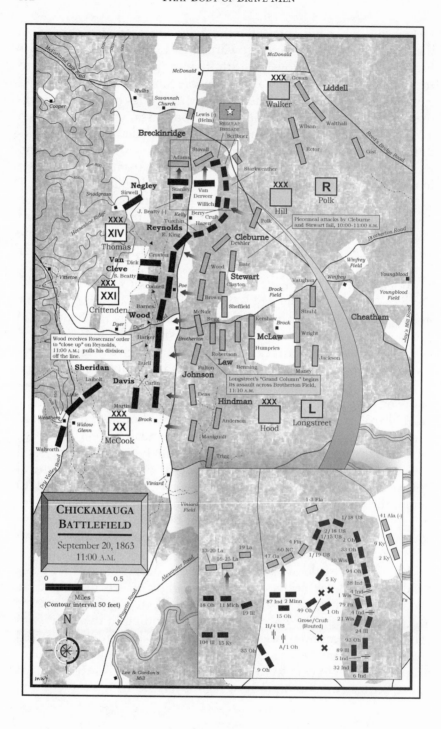

CHICKAMAUGA
BATTLEFIELD

September 20, 1863
11:00 A.M.

0   0.5

Miles
(Contour interval 50 feet)

N

104th Illinois, and had them retrace their steps back to Kelly Field; his other two regiments scattered and were effectively out of the battle for the rest of the day. Having gained a position on the La Fayette Road, the next task for Breckenridge was to start rolling up the Federal position at Kelly Field. After a pause to regroup following the easy victory over Beatty, the two Confederate brigades moved south toward Baird's division. Stovall's Brigade moved on the east side of the road, crashing into the regulars and Dodge's brigade at eleven o'clock. Dodge's regiments, having neither fortifications nor much resolve, fired a single volley and fell back. The regulars and their barricades were made of stiffer material than Dodge's men, and King's troops put up a fight as Stovall's line approached. The 1st & 3rd Florida advanced against 1/18th Infantry. Smith's line put out a "galling fire" according to the Floridians's commander, but the Southerners endured the punishment and continued to slowly advance.[38]

After smashing Dodge's line, three of Stovall's regiments gained the edge of Kelly Field. General King moved the 18th Infantry's 2nd Battalion forward to protect the left of the 1st Battalion, and also ordered 1/15th and 1/19th to deploy from their reserve positions to cover the brigade's exposed left flank. Stovall's assault was so severe that some of the 18th Infantry's troops began to fall back. At this juncture, the 18th received a one-man reinforcement. Private William J. Carson, the 15th Infantry bugler who had helped rally the regulars the previous day, picked up a discarded musket, ran forward, and designated himself a solitary provost guard for the frontline battalions. He ran up and down the line like a man possessed, sending sulkers back to the ranks, even refusing to allow an officer to pass. Carson's efforts were not enough, and more troops began to leave the frontline positions. The bugler then resorted to the successful tactics he had employed the previous day at Jay's Mill: "I threw down my gun rushed out some 30 yards to the color bearer of the 18th and said to him Let us rally these men or the whole left is gone. The brave fellow stopped and waved his flag I sounded to the colors. The men cheered. They rushed into line. Still sounding the rally, I passed back and forth of the forming line, and what a few minutes before seemed a hopeless disastrous rout, now turned out to be a complete victory. The retreat had been checked and the enemy driven back with awful slaughter. So severe was their repulse, that within a few minutes we were firing toward our rear into the enemy who were pressing Beatty's troops back." Carson would be captured later in the day and spent the next three months at Pemberton Prison in Richmond. He was ill throughout his captivity and, upon exchange in early 1864, weighed a mere sixty-four pounds. Years after the war, the bugler received the Medal of Honor for his actions at Chickamauga.[39]

Severe fighting took place for about fifteen minutes. The 18th Infantry skirmishers were able to fall back to the brigade's line, but their counterparts from the 19th Regulars on the left were cut off and destroyed in the melee. "we held them for as long as we could and then fell back," remembered Lieutenant Carpenter of his experiences in that deadly forest. "they got between us and the brigade, so we could not join the Brigade at all, which was off to the right of us. they were fighting hard. we had lost all but 6 of our company and now had to fight any where we would fight in one place and then in another." The 1st & 3rd Florida's colors advanced to within a dozen paces of the 18th Infantry's line. Receiving fire from the front, left, and rear, the 18th Infantry battalions and provost guard Carson retired back to the brigade's third line, but Stovall's troops withdrew at about this same time. Van Derveer's brigade, just up from Poe Field, made a timely appearance and led the effort against Stovall along with a few stray regiments from Willich's and Berry's brigades. They counterattacked Stovall and threw the Southerners out of Kelly Field. West of the La Fayette Road, Stanley's brigade from Negley's division, Wood's long-anticipated relief of Negley at Brotherton Field having finally been accomplished, meted out a similar fate to Adams's Brigade of Louisianians. Breckinridge's tired ranks fell back to the McDonald Farm and regrouped. Colonel William Grose's brigade and remnants of Dodge's regiments took up positions on the Regular Brigade's left.

King's brigade suffered heavy casualties, particularly among the 18th Infantry battalions. As the fighting abated, Lieutenant Edgar Wilcox learned that his cousin Lieutenant Lucius Brown had been hit—the man who the month before had proclaimed that the enemy "may pick me off a dozen times" before he would remove his shoulder straps in battle. Not being able to leave his own company, Wilcox detailed a sergeant and four men to carry Brown rearward. The men took the bleeding officer to a field hospital and the sergeant reported to Wilcox that Brown had been hit a half dozen times, the most serious wound having broken one of Brown's legs.

Despite the multiple injuries, Brown "was cheerful and did not think his wounds serious."[40]

* * *

Prior to eleven o'clock on September 20, Thomas's position at Kelly Field was the only threatened portion of the Federal line, which focused Rosecrans on shifting every available unit northward to Thomas's aid. George Thomas was also moving whatever troops he could find to support Baird's division on the left. At some point after ten o'clock, but before Van Derveer's brigade arrived at Kelly Field, Thomas sent one of his aides, Captain Sanford Kellogg, in search of General Brannan bearing orders for that division to again move to the XIV Corps's left flank, still not realizing that Brannan was in line at Poe Field. Kellogg located Brannan and transmitted Thomas's order. Brannan again conferred with General Reynolds, and the two agreed that Brannan should comply with Thomas's order. The matter seemingly settled, Kellogg prepared to leave. Before he did so, Reynolds requested that Thomas and Rosecrans be made aware that his own division's flank would be unsupported upon Brannan's departure. Kellogg then galloped to Rosecrans's headquarters on the west side of Dyer Field. After listening to Kellogg's report that Brannan was heading for Kelly Field and Reynolds needed support on his right, Rosecrans instructed one of his aides to send a note to General Wood, the commander of the next division in the line, to close the gap on Reynolds's right. The order instructed Wood to "close up on Reynolds as fast as possible, and support him."

Unbeknownst to anyone at Rosecrans's headquarters, Brannan had not in fact moved; he had decided once again to remain where he was at Poe Field instead of creating a dangerous gap in the Federal line. Thomas J. Wood was one man who did know Brannan was still there. After receiving Rosecrans's order to both "close up on" and "support" Reynolds (instructions that were tactically self-contradicting), Wood choose not to seek clarification and followed his instructions to the letter, even though he knew that Brannan was between his troops and Reynolds—Wood had been on the receiving end of a number of Rosecrans's outbursts for failing to follow orders, the most recent occurring only a few hours ago, and was not about to hand the commanding general another opportunity. Knowing full well that obeying the order as written would open a

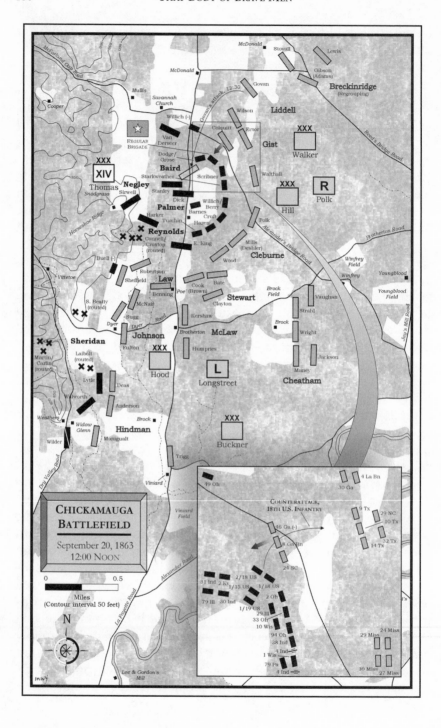

CHICKAMAUGA BATTLEFIELD

September 20, 1863
12:00 NOON

0   0.5

Miles
(Contour interval 50 feet)

N

gap in the line and invite disaster, Wood pulled his troops out of line and began to march around Brannan in an attempt to close up on Reynolds. Wood could not have been more satisfied as the movement began. Rosecrans had treated him in a very shabby manner, and Wood knew that the ambiguous order from army headquarters meant the obnoxious Rosecrans would take the blame for the consequences of Wood's actions. As Wood's troops filed northward, eight brigades from Longstreet's Left Wing of the Army of Tennessee, nearly 11,000 men, were forming for an attack on the very position Wood was evacuating. Shortly after eleven o'clock, Longstreet's troops poured through Wood's position, now empty of Federals save for a few skirmishers, an attack that ultimately sealed the fate of the Army of the Cumberland in this battle. So goes the oft-told account of Wood's actions at Chickamauga.[41] But there is more to the story.

The "Wood the Vindictive" theory does not hold up under close scrutiny. Was Rosecrans's order confusing? Yes. He issued it in response to Captain Kellogg's report that Brannan was moving and Reynolds needed support. The Army of the Cumberland's efficient chief of staff, James A. Garfield, was, at that critical moment, busy issuing additional orders, instructions that were putting in motion other elements of Rosecrans's army to aid Thomas. Major Frank S. Bond, an aide-de-camp who normally did not write such orders, drafted the message to Wood. Had either Rosecrans or Garfield reviewed the order before it was sent to Wood, they undoubtedly would have clarified its ambiguities and made compliance conditional upon the departure of Brannan, but neither of them did so. Should Wood have sought clarification before he executed the order? Again, yes. At this point, another player enters the scene: Major General Alexander McCook.

Corps commander McCook happened to be with Wood when the order to move was received. Although Wood's division was assigned to Crittenden's corps, as a corps commander it was incumbent upon McCook to function as a forward-based set of trusted eyes and ears for the army commander, one who ensures that instructions from higher headquarters are executed in accordance with operational realities. It should have been obvious to McCook that the order to Wood did not mesh with reality; McCook should have put its execution in abeyance until Rosecrans had been made aware of the potential consequences. He did not. Wood would later claim that

McCook agreed to fill the void in the line at Brotherton Field, but McCook would vehemently deny it. It is not surprising that little can be gleaned from self-serving reports and testimonies. There can be no doubt, though, that Wood would have stayed put had McCook instructed him to do so. At the very least, McCook acquiesced to the move, thus failing to carry out his inherent duties as one of the Army of the Cumberland's senior leaders.

Did Wood have such an intense dislike of Rosecrans that he would invite battlefield disaster to carry out a personal vendetta? It is hard to believe so. Rosecrans's intent to reinforce the left on September 20 at almost any cost was well communicated throughout the Army of the Cumberland. An order to move north and aid Thomas was not unexpected by any division commander on the southern half of Rosecrans's battle line that day. Most elements of McCook's and Crittenden's corps had either moved north or were in the process of receiving orders to do so by the time Wood received his orders. Being a professional soldier with more than eighteen years in uniform, Wood knew how to follow an order. He also knew that occasionally being chewed out, even unjustly, came with the job. And if Wood were indeed bent on bringing about Rosecrans's ruin through defeat on the battlefield, why then did Wood later fight with such tenacity that very afternoon at Horseshoe Ridge? He also was never officially sanctioned for his actions at Chickamauga (other than a few lines buried in Rosecrans's official report), never requested a court of inquiry to probe the matter, and continued to actively serve in positions of increasing authority through war's end. On this final point the same cannot be said of either William Rosecrans or Alexander McCook.[42]

On September 20, it did not really matter upon whose shoulders the blame should rest; the bottom line is that 11,000 Confederates were pouring westward across Brotherton Field. Stewart's Division on the right of Longsteet's column and Hindman's Division to the left also advanced. The southern portion of the Federal line crumpled before the onslaught. The two brigades of Jefferson C. Davis's division were routed, as were Brannan's men, Colonel Samuel Beatty's brigade of Van Cleve's division, and the southernmost brigade of Wood's northward-marching column, Colonel George P. Buell's. Sheridan's division near the Widow Glen House was also forced back. About half of the Army of the Cumberland was soon streaming through the ridges toward Chattanooga. Rosecrans went with them.[43]

Union troops at Kelly Field were unaware of the disaster occurring just to their south. For the time being, they had no trouble dealing with the attacks on the northern end of the Union battle line, for Bragg and his subordinate commanders still had serious coordination problems and continued to attack Thomas's line in piecemeal fashion. After the failure of Breckinridge's and Cleburne's attacks, General Polk and his immediate subordinate, corps commander Lieutenant General Daniel H. Hill, attempted to bring additional forces to bear against Kelly Field. Available to them were the four brigades of Walker's Reserve Corps and also the fresh brigade of Brigadier General States Rights Gist, just up from Mississippi after a lengthy rail journey. Walker's own division of two brigades was without a commander, so Walker tapped Gist to command the division, consisting of Gist's own brigade plus those commanded by Ector and Wilson. Colonel Peyton Colquitt of the 46th Georgia assumed command of Gist's Brigade.[44]

Anxious to continue the attack after the repulse of Helm, General Hill ordered Gist to send in Colquitt's Brigade against Kelly Field and support him with Wilson and Ector's troops. Although he stood little chance of success against Baird's breastworks, about noon Colquitt led his brigade forward. Colquitt's line drifted westward during its approach march. The brigade's left-flank unit, the 24th South Carolina, ran into the Regular Brigade, while the rest of Colquitt's line was too far to the right to give the South Carolinians much support. The results were predictable. The 18th Infantry raked the 24th South Carolina with a "most destructive and well-aimed fire" before Colquitt managed to wheel his other units into position to help. As the Confederate line moved closer, Grose and Dodge on the Regular Brigade's flank decimated the ranks of the 8th and 46th Georgia. When Colquitt attempted to rally his Carolina regiment in front of the Regulars, a sharp-eyed regular infantryman dropped the colonel with a fatal shot.

Sensing that the enemy was about to crack, General King ordered the 18th Infantry battalions to charge. The Regulars leapt over their short breastworks and, with a yell, scattered the remnants of Colquitt's Brigade. Smith's and Haymond's battalions pursued the fleeing Southerners beyond the Alexander's Bridge Road before the Confederates were able to form a semblance of a line. The 18th

Infantry's sudden assault meant few if any of the fleeing Southerners had had a chance to reload; Colquitt's men could only watch for a few seconds as the blue-clad swarm closed the distance. The regulars then showed what they were capable of, even after a day and a half of intense combat. Unlike their opponents, the regulars' Springfields were loaded. Smith and Haymond brought their men to a sudden halt, bellowed out orders to fire, and a devastating volley slammed into the enemy line. The 18th U.S. followed that up with another charge. The fighting became personal, with rifle butts and bayonets dominating the action. The surviving Confederates fled, but still the regulars would not quit. The two battalions reloaded, advanced a short distance, and sent another volley into their enemy's backs. The tables began to turn on the 18th U.S. at this point, for a new Confederate force emerged from the distance. The remaining two brigades of Gist's Division were moving up to support Colquitt and would have been more than enough to overwhelm the sweating, exhausted regulars had Smith and Haymond pushed their regulars any further. The 18th Infantrymen headed back to their fortifications as quick as they could, King moving the 15th U.S. to the front and placing the winded 18th in reserve. The general commanding the Regular Brigade considered the charge against Colquitt to be "the most gallant act of that day's engagement."[45]

With Gist's attack stymied, Hill and Walker turned to the only other Confederate force in the area, Liddell's Division. Liddell's available force had dwindled to just a single brigade, for while the regulars were punishing Colquitt, Polk had dispatched Walthall's Brigade to support Cleburne. That left Govan's Arkansas Brigade, the men who had overrun the regulars the previous day. In a belated attempt to support Colquitt's rapidly disintegrating command, Hill ordered Govan to move around the end of the Federal line and approach Kelly Field from the north, much as Adam's and Stovall's Brigades had done earlier in the day. Colquitt's troops were already straggling rearward by the time Govan raised the late Major Coolidge's sword and waved his own regiments forward. After brushing aside two of Willich's regiments on the southern fringe of the McDonald Farm and narrowly avoiding Van Derveer's brigade, Govan advanced as far as the edge of the timber bordering Kelly Field. The Southerners routed the defenders posted west of the road, the worn out brigades of Colonels Timothy Stanley and George Dick, and then swung around to attack Kelly Field from the rear.

Although Govan's total force was small, its presence in the rear of the Kelly Field line posed an annoying threat that would have to be dealt with.[46]

Govan's Arkansans were again flanking King's troops. Captain Dod's 1/15th U.S. had occupied the brigade's front breastworks only a short while before the captain decided to fall back. "I perceived two regiments of the enemy marching in double-quick time to my left," the battalion commander reported. "I waited until they commenced fire and were pouring an enfilading fire down my ranks— which it was impossible for me to return—when I gave the order to rise up, and the battalion marched [back]...under a terrific fire as steadily and in as good order as if on drill or parade." Seeing the 15th Infantrymen retreating, the Regular Brigade's adjutant, Captain John W. Forsyth of the 18th Infantry, ran forward and told Dod that the line was "ordered held at all hazards." Dod understood the order but argued that without support on the left the ground was too hot to occupy. Forsyth ordered the battalion to return to the forward position anyway, promising Dod that some left flank protection would be sent up as soon as possible. Dod's battalion returned to the front.[47] Other Federal troops were also on the move. Colonel Sidney Barnes's brigade of Wood's division was in the area and Baird threw it against Govan. He also faced about some men of Scribner's brigade and sent them in. Some of Willich's regiments joined the fray. The combined assault finally pushed Govan out of Kelly Field. A few regulars pitched in against Govan, partial repayment for Jays's Mill. The sights before him fascinated Captain Haymond, whose 2/18th Infantry had just recently arrived at the rear line of the Regular Brigade's position when Govan made his appearance:

> The enemy...swept around to our left driving everything before them, until they reached the edge of a large cornfield across which a fresh division of our troops were advancing in line of Battle. The fate of the Army depended upon the possession of this field, and of course the result was eagerly watched. The enemy advanced to meet our men and the scene that took place in that field was the most thrilling and grand that I ever saw. The very trees seem to wave to and fro under the terrific fire of musketry, and the earth trembled under the roar of artillery. Capt. Smith and myself with the colors of our Battalions and but a few men, joined in the melee and assisted in sweeping the enemy through the cornfield into the woods beyond. In this part of the field they were now thoroughly beaten and the

field for many hundred yards was strewn with their dead and wounded.[48]

What was left of Barnes's brigade took up a position on the regulars' left. Although Baird had managed to once again keep Kelly Field clear of Confederates, the Federals were reaching the end of their endurance and the bottom of their cartridge boxes. General King sent Sergeant James E. Patten of the 18th Infantry to the rear with a squad of men in search of ammunition, hoping they would return in time. Additional troops as well as cartridges were needed to defend Kelly Field, but Thomas was now shifting units to Snodgrass Hill and Horseshoe Ridge, due west of the field, in an attempt to stem Longstreet's breakthrough. Units that had earlier played key roles shoring up the lines at Kelly Field, Van Derveer's brigade and others, were now needed elsewhere. Stanley's brigade also headed westward, as would Hazen's brigade of Palmer's division.[49]

Bragg had routed half the Federal army and was on the verge of a decisive victory. All that remained was to crush the Federal positions at Kelly Field and Horseshoe Ridge. Thomas's makeshift line on the ridge held out against heavy attacks until after sundown, thanks in large part to the nick-of-time arrival of three brigades from Major General Gordon Granger's Reserve Corps. While men on both sides fell in droves on the ridge, Kelly Field remained relatively calm. "We lay quiet and listened to the roar of the Battle trying to tell by the sound of the firing who was being driven," Captain Haymond recalled. "The firing at this time was the heaviest I ever heard. It was a continuous roll of musketry." Action at Kelly Field was confined to skirmishers for much of the early afternoon, although that contest was dangerous enough for some. Between one and two o'clock, a Confederate sharpshooter put a bullet in the brain of Colonel Edward A. King, commander of a brigade in Reynold's division, as King was dismounting behind his brigade line. The former lieutenant colonel of the 19th U.S. Infantry was dead before he hit the ground.[50]

Bragg sent repeated orders to his commanders opposite Kelly Field to attack, but lackluster leadership and muddled chains of command prevented the Southerners from moving out until late in the day. Polk moved Cheatham's Division, which had been largely idle most of the day, to the Confederate right at two o'clock.

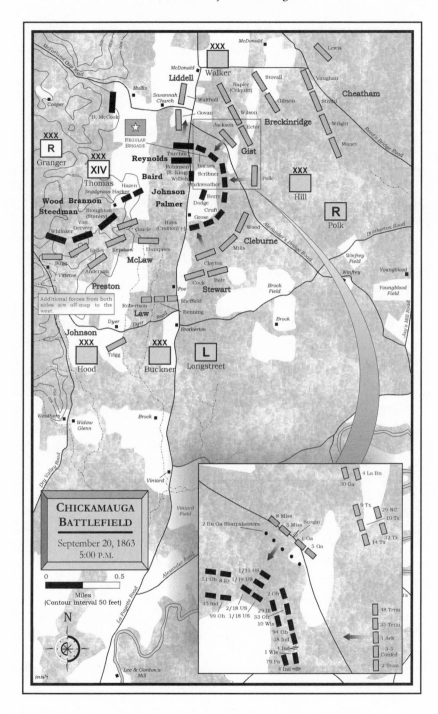

CHICKAMAUGA
BATTLEFIELD

September 20, 1863
5:00 P.M.

0   0.5
Miles
(Contour interval 50 feet)

Cheatham moved in behind the reformed divisions of Lidell, Gist, and Breckinridge with four brigades. Bragg had earlier detached Cheatham's fifth brigade, commanded by Brigadier General John K. Jackson, to fill the gap in the line between Breckinridge and Cleburne, the same task given earlier to Walthall's Brigade. Thus it was that Jackson's lone brigade ended up leading the effort against Baird's line when the final Confederate attack on Kelly Field began at five o'clock that evening. There was plenty of help for Jackson in the vicinity. While Liddell's Division swept across the McDonald Farm, a reinforced battalion of Confederate artillery, a total of twenty guns, pounded Kelly Field from the south. Stacked up behind Jackson were nine additional brigades of the Confederate Right Wing. Meanwhile, Cleburne and Stewart were poised to once again advance toward Palmer and Johnson's men on the southern portion of the Federal line.[51]

Behind their bullet-splintered barricades, the regulars knew the afternoon's respite would eventually end. Few Federal brigades at Kelly Field had seen as much action on September 20 as had the regulars—standing fast against the assaults of Helm, Stovall, Colquitt, and finally Govan. As they heard Jackson's Brigade approach, they prepared for the next round. Jackson advanced his five regiments and Captain John Scogin's Georgia Battery toward the 15th Infantry's frontline position. The Confederate brigadier reported that Captain Dod's battalion, supported by the 4th Indiana Light Battery and other units to the Regular Brigade's right, put up a stiff fight: "The brigade, with the battery in the center, moved forward in splendid style about 100 yards, when the enemy opened a galling fire from the front and left flank, enfilading the entire line with canister and small-arms. The engagement now became terrific and the position of my brigade extremely critical." As the battle raged, Captain Dod noticed that one of his companies was falling back off the line. Mindful of his recent dressing-down from Captain Forsyth, Dod rushed to the unit. It was E/2/15th U.S., the new company that Colonel Oliver Shepherd had cobbled together at Fort Adams the previous May. The unit had performed well during its baptism of fire, although its commander, Lieutenant Samuel S. Holbrook, had been captured on September 19. The next day, 1st Sergeant John Marrs, a veteran of the prewar regulars who had been cited for gallantry as a corporal with the 15th U.S. at Shiloh, led the formation.

Battle Monument at West Point

Oliver Lathrop Shepherd
Lieutenant Colonel, 18th U.S. Infantry,
1861-1863
Colonel, 15th U.S. Infantry,
1863-1870

George Henry Thomas
2nd (5th) U.S. Cavalry, 1855-1863
Brigadier & Major General of
Volunteers, 1861-1863
Brigadier & Major General, U.S. Army,
1863-1870

Richard W. Johnson
Captain, 2nd (5th) U.S. Cavalry,
1855-1861
Brigadier General of Volunteers,
1861-1866

Henry Beebee Carrington
Colonel, 18th U.S. Infantry, 1861-1869
Brigadier General of Volunteers,
1863-1865

John Haskell King
Major, 15th U.S. Infantry, 1861-1863
Brigadier General of Volunteers,
1863-1865

Frederick Phisterer
Sergeant Major, Lieutenant, & Captain, 18th U.S. Infantry, 1861-1866
(photographed in 1867 at his marriage to Ms. Isabel Riley)

Edgar Romeyn Kellogg
Private, Sergeant Major, & Lieutenant,
16th U.S. Infantry, 1861-1866
(post-war photo)

Frederick Townsend
Major, 18th U.S. Infantry, 1861-1864
(photographed in 1861 while serving as
colonel, 3rd New York Volunteer Infantry)

Adam Jacoby Slemmer
Major, 16th U.S. Infantry, 1861-1864
Brigadier General of Volunteers,
1863-1865

John Phillip Sanderson
Lieutenant Colonel, 15th U.S. Infantry,
1861-1863

Edward Augustin King
Lieutenant Colonel, 19th U.S.
Infantry, 1861-1863

Arthur Brigham Carpenter
Sergeant & Lieutenant, 19th U.S.
Infantry, 1861-1866

Henry Blanchard Freeman

First Sergeant, Lieutenant, & Captain,
18th U.S. Infantry, 1861-1866

Lovell Harrison Rousseau

Brigadier & Major General of
Volunteers, 1861-1865

Brigadier General, U.S. Army,
1867-1869

William Rufus Terrill

Captain, 5th U.S. Artillery, 1861-1862

Brigadier General of Volunteers, 1862

Francis Luther Guenther

Lieutenant & Captain, 5th U.S.
Artillery, 1861-1882

(post-war photo)

The 15th Infantry Band

Charles Augustus Wickoff
Lieutenant & Captain, 15th U.S.
Infantry, 1861-1866

Alfred Lacey Hough
Captain, 19th U.S. Infantry,
1861-1866

**Robert Erskine Anderson (R.E.A.)
Crofton**

Lieutenant & Captain, 16th U.S.
Infantry, 1861-1868

Colonel, 15th U.S. Infantry,
1890-1894

Edward Lewis Mitchell

Lieutenant, 16th U.S. Infantry,
1861-1862

James Harrison Gageby

First Sergeant & Lieutenant, 19th U.S.
Infantry, 1861-1866

Henry Douglass
Captain, 18th U.S. Infantry, 1861-
1869

John Henry Knight
Lieutenant & Captain, 18th U.S.
Infantry, 1861-1870

Amos Fleagle
Sergeant, 18th U.S. Infantry, 1861-1863

George Washington Smith
Captain, 18th U.S. Infantry, 1861-
1866

James Voty Bomford
Lieutenant Colonel, 16th U.S. Infantry,
1862-1864

(post-war photo)

Howard Burnham
Lieutenant, 5th U.S. Artillery,
1861-1863

Phillip Sydney Coolidge
Major, 16th U.S. Infantry,
1861-1863

Henry Haymond
Captain, 18th U.S. Infantry,
1861-1870

Robert Ayres
Lieutenant & Captain, 19th U.S. Infantry,
1862-1871

(post-war photo)

Albert Baldwin Dod
Captain, 15th U.S. Infantry, 1861-1864

Isaac D'Isay
Private, Sergeant, Sergeant Major, & Lieutenant,
18th U.S. Infantry,
1861-1866

Roland W. Evans
Color Sergeant, 1/18th U.S. Infantry, 1861-1864

William Henry Bisbee
Private, Sergeant, Sergeant Major, & Lieutenant, 18th U.S. Infantry, 1861-1866
Brigadier General, U.S. Army, 1901-1902
(photographed in 1895 while serving as major, 8th U.S. Infantry)

John H. King
Brevet Major General, U.S. Army

Andrew S. Burt
Lieutenant & Captain, 18th U.S.
Infantry, 1861-1866

Frederick Townsend
Major General, New York National
Guard, 1880

Oliver L. Shepherd
Brevet Brigadier General, U.S. Army

Frederick Phisterer
Colonel, New York National Guard,
1894

The Regular Brigade Association of Survivors
Stones River National Cemetery
September 17, 1895

(William J. Carson, the 15th Infantry musician awarded the Medal of Honor for his actions at Chickamauga, is in the second row, standing sixth from left)

Marrs had faced his company about and was marching it toward the brigade's second line when Dod noticed the movement. Marrs marched backwards, facing his men with his rifle at right shoulder shift as he steadied the raw troops. Captain Dod ran up to Marrs and told him to halt. The first sergeant halted his line, faced about, crisply brought his rifle to present arms, and calmly asked: "Does the commanding officer know we are out of ammunition?" Dod told him no ammunition was to be had, but the company could not fall back. Marrs had his men fix bayonets, faced them about, and moved them back into line. The rookies of E/2/15th U.S. became veterans at Kelly Field, the new troops returning to the front and expending their last rounds at Jackson's line. Their first sergeant was killed while they did so. Captain Dod wrote a fitting epitaph for Marrs in the battalion's report on the battle: "The cool, soldierly bearing of this man under the terrific fire of Sunday evening was most commendable."[52]

The life span of a soldier serving on a color guard in the Civil War was considerably shorter than that of his peers. Paul Fisher was tempting fate at Kelly Field. He had been promoted to sergeant in January 1863 and selected as color bearer of 2/18th U.S. for his heroism in helping Frederick Phisterer and William Bisbee save 2/18th's colors at Stones River. He had carried his unit's national flag ever since. Fisher had survived the fighting at Jay's Mill, but was severely wounded as the struggle raged between the regulars and Jackson's men. When Fisher was hit, the surviving members of the color guard, two corporals, headed for cover instead of retrieving the flag. Corporal Robert Kennedy saw Fisher go down and rushed to the spot. The corporal was having a busy day. By his own count, he fired more than 200 rounds on September 20, picking up discarded Springfields as each in turn became fouled with powder residue. His company had been whittled down to just a handful of men, and by late afternoon Kennedy and Lieutenant Rufus C. Gates were the only leaders in C/2/18th U.S. still fighting. Kennedy picked up the flag, grasping it with one arm while awkwardly loading and firing with the other, resolving to be the color bearer if neither of the color corporals was up to the task. The color guards eventually found some courage, and one of them requested that Kennedy hand over the flag. Kennedy refused until Lieutenant Gates intervened. "Kennedy, give them the flag," Gates ordered. "You are the only [non]commissioned officer in the company now, and if anything

should happen to me, you will have to take charge of the company."
Kennedy reluctantly handed over the colors, but warned the color
guards that he would shoot them himself if they abandoned their
posts again. Kennedy recalled that the corporals then "stood like
men all afternoon."[53]

Baird received orders to withdraw from Kelly Field at the height
of Jackson's attack. Rosecrans had arrived in Chattanooga at mid-
afternoon following his flight from the battlefield. Not having
accurate knowledge of Thomas's stand at Horseshoe Ridge and
Kelly Field, Rosecrans ordered Thomas to withdraw to Rossville,
about three miles northwest of Kelly Field, with whatever could be
extracted of the Army of the Cumberland from the battlefield. If
that bloodied army was going to prevent Bragg from advancing all
the way to Chattanooga, the place to do it was atop Missionary
Ridge at Rossville Gap. Thomas had planned on withdrawing come
nightfall anyway, and upon receiving Rosecrans's order at 4:30 P.M.
decided to comply immediately, although withdrawing while in
contact with the enemy would be hazardous. He ordered the troops
at Kelly field to begin withdrawing first, followed by the defenders
of Horseshoe Ridge. The divisions at Kelly Field would fall back
starting with the troops on the south. Baird's division would be the
last to leave that portion of the battlefield.[54]

The opposition sensed the Federal retreat as the units to Baird's
right abandoned their positions. Confederates all along the line
began to swarm over the Union fortifications. Palmer's men pulled
out first and in good order; they marched northward past the regulars and routed Lidell's division at the McDonald Farm, opening the
road to Rossville. After Johnson's Division headed for the rear, Baird
sent staff officers to his three brigades and ordered them to retire.
Continuing the right-to-left sequence, Starkweather's brigade pulled
off the line first, followed by Scribner. By the time General King gave
the regulars the order to withdraw, Kelly Field was a scene of
absolute devastation. Much of it was on fire. Shattered guns, caissons, and dead horses littered the ground. Retreating Federal troops
streamed in many directions. Victorious Confederates seemed to be
everywhere as they stormed the breastworks. King attempted to
withdraw his men as cohesively as possible. He ordered the brigade's
multiple lines to fall back starting with the forwardmost, each withdrawal to be covered by the rear lines. The 15th Infantry in the
frontline was thus the first of King's units to run through the killing

field. "In falling back we discovered that we had been almost surrounded," recalled Lieutenant William Heilman, commanding C/1/15th. "My company was in the centre and we hardly knew what direction to take. At length we got under cover of the woods when it was found that all the officers to my right and a large number of men had been captured. As we fell back we were heavily fired into and the ground was covered with the dead and wounded of both armies. We were crowded very closely [by the enemy] and fell far back, being entirely out of ammunition."[55]

Confederates of Maney's and Gibson's Brigades passed through Jackson's Southerners and occupied the 15th Infantry's abandoned line. Troops from Brigadier General Lucius E. Polk's Brigade of Cleburne's Division, having passed through Starkweather's vacant position, came up on the Regular Brigade's right. Additional Southern troops moved around King's left. Scogin's Battery raked the remaining regulars with canister. John King's plan for an orderly retrograde movement degenerated into a whirlwind of vicious close combat, narrow escapes, and sudden surrenders. Although it is hard to determine the exact sequence of events as the regulars' position collapsed, it appears that most of the 16th and 19th U.S. fell back as the 15th retreated through the 18th's lines. "We retreated across the open field which for a while made us a fine target," Van Zwaluwenburg of the 16th U.S. recalled, "and we lost heavily, a few of us managed to cross that fatal field, which was raked right and left by shot and shell, grape and canister. All order, and formation seemed to be lost. It was every one for himself." Captain Crofton's horse was killed (his fourth mount to die in battle), but the 16th Infantry's commander made it through to safety. With most of the brigade heading for the rear, the 18th U.S. alone now faced the full fury of the enemy assault. The battalion commanders, Captains Smith and Haymond, ordered their men to fall back largely in accordance with King's plan. According to Captain Smith, part of 1/18th U.S. maintained some sort of cohesion as they escaped across Kelly Field: "Over a wide corn-field, under a terrific fire of musketry, canister, and spherical case shot, my men steadily and slowly followed their color, when, gaining the woods, they faced about, fired, and moved to the rear, where, as ordered, I reported to the general of brigade." By this point in the struggle, it appears that Smith and Haymond had control of only a small portion of their battalions. Haymond conceded that after crossing the field he and Smith only "collected what men we could" and then continued to the rear, where they came upon General King and received orders to make for Rossville.[56]

Many 18th Infantrymen remained at the breastworks, unknowingly covering the movement of their comrades. Shortly after the war, Major Caldwell had the regiment's surviving officers who had been captured at Chickamauga write reports about their experiences. From these fascinating documents one can glimpse snapshots of what was probably the last organized Federal resistance on the Kelly Field line. Few of the regulars knew who was in command; all were confused about when and if they should fall back. Captain Tenedor Ten Eyck was probably the senior man remaining: "an officer reported to me for orders, stating at same time, that he believed I was the ranking officer present, and as we were immensely out numbered by the enemy, advised me to give the order to retreat. My men were holding their position firmly at this time and I had received no order to retire the command. Therefore I declined following this advise and maintained my position under a heavy fire of Infantry and Artillery, until after sunset, when being flanked both on the right and left, we were driven from our works and captured by the enemy."[57]

In the confusion, at least part of the 18th fought outside of Captain Ten Eyck's control. Lieutenant Rufus Gates of C/2/18th U.S. claimed that about five o'clock he assumed command of the 18th Infantry as senior officer present. "The enemy pressed us hard," Gates remembered as he wrote his report at Camp Thomas on May 20, 1865, "but the temporary works erected during the morning of the 20th enabled us to hold the enemy, greatly superior in numbers, in check, as well as keep him ignorant of our real strength." At sundown, the horde of Confederate troops to the front and on both flanks made Gates realize that further resistance was futile. "I...at once gave the command to retreat," Gates continued:

> The Detachment fell back through an open field; the enemy at the same time opened a heavy fire of Musketry and Artillery upon us, causing the Battalions to lose their organization soon after retreating. The enemy had, unknown to me, previously gained a position about one fourth of a mile in our rear, and finding ourselves surrounded, each man surrendered, I think, because he found escape impossible, and resistance vain. ...At the time I assumed command, the two Battalions numbered about 130 men. A small number broke

from the right of the 1st Batt., and a few from the 2nd Batt., perhaps about 20 men in all, and fled to the rear soon after I took command. ...The number captured was about 80.[58]

Sergeant Major Isaac D'Isay of 1/18th U.S. experienced the same fate. With Captain Smith heading rearward and no other officers present, the Dutch-born sergeant major became the ranking man of the battalion remaining on the line. He was not sure about what to do: "A few minutes after I saw portions of our troops on the right and the left of our Brigade falling back the thought occurred to me at the time, that we should also fall back, but having no command to that effect, we continued to hold our position." Lieutenant Gates soon appeared and told the sergeant major that the battalions were flanked and had better pull out now. D'Isay's tenure as a battalion commander then came to an abrupt end:

> The Detachment then instantly began to retreat, but owing to the terrible fire poured into us from the front, and flank...and having no support, we were unable to preserve Battalion and Company organization, each man seeking to escape for himself, knowing that further resistance would be entirely in vain. We had to cross a large cornfield, on the other side of which, I supposed our lines still existed. I had succeeded in getting half way across, when a squad of rebel cavalry men rode up to me, and demanded my surrender. I could not realize my true situation at first, and hesitated, but seeing the threatening appearance of several revolvers, pointed at my head, I yielded to their demand. My astonishment and surprise can be better imagined, than described, when I saw the rebel lines formed upon the ground, which I had supposed was still held by our own troops.[59]

Robert Kennedy was part of the Gates-D'Isay contingent and met a similar demise as he crossed Kelly Field. The corporal was completely out of ammunition and all the discarded cartridge boxes within reach were likewise empty when Lieutenant Gates put out the word to run the gauntlet. Kennedy sprinted for safety. He made it away from the firing line, through the timber, and into Kelly Field, but then bumped into an officer from an Illinois regiment who was directing troops to support a nearby battery. Kennedy complied but found a surprise in store upon reaching his destination: "When we got up to the battery we found it was occupied by the enemy and two lines of Rebel infantry around it. It was then we received the order, 'Throw down your guns, you Yanks'. ...We were then marched back past the Rebel field hospital where there were the most ghastly sights I ever saw. Doctors were amputating limbs of the wounded. We lay in the woods all night and the next day were marched back to Dalton's Mills. This was the last battle in which I took part.'[60]

Some of the regulars made it across Kelly Field and into the hills beyond, but many from all the battalions were captured. Brigadier General Lucius Polk, sweeping into the Regular Brigade's position from the right, asserted that during the final assault on Kelly Field his brigade captured "more than 200 prisoners—all of them regulars." Lieutenant Alfred Townsend and a group of men from G/1/18th escorted Color Sergeant Rowland W. Evans off the line when Captain Smith fell back, safeguarding the colors of 1/18th U.S. and making good their escape. The color guards of 2/18th U.S., Corporal Kennedy's threat looming over them, were not as fortunate. They stood their ground and were captured along with the battalion's precious flag. The Regular Army had not lost any colors in battle through the first twenty-nine months of the war, but that streak appeared to be over on September 20, 1863.[61]

General King and his staff attempted to assemble what remained of the brigade while continuing to head toward Rossville in the gathering gloom. As he made his way through the throng of men fleeing northward on the Rossville Road, he noticed a determined-looking group of soldiers heading southward, back toward the battlefield. They turned out to be Sergeant Patton and the detail of regulars that King had sent in search of ammunition during the afternoon. Patton had located a few crates of cartridges and was dutifully attempting to follow his orders. "The command has retreated toward Rossville," King informed the sergeant. "Gather up what men you can and follow on after." King and Sergeant Patton could lay their hands on only a few regulars, among them the Smith-Haymond contingent of 18th Infantrymen. Whatever attempt the brigade made to reform was quickly overwhelmed. Once off the field and sheltered from enemy fire, the regulars and the rest of the Kelly Field defenders continued to scatter to all points save toward the enemy. A few fell in with other commands. Some who successfully traversed Kelly Field still never made it to safety, such as Lieutenant Charles F. Miller of the 19th Infantry. He had been wounded in both legs early in the day but was still conscious at dusk. Soldiers from E/1/19th U.S. carried their officer through the final fire and about two miles further toward Rossville. Miller's pain became so acute that he could be moved no further; he ordered his men to leave him beside the road. Miller was captured during the night and died of his wounds two days later. "he was a young man about my own age, liked by all who knew him," Arthur Carpenter wrote after learning Miller's fate. "his papers promoting him to 1st Lt. had just arrived from the War Department at Washington, but the poor fellow did not get a chance to see them."[62]

The road to Rossville was jammed with the broken remnants of the Kelly Field defenders as darkness descended on the battlefield. Thomas's troops from Horseshoe Ridge were also moving north, having pulled off their line after sunset. Throughout the chilly night and into the next morning, commanders gradually regrouped units and gathered in scattered formations. General Crittenden of the XXI Corps came across a regular officer, probably Captain Andrew Burt of Rosecrans's staff, during the corps commander's exodus from the battlefield: "On reaching the crest of the next hill I found only a small number of men, less than 100, who had been rallied by a captain of the Eighteenth Regulars, as he told me, and whom he kept in line with great difficulty." Lieutenant Edgar Wilcox had better luck than Burt, reigning in twenty regulars with the assistance of a sergeant from G/3/18th U.S. and a corporal from 2/18th's Company H. Things began to improve somewhat the next morning. Lieutenant James Powell of the 18th U.S. reported to General King shortly after daylight at the head of a small mixed group of regulars. The Regular Brigade subsistence officer, Lieutenant Samuel S. Culbertson of the 19th U.S., pulled into Rossville at daybreak with a much-needed train of provisions. There were so few of the brigade's troops present that Culbertson had enough rations left over to distribute food to Major General Philip Sheridan's entire division as well as Battery I/4th U.S. of Van Derveer's brigade. Another welcome event happened later in the day, as Major General Lovell Rousseau finally arrived on the scene and resumed command of his old division from General Baird.[63]

By sunrise on September 21, the skeletal remains of the formations that had defended Kelly Field and Horseshoe Ridge were on Missionary Ridge astride Rossville Gap. Baird's division held the gap itself and the general placed the remnants of the Regular Brigade at the point of greatest danger, blocking the Rossville-Chattanooga Road. Another Confederate attack may have taken this line also, but

Bragg was content with resting his own tired troops and collecting up abandoned Federal equipment from the bloodied fields west of Chickamauga Creek. A contingent of Forrest's cavalry advanced up the Rossville Road on the morning of September 21, but fire from the regulars kept the Southern horsemen at a distance. One of Forrest's batteries shelled the Union position during the afternoon and that was the extent of Confederate pursuit of the battered Army of the Cumberland. The Regular Brigade was on the receiving end of this last shellfire. Lieutenant Wilcox witnessed the incoming rounds: "About 4 P.M. enemy commenced to shell the road and the ord[nance] train some 500 yds down the road started to the rear. Shells burst unpleasantly near and [I] concluded [I] better follow suit. shell burst in road front of me some distance but a piece hit me on left knee—but so spent it made no injury." Other regulars were not as fortunate. Five of them were wounded during the barrage, the only Federal casualties of the day. They are the final names on the long list of Union soldiers maimed at the Battle of Chickamauga.[64]

Lieutenant Henry Freeman's journey from Chickamauga eventually ended at Richmond's infamous Libby Prison. During the first two months of his captivity, he saw at various places more than 200 other prisoners from the Regular Brigade. Not knowing what had happened to the regulars at Kelly Field, he feared the worst. "I believe the Regular Brigade is very nearly wiped out," Freeman wrote in a November 17 letter to a fellow 18th Infantry officer. Freeman's statement was unfortunately more accurate than the lieutenant probably realized. The Army of the Cumberland suffered more than 16,000 casualties along the banks of Chickamauga Creek, making the clash the bloodiest battle in the Western Theater. Fifty-six percent of the Regular Brigade's members were on the casualty rolls, the highest percentage of loss of any Federal brigade on that field. Forty-nine of the brigade's eighty-five officers were killed, wounded, or captured. Fewer than 600 of the enlisted troops came through unhurt. The 19th Infantry's casualties tell a shocking story. Of the fourteen officers and 190 enlisted men who entered the battle, just three lieutenants and fifty-one troops were fit for duty two days later. Casualties in A/1/19th U.S. were 100 percent. Captain Verling K. Hart, Lieutenant James Gageby, and five soldiers from this company were captured. The rest of the unit's thirty-one troops were wounded or dead.[65]

Rosecrans withdrew Thomas's force from the Rossville line on the evening of September 21. Baird's division, now led by its old commander Lovell Rousseau, covered the retreat and arrived in Chattanooga during the wee hours of the next morning. The establishment of Rosecrans's bloodied army there was a significant accomplishment, for the capture of Chattanooga had been the campaign's immediate objective. While the tactical defeat at Chickamauga was a serious setback for the Union war effort, Bragg's victory was a hollow one as long as Chattanooga was in Federal hands. The Army of Tennessee had also been gutted, losing between 15,000 and 20,000 men that the Confederacy would be hard-pressed to replace. Chattanooga's fate was still in the balance as the opposing forces regrouped after the bloodletting of September 19 and 20. "Our Brig. has fallen back to the fortifications in the edge of the town & there will probably be a heavy fight tomorrow," a sick and lame Lieutenant Edgar Wilcox scribbled in a note to his sister a few hours after arriving in Chattanooga. "Our Brig. is now all cut to pieces and numbers about 200 men but they will fight to the last & you may bet I will be with them if I am able to stand up." More than two months would pass before Wilcox's expected "heavy fight" for Chattanooga took place, and seven months would transpire before a Federal army again ventured deep into Georgia.[66]

The Army of the Cumberland was defeated at Chickamauga, but the actions of a handful of Union formations prevented that defeat from being far worse. Many of these events have been chronicled in detail over the years, such as the delaying actions of Union cavalry guarding the Chickamauga crossings, the Federal counterattacks at Kelly Field, and the timely arrival of Gordon Granger's Reserve Corps on Horseshoe Ridge. The Regular Brigade's stand at Kelly Field ranks just behind these more familiar events. By never budging from its position throughout the day, the regulars provided Federal counterattacking units at Kelley Field with a firm anchor upon which to base maneuvers. Standing fast while the rest of the field's defenders withdrew helped to prevent a disorganized retreat from becoming a complete rout. "It was a juncture when failure on the part of any one, there engaged, to do his full duty would have brought infinite disaster to our cause," General Absalom Baird wrote years afterward about the Regular Brigade's stand on the left of the line. "Viewed in the light of to-day, we know that had the point we held [at Kelly Field] been lost our army would have been scattered into the mountains and a race for the [Tennessee] River would have followed. The rebel forces would have occupied the line of that river in triumph and it would have been necessary to raise a new army in the north to confront them." That the regulars accomplished these feats on September 20 in the aftermath of the pounding they had received the previous day makes their actions all the more noteworthy.[67]

* * *

Private Richard C. Price spotted the silken cloth and recognized it immediately. A member of C/2/18th U.S., Price had been captured during the retreat on September 20. Near the camp where the private ended up that evening, his captors had unwisely deposited captured Union flags. When the guards weren't looking, Price crept over to the pile of frayed banners and grabbed his battalion's colors, which had been lost during the horrific last moments on the Kelly Field line earlier that day. He tore the flag from its staff, ripped it into small pieces, and distributed the scraps amongst fellow captive 18th Infantrymen. By the narrowest of margins, the Civil War regulars maintained their streak for at least never permanently losing a flag in battle—a record that stood untarnished as the guns fell silent in 1865.[68]

Chapter 9:

The Chattanooga Campaign

"You Know How the Regulars Are"

It was a thoroughly battered Regular Brigade that arrived in Chattanooga. Similar to the aftermath of Stones River, the battalions would have to be reorganized and then built back up to strength. But unlike the previous January, the Army of the Cumberland in September 1863 remained in close contact with Bragg's Confederates. The rebuilding process had hardly began before the regulars were called upon to again form line of battle and close with their enemy. By the spring of 1864, the regular battalions would be stronger numerically than they had ever been, but they soon discovered that their manpower, character, and battlefield role had changed much from the previous year.

* * *

Lieutenant Lucius Brown of the 18th Infantry was one of the many wounded officers left behind on the Chickamauga battlefield. The Federal field hospital to which he had been carried on September 20 was captured later that day. The Confederate medical service was overwhelmed with caring for Southern wounded, and Federal injured like Brown received little care. Although Brown had initially thought the half-dozen wounds he acquired during the desperate struggle for Kelly Field were not serious, after lying unattended for five days he was close to death. To relieve Southern surgeons from the burden of caring for enemy soldiers, Bragg allowed Federal troops access to the battlefield during the following weeks to recover Union casualties.

Lieutenant Brown was brought into the Chattanooga lines under one of these flags of truce. He lingered eleven more days before finally succumbing to his wounds, yet another regular officer for whom Chickamauga was the final campaign.[1]

Chickamauga had been the final campaign for all too many of Lieutenant Brown's comrades. Many of these casualties were the new officers who had reported for duty with the Regular Brigade at Murfreesboro, such as Lieutenant Michael B. Fogarty of the 19th Infantry. This Irish-born officer was one of the 19th's original civilian appointees. He served one year on recruiting duty and another as regimental adjutant in Indianapolis and Fort Wayne before joining 1/19th U.S. in the field just prior to Chickamauga. Fogarty was killed in action on September 20, and his conduct left a deep impression on Arthur Carpenter: "Lieut Fogarty was killed, shot through the heart. he was superb, grand. no braver and gallant an Officer, or man was on that field during the battle. no braver man ever fought before, and he was as good as he was brave. he scorned to do a mean act. we feel his loss much."[2] All but three of the 19th Infantry's officers at Chickamauga had been killed, wounded, or captured. Carpenter wrote more about Fogarty than any of the others, a man with whom he had closely worked for less than two months. The record of Michael B. Fogarty today is little more than a few scattered references, but for a short time this lieutenant was a role model for whom subordinates and peers had the utmost respect. The same could be said for Lieutenant Howard Burnham of Battery H. Joshua Fessenden wrote to Burnham's father six days after the battle:

> Your son joined the Battery the 1st of June; closely associated since that time I knew him very intimately. He was a fine officer, always looking out for his men, and much esteemed by them. He fell at his post, gallantly fighting his Battery, against overwhelming numbers of the enemy. ...While he lived he fought his guns well; that they were lost is no fault of his. ...Fifty-one men were killed and wounded, and more than one-third the horses were shot. This will attest the severity of the fire we were under.
>
> It would ill-become me, a stranger to you, to offer any words of sympathy. At such a time as this, mere words are of no avail. Your son died the most glorious of deaths, for he fell fighting his country's battles, his face to the foe. By his death our Regiment loses one of its superior officers, the country a brave and good man.[3]

Whatever impact leaders such as Fogarty and Burnham would have made on the Regular Army had they survived will never be known. The price paid at Chickamauga was indeed steep.

Chattanooga was the northernmost point Federal wounded like Lieutenant Brown could reach for the time being. Bragg cautiously followed Thomas's retreat from Rossville and laid siege to Chattanooga on September 23. With Confederates ringing Chattanooga from Lookout Mountain in the west to the north end of Missionary Ridge in the east, the Army of the Cumberland was bottled up in the town with the Tennessee River at its back. The first order of business for Rosecrans's bloodied army was to ensure Chattanooga's security. Everyone, even teamsters and other rear-echelon personnel, pitched in on improving existing fortifications and constructing additional works. The provost guard of Rousseau's division, C/1/19th U.S., took its turn working the lines with the rest of the Regular Brigade. Sergeant Tarbell and his company mates dubbed their handiwork "Fort P.G."[4]

Besieging Southerners were close by in their own field works. Informal truces between pickets were commonplace on many Civil War battlefields, but such was not the case at Chattanooga for the first few days of the siege. After the intense combat of the previous week, neither side wanted to give the other a moment's rest. Lieutenant Carpenter recalled that picket duty could be dangerous: "We have skirmishes on the picket line most every day. A rebel sharpshooter killed one of our sentinels the other night. one of our men saw the flash and watched for him until morning. as soon as the clear morning appeared, he espied Mr. Rebel sharpshooter and brought him down. some of the rebel pickets came out to get his body. when one of them tumbled over, 'that will do' says our man, and took a chew of tobacco with a feeling of great satisfaction." Jacob Van Zwaluwenburg recorded a similar observation: "The enemy pickets were often posted within gunshot of our pickets, after the battle and shots were exchanged continually, so that a sentry posted in the early morn had to dig a trench to protect himself from the enemys fire and stay there all day."[5]

The hard feelings abated somewhat by the beginning of October. Carpenter then noted that the sentinels "exchange papers, and even go down between the lines and have a social talk about matters & things, make agreements not to shoot each other when on guard." With peace between the pickets, the main hazard became enemy

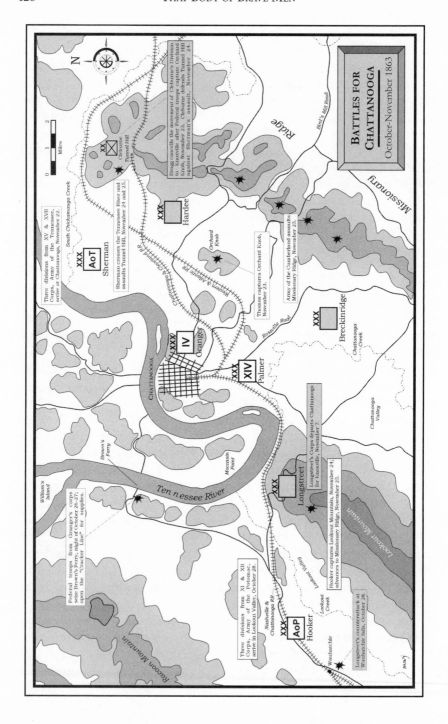

BATTLES FOR
CHATTANOOGA
October–November 1863

Bragg cancels the movement of Cleburne's Division to Knoxville after Federal troops capture Orchard Knob, November 23. Cleburne defends Tunnel Hill against Sherman's assault, November 24.

Three divisions from XV & XVII Corps, Army of the Tennessee, arrive at Chattanooga, November 22.

Sherman crosses the Tennessee River and assaults Tunnel Hill, November 24 and 25.

Thomas captures Orchard Knob, November 23.

Army of the Cumberland assaults Missionary Ridge, November 25.

Longstreet's Corps departs Chattanooga for Knoxville, November 7.

Federal troops from Granger's corps seize Brown's Ferry, night of October 26–27; open the "Cracker Line" for supplies.

Three divisions from XI & XII Corps, Army of the Potomac, arrive in Lookout Valley, October 28.

Hooker captures Lookout Mountain, November 24; advances to Missionary Ridge, November 25.

Longstreet's counterattack at Wauhatchie fails, October 28.

artillery fire. A heavy field gun on Lookout Mountain was the only piece that could reach the regulars' part of the line. Carpenter recalled that this weapon occasionally generated some excitement, if not many casualties:

> Our brigade lies right around Gen Rousseau's Hd Qrs. Gen Rousseau & Gen King have their Head Quarters in two houses, which with our camp all around, presents a very conspicuous sight to the rebels. they commenced throwing their shells at Gen Rousseau's house about noon when the men were all in line to answer roll call. the first shell came over and struck right in the centre of our camp a little to the left of Gen Rousseau it was a percussion shell, and stuck on a rock and exploded beautifully. Very fortunately no one was injured. the next shot passed right over Gen Rousseau's house and struck right in front of the door of Gen King's house, about 4 feet behind a man who was carrying water, as the shell struck the ground he fell water and all, kicked with his legs to see if he was alive and then got up and walked off.[6]

With the enemy controlling Chattanooga's river and rail approaches, the Army of the Cumberland's lifeline consisted of a narrow, twisting road up and over Walden's Ridge north of town. Desperately needed supplies and reinforcements had to travel more than fifty miles on this difficult route from the Federal depots at Bridgeport and Stevenson. Only a trickle got through, but part of that trickle was a battalion of regulars. On October 2, Major John R. Edie reported to the Regular Brigade's camp at the head of a begrimed and exhausted column of troops: the 2nd Battalion, 15th U.S. Infantry. Their journey had been a long one, covering more than 400 miles by river steamer, railroad, and foot in just less than two weeks.

When Oliver Shepherd took command of the 15th U.S. in May 1863, he knew that the Regular Brigade would put 2/15th's services to good use; it would certainly be a better use of regular manpower than having the battalion continue with its garrison duty in Grant's Department of the Tennessee. Shepherd started working through the red tape and requested an assignment to the Army of the Cumberland for Edie's Memphis-based troops. General Grant was understandably reluctant to part with a battalion of regulars (he had only three in the Army of the Tennessee, the others being 1/13th U.S. and a small contingent of the 1st Infantry), but finally relented. On September 20, the day King's regulars were defending Kelly Field,

2/15th U.S. boarded a northbound steamer at the Memphis docks. The craft docked at Louisville five days later and Edie's troops started toward the front via the Louisville & Nashville Railroad. The battalion arrived at Bridgeport on September 28, the starting point for its difficult overland march to Chattanooga. For most of the trip, Edie's command accompanied a huge mule train of more than 800 wagons, Rosecrans's most ambitious attempt to force supplies into Chattanooga. The regular battalion separated from the train on the morning of October 2, taking a more treacherous but shorter footpath over Walden's Ridge for the final leg of the journey. Moving along that separate route spared 2/15th U.S. from the rest of the column's fate. Confederate Major General Joseph Wheeler crossed the Tennessee River north of Chattanooga at the head of the Army of Tennessee's Cavalry Corps on September 30, setting out on a raid of Federal communications. His first prize was the wagon train strung out along Walden's Ridge. The raiders captured the entire train and destroyed what they could not carry. Edie's battalion avoided the confrontation, but the unit's equipment was put to the torch with the rest of the convoy. The battalion quartermasters escorting the baggage, Lieutenant Charles Lord and nineteen soldiers, were captured.[7]

Edie's tired troops limped into Chattanooga with little more than what they could carry. "Everything belonging to my Officers was destroyed by the Rebels," Edie complained to the department adjutant a few weeks later. "Since our arrival here we have been compelled to trespass upon the kindness of friends for all the necessaries of life, and as the things we need can not be bought or otherwise procured here, I know of no other way of supplying our wants." At least the battalion was well supplied with ammunition. A few days after venting his equipment complaint, Major Edie reported that his unit "has been supplied with a sufficient amount of ammunition, each enlisted man having forty round in his Cartridge Box and there is a surplus of 5,000 rounds remaining."[8] Carrying live cartridges was a new experience for the battalion. Edie informed department headquarters that it would be a good idea to put some of that surplus to use:

> Head Quarters 2d Batt. 15th Infy.
> Chattanooga, Tenn.
> Nov 20th 1863

Lieut. Col C. Goddard
 A.A. Genl
 Department of the Cumberland
Colonel

I have the honor to request that permission be given me to practice the men of this Command, for a few days, at Target firing. They have had some practice in firing with blank cartridges, but have always been stationed at points where Target firing was strictly prohibited. I respectfully suggest that if the permission be given, it would render this Battalion much more efficient in action than it would be without such practice.

I have the honor to be
Very Respectfully
Your obt servt

JOHN R. EDIE
Major 15th Infy
Com'g Batt.[9]

While Edie's troops may not have been skilled marksmen, the Regular Brigade still desperately needed the 198 officers and men of 2/15th U.S. who survived the trek from Bridgeport. Even after the return to duty of lightly wounded troops and a few others who had been listed as missing in action after Chickamauga, King's battalions still counted less than 800 men in ranks at the end of September. The battalions of the 16th and 19th Regulars were so low in numbers that King combined them into a single battalion of four composite companies, commanded by the sturdy R.E.A. Crofton of the 16th Infantry.[10]

After the decimation of the Regular Brigade's officer corps at Chickamauga, the question of who would lead the battalions had to be addressed once again. There were plenty of officers holding regular commissions who had not yet experienced field service with their regiments. General King sent numerous requests to the War Department to have at least some of them sent to Chattanooga:

Head Quarters 2nd Brigade
1st Division 14th A.C.
Chattanooga Dec 29th 1863

Gen L. Thomas
 Adjt Gen U.S.A.
 Washington D.C.

General

I have the honor herewith to forward the names (with rank, regiment, whereabouts, etc. etc.) of officers, belonging to the different regiments of Regular Infantry serving in this Department, whose services are required to render the Battalions under my command efficient and useful.

The allowance of Field Officers to each one of the new Regiments is such that it would give to the four regiments serving in this Brigade a total of twenty. I think that out of the above number, I should have at least one to command each of my Battalions, but if so large a number cannot be spared, from the arduous duties they are now rendering the Government in the cities of the north, I would respectfully request that I be allowed one to each Detachment of two Battalions.

I have at present, only one Field Officer serving in the regular regiments of my Brigade, with two more making a total of three, I would have a Field Officer as above to each Detachment.

In one of the battalions I have five Second Lieutenants for duty and four out of the five are commanding companies.

Some of the officers named on the enclosed papers have never seen any field service, their companies being commanded by Lieutenants. I think unless it is intended to have two distinct sets of officers, one to undergo all the privations and hardships of the service in the field, the other to do fancy and light duty near and at their homes, that the officers now absent...be ordered to their respective commands at once, so that officers who are now and have been on duty at the front, since the organization of their respective regiments, may be allowed to see their friends, at least once more. All that I ask is simple justice, that those who have nearly worn themselves out in the field, may be allowed a little rest.

In conclusion I have to state that unless I get more officers, my battalions of regulars will not come up to the standard. One officer to a company is not sufficient.

I am General,

Very respectfully Your obt servant,

JOHN H. KING
Brig Gen commanding[11]

A number of regular officers were ordered to Chattanooga during the winter of 1864-1865, but most of them had already served many months in the field; those regulars who had managed to get themselves placed on detached service early in the war seemed untouchable. In a way, the Regular Brigade now benefited from its officer exodus of the previous spring, for those reassignments had preserved a core of competent leaders who otherwise might have ended up buried in northern Georgia or languishing alongside Henry Freeman in Libby Prison. Having forged personal ties to their men and units in the field, these old hands eventually felt the tug of regimental pride pulling them back into ranks. Officers such as Frederick Phisterer, William Fetterman, Jacob Kline, William Bisbee, John Henry Knight, and Edgar Kellogg all reported to Chattanooga during the coming months. Captain Andrew S. Burt of the 18th Infantry, on staff duty the entire war thus far, requested duty with his regiment shortly after Chickamauga and relinquished his post as assistant inspector general on Rosecrans's staff. Captain George Smith welcomed the assignment of this competent leader, placing Burt in command of Company B, 1st Battalion. Lieutenant Edmund D. Spooner of the 5th Artillery, a veteran of many campaigns with the Army of the Potomac, was assigned to Battery H to replace the late Howard Burnham.

The assignment of these officers did not fill all the empty billets, so the usual practice of commissioning proven sergeants was resorted to again during the last months of 1863. Prominent among this latest batch was Sergeant Major John U. Gill of 2/18th U.S., who had served as the Regular Brigade's sergeant major from the unit's formation. He donned lieutenant straps on October 31. The Prussian first sergeant of B/1/16th, Peter Joseph Cönzler, had been recommended for a commission after his good service at Stones River. The approved paperwork finally came back from the War Department and the new lieutenant took command of F/1/16th on October 29. First Sergeant Ezra P. Ewers of E/1/19th U.S. was also commissioned in October. A veteran of Shiloh, Stones River, Hoover's Gap, and Chickamauga, Ewers embarked on a commissioned career at Chattanooga that would last into the twentieth century. During the next forty years, he would rise to command the 10th U.S. Infantry and also serve as a brigadier general of volunteers during the Spanish-American War.[12]

Another familiar face reported for duty with the regulars at Chattanooga in early October 1863—Captain Frank Guenther. While commanding Battery I/5th U.S. Artillery in Washington during the summer and autumn of 1863, Guenther had been chafing for a chance to return to Battery H. Shortly before Chickamauga, he and Captain Kensel agreed to try to switch commands. "I have been connected with Battery 'H' 5th Arty during the whole of its service in the field," Guenther wrote the War Department on September 11, "and have commanded it the greater part of the time. My service with the battery has been of such a nature that I desire exceedingly to retain Command of it." The adjutant general approved the switch on September 17 and a few weeks later a travel-worn but happy Captain Guenther arrived in Chattanooga.[13]

Private Charles V. Bogart's uncle, Private Trine Swick, was killed at Chickamauga. The 18th Infantryman wrote to his own mother with the sad news of her brother's death on September 28. He tried to cheer her up by relating a rumor about the Regular Brigade's next move: "the word is now that this Brigade is a going north to recruit. in the brigade there is a bout 300 or 350 left where there ought to be 4000 or 5000." But the Regular Brigade's manpower shortage was not unique. Five months of campaigning in 1863 had reduced many of the Army of the Cumberland's regiments to mere shadows of full-strength units, and another major reorganization took place in the weeks following Chickamauga. The centerpiece of the reorganization was the breaking up of XX and XXI Corps, and Negley's division of Thomas's corps, units whose commanders had fled the Chickamauga battlefield perhaps a bit too hastily on September 20. Some of their brigades were consolidated with the Reserve Corps to form the new IV Corps. Others were sent to the XIV Corps. Three regiments from Colonel Timothy R. Stanley's brigade of Negley's old division were grafted into the Regular Brigade and the consolidated unit was designated the 2nd Brigade, 1st Division, XIV Corps. Joining the regulars were the 11th Michigan, 19th Illinois, and 69th Ohio, veteran organizations that had all fought well at Chickamauga. John King retained brigade command and divided the unit into two "demi-brigades," one volunteer, the other regular. Major Edie took charge of the regular battalions. Captain William S. McManus, a New Yorker commanding B/2/15th U.S., moved up to take Edie's place in command of the 15th Infantry's 2nd Battalion. William L. Stoughton commanded the state regiments. A former U.S. District Attorney, Stoughton was colonel of the 11th Michigan and during the previous two years had developed into a talented, respected commander. After Colonel Stanley was wounded at Chickamauga on September 20, Stoughton played a key role in the struggle for Horseshoe Ridge while temporarily commanding Stanley's brigade.[14]

The Army of the Cumberland's senior leaders likewise experienced many changes of assignment at Chattanooga, a general's performance at Chickamauga being a determining factor on whether he remained or was sent elsewhere. Alexander McCook and Thomas Crittenden had never really performed up to par as corps commanders. After Chickamauga they were shelved for the remainder of the war. Gordon Granger, who performed well in command of the Reserve Corps at the September battle, took charge of the IV Corps. Three division commanders and eleven brigade commanders also made their exits from the Army of the Cumberland after Chickamauga, as did William Rosecrans. From the spring of 1863 onwards, "Old Rosy" had not been highly thought of in Washington. Chickamauga did much to seal his fate, and after he sent alarming messages to Washington hinting that Chattanooga might have to be abandoned, Secretary of War Stanton authorized Grant, commanding the new Military Division of the Mississippi, to fire Rosecrans and replace him with George Thomas. Grant did so on October 19.[15] Thomas's elevation to army command was welcomed by many of his soldiers, including the 18th Infantry's Captain Henry Haymond, who in a letter home explained that in the aftermath of Chickamauga, Thomas was the man of the hour:

> To Genl. Geo. H. Thomas the Army of the Cumberland owes its safety. He remained on the field until late at night and conducted the retreat in a manner becoming the great and able man that he is, while others higher in authority were in Chattanooga, nine miles away by 4 o'clock P.M. and before the hardest fighting had commenced. Genl. Thomas has always commanded the respect and confidence of the Army to a greater extent than any man in it. Today he is its idol. There is nothing about him to create enthusiasm, but there is everything to inspire a confidence that he will not make a mistake. He is quiet almost taciturn in his manner, says but little but is pleasant and affable, when addressed. He is a soldier—Rosecrans in not, but is a seeker of popular favor.[16]

Lovell Rousseau was the logical choice to succeed Thomas as commander of the XIV Corps. The Kentuckian had much in his favor: he was the Army of the Cumberland's senior division commander, had always performed well in battle, and was revered by his men. Unfortunately, Charles A. Dana disagreed with these facts. A journalist by profession, Dana was an assistant secretary of war and confidant of Secretary Stanton. Dana was sent to hot spots in the war to provide information to the War Department on Union generals. He had been with the Army of the Cumberland since the Middle Tennessee Campaign and for some reason disliked Rousseau, calling him an "ass of eminent gifts" and reporting that the XIV Corps would be better served by virtually any other general. Rousseau's soft stance on slavery did not endear him to Washington radicals. Secretary Stanton also had an unfavorable opinion of Rousseau, formed during the latter's visit to Washington the previous August. Stanton denied the Kentuckian command of a corps but did not stop there. He removed Rousseau from the Army of the Cumberland. Rousseau was assigned to Nashville as commander of the District of Middle Tennessee, an administrative posting that effectively ended Rousseau's military career. Major General John M. Palmer, a division commander with average credentials from the defunct XX Corps, took over the XIV Corps on November 12. Rousseau, a self-educated soldier who had evolved into a consummate professional, swallowed his pride and left without protest.[17]

Rousseau wanted the Regular Brigade to accompany him to Nashville and serve in the city's garrison. King's troops were all for it, but General Thomas kept the battalions in Chattanooga. On the morning of November 13, the regulars of the division provost guard fell in and presented arms. Rousseau inspected Captain Williams's C/1/19th U.S. for a final time and then said farewell:

> A year and a half ago I succeeded the gallant and patriotic General O.M. Mitchel in the command of the third Division—now the first, of the fourteenth Army Corps.
>
> In yielding up my command for one in another field of duty, I feel that I am severing one of the strongest ties that can exist between friends and brothers in arms.
>
> In taking leave of those who have dared danger and death by my side,—who, without murmur, have borne the "pitiless peltings" of the elements, and bravely breasted the storm of battle,—I must be allowed to say, I feel honored in having commanded you.
>
> I leave you with regret—with heartfelt sorrow—for there is not an officer nor soldier of my command to whom I do not feel grateful for his gallantry and soldierly bearing. In the future, as in the past, I know your services and your chivalric deeds will challenge the admiration of your countrymen; and I shall exult then, as now, in the recollection that once you were called "Rousseau's Division."
>
> Good-by, my brave comrades in arms, and may God bless you![18]

With scarcely a dry eye in the ranks, the general mounted up and departed. Except for brief service at the head of an ad-hoc cavalry division during the Atlanta Campaign, and later during the 1864 Confederate foray into middle Tennessee, Rousseau's days in the field were over.[19]

John King would have moved up to take command of Rousseau's division under normal circumstances, but there were plenty of generals senior to him lurking about Chattanooga, hoping for a job after the dust settled on the reorganization. General Thomas selected Brigadier General Richard W. Johnson to replace Rousseau. Johnson had capably led a division of McCook's old corps at Chickamauga, a unit that had been attached to Thomas's command for the fighting at Kelly Field. The old 2nd Cavalryman was pleased with his assignment to command of the XIV Corps' premier division, as were many of the regulars. Arthur Carpenter commented: "we all regretted the departure of Gen. Rousseau, but Johnson is a good general." Experienced commanders also took charge of the other two divisions of Palmer's corps. Absalom Baird was justly rewarded for his Chickamauga performance and received the corps' 2nd Division as his own. Brigadier General Jefferson C. Davis, who had commanded a division in McCook's corps during the recent campaign, led Palmer's 3rd division.[20]

The prospect of giving orders to John King made Richard Johnson uncomfortable. When Johnson had been a wet-behind-the-ears lieutenant reporting for duty in Texas back in 1851, the officer he reported to for orders had been none other than Captain John King of the 1st U.S. Infantry. Johnson recalled that at Chattanooga King cleared up the new division commander's apprehensions shortly after the change of command:

> I was appointed a brigadier-general before [King] was, and hence in the volunteer service I was his senior and entitled to command over him. I called on him at once and expressed my regret that we were brought together under such circumstances. It is due to him to say that he regarded the final triumph of our arms of much more importance than any question of rank, and he was willing and glad to serve in any capacity where he could be of service to his country. His ready compliance with all instructions from division headquarters, and the gallant and skilful management of his command showed him to be a true soldier in every sense of the term. So the fear I had of the possibility of a lukewarm support on his part proved

unfounded, and our official intercourse was as pleasant as our social intercourse had been in years gone by. This service with King is one of the pleasant memories of the war.[21]

The removal of Rosecrans and Rousseau signaled a shift in status for the regulars. These two officers had been instrumental in the formation of the Regular Brigade and in forging the regulars' special role in the Army of the Cumberland. After their departure, the regulars found themselves without a high-ranking advocate in their immediate chain of command. George Thomas knew the value of regular troops and of what they were capable, but after his promotion to army command he appears to have paid less attention to them. He realized as well as anyone that sending the regulars to the hottest part of a battlefield time after time had resulted in his having regular battalions that now consisted of just a few score lucky survivors. Since regular units were short of manpower to begin with and the prospects for rebuilding them with quality recruits were dim, continuing that practice in the future would result in the regulars being so weak that they would no longer be able to perform a significant role. As a career regular officer himself, Thomas realized that fighting the regulars into extinction would not serve the nation's long-term interests. He also realized that many of his volunteers were now well-trained veterans themselves, much different from the armed mob he had commanded in Kentucky during 1861. To bring the war to a successful conclusion required many thousands of competently led and motivated troops, not just a single elite brigade of regulars. The regular battalions in the Army of the Cumberland would continue to have a reputation for being dependable, experienced organizations, but there were now many units claiming such status. While the regulars would no longer serve as the army's special reserve force, they were still an important part of Thomas's command. He did not want them to sit out the war with Lovell Rousseau in Nashville.

Colonel Benjamin Scribner was glad General King and the regulars remained in Chattanooga. Scribner had led the 38th Indiana in the early days of the war and commanded a brigade in Rousseau's division at Chickamauga. Three regiments from Negley's division had been added to Scribner's brigade after the battle, with Brigadier General William P. Carlin in command of the combined unit in Johnson's division. Like many volunteers early in the war, Scribner had been skeptical about the regulars and their professional officer corps: "Then they were impatient, irritable and abusive, and if profanity was included in the course of study at West Point, I am sure that the Army of the Cumberland had their share of the prize scholars in this branch." After a few campaigns, Scribner came to respect the regulars for both their fighting abilities and their knowledge of military matters. While building fortifications at Chattanooga, Scribner was ordered to send to division headquarters a 200-man detail fully equipped with axes and shovels. Such tools were in short supply. "Had the earth been demanded," the colonel exclaimed, "I would have been able to respond to it as I was to fill the requisition for the required implements." Scribner went to the right man for advice: "In my dilemma I consulted Gen. King, whose advice at once relieved my anxiety. He said, [']just take the blank form and make a requisition upon the division quartermaster for the implements called for, which in all probability he will not have on hand, but have him indorse that fact upon the paper, and you will thus have something to show if any explanations are needed for your failure to obey the order.['] In matters like this and concerning boards of survey, I was kindly assisted to understand the army regulations by friends among the regular brigade."[22]

More than tools were hard to find in Chattanooga that autumn. With just a pitiful amount of supplies making it over Walden's Ridge, the Army of the Cumberland was in poor shape. Rosecrans's men were shabby enough after marching from Nashville to Chattanooga with a two-day stop at Chickamauga. "I am about the hardest looking case this morning you ever saw," Henry Haymond wrote his father on September 25. "My boots and blouse have not been off for six days, and I scarcely ever wash my face. I have no blanket but sleep soundly at night in the dust." Most serious was the lack of provisions. Much of Rosecrans's army had been on short rations since the retreat from Chickamauga. By the middle of October, the situation was grim. A hungry Jacob Van Zwaluwenburg recalled: "Often the rations given me to last three days I could have eaten all in one meal. I often went to the Hospital slaughter yard, and once secured a hoof as part of the waste. I took it to our tent, cut it up fine, stewed it a long time, ground a cracker up fine, stirred that in which made us a good meal."[23]

Even when Confederate cavalry did not harass the Federal wagon trains moving between Stevenson and Chattanooga, the journey was still hazardous. Lieutenant Daniel Benham, quartermaster of the

18th Infantry, led a train of twenty-one empty wagons out of Chattanooga on the afternoon of October 14. It took the column a full week to traverse Walden's Ridge and cross the Sequatchie River. Upon arrival at Stevenson, Benham reported the arrival of the train to the provost marshal of the depot. The lieutenant was warned not to attempt the return trip with full wagons unless the mule teams pulling the vehicles were doubled to eight animals each. Benham searched in vain for eighty-four additional mules, finally deciding to abandon ten of his wagons and use the spare mules to double the other teams. After loading up with provisions, the diminished train was on the road back to Chattanooga on October 24. Benham reported that the journey was difficult: "[I] abandoned one wagon in the Sequatchie Valley, it having two wheels broken, and otherwise damaged. Lost quite a number of mules, they having died on the roads." The teamsters had to lighten the loads to compensate for the lost mules. The train straggled into the camp of King's brigade on November 1, ten partially filled wagons instead of the expected twenty-one full loads. "we are getting along fine except for grub," Private Bogart wrote four days later. "that is pretty hard to get. there is 100s of horses dying every day. the Battery in our Brigade has lost most all of its horses for the want of something to eat."[24]

While Benham's convoy was making its way to and from Stevenson, a soldier was being transported to Chattanooga courtesy of a different wagon train: Private John A. Mallory of B/3/18th U.S., the regular who had been convicted of fleeing the battlefield at Stones River. Mallory had served his required six months' confinement in a Nashville military prison, at the conclusion of which he was ordered back to his unit for execution of the final part of his sentence. He made the bumpy ride over Walden's Ridge in mid-October in the back of a wagon with a ball and chain around his ankle. On the morning of October 27, Captain Haymond formed the 18th Infantry's 2nd Battalion into a single line of two ranks. Private Mallory, in full kit and with a now too-large hat perched atop his freshly-shaven head, was posted in front of the unit. Adjutant John Lind read aloud Mallory's crime as Sergeant Major John Gill marched up to the prisoner. Gill relieved Mallory of his rifle, and also stripped him of waist belt, bayonet, and cartridge box. The sergeant major knocked the cap off Mallory's head and cut the four eagle-adorned buttons from the prisoner's sack coat. After Mallory had been divested of all the trappings of a soldier, Captain

Haymond ordered the battalion's front rank to march forward three paces and face about. With the battalion's drummers playing a long roll, Mallory slowly walked between the two ranks. As he came abreast of each two-man file, the soldiers executed an about face and turned their backs on him. Mallory's "Drumming Out" marked the end of his service in the Regular Army. He left Chattanooga that same day, a Civil War veteran who for the rest of his days probably did not speak very much about his wartime experiences.[25]

* * *

The War Department was rushing reinforcements to Chattanooga, a contingent of Sherman's Army of the Tennessee from Mississippi (four divisions from the XV and XVII Corps) and also the XI and XII Corps from the Army of the Potomac under Major General Joseph Hooker. Without a reliable supply line these additional troops would be of little use. George Thomas began fixing the dire supply situation shortly after assuming command. Inheriting a plan that Rosecrans had already approved, in the early morning darkness of October 26 Thomas launched a daring river-borne assault on Brown's Ferry west of Chattanooga. Simultaneously, Hooker's troops crossed the Tennessee River at Bridgeport and seized Lookout Valley. The two forces linked up west of Lookout Mountain, throwing back a weak counterattack at Wauhatchie during the night of October 28. With the capture of Brown's Ferry, Federal quartermasters could avoid the treacherous route over Walden's Ridge. The small steamers *Paint Rock* and *Chattanooga* were hauling supplies from Bridgeport to Brown's Ferry by the end of the month. From there, provisions went by way of a short wagon road across Moccasin Point and over a pontoon bridge the rest of the way into Chattanooga. The "Cracker Line" was secure.

Ulysses S. Grant supervised these operations in person. The newly appointed commander of the Military Division of the Mississippi, responsible for the Union's war effort in the Western Theater, arrived in Chattanooga on October 23. As soon as Sherman's troops arrived, Grant planned to attack Bragg and lift the siege. His plan had Sherman attacking the enemy's right flank at Tunnel Hill while most of Hooker's troops moved from Lookout Valley through Chattanooga to reinforce Thomas. Grant initially planned only a supporting role for Thomas's Army of the Cumberland. Only after Sherman had crushed Bragg's flank would

Thomas move against Bragg's center along Missionary Ridge. The mission of Thomas's army was sound in a military sense, but Grant was at least partially motivated by other concerns. He had a low opinion of the Army of the Cumberland's morale and fighting abilities in the aftermath of its defeat at Chickamauga. In addition, Grant's personal relations with Thomas had been only as cordial as professional decorum dictated ever since Henry Halleck briefly replaced Grant with Thomas as commander of the Army of the Tennessee during the Corinth Campaign.

While the Union forces in Chattanooga waited for Sherman's column to arrive, the regular battalions bid farewell to Captain Guenther, Lieutenant Spooner, and Battery H. A number of batteries in Thomas's army were attached to units slated to attack Tunnel Hill, the 5th U.S. Artillerymen among them. During a subsequent overhaul of the artillery organization in the Army of the Cumberland during early 1864, Battery H was assigned to the regular artillery brigade of the Nashville garrison. Guenther's battery would remain in middle Tennessee for the duration of the war.[26]

* * *

Frederick Phisterer hung on to the swaying freight car for all he was worth, the icy wind of the predawn darkness chilling him to the bone. The 18th Infantry lieutenant wanted to get to Bridgeport as soon as possible, and the first thing heading south on November 25 was a fully loaded cargo train. Phisterer had to ride on top. He had spent the previous night sleeping on the floor of the depot at Decherd Station, scrounging up a few stray apples for breakfast early the next morning. His Spartan room and board were a definite change from what had been his fare for the previous seven months. Since April 1863, Phisterer had been detailed on a staff assignment at Camp Thomas. The lieutenant's administrative duties ended on November 7 with orders to proceed to Chattanooga for duty with his regiment. The train pulled into Bridgeport at daybreak. Stiff and cold, Phisterer jumped down from his frigid perch and searched for a way to complete the final leg of his long journey. Luck was with him, as a steamer at the Bridgeport landing was about to depart on a trip upriver to Brown's Ferry. Hopping aboard, Phisterer relaxed for a few hours as the boat churned up the Tennessee. It was the only relaxation he would receive on an otherwise eventful day.[27]

The day prior to Phisterer's arrival, Grant had unleashed the attack on Bragg. Although the offensive had thus far not unfolded exactly as planned, it would eventually generate spectacular results. On November 22, Federal observers noticed enemy activity that seemed to indicate Southern troops were leaving Chattanooga. This was Cleburne's and Buckner's Divisions beginning a movement to reinforce Longstreet, then operating miles to the northeast near Knoxville, but the Northerners could only discern that some sort of withdrawal was taking place. Rumors reached General Grant the next day to the effect that the Confederates at Chattanooga were calling off the siege and retreating southward. Worried that Bragg's army might withdraw prior to Sherman's attack, which would finally get under way the next day, Grant ordered Thomas to conduct a strong reconnaissance toward the center of the Confederate line along Missionary Ridge to confirm or deny the rumors. George Thomas employed almost half of the Army of the Cumberland on this "reconnaissance" and seized a low, craggy eminence about half way between the lines known as Orchard Knob. The operation verified that the enemy was still present, but unfortunately also spurred the Confederate high command into action. Alarmed that the seizure of Orchard Knob might be the preliminary step of a larger offensive, Bragg recalled Cleburne's Division and held it in readiness to respond to the next Federal move. Nervous Confederate generals also began to think that perhaps an attack on Missionary Ridge would take place soon. The ridge's natural strength had lulled Bragg into thinking the Federals would never contemplate attacking it. The Southerners had not even constructed significant fortifications on this high ground during the two months they had been staring down at the Federal army in Chattanooga. They belatedly started doing so on the evening of November 23.[28]

Attacking Missionary Ridge was indeed part of Grant's overall plan, but an assault there would take place only after Sherman's command had seized Tunnel Hill and turned Bragg's right flank. Sherman's operation got underway prior to daybreak on November 24, a day marked by fog, low clouds, and intermittent rain. Three divisions from the Army of the Tennessee, with Davis's division of Palmer's corps nearby in support, crossed the Tennessee near the mouth of South Chickamauga Creek, a move that caught Bragg completely off guard. Instead of immediately moving inland to press his advantage, however, Sherman had his forces advance only a short distance from the river and dig in. He was well short of Tunnel Hill, the delay providing Bragg enough time to shift Pat Cleburne's crack troops to oppose Sherman's advance. When Sherman pushed his own men forward early in the afternoon, Cleburne stopped them dead in their tracks.[29]

While no progress was made on the Federal left, the right was a different story. Grant at first had envisioned only a limited role for Hooker in the overall Federal plan. A few days before the attack, Grant had detached from Hooker the XI Corps (three divisions under Major General Oliver O. Howard), moved these troops into Chattanooga, and placed them under George Thomas's immediate command. The only units that remained under Hooker were a single division of the XII Corps and a small division temporarily attached to Hooker from Granger's corps (two brigades under Brigadier General Charles Cruft). Events that took place the day prior to Sherman's attack on Tunnel Hill caused Grant to recast Hooker's role in the upcoming battle. First, the Confederates floated down-river some heavy rafts that seriously damaged the pontoon bridge at Brown's Ferry. Heavy autumn rains had raised the Tennessee River sharply and put the bridge under enormous strain; the impact of the enemy rafts broke the pontoon span on the afternoon of November 23. Stranded in Lookout Valley with Hooker was Brigadier General Peter J. Osterhaus's division of the XV Corps, one of Sherman's divisions that had just marched up from Bridgeport. Also on November 23, Thomas's signalers intercepted and decoded a message from Confederate Major General Carter L. Stevenson, whose division was responsible for defending Lookout Mountain, that stated a Federal attack was expected against the Confederate left. Since the enemy was watching the Lookout area closely, Grant ordered Hooker's larger-than-expected command to make a demonstration against Lookout Mountain in support of Sherman's simultaneous attack on the opposite flank. Hooker, who had long wanted to push the opposition off that dominating piece of terrain, seized the initiative and turned the demonstration into a full-scale attempt to capture Lookout Mountain.[30]

The regulars had a close up view of the struggle for Lookout, having been on picket duty in the valley east of the mountain since the morning of November 22. Colonel Marshall F. Moore of the 69th Ohio was in temporary command of King's brigade at this time, John King being sick after contracting one of the many diseases infesting Chattanooga's squalid camps. The brigade's regulars and volunteers covered the entire XIV Corps front, from the mouth of

Chattanooga Creek to a position just short of Orchard Knob. The regulars manned the western portion of the line near the creek, at the base of Lookout Mountain. Despite the intense fighting going on all around, on November 24 the picket lines were relatively peaceful. That evening, as the struggle for Lookout Mountain was reaching its culmination, Private Jacob Van Zwaluwenburg went down to Chattanooga Creek to fill his canteen. A Confederate sentinel appeared on the far side. "Hello Yank," the Southerner said, "how do you like this war?" The Dutchmen replied that he wished it were over, a point upon which both men agreed. Van Zwaluwenburg recalled that they had "quite a talk about the wrongs of war and agreed that all war was wrong." As the two enemies parted, they heard the dull sounds of firing drifting down from above. Glancing up at Lookout Mountain's towering eminence, the Confederate told the regular "they can never take that position" and then disappeared into the gloom.[31]

Contrary to the Confederate picket's claim, as dusk gathered on November 24, Hooker seized Lookout Mountain in the celebrated "Battle Above the Clouds." The next day, Grant ordered Sherman to renew the left-flank attack on Tunnel Hill while Hooker was to continue rolling up Bragg's right. Neither force made much progress during the morning of November 25. To jumpstart the stalled offensive, during the early afternoon Grant ordered Thomas to advance the Army of the Cumberland toward Missionary Ridge.

Lieutenant Phisterer disembarked at Brown's Ferry a few hours before Thomas received the attack order. The lieutenant made his way across Moccasin Point and through Chattanooga. He walked to the regulars' camp, which was deserted except for some troops on detail, and ran into Lieutenant Dan Benham, the 18th Infantry quartermaster. Benham greeted his old friend warmly, but did not have time for an extended chat. He explained that the brigade had been on picket duty for the past three days and had been recalled a few hours ago. It was now formed in line-of-battle and it appeared that an attack would take place soon. Benham, Commissary Sergeant Joseph Livsey, and Quartermaster Sergeant John W. Price were about to head for the front. Phisterer quickly drank some coffee, mounted a borrowed horse, and galloped alongside Benham down the Chattanooga-Rossville Road.[32]

They were riding toward the right flank of Thomas's battle line. Two divisions from Granger's corps, Wood's and Sheridan's, held

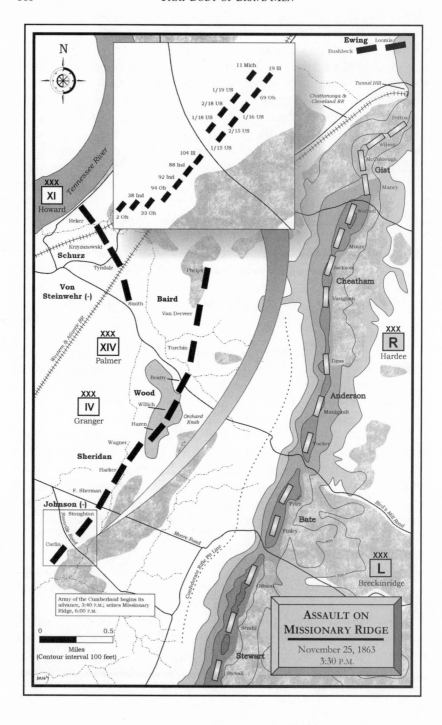

Army of the Cumberland begins its
advance, 3:40 P.M.; seizes Missionary
Ridge, 6:00 P.M.

0   0.5

Miles
(Contour interval 100 feet)

ASSAULT ON
MISSIONARY RIDGE

November 25, 1863
3:30 P.M.

the center while Baird's division of Palmer's corps, which had been sent to Sherman's aid but had recently been recalled, held the left. Brigadier General Richard W. Johnson's division was on the right with two brigades in line (his final brigade, Brigadier General John C. Starkweather's, had been retained as a reserve in the Chattanooga fortifications). Johnson arrayed his men in line-of-battle a few miles outside of town during the early afternoon, facing Missionary Ridge from a narrow patch of woods astride the Rossville Road. Brigadier General Carlin's brigade was on the right, with the mixed brigade of regulars and volunteers on the left. King's brigade changed commanders while waiting to for the attack to commence. Colonel William L. Stoughton of the 11th Michigan, the senior officer in the brigade next to General King, had been absent for the past few weeks, but reported for duty just as Colonel Moore moved the brigade into line adjacent to Carlin. Stoughton took over, with Colonel Moore taking command of the brigade's left wing of volunteer regiments. In the right wing, Major John Edie formed the regular battalions with the front rank consisting of the 15th Infantry battalions on the right and the 16th Infantry on the left. The 18th and 19th Infantry formed Edie's second line. The regulars were waiting for word to advance as a small group of horsemen approached from the right rear. Benham, Phisterer, and the two staff sergeants dismounted near the 18th Infantry. Captain George Smith, commanding the 18th Infantry Detachment, was happy to see Phisterer again and assigned the lieutenant to Company A of Captain Haymond's 2nd Battalion. The new company commander barely had time to say hello to his troops. About ten minutes after Phisterer's arrival, six cannon on Orchard Knob were fired in succession, the Army of the Cumberland's signal to advance. An aide from General Johnson galloped over to Stoughton's Brigade and relayed a message to its commander. "The general commanding sends his compliments," the staff officer informed the Michigan colonel, "and directs you to charge to the hill."[33]

The Federals faced a daunting task. Missionary Ridge loomed ahead, enemy infantry and artillery dotting its crest 500 feet above the Tennessee River flood plain. Additional Confederates were dug in at the base of the slope. Between the opposing lines stretched about a mile of open or sparsely covered ground. Ahead of the regulars on Missionary Ridge was the Confederate division of Major General Alexander P. Stewart, which included many of the Tennessee regiments that had fought so furiously against the regulars in the cedars at Stones River. With the exception of the recently arrived troops of 2/15th U.S. and a few others, all the regulars were veterans of Chickamauga. There was no doubt in their minds about what was in store: a whirlwind of shot and shell cutting through their formation, many comrades being hit before they ever reached the ridge.

The regulars and the rest of the Federal army at Chattanooga were about to find out that the Confederate position was not as strong as it appeared. The fortifications on the ridge were not well planned and the disposition of the troops manning them bordered on ludicrous. Bragg kept half his infantry in rifle pits at the base of the ridge, ordering them to fire a single volley if attacked and then fall back on the main line at the top. It was not clear to anyone what good this would do, and the troops manning the lower line were unsure about what was expected of them. Cold, hungry, tired, and confused (in terms of logistics, the Confederate troops surrounding Chattanooga were no better off than their opponents), many of the soldiers defending Missionary Ridge had little fighting spirit.

There was no dearth of spirit in the blue-clad ranks on the wide plain facing the Confederate positions. After being cooped up in Chattanooga for two months, the Army of the Cumberland was spoiling for a fight. But there was some confusion among the Federal troops also. Grant had ordered Thomas only to advance to the base of Missionary Ridge and capture the first line of Confederate rifle pits, hoping the move would prevent Bragg from sending additional forces northward against Sherman. As that order hurriedly made its way through the various corps, divisions, and brigades, most Federal commanders thought they had been ordered to either take the ridge itself or that they were to do so after taking the lower line of rifle pits.[34]

Confused or not, the first step was to reach the base of Missionary Ridge. The Federal line advanced at 3:40 P.M., Thomas's four divisions totaling about 24,000 troops in eleven brigades. Major Edie gave the regular battalions the command to move forward and the lines lurched into motion, the nervous regulars picking their way through the sparse trees while trying to maintain proper alignment. At the edge of the wood line, the battalion commanders briefly halted their commands, dressed up the ranks and had their men fix bayonets. The battalion commanders then yelled: "Forward! Double quick! March!" With their rifles at right shoulder shift, the regulars emerged into the open. Confederate artillery replied to the advance with a deluge of projectiles. "We moved so rapidly," recalled Private J.N. Stanford of A/2/18th U.S., "their shells burst to our rear, sometimes so close as to make it uncomfortable, to say the least." The enemy fire was erratic and casualties few as the regulars advanced. Nervous Confederates at the base of the ridge in front of Edie's battalions, elements of the 4th and 5th Tennessee of Brigadier General Otho F. Strahl's Brigade, fired some scattered shots and then headed for the crest. The story was the same along the entire Union line: the enemy manning the lower line of rifle pits fled. Jubilant Federals, not realizing their opponents were following orders, cheered and ran even faster. "You better believe I done some tall running till I got to the hill," remembered Sergeant Philip Lyman, a company mate of Stanford's in Captain Haymond's battalion.[35]

Plunging fire from enemy positions on the crest was more effective as the Federals advanced closer to the ridge. Private Stanford, having successfully traversed what he thought was the most dangerous ground, was knocked over and dazed by a bursting shell when he was within fifty feet of his destination. Captain Crofton, commanding the composite battalion of the 16th and 19th U.S., had yet another horse shot out from beneath him when he approached within a few strides of the rifle pits (the mount was the fifth that Crofton lost during the war, which must have been something of a record for an infantry captain). Skirmishers from the 15th Infantry battalions quickly cleared the rifle pits in front of Missionary Ridge. The rest of the regulars, winded from the sprint, consolidated the position a few moments later. Many Federal units, believing their orders were to continue to the crest, moved past the rifle pits and immediately began the difficult assent of Missionary Ridge. "Come on boys follow me!" Captain Smith bellowed out to his 18th Infantrymen, digging spurs into his horse's flanks and springing forward up the steep hillside. "The command was obeyed with the zeal and alacrity which these gallant troops have ever shown," Smith reported, "and the line pushed onward and upward, exposed to a galling fire from an earth-work about half way up the side of the ridge." Smith soon had to abandon his horse as the ground slope became too great. "If you could have seen the places we charged up you would have said we could not have got up at all," Sergeant Lyman proudly wrote his parents the next week, "but we got up and did not lose a man out of our company. ...We first stuck to the Ridge like leaches, the shells would burst over head, some times they would come in two feet of our heads and burst but we would hug the ground and stumps so close that they could not hit us at all."[36]

A rare event during the Civil War occurred at Missionary Ridge that afternoon, a successful uphill assault against an entrenched enemy. In some places, Southern troops retreating from the baseline positions obscured the fire of the Confederates on top, allowing Federal troops to advance up the ridge quickly and, occasionally, with few casualties. Making the enemy's task even more difficult was the poor quality of the upper fortifications. Hastily thrown up during the previous day and a half, most of the works were incorrectly sighted and not very strong. The men retreating from the rifle pits arrived at the upper positions in an exhausted condition. Most of them continued rearward after reaching the top, with many of their comrades from the upper fortifications joining them in flight. Even so, Johnson's division encountered some of the worst conditions among the attacking Federals. They had to run a longer distance to reach the ridge, and having been on picket duty for more than seventy-two hours immediately prior to the assault Stoughton's men were in need of rest before the advance even began. In addition, Stewart's Confederates had constructed an additional fortified line about halfway up the slope.

The regulars took a breather after rooting the enemy out of this intermediate position. Like all the attacking units struggling up the slope, the regular battalions were badly intermixed at this point, formation and cohesion evaporating amidst the steep and broken terrain. Confederates on the crest, their line of fire now clear of friendly forces, fired more effectively. Union casualties increased. Private Stanford remembered firing back despite the opposition and poor terrain: "Away we went, dodging from stump to tree, rock or whatever would protect us, and now and then clinging to bushes to help us up (for it was very steep in places), and cracking heads wherever they showed themselves above us. ...As my regiment reached the top the Johnnies lay down and stuck their guns over the works and shot them off without looking up." Captain John Henry Knight, commanding a company in 2/18th U.S. and shouldering a Springfield rifle as he ascended the slope, was elated that friendly casualties were not heavy during the assault: "Of course I had many hair breadth escapes—ball and canister were just rained down into our faces and many, many a poor fellow tumbled backwards down the hill, though I was surprised to see so few killed or wounded. I had but two or three men injured coming across the open field where they could have mowed us down like grass. After the men got to the hill they could protect themselves behind trees and rocks."[37]

While checking on what troops of the 18th Infantry he could locate amidst the confusion, Captain Smith came to Lieutenant Phisterer's position. As they talked, a piece of shell struck the lieutenant in the right breast and knocked him over. "Smith asked if I was hurt, I said, I'll see, put my hand under my coat and found the place...took my hand out and it was not red. I have heard of men being saved by bibles, prayer-books and cards even; I was saved by a package of bills I carried in a pocket book inside of my overcoat. The bills had been given me by our sutler at Columbus to give to the parties concerned. While resting I saw our line to the left halfway and advancing up the ridge, and in the plain below our second line crossing in double time with colors flying." Phisterer continued climbing, perhaps glad he had a legitimate reason for losing the sutler's paperwork. Nearby in the 16th Infantry, Private Van Zwaluwenburg also turned around and glanced toward the Tennessee River. Like Phisterer, he was impressed by what he saw: "I looked back a moment and counted eight lines of battle of our boys marching steadily to our support. The 11th Mich was on our left. they went up the ridge in the shape of an inverted V with the colors at the apex. I saw the colors go down a number of times, but were raised at once by some strong arm. It is strange what pride men take, under such circumstances in keeping the colors up. Plenty men will quickly face almost certain death rather than see the colors touch the ground."[38]

The eyesight of the Southerners on top of Missionary Ridge was just as good as that of Phisterer and Van Zwaluwenburg. The sight of the legions that Thomas was hurling against Missionary Ridge was enough to cause many of the ridge's defenders to think twice about standing their ground. Sheridan's division to the immediate left of Johnson's troops had already gained the summit by the time Stoughton's Brigade approached the top, causing many of the defenders on Johnson's front to flee. Some resolute Confederates still remained as the regulars neared the end of their exhausting climb. Captain Anson Mills found himself crawling upward directly toward an enemy battery. "Half second fuze!" the chief of the piece called out, meaning the shell would explode a half second after leaving the muzzle. Mills hugged the earth, the shell exploding nearby but fortunately not hurting anyone. His ears ringing, the captain led the troops near him the short distance remaining to the top.

The shell fired at Mills was one of the Confederates' parting shots. The first soldier of Edie's battalions over the top was Sergeant James A. Elliot of A/1/18th U.S. Infantry. Jumping over a breastwork, Elliot single-handedly rounded up two Confederate officers and ten men as prisoners. Lieutenant John Gill, leading from the front in the best tradition of an ex-sergeant, was the first officer of the regular battalions to gain the summit. Elliot and Gill were joined a moment later by a swarm of regulars. Sergeant Elliot's exploits were repeated many times over. After mounting the crest, Private Stanford suddenly found himself face to face with a group of armed Confederates. "We surrender; don't shoot!" one of them called out as the sweating, excited Federal soldier jumped into their midst and took aim. Stanford and his companions disarmed this group and then turned their attention "to those who were making Maud S time down the side of the ridge, and persuaded a few to stop and rest." While some hard fighting took place on top of the ridge, the enemy for the most part had fled or was attempting to do so as the regulars gained the summit. By shortly after 5:00 P.M., most of Missionary Ridge was in Federal hands.

From general to private, the Federal army at Chattanooga was amazed by the victory. The advance to the top of Missionary Ridge and the resulting Confederate collapse had been so unexpected that few of the victorious commanders knew what to do next. Major General Phillip Sheridan led his division on a brief pursuit in the gathering darkness, but otherwise, Federal units bivouacked on top of the ridge amidst abandoned Confederate camps. Their main problem that night was transporting rations and ammunition up the steep slope and casualties back to Chattanooga. By morning, the regulars had been issued 3 days' rations and 100 rounds per man.[39]

The Federal pursuit began in earnest on November 26. Johnson's division led the XIV Corps' column marching southeastward from Missionary Ridge on the Bird's Mill Road. Repairing bridges over South Chickamauga and Pea Vine Creeks delayed the advance for many hours. It was dusk by the time Johnson's men crossed the Pea Vine and began to catch up with Bragg's fleeing troops. After crossing the creek, the road forked as it headed into Georgia. The left branch led to Graysville while the other went to Ringgold. General

Johnson sent a brigade down each road, Carlin left and Stoughton right. Troops of Carlin's advanced guard heard what they thought was a column moving on the road some distance to their front. In the gathering darkness, they could not be sure whether the troops were friendly or enemy. Word was sent to Stoughton's Brigade to be on the alert. Stoughton's men had meanwhile continued their own cautious advance. They eventually saw campfires flickering around a road intersection a short distance to the front. A company of skirmishers from 2/15th U.S. under Lieutenant Robert Harrison scouted the area and returned with a courier from General Bragg in tow and word that an enemy camp was ahead, in which could be seen some limbered artillery pieces. Stoughton quietly formed his brigade into line. The Confederates, members of Stewart's Division again, had no chance to react to the sudden ambush. "On approaching the road we surprised and captured his pickets," Colonel Stoughton reported, "and learning his position moved promptly forward and made a vigorous attack." The assault was so vigorous that it even startled Brigadier General Carlin: "There broke out on the still air a most frightening roar of musketry about 300 yards down the road towards Ringgold. It seemed to come from at least an entire brigade. It must have been heard for miles around in all directions. It turned out that it was Stoughton's Brigade, which had learned the location of a Confederate command bivouacked temporarily alongside of the road. There was no return to that fire. Stillness returned as suddenly as it had been broken."[40]

Stoughton's nighttime assault scattered Stewart's men. Captain Andrew Burt led forward B/1/18th U.S. to the abandoned position, capturing an artillery piece from Captain T.B. Ferguson's Battery and several prisoners. Skirmishers from the 16th Infantry claimed another gun, while the 11th Michigan took two others. In addition to the cannon, the haul from the skirmish totaled four caissons, a battle flag, and more than sixty prisoners. The noise from the attack also frightened a party of Confederates then attempting to cross East Chickamauga Creek at Graysville. Fearing that the Federals were close, they dumped some artillery pieces into the creek and hurried on to Ringgold "in great confusion and fright." Following the engagement, Stoughton marched his command to Graysville, where it linked up with Carlin's brigade and passed a quiet night.[41]

Hooker's troops suffered a bloody repulse the next day while attacking Cleburne's Confederate rear guard at Ringgold Gap.

Johnson's division marched from Graysville to Ringgold that morning and stood in readiness to support the Federal assault, but Hooker broke off the frustrating battle without calling Johnson forward. The fighting at Ringgold ended the Federal pursuit of Bragg and closed the book on the Chattanooga Campaign. Bragg's army suffered about 6,600 casualties, including more than 4,000 captured. During late November, the demoralized Army of Tennessee gathered at Dalton, Georgia, about twenty miles to the southeast, while Federal troops secured the approaches to Chattanooga. Johnson's division returned to Chattanooga on November 29. The November battles had cost the North about 5,800 troops, but the combined Union armies had routed their opposition and lifted the siege of Chattanooga. Newly promoted Lieutenant Peter Cönzler of the 16th Infantry died on Missionary Ridge, and fifty-seven other regulars were killed or wounded in the short campaign. The newcomers of 2/15th U.S. earned praise from General Johnson: "A small battalion of the Fifteenth U.S. Infantry, never under fire before, acted like veterans."[42]

Not everyone agreed with Johnson's opinion of the regulars. Debates about the relative fighting abilities of volunteers and regulars had been taking place since 1861, with the regulars in the early months of the war usually coming out ahead due to their more thorough training, superior equipment, and tougher discipline. By late 1863, though, many volunteers had gained through experience much of what they had earlier lacked. The dividing line between citizen soldier and military professional had become quite narrow. In many cases it was nonexistent. If volunteers had not seen the need for regulars early in the war, they considered professional soldiers to be even more unnecessary two years later. If a regular soldier or unit was disciplined for performing poorly—a common enough occurrence given the high standards of the Regular Army—the incident was sure to be told and retold around many a volunteer's campfire that evening. Despite numerous examples to the contrary, it was a foregone conclusion to some volunteers that regular troops were unreliable and would not fight hard. During the brief stand at Rossville Gap immediately after Chickamauga, Sergeant Major Levi A. Ross of the 86th Illinois Volunteer Infantry had been near enough to the Regular Brigade's position to observe the attack of Forrest's cavalry. "Up on the Rossville road the Johnnies made a charge today," Ross entered into his journal on September 22, 1863, "but were repulsed with loss by a brigade of Regulars, [although] as a rule the Regular soldiers are less efficient and reliable than the volunteers." Private Oliver Lyman of the 18th Regulars had heard his fill of these snide comments. Writing to his brother Luke, who was convalescing in a Cincinnati hospital (still battling the rheumatism he had been stricken with the previous summer), Oliver closed out his description of the Battle of Missionary Ridge with an admonition: "Luke you know how the regulars are when they get started, if anyone tells you the regulars run kill the d[umb] a[ss] liers for they never went into a battle yet for what there was some d[umb] a[ss] volenteers says they run. The next one tells me so I will bruise his..."[43]

For the rest of their days, Federal soldiers who participated in the assault of Missionary Ridge would look back with pride on what they accomplished. The rejuvenated spirit of Private Charles Bogart leaps from a letter the regular wrote twelve days after the battle: "the rebs held the mountain but now we have it. the rebs threw a number of shells in our camp from that mountain but if they shell us now they will have to build a larger gun than ever was made yet." The Army of the Cumberland went into winter quarters during the first week of December 1863. Active operations came to a temporary halt.[44]

* * *

John King received another promotion in 1863 in addition to becoming a brigadier general of volunteers. On the first day of June he was promoted in the Regular Army to lieutenant colonel, 14th Infantry Regiment. Captain Albert Tracy of the 10th Infantry was promoted to King's former slot as a major in the 15th Infantry. Tracy's service had been extensive and varied prior to being assigned to the 15th Infantry, seeing action with the regulars in the Mexican War and then serving as the adjutant general of the state of Maine for seven years. He reentered the regular service as an officer of the 10th Infantry in 1855 and participated in the 1857–1858 Utah Expedition. During the first two years of the Civil War, Tracy had served as a staff officer and colonel of volunteers in Missouri and Virginia. None of these experiences really prepared 1/15th's new commander for the sights that greeted him upon reporting for duty at Chattanooga on December 31, 1863: "I must say that I never beheld so much suffering and misery from want of food and clothing as I saw in the camps of the Federal troops at Chattanooga from the date of my joining until the opening of [the rail line in] February,

1864. For tents, a few blackened specimens were left, but there were not wanting instances where soldiers were compelled for want of covering to burrow in the side of the hills like animals to escape the piercing inclemencies of the weather. It was only when we opened the newspapers, which now and then reached us from the North, that we felt assured that the men at Chattanooga were amply fed and eager for battle."[45]

Meager rations were on Lieutenant Edgar Kellogg's mind a few weeks prior to Tracy's arrival as the 19th Infantry officer searched through his provisions for something to eat. Whatever he came up with would have to be split three ways. His brother, Captain Sanford C. Kellogg, had come for a visit and had brought along a distinguished two-star guest. George Thomas had a familial connection with the Kellogg brothers that stretched back to the previous decade. The 18th Infantry's Captain Lyman Kellogg, elder brother of Sanford and Edgar, was a member of the West Point Class of 1852. A number of times during the springtime, just prior to Lyman's graduation from the academy, one of his aunts, Mrs. Abigail Paine Kellogg, visited him at West Point. Abigail Kellogg, the widow of a wealthy merchant who lived in Troy, New York, had two daughters who often accompanied her while visiting her nephew. One of them, Francis, was introduced to then-Brevet Major George Thomas, a highly eligible bachelor on the West Point faculty who taught artillery and cavalry tactics. The two were married in November 1852. The Kellogg brothers were thus able to claim that their aunt was the mother-in-law of the Army of the Cumberland's commanding general. The family ties resulted in Sanford Kellogg serving as one of Thomas's aides-de-camp. Shortly after Edgar recovered from his bout with malaria and returned to field duty with the 16th U.S. in December 1863, General Thomas was making a morning inspection of the lines. At the 16th Infantry's position, Captain Kellogg introduced the general to his brother. Sanford whispered to Edgar that the general had not yet eaten that morning, and asked if the regulars could provide breakfast. Lieutenant Kellogg tried to find something for the impromptu meal but could scrounge up very little. "I gave the gentlemen the best," Edgar Kellogg remembered with a hint of embarrassment, "which was all that I had, and it was coffee without sugar (it seems unnecessary to state that I had neither cream nor milk) and a rather limited quantity of hard bread." The meal quickly over with, Thomas and his aide continued on their rounds.[46]

The lack of fare on Kellogg's table was a common occurrence in the Army of the Cumberland that winter. Enough food to prevent starvation made it into Chattanooga, but little more. The makeshift overland-waterborne supply route to the town simply could not handle a sufficient volume of supplies. Work on the damaged rail line from Stevenson to Chattanooga continued nonstop, although foul weather and rugged terrain delayed the line's opening until February. All in all, it was a miserable beginning to 1864. With both firewood and adequate shelter fast becoming rare, the troops in Chattanooga suffered greatly from the weather. A cold front blew through the Chattanooga area with a vengeance during the first week of January. A tree was blown over onto a tent in 2/18th's camp on New Year's Day, severely injuring two soldiers. Private Austin Murphy, an Ohioan serving in H/1/18th, recorded in his diary the next day that it was "very cold and frosty. I had to go out and grub up stumps for to get Wood to burn to keep from freezing." One lucky squad of regulars obtained good canvas to sleep under through pressing into service a tent marked "40th Alabama," which they had found on Missionary Ridge.[47]

The regulars continued their routine of formal Sunday inspections despite the weather, even though the regulars' uniforms during those weeks were in many cases the same clothing that had been on their backs during the Chickamauga Campaign. Some fresh clothing was available from regimental sutlers, but prices such as sixteen dollars for a pair of trousers and up to sixty for a frock coat meant that only a few officers could afford to buy replacement items. Lieutenant Arthur Carpenter wrote that supplies were still scarce as late as January 6: "Provisions are not plenty yet, nor will they be so until the railroad is through. horses and mules are dying off every day for want of forage, and what are alive are nothing but skin and bones, so weak that they can hardly hold themselves up. we are short of wood for want of teams to haul it from the woods to our camps, everything in the shape of wood within two miles has been used. Chattanooga is a cold and desolate place." The supply situation improved with the opening of the rail line in February. One of the regulars remembered that the arrival of that first train caused quite a stir: "Hundreds of our boys rushed out and met the first provision train as it came in sight around moccasin point. some tore the doors open and thru out boxes of crackers and barrels of pork. as soon as the train reached the depot, guards kept the men away, and we soon received our regular rations." The Army of the Cumberland was gradually put back in fighting trim.[48]

The pace at Chattanooga was slow and monotonous for most of January and February 1864. When this was combined with the whiskey that was more readily available with the opening of the rail line, there were always some regulars in trouble for one reason or another. "My everyday life has nothing new," Captain Andrew Burt wrote his father on February 5. "The daily round of duty is varied at short intervals by some one being put in arrest. When whiskey is attainable there is a merri making. ...Ye Gods save us but the amount of Liquor drunk in the army. It seems to be a given scorn of existence."[49] Some officers who could be spared from duties took advantage of the slow times and went home on leave. Arthur Carpenter wished he were one of them, but wrote home on January 30 that there was no chance of his seeing his family anytime soon:

> There is no prospect yet for a leave of absence. ...If I was a scape-goat or a staff officer, I could go home every 6 months. but as I am a line officer on duty everyday—dozing on rocks or in mud-puddles—while on picket and staff officers are in some house sleeping on some cot or feather bed (generally the result of thieving), for this reason I must be bound down and kept in the field year after year, put into the hottest of the fight, doing all the hard and dangerous work, getting no reward but the recommendation of your own conscience, getting no *brevet* (none but staff officers and those who do the least work get brevets) and now after considering such a state of affairs, where shall we look for aid to remedy the evil?. ...I wish I had control of the lightning for 24 hours.[50]

The lieutenant apologized for his tirade two weeks later: "There is nothing so dull as the monotonous routine of camp life and yet when we are engaged in the different scouting expeditions, we are complaining because we cannot be left in camp. ...it is universaly the custom of soldiers to be always grumbling. If my letters partake of anything of that spirit, you must make allowance for the force of habit."[51]

While performing occasional picket duty, relaxing, and grumbling were the main pastimes for most troops at Chattanooga during the first months of 1864, such was not the case in Major Edie's 2/15th U.S. Infantry. The regulars had been called upon to furnish a battalion for post guard at Chattanooga. General King, healthy again and back in command, gave the assignment to Edie's battalion. After a few weeks of guard duty, Edie believed his battalion was not nearly large enough. Knowing it was difficult to keep troops drilled to Regular Army standards under the best conditions, Edie wrote a letter to Chattanooga's post commander, Brigadier General James B. Steedman, with his concerns:

> I desire respectfully to call Your attention to the fact that the enlisted Men of my command are required to perform duties of so arduous a character that it will be impossible to keep them in that state of discipline and drill calculated to render them efficient when ordered to the front.
>
> There are a few more than two hundred men reported daily for duty. I take but six of them for my Camp guard, and the guard duty I am called upon to do for the Post forces me to put one half the command on duty every day, this give the men but one night in bed. It leaves me no Companies to drill, and is gradually wearing out the men. This state of things has continued now for about a month and I hope it may be so changed as to allow at least two consecutive nights of rest to the men.[52]

Steedman eased the regular battalion's duties by shifting some of its details to units assigned to similar duties at General Thomas's department headquarters. Even these new arrangements did not allow 2/15th U.S. much training time. When the tour of duty ended in April, Major Edie began drilling his companies at a fast pace.

Manpower was a difficult issue throughout the Union Army that winter. The volunteers who had enlisted in the spring and summer of 1861 had done so for three years, meaning their enlistments would expire just as the 1864 campaign season got underway. The government offered cash bounties and furloughs as an inducement for them to reenlist, designating regiments as "Veteran Volunteers" if 75 percent of their members reenlisted. About 136,000 of the Union Army's eligible volunteers reenlisted under this program, thus securing a vital pool of experienced manpower for the rest of the war. The great number of volunteer troops who decided to stay in uniform impressed Lieutenant Carpenter: "several regiments have gone home on 20 or 30 days furlough, by reenlisting as Veteran Volunteers. nearly all of the Volunteers of this army are reenlisting. It shows forth in all its brilliancy the noble spirit of patriotism which they have, and which carries them through all the self sacrificing duties of a soldier." The 69th Ohio of King's brigade "veteranized" through this process and its soldiers spent a few precious weeks at home as a result.[53]

Not enough troops of the 11th Michigan or 19th Illinois chose to reenlist for those units to qualify as veteran regiments. They remained in Chattanooga the entire winter, although these soldiers certainly looked forward to the coming summer when they would muster out of the service. The regulars were not given a choice in the matter and could only watch with envious eyes as the volunteers went home on furlough, for a different set of policies covered regular reenlistments. They were offered a Federal cash bounty identical to that of the volunteers for reenlisting but no official mention was made of a furlough. Furthermore, the general order laying out the terms under which regulars could reenlist would expire in June 1864. Frederick Phisterer investigated this issue in 2/18th U.S. and discovered that there were serious problems with regular reenlistment policies. He sent word back to Major Caldwell at 18th Infantry Headquarters in Columbus that something would have to be done:

> General Orders No 190 War Dept Adjt Genl Office June 25th 1863 orders "a bounty of $400 shall be allowed and paid to all the men, now in the Regular Army, whose terms expire within one year from this date and who shall re enlist at any time within two months before the expiration of their present term of service."
>
> There being no men in the 18th U.S. Inf., whose terms will expire before the 25th of June 1864, which I believe to be the case in all the new Regiments of the Regular Army, I would respectfully suggest, that, if you see proper, the attention of the War Department be called to this fact, the more so as at present quite a number of men of this Battalion are willing to re-enlist for five years under the bounty offered in the above mentioned order.
>
> An order "allowing all men enlisted in the regular army in 1861 and 1862 to re-enlist for five years with the offer of a $400 bounty and a furlough for 30 days" would be a great inducement for those men to re-enlist.[54]

The War Department staff officer who drafted General Order 190 back in the summer of 1863 failed to realize that most of the regulars who enlisted in the summer of 1861 did so for five years, not the volunteers' three. These regulars would be in ranks well into 1866 and thus were not eligible to reenlist anytime soon. The majority of regulars who were serving three-year terms had enlisted in the autumn and winter of 1861. As Phisterer noted, none of the three-year regulars would be eligible to reenlist prior to June 25, 1864, the date the incentives of General Order 190 would expire. General King was alarmed by this situation and wrote to the War Department for guidance. Adjutant General Lorenzo Thomas replied in early January 1864 that all regulars who had signed five-year enlistments in 1861 would have their terms summarily reduced to three years. The War Department attempted to further clarify the issue a few weeks later in a general order. All regulars whose terms of service would expire in 1864 were authorized to reenlist prior to the first of March and receive a bounty of $300. The bounty was later increased to $402. It was not until June 20 that Congress brought official relief to the five-year regulars of 1861. The original enlistment of these troops was summarily reduced to three years, and they were authorized to reenlist for another three years provided they did so prior to the first of August.

Confusion still remained about the length of service and the possibility of a furlough. The last action Congress took on the term of service was in July 1861, when the lawmakers had fixed the regular term at five years for all enlistments taking place after January 1, 1863. A War Department general order dated February 20, 1864, mentioned a three-year term for veterans reenlisting for regular service, but without legislative backing, many regulars thought they may in fact have to serve the longer term. Another fine point of the regulations was that furloughs for regulars who reenlisted were not automatically granted; requests had to be approved by the War Department, which meant a lengthy delay as paperwork traveled from the field to Washington and back. Rumor had it that whatever furlough the regulars would receive could be taken only after the war was over. "Well the bounty for reenlisting in the regulars is not very high yet," Oliver Lyman wrote on January 29, 1864, "they offered the same as the volunteers but for the term of five years, and thirty days furlough, but the boys said they thought the furlough was on the far end [of the war] and couldn't see it. ...there is not green backs enough to get me for five years longer." The furlough issue was so important that Major Tracy telegraphed Colonel Shepherd about it on February 4: "3/4 of 1st Battalion will re-enlist if granted 30 day furlough. Please advise War Department." Shepherd duly advised the War Department, but received no reply.[55]

Despite these exertions, the Regular Army's reenlistment effort turned out to be a dismal failure during 1864. Perhaps the greatest impediment to regular service at this point in the war was the fact that regulars had to sign away three (perhaps five) years of their lives regardless of how long the conflict might last. As it then appeared that the war might not continue more than a year or so, service in the peacetime army at the conclusion of the Civil War was what any regular was facing if he reenlisted. This was another major difference from the term of service for volunteers. State troops signed up for three (sometime fewer) years or the duration of the war, whichever was shorter. Jacob Van Zwaluwenburg was considering reenlisting in the 16th U.S. until his older brother reminded him of this fact. Garret Van Zwaluwenburg's 2nd Michigan had become a veteran regiment. The brothers saw each other for the first time in almost three years while Garret was passing though Chattanooga at the end of his furlough. When Garret told his younger brother that he had signed on again, Jacob replied that he was considering a similar move. "He urged me not to re-enlist," Jacob recorded in his memoirs, "for I was a member of the regular army and would have to serve a full term in the u.s. army while he, as a volunteer member, could go home at the close of the war, which certainly would be finished in a year. ...We had a hurried, happy visit, and I never saw him again." Garret Van Zwaluwenburg would lose an arm at the Battle of the Wilderness in Virginia on May 6 and died of his wounds a few weeks afterward. Jacob heeded his brother's advice and did not reenlist in the Regular Army. Some regulars signed up for another term but not many. During the first 10 months of 1864, reenlistments totaled 129 in the 15th U.S., 51 in the 16th U.S., and but 34 in the 18th Infantry. The total for the entire Regular Army was a slim 916. Facing the possibility of a five-year hitch, an uncertain furlough, almost certain service in the post-war army, and the rough life of the regulars, most of the veteran troops in the Army of the Cumberland's regular battalions had an attitude similar to that of the 19th Infantry's Eli Tarbell: "Lieut Edwards asked us to reinlist but no one in our Co. Will, we have inspection Every Evening." Incredibly, not a soul in the 19th Regulars agreed to reenlist during this ten-month period.[56]

* * *

The relaxing pace of life at Chattanooga ended temporarily in February 1864. On the 10th of that month General Thomas

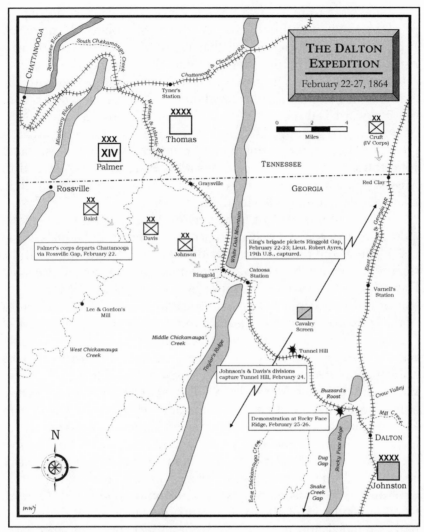

THE DALTON
EXPEDITION
February 22-27, 1864

CHATTANOOGA

Tennessee River

South Chickamauga Creek

Chattanooga & Cleveland RR

Tyner's
Station

Western & Atlantic RR

Missionary Ridge

XXXX
Thomas

0   2   4
Miles

XX
Cruft
(IV Corps)

XXX
XIV
Palmer

TENNESSEE

Rossville

Graysville

GEORGIA

Red Clay

XX
Baird

Palmer's corps departs Chattanooga
via Rossville Gap, February 22.

XX
Davis

White Oak Mountain

XX
Johnson

King's brigade pickets Ringgold Gap,
February 22-23; Lieut. Robert Ayres,
19th U.S., captured.

East Tennessee & Georgia RR

Ringgold

Catoosa
Station

Varnell's
Station

Lee & Gordon's
Mill

Middle Chickamauga
Creek

Taylor's Ridge

Cavalry
Screen

West Chickamauga
Creek

Tunnel Hill

Johnson's & Davis's divisions
capture Tunnel Hill, February 24.

Buzzard's
Roost

Crow Valley

Mill Creek

N

Demonstration at Rocky Face
Ridge, February 25-26.

DALTON

East Chickamauga Creek

Rocky Face Ridge

Dug
Gap

XXXX
Johnston

Snake
Creek
Gap

mwj

received reports stating that the Confederate army at Dalton, now
commanded by General Joseph E. Johnston, was detaching large
amounts of troops for service in Mississippi and east Tennessee. Ever
mindful of the latter region's security, Grant ordered Thomas to proceed to Knoxville on February 13 with as much of the Army of the
Cumberland that could be safely spared from Chattanooga's
defense. Thomas found it difficult to comply. His army then had a
great many regiments absent on veteran furlough and also still had

not come close to replacing all the horses and mules lost during the previous four months. Grant canceled the planned move on February 14 after determining that Knoxville was sufficiently garrisoned by the troops already there. Since Thomas had begun preparations to move, Grant gave him a mission more in line with the Army of the Cumberland's capabilities. Thomas was ordered to move toward Dalton and threaten Johnston's position there, "the object being to gain possession of Dalton and as far south of that as possible." Grant hoped this limited offensive would at least cause Johnston to recall the troops that had been recently dispatched to Mississippi, where Sherman's Army of the Tennessee was engaged in a large-scale raid toward Meridian.

Thomas's operation got underway on February 22 with General Palmer of the XIV Corps in immediate command, Thomas being bedridden at the time with a case of neuralgia. Palmer directed the three divisions of his corps, commanded by Johnson, Baird, and Davis, to move from Chattanooga toward Dalton by way of Ringgold Gap. A fourth division, Brigadier General Charles Cruft's of the IV Corps, headed toward Dalton from its station northeast of Chattanooga at Cleveland, Tennessee. King's brigade led the column out of Chattanooga. Only one of the brigade's volunteer regiments accompanied the regulars on this excursion, the 19th Illinois under Lieutenant Colonel Alexander W. Raffen. Five of the six regular battalions rounded out King's command, with Major Edie's 2/15th U.S. remaining behind on guard duty in Chattanooga. Major Tracy led 1/15th U.S., this being his first field experience in the Army of the Cumberland. Shiloh veteran Captain Robert Peabody Barry commanded the 16th Infantry, Barry having replaced Captain Crofton the previous month, when Crofton headed for Ft. Ontario to take command of the 16th Infantry's headquarters. Barry had been wounded and captured at Stones River, but had since been exchanged and was back on duty. Captains Smith and Haymond continued to command the 18th Infantry Battalions. Captain James Mooney led 1/19th U.S., a native Englishman who had spent the first two years of the war on staff duty before taking command of E/1/19th U.S. just prior to the Middle Tennessee Campaign. A timely illness had spared Mooney from experiencing Chickamauga. He was healthy again in November and took command of the battalion the following month.[57]

The column moved out at five in the morning. With Colonel Thomas J. Harrison's 39th Indiana Mounted Infantry covering the movement, the regulars passed through Rossville Gap in Missionary Ridge. General King deployed skirmishers from Captain Mooney's 19th U.S. to support the cavalry, but the column encountered no resistance. Constructing a footbridge across West Chickamauga Creek, four miles beyond Rossville, briefly delayed the advance, but the column managed to reach the small town of Ringgold, eighteen miles from Chattanooga, by three that afternoon. The tiny Confederate garrison fled with the approach of the Indiana mounted troops. King's brigade arrived on the scene shortly afterward. Remaining largely stationary in Chattanooga for almost five months had resulted in the regulars being in poor marching form. One of them recalled that they arrived in Ringgold "with blistered feet, tired and weary" after what was in reality an easy movement on a day of mild weather. They had little time to rest, for General Johnson posted King's brigade as a picket line on the high ground at Ringgold Gap, a half-mile beyond the town, while the balance of the column closed up. "[W]e felt very bad at having to go on picket on the ridge after the hard march during the day," Lieutenant Carpenter lamented. "but it was so ordered and we had nothing to do but to comply."

White Oak Mountain and Taylor's Ridge, flanking Ringgold Gap to the north and south respectively, was the sight of Pat Cleburne's skillful repulse of Joseph Hooker on November 27. After trudging up the 400 feet of elevation to the top of the ridgeline, the regulars and 19th Illinois had a clear view of the valley below. A force of dismounted Confederate cavalry formed a hasty line blocking movement on the Ringgold-Dalton Road near Catoosa Station, a mile down the Western & Atlantic from Ringgold. Fortifications were just visible four miles further to the southeast on Tunnel Hill,[58] the obligatory name of the high ground and nearby settlement containing a passage for the Western & Atlantic Railway. General King placed the 15th and 19th U.S. south of Ringgold Gap on Taylor's Ridge, the 18th Infantry battalions in the gap itself, and the 16th U.S. and 19th Illinois to the north on White Oak Mountain. The commanders posted strong picket forces forward of the crests with supporting troops to the rear. They then settled down for a hopefully uneventful night, which it was for the most part. A patrol of enemy cavalry advanced into Ringgold Gap during the darkness, but a few shots from the 18th Infantry's forward sentinels sent the intruders back toward Catoosa Station. Another probe took place just prior to dawn along the 15th Infantry's line on Taylor's Ridge, with a volley from Major Tracy's men keeping the Confederate scouts at a respectable distance.

The regulars' only loss during the night occurred in the 16th Infantry's sector. Captain Barry's battalion was still short of officers, so Lieutenant Robert Ayres of the 19th U.S. volunteered to assist in the posting of 1/16th's pickets. While riding forward of the picket line to get the lay of the land, Ayres became disoriented in the darkness and disappeared. His fate was a mystery until the next morning, when local citizens informed the regulars that they had seen a detachment of Confederate cavalry escorting a captured Federal lieutenant southward. General Johnson was saddened when he heard the news. Although the general had met Ayres's father-in-law, Benny Havens, only a few times while a Military Academy cadet, Johnson remembered hearing of the tavern keeper "so frequently while at West Point that even his son-in-law seemed dear to me, and I was sorry that he had determined on making a trip through Georgia in advance of the main army."[59]

Johnson's division moved out shortly after daybreak on February 23. Carlin's brigade had the advance, followed by King's and Starkweather's brigades, the latter temporarily under Colonel Henry A. Hambright's command. Colonel Harrison's mounted infantry again covered the movement. The Indiana horsemen encountered a small body of enemy cavalry at Catoosa Station. A running fight took place as the Southern cavalry retreated three miles to Tunnel Hill. Completed in 1850, the tunnel there is 1,447 feet in length and was the first such structure in operation south of the Mason-Dixon line. Connecting as it did rail systems from the lower Atlantic seaboard to the Mississippi River, for the first half of the war it was one of the key transportation points in the Confederate States. In the shrunken Confederacy of early 1864, its status was reduced to being just another piece of high ground to be seized or defended.[60]

The enemy horsemen countercharged Harrison's men as the Federals approached Tunnel Hill. General Carlin moved up his brigade, reinforced with the 19th Illinois from King's brigade, to support the mounted infantrymen. Harrison and Carlin advanced again, outflanking a Confederate blocking force and chasing the enemy through the town of Tunnel Hill. On approaching the tunnel itself, fire from two Confederate Parrot rifles positioned on the heights above halted the Federal advance. Johnson had no artillery with which to reply. The lack of horses in Chattanooga meant that Johnson's column had just a single section of guns available. Even these were of no use, for the negligent commander of the two pieces had failed to bring along much forage for his animals and they had given out at Ringgold. With darkness approaching, Johnson consolidated the division at Catoosa Station.[61]

Johnson employed the same tactics the following day. Initially he had the same results. Carlin's brigade advanced unopposed through the town of Tunnel Hill, but artillery fire again halted the movement as the Federals approached high ground beyond the town. With plenty of daylight remaining for this round of fighting, Johnson deployed King's and Hambright's brigades to flank the enemy position. The regulars advanced onto the high ground north of the Western & Atlantic's tracks. A few enemy pickets fled as the regulars gained the crest. Down near the railway, the 39th Indiana Mounted Infantry also attempted to advance. From his vantage point nearby, 19th Infantryman Arthur Carpenter described what happened next: "As we went to the hill the enemy opened their two parrots again on the cavalry. we were so far to the left as to be out of range. ...we advanced to within 500 yds of the ridge then halted. the cavalry could do nothing & were driven back in confusion[,] the shells of the enemy having a telling effect on them. I saw one horseman hit with a shell. he was knocked to pieces and the horse turned a complete somersalt. It seemed as though they could throw their shells where they pleased."[62]

General Palmer arrived on the scene and deployed Davis's division to King's left, extending the Federal flanking effort against Tunnel Hill even further. The Federal forces converging on Tunnel Hill dwarfed the Southern cavalry screening the region. "The position was easily taken," reported General Johnson, "and the enemy was soon in full retreat, followed by Davis's division, supported by King's brigade." The regulars clawed their way up the northwest side of Tunnel Hill, a 500-foot climb. They descended into the valley beyond and bedded down for the night.

The Federal movement toward Dalton had thus far not encountered much sustained resistance, but upon moving forward from Tunnel Hill, General Palmer's forces came face-to-face with the Army of Tennessee's main position. Little more than a mile from where King's regulars camped on the evening of February 24, Johnston's Confederates occupied a position that was as tough as its name suggests: Rocky Face Ridge (so called because of the sheer rock palisades that dot the ridge's western slopes). At the ridge's highest point it rose to a height of more than 1,600 feet and dominated movement throughout the region. Confederates were strongly entrenched on Rocky Face and also in Crow Valley to the northeast, covering the western and northern approaches to Dalton. Rocky Face Ridge was traversable only through three gaps. The most direct of these, through which passed the Western & Atlantic tracks as well as the Dalton-Ringgold Road, was Buzzard's Roost (also known as Mill Creek Gap and Kinyan's Gap). Strong fortifications covered Buzzard's Roost, while the flooding of Mill Creek obstructed the passage itself. "The position of the enemy was very strong," Lieutenant Carpenter recalled of his view of Buzzard's Roost. "they had breastworks and masked batteries in the gap, and the rocky cliffs were lined with sharp shooters." The second gap through the ridge, man-made Dug Gap, was about six miles south of Buzzard's Roost, while the third and final passage, Snake Creek Gap (actually a long defile), was even further to the south.

On February 25, Davis's division probed toward Buzzard's Roost and skirmished with its defenders throughout the day. At dusk, Johnson moved forward King's and Hambright's brigades and relieved Davis's troops. "[W]e...could have no fires," Carpenter continued, "and had to be on the alert all the time. a cold chilly wind sprung up, which made us all shake as though we had the 'ager,' but we stood it manfully." The night passed quietly, the regulars getting what rest they could while steeling themselves for the coming day of cat-and-mouse skirmishing.[63]

Sporadic firing commenced with the sun's rising over Rocky Face Ridge. Lieutenant Edgar Kellogg's F/1/16th U.S. held the left of the 16th Infantry's line, positioned astride the Western & Atlantic tracks facing Buzzard's Roost. Four of his men occupied what appeared to be an ideal position adjacent to the railway embankment, an excavated area that provided cover as they sniped at the Confederates. But it was just a matter of time before the enemy higher up on Rocky Face Ridge took note of the regulars' position. "They had been there an hour or more," Kellogg remembered, "when suddenly we heard what seemed more like a volley than the individual firing of skirmishers, and three of these men found themselves wounded, one of them severely hurt. Some Confederates had climbed one of the mountains to a point where they got a clear view of the interior of this ready formed rifle pit and they soon made it untenable with their plunging fire, but we held the rest of our line intact."[64]

Major Albert Tracy was in charge of the regulars to the left of the 16th Infantry's position, his own 1/15th U.S. and also Captain Haymond's battalion of 18th Infantrymen. The major's post-battle report, one of the few written about this operation by a commander below the brigade level, gives details of an eventful day in the highlands of northwest Georgia:

> The morning of the 26 opened with lively skirmishing, which continued with greater or less severity during the day. The enemies sharpshooters being able to reach at nearly every point, the hills held by both the pickets or skirmish line and the reserve. One man— name not reported to me—was Killed out of the battalion of the 18th on my left. In my own battalion casualties none. Good service was done by twenty men of the 1st Battalion under an officer posted subsequently to my arrival. At the foot of the hill, to the right, others of my command were thrown out as sharpshooters on a low knoll to the right and front, aiding effectually to clear the enemy from guns posted on an opposite eminince, and to drive back stray parties along the rail-road or elsewhere.[65]

Arthur Carpenter's recollections of February 26 do not include being able to fire back as effectively as Major Tracy's 15th Infantrymen. The height advantage Rocky Face Ridge afforded the enemy meant the regulars, at least as far as Carpenter could discern from the 19th Infantry's line, spent most of the day hiding: "so we stood behind trees and peeped at them carefully, to see them shoot at us. every tree behind which a sentinel stood was completely barked with bullets. we had no men hurt though many had very narrow escapes."[66]

While the regulars' casualties were light, the skirmishing at Buzzard's Roost resulted in the loss of about 300 men in the 4 Federal divisions. General Thomas, now present at the front, determined that the Confederate position near Dalton was still quite strong despite the recent detachment of troops from the Army of Tennessee. An assault on this bastion was out of the question. Word reached the Union lines that two of Johnston's recently detached divisions had been recalled to Dalton, so Thomas considered his mission to be accomplished. He decided to move his forces back to

Chattanooga, but not before Colonel Harrison's 39th Indiana Mounted Infantry brought Thomas some interesting news. Harrison's men had occupied Dug Gap in Rocky Face Ridge during the night of February 25–26. The pass was unguarded that night and the route through it led far to the rear of Johnston's position. The Hoosiers were forced out of the gap on the morning of the 26th, although they had remained there unmolested for a considerable amount of time. To General Thomas the implications were clear: Johnston was so fixated by the situation at Buzzard's Roost and Tunnel Hill that the Confederates had failed to adequately secure their left flank. Thomas was shrewd enough to know that he could not count on finding Johnston negligent about defending Dug Gap when next a Federal army approached Dalton, but perhaps the final gap in Rocky Face Ridge to the south, Snake Creek, was likewise undefended and could serve the same purpose. This issue weighed on Thomas's mind as he issued orders for a withdrawal from the Buzzard's Roost area on the night of February 26.[67]

Lieutenant Edgar Kellogg had more immediate concerns on his mind that night. About 100 yards in front of the left portion of Kellogg's picket line was a wooden shack occupied by a squad of Southern sharpshooters. They had been making life annoying for the men of F/1/16th U.S. all day. Shortly after nightfall, but before receiving the withdrawal order, Captain Barry sent a company forward to relieve Kellogg's men from their exposed position in front of the gap. The commander of the relief company, instead of properly coordinating his actions with Kellogg, instead simply started to post his men and send the ones he could find from Company F back to the rear. He assumed the structure in front of the lines was in friendly hands and sent a corporal and two privates to the building to relieve what he assumed were some of Kellogg's men. "The Confederates in the house saw that the 'Yankees' were making a blunder and kindly took them in," Kellogg recalled. "Some of the unusual sounds from my left reached my ears, and suspecting that 'some one had blundered' I made quick provision against further loss from ignorance or carelessness." The night had quieted down again by the time General King told his battalion commanders to start pulling back. Carlin's brigade and Harrison's troopers covered the withdrawal from a position near Tunnel Hill. Lieutenant Frederick Phisterer remembered that "about midnight [we] evacuated our position and stole away in the dark; it was an anxious time, and my care was to stop every possible noise, as we were all that was left in the Gap; we got off and out of the hills, reached our cavalry, which was to hold position as rear guard, and marched back to Catoosa Station."

Johnson's division continued the retrograde movement the next morning, marching to Tyner's Station, a stop on the Western & Atlantic due east from Chattanooga and about three miles from Missionary Ridge. The excursion to Dalton had done much to lift Lieutenant Carpenter's spirits: "thus ends our three days scout. I am very well. such trips seem to do me good." To facilitate communication with Baird's division, which had remained at Ringgold, Johnson moved his command to Graysville five days later. The regulars' baggage and camp equipment was brought out from their old camps near Chattanooga and the familiar routines of camp life began once more. But it would not be long before the regulars would again gaze upon the heights of Rocky Face Ridge.[68]

* * *

King's regulars spent March and April 1864 preparing themselves for the upcoming campaign. Dress parades and target practice became part of the weekly routine. A surprise awaited the regulars at the conclusion of their parade on Sunday, April 3: crates containing factory-fresh Springfield rifles were deposited in the various battalion camps, replacements for the worn-out weapons that some of the regulars had been using for more than two years.[69] Major Tracy wished additional trained troops had shown up along with the rifles. Except for Major Edie's 2/15th U.S., the regular battalions as late as mid-March were still limping along with just the troops who had managed to survive Chickamauga and Missionary Ridge. The continuing lack of troops in 1/15th U.S. so frustrated Major Tracy that he sent a long dissertation up his chain of command:

> Head Quarters 1st Batt. 15th Infy.
> Graysville Ga. March 18, 1864.

Capt. J.W. Forsyth
A.A. Genl,
1st Div. 14 A.C.

Sir,

    I have the honor to submit for endorsement of the proper intermediate commanders to the War Department the following Special

Report of the condition and history of the battalion under my command—having in view its temporary withdrawl from field service for the purpose of thorough re-organization and recruitment.

In addition to minor affairs and skirmishes, the battalion participated honorably in battles of Shiloh, Stone River, Chickamauga, Mission Ridge, and Ringgold, taking part lastly in skirmish at Kinyan's Gap in the late advance towards Dalton, Ga.

It has had Killed and wounded in these several engagements 11 officers and 181 men. Loss in addition to killed in battle, by died of wounds and disease, one officer and 76 men. Loss by prisoners of war now in rebel hands 3 officers and 74 men. Grand aggregate of loss since entering the field 398. Now absent sick in hospital or elsewhere, from wounds or disease 1 officer and 72 men. Absent detached by War Department or other proper authority, rendering them incapable for present duty with battalion 8 officers and 23 men. Of nine officers present two (being Captains) are, by surgeons certificate, non-effective for active field service by reason of wounds received in action. Having seven officers—inclusive of Field and staff—for all duties. Of number of enlisted men present twelve are musicians (boys, being untaught, and without instruments, none having been at hand to obtain) are worthless for any important purpose. Of other enlisted men 40 are non-effective by surgeon's certificate. ...Present enlisted strength inclusive of sick, confined, on daily duty, etc., 124.

On the late march towards Dalton, all the companies of the battalion were consolidated into two—this measure being indispensable for any practicable field purpose. Deducting at that time non effectives left behind to guard Camp & men absolutely necessary to Qr. Master on the march (teamsters, blacksmiths, etc.) and to Hospital as acting steward and attendant, and adding two of the strongest Musicians to carry muskets, and the battalion gave average battle front of about forty files, *not one full company*. With this presentation of the numbers and condition of my command, I respectfully suggest so far as I may be permitted to do whether...it be well to hold the battalion for further present duty in the field, or whether...it might not be equally for the interest as well as the economy of the government, and of the service, to order the whole to such point as will be most convenient for thorough re-construction of companies, discipline and fitness for further effective service.

Trusting further that the General Commanding will accord to me credit for the desire only to present in a simple and truthful manner the points upon which I have treaded, with a general view to the best interests of my command.

I have the honor to be, Captain
Very Respectfully
Your obdt. servt.
ALBERT TRACY
Major 15th Infy.
Comdg. 1st Batt.[70]

The 15th Infantry's records that survived the war do not reveal how far up the chain Tracy's cry for help was heard. Needless to say, the battalion was not withdrawn from the field. The "interest of the government" that winter was to prepare to place maximum military pressure on the Confederacy during 1864. For that task it would need every unit available, even a formation as pitifully weak as the 1st Battalion of the 15th U.S. Infantry. Tracy's concerns, though, are understandable. For professional army officers, the Civil War was not simply a diversion from a civilian occupation and family. Military service provided Tracy and his peers with their livelihoods. The welfare of an officer's regiment was synonymous with an officer's job security. To have been a regular officer in one of the largest armies in the history of the world at that time and yet belong to a regiment that could barely scrape together a company of troops was demoralizing to the extreme. These career soldiers also realized that the winds of change would blow at gale force after the war. A regular regiment that existed only on paper would be all too easy to erase completely. And being a supernumerary officer of a defunct regiment in a demobilizing army did not constitute particularly bright career prospects. Concerns such as these are what compelled Tracy to spend most of the hours of a short winter day composing a plea for assistance, even though he knew the impact of his effort would probably be nil.

Some help was on the way even as Tracy wrote his concerns, for the Regular Army's five-year term of enlistment had finally come to end. Oliver Shepherd, the only regimental colonel of the Regular Army actually serving at a regimental headquarters, was largely responsible for effecting the change. While struggling to find recruits during the last half of 1863, Shepherd had sent letter after letter to the War Department in an attempt to focus the bureaucrats on this issue. The colonel made his final plea in late November:

Hd. Qrs. 15th Inf..
Fort Adams, R.I.
November 17, 1863

Brig. Genl. L. Thomas
   Adgt. Genl. U.S.A.
   Washington, D.C.

General,

   I respectfully submit and recommend that the provisions of general orders...authorizing Volunteers to re-enlist for the term of three years, be extended to the Regulars.

   Most of the Regulars now in service have a term of three years, dating in 1861, and consequently they will go out of the service next Spring and Summer. Authority for them to re-enlist for the term of three or five years, which it is supposed they would do in order to secure the Bounty of $402, would tend to their continuance in the Regular Service, which otherwise would not be, while there are such enormous bounties offered to Volunteers.

   I deem it proper also to recommend that the term of service be altered by the next Congress, from the term of five years to three years.

   At the close of the Florida Indian War, in 1843, it was thought that the term of enlistment, increased from three to five years, would prove beneficial to the service, but from my own observation I must disagree, because of the less frequency of re-enlistments, and the inferior quality of recruits, thereby losing the efficiency of old soldiers as the basis of discipline and Esprit-de-Corps.

   I am induced to make the foregoing recommendations on account of the discouraging slowness of recruiting, caused by the long period of Enlistment, five years. Nine tenths of those coming to the [recruiting] rendezvous are deterred from enlisting by the long period of five years. Many men besides who have been serving with the Volunteers have a desire to enter the Regular service but cannot endure the five years.

> I am Sir
>   Very Respectfully
>   Yr. Obdt. Sevt.
>
> O.L. SHEPHERD
> Col. 15th Inf..
>   Comdg.[71]

The lone voice was finally being heard. Two weeks after Shepherd sent this plea to the War Department, Assistant Adjutant General Edwin D. Townsend submitted a recommendation to the secretary of war:

Much solicitude is felt in regard to the reduced ranks of the Regular Army. Comparatively few recruits are now enlisted for it, partly because of the greater bounties paid to volunteers by States, counties, and associations, and partly owing to the term of service being five years instead of three. The official reports of battles have invariably spoken in high terms of the good conduct of the regulars wherever they have participated, and their thinned ranks after each encounter bear testimony that they are in no wise behind our gallant volunteers in steadiness and unyielding bravery under fire. It is earnestly recommended that such inducements as may be deemed effective and proper may be offered by Congress for enlistments in the regular regiments, and, among others, that the term be fixed for three years for all enlistments made during the present war.[72]

Congress reduced the term of Regular Army enlistment to three years in a joint resolution dated January 13, 1864. It took until February for the news to spread to all regimental depots, but at that point recruits started to line up. Another factor in this equation was the Federal draft. Although relatively few men entered the Union Army by being drafted, the Enrollment Act of 1863 set in motion machinery at the federal, state, and local level that focused communities on filling their enlistment quotas during a time when volunteerism was on the wane nationwide. With the $402 bounty authorized in August 1863 and the return of the three-year term, the Regular Army in 1864 offered citizens a viable alternative to being drafted. Significantly, men who joined the regulars in 1864 counted against a community's volunteer enlistment quota. Draft calls took place in March, July, and December 1864, and during those 3 months 7,354 men joined the regulars, a three-month total that exceeded the enlistments of the entire previous year. During the first four months of 1864, more than 1,300 men signed on for service with the four regular infantry regiments serving in the Army of the Cumberland. Some of these recruits began to arrive at Graysville starting in late March, finally making up for the regulars' Chickamauga losses. Major Tracy's manpower concerns eased somewhat as his battalion soon numbered almost 400 troops. At the 19th Infantry's headquarters in Ft. Wayne, Michigan, Company D/1/19th U.S., which had been broken up after Stones River, was reconstituted with recruits in April 1864 and prepared for shipment to the field.[73]

The motivations of most of the men in these levees, signing up simply to receive bounty cash or as a way to avoid the social stain of being drafted, were much different than the troops who had donned uniforms earlier in the war. Many 1864 enlistees would have been considered substandard material for a volunteer regiment; in a regular outfit they were even more so. Captain Barry of the 16th U.S. was so disgusted with the quality of the fresh manpower assigned to his battalion that he conducted a special board of examination to determine the fitness of his new soldiers. Barry found most of them lacking, as he described in a letter to the War Department:

> Hd Qrs 1st Battalion 16th Infantry
> Graysville Ga
> March 25th, 1864

Adjt Gen L. Thomas
War Department
Washington City

Sir:

I have the honor to enclose herewith the proceedings of a Board of Inspection of recruits lately received from Ft. Ontario, Oswego New York.

The assembling of the Board by me may not have been exactly according to Regulations. Still, I deemed it the best and surest method of calling your attention to and so stopping the enlistment, under the stimulant of high bounties, of old men cripples and boys as *Soldiers* into our Regiment.

Several of the recruits examined by the Board were only passed by a liberal construction of the Regulations governing the Recruiting Service in War Times, but the enlistment as *Soldiers* of the men named in the accompanying report, was such glaring injustice to the Government and injury to the Regiment, that mere justice demanded a Special report in their case.

I would especially recommend that the five boys named be Sent to Ft. Ontario. They are no use here—have no opportunity of learning Music, while being reported as Soldiers they make the other men do duty for them, evidently an injustice to the Soldiers of the command.

> I remain
> Your obdt svt
>
> R. PEABODY BARRY
> Capt. 16th Infantry
> Commanding Batt & Detach.[74]

As the new manpower poured into the regular battalions that spring, the regulars' lack of officers became readily apparent. With so many officers serving on staff duty, manning recruiting stations, and holding volunteer commissions, the regulars' officer corps in the field had been pared down to the bone. Captain George Smith thought something would have to be done soon and sent a recommendation to Department of the Cumberland headquarters:

> Head Qrs. Detachment 18th Inf..
> Graysville Ga
> April 3rd 1864

Brig Gen W.D. Whipple
    A.A.G. Dept. Cumberland

General

I have the honor respectfully to submit to you that there is a great want of Officers in this Regiment; that already since its organization there have been forty Second Lieutenants appointed from the ranks, and that material is exhausted, whilst there is not a Second Lieutenant in the Regiment.

As many young officers of the Volunteer Army are anxious to enter the Regular Service, I would respectfully recommend that an Examining Board be appointed of Officers in this Brigade, to convene within its limits for the examination of meritorious young officers of the Volunteer Service (not above twenty five years of age) who may be recommended by their Regimental Commanders to appear before it as applicants for Commission in the Regular Service.

> I am Sir
>   Very Respectfully
>   Your obedient servant
>
> G.W. SMITH
> Capt. 18th U.S. Inf.
> Comd'g Detcht[75]

Volunteers commanders and state politicians undoubtedly would have put up the same resistance against transferring officers to the regulars that they had when ordered to transfer troops during the winter of 1862–1863. But the main problem with Smith's recommendation was that there was no shortage of regular officers on paper. It was irrelevant to the War Department that so many of them were on duty elsewhere. Generals King, Johnson, Palmer, and Thomas duly forwarded Smith's recommendation to Washington, where it was carefully filed away. Smith was so disillusioned that he attempted to transfer to the regular cavalry—specifying in his request that he desired a field command—but was informed that there were no vacancies available.[76]

In addition to the new recruits, four additional companies of regulars also joined King's brigade at Graysville. One of these companies was Captain Solomon S. Robinson's A/2/16th U.S., the regulars who had been pulling garrison duty at Columbus, Kentucky, since June 1862. The three companies of 2/16th U.S. that had been assigned to the Regular Brigade during 1862 and 1863 had been temporarily attached to 1/16th, but with the arrival of Robinson's command, the four companies together were substantial enough to warrant 2/16th's establishment as a separate battalion. Captain Barry took command of the unit. Captain Alexander Stanton replaced Barry in command of the regiment's 1st Battalion, Jacob Van Zwaluwenburg's old company commander who had experienced so many difficulties while drilling his troops at Murfreesboro the year before. Stanton had been captured at Chickamauga along with most of the 16th Infantry's officers, but was exchanged and back on duty with the 16th U.S. by April 13 (being a nephew of the secretary of war had evidently served him well). He returned just in time to see General Johnson select the captain's old command, D/1/16th U.S., as the provost guard at division headquarters.

The other three new companies were all 15th Infantry outfits, tangible results of Colonel Oliver Shepherd's effort to fully organize the 15th Infantry's three battalions. Two of the units, A and B of 3/15th U.S., were attached to Major Tracy's 1st Battalion. The recruits were weak on basic soldiering skills, not to mention company and battalion tactics, so on April 27 Major Tracy ordered up extra drill for them: "In addition to drills as now ordered the recruit companies of the 3d Battalion will drill daily in squad drill and the manual of arms from 7 to 71/2 A.M. ...This drill will be conducted by non-com'd. Officers, under direct supervision of a commissioned officer of each company. Afternoon drills will be mainly skirmishing with the proper bugle calls."[77]

Major Edie's battalion contained the final new company, F/2/15th U.S. Infantry. Having spent so much time on guard duty recently, the major kept his troops drilling in the field every day the weather permitted. One of the battalion's company commanders discovered that a regular unit's training regimen could still amuse at least some volunteers. Edie discreetly handled the situation by sending a note to Colonel Stoughton:

> Hd Qrs. 2nd Batt. 15th Infantry
> Graysville, Ga.
> April 23d 1864

Commanding Officer
11th Michigan Vols

Sir,

I regret to be under the necessity of complaining to you of the conduct of some of the men of your command. The officer in command of Co. "D" of this Batt. reports to me, that whilst engaged in drilling his co. this, and previous, mornings he and his command were much annoyed by some of your men, who, standing in the edge of your camp amused themselves, by shouting a repetition of the orders given, and by applying opprobrious epithets to the men drilling.

[I believe] that it is only necessary to call your attention to these acts of discourtesy, to have them stopped. I have thought it best to resort to this mode of ending the annoyance.

> Very Respectfully
> Your obedient Servant
>
> JOHN R. EDIE
> Maj. 15th Infy
> Com'dg[78]

Unlike the charged atmosphere in 1862 when troops had rioted against the 18th Infantry, by 1864 most volunteer officers—if not all their men—knew the value of training and discipline. Stoughton reigned in his soldiers and 2/15th U.S. trained without further interference.

While at Graysville, King's brigade was responsible for performing outpost duty on Taylor's Ridge at Parker's Gap, due east from Graysville and about five miles north of Ringgold, to ensure that the enemy did not use the route in an attempt to outflank Baird's division at Ringgold Gap. A battalion would periodically spend a two-day tour of duty there. Substantial encounters with hostile forces were rare (although a sharp skirmish involving H/1/18th U.S. took place on April 14), but the experience at least provided the raw troops with some field time. The regulars knew a great campaign was about to commence and struggled to get ready. When not on outpost duty, they drilled and conducted target practice at a fast rate. Some of the regulars sharpened their shooting skills to a great extent. "[T]he company was out shooting at a target to day," Private Austin Murphy recorded in his diary on April 22, "but it was further off than it had been we shoot 300 yards today. I made a splendid shot."[79] Arthur Carpenter wrote details of his own daily routine in a letter dated April 14:

> we have to be up at 6 every morning and drill the Skirmish drill an hour, and from 91/2 o clock to 11 we have target practice. In the afternoon from 2 till 4 we have Battalion & Company drill. from 51/2 to 61/2 Inspection and Dress Parade, and between these drills & exercises we have to attend to Company matters official Business etc. So you can see that our time is pretty well occupied. ...Our battalion is camped about 300 or 400 feet above the rest of the Division on top of the ridge. we have just room enough for the camp and a drill ground. The views from our camp are splendid. we can see toward the west Mission Ridge & Lookout Mountain & Waldon's Ridge the other side of the Tenn River, extending for miles northward. toward the east we can see Taylors & White Oak Ridges— Ringgold, and far in the distance Buzzard Roost looms up showing a ragged outline against the deep blue horizon. toward the south we can see the mountain peaks around Lafayette & Rome. Here we have the benefit of the Mountain breezes, wafted to us across the intervening valleys.
>
> We are all enjoying excellent health, and always ready to fight. And we are hoping that we shall have a chance this summer to close this war. As soon as the weather permits operations will commence.[80]

As the regulars made final preparations for an excursion to their next battlefield in Georgia, a few made a trip back to the site of their first Georgia combat. A detail of forty-four regulars with seven mule teams departed Graysville on April 28, bound for Chickamauga. Their mission was to locate the bodies of any dead comrades still on the battlefield and transport the remains to Chattanooga for re-internment in the town's new national cemetery. Although more than eight months had transpired since the battle, the landscape along Chickamauga Creek still bore vivid wounds. The many newcomers on the detail could only stare in disbelief at the sights greeting their eyes at Kelly Field. Lieutenant Carpenter recorded what they saw: "Notwithstanding the horrid Spectacle that meets the eye at every step it is interesting to go over that field. graves are scattered for miles over that ground, pieces of shell, and solid shot, are lying all over the ground. broken caisons & Limbers point out the places where batteries fought, being taken & retaken, time and again, trees cut to and split to pieces, show what a storm of lead & iron fell on those memorable days. I wondered often as I gazed on the spots where I stood those days, and saw hardly a spot but what was struck with a bullet. how I could ever come out a live, but a God rules over all whose works are mighty."[81]

The regulars concentrated their efforts in the woods to the west of Jay's Mill. The old hands on the detail had no trouble locating the spot. They noticed some shallow graves near where the brigade had been overrun, and also four bodies that were still above ground. The unburied bodies consisted of just bones and tattered, bloodied uniforms. One of the region's four-legged predators had haphazardly scattered one set of remains; a weathered sack coat and forage cap among the bones identified this poor soul as having been a sergeant of the 18th Infantry. Another body was that of a corporal in the same regiment, but the final two were unidentifiable. The regulars gathered up the remains and took them to Chattanooga. The four deceased regulars were laid to rest in the cemetery as twenty-six coffins were loaded onto the wagons. The detail returned to Chickamauga the next day, filling the coffins with the remains from the shallow graves near Jay's Mill. The fallen were laid to rest later that day in Chattanooga with as much ceremony as the small detail could muster.[82]

Only a few of the regulars present in Chattanooga that day had also witnessed the burials at Stones River, when the entire Regular Brigade had rendered full military honors in a torchlight ceremony. Much had happened to the regulars, the war, and the nation during the sixteen months since the battle near Murfreesboro. After the costly battles in Georgia, Mississippi, and Pennsylvania that occurred during 1863, the focus now was to end the war as soon as possible by taking the struggle deep into the Confederate heartland. For the time being, a few soldiers and a simple ceremony were all that could be arranged to honor those who had fallen.

There were more than 2,100 men answering roll in the ranks of the seven regular battalions during the first week of May 1864, the highest strength the Army of the Cumberland's regulars ever attained. Many of these troops had been in camp a few weeks at most and were regulars in name only. Unlike the previous year prior to the Middle Tennessee Campaign, the veteran regulars did not have most of the first eight months of the year to mold the newcomers into some semblance of bonafide professional soldiers. Training would have been sporadic even if time had been available, for there were just fifty-five officers present to fill the command and staff positions of a brigade headquarters, seven battalions, and forty-eight companies. Stones River veteran James Biddle of the 16th Infantry returned to the field in early May and resumed command of his old company, B/2/16th Infantry. "Found my company much changed," the captain noted in his diary, "mostly composed of recruits, the old men being either killed or gone home. The Regular Brigade no longer exists."[83]

The Army of the Cumberland made its final preparations for the impending offensive. The IV Corps, now commanded by Major General Oliver O. Howard, gathered at Cleveland, Tennessee. Joseph Hooker's new XX Corps, formed out of the Army of the Potomac contingent that had been sent to Tennessee the previous October, rallied in Lookout Valley. King's brigade packed up its camp equipment at Graysville on May 3 and headed for Ringgold, the final staging area of Palmer's XIV Corps. Private Murphy of the 18th Regulars recalled that it was an exciting day: "This morning we have marching orders to leave we will go to ringold to reorganize the old corps and get the divisions all together. We will have a nice day to march in it is a nice breeze." Private Charles Bogart wrote a letter home to his mother on May 5, informing her of the regulars' new address: "we came here on the 3rd. we are expecting every moment to get orders to go and our whole army Corps is here now together ready for the word Go." The word would come soon enough. The Atlanta Campaign got underway less than forty-eight hours after the 18th Infantryman posted his letter, a campaign that would be different in many ways from any the regulars had endured thus far.[84]

Chapter 10:

The Atlanta Campaign

"No Troops Ever Fought Better"

The evening of May 6, 1864, was memorable for the troops at Ringgold. Orders had come down earlier in the day from General Thomas to move out at daybreak and seize Tunnel Hill, the opening move of the campaign for Atlanta. A soldier in the 37th Indiana of Brigadier General Richard Johnson's division sorted through his equipment and discarded items he would not need on the march. Shortly after sundown, he broke some candles into small pieces and lit them around his tent. The Hoosier's companions followed suit, some placing candles in nearby trees. Other units, including the regular battalions, joined in and soon an array of candle-powered constellations too numerous to count dotted the hills and valleys around Ringgold, the troops taking in the sight while silently contemplating what the fortunes of war had in store for them.[1]

The number of candles lit that night was a good indication of the martial might that the United States had assembled in southeastern Tennessee and northwestern Georgia during the spring of 1864. These forces constituted one of the Federal columns under the overall command of newly promoted Lieutenant General Ulysses S. Grant, who had become general-in-chief of the Union Army in March 1864. Grant's campaign plan for 1864 envisioned five separate armies bringing simultaneous pressure to bear on the Confederate war machine. While Grant himself would accompany George Meade's Army of the Potomac in Virginia, smaller Union forces would operate in Louisiana, on the Virginia Peninsula, and in the Shenandoah Valley. William T. Sherman now commanded the main Union Army in the West, the Military Division of the Mississippi. Grant ordered Sherman "to move against Johnston's army, to break it up, and to get into the interior of the enemy's country as far as you can, inflicting all the damage you can against their war resources." Sherman set his sights on Atlanta.

Sherman's field forces numbered about 110,000 troops. Thomas's Army of the Cumberland accounted for almost two-thirds of Sherman's manpower, with the balance consisting of Major General James B. McPherson's Army of the Tennessee and the Army of the Ohio under Major General John M. Schofield. Despite the preponderance of forces under Thomas's control, the Army of the Cumberland was destined to play a supporting role for much of the upcoming campaign. Although Sherman and Thomas were on good terms personally (they had roomed together as cadets at West Point), to an extent Sherman shared Grant's low opinion of the Army of the Cumberland's capabilities. Sherman was also still smarting from Thomas's success and his own defeat five months earlier on Missionary Ridge. In the movement against Atlanta, Sherman planned to use his former command, McPherson's Army of the Tennessee, as the main effort.

Sherman had to revise his plan for the campaign's opening moves at the last moment. Confederate General Joseph Johnston's Army of Tennessee had remained near Dalton throughout the spring. Knowing that the Confederate defenses at Rocky Face Ridge and Crow Valley were too strong to assault directly, Sherman wanted to outflank Johnston to the south and threaten his communications with Atlanta. The first version of the Union commander's plan was quite daring, involving a wide flanking movement to Rome, Georgia, by the Army of the Tennessee. Had all nine of McPherson's assigned divisions been available, the Army of the Tennessee would have been strong enough to undertake such an independent operation. But two of McPherson's divisions had been sent to Louisiana in early March to participate in the ill-fated Red River Campaign. This force, commanded by Brigadier General A.J. Smith, became bogged down in that operation and in late April Sherman learned that it would not be available for the start of operations in Georgia. Two additional divisions from McPherson's army were also absent, their regiments home on veteran furlough. With only five divisions immediately available, Sherman canceled the march to Rome.

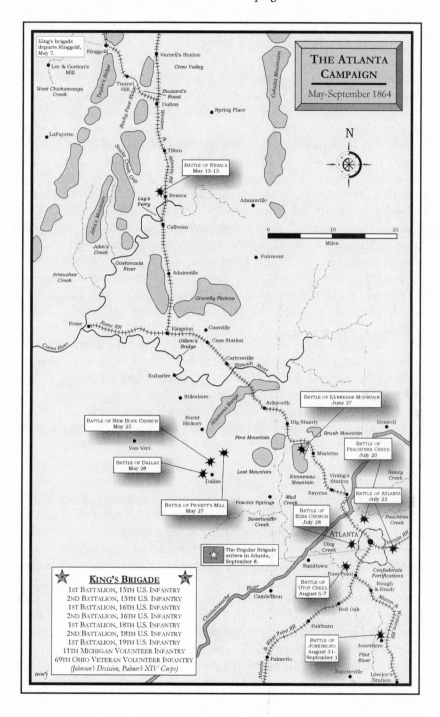

King's brigade departs Ringgold, May 7.

THE ATLANTA CAMPAIGN
May–September 1864

BATTLE OF RESACA
May 13-15

BATTLE OF KENNESAW MOUNTAIN
June 27

BATTLE OF NEW HOPE CHURCH
May 25

BATTLE OF PEACHTREE CREEK
July 20

BATTLE OF DALLAS
May 28

BATTLE OF ATLANTA
July 22

BATTLE OF PICKETT'S MILL
May 27

BATTLE OF EZRA CHURCH
July 28

The Regular Brigade arrives in Atlanta, September 8.

BATTLE OF UTOY CREEK
August 6-7

BATTLE OF JONESBORO
August 31-September 1

KING'S BRIGADE

1ST BATTALION, 15TH U.S. INFANTRY
2ND BATTALION, 15TH U.S. INFANTRY
1ST BATTALION, 16TH U.S. INFANTRY
2ND BATTALION, 16TH U.S. INFANTRY
1ST BATTALION, 18TH U.S. INFANTRY
2ND BATTALION, 18TH U.S. INFANTRY
1ST BATTALION, 19TH U.S. INFANTRY
11TH MICHIGAN VOLUNTEER INFANTRY
69TH OHIO VETERAN VOLUNTEER INFANTRY
(Johnson's Division, Palmer's XIV Corps)

Sherman instead adopted a plan earlier proposed by George Thomas: outflank Johnston's Dalton fortifications by sending a column through Snake Creek Gap. Thomas had been pushing for such a course of action ever since the February reconnaissance and skirmishing in front of Buzzard's Roost. Thomas wanted to send the Army of the Cumberland through the long defile that skirted the southern end of Rocky Face Ridge while the balance of Sherman's forces fixed Johnston's attention in the Buzzard's Roost-Dug Gap region. After traversing the undefended gap, Thomas's army would advance to the town of Resaca. Capturing this hamlet fifteen miles south of Dalton was the key to the operation, for at that point the turnpike and railroad from Dalton crossed the Oostananula River. With the crossings in Union hands, the Confederate army on Rocky Face Ridge would be cut off from Atlanta. Sherman agreed to the plan in principle, but made a major modification to it by designating McPherson's much smaller Army of the Tennessee as the force that would make the march through Snake Creek Gap. Thomas and Schofield would conduct the diversionary moves in front of Dalton. Sherman also ordered McPherson to simply break the rail line somewhere north of Resaca and then "fall back to a strong defensive position near Snake Creek, and stand ready to fall on the enemy's flank when he retreated." This was a far cry from George Thomas's vision of a powerful column emerging from the gap and storming Resaca, but it still stood a good chance of success as long as McPherson moved aggressively. It remained to be seen whether McPherson would act aggressively with just five divisions under his command.[2]

* * *

Only one regiment of volunteers marched with the regulars in John King's brigade at the start of the campaign, Colonel Stoughton's 11th Michigan. The 19th Illinois had been reassigned to Baird's division, while the 69th Ohio had not yet returned from its veteran furlough. King's regular commanders were all experienced veterans, although three of the battalions had experienced recent command changes. Captain Henry Haymond, who had commanded 2/18th U.S. ever since Captain John Thompson's death at Hoover's Gap, had left the brigade in early March for a recruiting assignment in Pittsburgh, Pennsylvania. The officer Haymond relieved there was Captain William J. Fetterman, who in turn reported to Graysville on March 31 and took command of

Haymond's old battalion. Fetterman had spent most of the previous year on recruiting duty, but he had experienced all of the 18th Infantry's 1862 marches and commanded A/2/18th U.S. at Stones River. Major Albert Tracy of 1/15th U.S. had been ill for a number of weeks and was granted sick leave on May 8, just as the campaign was getting underway. With Tracy absent, Major John Edie of 2/15th U.S. took overall command of the regiment's field detachment of two battalions. Captain Albert B. Dod, commander of 1/15th U.S. at Chickamauga, took charge of that battalion once again. Captain William S. McManus, who led 2/15th U.S. up Missionary Ridge, replaced Major Edie in immediate command of the 2nd Battalion.[3]

The regulars moved out from Ringgold early in the morning on May 7, following the familiar route through Catoosa Station to Tunnel Hill. Brigadier General Jefferson C. Davis's division led the XIV Corps' column, so the regulars and the rest of Johnson's division had an easy march. Johnson deployed his men into line-of-battle to support Davis as the latter drove some enemy pickets from Tunnel Hill, but Davis did not require assistance. King's brigade bivouacked for the night near the railroad tunnel. After General Palmer received a report that evening stating that an enemy infantry column was lurking in the valley between Tunnel Hill and Rocky Face Ridge, he warned Johnson to "Push out a strong line of skirmishers well to your right." General King positioned Captain James Mooney's 1/19th U.S. forward on the main road leading to Buzzard's Roost. Mooney, in turn, sent out two companies that evening to reconnoiter further eastward, but they reported no enemy forces deployed outside of the main Confederate positions.

So far everything had gone smoothly, although McPherson's army had not yet reached Snake Creep Gap in force as Sherman had desired. Sherman ordered Thomas to continue moving forward the next day. The Army of the Cumberland was to "threaten the Buzzard Roost Pass" and, if possible, get a force on top of Rocky Face Ridge. The Army of the Cumberland continued to close on the Confederate position during the next two days. By the morning of May 9, King's brigade was in a reserve position in front of Buzzard's Roost, the same ground it had occupied during the February skirmishing. Although Sherman's plan did not call for an actual assault on Buzzard's Roost, the Federal troops deployed here had to make their presence felt. Carlin's brigade of Johnson's division managed to claw its way up a good portion of Rocky Face Ridge immediately south of Buzzard's Roost. Johnson ordered King's brigade across Mill Creek to support Carlin if needed, but the severe terrain toward the top of the high ground prevented Carlin's men from reaching the summit. Federal forces north of the pass had better luck. A brigade from Howard's corps led by Brigadier General Charles G. Harker (who also held a regular commission as a captain in the 15th U.S.) reached the top of Rocky Face Ridge and cleared off enemy skirmishers from almost a mile of the ridgeline. This day also saw the heaviest fighting of the campaign thus far. A few miles south of Buzzard's Roost, Confederates led by Pat Cleburne bloodily repulsed an attack on Dug Gap delivered by Brigadier General John W. Geary's division of Hooker's XX Corps.[4]

Sporadic skirmishing took place in front of Buzzard's Roost for another forty-eight hours. King's brigade was within range of Confederate batteries and sharpshooters, so there was some danger to the regulars. Being subjected to random enemy fire was also nerve racking for King's troops. "I think we did not fire a shot," the 16th Infantry's Edgar Kellogg recalled of his second excursion to Buzzard's Roost, "but were for many hours compelled to passively submit to annoyance from sharpshooters on the mountains above us, and beyond the reach of our rifles. ...Towards evening the nerves of some of us seemed to need an opiate." The lieutenant took it upon himself to relieve some of the strain:

> I was sitting on a fence rail with two or three other officers, dining al fresco. I have never been much addicted to playing practical jokes, but, at the crack of a rifle away up on the mountain, temptation was too strong for me. Putting my mouth close to the ear of the gentleman next to me, I imitated the hissing, spitting sound made by a bullet passing close to one's head.
>
> The effect was surprising—yes, uplifting—but scarcely so in a moral sense, for the victim, when he returned to earth, challenged me to a fist combat. But I persuaded him to accept an apology and deny himself the fleeting pleasure of marring my anatomical comeliness.[5]

The nervousness of Kellogg's would-be assailant is understandable. "My loss from the enemy's artillery in this affair was unusually heavy," General Johnson reported, "the battery on Chattoogata Mountain [Rocky Face Ridge] and one near their left, and which I judge to be on the eastern slope of Rocky Face, burst their shell among us with remarkable accuracy." The regulars lost ten men during the skirmishing, but King's brigade was actually stronger by the time it left Buzzard's Roost. On May 11, the 69th Ohio Veteran Volunteers rejoined the brigade, Colonel Moore having 23 officers and 324 men present for duty. Four additional officers and forty-five recruits for the 16th U.S. Infantry also reported in, providing Captains Stanton and Barry with a welcome infusion of manpower for their battalions. These troops barely had time to acquaint themselves with their surroundings before a new set of orders came down. On the afternoon of May 11, King's brigade and the rest of Palmer's corps pulled back from Buzzard's Roost, elements of Howard's corps assuming responsibility for their former positions.

Early the next morning, the Army of the Cumberland, less Howard's command, marched southward to follow the Army of the Tennessee's route through Snake Creek Gap. The initial main effort of Sherman's offensive, McPherson's flanking march, had gotten off to a rough start. McPherson's movement through the gap on May 9 had indeed caught the Southerners by surprise, but the Federal column that debauched from the gap's southeastern end was hamstrung by a lack of combat power. McPherson sent only Brigadier General Grenville M. Dodge's XVI Corps (two divisions) through the gap, keeping Major General John A. Logan's XV Corps at the north end of the gap to secure the rear and flank of the movement. Dodge detached one of his divisions as further flank protection at a crossroads two miles west of Resaca. Thus only a lone Federal division continued advancing toward the town. It was not strong enough to overcome Resaca's 4,000 defenders and extensive fortifications, so McPherson called off the advance and consolidated a position well short of his objective. The Army of the Tennessee was largely idle during the next two days, except for constructing fortifications, for McPherson convinced himself that the Confederates were about to attack him with overwhelming force. With McPherson stymied, Sherman decided to send additional forces through Snake Creek Gap and again try to outflank the enemy, this time by capturing the rail bridge over the Oostanaula River at Resaca.[6]

Once Johnston realized that the bulk of the Union Army was heading for Snake Creek Gap, he pulled his forces out of the Buzzard's Roost-Dalton area and headed south to block the Federal flanking movement. By a narrow margin, most of Johnston's army reached Resaca and set up defensive positions before Sherman was able to attack. Preliminary skirmishing began on May 13 as Sherman's army continued to gather west and north of the Confederate positions covering Resaca. Palmer's corps passed through Snake Creek Gap during the night of May 12–13. King's brigade was re-supplied with ammunition and rations at daybreak. The road leading out of the gap was so crowded that it was nearly noon before Johnson's division was able to advance to its position in the Union battle line. Johnson deployed his brigades to the left of the main road leading from the gap to Resaca, with Carlin and King in front and the division's third brigade, now commanded by Colonel Benjamin Scribner, held in reserve. Johnson's line moved about four miles toward Resaca, "over a very broken and heavily wooded country," the last mile of which a running fight was kept up with Confederate skirmishers. It then came upon the main Confederate position, a four-mile battle line starting along the Oostanaula west of Resaca and arching off to the hills in the north. Johnson halted his line and shortly thereafter received orders from General Palmer to move two miles northward to the XIV Corps's new position.[7]

Upon arrival the next day of Howard's corps from Dalton, Sherman ordered an attack. The Union commander erroneously believed that Johnston was about to continue moving southward. To pin down the Confederates, Sherman ordered the three northernmost Federal corps, which included Palmer's XIV, to advance against the enemy line. Richard Johnson moved King's and Carlin's brigades into line at nine o'clock in the morning, with Scribner again in reserve. The division then made another slow movement over heavily forested and rugged terrain, making it difficult for Johnson to maintain contact with Baird's division on his left. After groping forward about a mile, the division came upon some open ground. A half-mile in front of Johnson's position on a low ridge waited the enemy, elements of Cleburne's and Major General William Bate's Divisions. The valley of Camp Creek lay between the lines, a swampy stretch of low ground laced with thick vegetation. General Johnson saw that closing with the enemy position over this ground would be difficult: "In front...was an open field of some 400 yards wide, sloping gradually down to a creek directly in my front. The general course of this creek in front of my line was nearly parallel to the enemy's works; the bottom was in some places miry with a considerable depth of water—in others quite the reverse, its crooked

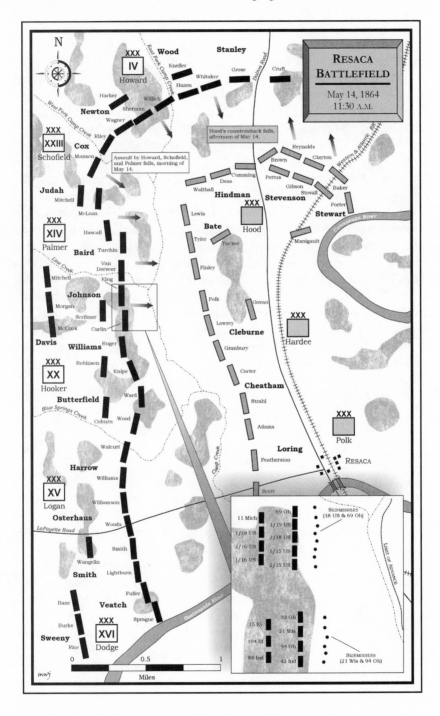

N

XXX
IV
Howard

Wood

Stanley

RESACA
BATTLEFIELD

May 14, 1864
11:30 A.M.

Knefler

Whitaker   Grose   Cruft

Dalton Road

Harker   Willich

Newton   Sherman

Wagner

Riley

East Fork Camp Creek

West Fork Camp Creek

Hood's counterattack fails,
afternoon of May 14.

XXX
XXIII
Schofield   Cox

Manson

Assault by Howard, Schofield,
and Palmer fails, morning of
May 14.

Reynolds

Brown   Clayton

Cumming   Pettus

Deas

Walthall   Gibson   Stovall
Hindman   Buker
XXX
Hood   Stevenson
Porter

Stewart

Western & Atlantic RR

Judah

Mitchell

McLean

XXX
XIV
Palmer

Baird

Hascall

Turchin

Van
Derveer

Lewis

Bate

Tyler   Tucker

Finley

Conasauga River

Manigault

Line Creek

Mitchell   King

Johnson

Morgan

Scribner

McCook   Carlin

Polk   Govan

Lowrey
Cleburne

Granbury

XXX
Hardee

Davis   Williams   Ruger

Robinson

XXX
XX
Hooker

Knipe

Butterfield

Ward

Carter

Cheatham

Strahl

Blue Springs Creek

Coburn   Wood

Walcutt

Adams

XXX
Polk

Harrow

Williams

Loring

Featherston

RESACA

XXX
XV
Logan   Osterhaus

Williamson

Woods

Camp Creek

Scott

LaFayette Road

Smith

Wangelin

11 Mich   69 Oh

SKIRMISHERS
(18 US & 69 Oh)

Smith   Lightburn

1/19 US

1/18 US   2/18 US

2/16 US   1/15 US

1/16 US   2/15 US

LIMIT OF ADVANCE

Fuller

Veatch

Bane

Burke   Sprague

Sweeny   Rice

XXX
XVI
Dodge

Oostanaula River

33 Oh

15 Ky   21 Wis

104 Ill   94 Oh

88 Ind   42 Ind

SKIRMISHERS
(21 Wis & 94 Oh)

mwj

0   0.5   1

Miles

channel filled in some places with a dense underbrush, in others
obstructed by fallen trees and drift. It afforded a serious obstacle to
the advance of troops in line."[8]

General Palmer instructed Johnson to move forward after Baird
did so. The wait lasted about ninety minutes, during which time
skirmishers from the 18th Infantry drove their Confederate counterparts across the creek while General King aligned his brigade. When
Johnson heard heavy firing off to his left commence at half past
eleven, the Kentuckian ordered King and Carlin forward. Carlin's
brigade on the left was closer to Camp Creek and crossed the
swampy ground before King's troops. Carlin pushed his men up the
slope on the far side toward the Confederate line. They did not go
far before intense fire brought them to a halt; Carlin lost more than
200 troops in the span of just a few minutes. Over in King's ranks,
meanwhile, a heavy skirmish line of the 18th Regulars and 69th
Ohio crossed the creek and advanced toward the Confederate line.
When General King saw how easily Carlin had been repulsed, he
halted his own advance. King ordered his regulars and volunteers to
dig in along the low ground of Camp Creek, an area that partially
sheltered the men from enemy fire. Carlin's regiments did the same,
and the attack in Johnson's sector was over just moments after it
began.

Up and down the line, the Federal attack on May 14 gained little, as did a Confederate counterattack later in the day on the north
end of the Federal position. Additional attacks on May 15 (none
involving the regulars) likewise produced few tangible results. Both
sides by now had learned the value of field fortifications. If frontal
assaults had been difficult early in the war, they were just about
impossible by 1864. The best way to dislodge an entrenched enemy
force was to maneuver it out of its fortifications. Sherman began to
do this while the fighting at Resaca began in earnest on May 14,
sending Brigadier General Thomas W. Sweeny's division of
McPherson's army southwest of Resaca to find a spot to cross the
Oostanaula. By early afternoon on May 15, Sweeny's division had
established a bridgehead across the river at Lay's Ferry.[9]

Although the regulars did not close with the enemy line during
the Battle of Resaca, their losses were beginning to mount. A new
and unwelcome feature of this campaign was the almost daily occurrence of casualties. Losses in a single day never matched what the
Regular Brigade had endured at Stones River or Chickamauga, but

constant exposure to hostile fire meant fewer and fewer men answered role call each morning. Richard Johnson witnessed a casualty while repositioning King's troops during the early evening of May 15, one of the many regulars to die an unheralded death on the road to Atlanta: "I was with General King. A halt had been made for some reason, and one of the regular soldiers lay down, with his head against an old, badly-decayed log, to take a short sleep. When the order was given to fall in, he did not move, and, on examination, he was found to be dead. An ordinary bullet had passed through the log and entered his skull, producing instant death."[10]

Captain Anson Mills squinted through the early-morning mist at the enemy position. The sun was starting to brighten the eastern horizon, providing enough light to silhouette any enemy soldiers who happened to be on top of the ridge to Mills's front. With a sigh of relief, Mills discerned that nothing was moving. He motioned for his company to follow as he cautiously advanced up the ridge on the east side of Camp Creek, toward the position that the previous evening had been crowned with Confederate artillery and bayonets. Reaching the top, they found only empty fortifications and refuse. The patrol moved down the opposite side of the ridge and pushed eastward until reaching the tracks of the Western & Atlantic Railroad. Turning south, Mills led his troops about a mile and a half further to the outskirts of Resaca. There they bumped into a group of twenty Confederates who were quite willing to surrender. From them Mills learned that the Southern army had retreated south of the Oostanaula River. The captain headed back for Federal lines with his bag of prisoners and the news.

General King had sent Mills and B/2/18th U.S. out on a predawn reconnaissance on May 16 to confirm rumors that the enemy had pulled out. Similar scouting parties elsewhere along the line returned with the same news: the enemy had stolen away after dark the previous night. Threatened by the Federal crossing of the Oostanaula at Lay's Ferry, Johnston abandoned the position on the north side of the river and retreated southward. King's brigade marched to Resaca and relaxed, relishing their first chance in nine days to be out of close contact with the enemy.[11]

* * *

The 18th Infantry gave a warm welcome that afternoon to Lieutenant William Bisbee, who finally returned to the field after spending the previous eleven months serving as a mustering officer in Boston, recovering from the rheumatism that had flared up during the Middle Tennessee Campaign. The veteran officer was assigned as adjutant of the 18th Infantry's 2nd Battalion. Captain George Smith had been serving as both the 18th Infantry's detachment commander (a position similar to Major Edie's role in the 15th U.S.) and commander of the regiment's 1st Battalion, while Lieutenant Phisterer was also double hatted as detachment adjutant and adjutant of the 2nd Battalion. Bisbee's assignment as 2/18th adjutant relieved Phisterer from many of his administrative duties and allowed Phisterer to concentrate on the operations of the detachment, which in turn enabled Smith to spend more time as commander of the 1st Battalion.

A few days after Bisbee's arrival, a new officer arrived to take command of the 16th Regulars—Captain Ebenezer Gay. Gay was virtually unknown to his men even though he had held a commission in the 16th since 1861. An 1855 West Pointer who ranked sixth in his class, Gay spent his first six years after graduation in the 2nd U.S. Dragoons. During the first three years of the Civil War, he was on detached service in various cavalry staff positions at the headquarters of the Department of the Ohio/Cumberland. Upon arrival at Resaca, Captain Gay reorganized his two-battalion detachment. The 16th Regulars had not been numerically strong at the beginning of the campaign, and by mid-May its strength was even worse, so Gay distilled the two battalions into a single detachment with all nine companies lumped together under his control. Captain Barry, former commander of 2/16th, took command of F/1/16th U.S., while Captain Stanton of 1/16th became Gay's second-in-command.

The 19th Infantry also experienced a command change. Captain Lewis Wilson linked up with 1/19th U.S. on May 22 and assumed command due to his seniority over Captain Mooney. Wilson is a somewhat shadowy figure who began the war as colonel of the 2nd Ohio Volunteers. He resigned that commission in June 1861 and accepted a captaincy in the 19th Regulars. Wilson spent some time in the field during 1862 as commander of D/1/19th U.S., although he always managed to be absent on other duties when important events (such as battles at Shiloh and Stones River) occurred. He was briefly present for duty at Murfreesboro prior to the Middle Tennessee Campaign, but ended up spending most of 1863 and early 1864 in a comfortable position at the 19th Infantry's headquarters in Michigan. It was undoubtedly frustrating for veteran officers such as Lieutenant Carpenter to be commanded by a man whose main wartime experiences were centered on field duty avoidance, particularly when the presence of such officers on the regiment's rolls delayed the promotions of more deserving lieutenants. Carpenter was probably happy when General King brought charges of misconduct against Wilson in June 1864, resulting in Wilson's resignation the following month. Captain Egbert Phelps briefly commanded 1/19th after Wilson's exit, although a few weeks later Phelps left the field due to sickness. The 19th Infantry would end the Atlanta Campaign as it began, with Captain Mooney in command.[12]

The physical and mental strain was heavy on everyone during the Atlanta Campaign. Unlike the Army of the Cumberland's previous campaigns, operations in 1864 did not cease after an encounter with the opposition. In recalling their experiences in north Georgia, many veterans remembered the campaign as a blur; the endless marching, frequent combat, and daily casualties seemed to all blend together. In his memoirs, Frederick Phisterer summed up nearly two weeks of operations that occurred during June 1864 in a single sentence: "moved to the right, to the left, to the front, placed in reserve, etc., fortified positions, and almost always under fire." Even Jacob Van Zwaluwenburg, who spent almost the entire campaign in a relatively safe position as a division provost, wrote little about it. As the veteran composed his memoirs years after the war he was able to write in detail about events that occurred both immediately prior to and after the Georgia fighting, but not much in between. The fast pace of operations meant that a prolific writer such as Arthur B. Carpenter could not find time to compose any letters during the first three weeks of his march into Georgia. The initial word his family received from him came in the form of a telegram the lieutenant sent on June 1: "I am all right so far, have not time to write details. I lost men out of my Company at Resaca. Good Bye."[13]

The nine days of maneuvering from Rocky Face Ridge to Resaca set the tone for what was to come. Sherman outnumbered Johnston by a good margin and could outflank the Confederates almost whenever Johnston made a stand. Johnston usually chose to delay the Federal advance for only a few days before falling back again, keeping the Army of Tennessee between Sherman's force and Atlanta. A Confederate captured by the 19th Infantry toward the end of the campaign gave about as good of an opinion as any about what the Southerners thought of Sherman's tactics: "As soon as he

[Sherman] gets in front of our army, he gets on a hill, stretches his wings around our flanks, and commands, Attention! Creation! Right Wheel! March! and then we 'uns have to get up and git."[14]

* * *

The war of maneuver continued on May 17 as Sherman's army crossed the Oostanaula and strove to catch up with the retreating Army of Tennessee. General Johnston briefly considered making a stand at Calhoun, six miles south of Resaca, but instead pushed his army seven miles further south along the Western & Atlantic to Adairsville. This position he likewise abandoned without a fight, finally deciding to offer Sherman battle eleven miles deeper into Georgia at Cassville. The Federal army arrived in front of Cassville on May 19, deployed, and bombarded the Southern position with artillery. Sherman planned to attack the enemy line the next day but this proved unnecessary. Two of Johnston's three corps commanders, Hood and Polk, doubted the wisdom of Johnston's decision to fight at Cassville and convinced their commander that further retreat was the only alternative. Shortly after midnight on May 20, the Confederate army abandoned Cassville and again slipped away in the darkness, this time heading toward the Etowah River. The head of Johnston's column covered the twelve miles to the river by daybreak. By mid-afternoon, the Army of Tennessee was safely across and moving further southward.

The regulars never came within eyesight of an enemy soldier during the march between the Oostanaula and the Etowah. While moving toward Cassville on May 19, Johnson's division was ordered to veer off to the southwest and seize Gillem's Bridge on the Etowah. The division's column reached the bridge in the late afternoon, but found Federal troopers from Brigadier General Kenner Garrard's cavalry division already securing the site. "I formed my lines here so as to cover all approaches and remained until morning," General Johnson wrote, "seeing nothing of the enemy." The regulars would soon enough see their opposition again. After crossing the Etowah, Johnston occupied a strong position about five miles south of the river in the rugged Allatoona Mountains. Sherman chose not to assault the Allatoona line. He instead moved southwestward and attempted to outflank it, even though doing so meant that Sherman's armies would be operating away from their rail supply line. In preparation for this difficult undertaking, the Federal army remained north of the Etowah for three days, sending sick and wounded soldiers back to Chattanooga and stripping down to the barest of logistical necessities. In his adjutant's journal for the 18th Infantry, Lieutenant Bisbee noted that on May 20 the regulars "Bivouacked near Cass Station and sent back the baggage reserving only one wagon to the battalion which from this time to the capture of Atlanta was seldom seen." According to James Biddle's diary entry of the following day, this captain, for one, was sorry to see the baggage depart: "When I left Chattanooga I had on a thin suit of flannel uniform & on the march, while passing through some under-brush, I tore off one [of] my trouser legs & as my under clothing is red I now have one red & one blue leg. No other clothing is to be had & my valise is somewhere near Tunnel-Hill."[15]

The combined Union armies crossed the Etowah on May 23, Johnson's division by way of Island Ford near Gillem's bridge. Sherman's march objective was the small town of Dallas, about six-teen miles southwest of Cassville, from which point he planned to move back eastward to Marietta. This movement would bypass Johnston's position in the Allatoona Mountains and, hopefully, cause the Confederates to again retreat. Johnston pulled out of Allatoona once he discerned what Sherman was up to, but instead of heading south to Atlanta, the Army of Tennessee moved toward Dallas to block the Union flanking maneuver. Late in the day on May 25, as the two armies struggled toward each other through this region's dense forests and rolling hills, part of Hooker's corps assaulted a small Confederate force commanded by Major General A.P. Stewart near New Hope Church. Sherman had hoped Hooker would brush this force aside and enable the Union Army to begin its march to Marietta, but Stewart skillfully held his ground. Throughout that night and into the next day, both armies rushed forces to the area and dug in. Instead of outflanking the Confederates, three days of tough marching to the Dallas-New Hope Church area had resulted in Sherman again confronting a for-tified enemy line.

The line of Johnston's smaller army could not go on forever. In an attempt to find the Confederate right flank beyond New Hope Church, Sherman sent Richard Johnson's and Thomas Woods's divi-sions (the latter from Howard's corps) northeastward on May 27. After moving through seemingly endless dense woodland for most of the day, the Federals came upon the end of the Confederate line near Pickett's Mill and attacked at 4:30 P.M. General Howard had

overall command of the operation and designated Wood's division
to conduct the assault. Johnson supported with Scribner's brigade
while holding King's and Carlin's troops in reserve.[16] In a confusing,
intense struggle over rugged terrain, four Federal brigades battered
themselves against Pat Cleburne's division, Johnston having rushed
the Irishman's troops to Pickett's Mill just in time to meet the Union
assault. Two brigades of Woods's division were decimated; about
100 of Scribner's men went down. The unfamiliar wilderness
restricted maneuver and the regulars were not committed to the
fighting. Lieutenant Kellogg remembered the day as a frustrating
one:

> Once during the day the Sixteenth formed line and dressed ranks,
> and as I aligned my company I found myself standing on a heart-
> shaped stone. Then, in obedience to someone's order, or a conflict of
> orders, we executed a series of movements to nearly every point of
> the compass–I really believe we "boxed" it–and at the termination
> of these erratic maneuvers I found myself "dressing" my company,
> and standing on the same heart-shaped stone, and facing precisely
> the same direction that I had about an hour before. Taking this last
> hour's work as a basis, I endeavored, with a somewhat addled brain,
> I must confess, to demonstrate mathematically just how long a time
> would be required for us to drive Johnston and his army off the
> southern end of Florida, and drown the whole outfit in the Gulf
> Stream. But no one would listen to me and I left the problem
> unsolved.[17]

The attack ended at sundown having generated little except
1,600 Federal casualties. Scribner's bloodied regiments fell back
through King's line shortly before midnight. King's brigade dug in,
expecting the enemy to follow up their defensive victory with an
assault of their own. King's and Carlin's commands were the only
fresh troops available, and they would have to bear the brunt of any
Confederate counterattack. Brigadier General Johnson, wanting to
be near the potential crisis spot, spent the night with John King. The
division's baggage train had not been able to make it through the
difficult terrain to the vicinity of Pickett's Mill, so the two generals
bedded down with a single saddle blanket as cover, a stone for a pillow, and nothing to eat.[18]

The expected attack did not materialize, although an enemy battery heavily shelled the area where King's brigade was positioned.
Lieutenant Carpenter recalled in a June 3 letter, the first he was able

to compose in Georgia, that "[t]he first night we were shelled by the rebels. one burst over my company, but fortunately hurt no one. they are very demoralizing however." Carpenter's fellow 19th Infantrymen Sergeant Eli Tarbell was not as fortunate: "About 4 oclock this morning a shell burst over our heads & wounded me in the right foot & John Howell in the side. I went to the rear Sit down behind a big tree, another Shell burst in the Top of that tree & I got out of that, met the hospital Stewad, he put me on his horse & took me out of reach of the Rebel Shells. The Roar of artillery & musketrey is deefning. It looks a little Scary for our Side just now." The Battle of Pickett's Mill was the end of the line for Eli Tarbell. The sergeant had received what American soldiers of the next century would call a "million dollar wound," serious enough to be evacuated off the front line, but not life threatening. Tarbell spent the rest of his enlistment convalescing in hospitals at Nashville and Louisville.[19]

Federal pioneers cut a trail through the woods during the darkness. By morning, provisions and ammunition were moving forward and casualties were heading for the rear. General Johnson had an orderly build a fire in a ravine to boil some coffee. Seeing the generals brewing up, some of the regulars nearby started fires of their own. "Soon a heavy column of smoke ascended above the trees," Johnson recalled, "revealing our exact whereabouts." The guns that had annoyed King's brigade during the night opened up again. Johnson was impressed, in a way, with the Confederate artillery's accuracy: "At this time King and myself were sitting on the stone which we had used for a pillow, with our faces buried in our hands and our hands on our knees. Suddenly the enemy opened with one or more batteries upon our position. I straightened myself up in time to see the effect of the first shot, which was to cut a soldier into two pieces; the second shot carried away the arm of Colonel Niebling of Ohio; the third shot grazed the talma of King and struck me just over the liver and disabled me. I was taken back to a safe place and King assumed command of the division. If he had had the same amount of curiosity that I exhibited he would have received the twelve-pound shell instead of myself." Richard Johnson would be out of action the better part of the next two months. King replaced Johnson in charge of the division and Colonel Stoughton assumed command of King's brigade.[20]

The regulars remained in their Pickett's Mill entrenchments a total of ten days. Facing a stalemate after the clashes at New Hope Church and Pickett's Mill, Sherman wanted to move his logistically strapped army back to its Western & Atlantic lifeline, but pulling forces off the firing line and laterally shifting them across the front was a hazardous and time-consuming affair. While Sherman repositioned his forces at the western end of the Federal line, King's division on the eastern flank remained in place. Although no large-scale attacks involving the regulars took place, the opposing lines were quite close, and heavy firing took place every day, along with a few localized assaults. Major John Edie recalled that during the stay at Pickett's Mill "[i]ncessant vigilance and resolute determination were all the time necessary to hold the position. The enemy kept up during these days a continuous and fatal discharge of musketry, shell, and canister. The casualties at this point were numerous." Arthur Carpenter used less colorful prose to express much the same sentiment: "our brigade has been in front all the time and has lost severly. our works are close to the rebel works, so that in some places no pickets or skirmishers are thrown out. we have to lay low or get picked off."[21]

Edgar Kellogg came close to being picked off more than once on May 28. His 16th Infantry company was on the left flank of the brigade, overlooking the ruins of Pickett's Mill on Little Pumpkin Vine Creek from an open, sloping field. The company's position in the field was very exposed and only the hasty fortifications dug the previous evening kept the regulars alive. "The...day was a hot one," Kellogg remembered, "and the Confederates, a short rifle shot away, hidden by intrenchment's, trees and bushes, sent their bullets with deadly precision over the top of my parapet, making it impossible for my men to leave their trench for any purpose except at the risk of almost certain death or wound." Captain Ebenezer Gay, commanding the 16th U.S., evidently was not aware of Kellogg's precarious position, for the detachment commander ordered Kellogg to take his company to another part of the line for picket duty. The sergeant detailed to convey Gay's order was no fool and knew that crossing the open field to Kellogg's position was an unhealthy endeavor. The courier shouted the orders to Kellogg while hiding behind a tree in the woodline to the lieutenant's rear. Kellogg likewise did not want to risk his company, but orders were orders. Wisely, the lieutenant decided to run the gauntlet with just a small group initially. He told his 1st sergeant and ten men to follow him up the hill: "With this squad of leading men I ran from cover. In an instant half of these men were shot down. I tried to assist those unhurt in carrying or dragging the stricken ones out of this death-trap, but as I stooped to help a poor fellow whose thigh had been shattered, the contents of the inside breast pocket of my coat, all the official documents, notes, memoranda for muster rolls, everything pertaining to my company fell out and into that bullet-beaten ground. I recovered every one of those papers, but while doing so it seemed to me that every bullet that struck the earth near me made a sound like that of a sledge hammer wielded by a Titan." Kellogg reported the results of his experiment to Captain Gay, who merci-fully countermanded the orders for picket duty. Kellogg ran back into the field and returned to his company's position. He dodged back and forth as he ran across the open space, amazed that he made it: "Perhaps the Confederates in front thought I had taken on a load of alcohol, and were for a moment lost in envious wonder as to where I got it, for only two or three of their bullets [were fired], and none hit me."[22]

The lines the two sides occupied were initially those they had ended up in upon conclusion of Howard's May 27 attack. Prior to his wounding General Johnson noticed that the layout of his divi-sion line was "an exceedingly bad one," but with the enemy so close, it was difficult to for either side to improve their positions. A Confederate picket post occupying a certain knoll in front of the reg-ulars' position was particularly annoying because it provided the enemy with a key observation point. The regulars deemed the posi-tion so important that they launched a night assault to capture it after sundown on May 29. They pulled off the raid flawlessly and without loss. Two companies of the 16th Infantry, A/1/16th and C/2/16th, silently crept out of their rifle pits in the darkness and tra-versed a portion of the distance to the knoll. With a yell, the regu-lars charged up the hill and captured the startled enemy sentinels occupying the area. The commotion was the signal for Captain William J. Fetterman to bring up 2/18th U.S., which ran forward and consolidated the Federal hold on the position. With the 16th Infantrymen providing security from enemy picket fire, Fetterman's battalion spent the rest of the night fortifying the knoll. They fin-ished their work by daybreak, at which time the 16th Infantry secu-rity force was withdrawn back to the main line. The capture of the knoll evidently irritated the enemy, for they kept it under heavy fire and, on May 31, launched a determined assault to recapture the lost ground. Fetterman's battalion repulsed the attack and inflicted numerous casualties on the assailants, although in doing so, 2/18th U.S. lost thirty-four men wounded. Lieutenant John I. Adair was among the injured, shot through the neck. Adair had been previously wounded at Chickamauga, so he was definitely lucky to be alive at this point. Captain George Smith noted in his campaign report that "The conduct of Captain Fetterman, in command of his battalion, in throwing up a salient and maintaining his position against repeated attempts to dislodge him by the enemy, is worthy of particular notice."

The heavy assault on the knoll was the exception rather than the rule in regard to the type of fighting that took place while the regulars occupied the trenches at Pickett's Mill. Most of their losses occurred randomly and in small numbers, but after ten days, the numbers began to add up. Among those killed were Lieutenant Joseph Cochran Forbes, an Englishman hailing from the Sandwich Islands and mustang officer of the 15th Infantry, and Sergeant Major Christopher Peterson of 2/18th U.S., "a gallant and faithful soldier," one of only two Regular Army sergeants major to die in battle during the Civil War (the other being Sergeant Major George W. Steever of the 13th U.S. Infantry). Sergeant James E. Patton replaced Peterson as Fetterman's sergeant major. The regulars gave as well as they received in terms of casualties. Lieutenant William Bisbee recalled that, after a few days, the enemy dead piled up around Fetterman's knoll "created an intolerable stench, causing sad diminution in our ranks on account of nauseating sickness."[23]

As Lieutenant Kellogg had discovered the hard way, the regulars' most hazardous undertaking was rotating men for picket duty. To keep losses to a minimum they quickly learned to change out pickets only at night. According to Captain Biddle, it was still dangerous work:

> May 31st. Had a quiet night, the Reb. batteries for the first time in four days not shelling us & we got some sleep. My company was detailed for picket line. When the lines are very close, as in this case we generally form the relief either in side or out side the brest-works, a detail of three or four men is then made for each rifle-pit & the men directed to go forward with as little noise as possible, so as not to draw the enemy's fire and occupy their respective pits. The old

line, on being relieved, comes back in the same way. As soon as every thing is quiet the officer on duty makes his round. The making of these was the most disagreeable duty we had, for besides the bullets, which, were not very dangerous in the dark we were in danger of missing the rifle-pits and walking into lines on the other side.[24]

Arthur Carpenter spent a disagreeable day and night on June 4 while picketing the 19th Infantry's line. "Lieut Leary & myself picked out a place behind a tree with a little work thrown up each side," Carpenter recalled. "the ditch was about half full of water. At daylight the firing commenced and we were compelled to lay down there all the time. bullets struck the tree and dirt all around us. and it was raining all the time too. we lay there in the rain, under fire, with nothing to eat or drink for 24 hours. Is not that suffering for your country?" Captain Wilson sent out another company that evening to relieve Carpenter's hungry and wet troops. The relief went smoothly until one of the regulars slipped on the muddy ground. He fell and made a great racket; vigilant Confederate pickets opened fire all along the line. Luckily, none of the regulars were hit and the relief continued without further incident. The Southern pickets were quick to react that night because the Army of Tennessee was again pulling out and falling back. Federal cavalry had occupied the Allatoona area on June 1, a move that caused Johnston to abandon the Dallas line and take up a new position in the mountains northwest of Marietta. With the enemy gone, Carpenter and Leary went out to their old picket post the next morning to inspect the tree behind which they had hidden. It turned out to be hollow and had a "large hole open toward the enemy."[25]

While the Federal army had been tactically defeated in most of the small battles on the Dallas front, Sherman gained a victory of sorts by maneuvering the enemy first out of the Allatoona mountains and then from the Dallas wilderness. When the armies again clashed later in June near Marietta, Atlanta would be but twenty miles away.

* * *

Constant exposure and daily skirmishes were slowly wearing down the Union Army as it approached Atlanta. Sherman was able bring additional units to Georgia from elsewhere in the theater, thus keeping his overall numbers up, but for those units that participated in the campaign from the start, the wear and tear started to show after only a few weeks. The 2nd Battalion of the 18th U.S. reported losing sixty-four troops from all causes during May 1864, more than 17 percent of the men who had marched out of Ringgold at the beginning of the month. Contingents of recruits arrived periodically to reinforce the regular battalions, totaling about 300 fresh troops during the duration of the campaign. Included in that number were two additional companies, both of which linked up with King's brigade during the latter part of May. Company C/3/15th U.S. was attached to Captain Dod's 1/15th, while the new iteration of D/1/19th joined Captain Wilson's battalion, meaning that, for the first time, 1/19th U.S. had its full complement of eight companies in the field. These reinforcements did not make up for the constant losses. Even if they had, the newcomers were of little practical use without proper training, time for which was hard to come by during the Atlanta Campaign.

Extracting the Federal army from the Dallas line and resuming the offensive was a slow process. Heavy rains hindered movement over the region's primitive roads. The bridge over the Etowah had to be repaired and supplies stockpiled before continuing. Sherman moved his headquarters to Acworth and gathered his forces. Stoughton's brigade moved on June 6 to Big Shanty, a station on the Western & Atlantic nine miles northeast of Pickett's Mill and seven miles up the tracks from Marietta. Johnston's Confederates were only a few miles away, occupying yet another series of fortified positions from Gilgal Church in the west to Brush Mountain in the east, again blocking Sherman's advance. The Federal army was glad to be out of the wilderness of the Dallas line and again near the railroad, in spite of the almost constant downpours. "I am well and confident of success," Lieutenant Carpenter wrote to his parents on June 8. "Our whole army is in good spirits." Spirits sank somewhat in the 16th Infantry the next day. One of the regiment's inexperienced troops accidently fired his rifle, wounding one regular and killing another.[26]

Sherman began advancing again on June 10. Rain that seemed like it would never end continued to slow the progress, as did the nearby enemy. The Federal army's glacial movement and fondness for digging in is well summed up in Captain McManus's report on the operations of 2/15th Infantry: "On the 11th instant advanced one mile, built works, and moved in the afternoon by the right of companies to the front, a distance of two miles, and built new works, behind which we lay until the 14th instant, when we advanced one mile and again built new works." A welcome event occurred on June 11: the bridge over the Etowah was put into operation and trains started bringing in much-needed supplies. The position the regulars occupied from the 11th to the 14th of June was directly to the right of the Western & Atlantic tracks (where they formed the left flank of the Army of the Cumberland, troops from the Army of the Tennessee being on the other side) and thus they were able to benefit immediately. William A. Gilday, a private in B/3/15th U.S., remembered when the first train arrived: "We had not seen cars for some time, and we gave a whole-hearted cheer. We knew that meant supplies and letters from home. The engineer responded with the whistle."

The train pulled up right next to the 15th Infantry's position. Grinning regulars eagerly assisted in off-loading the cargo. Just up the tracks on Pine Mountain, a fortified hilltop in front of the enemy main line, Confederates also noted the train's arrival and concurrent cheering. They lobbed a few shells through the rain at the regulars during the unloading, but never quite got the range. Someone on the Federal then side came up with a daring idea as the train was emptied. To get a fix on the enemy artillery's position, it was suggested that the train proceed down the tracks a bit and draw additional fire. The engineer was intrigued by the notion and agreed to give it a try. The locomotive and one boxcar were uncoupled from the rest of the cars and "started fast" toward Pine Mountain. Southern gunners duly opened fire and the engineer suddenly realized that a shooting gallery was perhaps not a safe place for either he or his locomotive to be. He slammed on the brakes and the train screeched to a halt, after which he reversed back toward Federal lines at top speed. Confederate shells followed him all the way, the only thing saving the train being that Civil War artillerymen did not often shoot at fast-moving targets. The episode at least provided the regulars with a good idea of where the enemy's guns were located. A Federal battery pulled into the 15th Infantry's position later in the day and opened up. The counterbattery fire seemed to be effective, for the opposing artillery was silent for the next two days.[27]

George Thomas advanced the Army of the Cumberland's lines about a mile closer to Pine Mountain on June 14. As Stoughton's brigade moved forward that day, a familiar officer reported for duty with the 18th Regulars, Captain Lyman M. Kellogg. Kellogg, the elder brother of both 16th Infantry Lieutenant Edgar Kellogg and General Thomas's aide Captain Sanford Kellogg, by virtue of seniority replaced Captain Smith in command of the two-battalion 18th Infantry field contingent. Kellogg had a strained relationship with many of the 18th Infantrymen and a somewhat checkered career both before and during the war, the marriage of his cousin to George Thomas notwithstanding. After graduating from West Point in 1852, Kellogg was assigned to the 2nd U.S. Infantry. His regiment did not then have any vacant lieutenant positions, so Kellogg occupied the lowly rank of brevet 2nd lieutenant for more than two years. He was a "real" lieutenant in the 2nd U.S. for only a year before he was transferred to the newly authorized 10th U.S. Infantry in 1855. Little more than four months after the transfer, Kellogg had enough of the peacetime army and resigned his commission. Ten months of civil life did not suit him either, so in 1856 he secured a new commission as a second lieutenant in the 3rd U.S. Artillery, the third regiment in which he had held that rank in an era when the typical officer spent his entire company-grade career in a single outfit. He was posted to the Pacific Northwest and served in Company A of the 3rd Artillery (one of Kellogg's non-commissioned officers was Sergeant Frederick Phisterer), but life in the "redlegs" did not work out for the ex-infantry officer. Although he was finally promoted to first lieutenant in 1858, he had a fondness for alcohol that got the better of him. Kellogg was cashiered in May 1860 for being drunk on duty.

As with so many former regulars, the Civil War provided Kellogg another opportunity for military service, at first as a captain in the 24th Ohio. After securing a regular captaincy in the 18th U.S. during the summer of 1861, Kellogg assisted Henry Carrington in recruiting the regiment and training its new officers. Oliver Shepherd was glad to have the services of a company commander with so many years of service, once remarking: "The Regiment is new, and has not enough officers in the grade of Captain, who understand well the duties of so responsible a commission. Captain Kellogg does understand them well and has the disposition & will to perform them in a strict & rigid manner."[28] The captain commanded D/3/18th U.S. at Corinth, but found himself in hot water again during July 1862. While the 18th Regulars were guarding the depot at Iuka, Kellogg began drinking again. He later disingenuously claimed that imbibing was almost an official duty:

Concerning my use of liquor, it is due to myself to state (and every officer and man in the regiment knows it to be the truth) that I made use of liquor for the space of only about five weeks—all the rest of the time I totally abstained and during these five weeks, when I did use it, I only used it as a medicine, on the advice of the regimental Surgeon, and after his oft repeated solicitation to do so. ...I had been for many months debilitated and ill—some of the time quite dangerously so—caused by exposure and the severity of my duties, and having no officer to assist my in the discharge of my Company duties, I simply made use of stimulates, as stated above, for the purpose of regaining my health, to obtain the necessary strength to enable me to perform those duties.[29]

Drinking on duty, even for supposed medicinal purposes, was a breach of discipline that Lieutenant Colonel Oliver Shepherd would not tolerate. Intending to teach Kellogg a lesson, Shepherd brought him up on charges. Shepherd went about it a little too publicly, ordering Kellogg's own 1st sergeant to seize the captain and escort him to quarters. Kellogg felt humiliated and tendered his resignation. Shepherd did not want to lose Kellogg and Kellogg did not in fact want to leave the regulars, but they were both proud, stubborn men and each expected the other to back down first and withdraw their paperwork. Unknown to both was a new regulation that authorized the president to summarily cashier any officer who resigned his commission while under official charges. Everyone was therefore mortified when in mid-August 1862, a special order from the War Department was received that dismissed Kellogg from the service. Had Kellogg's resignation been accepted, he had planned on securing a volunteer commission. Being dismissed changed everything, since it was doubtful that any governor would hand out a commission to a former regular who had been dismissed under a cloud of controversy. Oliver Shepherd and George Thomas both wrote the War Department and urged revocation of the dismissal, but Washington held firm.[30]

Lyman Kellogg was resilient. He returned to his home in Ohio and began the laborious task of convincing the War Department to reinstate his commission in the 18th Infantry. After almost two years on the sidelines, the adjutant general did so on June 1, 1864, and the new/old captain headed for Georgia. Kellogg's men accorded him a certain amount of respect due to his twelve years of on-again-off-again soldiering, but his "strict & rigid manner," which had worked well in 1862, was out of step with the soldiers of 1864. Some 18th Infantrymen hated the captain so intensely during the Atlanta Campaign that they would sometimes intentionally walk in view of the enemy near Kellogg's position, hoping to bring down artillery fire on their commander. But no one doubted Kellogg's courage; it was a virtue he would display a number of times on the march to Atlanta. Lieutenant Bisbee once commented: "Captain Kellogg was always ready for a fight (his only good quality), but there was no frolic in his makeup."[31]

The day after Captain Kellogg's arrival, the Confederates evacuated Pine Mountain. Two days of inconclusive skirmishing and artillery bombardments followed at Gilgal Church and Mud Creek as Sherman's forces again closed with Johnston's fortifications. Johnston then fell back to a much stronger position at Kennesaw Mountain, the last significant piece of high ground north of the Chattahoochee River, where the heaviest fighting of the Atlanta Campaign thus far would soon occur. The regular battalions began a five-day tour of duty in the frontline trenches at Kennesaw on the evening of June 22, the same day that the weeks of rain finally came to an end. Arthur Carpenter continued his streak of narrow escapes the next night: "After dark last night our brigade moved to the front and relieved a Brigade of the 4" Corps. Picket firing is incessant. At 4 P.M. the rebels commenced shelling us, which lasted 2 hours. the shells came very close. one struck the breast works in front of me, and fearing that the next one would come through, I moved behind a tree. I had no sooner got there when one struck the tree about 4 feet above my head, passing clear through. the tree was a red oak 15 inches through. I was stunned for a while. fortunately no one was hurt."[32]

Enemy artillery also paid close attention to Lieutenant Edgar Kellogg's position. Captain James B. Mulligan of the 19th Infantry, a brigade staff officer, came up to the front to deliver an order to the 16th Infantry. After giving the message to Captain Gay, Mulligan stopped for a brief chat with Lieutenant Kellogg. He asked Kellogg for some pipe tobacco and was soon puffing away when a shell struck the top of a nearby oak tree, crashed to the ground, and exploded. The two officers were knocked down and stunned by the blast. The lieutenant thought he had been hit, but in a few moments regained his senses and discovered that everything still worked. Kellogg recalled that "Soon the Captain arose in the smoke, unhurt also, but his pipe was empty, and when I requested him to refill from my pouch he declined, without unnecessary thanks, and left that part of the field."[33]

Additional maneuvering and small-scale attacks, most notably by Hooker's corps at Kolb's Farm on June 23, led Sherman to believe that the Confederate line was stretched thin. With the soggy ground hindering movement for at least a few more days, Sherman decided to launch a frontal assault on June 27. Elements of McPherson's and Thomas's armies advanced shortly after eight o'clock in the morning and in two hours of heavy fighting got nowhere. The dug-in Confederates easily repulsed the attack, inflicting 3,000 Union casualties while suffering less than a third of that number in return. Among the Federal dead was Brigadier General Charles D. Harker, captain of the 15th Infantry, who was mortally wounded at the head of his brigade. The only unit of Palmer's corps that participated in the attack was Jefferson Davis's division, so King's division and the regular battalions were fortunately spared the ordeal of assaulting the Confederate works.[34]

While Thomas and McPherson's men were battering themselves against Southern fortifications, elements of Schofield's army began working their way around the Confederate left flank to the south. Sherman reinforced this success on July 1 by sending McPherson's army around Johnston's southern flank also. Finding themselves flanked yet again, the Confederates abandoned the Kennesaw line and fell back during the evening of July 2. With the enemy works at Kennesaw now empty, Thomas put the Army of the Cumberland in motion on the morning of July 3. Palmer's corps advanced on the main road to Marietta. "As soon as we could get our coffee, we started in pursuit," Arthur Carpenter wrote, "and were soon in Marietta, where we rested an hour or two. Marietta is a very pleasant little place. there are some grand estates in the suburbs, but all is deserted. I saw only about 5 or 6 families who had remained. After we had rested we continued the pursuit our Brigade in advance."[35]

Sherman had thought that upon abandoning Kennesaw Johnston would head for the far side of the Chattahoochee, but instead the Confederates retreated to a point just a few miles south of Marietta and dug in again. Sherman doubted the initial reports he received that stated the Confederates were still north of the river. In the early afternoon, he set out to take a look for himself. Accompanied by just a single aide, he ventured a few miles south on the road from Marietta. A few moments later, Stoughton's brigade led the XIV Corps's advance south from Marietta, heading out on the same road down which Sherman had disappeared. After marching a short distance, troops of 1/15th U.S., at the head of the brigade, heard the thundering sound of multiple horsemen approaching. Captain Dod quickly deployed his battalion from column into line and waited. Two Federal officers, one obviously a general, came galloping around a bend in the road toward the regular battalion, a group of Southern horsemen in hot pursuit. The Confederates pealed off and headed back upon seeing a line of blue-clad infantry ahead. As for Sherman and his aide, they slowed to a canter upon approaching Dod's line, not wanting to make an undignified dash through the regulars. "Sherman looked confused," one 15th Infantrymen recalled, "and we just smiled as he rode by." The general commanding the Military Division of the Mississippi was at least not confused anymore about which side of the river the Confederates were on.

John King and William Stoughton found this out for themselves shortly thereafter. Four miles south of Marietta, King and members of his division staff were riding about a hundred yards in front of Stoughton's brigade, for some reason not realizing that Stoughton's command was leading the Army of the Cumberland's advance at this point. A scattering of close-range rifle fire erupted, causing King and his staff to spur their mounts back to the brigade's main body. "Had the Rebs. not fired when they did," James Biddle wrote, "Genl. King...would have gone right into the enemy's rifle-pits. One of the balls struck me two inches below the knee & though the skin was not broken the leg turned black to the heel." Colonel Stoughton rode forward to King at the sound of the shots. "I thought other troops were in advance of us!" King exclaimed to the colonel. Before the two officers could dwell on the subject, George Thomas appeared and cleared things up. "You are the advance," the Army of the Cumberland's commander said to General King. "Throw out two or three companies of...skirmishers, and continue to push right along as you have been doing. Hooker is on the right and Howard is on the left. Keep things steadily moving and if the rebels cause you too much trouble order up some of the artillery." General King heeded Thomas's advice, deployed his division into line of battle, and advanced cautiously while feeling out the enemy fortifications.

Captain Biddle was among the lead troops: "Four companies of our regiment were thrown out to feel the enemy & to see if he were in force. We soon discovered, by the long line of entrenchments that a large part, if not all his Army was in our front. Our brigade advanced skirmishing about two hundred yards and held our position." Stoughton's brigade had come up against the Confederate army's latest position, the Smyrna Line. Earlier in the war, an attack would have quickly followed, but the 1864 technique was to bring up artillery and dig in, much as General Thomas had instructed. The regulars spent a sleepless night moving dirt and stacking logs, as did thousands of their peers.[36]

The next day's fighting has been variously labeled the Battle of Smyrna, the Battle of Ruff's Station, and the Battle of Neal Dow Station. For the regulars, it was little more than an artillery duel with opposing batteries slugging it out most of the day. After skirmishers drove in some enemy outposts and Stoughton moved his brigade forward about 300 yards, the infantry could only hug the earth and watch. Frederick Phisterer came about as close to an enemy shell as one can and still live to tell about it: "I took a walk of inspection to our extreme right and while conversing with the officer in command there, both of us of course lying down, we saw a shell strike the ground in front of our line, jump over a little fence there and roll towards us, we kept low, it passed right between us and we hugged the ground still more." The lieutenant braced himself for the inevitable. After some breathless seconds, he worked up enough courage to take a glance to the rear. The shell was lying just a few feet from his boots. He again buried his head in the dirt, but found himself still alive after another minute. Collecting his wits, Phisterer crawled back to the shell and discovered that its fuse had fallen out. "Those were anxious moments," he later wrote with considerable understatement.

Other regulars were not so lucky. Confederate artillery fire killed eight and wounded eleven during the day. A single shell exploding directly on the 16th Infantry's position inflicted half of the regulars' losses. Colonel Stoughton was also hit, severely wounded during an early-morning reconnaissance. An explosion mangled his right leg to such an extent that it later had to be amputated. All in all, it was an eventful 4th of July. "If celebrating on the fourth consists in firing cannon we had plenty of it," Arthur Carpenter wrote home a few days later, "but I only wished the rebs had pointed their cannon the other way." Edgar Kellogg remembered the battle as "the liveliest anniversary of the Declaration of Independence I have ever seen."[37]

Colonel Moore of the 69th Ohio took charge of the brigade after Stoughton was wounded, but was in command only a week and a half. Colonel Benjamin Scribner, commanding the 3rd Brigade of King's division, had fallen ill with dysentery and was unfit for duty. There were no regimental officers in Scribner's brigade with enough rank and experience to take Scribner's place, so Moore took command of it on July 15. The 69th Ohio went with its commander and served in Moore's brigade for the rest of the campaign. John King was fortunately available to resume command of his old brigade when Moore departed, Richard Johnson having meanwhile returned to division command after recovering from his wounding at Pickett's Mill.

The regulars advanced to a new position during the evening of Independence Day, building additional fortifications. Their labor was wasted, for the Confederates were falling back toward a new line on the Chattahoochee. This latest Southern line was an ingenious series of fortifications on the river's north side that had been quickly constructed the previous week by a force of slave laborers under the direction of Brigadier General Francis A. Shoup, Johnston's chief of artillery. The worn-out soldiers of King's division advanced a few miles on July 5 before General Palmer had another division take the lead. The regulars shifted about a mile to the vicinity of Vining's Station. None of the Union troops moved very far after discovering that the Southerners were dug in again and ready for battle. Sherman halted his men for a few days, waiting for the rails to be put in running order below Marietta and for the rain-swollen Chattahoochee to moderate somewhat while also scouting out crossing points beyond Johnston's flanks. From a piece a high ground immediately to the rear of the regulars' position, they could see the church spires and rooftops of Atlanta in the distance, nine miles away. "I have no doubt that the citizens [of Atlanta] are looking at our camp fires to night," one of the regulars wrote on July 5.[38]

"The cars are up with us now," Lieutenant Carpenter noted a few days later. "an engine run down near our Picket line this morning and commenced whistling to the rebs. It did not seem to please them much, as they opened a brisk picket firing." The Confederates were even less pleased to find out that the previous evening, forces from the Army of the Ohio had crossed the Chattahoochee upriver at Isham's Ford. The next morning, Federal cavalry crossed the river at a point near Roswell. The Confederates withdrew the next night and by the morning of July 10 were south of the Chattahoochee. Thomas instructed his corps commanders to throw forward a line of skirmishers and occupy the abandoned enemy works to their front. A contingent of regulars went forward at daylight, troops of 2/15th U.S. collecting up nine prisoners. Arthur Carpenter was glad that his first close view of Shoup's fortifications occurred after the enemy had abandoned them:

> Their line of works, which they left constructed about a mile and one half this side of the River, surpass any that I have ever seen as regards strength & durability. They evidently have been in process of construction for several months, and a great amount of care & attention has been paid to them. ...The rebels in building their works here, constructed round houses on the highest points, so as to enfilade their own lines and pour a destructive crossfire on us if we attempted to storm them. about four rods from their works they had a abatis of sharp pointed sticks and brush that would effectively break & disorganize any line of battle that attempted to get over them. By our movements they were compelled to evacuate without firing a shot. The effect of this on the Morale of their army must be awful. By what system of lying or by what allurements their leaders manage to hold them, and keep an organized army, I cannot imagine.[39]

* * *

The losses the regulars had incurred during two months of difficult campaigning took a variety of forms. Fatigue and disease would have taken their toll under the best of circumstances, but the climactic conditions of May and June compounded these problems. When they were not baking in the sun and dropping from heat exhaustion, torrential rains were soaking them to the bone. Occupying fetid and waterlogged fortifications much of the time caused dysentery and typhoid to periodically spread at epidemic rates. Lieutenant William Leary, Arthur Carpenter's companion on picket duty at Pickett's Mill, was evacuated to Chattanooga due to typhoid on June 9. He died of the disease on July 11. Desertions also thinned the regulars' ranks, as some of the recruits who had been rushed to the front in March and April decided that the Atlanta Campaign was more than they had bargained for. Their numbers did not amount to much: three at Resaca, nine during the difficult times in the trenches at Pickett's Mill, a few more near Atlanta. Since it was difficult for a deserter to make it back to Northern territory from the middle of the deep South, the fact that a few soldiers attempted to make the journey is a good indicator of the physical and mental demands this campaign made on them. While most of those who disappeared were men who had spent little time in uniform, some veterans also choose this avenue of escape. Sergeant Major James R. Bruce of 1/15th U.S. was left behind sick at Resaca in May. He was eventually transferred to a hospital in Chattanooga, at which place he evidently made a full recovery from whatever had been ailing him. He deserted on September 24.

Enemy action, disease, and lack of resolve were, however, not the most serious sources of loss for the regular battalions in 1864. Starting in July, many regulars started to be discharged. These were the men who had rushed to the colors in the summer of 1861, the original five-year New Army regulars whose enlistments the War Department had commuted to three years the previous winter. Except for the few who had reenlisted, their terms of service were rapidly coming to an end. In July and August 1864, while the campaign for Atlanta was approaching its culmination, more than 275 regulars in the Army of the Cumberland were discharged. The 18th Infantry was hardest hit by these losses, accounting for 151 of the total, a result of that regiment having had such a successful recruiting effort during the early months of the war. Even the 19th Infantry, whose 1861 recruiting program lagged behind the other regiments in the Regular Brigade, lost the services of thirty-eight men through discharge near Atlanta. "This Detachment [18th U.S.] has now only 350 effective men," Captain Lyman Kellogg complained to the adjutant general on August 14, "and by the end of September, it will not have probably over 100—the terms of service of many of the men daily expiring." The departure of these troops was particularly damaging. They were not inexperienced newcomers like most of those who had deserted, but rather were the toughest and most experienced veterans in the regular battalions, the men who had marched from Louisville to Corinth and back again, from Nashville to Chattanooga, and deep into the heart of Georgia. In many cases, they were senior non-commissioned officers, the only real leaders many of the companies had by this point in the war.[40]

Volunteer regiments that had not "veteranized" were also starting to leave the Union Army during the summer of 1864, but the
process of their departure differed vastly from that of the regulars.
Although regulations varied slightly from state to state, most volunteer regiments established a common discharge date for all of the
unit's troops that had been present in 1861 when the regiment was
mustered in for Federal service. As a result, the discharge of a volunteer unit was predictable and planned. Typically, weeks before a
regiment was due to muster out, it was pulled off the line and sent
to a camp in its home state, where the troops were honored with
parades and speeches by local dignitaries. From there, the volunteers
received their discharges and went en masse to their homes, which
were usually concentrated in the same locality. There they rightly
received another hero's welcome. A regular's departure from the
army was a much more subdued event. He served with his unit in the
field until the very end, until the final morning when he woke up and
could proclaim that he was a civilian once again. He then gathered
up his belongings, signed some papers with his company officer, bid
farewell to comrades, and hitched a ride on a northbound train. He
eventually arrived at his home in Michigan, Indiana, or elsewhere,
not as a conquering hero, but rather as just a solitary, anonymous
soldier in a faded blue uniform, welcomed by his family if he had
one, noticed by few others. Few people knew he had served in the
Regular Army, and certainly fewer still were interested in learning
about his wartime experiences, not when the invariably legendary
exploits of the local volunteers were fast becoming immortalized in
story and song.

* * *

There remained much work to be done near Atlanta in the
summer of 1864. Although by July 10 the Confederate army was
on the south side of the Chattahoochee and Federal troops had
crossed the river in force at a number of points, Sherman did not
immediately press forward. The Federal commander dispatched
cavalry columns to break the rail lines into the city while the
opposing armies faced off near the Chattahoochee. When the cavalry raids were finished, Sherman planned to send the Army of the
Tennessee to the east of Atlanta while Thomas's and Schofield's
troops advanced directly toward the city from the north.[41]

The regulars had their first extended break of the campaign,
remaining near Vining's Station until July 17. Major Edie reported

that occasional picket duty along the river kept his troops busy, as did the enemy's artillery, "an occasional shot passing through our camp." The excess baggage and equipment that the regulars had turned in prior to crossing the Etowah River back in May finally caught up with them on July 16. The items "were most welcomely received," remembered Captain McManus of 2/15th Infantry, "as the officers suffered great inconvenience from want of clothing, company papers, &c." It goes without saying that the captain's troops had suffered just as much if not more. The brigade's organization was trimmed down considerably at Vining's Station. Colonel Moore and his 69th Ohio departed for Scribner's brigade on July 15, while Captain Kellogg overhauled the organization of the 18th Infantry. There were now only about 300 men present for duty in Kellogg's two battalions, so he consolidated them into a single unit. Kellogg took direct control of all sixteen companies with Lieutenant Phisterer as his adjutant, meaning ex-battalion commanders George Smith and William Fetterman were both relegated to commanding companies that consisted of, at most, a few dozen men. Both would soon find duties more in line with their capabilities. Fetterman became General King's adjutant on the brigade staff, while Captain Smith, leader of the 18th Regulars since the Middle Tennessee Campaign, took a position on General Johnson's division staff. Only the 15th Regulars would continue to maintain a multi-battalion organization when the Federal army resumed its advance on Atlanta.[42]

The regular battalions and the 11th Michigan, with Brigadier General King back in brigade command, crossed the Chattahoochee by way of a pontoon bridge at Pace's Ferry at four o'clock in the afternoon on July 17. Most of the Army of the Cumberland pushed across the Chattahoochee that day, with the lead division of Palmers's corps, Davis's, encountering some resistance. Richard Johnson deployed Moore's and Carlin's brigades (the latter temporarily commanded by Colonel Anson McCook) in support of Davis while keeping King's brigade in reserve. The Confederates fell back, but Johnson's division was able to advance only about a mile south of the river before nightfall. The advance resumed the next morning, with McCook's brigade skirmishing as it led the way down the Buckhead and Howell's Ferry Roads to Peachtree Creek. Although the Peachtree as a watercourse was rather shallow, it was steeply banked and lined with dense vegetation, making it a serious obstacle. The enemy troops contesting McCook's advance destroyed the bridge at Turner's Mill over the Peachtree; this and enemy artillery fire held up the advance. The regulars were able to rest on the 19th, for repairing the bridge took all that day and into the night.

By then, word had spread throughout Sherman's army that the aggressive John Bell Hood had replaced Joseph Johnston in command of the Army of Tennessee. The Union Army would soon find out that their opposition would no longer sit passively while the Federal host advanced. Perhaps this time around the Confederates would be doing the assaulting and dying, a situation that suited the Northerners just fine. "We thought Hood would be more aggressive than Johnston had been," Lieutenant Kellogg remembered, "and in his eagerness to punish us would give us an opportunity to meet him on equal terms." Hood did not disappoint the lieutenant, although the regulars did not have an opportunity to inflict much punishment during their next engagement, the Battle of Peachtree Creek.[43]

King's brigade crossed the Peachtree at Turner's Mill early in the morning of July 20, advanced a short distance, went into line, and began to dig in. Palmer's corps was on the right of Thomas's line, with Hooker's corps and a division of Howard's corps to the left. Late in the afternoon, about two-thirds of Hood's army launched a furious assault on the Army of the Cumberland's left flank. General Johnson deployed King's brigade in a patch of low ground between the division's first and second lines, with orders to move forward from there should the need arise to reinforce McCook's brigade. King's men were grateful that they never had to move forward that day. Captain James Biddle, a veteran of Stones River, could not recall more intense fire: "At 4:00 P.M. we were ordered in to line across the road in the rear of front line. Hardly were we placed when the enemy opened a terrific fire, shell, grape & canister (the worst fire I was ever exposed to) the very air seemed to be alive with pieces of shell & bullets, the ground was torn up with unexploded shells, big trees were cut half off & the line of breast-works in our rear was knocked to pieces. The most curious part of all this firing was that 6 or 7 of our men were all the injured we had."[44]

After three hours of combat, Thomas's men prevailed and the Southerners retired to their line of departure. There were about 2,500 fewer Confederate soldiers manning those lines as night fell, while Thomas lost about 1,900, mainly from Hooker's corps.

McCook's brigade of Johnson's division lent a hand in repulsing the extreme left of the enemy attack, but Moore's and King's brigades ended up being spectators only during the battle. Captain E.T. Wells, Richard Johnson's adjutant, was severely wounded in the battle, creating the vacancy on the division staff that the 18th Infantry's Captain George Smith moved up to fill. Johnson was happy to have Smith on the staff, for he thought the captain was one of the division's "best and bravest commanders." Smith quickly proved to be an excellent staff officer also. "When orders were to be sent to a distant and dangerous part of the field," General Johnson later recalled of George Smith's staff performance, "they were usually intrusted to him feeling assured that if he was not killed the orders would be delivered." As Smith assumed his new duties, King's brigade moved two miles to Thomas's left during the evening of July 20 to guard the Army of the Cumberland's eastern flank. The 15th Infantry battalions were detached to guard the Turner's Mill bridge. King's remaining regiments had such a large swath of terrain to cover that each company was responsible for more than three times its normal frontage. "We were ordered to throw up breast-works," Biddle continued, "but from the lack of men this was slow work, then too the men we could put to work were so tired that they went to sleep with the spade in their hands." King's brigade rejoined Johnson's division the next morning. The regulars spent July 21 in the familiar routine of digging, picketing, and, in the late afternoon, a short movement to a point near the Western & Atlantic tracks, after which they began the routine again.[45]

Hood launched another attack on July 22, this time against McPherson's Army of the Tennessee east of Atlanta. During a day that saw combat even more intense than that of Peachtree Creek, Hood again failed to accomplish his intended rout of the Union forces to his front, although a Tennessean managed to shoot and kill General McPherson. General Howard gave up command of the IV Corps and replaced McPherson, while Major General David S. Stanley took command of Howard's old corps.

Sherman knew he could not easily pierce Atlanta's strong defenses, even when manned by Hood's battle-thinned army. His next plan involved a wide flanking movement by the Army of the Tennessee that would carry it from east of Atlanta to the western side. Once there, Howard would try to break the railroad between East Point and Atlanta, Hood's last remaining lifeline into the city.

Sherman also dispatched his cavalry on a raid to cut the railroad at Macon, hoping that arm would be more successful in this effort than it had been previously. While preparations for these moves began, both armies occupied and strengthened their respective fortifications. The Confederate late-July attacks had disrupted Sherman's timetable for capturing Atlanta, although the price the Army of Tennessee paid in doing so was high.[46]

The regulars remained in largely the same location north of Atlanta from July 22 until August 3. Although the opposing lines were not as close together as they had been at either Pickett's Mill or Kennesaw, there was enough activity each day to keep the regulars busy. Major Edie reported that "During these twelve days all the battalions composing the brigade were engaged at different times on the picket and skirmish line, and in the face of fire engaged in steadily forcing the enemy back from our front." One of the more strangely worded orders to force the enemy back came down on July 27, when Captain McManus's 2/15th U.S. was instructed to "worry the enemy and attract his attention to the front." The regular battalion duly complied, driving in the enemy pickets to its front and remaining in no-man's-land the rest of the day. The enemy was worried enough about the foray to pound the regulars with artillery; three soldiers and Lieutenant Mason Jackson were wounded before McManus's battalion returned to friendly lines at nightfall.

The soldiers who had marched from Chattanooga to Atlanta were largely desensitized to the sights of a battlefield after more than ten weeks of campaigning. Lieutenant Carpenter's parents must have been shocked by what he wrote on July 26: "one of our batteries & a rebel battery are amusing themselves at the present moment in firing at each other. It is more funny for them than for the troops around, but then soldiers don't mind seeing one anothers heads taken off. Our breastworks are 10 feet of solid earth, we have to make them thick where there is much artillery." Enemy artillery was not the only hazard. On July 30, a short round from a Federal piece landed amidst the 18th Infantry, ripping off a sergeant's leg and injuring nine other regulars. Lieutenant Bisbee was discussing the situation with Captain Anson Mills when another round impacted nearby—friendly or enemy, no one knew this time. The shot splintered a twenty-inch thick pine tree that the two officers were standing beside and knocked them down. Both were sent sprawling amidst a shower of splinters. Another nearby explosion quickly followed. Bisbee remembered that "something stubborn and blunt struck my leg, entitling me to a day or two limping spell, but not a furlough so highly prized by some and hardly to be despised by any, as we had now been over three years trying to...kill the enemy and go home." Bisbee's attitude had changed considerably from the summer of 1863 at Hoover's Gap, when he had been mortified that sickness had forced him to ride in an ambulance. Captain Albert Dod, 1/15th U.S., had also had a change of heart. He resigned his commission on August 1 and was granted a leave of absence pending its acceptance. Captain James Curtis, a solid veteran who had been wounded at Shiloh while leading H/1/15th U.S., took command of the battalion.[47]

* * *

"We moved from our place in the trenches yesterday," Lieutenant Carpenter wrote on August 4. "We are in rear of the right flank of our grand Army. ...For the last few days we have been moving troops to our right. ...there is no enemy immediately in our front here, and it is quite a relief to be for a few hours out of the sound of muskets and cannon." The lieutenant's comments about troop movements were not quite correct, for by August 4, Federal forces had been shifting to the right (that is, to the west and south of Atlanta) for more than just a few days. Howard's Army of the Tennessee started its end run on July 27, a movement that caused 2/15th U.S. and other Federal units that day to "worry" the enemy to their front while Howard's men took to the roads. Hood countered by sending one of his own corps, led by the newly arrived Lieutenant General Stephen D. Lee, to the west of town. The next day, Lee transformed the movement into a spoiling attack against Howard's column, an action known as the Battle of Ezra Church. Poor battle handling again plagued the Confederates. Lee's piecemeal assaults generated nearly 3,000 Southern casualties, nearly five times as many men as Howard lost. Despite the carnage at Ezra Church and elsewhere, Hood's effort was successful in that it thwarted Sherman's plan to have Howard's army swing around to East Point before the Confederates could react. The latest Federal cavalry raid also came to naught, so it appeared that Sherman's efforts were getting nowhere fast by the end of July.[48]

With Howard's army bogged down, Sherman decided to have another force move toward East Point, extend the Federal right flank, and break the railroad. He gave the mission to Palmer's XIV

Corps and the XXIII Corps from the Army of the Ohio. General Palmer did not like these instructions, for they placed his corps under the overall command of Major General Schofield, commander of the Army of the Ohio, but technically Palmer's junior in rank. A bizarre series of events then transpired in which Sherman and Palmer argued about protocol and dates of rank while the offensive's timetable became hopelessly disrupted. As the argument continued, Palmer's instructions to his subordinate commanders seemed to be worded in such a way as to barely comply with Sherman and Schofield's designs. Thus on August 4, the day that Sherman had ordered an "all-out offensive" toward East Point and the railroad, Palmer told Baird to simply conduct a "reconnaissance" in that direction. Baird sent out a single brigade, which found the enemy strongly posted to its front and then returned to its start point. Similarly, Richard Johnson also dispatched forward just a portion of his command. The only action Johnson mentioned in his campaign report for August 4 was that "King's brigade made a reconnaissance to the right and returned." King deployed skirmishers from the 15th and 18th Regulars as the brigade neared the enemy line. Edie's and Kellogg's troops drove in a few enemy pickets, at which time King led the brigade back to the fortifications it had occupied the previous night. Similar events occurred during the next two days, with Sherman and Schofield exhorting the XIV Corps to attack and Palmer doing nothing of the sort. James Biddle's diary entry for August 5 confirms that Palmer's orders contained not a hint of aggressiveness: "At 4 P.M. we went out to reconnoiter some Confederate works in our front with orders to try & carry them if not too strong. Must have been too much for us as we marched back with out firing a shot & took position in rear of Genl. Schofield's lines."[49]

The flap over rank resulted in Palmer tendering his resignation late in the day on August 6. Sherman had never thought much of Palmer anyway and was glad to be rid of him. Palmer's senior division commander, Richard Johnson, took temporary command of the XIV Corps, but Sherman was concerned that Johnson would not be any more aggressive in attacking than Palmer had been. John King resumed his familiar role as second-string commanding general of Johnson's division, although King's own brigade was also scrambling for leadership at this point. With the one-legged Colonel Stoughton evacuated and Colonel Moore in charge of Scribner's brigade, there were only two field-grade officers remaining in the brigade from which to choose. Lieutenant Colonel Melvin Mudge of the 11th Michigan was the next-ranking officer, but he had been severely wounded in the left forearm at Chickamauga. Although present in the current campaign, he was sick much of the time, had a useless left hand, and possessed little stamina. That left Major John R. Edie of the 15th Infantry as the only officer available to assume command of the brigade.

The new corps, division, and brigade commanders took over amidst the Battle of Utoy Creek. Hood used the delay caused by Palmer's concern about ranking Schofield to rush reinforcements to the threatened area. Instead of flanking the enemy and advancing to the rail line, the Federals found themselves once again attacking prepared defenses head-on. Elements of two divisions from Schofield's XXIII Corps attacked on August 6 but accomplished little. With Palmer now out of the way, Sherman wanted the XIV Corps to make a strong attack on the morning of the 7th, but newly installed corps commander Richard Johnson was not able to get the movement underway until mid-afternoon. When the attack finally commenced, it consisted of little more than King's division.[50]

Looking over the battleground, veterans in Edie's brigade might have thought they were re-fighting the Battle of Resaca. The opposing lines occupied low ridges, a quarter-mile of open ground and a shallow stream separating them. Stovall's Brigade, old antagonists of the regulars from both Kelley Field and Missionary Ridge, manned the opposing Confederate line. The terrain the Southerners occupied was heavily wooded, a line of rifle pits along the wood line and the main entrenchments farther back in the trees. Major Edie deployed the entire 18th Infantry as a heavy skirmish line. The line of battle consisted of the 15th Infantry battalions on the left and the 11th Michigan on the right. The 16th and 19th U.S. remained in reserve within the Federal fortifications. Edie led the brigade forward at 1:00 P.M.[51]

But not all of the brigade's troops followed the major over the top. The 11th Michigan had chosen not to reenlist the previous winter and was scheduled for muster out within a matter of weeks. All of the regiment's troops were gripped by an understandable reluctance to be the last man of the unit to be killed in action. When the regular battalions went forward, the Michiganders stayed in place. Major Edie was too busy to do anything about the regiment's

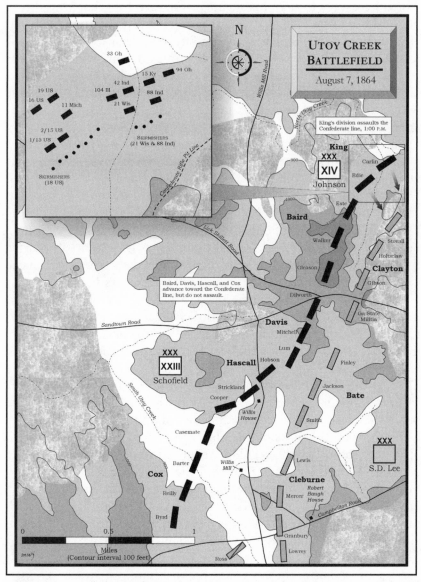

reluctance, and the 11th Michigan's commander, Lieutenant Colonel Mudge, outranked him anyway. The sickly Mudge, on duty for the first time in weeks, rose to the occasion. He drew his sword while mounting a breastwork in front of his men. With his back toward enemy sharpshooters and bullets whizzing by, the colonel found the words necessary to urge his regiment forward for what would turn out to be its final charge: "Men, you have always done well. For almost three years you have stood nobly at your posts and have performed every duty that has been required of you. Yonder are the rebels. You are again called on to meet them in battle. The regulars on your left have already gone and there they are, nobly struglling with the foe. Do you see that gap to their right? Do as well as they are doing; go as far as they have gone—Aye, and go farther. Let not a man shirk from duty!" General King made a timely arrival at the 11th Michigan's entrenchments and bellowed: "Move right forward! Every man!" Mudge also gave the command to move out. Extorted from front and rear, the Michigan soldiers found their courage and went forward.[52]

While the bravery of Mudge's troops was commendable, a number of them probably had second thoughts as they belatedly started their advance. Enemy fire was intense as Edie's troops advanced toward the woodline, the heaviest fire the regulars had faced since Chickamauga. Captain Curtis of 1/15th U.S. took a bullet in the mouth the moment he rose up out of cover on the line of departure. Captain Horace Jewett, an experienced campaigner who had commanded A/1/15th U.S. at Shiloh and Stones River, took his place and led the battalion out into the killing field: "we were subjected to a direct[,] oblique and enfilading fire of both artillery and musketry from the time we left our works." With the 11th Michigan lagging behind, Edie shifted the 15th U.S. forward and to the right, bringing it on line with the mass of 18th Infantry skirmishers. Casualties littered the ground as the regulars advanced under, to quote Captain McManus, "a destructive fire from the well-filled rebel rifle pits," but they continued on despite the heavy losses. The loss in Captain Jewett's 1/15th U.S. was particularly heavy, the battalion suffering more killed and wounded troops in this single charge than it had at either Shiloh or Chickamauga, only slightly less than Stones River. Edie's regulars then performed a feat that was becoming increasingly rare by this point in the war: they pressed home an attack against a dug-in enemy. The regulars in the Atlanta Campaign may have not possessed the same swagger and panache their predecessors had displayed during the early years of the war, but the regulars on August 7, 1864, proved they were still a cut above many of the soldiers on either side.

Stovall's Georgians, the troops filling the rifle pits in front of the regulars, were surprised by what they saw in the open field to their front. Despite cutting down so many of the Yankees charging toward them, the blue line continued to close the distance. Many of the Southerners threw down their smoking rifles and raised their hands in surrender as the regulars came within bayonet range. Captain Robert B. Hull of the 18th U.S., Kellogg's second-in-command, reported that his regiment "captured in prisoners greater in number than its own strength, taking several companies entire with their officers and while in the act of re-forming their lines." The 15th U.S. also captured a large number of prisoners in relation to its strength, the regulars of 2/15th U.S. alone taking ninety-five. There were so many enemy troops captured and so few regulars available to guard them that Edie had to send the prisoners unescorted toward Federal lines. To the later disgust of the regulars, other units collected up these prisoners and claimed them as their own, although no unit of Johnson's corps at Utoy Creek matched the advance of Edie's brigade.[53]

The regulars did not have time to escort the captives rearward because they still had work to do. Although they had captured the first line of rifle pits at the wood line, the main enemy line was still deeper in the forest. Despite the fact that the regulars had already accomplished more than was reasonably expected of them, they kept going. Captain Kellogg, always at his best when bullets were flying, took charge:

> After the first assault I took advantage of a ravine beyond the open field over which we had driven the enemy to reform the line, which had become partially disorganized owing to the difficulties of the ground and the very severe flank and front fire, both artillery and musketry, which had been playing on us while driving the enemy across the open field. After I had reformed I again moved forward with the Eighteenth and the Fifteenth Regulars, driving the enemy into their main works and arriving with my line, composed of the regular regiments above mentioned, to the abatis close to the enemy's main works. The Eleventh Michigan, during the second assault, remained in position, protecting my right.[54]

Advancing to the abatis in front of the Confederate position was about all the regulars could do. They were the only Federal troops who advanced even that far. The regulars who were still on their feet were completely exhausted and low on ammunition. Major Edie

ordered them to fall back to the rifle pit line, but Lieutenant Bisbee
and a few others found it difficult to comply. He and a handful of
18th Infantrymen had worked their way right up into the abatis and
the guns of an enemy battery were just forty yards away; falling
back at this point was more dangerous than staying put. Between
cannon blasts, Bisbee thought he heard sounds of the enemy preparing to pull out. He called out in a low tone to an Irish private nearby
named Hanlon, telling him to get word to Captain Kellogg that the
balance of the regiment should be brought forward. Instead of
bringing forward the regiment, Hanlon brought back a message for
Bisbee from Kellogg: "Rejoin your battalion, sir!"

"That old tyrant Kellogg, as if I was a deserter!" Bisbee thought
to himself.

"Leftinint," Hanlon whispered in his Irish brogue, "I'll soon be
down there wid ye."

"Stay where you are," Bisbee cautioned. Despite Kellogg's order,
returning to the 18th Infantry's position was something Bisbee
could not do. He and his comrades remained hidden until nightfall,
at which time they snuck back to their regiment's position. The rest
of the 18th Regulars, believing Bisbee's squad had been captured,
were relieved to see them again. The lieutenant then had a chance
to see some of the 125 Confederates that Edie's brigade was "officially" credited with capturing that day. He was not impressed with
his former antagonists: "Some of [the enemy] seemed more inclined
to surrender than fight longer in a cause growing more hopeless day
by day. I shall never forget how meek and unwarlike many of them
looked in giving up when they could easily have joined their commands with diminished danger. Evidently they preferred a Northern
prison to the rebel ranks on short rations."[55]

Major Edie had meanwhile consolidated his brigade's hold on
the rifle pits, bringing forward the 16th and 19th Infantry. The regulars and 11th Michigan worked throughout the night transforming
the light Confederate works into proper fortifications. "There were
several dead rebels lying in the pits," Lieutenant Carpenter recalled,
"and in building our works we threw the dirt over them without
any ceremony. such is the lot of those who fight against their country."[56]

The XIV Corps did not have much to show for the Battle of Utoy
Creek except a small bag of prisoners and an insignificant advance.
Carlin's brigade made a gain similar to Edie's, taking the first line of

rifle pits to its front. The hastily planned and unsupported attack then sputtered to a halt. For their efforts, Edie's assaulting units suffered horribly. The 15th and 18th U.S. lost 149 troops between them, with 1/15th U.S. reporting twelve killed and fifty-nine wounded. One out of every four 18th Infantrymen present on the field was hit. Casualties in the 11th Michigan were not as heavy, but fifteen of the short-timers had their final muster a few weeks early. Another fifteen were wounded. Sherman, Schofield, and others attributed the failure at Utoy Creek to a lack of aggressiveness on the part of the XIV Corps.[57] Some of that criticism was justified, although the regulars took exception to it. Lyman Kellogg had heard enough by the time he wrote his report on the engagement. In his zeal to set the record straight, the captain can perhaps be forgiven for overestimating the results that the battle might have obtained:

> Had I been supported and the enemy attacked by the division on my right and by the brigade on my left, as I had been told would be the case, I am of opinion that the main line of works around Atlanta would have fallen on the 7th of August. The forces under my command had been engaged from 1 P.M. until nearly dusk; nearly one-third of my men had been put *hors de combat*, and I was almost entirely out of ammunition, not having had time to send to the rear for it, so that had I finally succeeded in entering the enemy's works I should only have succeeded in turning my remaining small force over to the enemy as prisoners. We, however, successfully advanced our main line about half a mile, intrenching and holding it, taking three lines of rebel rifle-pits and capturing a large number of prisoners, 300 of them being credited to my command. ...This assault was most successful and brilliant, and due credit should be given to whom it was mainly owing, viz, the Eighteenth and Fifteenth Regulars.[58]

Although the regulars were proud of what they accomplished at Utoy Creek, some of them were reaching the end of their endurance. An 18th Infantry general order published the day after the battle reveals that troops of the 11th Michigan were not the only ones who displayed a reluctance to follow orders on August 7:

> Head Quarters Detcht 18th U.S. Inf..
> before Atlanta Ga August 8th 1864

General Orders
No 7

I. Corporal Wm Beesly of Company "G" 3rd Batt. is reduced to the ranks for disobedience of orders.
II. Sergeant Maklon Peters of Company "D" 1st Batt. is hereby reduced to the ranks for not going into action when so ordered.
III. Sergeant R.W. Evans of Company "F" 1st Batt. is hereby reduced to the ranks for conduct prejudicial to good order and military discipline, on the 7 inst.
IV. Sergeant W.E. Grandall of Company "G" 1st Batt. is reduced to the ranks for not going into action with his company on the 7 inst.

By order of
Capt. L.M. Kellogg Commdg
FREDERICK PHISTERER
1st Lieut 18th U.S. inf..
Adjt Detcht.[59]

* * *

In the aftermath of Ezra Church and Utoy Creek, Sherman realized that he could neither assault Atlanta's fortifications directly nor flank the Confederate line in an attempt to stretch it to some theoretical breaking point. Sherman next tried to bombard Atlanta into submission. As Federal guns pounded the city and its defenders, the Union commander dispatched another round of cavalry raids against the railroads to the south of Atlanta. King's division remained near the Utoy Creek battleground for nineteen days. Arthur Carpenter's letter of August 14 indicates that the grueling campaign may have been wearing out the Confederates in Georgia a bit faster than the Federals:

> We are now in front, about 200 yards from the rebel works, with the port holes of their batteries frowning upon us. But they have not used any Artillery on us yet. Our batteries are in such good positions that they make it too hot for the rebels, so they keep very quiet.
> The picket firing has subsided a great deal lately, and some days hardly a shot is fired. And occassionaly our pickets meet the rebel pickets half way and trade coffee for tobacco. But I think the rebel authorities will stop that, for a great many of them have deserted and come into our lines within the last 3 or 4 days. ...Such facts indicate strongly that they are in a state of demoralization.[60]

Although the men in Sherman's armies may not have been demoralized, trench warfare was hard on both friend and foe. James Biddle wrote on August 17: "sitting so long in the trenches, always dirty & generally wet, has broken the men down more than the previous hard marching."[61]

Additional command changes occurred during late August. Sherman arranged for the aggressive Brigadier General Jefferson C. Davis to take command of the XIV Corps on August 22, naming Richard Johnson as the Chief of Cavalry for the Military Division of the Mississippi. Exposure, nagging wounds, and poor health forced John King from the field on August 17. Brigadier General Carlin took command of King's division. In Edie's brigade, the lack of troops in the regular battalions caused some of the units to undergo further reorganizations. The sixteen companies of Captain Kellogg's 18th U.S. averaged less than fifteen men each in the aftermath of Utoy Creek. Since Henry Carrington's supply of recruits in Ohio had dried up long before, on August 11 Kellogg consolidated his command into eight composite companies. No unit of the XIV Corps had suffered heavier casualties at Utoy Creek than had Captain Jewett's 1/15th U.S. Infantry. He temporarily disbanded A/1/15th and E/1/15th on August 22, assigning their surviving six non-commissioned officers and twenty privates to the battalion's remaining four companies. The regulars bid farewell to the 11th Michigan on August 27 as the last volunteer regiment in Edie's brigade headed for Chattanooga. Six week later in Michigan, the regiment mustered out of Federal service. The 2nd Brigade, 1st Division, XIV Army Corps again consisted exclusively of regular troops.[62]

The number of officers present for duty in the regular battalions was now dangerously low. Major Edie tactfully tried to make General Carlin aware of this fact: "There is not a sufficient number of officers with the command to enable the brigade to operate as effectively as it could if more were present." Although Lieutenant Forbes of the 15th U.S. had been the only regular officer killed in battle thus far during the campaign, numerous others had been wounded and many more were on the sick rolls. Some had resigned, some were assigned to staff duty, and a few others, Captain Ebenezer Gay among them, had been granted leaves of absence for various reasons. When a few new officers for the 16th Infantry reported for duty back in May, Captain Biddle had then predicted: "These men will not stay long as they belong to a class of officers who always get sick when there is any fighting to be done. This class is larger than one would think." By late August, the captain noted that "Nearly every officer who started with us from Tunnel Hill has gone home on sick leave." There was the usual crop of non-commissioned officers willing to step forward and swap out chevrons for shoulder straps, but the non-stop operations meant that no paperwork requesting battlefield commissions had yet started on the lengthy journey to the War Department. By early September, Captain Mooney's 1/19th U.S. had only five officers present for duty; Captain Jewett's 1/15th had but four.[63]

Frederick Phisterer also left the field. It was a tough decision. He had lately come of age according to German law and was due to receive a large inheritance, but if he was not present in a German court during October 1864, he would lose everything. Phisterer became increasingly discouraged as the Atlanta Campaign went on for week after week with no end in sight. He eventually felt he could delay no longer:

> Camp Detachment 18th U.S. Infty
> Before Atlanta, Georgia
> August 15th, 1864

Brig. Gen'l L. Thomas
    Adjutant General U.S. Army
    Washington, D.C.
General

I have the honor respectfully to tender the immediate and unconditional resignation of my commission as 1st Lieutenant in the 18th U.S. Infantry. ...I have served the United States as an Enlisted Man and Commissioned Officer for over eight years and had intended to make application for a leave of absence for four or more months at the end of the present campaign, but as the campaign lasts longer than I calculated and my time is getting too short to await the close of it, I am compelled to resign, not being able to afford the losses, which my absence from Germany in October 1864 may entail upon me. I therefore respectfully request, that my resignation may be accepted as soon as practicable.

> I have the honor to be, General, Very Respectfully
> Your Obedt Servt,
>
> FRED' PHISTERER
> 1st Lieut 18th U.S. Inf.
> Adjt Detcht 18th Inf. in the field.[64]

Phisterer's chain of command was not going to permanently lose the services of this officer if it could be helped. Captain

Kellogg, Major Edie, General Johnson, and General Thomas all urged the War Department to grant Phisterer a leave of absence in lieu of the resignation. From faraway Albany, New York, Major Frederick Townsend also weighed in: "I desire to say from two years of experience with him in the field, that he is uncomparably the finest officer of his grade in the 18th U.S. Inftry, and that I should very much regret to learn that his resignation had been accepted." The War Department agreed and Phisterer was granted an extended leave with permission to visit Europe. He was most likely the only lieutenant in the Regular Army to travel overseas on leave during the Civil War while his regiment was actively campaigning. William Bisbee took Phisterer's place as adjutant of the 18th Infantry's field detachment.[65]

Frederick Phisterer would regret for the rest of his life that he did not hold out in the field about two more weeks, for the Regular Brigade's next battle proved to be its last. The War Department had been wrestling with the question of what to do with the regulars for some time. Regular regiments had never been able to find enough recruits to fill their ranks. When that was combined with heavy battle losses, by 1864 the regulars had a nearly insurmountable manpower shortage. While many volunteer regiments also contained just a small number of troops by mid-1864, the postwar existence of state units had never been an issue. The regulars, on the other hand, would be needed after the war—and needed in large numbers. In addition to performing their traditional duty of serving as the nation's constabulary on the Western frontier, a strong force of regulars would have to garrison the former Confederate States for an as yet indeterminable amount of time. The Regular Army of 1864 was in no way ready to carry out these important tasks, nor would it be for some time to come. Few of the regulars had reenlisted. Battle losses, disease, desertions, and discharges were constantly eating away at the number of regulars who remained. With the end of the conflict at last a glimmer on the horizon, the War Department did not want regular units, the permanent military establishment of the United States, to be in such a critical condition as the fighting ended that they would require a lengthy postwar rebuilding period. If at least a cadre of veterans could be preserved, filling the regiments with recruits after the war was over would be a fairly simple process.

This manpower problem was particularly acute in the smaller regular infantry regiments of the Old Army, which had only ten companies instead of the twenty-four authorized in the New Army organizations. The battered remnants of most of the small Old Army regiments that had been serving with the Army of the Potomac were withdrawn from active service during the autumn of 1863 following the Battle of Gettysburg. The larger size of the New Army regiments enabled them to stay in the field into 1864, but only through fleshing out their ranks with the dregs of society. By the latter half of that year, the New Army regiments were also approaching combat ineffectiveness.[66]

* * *

The Federal cavalry raids of August had again failed to disrupt the supply lines keeping the Confederates alive in Atlanta. Sherman came to the realization that mounted troops alone were not sufficient for this task and decided to send his entire army south of the city to do the job. Leaving the XX Corps to man a bridgehead on the south side of the Chattahoochee, the balance of the Union Army began a sweeping movement to the west and south on August 25. Major General John Logan's corps from the Army of the Tennessee led the march. The Regular Brigade pulled out of its position the next night, which was a difficult movement according to Captain Biddle:

> Just about dark we were sitting by our camp fire thinking about nothing when orders came that we were to march at once. We pulled down our shelter tents & were off by 8 o'clock. Leaving a skirmish line behind us, with orders to hold the line until day light, the night was one of the darkest I ever felt, can't say saw, the rain had been falling most of the day making the roads almost impassable. We went stumbling along for about a mile or so, with the enemy, who appeared to be aware of our movement, shelling us but doing no harm when we came to the rear end of our wagon train stuck in the mud & unable to move. We halted for some time but finding that the wagons could not be got on & having orders to be in position by a certain hour, we passed on & after a march of about 4 miles, took possession of the earth-works of the 23d corps, that corps moving to the right.[67]

The regulars marched three miles that night, rested the next morning, and continued marching the following afternoon. On the night of August 28 near the hamlet of Red Oak, the regulars reached the line of Atlanta, West Point, and Montgomery Railroad, one of the two railroads that went through East Point and from there into Atlanta. While a contingent of regulars kept harassing Confederate cavalry at bay, from dawn on August 29 until the afternoon of the next day, the balance of the Regular Brigade had their first and only experience in creating what would become one of the enduring symbols of the Civil War in Georgia: "Sherman's neck ties." Private William Gilday of the 15th Infantry described how they went about it: "We destroyed the railroad to West Point, each company taking its own length of track; the rails were torn up and the ties used for heating and twisting the rails. It was a contest between the different companies to see who could take up their part first. It was a straight level track, and as far as we could see either way the troops were at work. As soon as this was accomplished we headed for the next line of railroad."[68]

The next line was the Macon & Western, the only railroad into Atlanta still in Confederate hands after the wrecking of the West Point line. The tracks of the Macon & Western were about fifteen miles due east from where the regulars had torn up their assigned section of track. Carlin marched his division ten miles eastward on August 30, bivouacking that night near the farm of a Mrs. Evans on the Fayetteville-Atlanta Road. Judging by General Carlin's report, August 31 was a frustrating day of much marching, but little actual movement for the regulars: "On the 31st the division marched to Renfroe's and remained there till near sundown, when I received orders from Major-General Thomas to move at once to support General Howard, who was then confronting the enemy near Jonesborough, which movement was made without delay. Being informed through General Howard's staff officer that he wished me on the Fayetteville road—that is, near Renfroe's—I countermarched to that place, where instructions were received from General Davis, commanding the corps, to proceed to my former camp at Mrs. Evans's and remain there that night."[69]

These conflicting orders are evidence of the confusion generated by the first day of the Battle of Jonesboro. On August 30, Logan's corps led the Federal advance toward the Macon & Western. After crossing the Flint River, Logan dug in his troops on some high ground overlooking the town of Jonesboro and waited for the rest of the army to close up. A little more than a mile from Logan's line lay the tracks of the Macon & Western. Southern troops were closing on the Jonesboro area while Logan's men dug. General Hood did not realize how large of a force Sherman had sent toward Jonesboro and dispatched only half of his own army, Hardee's and Lee's Corps, to deal with the marauding Federals. The Confederates assaulted Logan's line on the afternoon of August 31, but Logan's men and their fortifications prevailed. Hood, misinformed of the day's events and unsure about Sherman's movements, then compounded the Southern defeat by ordering Lee's troops back to Atlanta. Only Hardee's Corps remained in the Jonesboro area, covering the western and northern approaches to the town.

While Confederate strength diminished in front of Jonesboro on August 31, Federal numbers increased with the arrival of three additional corps, Davis's XIV Corps among them. After crossing the Flint River, Stanley's IV Corps reached the line of the Macon & Western near Rough & Ready, seven miles up the tracks from Jonesboro, in the late afternoon. Stanley's troops spent the rest of the day fortifying and tearing up track, not ceasing the latter activity until three o'clock the next morning. General Davis pushed Baird's division forward to the Macon & Western also. Baird reached the rails at a point about four miles north of Jonesboro. While a contingent of Baird's men began to destroy the rails, Baird entrenched his division just west of the tracks on the Jonesboro-Rough & Ready Road. Carlin and the regulars had meanwhile conducted their evening countermarches and ended the day back at Mrs. Evans's.[70]

Sherman ordered the Army of the Cumberland to attack the next day. He instructed Thomas to get the rest of Davis's corps across the Flint River, link up with Baird and Stanley north of Jonesboro, and then advance south toward the Confederate position. The regulars prepared for battle as the sun rose on September 1. Major John Edie wrestled with a manpower problem while his troops finished their meager breakfasts and fell in. For once, too few troops was not the main problem, although only about 1,200 regulars were present for duty in the battalions, with details and guard duty reducing the brigade's effective strength to little more than 1,000. Edie's concern was that ninety-one of his troops, a contingent of 19th Infantrymen, were fresh from that regiment's depot in Michigan. Even if the veteran sergeants in charge of the newcomers could prod them forward to participate in an attack—it was highly unlikely that the recent civilians possessed the courage necessary to move out on their own—the major knew they probably would not advance far. A situation like that would be more trouble than it was worth, and Edie made up his mind to leave the recruits behind if the regulars were ordered into an assault.

The major anticipated receiving that order sometime later in the day as he led the Regular Brigade toward the battlefield. Davis's corps marched northeastward after crossing the Flint, moved around the Army of the Tennessee's left, and then headed due east for a linkup with Baird's forward-deployed division and Stanley's corps, the latter of which was supposed to be moving down the rails from Rough & Ready. Davis's column soon arrived at Baird's position and then headed south with General Carlin's division in the lead. After encountering friendly pickets from Howard's army, General Davis learned that the Confederate line was not far in the distance. He did not want to proceed further until he knew Stanley's corps was on the XIV Corps's left as planned. He ordered Carlin's division (less one brigade, which had remained on the west side of the Flint River guarding the Army of the Cumberland's baggage train) to move directly eastward to the railroad and see if Stanley was nearby. Carlin sent Moore's brigade forward, with the 16th Infantry attached as skirmishers. The rails were about a mile and half through the woods to their front. Captain R. Peabody Barry, again commanding the 16th after Captain Gay's departure on leave the previous month, ordered his men forward. As Barry's regulars plunged into the woods and advanced toward a stream near the railroad bed, they came under fire from enemy pickets.[71]

The 16th Infantry's Captain Solomon S. Robinson was quite hard of hearing after three years of his second war. A veteran of the Mexican War, where he had served as a 1st sergeant in an Ohio volunteer regiment, at Jonesboro Robinson was second-in-command of the 16th Infantry field detachment. The captain had halted his horse in front of a split-rail fence as the battalion deployed to deal with the enemy skirmishers. As Lieutenant Edgar Kellogg ran by and began climbing over the fence, Robinson yelled: "Are the Rebels shooting any?" Kellogg's courage had carried him safely through from Shiloh to Atlanta, but he desired more after some bullets struck the fence near him. "Someone is, sure," Kellogg replied, "and I'd give a thousand dollars for your ears." Kellogg could keep his money, for he and his companions had more than enough courage to prevail in this small exchange. The enemy contesting their advance was a weak force of dismounted enemy cavalry supported by a single artillery piece. They had been watching northward for Stanley's advance, and thus Carlin's movement out of the west took them by surprise.

At the sound of the firing, Carlin ordered Moore and Edie to move their brigades forward. The Regular Brigade also encountered some enemy pickets, but it was all over by the time the unit reached the railroad bed. Colonel Moore's brigade was already in position by the time Edie's arrived. The major aligned the regulars beside the colonel's regiments. Captain Berry's men brought their prisoners through the Regular Brigade's position, en route for the rear. "We teased them about being captured," 15th Infantryman Gilday recalled, "told them that after awhile we would get the whole of them. They got mad as bears and told us we would get ours, as the whole of Hardee's Corps, that never was whipped, was ready for us. We told them this was the Regular Brigade that never was whipped, and we would lick Hardee good this time" (Gilday was one of the young regulars who had enlisted in 1864; evidently no one had bothered to inform him about what had happened to the regulars at Chickamauga).[72]

Carlin's division consolidated its position near the railroad bed, but Stanley's corps was nowhere in sight. The main Confederate line guarding Jonesboro was not far away, and about an hour after arriving at the rails, one of Carlin's staff officers noticed a hill to the south that could serve as an excellent artillery position. Carlin concurred and ordered Captain Mark H. Prescott's Battery C, 1st Illinois Light Artillery, into action. The division commander noticed that "Prescott moved to [the hill] as rapidly as his horses could go, unlimbered, and opened his guns, which created great havoc among the rebels." The 15th U.S. went forward as support for Prescott, Private Gilday among them: "The enemy were bringing field artillery into position, and the battery immediately opened fire. As they were only a quarter of a mile off, every shot took effect and their guns were put out of action; other guns were being brought up but were knocked over as fast as they appeared. Their line directly in our front was in the woods, and they got some guns in position there, as they could not be seen."

General Carlin concurred with the private's evaluation of Prescott's effectiveness: "It may here be stated that much of the success later in the day was due to the execution of this battery, both

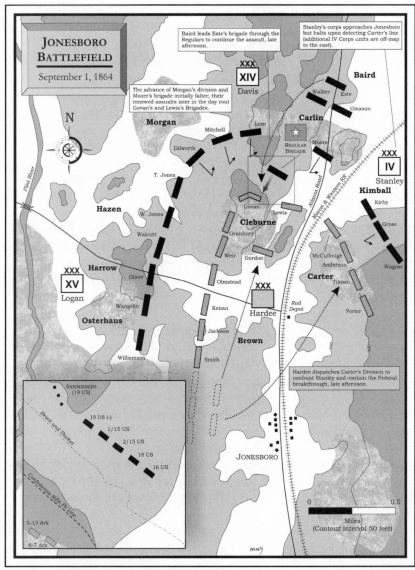

JONESBORO
BATTLEFIELD

September 1, 1864

Baird leads Este's brigade through the Regulars to continue the assault, late afternoon.

Stanley's corps approaches Jonesboro but halts upon detecting Carter's line (additional IV Corps units are off-map to the east).

The advance of Morgan's division and Moore's brigade initially falter; their renewed assaults later in the day rout Govan's and Lewis's Brigades.

XXX
XIV
Davis

Baird

Walker   Este

Gleason

N

Morgan

Mitchell

Lum

Carlin

Moore

XXX
IV
Stanley

Dilworth

REGULAR
BRIGADE

Kimball

Kirby

T. Jones

Hazen

W. Jones

Govan

Lewis

Cleburne

Granbury

Grose

Walcutt

Weir

Gordon

McCullough

Anderson

Wagner

XXX
XV
Logan

Harrow

Oliver

Olmstead

XXX

Carter

Tilman

Wangelin

Kenan

Hardee

Rail
Depot

Porter

Osterhaus

Jackson

Brown

Williamson

Smith

Hardee dispatches Carter's Division to confront Stanley and contain the Federal breakthrough, late afternoon.

SKIRMISHERS
(19 US)

19 US (-)

1/15 US

2/15 US

18 US

16 US

JONESBORO

5-13 Ark

6-7 Ark

0   0.5

Miles
(Contour interval 50 feet)

mwj

on the infantry and artillery of the rebels." Captain Mooney's 1/19th was also deployed to the south, serving as skirmishers to cover the division's anticipated movement toward the enemy line. Mooney's battalion was also ordered to cover a large gap between Carlin's division and Colonel Thomas J. Morgan's division (Davis's former command).[73]

While Prescott's gunners began to pound the enemy line, General Thomas linked up with Davis on the Jonesboro Road. He told Davis that Stanley's men may have, in fact, already passed Carlin's division and ordered Davis to resume the advance southward. Carlin, in fact, had already figured this out for himself, having sent the 21st Ohio on a reconnaissance east of the tracks. The Ohioans located Stanley, whose corps had indeed already approached Jonesboro on the eastern side of the railway. Davis's corps then moved out toward the Confederate lines, Carlin on the left, Morgan on the right. Baird's division was in reserve, echeloned to the left behind Carlin. General Carlin was glad that the corps was at last moving in a decisive direction: "Finally my division was placed where Thomas wanted it. It, or at least two brigades of it, were to move south, to the west of the railroad, and assault the enemy's works. The brigade of Regulars...was on my right. The brigade commanded by Colonel Marshall F. Moore was on the left. For a hundred yards or more we passed through underbrush and then came into open but broken ground."[74]

Carlin's battle line actually moved through thick woods for about a mile before arriving at a broad open field. Enemy fortifications occupied high ground on the far side. If anything, the terrain the Regular Brigade was about to cross was even more difficult than what the regulars had encountered at either Resaca or Utoy Creek. The field was anywhere from 300 to 800 yards across (estimates vary, but the regulars certainly had to traverse a wider swath of land than they had in either previous battle). A creek and low ground ran laterally across the front. Worst of all, much of the field was covered with thick brush and vines. Walking through the vegetation was hard enough; maintaining alignment in a battle formation would be close to impossible. Little did they know it at the time, but as the regulars peered across the obstacle-laden field they were staring at the position of Brigadier General Daniel C. Govan's Arkansas Brigade—the same unit that had broken and scattered the Regular Brigade near Jay's Mill on the first day of Chickamauga. Govan's regiments occupied an angle in Hardee's entrenchments, formed as the Confederate line bent southward to cover Jonesboro's western approaches. That angle was the focal point of the XIV Corps's attack.[75]

The 15th U.S. departed Prescott's artillery position and linked up with the Regular Brigade as Carlin's line approached. General Carlin ordered his division forward at three o'clock in the afternoon. On the Federal left, Stanley's men did not expect to encounter much in the way of opposition, for they thought the Confederate line ended near the railroad and that the IV Corps was therefore beyond the enemy's right flank. In this they were mistaken. Hardee's line, although not overly strong, extended far to the east of the railroad. Shortly after Stanley's corps began its advance, it encountered enemy skirmishers and breastworks where none should have been. That was enough to stop the IV Corps. Stanley's advance halted and his men dug in.

The regulars had meanwhile advanced in a single line, the 16th U.S. on the left, the 18th U.S. in the middle, the 15th U.S. on the right, and ninety-one recruits remaining behind in the rear. The 19th U.S., previously deployed as skirmishers, continued in that role. The regulars waded into the vegetation, "an almost impenetrable undergrowth of vines and bushes," in the words of Captain Jewett, and advanced at what must have seemed like a snail's pace, particularly on the left portion of the brigade's line where the vegetation was heaviest. Despite Captain Prescott's earlier counterbattery fire, there were still some Southern guns in action. Govan's line included two artillery batteries; the fire of these pieces and Govan's supporting infantry ripped into Carlin's line. Moore's brigade on the regulars' left was subjected to both this fire and an unexpected crossfire from the enemy line on the far side of the railroad. A brigade of Stanley's corps was supposed to support Moore's eastern flank, but with Stanley's men holding in place for the moment, these troops were nowhere to be seen. Moore's brigade barely advanced before halting. Morgan's division on the regulars' right likewise halted shortly after the attack commenced, preferring to instead construct hasty rifle pits in a fortuitously sited ravine. The difficult terrain disrupted the alignment of the 19th Infantry's skirmish line. The four companies of Mooney's battalion that were covering the gap between Carlin and Morgan halted when Morgan's division ceased its advance. Mooney told his battalion quartermaster, Lieutenant John J. Wagoner, to take charge of this stationary contingent. Mooney himself gathered in his remaining five companies, totaling 118 men, and formed them to the right of the 15th Infantry. Unsupported and alone, the Regular Brigade continued forward. It was Utoy Creek all over again.[76]

"Such a sight I never seen nor do I ever want to see again," Private David Melville thought to himself as he looked over the Jonesboro battlefield. The private was lucky that all he had to do that afternoon was sit back and watch, for he was one of the 19th Infantry recruits left behind at the line of departure. Melville's comrades in the field to his front were having a much tougher time of it. Some of the regulars were hit as soon as they emerged from the tree line, but, at first, advancing was actually their safest option. The forward Confederate positions were too far back on the far ridge line to place effective fire on the low ground in the middle of the field. The closer the regulars came to the stream, the safer they therefore became. In contrast to the men of Morgan's division, the regulars did not halt and cower as soon as they came upon some cover. Captain Jewett believed they continued on because each regular seemed to be "stimulated with the idea that upon his individual efforts depended our final success." General Carlin was nearby and did what he could to ensure that Edie's troops kept going: "I was near the Regular brigade. Coming to a little stream, perhaps 200 yards north of the enemy's works, I ordered...Edie to assault the enemy's position and take it."[77]

After crossing the swampy ground and advancing up the slope on the far side of the valley, where the vegetation was not as thick, the pace of the regulars' advance increased. So did the amount of incoming projectiles. "The officers and men...rushed gallantly up the hill in the face of a galling fire," Major Edie reported, "and before support of any kind was given them, succeeded in driving the enemy from their front line of works." With no flank support as he advanced up the ridge, Captain Mooney detached two companies of 19th Infantrymen and sent them to the right to take care of some enemy skirmishers in a ravine that were placing oblique fire down the brigade's line. The detachment made short work of the threat, returning to their battalion with twelve prisoners in tow. The rest of the brigade had meanwhile continued to advance.

As the regulars approached the top of the ridge, they received their first clear view of what they were going up against. The forward line of rifle pits, the occupants of which had been making the advance difficult for the regulars, was just the first of three separate lines of breastworks that Govan's Brigade occupied. Edie's horse was hit as the brigade staggered up the hill, but the major escaped injury. Captain Lyman Kellogg of the 18th Infantry had also remained mounted, urging his men forward. The captain's enthusiasm got the better of him, for he applied his spurs, jumped a parapet, and landed amidst Govan's men. He was quickly unhorsed, a bullet lodged in an arm. His sudden appearance startled nearby Southerners to such an extent that he was luckily able to stagger to his feet and avoid capture. Seeing their commander shot inside the enemy position, the 18th Infantrymen hesitated. This hesitation rippled through most of the brigade, with the 15th and 19th ceasing movement at the very moment when the attack should have been pressed home.[78]

It was not a good day for the Kellogg family. At about the moment Lyman was getting himself shot, his brother Edgar was closing with the enemy's first line. Lieutenant Kellogg commanded two companies of the 16th U.S. on the brigade's left flank. Seeing most of the regulars to his right faltering to a standstill and taking cover, Kellogg called out to Lieutenant St. Onge, the battalion's quartermaster, asking if a command had been given to halt. "I don't think there is—I have not heard any!" St. Onge yelled back. Kellogg kept his men moving: "My own regiment—except my two companies—and others, stopped for a short time when within ten to fifteen rods of the enemy's line, but my two companies kept on, drove the enemy from their works in my front." Kellogg's position in front of the brigade's temporarily halted line was exposed to deadly crossfire. The 16th Infantry's adjutant, Lieutenant Charles Hotsenpillar, took it upon himself to recall Kellogg's men. Hotsenpillar somehow galloped up to Kellogg's position unscathed and told the company commander to fall back.

"Is that an order?" Kellogg demanded.

"No, but you will be captured if you stay here."

"We can hold what we have," Kellogg replied. "Go back and bring up the regiment."[79]

Help was on the way. Captain Robert Hull had taken command of the 18th U.S. and urged it forward. Other commanders got their men on their feet and pushed them up the slope. The Regular Brigade closed the distance to the rifle pits and the fighting then became a vicious hand-to-hand struggle. "One Johnny caught hold of my gun and tried to pull me over," 15th Infantryman Gilday recalled, "but I had the big end [i.e., the butt of the rifle] and my foot on the head log. I gave a sudden pull and wacked him over the head and then gave my attention to others." Meanwhile, Edgar Kellogg's luck ran out: "My men were steady, and I walked back and forth behind them from right to left, praising and encouraging them. About a dozen Confederates jumped over the works a few rods to my right and began to enfilade my men. I was returning towards the right of my line when one of this bunch of Confederates sent a ball through my right hip. It did not occur to me that I was knocked out, and I managed to nearly regain a standing attitude, but I fell again, and then realized that I was severely wounded." Kellogg remained in command until the balance of the 16th came forward. In his later years this tough old veteran would be quick to point out that when shot at Jonesboro, he fell forward, facing his adversaries.[80]

The Regular Brigade had captured a portion of Govan's forward line, but the main Confederate position was still further ahead in the woods. Some of the regulars attempted to continue the advance, but a volley from Govan's still-intact second line quickly dissuaded them of that notion and the regulars fell back to the rifle pit line. Govan followed up his rifle fire with a charge of his own and the Arkansans surged toward the regulars. Edie knew his worn-out troops would not be able to withstand a determined assault. He ordered them to abandon the captured rifle pits and fall back a short distance down into the valley out of which they had just advanced. Most of them responded, although some, in particular from the 19th Infantry on the right flank, never received the order and held their ground. Govan's troops closed the distance and quickly overwhelmed the few regulars remaining in the fortifications, capturing twenty-six from 1/19th U.S. and twenty more from the other battalions. The regulars who retreated into the valley found themselves in a sheltered position, but pinned down, too weak to advance, but unable to fall back. Their own fire was still effective and it was difficult for the Confederates to rise up and draw a bead on the regulars. "[W]e had a battery in front of us," remembered Arthur Carpenter, "but we were so close to it that the rebels could not work it." Another of Edie's troops recalled: "Every man who showed his head above only did so one time." Private Gilday was one of the regulars who made it to the temporary shelter: "Here we were out in the open field, in the hot sun, one brigade against a corps strongly entrenched with a few rounds of ammunition and none in sight. We could not go to the stream for water, as to rise up was to be shot. Our position was a critical one, but we determined to hold it if possible until reinforcements came up."[81]

As Gilday noted, the actual assault force of the Army of the Cumberland's two-corps attack on the second day of the Battle of Jonesboro had thus far consisted of exactly one brigade, Major Edie's regulars. Reinforcements were coming. It had taken about an hour, but General Davis was finally able to get his corps moving again. Moore's brigade on the regulars' left and Morgan's division on Edie's right resumed the advance. Not wanting to lose what the regulars had gained, General Davis ordered Colonel George P. Este's brigade from Baird's reserve division to move forward and renew the assault beyond the regulars' hard-won position. What followed is one of the few examples in the Civil War of a successful reinforcement of a stalled attack. Personally led by their division commander (an action for which Absalom Baird would one day receive the Medal of Honor), Este's brigade advanced across the field and swamp, following the route the regulars had taken earlier in the afternoon. With fire from the regulars pinning down Govan's forward troops, Este was able to advance unchecked right up to the edge of the enemy position. Baird halted the brigade fifty yards behind Edie's line and had his men strip off their knapsacks and fix bayonets, "so as to be ready for heavy work." The regulars warned Este's Ohioans, Kentuckians, and Indianans that the Southerners had at least two lines ahead and that some regulars may be still holding out in a portion of the first. Baird gave the word to advance. The regulars cheered as Baird's troops walked through Edie's line, continued up the slope, and disappeared from sight.

The regulars had already pushed Govan's regiments to the breaking point. The Arkansans began to give way in the face of Baird's assault. Baird proudly reported: "The rebel troops, confident in themselves and in their ability to hold their works, were totally unprepared for a charge of this kind, and were taken completely by surprise. They delivered a single volley, and before they could reload found our men in the trenches with them, bayoneting all who did not surrender." Este's brigade continued to advance into the main Confederate works. Moore's brigade and elements of Morgan's division joined them there. Federal numbers carried the day for the moment, although heavy fighting inflicted casualties among these assaulting units at rates just as heavy as the regulars had suffered. In addition to scattering Govan's Brigade, the Federal assault shattered the Kentucky Orphan Brigade to Govan's right. Hundreds of Confederates surrendered, and many more fled. The

Federal breakthrough was eventually contained as General Hardee rushed reinforcements to his threatened northern flank, but the XIV Corps at Jonesboro had executed the most successful assault of the entire campaign for Atlanta.[82]

One of the regulars' own was among the victorious troops occupying Govan's line. Henry Mizner had held a regular commission as a captain in the 18th Infantry since 1861 and commanded F/3/18th U.S. at Stones River. In early 1863, he secured a volunteer appointment as colonel of the 14th Michigan Infantry. At Jonesboro, Mizner's regiment was part of Morgan's division and among the first to break through the Confederate line. One of Mizner's sergeants captured General Govan. The sergeant took the captive to see Colonel Mizner, to whom the general handed over his sword. The blade was well traveled. "I surrendered my brigade," Govan later remarked, "with a sword bearing the name of Major Sidney Coolidge, 16th United States Infantry, that I had obtained at the battle of Chickamauga in September, 1863." Mizner also collected from Govan a pair of "very handsome" spurs that had been captured during the Mexican War by Govan's father, a veteran of that conflict. Now it was Govan's turn to point out that his troops had never before been broken. Chickamauga was avenged.[83]

After Baird's men advanced through the Regular Brigade, Major Edie got his own weary troops on their feet and marched them back to Federal lines. They linked up with the 19th Infantry recruits and refilled cartridge boxes. The regulars returned to the lines later during the early evening next to Colonel Moore's brigade, constructing fortifications well into the night. The Federal defensive measures were not necessary, for General Hardee's battle-weary Confederates had no intention of attacking. Hardee withdrew that night six miles southward to Lovejoy's Station. On the morning of September 2, the Northerners discovered that the enemy was gone. Sherman pursued Hardee to Lovejoy's, leaving Davis's corps as a rear guard at Jonesboro while the Federal army moved further south.

The Battle of Jonesboro itself had no real bearing on the ultimate outcome of the Atlanta Campaign. Sherman's purpose in moving south of Atlanta was to destroy the railroads leading into the city. His troops were able to do that prior to the fighting on the first day of September. Sherman's handling of the Federal assault at Jonesboro was not particularly brilliant, using less than half of his available force to attack Hardee's line. Regardless of either the status of the two rail lines leading into East Point or the outcome of the Jonesboro fighting, the mere presence of Sherman's army south of Atlanta had convinced General Hood that the Confederate hold on the city was untenable. The Southerners evacuated Atlanta shortly after midnight on September 2. Union troops from the XX Corps marched in later that day.[84]

At Jonesboro on September 1, the Regular Brigade again paid a heavy price. Nearly one-fifth of the regulars who participated in the assault were killed, wounded, or missing as night fell. The brigade's line at the start of the battle consisted of just 32 officers and 889 troops, most of the men having been in uniform less than a year, led by a junior field-grade officer who was a West Point dropout. They represented the sum total of infantrymen the Regular Army contributed to the final phase of the Atlanta Campaign, a campaign now widely considered to have been one of the war's most decisive due to its positive effect on Abraham Lincoln's reelection in the 1864 presidential race. The strength of Edie's minuscule brigade of regulars in no way resembled the Iron Column that Winfield Scott had hoped the regulars in the Civil War would become. Despite the dedicated efforts of officers such as Oliver Shepherd, Stephen Carpenter, John King, and many others, the Union Army's professional soldiers by mid-1864 were not a particularly awe-inspiring sight.

But the regulars made an impact far beyond simple numbers. Their performance at Jonesboro was best summed up by General Carlin, who, according to Captain Biddle, paid Edie's troops a fine tribute: "In the evening after the fight was over General Carlin…rode along our lines & told us that the charge of the regulars was the most magnificent thing he had ever seen, that the rest of his division had done well but the fighting of the regulars was superb." Major Edie incorporated Carlin's comments into the Regular Brigade's official report: "I but quote the language of a distinguished division commander, who witnessed the progress of the battle, when I say that 'No troops ever fought better or more bravely.'" The usually taciturn George Thomas was also impressed with the overall effort: "We have won a great victory. I never saw such a charge." Although the Battle of Jonesboro had little impact on the final outcome of the Atlanta Campaign, that fact should not diminish the Regular Brigade's role in the September 1 fighting, which paved the way for much of the XIV Corps' tactical success.

Viewed in that light, in a small way Scott's plan for the Iron Column of regulars may indeed have finally been realized.[85]

Victory celebrations swept the North. Far away from Atlanta, at New York's Ft. Ontario on the Niagara River, Captain R.E.A. Crofton ordered the 16th Regulars of the post's garrison to don their frock coats and shoulder scales on Saturday afternoon, September 3. The local paper had given the nearby town of Oswego due warning that Crofton's regulars would stage a full dress parade that evening and fire a salute in celebration of recent events in Georgia. The Monday morning edition of the *Oswego Daily Palladium* reported that the ceremonies came off flawlessly: "West Oswego was fairly taken on Saturday evening. We capitulated, surrendered with good grace to Capt. Crofton of the 16th U.S. Infantry, who with a battalion of infantry marched over from the fort and planted their colors in the West Park. The demonstration and a salute of 100 guns which was fired, was in honor of the occupation of Atlanta by the Federal forces. All were jubilant over the event, and deemed the demonstration on the part of the 'regulars' as a fitting reflection of the general joy."[86]

A few more victories like Atlanta and the United States would no long have had a viable Regular Army. Major Edie's troops remained in Jonesboro until September 6, when they marched a few miles and bivouacked near the site of the September 1 battle. The regulars joined the rest of Sherman's triumphant forces in marching northward to Atlanta the next day. The soldiers of the Regular Brigade did not realize it at the time, but they would never again march southward during the Civil War.

Chapter 11:

Lookout Mountain

"The Character of the Regulars Must Certainly Suffer"

The autumn of 1864 marked the end of the line for the Regular Brigade. They had given their all during the Georgia campaign, but the march and battles of the previous months had so weakened the battalions that they were now at a critical point. Were they to continue on and fight to extinction, or would the War Department finally take an interest in their long-term prospects? The answer turned out to be a compromise, and the battalions spent the last winter and spring of the war in Chattanooga. They were rebuilt through another infusion of fresh manpower, but making regulars out of these latest recruits was one of their greatest challenges.

* * *

The Regular Brigade arrived in Atlanta on September 8. The most notable event of the day was the receiving of a ration of soft bread that evening, the first such delicacy the regulars had eaten in almost four months. The new surroundings did not impress Captain Biddle: "our camp is on high ground & should be healthy, but is the dirtiest place I ever got into, from having been so long occupied by Confederate troops. We are hard at work trying to clean up, but from present looks it may be a week before we can get rid of the bad smells." The 16th Infantry officer was presumably pleased when, on September 10, Major Edie led the regulars to a new camp about two and a half miles southwest of the city near the village of Whitesides, where the weary survivors of the campaign finally rested. A different sort of resting commenced the next day, as a paymaster arrived and paid the regulars their back pay. "Money is plenty & the men will soon be drunk," Biddle scribbled in his diary on September 11. "I don't blame them, after the hard times we have had, I should not mind doing the same thing myself if I could find some thing better than Sutlers whiskey." For the next ten days, the captain's diary is strangely silent. Perhaps he was just busy. Since reports, returns, and other paperwork had been largely neglected for almost four months, administrative tasks meant officers and sergeants on staff had little free time. "I have to write from morning till night," Arthur Carpenter complained in a short letter on September 14, "making out Pay Rolls and Company Papers so I cannot write more now." The regulars' hard work did not go unnoticed. The inspector general on General Carlin's division staff reported: "The camp of the 18th U.S. Infantry near Atlanta [is] especially commended for neatness and their books and records worthy of especial note."[1]

Sick and wounded soldiers also needed attention. Captains Anson Mills and Andrew Burt visited some their men in a nearby field hospital. Walking into a large tent containing perhaps seventy-five recuperating soldiers, Burt was incensed to read large placards on the inside walls adorned with such inspiring messages as "Are you prepared to die?" and "Prepare to meet your God," products of a well-intentioned but somewhat misguided religious society. Burt tore down the signs and stamped them underfoot, yelling "Never say die, men! Never say die!" A critically wounded sergeant of the 18th Regulars responded in a weak voice, saying to no one in particular: "If more officers like this visited us, there wouldn't be so many of us die."[2]

Some officers who had departed during the campaign rejoined their battalions in Atlanta. Captain Ebenezer Gay resumed command of the 16th Infantry in mid-September. An officer that no one had expected to see any time soon appeared in the 19th Infantry's camp on September 19. Lieutenant Robert Ayres, the adjutant of 1/19th U.S. who had been captured during the February reconnaissance to Dalton, in July had escaped from a Confederate prison at Macon, Georgia, and made his way to friendly lines north of Atlanta. After a thirty-day leave, he reported for duty, despite a frail condition and continuing poor heath. His sufferings while a prisoner had embittered him toward everything Confederate. Ayres told his comrades that the Southerners were "devoid of all humanity, lost to all honor." He added that he would never again take an enemy prisoner.[3]

None of the battle-worn, skeletal regular battalions would be able to do anything meaningful on a battlefield in the foreseeable future. While many Union regiments had sustained heavy losses from Rocky Face Ridge to Jonesboro, the regulars once again attracted more than their fair share. Judging from casualty figures published in the *Official Records* (which is the best source available, although it is not 100 percent comprehensive), the 261 battle casualties that the 15th U.S. suffered from May to September 1864 was the highest volume of losses any Federal regiment sustained during the Atlanta Campaign. The 18th Regulars were not far behind, losing 231 troops to enemy action. Captain Thomas H. Norton's company of 2/15th U.S., which had begun the campaign at nearly full strength with 100 men present for duty, by early September counted just one corporal and eight privates still in ranks.[4]

No casualties occurred during the occasional picket duty the Regular Brigade performed near Atlanta, but further discharges were constantly thinning its ranks. More than 200 veteran troops received their discharges and left the brigade during September 1864. With so few troops to command, some regular officers were granted leaves of absence during the stay in Atlanta. A few others decided it was time to resign their commissions. With no replacement officers or troops arriving to take their places, something would have to be done soon or the ranks of the Regular Brigade would eventually be whittled down to nothing. Captain Jewett felt compelled to make the War Department aware of 1/15th's frail condition in the aftermath of the Atlanta Campaign:

> Head Quarters 1st Batt. 15th Infantry
> Atlanta Ga. Sept 20 1864

> Brig Genl L. Thomas
> Adjutant General U.S.A.
> Washington D.C.

> General

> I respectfully report that the Strength of the 1st Battalion Fifteenth Regiment of Infantry present and absent at this date is Two Hundred and Two (202) enlisted men. Out of this number there are Eighty two (82) present for duty. Seventy seven (77) absent sick, "mostly wounded," and Forty three detached on various duties.

> The enlistment of most of these men expire before the end of next month, with the exception of Forty six (46) who have re-enlisted.

Out of this number Sixteen (16) are absent for various causes, "mostly wounds." This Battalion has attached to and serving with it three (3) Companies of the 3rd Battalion representing a total of enlisted present and absent Two hundred and Thirty eight (238) men, present for duty One Hundred and Thirty nine (139) about two thirds (2/3) of the command present.

In view of these facts I have therefore respectfully to request that the station of the 1st Battalion with its Staff and non-commissioned staff be ordered to the Head Quarters of the Regiment as a Regimental Recruiting Party.

If this battalion could be ordered away before the enlistment of all the men expire, a good many of these men could be induced to re-enlist, and by sending them out as Recruiting Parties from Regimental Depot to localities in which Regiments have been mustered out with whom they have been serving, They would undoubtedly obtain a good many recruits who have served one term of enlistment.

I make this request with a firm belief that its compliance with would be for the interest of the Regiment and of the Service, and that a double number and a better quality of recruits would be obtained for the field.

I would further add that the Major and the Adjutant are absent, the first from Sickness and the last from wounds received in action, and that the non-commissioned staff is reduced to a Hospital Steward and Quarter Master Sergeant whose time expires next month, and that could this command be ordered to Fort Adams, "D" Company of the 3rd Battalion could be relieved and ordered to the Field and the 3rd Battalion could have a distinct organization.

> I am Sir
> Very Respectfully
> Your Obdt. Servant
> HORACE JEWETT
> Capt 15th Infantry
> Comdg 1st Battalion[5]

Oliver Shepherd heartily agreed with Jewett's request, and tried to prod the War Department into action by requesting that at least the soldiers in Jewett's battalion who had recently re-enlisted be ordered to Ft. Adams: "The parties now at the various Rectg. Rendezvous are nearly all composed of Invalid Soldiers of the Regiment...who take but little, if any, interest in procuring recruits for the Regiment. ...The few re-enlisted men of the 1st Batt. asked for, would probably take great interest in Recruiting, and it is hoped that the Department may deem [it] proper to order them here." The answer Shepherd and Jewett received was predictable; nothing would be done: "Troops cannot be withdrawn from Genl Sherman's command at the present time."[6]

But these and other similar requests did not fall on completely deaf ears in Washington. Plans were in the works to withdraw the regulars from active campaigning and allow them to recuperate. In the East, the regulars of the V Corps would head for the rear by early November 1864 after the Siege of Petersburg began in earnest (although a few companies of the 4th U.S. continued in the field as guards at Grant's headquarters). In the West, it was thought that perhaps the Regular Brigade could leave the field now that Atlanta had fallen. As events turned out, the Regular Brigade had new marching orders just eight days after Captain Jewett made his request, but operational concerns ultimately dictated the regulars' next destination. The war had continued while Sherman's armies rested in Atlanta. After Sherman withdrew from Lovejoy's Station for the final movement to occupy Atlanta, Hood regrouped the Army of Tennessee near Palmetto, about twenty-five miles southwest of Atlanta on the Atlanta-Montgomery Railway. Since Hood's army was not strong enough to directly threaten Sherman's hold on Atlanta, Hood decided to advance the Army of Tennessee toward Chattanooga and disrupt Federal traffic on the Western & Atlantic. Simultaneously, Major General Nathan Bedford Forrest's cavalry would move from Mississippi into middle Tennessee and destroy the rail lines that connected Chattanooga with Nashville. The Confederates hoped these multiple threats to Sherman's lines of communication would prevent Sherman from advancing deeper into Georgia, perhaps forcing the Federals to abandon Atlanta and withdraw northward.

Forrest's raid got underway first, with close to 4,500 Southern cavalrymen crossing the Tennessee River near Waterloo, Alabama, on September 21. The raiders moved northeastward, capturing a small Federal garrison at Athens three days later. Forrest then began working his way along the Central Alabama Railroad. The Southerners destroyed large sections of the line, severing one of the two routes used to move freight from Nashville to Chattanooga. Major General Lovell Rousseau at Nashville positioned a scratch blocking force of 3,000 men at Pulaski to contain the Confederate raid. The two forces skirmished on September 27, after which

Forrest pulled back and headed toward Tullahoma to strike the Nashville-Chattanooga line. To counter this threat, Rousseau's men at Pulaski went by rail through Nashville to Tullahoma, while James Steedman moved westward from Chattanooga with 5,000 men of that town's garrison.[7]

Sherman ordered Thomas to Nashville. The Army of the Cumberland's commander was to take command of Union forces in middle and eastern Tennessee and coordinate the actions necessary to contain the Confederacy's "Wizard of the Saddle." Thomas had already taken some initial steps to shift forces northward. As Forrest crossed the Tennessee River, Thomas knew that Steedman's troops in Chattanooga would eventually be involved in the chase. He ordered Brigadier General John Newton's division of the IV Corps to head northward from Atlanta and bolster Chattanooga's garrison. Newton's men arrived in the town on September 26. The Army of the Cumberland's commander also ordered the Regular Brigade north. "It seems that our Brigade is to be sent to Lookout Mountain to do garrison duty," Lieutenant Carpenter wrote on September 22, the day after Forrest's raid began. "I do not know for certain, but every one who should know seems to think so." Captain Biddle's diary picks up again that same day: "We are still in the same camp. Nothing is being done except drilling the men & getting into some shape after the exertion of a long campaign. There is a report in camp that the regulars are to be sent back to Chattanooga."[8]

The rumors were indeed true. A change of base to Chattanooga would allow the weak regular battalions to garrison that vital spot, while at the same time incorporating into their ranks any new recruits their regimental depots could send south. The Regular Brigade broke camp on September 28 and by late morning was loaded onto box and platform cars at the Atlanta depot. At 11:00 A.M., the regulars pulled out of the stations and headed north. The train halted that afternoon near Marietta, and Major Edie took advantage of the delay to order details from each regiment to a nearby warehouse, in which was stored some of the regulars' camp equipment. The halt did not last long, for the men had just left the train when it started to move again. Some of the regulars ran after the cars and managed to jump on, but others were left behind and had to complete the journey to Chattanooga on their own. Further delays were encountered ascending the heavy grade of the Allatoona Mountains later that afternoon, rain having made the rails slick. The cars had to be split up and hauled in short segments over the high ground. The last of the cars arrived in Chattanooga on the morning of October 1. Major Edie then marched the brigade five miles to the top of Lookout Mountain. The battalions established camps just south of the ridge's northern terminus.[9]

The first order of business for Major Edie's troops was improving the defensive works on the mountain. Remnants of earlier fortifications remained, constructed by the Confederates after Chickamauga and then worked on by Hooker's troops following the Federal capture of Lookout Mountain in late November 1863. Not much had been done since. The Army of the Cumberland's Engineer Brigade had been stationed on top of Lookout since the winter of 1863–1864, but the engineers had put most of their energy into maintaining bridges across the Tennessee River and constructing hospital buildings in the Chattanooga area. The engineers had been sent to Tullahoma on September 27 to help secure that depot against Forrest, their place on the vital mountain being taken by a brigade from Newton's division. Newton's brigade rejoined its parent division in Chattanooga upon the Regular Brigade's arrival. Between picket duty and manual labor in the damp autumn weather, the regulars surely missed their comfortable camps near Atlanta. Private David Melville of the 19th Infantry did not recall fondly his first few weeks in southeastern Tennessee: "Our brigade was ordered back to Lookout Mountain in Tennessee to do picket duty. It was hard duty. We would be out every other night and day. No shelter nor cabins; nothing but a little tent. So we would put it up and lay down upon a few leaves with our blanket and overcoat about us."[10]

* * *

The war swirled around the regulars as they fortified Lookout Mountain. George Thomas arrived in Chattanooga a day ahead of the Regular Brigade, at the van of Morgan's division of the XIV Corps. Morgan's troops soon moved on to northern Alabama. Thomas himself also did not tarry long in Chattanooga, reaching Nashville on October 3. By that date, Forrest's Tennessee raid was winding down. Thwarted from breaking the Nashville-Chattanooga Railway by the strong columns Thomas had dispatched to the region, on September 29 Forrest called off his advance on Tullahoma and started heading southward. After causing further mischief near Spring Hill and Columbia, by October 6 the Confederate raiders were again south of the Tennessee River in Alabama.[11]

John Bell Hood had meanwhile been busy in Georgia. On September 29 the Army of Tennessee crossed the Chattahoochee River and headed north. By October 4, Confederate troops were north of Atlanta near Lost Mountain, Ackworth, and Big Shanty, where they captured small Federal garrisons and destroyed sections of the Western & Atlantic. Sherman countered by moving the bulk of his Atlanta-based forces to Marietta, leaving a single corps to cover Atlanta. Hood retired further north in front of Sherman, reaching the Dalton-Resaca region on October 13. The Confederates remained in this area only about forty-eight hours. Having destroyed twenty-four miles of track near Big Shanty and another twenty between Tunnel Hill and Resaca, Hood considered his mission accomplished and moved southwestward into Alabama. The Army of Tennessee regrouped at Gadsden on October 20.[12]

The Western & Atlantic was out of commission for the time being, but Sherman was not concerned. The Federals had cautiously followed Hood after the Southerners moved to north Georgia. Reaching Resaca late in the day on October 14, only minor skirmishing took place as Hood's men slipped away. The Federal army followed Hood into Alabama, taking up a position about thirty miles from the Confederate position. Sherman had no intention of chasing Hood any further. Frustrated by having to guard a lengthy supply line and reacting to Confederate threats, the Union general had been wanting to abandon Atlanta completely and conduct a grand raid to somewhere on the coast, making "Georgia howl" in the process. General Grant gave Sherman preliminary approval for the scheme on October 11. During the last week of October, Sherman dispatched Stanley's IV Corps and Schofield's XXIII Corps to Nashville, where they reported to George Thomas. Sherman took his four remaining corps and headed back to Atlanta. Pausing only long enough to destroy everything of potential military value in and around the city, Sherman's men set out for Savannah on November 15. After marching virtually unopposed through the heart of the Confederacy and blazing a swath of destruction in the process, by mid-December Sherman was approaching the Georgia coast. The Confederate garrison of Savannah evacuated the port city on December 20 and Federal troops took possession of it the next day, completing one of the war's great epochs.[13]

Hood moved in the opposite direction while Sherman's juggernaut cut its way across central Georgia. Hoping that a Confederate thrust into middle Tennessee would draw Sherman out of the Deep South, Hood decided to advance toward Nashville and confront Thomas. The Army of Tennessee moved westward from Gadsden on October 21, and by the beginning of November was astride the Tennessee River near Tuscumbia and Florence. After pausing three weeks in a vain attempt to accumulate adequate supplies for an offensive, on November 21, Hood's army sallied forth. Federal garrisons in northern Alabama and southern Tennessee retired in front of the enemy advance. Hood hoped to catch these Union troops before they crossed the Duck River at Columbia, but by the time the Southerners arrived at Columbia on November 28, most of the Federals had made it to safety. Major General John Schofield gathered in the scattered Union troops on the north side of the river and prepared to delay Hood's advance as long as possible.[14]

Schofield's delay turned out to be a short one, for Hood's army crossed the Duck on November 29 and came close to capturing Schofield's entire command eleven miles north of Columbia at Spring Hill. Escaping the trap through Confederate bungling and Federal good luck, Schofield retreated further northward to Franklin. Hood followed and attacked the Federal position there during the afternoon and early evening of November 30. After a series of bloody, futile assaults that cost Hood nearly a third of his army, Schofield fell back again. The Federal army covered the remaining miles to Nashville by noon on December 1. Hood's battered Army of Tennessee followed, taking up a position on the southern outskirts of the Tennessee capital and confronting the numerically superior Union forces hastily gathered there.

George Thomas assumed field command of Federal troops in Nashville following Schofield's retreat from Franklin. Thomas spent two weeks organizing his forces, perfecting his plans, and waiting out a nasty ice storm. The delay caused an impatient Ulysses Grant to issue an order on December 15 relieving Thomas of command, but downed telegraph lines and a quick-thinking officer on Secretary Stanton's staff prevented the message from being delivered. That same day, Thomas unleashed an attack that shattered his Confederate opposition. That portion of Hood's command not captured or destroyed outright retreated a few miles southward. Another Federal assault on December 16 pushed the Army of Tennessee past the breaking point. The remnants of Hood's army streamed back toward Alabama, harried by Thomas's mounting of the Civil War's most determined post-battle pursuit. The Battle of Nashville was one of the war's most complete victories, and the Army of Tennessee was finished as a significant military force.[15]

* * *

The threat of a substantial enemy advance toward Chattanooga permanently receded with the end of Forrest's raid and Hood's subsequent defeat at Nashville. The regulars continued to perfect the Lookout Mountain fortifications, although much of the impetus for the work waned as 1864 came to a close. In terms of moving the regulars to a location where the battalions could be recuperated back into effective fighting units, in retrospect, the move to Chattanooga was a half-measure that put the regulars in a position of little utility. The battalions were no longer part of the Union field army, but neither were they back at their regimental depots where proper recruitment and training could take place. The regulars had been relegated to what turned out to be a backwater garrison where their combat skills eroded and veterans had little incentive to reenlist, all the while contributing little to the Federal war effort.

From the documentary evidence available, it seems that no one really knew what to do with the regulars at this point. They were to occupy Lookout Mountain, secure that place, and beyond that, fend for themselves. A sense of lethargy set in from Major General James Steedman, commander of the District of the Etowah and the Chattanooga garrison, down to the Regular Brigade staff. At the end of October, Captain Ebenezer Gay told the brigade adjutant that even such a basic necessity as adequate clothing was being neglected:

> Head Qrs Detacht 16th Inf.
> Camp at Lookout Mountain, Ga

Capt Wm J. Fetterman
A.A.G. Brigade Regular Troops

Sir:

This regiment has been here over one month during which time repeated applications, estimates, and requisitions have been made for clothing. The men of this Command are suffering for want of it. As there is an ample supply of clothing in Chattanooga which can be readily drawn by the Brigade Quartermaster, I would respectfully request that he be directed to draw it and that if the transportation of the Brigade is so limited that it cannot be transported to this

Camp that I may be allowed to march my men to Chattanooga and receive it there.

That Soldiers should be without the necessary clothing at this Season of the Year, when an abundance can be obtained at a point 5 miles distant I consider as exhibiting a shameful state of inefficiency in the Quarter Master Department which by all means should be investigated.

> I have the honor to be, etc.
>
> EBENEZER GAY
> Capt. 16th Infy
> Com'dg Detcht[16]

Clothing was only one of Captain Gay's concerns. Most of the brigade's horses, wagons, and camp equipment had been left behind in Atlanta. The damage to the Western & Atlantic would be repaired by the end of October, but, in the meantime, it was impossible to transport the Regular Brigade's heavier supplies to Chattanooga. On October 23, Gay sent a request for horses to the department adjutant in Nashville: "I have the honor to enclose a requisition for three horses. Without those horses my regiment is inefficient. With them I think I can do good service. The Endorsement of the Brigade Commander shows that he has been active in the matter, without success."

No horses had shown up as of two weeks later, but Captain Gay had been complaining loud enough that on November 10 he was tasked with superintending the completion of Lookout Mountain's fortifications. Gay knew full well that neither sufficient manpower nor the equipment necessary to the job properly was on hand, so he requested a huge detail for the task, consisting of 3 officers, 8 sergeants, and 200 troops (all properly clad), and asked for spades, picks, crosscut saws, a total of ninety axes of three different varieties, ten mule teams, and twenty yoke of oxen. The captain renewed his bid for a horse: "It will also be necessary for me to be mounted, and I have the honor to apply for a Serviceable horse with Saddle and Bridle." Gay was told that none of the equipment was available and he would have to make do with what he had, which was practically nothing. The situation was so frustrating that on November 13, the captain headed home to New Hampshire on a leave of absence. He had to walk the five miles between the top of Lookout Mountain and the Chattanooga rail depot, for he still had not acquired a horse.[17]

Ebenezer Gay was not the only regular officer leaving Chattanooga. Others who were similarly fed up with the regulars' lack of purpose also left. Some secured positions on Steedman's staff, others resigned, a few more took leave. Lieutenant Arthur B. Carpenter was among the lucky officers in the latter category. He headed home to Indiana during early October for a well-deserved month off. James Biddle resigned his commission in the 16th U.S. Infantry effective September 30; on October 12, he made the final entry in his diary: "This is the end of my army life, and I am going home to my wife and babies."[18] The War Department also authorized three additional officers from each regiment to be placed on recruiting duty. The departure of officers was so severe that after a few weeks in Chattanooga, there were hardly any left. Captain John W. Young, the ranking officer of the 15th U.S. then in the field, tried to explain the situation in a letter to the War Department. The lengthy document is significant in that it illustrates how the remaining officers were so strongly dissatisfied with their situation, and also how they closely tracked peers who served in more comfortable assignments:

> Hd Qrs. 15th U.S. Infty in the Field
> Lookout Mountain
> Oct 23rd 1864

Brig Genl L Thomas
   Adjutant General U.S.A.
   Washington, D.C.

General:

   I would respectfully call your attention to the condition of this detachment, of the 1st, 2nd, & 3rd Battalions of this Regt, as to commissioned officers. There are present with Six Companies of the Second Battalion:

T.H. Norton	Capt. Comd'g
Irvin W. Potter	1st Lt. & Batt. Q.M.
R.M. Harrison	2d Lieut & Act. Adjt.

And with 8 Companies of the 1st & 3d Battalions:

John W. Young	Capt. Comd'g
Horace Jewett	Capt. Comd'g Co. "B" 3d Batt.
Sol. E. Woodward	1st Lt. & Q.M.
James Y. Semple	1st Lt. & Act. Adjt.
John Williams	2d Lt. Comd'g "G" Co. 1st Batt.

This gives but 2 officers to command 14 companies. The men of the 3d Battalion especially, are ignorant of the drill necessary to make them effective, never having received instruction in the School of the Battalion, except under the fire of the enemy, in the late Georgia Campaign. It needs neither words nor argument to convince you that it is impossible to render these Companies Efficient without additional Officers. The Regular Brigade had been stationed on this mountain to recruit its men, to add to its numbers and to perfect it in drill & discipline. It is now engaged in preparing winter quarters and in repairing and extending the defensive works. I trust I may not offend in urging that the following named Officers may be sent to "join their Regt. in the field without delay"

Capt. W.R. Brown, Mustering & Recruiting Philadelphia Penn, *under* Capt. W.B. Lane, 3d Cav, has only served with his Regt. at Post.

Capt. Henry Keteltas, on duty at Provost Mar Gen'l Office, Washington D.C.

Capt. Joseph S. York, on Recruiting Service, Harrisburg Pa, has not been in the field for 22 months.

Capt. James Curtis, Ordnance Dept. Nashville Tenn, where there are 3 Regular Officers, has entirely recovered from wound.

Capt. Joseph R. Payton, Mustering & Disbursing, Nashville Tenn, has never been in the field.

Capt. David R. Meredith, Mustering, Disbursing & Recruiting, Elmira N.Y.

Capt. Price R. Stetson, A.D.C. to Gen'l Hooker, Cincinnati Ohio by *Dept Cumberland Order*, has served but 3 weeks with his Regt. in the field.

Capt. Henry C. Gapen, Fort Adams R.I.

1st Lt. Edward McB Timoney, Fort Adams R.I.

1st Lt. Federick D. Ogilby, Fort Adams, R.I., has not served with his Regt. in the field for 18 months.

1st Lt. George H. Tracy, Asst. Com. Musters 1s Div. 14th A.C., Gen'l Carlin. Cannot his place be filled by a Vol. Officer?

1st Lt. Charles A. Wikoff, Fort Adams, R.I.

1st Lt. Charles McLord, Recruiting Poughkeepsie N.Y. Served 6 months with Regt. at Memphis Tenn.

1st Lt. Geo. W. Fetterman, Mustering Service in Indiana. Served but three months with his Regt. at Memphis, Tenn.

1st Lt. Wm B. Occleston, Fort Adams R.I., Recruiting, has not served with his Regt. in the field for 22 months.

1st Lt. Wilbur F. Melborne, Mustering & Recruiting Harrisburg Pa. Served with his Regt. 1 year at Memphis Tenn.

1st Lt. Robert P. King, on leave, expired, no notice of renewal, Phila Penn.

1st Lt. Geo K. Sanderson, Asst Com Musters Chattanooga Tenn, has not served with his Regt. in the field for 18 months.
1st Lt. Geo H. Burns, Recruiting Reading Pa, has not served with his Regt. in the field for 18 months.
2nd Lt. Wm H. Heilman, Recruiting Phila Pa, has not served *assisting* Capt. Brown 15th Infy.
2nd Lt. Alfred Hedburg, Jackson Mich, Draft Rendezvous.

All of the above named Officers are fit for the kind of duty to be performed at this post. The laborious and fatiguing march is dispensed with. The duties are but those of the school, the camp & the Grand Guard. The invigorating, the health-giving air of the mountain has made it justly celebrated among the records for Invalids. It has been chosen as the location of Extensive Hospitals for this Army; Where war-weary officers are sent to recuperate their impaired vigor of body and when the disease is of the mind it is dispelled during *a very short stay* amid the grand, the magnificent scenery of this Historic ground, where but a few months ago, thundered "above the clouds" the guns of Hooker, and marched to glorious Victory the irresistible Battalions of Thomas, of Sherman, and of Grant.

I trust that the Dept. will not prevent the above named officers from enjoying these advantages, so that, with renewed health, when spring time comes, they may be returned to their present duties or *continued in the field* (as the Dept. may Elect) to be of service to their Country, an honor to their Country's cause, to gather Laurels for themselves, imperishable as this Monte-Sano.

Very Respectfully
Your Obt Servant
JOHN W. YOUNG
Capt Comd'g[19]

Some officers returned to duty at Lookout Mountain in the coming months, but not nearly as many as Captain Young desired. In early 1865, a rather disgruntled captain of the 15th Infantry showed up on the mountain—Peter T. Swaine. Colonel Swaine's 99th Ohio Infantry was consolidated with the 50th Ohio in December 1864, leaving Swaine without a command. As soon as he received word of his impending fate, Swaine wrote to Horatio Wright, the general who had engineered Swaine's volunteer commission during the Kentucky Campaign, and asked for help:

I was officially notified yesterday that my regiment was consolidated and that I fall back to my rank in the Regular Army (Captain). ...it is urgent that I should be promoted [to brigadier general of volunteers] without waiting longer for others. I have been in the Army nearly thirteen years, have been a Colonel of Vols. two years and a half, participating in the greatest battles of the War, Shiloh, Stone River, Chickamauga, and all of Sherman's battles in the Atlanta Campaign, and have frequently been specially mentioned in the reports of my superiors for promotion. I have been in Command of a brigade most of the time I have been a Colonel, and when I had the honor of serving with you in Kentucky I commanded a brigade by the express wishes & request of all other Colonels in it who were all my seniors in rank.

I can conscientiously say to you that I not only can fill the position, but I believe I have earned it. Should the Secretary of War or the President wish to know anything further in regard to my military history I would respectfully refer them to my record in the War Dept.[20]

More than a good record in the War Department was sometimes necessary to become a brigadier general of volunteers during the Civil War. Many regular officers who like Swaine had accepted command of volunteer regiments eventually discovered that they were facing a glass ceiling. A governor early in the war may have been eager to appoint a regular officer to command a state unit, but most of those regulars did not have the political pull usually required to strap on a star. Swaine's bid for promotion went nowhere. The captain reported to Chattanooga and was placed on the Regular Brigade's staff. Colonel Henry Mizner's volunteer service came to a similar end. Mizner's 14th Michigan Infantry had mustered out of the service shortly after the Battle of Jonesboro, so Mizner reverted back to his regular rank of captain and reported to Chattanooga on October 17. Captain Lyman Kellogg showed up shortly thereafter, having recovered from his Jonesboro wound (the 18th Regulars dubbed Mizner and Kellogg "beauty and the beast"). Captain Alexander Chambers, another officer assigned to 2/18th, also reported for duty in October. Chambers had served as colonel of the 16th Iowa Infantry from early 1862 until mid-1863. He then served eight months as a brigadier general of volunteers, but the Senate never confirmed his commission and the captain was forced to turn in his stars in April 1864. Despite Chambers's former rank, Mizner held the ranking regular commission in the 18th U.S. and assumed command of 2/18th. He ended up commanding the entire 18th Infantry field detachment, for on October 23, the companies of

1/18th and 3/18th were temporarily broken up and their few remaining personnel transferred to the 2nd Battalion.[21]

By late November, the regulars had transformed the summit of Lookout Mountain into a bastion that would be difficult to assail. With the positioning of a battery of four guns from Chattanooga's garrison on the summit, the work was complete. "There has been a great many rumors that Wheeler's Rebel Cavalry is prowling about with the intention of taking this mountain," Lieutenant Carpenter wrote home on December 4, shortly after he reported for duty at the conclusion of his leave, "but he will have a sorry time at it if he undertakes the job. We would want no better fun."[22]

Cold weather was closing by this time and the regulars turned their attention to constructing winter quarters. They put to good use an old sawmill the Engineer Brigade had left in place on the mountain, churning out enough fresh lumber to house all the regulars in wooden huts. Captain Mizner's 18th Infantry constructed a rather smart-looking camp that probably would have made Henry Carrington proud, even if it did not match Camp Thomas's mathematical precision. "For the first time in three years we felt fairly at rest and peaceful," recalled Adjutant William Bisbee. "Our camp was two miles back from the point of the mountain, on the crest, our regiment some half mile from the 15th, 16th, and 19th. The ground being heavily timbered, trees were cut away, stumps uprooted and log huts constructed. Regular picket duty was kept up, large details were sent to town to guard warehouses, supply orderlies and for fatigue work in handling supplies by wagon, six miles from Chattanooga. ...I built a double room log house, one for an Adjutant's office, the other for living purposes. ...No one can know how fully I enjoyed my eight by ten foot office with its cozy fireplace of which I made good use."[23]

The 18th Infantry erected a number of other structures in addition to Bisbee's office, including the regiment's inevitable guard house, six headquarters buildings, eight sets of officers' quarters, additional quarters for 2/18th's sergeant major and non-commissioned staff, and eight barracks buildings. The barracks were designed to house a company each and contained an orderly room, five large bays for the troops, and a separate room for the company 1st sergeant, each complete with a fireplace. A covered porch sixty feet long extended down the side of the building opposite the fireplaces. Another large structure was the sutler's store, which was strategically sited at the opposite end of the camp from the company barracks, near the officers' quarters. Lieutenant Bisbee recalled that this building was a popular place: "The Sutlers was a nightly resort, old war songs were then new, and everyone could sing or thought he could."[24]

A number of officers' wives made their way to the Regular Brigade's camp on Lookout Mountain to be with their husbands during the winter of 1864–1865. "Lt. Lattimore has his wife here," Arthur Carpenter noted. "I think she is a very fine lady. they live in a large log house, with three rooms, and are very comfortably situated. I have spent two or there evenings pleasantly there. Mrs. L. plays the guitar and sings. Several officers of the Brigade have there wives here with them."[25] One of the first ladies to arrive was Elizabeth Reynolds Burt, wife of Captain Andrew Burt of the 18th Infantry. She met her future husband while serving as a volunteer nurse in a Cincinnati hospital during early 1862, the facility in which Lieutenant Andrew Burt recuperated from the wound he had received at the Battle of Mill Springs. Later the following summer, the lieutenant was able to take some leave after escorting the remains of Colonel Robert McCook to Cincinnati. He proposed to Elizabeth and the two were married in September 1862. Elizabeth Burt made the hazardous journey from Cincinnati through Nashville to Chattanooga in early December 1864, barely avoiding Hood's advance into middle Tennessee. She would turn out to be an exemplar of nineteenth-century army wives, accompanying her husband to remote posts throughout his lengthy career and keeping a detailed journal of her experiences. She was pleasantly surprised by her wartime room and board in Tennessee:

> As the regiment was now living on Lookout Mountain in log cabins built by the soldiers, it did not take long to prepare one for me. Our old friend, General Bisbee, then a lieutenant and adjutant of the regiment, kindly placed one room at our disposal, to which another was speedily added by the men of Company F.
>
> This was my first army home, and consisted of two rooms of logs, chinked with mud. The floors and all wood work, except window frames, were of unplaned boards. A half window sash in each room afforded light. A leather latch string was the fastening of the door. When it hung out, we were ready for visitors; drawing it in secured us from intrusion.
>
> Behind these rooms was a tiny kitchen, where a soldier was installed as cook, doing his best to please the Captain and the

Madam. There was little from which to supply variety for the table
and I began with ambitious ideas of making new dishes; but found
cooking by a fire in the open air with a camp kettle and Dutch oven,
so very different from using a stove, that I was soon obliged to
acknowledge the soldier's superior skill as a camp cook. In time we
became resigned to eat what he would give us from the meager variety of food; beef, sometimes, and potatoes when they could be purchased from the Commissary, as well as beans, rice, hard tack, flour,
coffee, dried apples, salt pork and sugar.

Flapjacks, mixed with water, flour and baking powder, when it
was to be purchased, was a breakfast luxury, served with sugar
syrup. Quite good biscuits were baked in a Dutch oven when it was
possible to obtain baking powder.[26]

The composition of the Regular Brigade was in a constant state
of flux during the waning months of 1864. Private Jacob Van
Zwaluwenburg was one of the many regulars who departed, for his
term of service expired on October 10. The 16th Infantryman gathered up his things that morning and began his solitary trek back
home to Michigan:

> There were no passenger trains from Chattanooga at this time, as
> the line to Nashville could not be fully protected; so when I got my
> discharge I got off the mountain and got aboard a freight car and
> took my chances. I was the only passenger. I climbed on top of the
> car, sat on my knapsack most of the way. The train was stopped
> about three miles from Nashville. I was glad to walk that distance
> and report to headquarters. There they gave me a ticket to
> Louisville, where I was paid the balance due me, including the $100
> bounty. Next day I made my way across the Ohio River and into free
> territory once more. I praised the good Lord to breathe the pure air
> of freedom, not menaced by Secesh bullets nor to hear the boom of
> hostile cannon.
>
> I secured a ticket to Kalamazoo via Indianapolis. There was no
> one to meet me, for I slipped into town unannounced. I left my
> knapsack at the Burdick House, one of Kalamazoo's oldest hostelries
> and started to walk the eight miles to the farm home of my sister. A
> farmer gave me a lift. I found my sister at home. She was overjoyed
> to see me, for she had made the prediction before I left for the front
> that she would never see me again.
>
> I went out to the field where my brother-in-law was husking
> corn. As I jumped over the fence, Karo, the shepherd dog that I had
> played with many times, came bounding toward me. Three years of
> absence had in no wise obliterated me from his memory.[27]

Of the original seventy-three men who enlisted in D/1/16th during October and November 1861, only Van Zwaluwenburg was still present to receive a discharge three years later.

Eli Tarbell, the 19th Infantry sergeant who had received the "million dollar" wound at Picket's Mill, was healthy again by the autumn of 1864. His enlistment was also up on October 10, but on that morning he was still in the convalesce barracks in Louisville. "I have looked for this date & traveld through rain & mud, Sunshine & Snow for 3 years waiting patintly for the 10th of Oct. 1864 to come around," Tarbell wrote in his diary. "3 years ago to day I put my name on Uncle Sams Book as a Soldier Boy & I was never Sorrey for it. I have passed through all kinds of hardships & have done my duty to the best of my ability & have got to go to Chatanooga to get my Dischrage." It was a two-day rail journey to Chattanooga. During an overnight stop in Nashville, the sergeant ran into other smiling regulars, discharged veterans who were heading north, including a few from C/1/19th, his own company. Tarbell arrived in Chattanooga early in the morning of October 12. After fortifying himself with a "good drink of beer" from a local establishment, he made his way to the brigade's camp. "Hard road to travel up the Mountain," Tarbell recorded later that day, "found the boys all well & glad to see me. Lieut. Edwards is Drunk, did not know me. Sergt. Frankhouser got some snaps & I got can oysters & we had a jolley good time. ...I don't know when I will get my discharge. Edwards is to drunk to make them out." Lieutenant Edwards had sobered up by October 14: "I got my discharge papers at 11 am & bid good Bye to the Boys & the Armey. ...Now I can say I am a free man for Sure, for I have my Discharge."[28]

Corporal Robert Kennedy of the 18th Infantry also received a discharge while his battalion was on Lookout Mountain. His return to civil life ended up being about six months delayed. After his capture at Chickamauga, Kennedy spent the next fifteen months in various Southern prisons, including five months at Andersonville. In December 1864, he was part of an exchange of sick prisoners that took place at Charleston, South Carolina. The scurvy he had contracted at Andersonville, along with a host of other ailments, probably made him sick enough to qualify for exchange, but just to be sure, he swallowed some tobacco and rubbed red pepper on his eyes immediately prior to the medical inspection. Kennedy was selected and soon turned over to the

Union fleet blockading Charleston. He was shipped to Annapolis, after which he took a thirty-day furlough at his home in West Virginia. At the conclusion of the furlough, he headed for Camp Thomas. Kennedy reported to Lieutenant Frederick Phisterer, who had just returned from his business trip to Germany and was serving as the 18th Infantry's regimental adjutant. Kennedy presented him with a tattered piece of silken cloth measuring about eight inches square, a remnant of 2/18th's national colors that had been captured and then recovered at Chickamauga. What became of the scrap at Camp Thomas is indeterminable. "I have always been sorry I did not know the value at the time of that relic," the remorseful corporal later wrote. "If I had I never would have parted with it." Kennedy attempted to secure discharge papers from Major James Caldwell, the post commander at Camp Thomas, but the major told Kennedy to return to Annapolis because exchanged prisoners were technically under the jurisdiction of the provost marshal there. The corporal made his way back to the East Coast. "After waiting five weeks longer I received my discharge on February 10, 1865," Kennedy wrote as he closed out his wartime memoirs. "This ended my experience as a soldier."[29]

Another regular captured at Chickamauga, Lieutenant Henry B. Freeman, also made it out of captivity in South Carolina. His journey was much more hazardous than Kennedy's, for Freeman turned out to be a determined, if somewhat unlucky, escape artist. His first escape attempt took place on the night of February 9, 1864, when Freeman participated in the famous mass tunnel escape from Richmond's Libby Prison. He and two companions made their way to the Appomattox River just below Petersburg, and managed to steal a small boat. Intending to float down the Appomattox, turn into the James River, and then head toward the open sea, they made it only as far as Fort Clifton, the main Confederate fortification covering the river approach to Petersburg. The boat unfortunately foundered on an obstruction in the river near the fort and the trio of escapees, who, according to a story in the *Richmond Enquirer,* were at this point "utterly exhausted and almost frozen to death," had no choice but to swim ashore and turn themselves in. After further incarceration in Libby, Freeman and the rest of Libby's population were sent to a prison at Macon. From there, many of the prisoners were sent by rail to Charleston during late July 1864. During a dark night on the journey through central Georgia, Freeman jumped from the train and headed through a stretch of swampland for what he hoped would be Federal lines. "After travelling 5 nights through the swamp, and suffering greatly from the want of food," Freeman recalled, "I made the Edisto River, about 5 miles from the mouth; while laying in the swamp waiting for darkness, I was seen by a white man, who informed the officer in command of a party of cavalry, the 2nd S.C., in the neighborhood, who at once started a detachment, with a pack of dogs, to hunt me up. After a chase of 4 hours, I was captured by the dogs, and by the men sent to Charleston."[30]

Freeman would not be deterred. Sent to Columbia, South Carolina, in late November 1864, he forged a parole pass and bluffed his way past some unsuspecting guards. He was on the lam for ten days, heading for Sherman's army in Georgia, when he was again captured. His captors took no chances with the troublesome lieutenant this time, binding him hand and foot while transporting him back to Columbia. Freeman's reputation was starting to get the better of him. In early December, an exchange of prisoners took place that included other regulars captured at Chickamauga, Captain Tenador Ten Eyck and Lieutenant Rufus Gates among them, but Confederate authorities were determined to keep their hands on Freeman and others who had attempted escape.

His next chance occurred in February 1865, as Sherman's army made its way from Savannah to Columbia. Receiving word that the prisoners were about to be transferred to Charlotte, North Carolina, Freeman searched for a place to hide. He discovered a way to pry loose a ceiling board in the prison's hospital, which allowed access to the building's sealed garret. With Sherman's artillery booming in the distance, sixteen prisoners took refuge in the hiding place while the camp's other prisoners were rounded up for movement north. Guards searched the hospital a number of times but overlooked the hidden prisoners, for there was no visible way into the garret. Freeman and his comrades remained hidden for two days, after which they made their way out of the abandoned prison and into the streets of Columbia. Freeman was among the last to leave the hospital building and heard shots ring out as he crept across the compound. He and a companion, a colonel, returned to the garret and remained until the next night. They emerged again, this time donning some Confederate garb they discovered in the hospital. They were not challenged as they slipped through Columbia and across the Congaree River, until a threatening voice called out "Come in

Johnnies, or I'll shoot!" The escapees complied and found themselves among troops of Major General Frank J. Blair's XVII Corps. After Freeman convinced his new captors of his true identity and changed out his rebel rags for a proper uniform, he was attached to the adjutant general's section of Blair's staff. On April 30, 1865, the lieutenant returned to Camp Thomas.[31]

* * *

While Henry Freeman's adventures in the Carolinas played themselves out that winter, contingents of new regulars arrived in Chattanooga. The four regimental depots had continued to receive fresh manpower while the Regular Brigade campaigned in Georgia and relocated to Tennessee, with a total of 1,550 new recruits signing on from May through October 1864. Company D/3/15th U.S. reported for duty at Lookout Mountain on October 13, allowing 3/15th U.S. to stand up as a separate battalion. Two companies of 2/19th U.S. arrived the following February, which turned out to be the last units assigned to the Regular Brigade during the war. Small batches of additional troops for the existing companies also arrived periodically, as did a new commander for the brigade. Major John Edie was promoted to lieutenant colonel of the 8th U.S. Infantry in November and headed for his new regiment's headquarters, Hancock Barracks in Baltimore. Taking Edie's place as commander of the Regular Brigade was the man who had served in that position longer than anyone else, Brigadier General John H. King. Three months of sick leave had been sufficient to recuperate the brigadier's health, and he resumed command of the brigade on November 14. With a general officer commanding again, the brigade's headquarters was established in one of the large mansions that dotted the summit of Lookout Mountain, the abandoned summer home of some lowland planter.[32]

The holiday season arrived shortly after the regulars finished their construction work. With Confederate operations in middle Tennessee during November curtailing rail traffic between Nashville and Chattanooga, Lieutenant Carpenter thought the regulars' Thanksgiving feast left much to be desired: "We never would know when Thanksgiving came here, if we did not read it in the papers. Perhaps sick soldiers got an extra potato. ...Our camps are now fixed for winter. we have plenty of fuel—good comfortable quarters. hardly enough to eat, but the road being blockaded between here and Nashville accounts for that." Provisions were flowing again by late December. In contrast to Christmas in 1862 and 1863, the former spent with a campaign looming in the immediate future and the latter cooped up in Chattanooga at the end of an inadequate supply line, some of the regulars celebrated the 1864 holiday in proper style. They received their first mail in more than a month on Christmas day, the best present soldiers in the field could have received short of an end to the war. After reading a newspaper column describing the Army of the Potomac's Thanksgiving, Arthur Carpenter again took up his pen: "I am very much obliged to the people north, for sending turkeys etc. to *the Army of the Potomac* for Thanksgiving. None of our Brig. got any. Well most of the men have good teeth, they can eat hard Bread. and then the Army of the Potomac ought to have something to stimulate them 'on to victory.' why! they have not completed their last spring's campaign yet, while the Army of the Cumberland has completed one, had a rest, and are nearly through another, sweeping everything before them. Our men out here want to get through, they have no time to slip for turkeys. Give the Potomac lads a few more, and sitting in trenches around Richmond will be fine fun."[33] At least the lieutenant was satisfied with his Christmas dinner, which consisted of "roast turkey, Beef, cove oysters, pie, cake, fruit etc." Elizabeth Burt was particularly proud of the meal she put together for her first army Christmas:

> As Christmas approached...my thoughts [began] to dwell upon the possibility of celebrating the day in some slight way. A dinner was all that seemed feasible and that was almost an impossibility, for what was a Christmas dinner without turkey?
>
> In an interview with the cook we concocted a plan to surprise the Captain. My mother had put fruit for a plum pudding in my trunk with the recipe by which to make it and the cloth in which to boil it. The cook made an eager search in the surrounding country for viands but returned with the report that there was not a turkey nor chicken to be begged or purchased, but a wee pig had been promised. A few eggs were bought as treasures and enough sweet potatoes for the dinner, with some apples to make sauce to accompany the pig. A little milk, too, had been promised. The prospect seemed so bright that I suggested to my husband that I would like to invite four officers to dine with us. He scorned the idea of my being able to prepare dinner for four guests—what could I give them for a Christmas dinner? At length, however, he yielded to my entreaties, when I asked him to leave all arrangements to me except providing me the evergreens and holly. The latter were easily supplied, making our

rooms very attractive in their decorations. Holly and red berries decorated the table.

A good beef soup was an appetizing course. Then came our wee pig with an apple in his mouth, apple sauce and sweet potatoes with rice, and beans baked beautifully and hot baking powder biscuit. Home made candy supplied the bon bons, and when the big round plum pudding was brought in with a sprig of holly on the top, a burst of surprise and delight rewarded my efforts. Coffee followed as usual, but in very primitive cups. Our guests pronounced my first Christmas dinner a complete success.[34]

The Burts's New Year's Eve was not quite as festive—sparks from their fireplace started a fire that gutted half of their hut. Elizabeth's trunk and wardrobe were luckily spared, meaning she was properly clad for a reception in January 1865. The citizens of Chattanooga, most of whom were Unionists or rapidly becoming so, hosted a New Year's social for the officers of the city's garrison. Most of the Regular Brigade's officer corps attended, although Mrs. Burt recalled that their uniforms were "not decorated with gold embroideries and glistening insignia, but bearing the marks of hard campaigning." General George Thomas was the guest of honor at the event, the laurels of his Nashville victory fresh in everyone's mind. "His commanding presence towered above those gathered about him," Mrs. Burt recalled. She was nervous as she approached the general in the official receiving line, but Thomas put her at ease when she was introduced.

"I am glad to meet the wife of Captain Burt, one of my good war captains who has served with me in the field since the Battle of Mill Springs. He did good work that day by his gallant ride under fire of the enemy."

"I thank you general," Elizabeth Burt replied, "you make me very proud."

It was an evening to remember, made even more festive because so many officers' wives were present for the dance.[35]

* * *

The holiday season was a break from the regulars' otherwise dull routine that winter. The battalions manned a picket line five miles out from their camps, pulling duty five days out of twenty. They constructed huts near the picket posts, so even this duty was not very arduous. Beyond that and work details in Chattanooga, there was not much to do. Private Solomon Stern of H/1/19th U.S. spent his days on Lookout carving himself an ornate pipe. He was evidently quite a craftsman, for he adorned the piece with mother-of-pearl inlays of the Federal coat of arms and an acorn, the latter being the official symbol of the XIV Corps. He also carved into it "37 days fighting for Atlanta" and fashioned a silver cap to protect the tobacco from the damp mist that swirled about the mountain almost every winter day. A bored Captain Arthur Allyn wrote his father about life in camp shortly after the veteran 16th Infantry officer returned to duty after some sick leave in early January 1865: "the camp is on the Summit of the Mountain and we can see Tennessee, Georgia, and North Carolina in the distance. When it is cloudy we are in the midst of the clouds and frequently at sunrise, you can see your shadow in them. We have fine water, a good location, plenty to eat and not much to do." Lieutenant William Bisbee had so much spare time on his hands that he painstakingly made out the 18th Infantry's 1864 annual return in great detail, often working on it well past midnight. The result of his effort was an official commendation from the War Department for preparing "the best return ever received."[36] Bisbee was proud of his achievement, although Captain Anson Mills remembered the adjutant's paperwork in a more revealing light:

> The beauty and symmetry of his reports was marked, but some apparently irrelevant figures excited my curiosity. Written in rather large figures in bright red ink was, "S-T-1860-X." Asked why he had made use of these particular letters and figures, he said he had copied them from a manufacturer's trade-mark for "Hostetter's Bitters," which, translated, read, "Started trade in 1860 with $10.00." He had noticed papers from Washington with red ink figures which he could not understand, and so interspersed the notations throughout his own reports, knowing that no one would understand them, but believing it would be assumed to be the result of much study and care!
>
> Sure enough, in due time Bisbee received a personal letter from the Adjutant General of the Army, complimenting him on the most perfect monthly returns ever submitted by any regular regiment.[37]

The war was occasionally visible from the regular's camp on Lookout Mountain. A band of Confederate guerillas under a certain John Gatewood infested the mountains of northwest Georgia. Sometimes resembling a lawless band of criminals more than a true military force, Gatewood commanded anywhere from 100 to 500 men. They occasionally tore up rail lines and captured wagon trains, but most of the time Gatewood's rag tag command just pillaged the countryside and ambushed stray Union soldiers. The commander of 1/15th U.S. reported that on March 23, 1865, he gave two of his men permission to go foraging in Chattanooga Valley. They encountered more than they bargained for: "they went out about four miles from the foot of the Mountain. About 12 O'clock M. they were surprised by the appearance of a party of men, about twenty five, supposed to be Guerillas, on foot, with a leader on horseback, who immediately advanced to capture them." One of the regulars was himself mounted and managed to escape. The other, on foot, took off into a nearby forest with guerillas close behind. The mounted regular returned to the scene a few hours later, but could find no trace of his companion. Local citizens informed him that men from Gatewood's band were prowling the area and had horses stashed in a nearby barn. The soldier returned to camp and reported what had happened. The missing regular turned up later that night, having outwitted his erstwhile pursuers.[38]

A certain amount of inactivity and boredom was the norm for units in winter quarters during the Civil War, although the campaign that would occur in the coming spring kept the units focused. The regulars' situation was more ambiguous during the 1864–1865 winter. The battalions were to incorporate fresh manpower and train, but they really did not know for what they were preparing. With the Confederacy's fortunes on the wane, the war would certainly be over sometime during the next year. The regulars in the West had not been employed during the Franklin-Nashville Campaign, although many other troops of Steedman's command were, and the notion gained steam that perhaps the Regular Brigade would sit out the rest of the war. With no immediate purpose spurring them on, motivating the new regulars to take their training seriously became extremely difficult. With so few officers or experienced sergeants remaining, the task was virtually impossible. Captain Thomas Norton, commander of 2/15th U.S. for most of the Lookout Mountain encampment, in early January 1865 sent the War Department yet another warning about the regulars' manpower and leadership:

H'dq'rs 2d Batt'ln, 15th U.S. Inf.
Lookout Mountain Tenn
January 11th 1865

Brig Genl L. Thomas
Adjt. Gen. U.S.A.
Washington City, D.C.

General,

The present condition of the 2d Bat. 15th Infy. is such that I feel warranted in directing your attention to the statement made below, and in requesting a consideration of the proposition herein submitted.

Companies "A" "B" & "C" of the Battalion are now being rapidly reduced by discharge of their men and on the 1st day of March, 1865, will number in strength as follows:

Co. "A"= 0 Sergts 0 Corpls 2 Musicians 3 Privates
Co. "B" = 0 "   0 "   1 "   36 "
Co. "C"= 3 "   1 "   1 "   34 "

Company "B", at the end of the same month, will be reduced to 1 Mus. And 9 Privates. Co. "C" will be nearly altogether discharged during the months of March and April.

I have also the honor to state that when the present non-commissioned officers of these companies shall have been discharged, it will be impossible to supply their places from the material of which the companies will then be composed, and for this reason, as well as from the reduction of strength, the companies will be rendered inefficient. Under these circumstances, therefore, I respectfully submit the following proposition and earnestly request that an order may be issued carrying it into immediate execution, Viz–

That Companies "A" "B" & "C" may be broken up and the men remaining in them on the 1st of March, 1865, be transferred, pro rata, to Companies "D" "E" & "F."

The men thus acquired, will about supply the places of those to be discharged from Companies "D" "E" & "F" during the ensuing three months, and will serve to make these companies effective, for field service much longer than they would be without the proposed transfer.

Should this proposition meet with your approval, I would further respectfully request that inasmuch as only three companies ("D" "E" & "F") will then remain to the 2d Battln, that the Battalion organization be temporarily discontinued and these companies attached to the 3rd Battln until such time as companies "G" & "H", 2d Battln (yet unorganized) may join the Regt, at which time the Battln organization can be resumed.

The reasons chiefly urged for the adoption of this measure are:

1st. That the Battln non-com. staff will have been discharged by the time contemplated for the transfer, and no competent non-com officers can be obtained from the Battln to fill the places.

2d. The advantage of gaining three com'd. officers to the line–the 2d Battln commander and his staff.

In addition, to the above it may be said that the efficiency of the 3d Battl'n will largely [be] promoted by the assignment of those companies, thus making it eight companies strong.

> I have the honor to be
> Very respectfully etc.
>
> THOMAS H. NORTON
> Capt. 15th Infy
> Comdg[39]

Washington's answer to this and similar proposals was to simply ship more recruits to Lookout Mountain. For instance, on December 29, 1864, the War Department ordered Colonel Oliver Shepherd "to forward, without delay, under proper charge, all recruits of the 15th U.S. Infantry...to join their regiment, now serving in the Department of the Cumberland." Shipping recruits to Chattanooga actually made the Regular Brigade's situation worse, for the men joining the Union Army by this point in the war were oftentimes far more trouble than they were worth. Some were pardoned Confederate prisoners, "galvanized Yankees" who swore an oath of allegiance and agreed to wear a blue uniform in exchange for ending their confinement. Being assigned to the Regular Brigade brought the former Confederates that much closer to home, and many shed their new Federal clothing and deserted as soon as they arrived on Lookout Mountain. At least two deserters, Private Peter Stroup of the 16th Infantry and Private Henry Black of the 19th, were apprehended while attempting to join Gatewood's guerillas. Stroup was caught when a local citizen betrayed the presence of a "soldier from the mountain" hiding in the woods of Lookout Valley who had failed to persuade a laundress to dye his blue clothing into a shade of gray.[40]

Real Yankees were sometimes not much more useful than the galvanized variety. From those whose motivation to serve consisted of bounty cash, to others who were paid to substitute for someone who had been drafted, to the draftees themselves, the men signing enlistment papers late in the war plagued the combat efficiency of many Northern regiments. A particularly vile breed were known as bounty jumpers, men who joined up with the intention of receiving an enlistment bonus and then deserting at their first opportunity. Desertion was a problem that hit the Regular Army particularly hard. Of the 278,044 Northern soldiers who deserted during the Civil War, slightly more than 21,000 were regulars. Similar to the statistics on courts-martial related earlier, the regulars also generated a disproportional amount of deserters, accounting for 7.6 percent of desertions yet representing only 3 percent of Union Army man-power. Ella Lonn, in her somewhat dated but still authoritative *Desertion During the Civil War*, states that a single factor was responsible for the Regular Army's higher desertion rate: "The con-clusion to which one is brought by a study of the desertion in the volunteer army for the entire war as compared with the regular troops is most surprising as it reveals a larger proportion where it would not be expected—in the regular army. In that branch of the service it reached the high rate of 244.25 per thousand, according to the provost marshal general, while it was but 62.51 in the volun-teers. One is forced to the inference that the men who enlisted in the regular service were far inferior in character to the troops furnished by the states."[41]

The regulars who enlisted during the first half of the Civil War (a number of whom were still alive in 1928 when *Desertion During the Civil War* was published) undoubtedly would have taken excep-tion to Lonn's conclusions. However, a label of inferior character is applicable for many of the men who joined the regulars in 1864 and 1865. A closer examination of the Regular Army's desertion statis-tics illustrates this difference between early- and late-war regulars. In the 19th Infantry a total of 677 men deserted between August 1861 and May 1865. Almost three-quarters of these desertions (491) occurred during the last seventeen months of the war. Relatively few soldiers serving in the field with 1/19th U.S. deserted during 1864; new recruits at Ft. Wayne and en route to the field account for 81 percent of the 1864 total. Late-war desertions were also a problem in the 15th Infantry. Nearly half of the 727 men who deserted this regiment between December 1861 and December 1864 did so in 1864, and 69 percent of the 1864 deserters were recruits at Ft. Adams, the regimental depot. A total of 158 soldiers from the Regular Brigade were tried by court-martial for desertion during the Civil War. One hundred-ten of those trials (70 percent) took place during a thirteen-month period between April 1864 and April 1865.[42]

These numbers indicate that the Regular Army provided the best possible environment during the war's last year for bounty jumpers and others who wanted to desert. It was much easier for such a man to slip away unnoticed after joining the regulars, where he was thrown together with strangers from many locations, than from the county recruiting rendezvous of a volunteer regiment, where many recruits knew each other. Even if a recruit planned to stay in uniform long enough to reach his battalion in the field, it was certainly much easier to desert from a quiet garrison like Lookout Mountain than from where the bulk of the Union armies were located that winter, the trenches around Petersburg or a bustling camp near Savannah. Brigadier General Philip St. George Cooke, commander of the Regular Army's General Recruiting Service, in summer of 1864 was fed up with the large number of men deserting before they reached their regiments. He published a general order on July 6 that outlined some preventive measures:

> The enormous amount of desertions among recruits calls for extraordinary zeal and energy to prevent it. It will not do for officers to quietly report the loss of nearly all their recruits. After using better care and judgment in selecting men of some character, they must hold them, and deliver them to the [regimental] depots, retaining the local bounties paid until thus delivered.
>
> Recruits, while at Depots, will be kept under strict guard in buildings and if necessary these will be vacated for that purpose, by putting permanent parties and invalid companies in tents.
>
> Furloughs leaves or permits to recruits, shall not be granted under any circumstances at any depot or rendezvous. Officers will treat every recruit as if he intended to desert whenever the opportunity offers.[43]

The Regular Army's high desertion rate resulted from a number of factors, including long terms of service, tough discipline, and the disinclination of some to serve in the army after the war. Instead of labeling all Civil War regulars as men of inferior character due to the Regular Army's high desertion rate, it is more accurate to say that men who were predisposed to desert joined the regulars in 1864 and 1865.

Even if they did not desert, many new recruits who reported to Lookout Mountain wanted to do anything but soldier to Regular Army standards. Knowing that by the late 1864 most regular infantry regiments had been withdrawn from field service, to avoid combat all a recruit had to do was join the Regular Army. Captain Norton's contention that by the first months of 1865 it would be impossible to obtain new sergeants "from the material of which the companies will then be composed" was putting it mildly. The regimental records from the war's last winter and spring mention numerous cases of indiscipline, everything from insubordination and neglect of duty to felonies such as robbery and rape. One pack of incorrigibles went so far as to ambush groups of peddlers making their way to the regulars' camp. "There are men in these battalions who disgrace the name of Soldier by robbing and plundering women of cakes, pies, and other eatables brought into our camp for sale," complained an officer of the 15th Infantry in March 1865. It should come as no surprise that some regulars contracted scurvy that spring due to a lack of fresh fruits and vegetables. Courts-martial and full guardhouses became a constant feature of life on Lookout Mountain.[44]

The officers and sergeants did what they could to train these unruly new privates, although the number of experienced non-commissioned officers constantly dwindled away. When given the choice of reenlisting and being responsible for training this rabble or accepting a discharge and heading home, the decision was easy for most of the veteran sergeants to make. Privates who had enlisted the previous winter and survived the Atlanta Campaign took their places, but these men had never really been properly trained themselves. Newly promoted Sergeant John H. Poland of the D/1/19th Infantry was his battalion's sergeant of the guard on the night of January 20, 1865. Poland discovered that three of his prisoners escaped during the night, but he did not bother to report the escape until after his tour of duty was over the next morning. Poland was brought up on charges of neglecting his duty. All he could say in his defense was, "I had been lately promoted to Sergeant, and this was the first time I has been in general charge of a guard, and from inexperience I did not consider it necessary that I should report the absence of the prisoners to the officer of the day until the morning." Poland was found not guilty, although he was admonished to quickly learn the duties of his rank. Captain Norton had sergeants like Poland in mind on December 18 when he complained: "The ignorance and carelessness exhibited by most non comm off of this command is inexcusable."[45] The captain noticed more ignorance and carelessness the next month:

Hd. Qrs. Det. 15th Infty
Lookout Mountain Tenn.
Jany. 5th 1865

Circular:

It has been reported to the Comd'g Officer that during a recent tour of Outpost duty, Seventeen men belonging to the 3d Batt. of the Regt. who had been posted as Sentinels on the Picket line, were found by the Officer of the Guard, neglecting their duties in the grossest possible manner. These men had built fires remote from their posts, and were discovered at night without arms, seated in Squads around them. This is not only a palpable neglect of duty but a practical violation of the 46th Article of War ["Sentinels found sleeping shall suffer death"], and the guilty men should properly be visited with the severest penalties of the law.

But as this is the first instance of such misconduct the Comd'g Officer is disposed to overlook it, but gives warning that a repetition of such glaring neglect will subject the offender to the full measure of punishment prescribed by the Articles of War.

By Order of Capt. Norton

J.Y. SEMPLE
1st Lieut. 15th Infty
Act. Adjt.[46]

Making do with barely-trained sergeants and few officers (and with most of the latter devoting a great deal of time to sitting on courts-martial), the battalions published detailed schedules of drill, guard duty, and fatigue details, with emphasis on school of the soldier and squad drill. Dress parades and Sunday morning inspections took place. As he tended to do throughout the war, Arthur Carpenter wrote a good description of the regulars' training regimen:

At morn when the first gray streaks of light are hardly perceptible, we have reveille. The Army is a good place to practice early rising. We have Roll Call at reveille. The Sergt. reports the company to me, and I report to the Adjutant. At 7 A.M. police call is sounded, and the camp is thouroughly cleaned. At 8 A.M. Sick Call is sounded, when the sick go to the Surgeon and get their "daily dose of poison." At 9 A.M. we have "Guard Mounting." At 10 A.M. to 11 A.M. company drill, and target practice. At 12 m. dinner Roll Call. At 2 P.M. drill which lasts until 5 P.M. At 5 on Sunday Inspection and dress parade. At 8 P.M. Tatoo Roll Call. 81/2 P.M. the Bugle sounds

"Lights out," and all seek repose...except those who have writing to attend to.[47]

The men made enough progress on basic tasks by the end of February that General King ordered the brigade to start conducting skirmish drill by battalions and battalion-level drill. He also stipulated that for target practice each man would fire four rounds at least four days per week. Target practice created new difficulties, for few of the troops had fired a weapon before. There were so many safety concerns that the 15th Infantry addressed the problem in a general order on March 13: "In order to prevent the chances of accidents among their men in loading, etc., Companies, or squads, will be formed in single rank upon the target ground. The men will also be required to reload their pieces in front of the Company or squad, before resuming their places in the ranks. A Non-Com'd Officer will be placed to superintend the loading, and to see that it be done properly, and that *all* the powder of the cartridge be emptied into the piece." Lieutenant Douglas Edwards of C/1/19th Infantry, the company commander whom Sergeant Eli Tarbell had noticed being drunk much of the time, was glad that at least one of his soldiers had little skill with firearms. After an argument with Private John Sheehy on April 3, 1865, the soldier attempted to shoot Edwards. Sheehy fired but missed, even though his intended victim was standing less than ten paces away. Sheehy reached into his cartridge box and was starting to reload for another try, when two of his company mates tackled him. It must have been hard for the Regular Brigade's leaders to believe that the ragged lines of unmotivated, undisciplined troops indifferently shooting at targets and at least one officer on Lookout Mountain in early 1865 were in any way related to the efficient soldiers who had produced lethal volleys at Shiloh, Stones River, and Chickamauga during the course of the previous twenty-two months.[48]

No one noticed these differences to a greater extent than did Major Albert Tracy of the 15th Infantry. During all of his previous military experiences—Mexican War regular, state of Maine Adjutant General, Civil War volunteer colonel—he had always dealt with troops that were at least motivated to do their jobs, even if they were not particularly skilled. While commanding 1/15th U.S. at Chattanooga during the winter of 1863–1864, his main problem was lack of personnel, not motivation and discipline. Having been on sick leave since May 1864, Tracy returned to duty in late January 1865 and assumed command of the 15th Infantry's field detachment. His many years as a staff officer gave him a fondness for paperwork, and the 15th Infantry's detailed records during Tracy's tour of duty on Lookout Mountain reflect this. The vast majority of Tracy's orders, letters, and circulars written during the three months following his return to duty dealt with disciplinary problems. On February 4, he wrote out instructions for the regiment's officer of the day, urging that officer to pay strict attention to regulations and guard mounting, "bearing in mind that this attention is the more necessary owing to inexperience on the part of many enlisted men present and expected to arrive." The 18th Infantry had known since arriving at Lookout Mountain that a regimental guardhouse would be a necessity; on February 24, Tracy belatedly came to the same conclusion. He ordered his quartermaster to "procure at the earliest moment such lumber and other material as may be necessary to erect a good and sufficient guard house." Ominously, Tracy also ordered him to "procure or have made such irons as may be necessary for prisoners confined for desertions or acts of felony."[49]

There were plenty of prisoners in the 15th Infantry's new guardhouse during the spring of 1865. Two of the building's more enterprising residents were Private Patrick Corcoran and Corporal Michael McFalls, who committed a crime truly unique in the annals of Civil War villainy. The two Irishmen were detailed as clerks for Company D/2/15th shortly after the regulars arrived at Lookout Mountain. McFalls happened to be a skilled forger. He could make copies of his commander's signature that were indistinguishable from legitimate ones. Sometime in early November, the pair removed a stack of blank discharge certificates from their company commander's desk, and used the papers to set up a home business of sorts, selling forged discharges and final statements for fifty dollars a set. Signing the papers with the signature of an officer of the 15th Infantry was no problem for McFalls, since in the course of his duties he saw handwriting samples from all of his regiment's officers. If a potential customer belonged to a different regiment, all the soldier had to do was hand over the required cash and a document bearing his own company commander's signature. Corcoran would make out the paperwork and McFalls, after a little practice, affixed what appeared to be bonafide signatures on all the documents. The two clerks even provided—at no extra charge—forged passes to get deserters off Lookout Mountain and into Chattanooga. At the rail depot there, discharge papers were the only documents needed to secure passage to points north. If a deserter could board a north-bound train a day or two before an officer on Lookout Mountain noticed that the man was missing, he was home free. The clerks had enough cash on hand after a few transactions to rent a room at the Crutchfield House Hotel in Chattanooga. They carried on the enter-prise from that point, which minimized the amount of time the fraudulent documents were vulnerable to prying eyes on Lookout Mountain. The business continued nearly five months and had expe-dited the desertion of perhaps two dozen regulars before 1st Sergeant Cain O'Connor of D/1/19th caught wind of what was going on. Posing as a potential deserter himself, O'Connor launched a carefully planned sting that landed McFalls and Corcoran in the custody of the Regular Brigade's provost marshal on March 22, 1865. The forgers were sentenced "to be shot with musketry" the next month after a court-martial convicted them of conduct preju-dicial and aiding desertion, but their sentences were commuted to lengthy terms of confinement at hard labor.[50]

Alcohol seemed to be at the root of most of the 15th Infantry's disciplinary problems. Major Tracy had to remind the regimental sutler on February 28, 1865, to "sell neither Ale, beer, nor any other article to any member of the guard, nor will he permit men on guard about his tent," and also pointed out that prisoners were not author-ized to consume alcohol. Marauding soldiers supposedly on guard duty were another headache. Tracy told the officer of the guard "that due protection will be afforded the sutler from any intrusion by members of the guard." The sutler's continued to be a hotbed of trouble, and on March 28, Tracy decreed: "Until further orders the Sutlers tent will be closed at tattoo, and except the Sutler or his Employees, no persons permitted therein until Reveille. A copy of this Order will be conspicuously posted in the Sutlers tent." The 15th Infantry's officers had no one to blame but themselves for the nightly closing of the Sutler, for on the night of March 27 they evi-dently staged quite a party: "The noise and disturbance by Officers in this Camp on the evening of the 27th cannot be passed without notice, and Officers are admonished that repetitions must necessar-ily lead to very prompt measures of suppression on the part of the Commanding Officer."[51]

An outbreak of scurvy, musicians who could not play a note, sergeants who did not know how to conduct basic drill and ceremonies, guards and prisoners who were indistinguishable—Tracy and the other leaders saw it all. Finally, on April 22 the major wrote to Fort Adams and told the regimental commander that he had seen enough:

> Hd. Qrs. Det. 15th Infty
> Lookout Mountain Tenn.
> April 22d 1865

Lieut. Sam'l R. Honey
 Act. Adjutant 15th Infty
 Fort Adams R.I.

Sir,

I have the honor to ask the attention of the Col Comd'g the Regt, to the class and character of men enlisted and sent as recruits to the Battalions of the 15th.

There are now in the guard house of this Detachment fourteen men who have already been tried for, and stand charged with offenses amounting to felonies, embracing desertion, stealing, highway robbery, forgery, rape, etc. Several men have already been tried, sentenced, and sent in irons to the penitentiary at Nashville, for crimes of the above description. Several have deserted in time to escape trial. It is well understood also that accomplices whom we are unable fully to identify or detect, must still be in Camp. Regular combinations have been found to exist for forging, and selling for considerable sums to parties wishing to get off, discharges and final statement papers, the blanks being stolen from Company desks or possibly printed elsewhere and sent hither for the purpose. Men have been detected in and tried for conduct so faithless as to quit their guard and go off with prisoners they were set to watch, and after getting the prisoners drunk, robbing them by sheer violence. Other parties, enlisted from rebel prisoners or refugees in the North, no sooner arrive with their high bounties in hand, than they desert with arms and get to their homes or join guerilla gangs. One man on orderly duty for a General Court Martial broke open a letter entrusted him to carry less than two hundred yards, and having taken a sum of money from it, made his escape in time to prevent apprehension. All these crimes and offenses as taken with the manner of their perpetration, indicate a class of men, either traitors or experienced and professional thieves and villains. All that discipline and watchfullness can do for their detection and apprehension is done from the General Commanding the Brigade, to every lesser commander or officer. But with a class so essentially vile and obtuse, it is a question whether either the interests or economy of the regiment or of the Government can be subserved or promoted. The character of the regulars for uprightness, discipline, and even a decent *morale* must certainly suffer under these conditions. I have felt it my duty to make special representation, leaving it for the proper authorities to determine whether any rule or system can be established such as shall obviate or lessen the evils complained of; such a system as, by furnishing recruits of a better class, shall relieve troops in the field from the common necessity of pursuing or reducing to order criminals, while regular duty is thrown upon honister men. While at the same time the Treasury becomes depleted to amount of bounty, pay, clothing, transportation, and to no practical end, either as regards efficiency of organization or the war yet in hand. Indeed as regards this latter view, the rebellion has been actually recruited by bringing into our camps men whose only objects have been to obtain bounties, outfit and transportation to their own neighborhood, or that of their friends, and then desert. Among the men thus deserting, pardoned rebels, canadians and English are conspicuous—though we have a few englishmen of good and faithful conduct.

Pardon the length of this communication, but it is made with a view to the best interests of the regiment and of the service.

Very Respectfully
ALBERT TRACY
Major 15th Infty
Comd'g[52]

The next significant piece of correspondence Tracy wrote was his request for retirement, which the War Department approved on May 6. John D. Wilkins, an 1846 West Pointer who had served with the Army of the Potomac's Regular Division as a captain in the 3rd Infantry, was promoted to major and took Tracy's place. Major Wilkins arrived on Lookout Mountain in early June.[53]

The war was all but over by the time Tracy sent his words of warning to Ft. Adams. Robert E. Lee's Army of Northern Virginia had surrendered at Appomattox Court House on April 9. The regulars would soon learn that Joseph Johnston's forces in North Carolina stacked their arms on April 26. Captain Allyn wrote on April 16 that news of the Union's military triumphs reached the regulars almost simultaneously with the shocking word of President Lincoln's assassination:

Amid the congratulations of a nation, while millions are rejoic-
ing at the very glorious successes of our arms, the merry peal of bells
and joysome roar of artillery is hushed at the news of our countrys
calamity. The bells are now tolling, and the sound of the mourning
minute gun but echoes the responsive grief of our Republic's heart.
The great, the good, the just has gone to rest. Fallen by an assassins
hands, when just at the pinnacle of fame. Well may a nation mourn.
Whatever the motive, the murderer's name is forever accursed. If
treason prompted, then little mercy may traitors expect at our
hands. ...Insanity alone can have prompted so disgraceful an act.
The feeling here is very very deep. Vengeance upon the traitor hearts
that conceived so cowardly a deed, is the universal sentiment here.
But may the great and wise God who rules the destiny of our race,
preserve the nation now and guide Abraham Lincoln's successor in a
path that will give us a quick and lasting peace though it be purchased at the price of the blood of every traitor who has borne arms
against our good country.[54]

"We are all in mourning for our beloved and good President,"
Arthur Carpenter wrote five days later from Ft. Wayne, where he
had been posted on recruiting duty. "The buildings are all draped in
mourning and our Garrison Flag is at half mast, with a deep border
of crape around it. We have to wear crape on our left sleeve and on
our swords, for six months by order of Lieut. Gen. Grant. Nearly
every building in the city is draped for mourning. I am heartily sick
of service up here and wish I was back in the Field."[55]

Lieutenant Carpenter's desire for a return to field duty might
have been tempered somewhat if he had known the conditions then
prevailing on Lookout Mountain. The Regular Brigade's desertions
and disciplinary problems increased during the weeks following the
cessation of hostilities. If the recruits had difficulty understanding
the necessity of training while the war was still underway, inspiring
them was even more difficult after they became members of a
peacetime army. The regulars' only excitement in the month of May
was the possibility of escorting Jefferson Davis on part of a journey
through Georgia and Tennessee. After Davis's capture by Federal
cavalry in south Georgia on May 10, he was packed off to Fortress
Monroe on the Virginia Peninsula for what would turn out to be
two years of incarceration. Security was tight as Davis made the
journey. At one point it was thought that Davis's route would take
him through Chattanooga; a "competent force" of regulars was
held in readiness to escort him upon his arrival at Dalton. Davis

ended up traveling to Savannah instead and was sent to Fortress Monroe via steamship, but being selected to guard the former president of the Confederacy was a fitting honor for a few score rugged, veteran regular troops, and a chance to escape the slack atmosphere permeating the Regular Brigade's camp on Lookout Mountain. For a few days, the martial spirit of the regulars that had been so prominent in 1862 and 1863 lived once again.[56]

What the commanders of the regular battalions wanted to do at this point was the same thing they had desired since the capture of Atlanta: return to their regimental depots, recruit up to strength, and train their new men as regulars should train. Captain Alexander Chambers, commanding 2/18th Infantry as of February, on May 17 sent forward yet another request to the War Department:

> Head Quarters 2nd Batt 18th US Infantry
> Lookout Mountain Tenn. May 14th 1865

L. Thomas
Adjutant General USA
Washington D.C.

General,

I have the honor to request in view of the speedy termination of hostilities in this Dept. and the facts embraced in the appended tabular Statement of the present effective condition of this Batt. that it be ordered to its Hd. Qrs. Columbus Ohio to recruit its depleted ranks. The Battalion has served constantly in the field since December 1861 and with one or two unavoidable exceptions has participated in every engagement in the Department under Major Genl. Geo. H. Thomas and it remains idle in its present Station only to see its old and tried Soldiers discharged day by day at the expiration of an honorable term while if the skeleton Companies now remaining were ordered North to join in a united effort to fill the regiment with our old men already discharged and from the Volunteer Army now rapidly going out, hardly a doubt can exist but that we might rapidly recruit to the maximum. The terms of service of our old and disciplined Soldiers will all expire within the next five months and could they be saved as a nucleus to the Regiment [this] would do more to promote the efficiency of the Service, than ten times their number of recruits.

I respectfully refer the General to our record of Service during the war and to the subjoined tabular Statement of our present condition:

Tabular Statement of effective Strength, 2nd Batt 18th U.S. Infty

		Absent					Present			
Total present & absent	Detached service	With leave	Sick	Confined	Total	Total strength	Not effective by Sickness arrest etc.	Effective Strength	Raw recruits	To be discharged in next 5 months
430	32	6	56	6	100	330	40	290	93	155

I would state that the above report includes the entire strength of the three Battalions of the Regiment, the 1st & 3rd Batts having been broken up and transferred to the 2nd last October by order of the War Dept.

I am very respectfully your obedient Servant
ALEX CHAMBERS
Capt. 18th US Infantry Comd'g Batt.[57]

The battalions of the Regular Brigade never returned to their Civil War depots. Rhode Island, New York, Ohio, and Michigan were among the last places the War Department desired regular infantrymen to be stationed during the summer of 1865. Dismantling the Union Army was a complicated process. While the War Department demobilized the Union Army's host of volunteers and the president and Congress hammered out the politico-military machinery necessary to administer the former Confederate states, the Regular Army waited. It was particularly galling for the regulars to sit out the Grand Review of the Union Army. When more than 150,000 Union soldiers marched down Washington's Pennsylvania Avenue on May 23 and 24, only a handful of men from the 3rd and 10th U.S. Infantry were present as representatives of the Regular Army's nineteen shattered infantry regiments. Since the regulars had also sat out the war's final 1864–1865 campaigns, the Civil War obscurity of the Regular Army was never greater than it was right at the very end.[58]

Unlike the volunteers who marched out of the army and back into civilian life that summer, the regulars' task was to train for whatever the future may hold. Transforming undisciplined, raw manpower into professional soldiers was a difficult undertaking, but it was a mission America's regulars usually performed well. In the years prior to the Civil War, there had always been present in every regiment a core of grizzled sergeants with up to a half-dozen or so service stripes on their sleeves who relished the task. By the summer of 1865, those men were not present for duty. They had either been killed or wounded during the previous four years, or had decided to get out of the army while they were still alive. Regular officers did what they could to make up the deficit. Many of them were looking forward to the opportunities that postwar army service offered. "My career is apparently fixed for some years," Captain Arthur Allyn wrote on August 5, "all centered in command of my Company, which I am very happy to say is the best Company in the Regiment here—but still capable of a great deal of improvement." A few weeks earlier, Major Wilkins, the 15th Infantry's latest field commander, had suggested to Colonel Shepherd that the 15th Infantry band be ordered to join the regiment's battalions on Lookout Mountain: "I urge this as a measure calculated to inspire the Enlisted men of the Regiment with an 'Espirit de Corps' neces-sary to bring [them] to the standard we all desire, and to vary the monotony of camp life." An army's transition from war to peace is never a simple process, but the U.S. Army's generally poor perform-ance in combat operations immediately following the Civil War can be traced back at least in part to its lack of experienced non-com-missioned officers in 1865.[59]

More than just the 15th Infantry's band would soon be departing Ft. Adams. In mid-August, the soldiers of the Regular Brigade learned their fate. All regimental headquarters were about to make their way southward. Since the U.S. Army did not then maintain tac-tical organizations larger than regiments during peacetime, the Regular Brigade was dismantled. Its four regiments were scattered across the former Confederacy and points north, part of the military muscle that would enforce Reconstruction laws and eventually escort the next round of expansion into the American West. George Thomas gave the Regular Brigade its orders to move on to other fields:

SPECIAL ORDERS   HQTRS., MILITARY DIVISION OF THE TENNESSEE
No. 56   *Nashville, Tenn. August 18, 1865*

. . .

III. The organization known as the Regular Brigade, is hereby broken up. The Regiments comprising the same are assigned to the several Departments as mentioned herein:

15th United States Infantry to the Department of Alabama. Commanding officer of the regiment will proceed with his command without delay to Mobile, Alabama, reporting to Maj Genl E.R. Woods, Commanding Dept., for duty.

16th United States Infantry to the Department of Tennessee. Commanding officer of the regiment will proceed with his command without delay to Nashville, Tennessee, reporting on arrival to the Asst Adjutant Gen, these Hdqtrs for assignment to duty as Hdqtrs Guards Military Division of the Tennessee.

18th United States Infantry to the Department of Kentucky. Commanding officer of regiment will proceed with his command without delay to Louisville, Kentucky, reporting on arrival to Maj Genl J.M. Palmer, Commanding Department, for duty.

19th United States Infantry to the Department of Georgia. Commanding officer of regiment will proceed with his command without delay to Augusta, Georgia, reporting on arrival to Maj Genl J.B. Steedman, Commanding Department, for duty.

Quarter Master Department will furnish the necessary transportation.

. . .

By command of Major General Thomas:

> HENRY M. CIST
> *A.A. Genl*

Official:
GEO. W. HOWARD
AAG[60]

Lookout Mountain was slowly demilitarized over the next few days as the battalions packed up their equipment and made their way to the Chattanooga rail depot. The last march of the Regular Brigade did not include brass bands, cheering crowds, or saluting dignitaries. The procession consisted only of professional soldiers doing their jobs, and it is the fate of America's peacetime regulars to do so without generating much in the way of public excitement or headlines. Some of the battalions boarded northbound trains at the depot, others headed south. All of them were embarking on the next chapter in the history of the United States Army.

Epilogue

"We are Few in Number, a Small Band of Comrades"

Yet after all, how little do we know of the history of this army, an army of which the country has every reason to be proud, and how few know anything of its formation and constituent parts.

> Frederick Phisterer
> *The Regular Army of the United States*
> 1893

I: The Regulars

The dawn of May 31, 1897, was dreary at West Point, New York. Low, heavy clouds skirted among the Hudson Highlands, scattering showers across the Military Academy. By late morning, the sky began to clear and the sun broke through the overcast. Anyone glancing northward up the Hudson River Valley from West Point that morning would have seen contrasting sunlight and shadow moving across the mountains that flank the river and form one of the most spectacular vistas in America. That person would have also noticed a temporary grandstand and rostrum near the trees lining the north side of the Plain, the Military Academy's parade field, the structures "covered by awnings of red and white striped canvas decorated with flags and trophies, the whole forming a very brilliant and beautiful mass of color."[1] Some members of West Point's Corps of Cadets looked upon the improving weather with much less enthusiasm. The brightening sky meant that a cancellation of outdoor ceremonies, secretly hoped for by many cadets, would not be forthcoming. Resigning themselves to the inevitable, the cadets began their familiar routine of ensuring that spotless uniforms, accouterments, and weapons were indeed spotless. The occasion was the dedication of Battle Monument, a tall granite monolith in the trees on the north side of the Plain.

It was a ceremony more than thirty years in the making. Credit for originating the idea that evolved into Battle Monument goes to Henry C. Hasbrouck, an 1861 West Pointer who served as a lieutenant in the 4th U.S. Artillery during the Civil War:

> I was ordered to West Point for duty in September, 1863, while north on sick leave. At that time all the officers temporarily on duty [at the Academy] had seen service in the field and many of them had been disabled by either wounds or sickness. All knew and appreciated the services of the regulars; and the merits and deeds of officers and men who had fallen were constantly recalled. These services were well known at the front, but received little recognition in the press, which, from local and State pride, made special effort to exploit the achievements of their own volunteers. We all thought the regulars were not receiving their just dues, and that their services should be better known and permanently commemorated. Soon after my arrival I suggested one night after dinner at the Mess a Monument at West Point which should have inscribed upon it a list of the battles and the names of all the officers and men of the Regular Army who had been killed or died of wounds received in action.[2]

Hasbrouck's idea was "well received" by other West Point faculty members. They formed a planning committee, mailed announcements, and raised funds. Six hundred-seventy Regular Army officers and 790 enlisted men donated $14,000 to the project during 1864, the money being invested in government bonds. The project was strangely dormant for the next twenty-four years, but was revived again in 1890. The market value of the bonds exceeded $60,000 by that time. Lieutenant Colonel James M. Wilson, superintendent of West Point from 1889 to 1893, pushed the project through to completion. An additional seven years were spent in selecting a design, constructing the monument, and melting down fifty captured Confederate artillery pieces, the latter being molded into bronze plaques upon which were inscribed the names of 188 officers and 2,042 soldiers of the Regular Army who had been killed during the war.[3]

The brightening skies on the last day of May 1897 meant that Battle Monument's dedication ceremony went as planned. The Corps of Cadets sallied forth across the Plain and took up its designated position around the grandstand. Carriages pulled up bearing Secretary of War Russell A. Alger, Justice D.J. Brewer of the U.S.

Supreme Court, retired Major General John Schofield, and Academy dignitaries. A series of dedication speeches followed, but the most memorable words spoken in connection with Battle Monument had actually been uttered almost thirty-three years earlier. A site dedication ceremony had taken place on June 15, 1864, upon the ground where the Academy's wartime faculty hoped would one day rest the Regular Army's Civil War memorial. On that date, the corps also marched across the Plain, but cadet gray was not the only uniform color on parade at West Point that day. Contingents of blue-clad troops and regimental bands from the 3rd, 6th, 7th, and 12th U.S. Infantry Regiments, and the 5th U.S. Artillery, also took part in the ceremony. All veterans of the Army of the Potomac's Regular Division, these combat-thinned, but still proud regular units had been assigned to garrison duty in the aftermath of their bloodletting at Gettysburg eleven months before. Thus, representatives of the Old Army, the New Army, and the Regular Army's future were all present as former general-in-chief and soon-to-be presidential candidate George B. McClellan gave the keynote address:

> We have assembled to consecrate a cenotaph which shall remind our children's children, in the distant future, of their fathers' struggles in the days of the great rebellion. This monument is to perpetuate the memory of a portion only of those who have fallen for the nation in this unhappy war—is dedicated to the officers and soldiers of the regular army. ...Each State will, no doubt, commemorate in some fitting way the services of its sons who abandoned the avocations of peace and shed their blood in the ranks of the volunteers.
>
> But we of the regular army have no States to look to for the honors due our dead. We belong to the whole country, and can neither expect nor desire the general government to make a perhaps invidious distinction in our favor. We are few in number, a small band of comrades, united by peculiar and very binding ties. ...West Point, with her large heart, adopts us all—graduates and those appointed from civil life, officers and privates. In her eyes we are all her children, jealous of her fame, and eager to sustain her world-wide reputation. ...Such are the ties which unite us, the most endearing which exist among men; such are the relations which bind us together, the closest of the sacred brotherhood of arms.
>
> It is therefore seemed, and it is fitting, that we should erect upon this spot, so sacred to us all, an enduring monument to our dear brothers who have preceded us upon the path of peril and of honor, which it is the destiny of many of us to tread.[4]

The concern that Hasbrouck, McClellan, and others expressed about the Regular Army's lack of recognition for its Civil War service turned out to be well founded, for history has not been kind to the Civil War regulars. As the guns fell silent, what little the public knew of the Regular Army centered on the fact that the regulars had not significantly participated in the war's final campaigns and, judging from the behavior of regulars at Lookout Mountain and elsewhere, the Union Army was probably better off without them. The favorable press coverage the Regular Brigade had received at Stones River and Hoover's Gap was but a distant memory. A popular notion took hold that the regulars were either "paper collar" martinets who did little hard fighting or were just a bunch of social outcasts looking for an easy dollar. Volunteers often portrayed regulars unfavorably both during the war and afterward, a way to highlight the virtuousness and skill of the citizen-soldier, and a common thread running through many volunteers' memoirs is a few lines pointing out how the regulars were just not very skilled soldiers. The situation became so irritating during the late nineteenth century that a number of regular veterans felt compelled to explain that the regulars had, in fact, shouldered their share of the fighting. Frederick Phisterer privately published a short account outlining the Regular Brigade's role at Stones River. John C. White, a Civil War veteran of the 10th U.S. Infantry, wrote a series of lengthy articles in *The Journal of the Military Service Institution of the United States* outlining the Civil War service of every Regular Army regiment. These and other efforts did not reach a wide audience in their time. They are largely unknown today.[5]

In James M. McPherson's landmark 1997 study on why men fought in the Civil War, *For Cause and Comrades*, it is difficult to recognize the few times when the author quotes members of the Regular Army. He anonymously labels Alfred Lacey Hough of the 19th U.S. as "a Pennsylvania officer." Arthur B. Carpenter of that same regiment is misidentified as belonging to the 19th Indiana, "part of the famous Iron Brigade." The only direct reference to the regulars occurs as McPherson quotes the writings of a volunteer who believed the regulars joined the Union Army for a job and paycheck rather than for the noble ideals of liberty, freedom, and justice that motivated state troops.[6] And yet, the citizens who joined the regulars during the war differed little from the volunteers. No one knew this better than the regulars themselves. William O. Crosby, who served as a sergeant in C/2/15th U.S., gave a short address on this subject at an 1892 gathering of Regular Brigade veterans. The aging former sergeant "spoke of the splendid record of the Regular Brigade, Fourteenth Corps, Army of the Cumberland,"

> and referred to the fact that meager praise was bestowed the regulars during the late war by the public press, while the deeds of volunteers were never overlooked, but were often enlarged by the fertile brain and imagination of the correspondent. He believed that no regular would wish to see obliterated even a paragraph honoring the volunteers, as the combined encomiums of the press did not, nor could not, overrate their patriotism and valor. However, he believed there had been misapprehension of the character of the material composing the regular regiments organized in 1861 by a special act of Congress. It was assumed that the men composing them were such as commonly enlist in time of peace, and that fighting, or military service, was their chosen occupation. Nevertheless, these new regiments were largely composed of students who left the institution of learning, clerks who quit the store and desk, mechanics who abandoned their tools, and farmers who left the peaceful quietude of the old farm, and placed themselves under the more rigid discipline of the Regular Army, believing thereby they could render more efficient service.[7]

Many volunteers during the Civil War, and most historians since, have overlooked the fact that the vast majority of soldiers who served in the Civil War Regular Army enlisted after the attack on Fort Sumter. The wartime regulars, more than 58,000 strong, joined the Union Army for the same reasons that volunteers went to war, be it to preserve the Union, abolish slavery, or just to participate in a great national event. The fact that more citizens choose to enlist in state regiments is irrelevant. It was simply the fortune—ill or otherwise—of a regular recruit to find himself in a unique organization, a unit whose standards of training and discipline set it apart from the Union Army's multitude of volunteer regiments.

In the end, though, the Regular Army was a misused weapon in the Union's arsenal. Particularly after Winfield Scott's retirement in November 1861, the War Department had difficulty articulating just what role the regulars were supposed to perform. Whether or not the Regular Army could have been put to better use, through either the formation of Scott's Iron Column or sprinkling all the regulars among the volunteers as cadre, is difficult to say. But with so many men deciding to join volunteer regiments instead of the regulars, and the regulars in the field sustaining heavy casualties, it was just a matter of time before the Regular Army was not able to make a significant contribution to the war effort. Military professionals today will recognize these circumstances as a breakdown in force management, the process by which operational requirements are translated into force structure and programs. With no mission requirements driving force structure, recruiting, and unit manning, no one was overly concerned about the nineteen regular infantry regiments being skeletal formations for much of the war and sitting largely on the sidelines by mid-1864. Maintaining a *corps d'elite* along the lines of Napoleon's Old Guard (with selective recruitment, higher pay, distinctive uniforms, and—most importantly—a firm mission and reason for being) would have solved this problem, but it is doubtful the War Department ever contemplated such a program given the democratic, anti-elitist nature of the soldiers making up the Union Army. General Rosecrans's proposal in early 1863 to form elite "Light Battalions" in the Army of the Cumberland was an effort to do exactly this, and the War Department stifled the scheme before it ever got off the drawing board.

The regular battalions in the Army of the Ohio/Cumberland were built from scratch in 1861 and were then rebuilt three times: in the spring of 1863 after Stones River, in the winter of 1863–1864 following Chickamauga-Chattanooga, and in the final months of the war after the Atlanta Campaign. This resilience was a significant feat given the recruiting obstacles in the Regular Army's path. Much of the credit for this accomplishment goes to two officers: Henry Carrington and Oliver Shepherd. Their performance as the respective colonels of the 18th and 15th Infantry Regiments illustrates what was possible for the regulars in the Civil War. No other regular infantry regiments had full time commanding officers comparable in experience and prestige to these two men, and competent leadership at the top made the difference for the recruiting efforts of the 15th and 18th Regulars. These two regiments accounted for more than 7,500 soldiers in Union blue between them, which means that nearly 13 percent of all Regular Army wartime enlistees were members of just these two regiments. If every regular regiment had a commander of similar ability and dedication, the Regular Army would have had the staying power to play a much more significant role throughout the war. That was not possible, since many of the Regular Army's best officers instead served with volunteer units. This was the price the United States paid for maintaining such a small standing army in the antebellum era, a practice that necessitated the use of a preponderance of state-based military organizations in the Union Army.[8]

With the North's manpower situation deteriorating as the war continued, each new iteration of the regular battalions had less Old Army distinction than its predecessor. By early 1864, the Regular Brigade was almost indistinguishable from any other brigade that had experienced more than two years of field service: it had a core of seasoned leaders, some veteran troops of varying degrees of efficiency, and raw, untried newcomers. Whatever need the Union Army had for professional organizations such as the Regular Brigade in the early years of the war was by 1864 supplanted by the on-the-job professionalization of the Union Army. General Schofield, standing before Battle Monument in 1897, made sure West Point's Corps of Cadets understood this: "The difference between the regular and volunteer exists only in name. The one, no less than the other, is a volunteer soldier, and the other, hardly less than the first, soon becomes, under the discipline of war, a regular soldier."[9] True enough, but perhaps a more robust and useful Regular Army could have substituted for some of the "discipline of war" that inculcated professional military values into the Civil War's volunteers. Certainly fewer volunteers would have perished during the learning process.

* * *

II: Regiments and Officers

In one form or another, the regular formations that served in the Army of the Cumberland are still part of the United States Army today, although tracing the history of American regular regiments is a difficult task. Congressionally mandated changes in the army's strength over the years resulted in extensive reorganizations of the army's regiments, sometimes done with little regard for regimental lineage, traditions, and identity. The first post-Civil War reorganization started in late 1866. With the rapid demobilization of the Union Army's volunteers, regulars were needed to occupy the former Confederate states and reestablish a strong military presence in the West. Recognizing that these demands would be heavy, Congress increased the army's size from 39,273 to 54,641—the only time Regular Army strength increased rather than decreased at the conclusion of a major conflict. Forty-five infantry regiments were authorized in 1866, a significant gain from the nineteen that had served during the Civil War. This increase was more apparent than real. All the regiments were manned in the traditional British style of the prewar regulars, each having ten companies. The nine regiments organized in 1861 lost their unique three-battalion organization. The twenty-seven battalions each became a separate regiment with the addition of a colonel, lieutenant colonel, and two more companies. The first battalion of each New Army regiment retained its 1861 designation, while the second and third battalions assumed completely new identities. As a result of this process, the four regiments that served in the Army of the Cumberland spawned eight new outfits:

Table E: Conversion From Battalions to Regiments, 1861-1870

Battalion (1861-1865)	Regiment (1866-1869)	Regiment (1870-Present Day)
1/15th U.S. Infantry	15th U.S. Infantry Regiment	15th Infantry Regiment
2/15th U.S. Infantry	24th U.S. Infantry Regiment	11th Infantry Regiment
3/15th U.S. Infantry	33rd U.S. Infantry Regiment	8th Infantry Regiment
1/16th U.S. Infantry	16th U.S. Infantry Regiment	2nd Infantry Regiment
2/16th U.S. Infantry	25th U.S. Infantry Regiment	18th Infantry Regiment
3/16th U.S. Infantry	34th U.S. Infantry Regiment	16th Infantry Regiment
1/18th U.S. Infantry	18th U.S. Infantry Regiment	18th Infantry Regiment
2/18th U.S. Infantry	27th U.S. Infantry Regiment	9th Infantry Regiment
3/18th U.S. Infantry	36th U.S. Infantry Regiment	7th Infantry Regiment
1/19th U.S Infantry	19th U.S. Infantry Regiment	19th Infantry Regiment
2/19th U.S. Infantry	28th U.S. Infantry Regiment	19th Infantry Regiment
3/19th U.S. Infantry	37th U.S. Infantry Regiment	3rd & 5th Infantry Regiments

This increase in army strength was short lived. Maintaining a large military establishment during peacetime was a financial burden that Congress was never willing to bear. Twenty infantry regiments were slashed from the force structure in 1869. Similar to the military downsizing that occurred after the War of 1812, the 1869 reduction wreaked havoc with regimental identities. As a result of the 1869 action, many regiments of the army today have no connection whatsoever with the nineteenth-century regiments of the same designation. The lineage of some regiments is so confusing that members of these units today often possess little accurate knowledge of their own regimental history.[10]

Some of the Regular Brigade's units emerged from the 1869 reorganization intact, while others were obliterated. The 15th Infantry was consolidated with the 35th to form the new 15th; the 18th Infantry was consolidated with the 25th to form the new 18th; the new 19th Regiment was a combination of the old 19th and the 28th. The battalions of the 15th, 18th, and 19th Infantry Regiments still serving in the U.S. Army today can trace unbroken lineages back to President Lincoln's May 1861 expansion of the Regular Army. The 16th Infantry was not so fortunate. In 1869 the 11th and 34th Regiments were combined to form the new 16th; the 2nd Regiment absorbed the 16th U.S. of the Civil War. The modern 2nd Infantry thus displays twenty-one Civil War battle and campaign streamers on its colors, a record number for an infantry regiment. Thirteen of them were awarded to the 2nd Infantry during its extensive service in the Army of the Potomac; eight more, earned by the 16th Infantry, were transferred to the 2nd in 1869. The 2nd Infantry Regiment today, part of the 1st Infantry Division in Germany, thus holds the distinction of having participated in most of the Civil War's major battles, its ancestors having fought in both the Eastern and Western Theaters.[11]

In addition to today's 15th, 18th, and 19th Infantry, traces of the Army of the Cumberland's regulars are visible elsewhere as well. The 11th Infantry Regiment, stationed at Fort Benning, Georgia, is the descendant of 2/15th U.S. and carries the nine Civil War streamers earned by Major Edie's battalion. The red acorn badge of the 1st Division, XIV Corps is part of the 11th Infantry's regimental coat of arms. The modern 9th Infantry Regiment, an element of the Korea-based 2nd Infantry Division, is another unit with a Regular Brigade past. It was consolidated in 1869 with the 27th Infantry, the old 2/18th U.S. of the Civil War. The eight Civil War streamers earned by William Bisbee, Henry Freemen, Frederick Phisterer, and the other members of this colorful battalion now adorn the flags of the 9th Infantry. The 9th actually benefited greatly from the 1869 reorganization—the old 9th spent the entire Civil War on the West Coast and, incredibly, did not of itself earn any battle honors from 1861 to 1865. Finally, today's 7th Infantry Regiment also has roots dating back to the western regulars of the Civil War. The 7th has seen more combat during its long history than any other regiment of the U.S. Army, having participated in every major American conflict from the War of 1812 through Operation Iraqi Freedom. Among the numerous battle and campaign streamers on the colors of the 7th Infantry (two battalions of which are part of the 3rd Infantry Division at Fort Stewart, Georgia) are fourteen from the Civil War. The 7th Infantry earned five of these during its limited service in New Mexico and Virginia. The companies of 3/18th U.S. that served in the field with the 18th Infantry's 1st and 2nd Battalions earned the other eight; the honors were transferred to the 7th as a result of the 1866 and 1869 reorganizations.[12]

* *

Battery H, 5th U.S. Artillery

While the Regular Brigade's infantry battalions experienced a turbulent organizational existence after the Civil War, their road was quite smooth when compared with that of Battery H. Army artillery went through numerous changes in the late nineteenth and early twentieth centuries while fielding new weapons and assuming new roles on the battlefield. From the Civil War until the present day, Battery H has endured no fewer than fourteen redesignations and reorganizations. At various times it served as a field artillery battery, coast artillery company, antiaircraft artillery gun battery, antiaircraft artillery missile battery, and rocket howitzer battalion. Today, Battery H exists in the form of the 5th Battalion, 5th Air Defense Artillery Regiment, part of the 2nd Infantry Division in Korea.[13]

Other than William R. Terrill, whose untimely death at Perryville in 1862 cut short what undoubtedly would have been a stellar career, Francis L. Guenther was the man responsible for Battery H's fine Civil War performance. The battery's field service ended in early 1864, when it was allocated to the Nashville garrison. Guenther departed Tennessee in October of that year for an assignment to the West Point faculty. He returned to the command of Battery H in 1866 and held that post for more than a decade. As a field-grade officer, Guenther spent further years at artillery garrisons up and down the Atlantic coast, and in the early 1890s commanded the post at San Francisco's Alcatraz Island. Guenther became colonel of the 4th Artillery Regiment in 1896. During the wartime expansion of 1898, he was appointed as a brigadier general of volunteers. He assumed command of a division at Camp Alger, Virginia, in May 1898, but suffered a nervous breakdown of sorts less than a week after taking command. He was diagnosed as "suffering from Neurasthenia caused by the worry and mental strain incident to the sudden assumption of new duties with greatly increased responsibilities." He was granted four months of sick leave to recover, although the army's surgeon general suggested: "General Guenther should resign his Commission as Brigadier General of Volunteers if he cannot stand the strain incident to the performance of the duties of a General of Brigade." Upon Guenther's return to duty in late 1898, the Spanish-American War was over, and he reverted to his prewar rank of colonel.[14]

A few more years of service remained for Frank Guenther. He capped off his lengthy career as the army's chief of artillery and commandant of the Artillery School at Fortress Monroe. As he approached mandatory retirement for reaching sixty-three years of age, by 1901 Guenther was the sole officer representative of the pre-Civil War Old Army still on the active roles. This was a fact not lost on the community of regular veterans, who lobbied to have Guenther promoted to Regular Army brigadier general before his retirement. Anson Mills and thirty-two other former members of the Regular Brigade wrote to the War Department on Guenther's behalf, as did retired Major General Alexander McCook and even former Confederate general officer Joseph Wheeler.[15] Anson G. McCook (another of Ohio's famed "Fighting McCooks"), who has served in Rousseau's division at Stones River as lieutenant colonel of the 2nd Ohio, wrote to Secretary of War Elihu Root:

> You will pardon me I am sure for bothering you in regard to my view as to filling one of the vacancies in the grade of Brig. Genl. when I tell you that the senior Colonel (I believe) is an old friend and comrade, Col Francis L. Guenther of the Artillery.
>
> We served together in the same [division] in the Army of the Cumberland under Rosecrans & Thomas, and Guenther as Captain of old Battery H, 5th Artillery was simply an ideal soldier. He never failed to be in the right place at the right time, and although a good many years have passed, his splendid conduct at the battle of Stone River, when the Enemy came charging out of the cedars and across the cotton field, can never be forgotten by those who saw him and his battery on that great day. He has been a faithful, devoted, unselfish soldier all of his life, and as he approaches the day for retirement, his services, it seems to me, entitle him to the promotion so dear to the worthy soldier.
>
> I hope that you can see your way clear to recommend him to the President when a vacancy occurs.[16]

"Full consideration will be given to what you say about Col. Francis L. Guenther, whom I know to be a very gallant officer," the secretary of war replied. "But there are thirty or forty officers, with similarly fine records, who want the same thing." Guenther's record, even taking into account his troubles during the Spanish-American War, was enough to best the competition for the coveted Regular Army star. He was promoted to brigadier general on February 21, 1902. The next day, his sixty-third birthday, he retired. General Guenther died on December 5, 1918.[17]

* *

The 15th Infantry Regiment

The 15th U.S. Infantry served on Reconstruction duty in Alabama and Georgia until the summer of 1868, when the regiment shipped out for duty in New Mexico and Texas. It served in the West until the turn of the century, seeing limited action in the Indian Wars. Following occupation duty in Cuba after the Spanish-American War, the 15th Regulars took part in the China Relief Expedition, a response to the Boxer Rebellion of 1900. The crisis was over by the time the regiment arrived in China. It was then sent across the South China Sea to the Philippine Islands, where it participated in the Luzon campaigns of the 1899–1901 Philippine War. Following stateside duty in California and Utah, and another tour in the Philippines, the 15th Infantry went back to China in 1912, where it joined a multinational peacekeeping force dispatched to China in an era of Chinese political instability and perceived threats to Western economic interests. The 15th remained in Tientsin until 1938, earning the nickname "the Old China Hands." During World War II, the 15th Infantry was assigned to the 3rd Infantry Division and campaigned throughout North Africa, Sicily, Italy, France, and Germany. It emerged from that conflict as one of America's most decorated infantry regiments, with Lieutenant Audie Murphy of B/1/15th Infantry taking honors as America's most decorated soldier. The 15th Infantry also served with the 3rd Infantry Division in the Korean War and battalions of the 15th today are still assigned to this division, stationed at Georgia's Fort Stewart and Fort Benning. In March and April 2003, they were among the leading forces that thundered into Baghdad during Operation Iraqi Freedom.[18]

A number of Audie Murphy's Civil War predecessors also went on to distinguished careers. Peter T. Swaine's frustration at not being promoted to brigadier general of volunteers during the Civil War continued afterward, for he knew that promotions in the peacetime army would again be maddeningly slow. It was not until December 1865 that Swaine finally received his first brevet: "I have the honor to accept the appointment of Major by Brevet for the Battle of Shiloh, and respectfully state for the information of the Hon. Secretary of War that having served in all the subsequent battles of importance of that Army: Stone River, Chickamauga, the Atlanta Campaign, most of the time as brigade commander, receiving the approval and recommendations of my superiors, I have as yet received no honorable notice of these services from the War Department." Persistence eventually paid off for Brevet Major Swaine. He went on to receive two more brevet promotions, to lieutenant colonel and colonel, for his good service at Stones River and also "faithful and meritorious service during the war." He received a full majority in the 16th Infantry during late 1865, became the lieutenant colonel of the 15th Regulars in 1874, and took charge of the 22nd Infantry as colonel in 1884. He retired in 1895. Peter's son William Maclay Swaine graduated from West Point in 1886 (a classmate of John J. Pershing) and saw combat in Cuba and the Philippines as a lieutenant in one of his father's old regiments, the 22nd Infantry. William outlived his father by only five years, dying from service-related disabilities in 1909. The elder Swaine's service record is all the more remarkable in light of the fact that he died in 1904 from complications associated with diabetes, a disease he suffered with most of his adult life.[19]

Charles A. Wikoff, the 15th Infantry lieutenant who was shot in the left eye at Shiloh, also went on to extensive post-Civil War service. He rose steadily in rank, becoming colonel of the 22nd Infantry in 1897. The next year he commanded a brigade assigned to Brigadier General Jacob F. Kent's division during the Santiago Campaign. Prior to embarking for Cuba, Wikoff ran into Lieutenant Colonel William Bisbee, 1st U.S. Infantry, in the lobby of the Tampa Bay Hotel. Bisbee was also bound for Cuba, and Wikoff remarked: "Bisbee, you and I are too old for this." Bisbee replied that he still felt fit, but Wikoff ended up tempting the fates of battle once too often. While leading his brigade toward the San Juan Heights on the morning of July 1, 1898, Colonel Wikoff was killed by Spanish artillery fire. The barrage was intense and the officer who assumed command of the brigade from Wikoff, Lieutenant Colonel William S. Worth of the 13th Regulars, was himself quickly wounded. The 24th Infantry's Lieutenant Colonel Emerson H. Liscum then took charge, but he lasted only about five minutes before also being hit. Next in line was Lieutenant Colonel Ezra P. Ewers of the 9th Infantry, the former first sergeant of E/1/16th U.S. who had been commissioned at Chattanooga during October 1863. He was luckier than his three predecessors and led the brigade through the remainder of the battle. Charles Wikoff was the ranking American killed in action during the Spanish-American War. The V Corps' post-Cuba rest camp at Montauk Point on Long Island was named Camp Wikoff in honor of the late colonel.[20]

* *

The 16th Infantry Regiment

The 16th Infantry spent its brief postwar existence garrisoning various points in Tennessee and Louisiana. With the consolidation of the 16th and 2nd Regiments in 1869, the story of the Civil War 16th U.S. comes to an end. Lost in this consolidation is the fact that a member of the 16th Regulars earned a Medal of Honor for Civil War service. Sergeant Major Augustus Barry received the honor in 1870, his citation reading simply: "For gallantry in various actions during the rebellion." Had Barry's regiment continued through the years with an unbroken lineage, the sergeant major today would probably be a revered figure among a pantheon of 16th Infantry heroes. Instead, the stories of his deeds are all but lost.[21]

Adam Slemmer served little more than five months in the field with the 16th U.S., but he left his mark on the unit through his leadership in organizing the regiment during the summer of 1861 and commanding 1/16th at Stones River. Although the leg wound he suffered at Stones River kept him on administrative duties for the balance of the war, Slemmer was promoted to lieutenant colonel of the 4th U.S. in February 1864. After the Civil War he served on a board that evaluated applicants for commissions in the expanded Regular Army of 1866. The next year he took command of Ft. Laramie in Dakota Territory (present-day Wyoming), at which place in 1868 he prematurely died of heart disease.[22]

After Stones River, Slemmer passed the baton of 16th Infantry leadership into Major Sidney Coolidge's able hands, only to have

Coolidge meet his demise at Chickamauga. Robert E.A. Crofton and Edgar R. Kellogg held the regiment together in the field for most of the war, and both went on to extensive postwar service. A promotion a decade came to the Irish-born Crofton after the war, pinning on major in 1868 and lieutenant colonel in 1879. In 1886, he became colonel of the 15th U.S. Infantry. With the requirements of frontier security finally on the wane by the late 1880s, the War Department began consolidating many of the army's far-flung units at larger posts east of the Mississippi. On May 29, 1891, Colonel Crofton presided over a full regimental formation and parade of the 15th Regulars at Ft. Sheridan, Illinois. It was the first time such an event had taken place in more than twenty years. The last time all the regiment's companies had stood together was in 1869 at Ft. Selden, New Mexico, the 15th U.S. then being under the watchful eyes of Colonel Oliver L. Shepherd. At the conclusion of the 1891 ceremony, Colonel Crofton had his adjutant read aloud a regimental general order: "The Colonel congratulates the regiment, that after twenty-one years it is again united. He is highly gratified at the soldierly appearance and good behavior of the companies recently joining headquarters. This indicates regimental pride and devotion to duty, which must produce good results. The present Colonel has served with the Fifteenth Infantry both in peace and in war, and knows there is no more gallant corps in the service. He is proud of his regiment and feels certain it will keep up, if not excel, its past record." Judging from the performance of the 15th Infantry during the twentieth century, this regiment certainly fulfilled Crofton's expectations.[23]

Major General Alexander McCook retired on April 22, 1895. Brigadier General Wesley Merritt replaced him in the two-star ranks, which meant a Regular Army colonel would be promoted to brigadier. A number of colonels intensely lobbied for the promotion, Crofton included. One of Crofton's strongest supporters was Absalom Baird, the division commander of the Regular Brigade at Chickamauga. Baird wrote to the secretary of war on Christmas Eve, 1894:

> In considering applications for appointment to the next vacancy in the list of Brigadier General's of the Army for which I understand nearly all the colonels of the line are candidates. I respectfully write you to consider the valuable service rendered by Colonel R.E.A. Crofton 15th Infantry at the battle of Chickamauga. He was then a

captain in the Regular Brigade which was a part of my division. On the first day of the battle the brigade of Regulars went into action under my personal supervision and I was with it until the moment when stuck by an overwhelming force, it was temporarily dispersed. Captain Crofton was in the midst of this fight and had a horse killed under him. His service was gallant soldierly and valuable. On the second day of that contest in which this brigade held a position of vital importance he conducted himself with gallantry and his service was valuable. I had occasion to make use of his services in sending him to Gen'l Thomas for reenforcements and he returned with two regiments that he conducted into action as I directed.

It is my opinion that any officer who passed through those trying two days, creditably deserves the gratitude of the country and for this reason I commend Col. Crofton to your notice.[24]

Despite this and other heavy-hitting recommendations, the promotion went to Colonel Zenas R. Bliss of the 24th Infantry. Colonel Crofton retired in February 1897. He lived in Washington until his death in June 1898.[25]

Edgar Kellogg also continued in the regulars after the war, serving more than twenty years in the American West. As lieutenant colonel of the 10th Infantry, he led that regiment through the Santiago Campaign. In January 1899, he become both colonel of the 6th U.S. Infantry and a brigadier general of volunteers. Kellogg's regiment was ordered to the Philippines the next month. He was advised not to travel to a tropical climate, for the malaria he had first contracted just prior to Chickamauga had flared up again while he was in Cuba. Kellogg was determined to go, and boarded the steamer *Sherman* in San Francisco with his command in March 1899. His health continued to deteriorate during the voyage, and the aging veteran had to be put ashore in Hawaii. He returned to the United States, but was never again strong enough to actively serve. Kellogg was promoted to brigadier general, Regular Army, on December 15, 1899, and retired the next day. Edgar Kellogg experienced many campaigns during his long career, but considered his Civil War service to be the most memorable: "Since I left the Sixteenth—the Civil War Sixteenth—I have served in five other regiments, and of my service in each of them I have many fond recollections, but the memories linked with the strenuous years of march and bivouac and battle with the Sixteenth are some of the dearest of those that cheer me as I go on to the sunset of life beyond the Great

Divide." The retired brigadier finished writing his Civil War reminiscences as the Guns of August thundered across Europe. He died on October 7, 1914, and two days later was buried in Woodlawn Cemetery, Norwalk, Ohio.[26]

* *

The 18th Infantry Regiment

The 18th Infantry avoided Reconstruction duty. Troops were needed to protect settlers and prospectors moving on the new Bozeman Trail through Dakota Territory to the gold mines of Virginia City in western Montana Territory. Colonel Henry Carrington used his still-considerable political influence to have the 18th Infantry picked for the assignment. His regiment would be the first contingent of regulars to penetrate the northern reaches of the Great Plains after the Civil War. After receiving levies of fresh troops in Louisville during late 1865, Carrington led the command west in the spring of 1866. The officers marching with Carrington included Captains Andrew Burt, Henry Haymond, Nathaniel C. Kinney, Tenador Ten Eyck, Joshua L. Proctor, and Thomas B. Burrows, along with Lieutenants John I. Adair, Isaac D'Isay, Frederick Phisterer, and Thaddeus Kirtland, Civil War veterans all. Carrington was ordered to scatter his battalions between far-flung posts in Dakota Territory and establish his headquarters in the eastern foothills of the Big Horn Mountains, a site he christened Fort Phil Kearny. The post's garrison, four companies of 2/18th U.S. and a troop from the 2nd U.S. Cavalry, was soon in dire straights as the Sioux Nation harassed the fort unceasingly in an attempt to shut down movement on the Bozeman Trail. Captain William J. Fetterman was part of the garrison, another Civil War veteran of the 18th Infantry, who arrived at Fort Phil Kearny in November 1866. On December 21 of that year, he unwisely led an eighty-man column into a Sioux ambush. Fetterman's entire command was wiped out.[27]

The Fetterman Fight, second only to the Little Big Horn as the worst army defeat of the post-Civil War Indian campaigns, has inextricably linked Fetterman's name to the military history of the American West. Less well known are this officer's Civil War experiences, although historians have used Fetterman's wartime exploits to explain the captain's rash actions in Dakota Territory. Many historians, most notably Dee Brown in *The Fetterman Massacre* and John

D. McDermott in a 1991 article that appeared in the journal *Annals of Wyoming*, contend that the captain's Civil War exploits were impressive and legendary. Brown states that Fetterman "was cited for gallantry at Stones River" and believes that by the end of the Atlanta Campaign Fetterman was a "breveted lieutenant-colonel" with a "brilliant" record.[28]

McDermott lionizes Fetterman to an even greater extent, asserting that the captain was chosen to command 2/18th U.S. during May 1864 as a reward for meritorious conduct at the Battle of Resaca. McDermott also claims that the captain's further great combat performance during the Atlanta Campaign resulted in Fetterman's being appointed as "Acting Assistant Adjutant General (AAAG) of the Fourteenth Corps." He summarizes Fetterman's wartime service as follows: "In looking back, Fetterman's Civil War career was impressive. Rising from company to battalion command, serving on the staff of the Fourteenth Corps, and being twice breveted for gallantry, the young officer gained a reputation for efficiency and courage as a member of a unit that had been in the thick of the fighting in the Civil War. ...With the exceptions of the battles of Chickamauga and Chattanooga, Fetterman had been through it all, and with confidence born of having been repeatedly shot at and missed, he was no doubt ready for more action against another foe in a distant land." These authors believe that a significant cause of the tragedy that befell Fetterman's command was Fetterman's arrogant desire to continue the spectacular combat career he had experienced during the Civil War.[29]

Actually, Fetterman's Civil War service was extensive, but not notably spectacular. While certainly brave and competent—it is hard to question the bravery of any regular who fought in the cedars at Stones River—Fetterman was certainly not the only regular officer in the Army of the Cumberland possessing those qualities. The captain's contemporaries did not mention him all that much during the war; it was only after his death that many remembered him as such an extraordinary combat soldier (particularly by his close friend William Bisbee in *Through Four American Wars*). Fetterman was not "cited for gallantry" in any official report on Stones River. He commanded 2/18th U.S. during the Atlanta Campaign because he was the battalion's ranking officer present for duty, not as a reward for supposed heroics at Resaca. Contrary to McDermott's claims, Fetterman never served on the XIV Corps staff. He was selected to be the adjutant of King's brigade in July 1864, but the only reason he was available for that posting was that he had lost his battalion command position during the consolidation of the 18th Infantry during the Atlanta Campaign. And officers were oftentimes selected to be adjutants more for administrative talent than due to aggressive frontline leadership ability.

Brown, McDermott, and others emphasize Fetterman's two Civil War brevets as evidence of his exceptional Civil War exploits. But Fetterman himself once asserted in an 1866 letter to Oliver Shepherd that the brevet for Atlanta was almost a "blanket" award, handed out to many regular officers who participated in that campaign. As for the Stones River brevet, the recommendation for this award was not submitted to the U.S. Senate until July 26, 1866, less than five months before his death, and Fetterman's name was just one of many on a long list. William J. Fetterman's reckless quest for glory in Dakota Territory resulted from many factors, prominent among them being his desire to make a name for himself and the contempt in which held Colonel Henry Carrington's lack of Civil War combat experience. It was not because Fetterman desired to continue a military career that included famous Civil War exploits. An overlooked factor in explanations of Fetterman's defeat is that he and his brother regulars had not received very much public attention during the Civil War. Fetterman therefore desired the headlines and recognition in 1866 that had eluded him while serving in the wartime Regular Army. He certainly accomplished that.[30]

The Fetterman Fight ended the careers of more than just Fetterman and his troops. The commander of the relief column sent out from Ft. Phil Kearny to Fetterman's aid was Captain Tenador Ten Eyck, the star-crossed 18th Infantryman captured at both Munfordville in 1862 and at Chickamauga the next year. While Ten Eyck was not responsible for the destruction of Fetterman's command, the action's controversy followed this captain until the end of his days. After an unsuccessful struggle with alcoholism, he resigned in disgrace in 1871. Congress passed a special act on September 29, 1890, that finally cleared him of any wrong doing in connection with the Fetterman Fight and restored him to the rank of captain on the Regular Army's roles. He honorably retired a week later.[31]

Henry Carrington viewed his command assignment in Dakota Territory as a career-enhancing move, a chance to belatedly acquire the field experience he had consistently sidestepped in the Civil War.

After the events of December 1866, questions about the Fetterman Fight dogged him at every step. Realizing his chances were slim for surviving the army reduction of 1869–1870 with his career intact, Carrington applied for a disability retirement. The War Department granted the request, even though Carrington's most serious medical problem was an accidentally self-inflicted gunshot wound in the thigh, which occurred in early 1867 shortly after he was replaced as commander of Ft. Phil Kearny. Carrington retired on December 15, 1870, having accepted a position teaching military science at Wabash College in Crawfordville, Indiana. He served there until 1878, when the War Department withdrew funding for the program. Carrington spent most of his remaining years as an author and historian at Hyde Park, Massachusetts, publishing some respectable works on Native Americans and the American Revolution, and also repeatedly revising his second wife's Ft. Phil Kearny memoirs. He served as a special agent for the U.S. Commissioner of Indian Affairs from 1889 through 1891, with assignments ranging from negotiating a treaty with the Flathead Indians of Montana to conducting a census of the Six Nations in Upstate New York. Henry Carrington died in 1912 and is buried in Hyde Park's Fairview Cemetery. He is one of only a handful of Union Army general officers who did not receive any brevet honors for Civil War service.[32]

Fortunately for the 18th Infantry, the events connected with Fort Phil Kearny are but a small portion of an otherwise illustrious history. Following many years and campaigns on the frontier, the regiment participated in the expedition that captured Manila in 1898 and, during the following decade, saw further extensive service in the Philippines. The 18th Infantry was the first American infantry regiment to arrive in France after America's entry into World War I in 1917. Shortly thereafter, the unit was assigned to the 1st Infantry Division, the vanguard of America's Army heading to Europe for both World Wars. With the "Big Red One" the 18th fought at Meuse-Argonne, defended Kasserine Pass, and stormed Omaha Beach. Variously assigned during the post-World War II era to the 1st, 8th, and 24th Infantry Divisions, battalions of the 18th Infantry reinforced the Berlin garrison during the 1961 Wall Crisis, patrolled Route 1 out of Saigon, and assisted in the partial destruction of the Iraqi Republican Guard in 1991. Troops of the 1st Battalion, 18th Infantry, are today stationed in Germany, again wearing the shoulder patch of the 1st Infantry Division.[33]

Many officers of the 18th Infantry not tainted by the Phil Kearny disaster went on to have successful postwar careers. Henry Douglass became colonel of the 10th Infantry in 1885, but chronic poor health limited his field service. He retired in March 1891 and died just fifteen months later. Andrew Burt eventually became a regimental commander also. He served under Colonel John King in the 9th Infantry from 1869 until 1883. After nine further years of field-grade service with the 7th and 8th Regiments (he was often heard to say during that time: "Captain of the 9th, major in the 8th, lieutenant colonel in the 7th, heaven help the 6th!"), Burt became colonel of the African-American 25th Infantry Regiment in 1892. He was appointed a brigadier general of volunteers during the Spanish-American War, but his brigade did not participate in that conflict's brief campaigns. Reverting to his regular rank of colonel, he led the 25th Infantry across the Pacific and served in the Philippine War for two years. He returned to the United States in 1901 and became a brigadier in the regulars on April 1, 1902. He retired two weeks later and lived in Washington until his death in 1915. Burt's son Reynolds graduated from West Point in 1896. As a disbursing officer for the U.S. Army Signal Corps, he signed the $2,500 check paid to the Wright Brothers in 1909 for the U.S. Army's first airplane. Reynolds Burt later became a general officer himself and commanded the 15th Infantry garrison in China during the 1930s.[34]

George Washington Smith was not present with the 18th Infantry in the Dakotas after the war, for he was not in the army while the saga of Ft. Phil Kearny played itself out. He resigned his commission in April 1866, a decision he came to regret. Dissatisfaction with the awarding of brevet rank after the war was the root of his discontent and his complaint was as a valid as anyone's. When the Regular Brigade headed north for Chattanooga in September 1864, Smith remained in the field as adjutant of Carlin's division. During the 1865 campaign in the Carolinas, Smith served as an aide-de-camp to Major General Jefferson C. Davis and saw action at the Battles of Averysborough and Bentonville. For all of that experience, not to mention being the only person who ever came close to filling the leadership vacuum existing in the 18th Regulars after Oliver Shepherd was put on the shelf, Smith ended the war with but a single brevet, for Chickamauga. He had been recommended for two additional brevets, but as far as he knew, they had never been approved. He wrote a letter to his congressmen in December 1865, stating his frustrations: "As a soldier by profession I have some bitter times when I see scores of men getting Brevets who have never seen one half the fighting I have." Four months later he decided to call it quits. "I have served thirty months of the war in the field," Smith complained to the War Department on April 16, 1866. "During the last two years and four months of the war I never asked for nor received a leave of absence, nor was I away from my duties in the field for one day; and the only leave I had throughout the war was to command a Regt of Volunteers." He resigned his commission five days later.[35]

Smith took up residence in Lawrence, Kansas, where he worked in his father's law office and commanded the local post of the Grand Army of the Republic. He was shocked when he glanced at a copy of the Army Register in August 1867 and found out that at some point after his resignation he had been awarded the brevet of lieutenant colonel for gallant and meritorious service during the Atlanta Campaign. His military aspirations slowly rekindled, and in June 1873 he applied for a Regular Army commission. Smith became a regular officer again, this time wearing the yellow shoulder straps of a cavalryman that had been his dream since 1861, but his resignation had cost him: he was a second lieutenant, not a captain and brevet lieutenant colonel. In August 1873, he reported for duty with the 9th Cavalry, one of the army's most famous regiments of "Buffalo Soldiers," and quickly proved to be the same industrious officer that he had been a decade earlier with the 18th Infantry. But peacetime promotions came very slowly, and he was still a second lieutenant eight years later while commanding a troop of cavalry during a skirmish with Apaches in the Membres Mountains of New Mexico on August 19, 1881. During the course of the action he was hit in the chest. His men begged him to dismount and seek cover, but Lieutenant Smith replied: "Never while breath is in me!" A second round struck him a moment later and he slid from the saddle, dead before he hit the ground. His remains were brought back to Lawrence, and he was laid to rest in Oak Hill Cemetery.[36]

William Bisbee probably saw as much action as any American officer did in the nineteenth century. Following extensive Civil War service, he participated in numerous campaigns of the Indian Wars. After serving in the Santiago Campaign as lieutenant colonel of the 1st U.S. Infantry, he took command of the 13th Infantry and led that regiment to the Philippines. Promoted to brigadier general in 1901, he spent a year commanding a brigade in the Philippine War prior to retiring in 1902. Bisbee then returned to his native New England and enjoyed a quiet retirement in Brookline, Massachusetts. He eschewed involvement with veteran's groups, but publicity found the aging soldier anyway in 1940, when he was awarded the Purple Heart Medal for his Civil War wounds and received a letter of commendation from President Franklin D. Roosevelt. When during the early days of the Second World War he was asked his opinion of the war in Europe, the veteran of four American wars replied simply: "I leave that to those better qualified." William Bisbee outlived all other officers of the Regular Brigade. He died at the age of 102 on June 11, 1942, and is buried in Arlington National Cemetery.[37]

Henry B. Freeman saw just as much action as Bisbee did in the years following the Civil War. Freeman was promoted to captain in 1866 and, four years later, transferred to the 7th U.S. Infantry, a regiment that saw extensive service during the Indian Wars. One of the chilling events of his tour of duty with that regiment was participating in the 1876 Sioux Campaign, during which Captain Freeman commanded the first contingent of infantrymen to reach the site of Lieutenant Colonel George Custer's defeat along the banks of the Little Big Horn River in Montana.

Freeman had a passion for marksmanship. His company won the coveted Army Trophy an unprecedented three years in a row during the 1880s. Many of his efficiency reports contained remarks similar to Colonel Henry C. Merriam's from 1890. The report required the rater to note if the rated officer "has shown any desire to go beyond the ordinary routine of his duty," and on Freeman that year Merriam wrote: "Nothing unless it be the art of teaching soldiers to shoot, in which he excels." Freeman's expertise with small arms landed him a position on the Magazine Gun Board, which convened in 1891 to select a modern replacement for the army's aging inventory of trap door Springfield rifles. Freeman was the board's leading advocate for the superb Danish-designed Krag-Jörgensen, a .30-caliber, bolt-action rifle with a five-round magazine that ultimately won the competition and was carried by the regulars in the Spanish-American War.

After spending thirty years as a company-grade officer, promotions came rapidly to Freeman in the 1890s. In 1891, he became a major in the 16th Infantry and was made lieutenant colonel of the

5th Infantry just four years later. He commanded the 5th regulars during the war with Spain, but his regiment was relegated to garrison duty in Florida while others embarked for Cuba. In October 1898, Freeman become colonel of the 24th Infantry. He took that regiment to the Philippines in 1899 and commanded a large district on the island of Luzon during the Philippine War. His performance in the Far East earned him the "highest praise" from the commander of U.S. forces in the Philippines, Major General Arthur MacArthur. Freeman retired in 1901 as a brigadier general, having been awarded the Medal of Honor in 1894 for rescuing Captain Henry Douglass during the retreat across the cotton field at Stones River. After a brief stint serving as an instructor with the Kansas National Guard at Leavenworth, he spent his remaining years living comfortably on an expansive ranch along the La Bonte River in Wyoming. General Freeman died in 1915 and is buried in Arlington National Cemetery. He kept detailed journals and wrote lengthy reminiscences of his military experiences, one of which was published in 1977 as *The Freeman Journal: The Infantry in the Sioux Campaign of 1876*, a classic account of frontier operations written from an infantryman's perspective.[38]

Anson Mills transferred from the infantry to the cavalry in 1871. He played a key role at the Battle of the Rosebud in 1876, leading two troops of the 3rd Cavalry on a wide flanking movement of Sitting Bull's warriors. Moving on to less hazardous duties, Mills was the American military representative to the 1878 Paris International Exposition and served on the Mexican-American International Boundary Commission from 1894 until 1914, a tribunal that adjudicated boundary disputes between the two nations. He became colonel of the 3rd Cavalry in 1892 and pinned on a general's star just prior to his retirement in 1897.

In the years following the Civil War, Mills made a name for himself as an inventor, taking out patents on items as diverse as bayonets, spurs, typewriters, and a tubular metallic pole for telegraph wires. He also launched a successful business career, although it took him some time to make a profit. With metallic cartridges quickly replacing the paper variety after the Civil War, Mills designed a woven cartridge belt that more comfortably carried small arms ammunition, a replacement for the infantryman's unwieldy cartridge box. Mills perfected the belt's innovative woven design and the machine to manufacture it by the late 1870s. He then formed the

Mills-Orndorff Cartridge Belt Company in Worchester, Massachusetts, with his brother-in-law Thomas C. Orndorff. The U.S. Army adopted the "Mills Belt" as its standard cartridge belt in 1880, although the small army of that era did not generate much in the way of orders. Mills cranked up production at the onset of the Spanish-American War, but the quick termination of that conflict resulted in Mills-Orndorff having no buyers, a pile of excess inventory, and mounting indebtedness.

Financial success for Mills came the next year, from across the Atlantic. When the Boer War in South Africa broke out in 1899, William Lindsey, an associate of Mills, bought the rights to manufacture Mills Belts in Great Britain. Lindsey was so confident that the British Army would want the belts that he set up a factory in London before anyone in Britain had even examined the product. Lindsey's confidence was on the mark, for as soon as Her Majesty's Quartermaster General, Lieutenant General Sir Henry Brackenbury, saw the belt he placed an immediate order. The field gear was extremely popular with British forces in South Africa, and the factories in London and Massachusetts were soon shipping Mills Belts and a number of variants as fast as they could be produced. By the time Anson Mills died in 1924, soldiers of many nations had worn Mills Belts on battlefields around the world. William Lindsey's subsidiary firm in London later became the Mills Equipment Company, Limited, which designed most the British Army's cartridge belts, packs, and other field gear for both World Wars.[39]

Along with Henry Carrington and Oliver Shepherd, Frederick Townsend was one of the key players who forged the 18th Infantry into one of the Regular Army's premier units of the Civil War. After Townsend's departure from the field during the spring of 1863, he spent the balance of the war on staff duty in New York. He was promoted to lieutenant colonel of the 9th Infantry in 1864, and after the war briefly served in California on the staff of the Department of the Pacific. Townsend resigned his commission in 1868 and returned to New York. He then had a successful business career, and became a trustee of a number of downstate colleges and universities. Townsend also remained active in the New York National Guard. The nation's widespread railroad strikes and labor unrest of 1877 exposed the decayed condition of most state militia forces, which in turn sparked a nationwide movement of militia reform and modernization. Large industrial states like New York led the way in this process, and to lead the state's effort it turned to men with professional military experience. Townsend become a National Guard brigadier in 1878; in 1880, he was appointed adjutant general of the state of New York, the same post he had held prior to the Civil War. "Most assuredly the time has come for the fancy soldier and the politician to step out from the Guard," Townsend bluntly declared in his 1880 annual report, "and the Guard to settle down to the professional work of the soldier." Townsend served as adjutant general three additional years, putting the New York National Guard on the road to becoming a force useful for both civil emergencies and national defense. The *Albany Times* reported in November 1889, eight years prior to his death in 1897, that Townsend had met with some success: "In this post [state adjutant general] he again turned his attention to a long cherished idea of further developing State troops, which, among other progressive measures, culminated in his establishing the 'Camp of Instruction' in Peekskill, and providing the service dress uniform for all the troops of the State. ...In the quietude of his handsome mansion on Elk street, General Townsend is enjoying the fruits of his well-earned military laurels, the respect and esteem of his fellow-citizens, and surrounded by all that makes domestic life pleasing and attractive."[40]

One of Townsend's first acts upon being appointed adjutant general in 1880 was to obtain for New York State the services of his wartime battalion adjutant, Frederick Phisterer. It was a position well suited to Phisterer's administrative skills, and he just happened to be in need of a job. Phisterer had been posted to Fort Phil Kearny as adjutant of the 18th Infantry in 1866, but fortunately departed the ill-fated fort five months prior to the Fetterman Fight for duty with the headquarters of the army's General Recruiting Service in New York City. Henry Carrington was sorry to see the officer he had commissioned in 1861 leave Dakota Territory:

> In parting with Capt. Phisterer, who has been identified with the 18th U.S. Infantry from its organization, and whose duties in the office and the field have signally honored his name and commander, my personal admiration and great respect, I am constrained to express my sincere regret at the separation, which, while it deservedly carries him into a higher grade of duty, deprives me of the cooperation of an officer, who has proved his entire devotion to the interests of the service, his regiment, and his colonel.

This assurance is a sincere tribute to his merit and he will be followed with my best wishes for even higher preferment, knowing that he will well deserve the confidence of his superiors, wherever he may serve.[41]

Phisterer was back on duty in Dakota Territory by late 1868, but his service in the regular army was coming to an end. With the downsizing of 1869, he decided the time was ripe to move on to other fields. He had a family to support and did not think he could properly do so on army pay. He also thought his stamina was not what it used to be, as he explained in his resignation request: "Having served in the Army as an enlisted man from 1855 until 1860, from July 1861 until October 1861, and as a Commissioned Officer ever since, my health is not firm enough any more to enable me to do my duty as an officer to my own satisfaction, while at the same time it is not impaired enough to entitle me to be retired, and my discharge will give the service the benefit of a more active man."[42]

Resigning his regular commission in 1870, Phisterer and his wife Isabel returned to Ohio (she was a native of Zanesville) and the ex-captain tried to earn a living without wearing a uniform. Similar to his job-hunting in 1855, Phisterer's business endeavors during the 1870s never bore fruit. He first attempted farming, then set up a sign-making shop, and finally ran a grocery store. He never managed to turn much of a profit. The weak American economy of that decade compounded Phisterer's problems and he sank deeper and deeper into dept. Soldiering was his natural calling, and seven years after leaving the regulars he began wearing a uniform again. He commanded a company of "citizens' police" in Columbus during the 1877 rail strikes. His unit was subsequently incorporated into the new Ohio National Guard. Phisterer continued in command of the company, receiving a captain's commission from the governor of Ohio. He served part-time in the Ohio Guard for a few more years, all the while still struggling in his civilian pursuits.

His big break came in January 1880. Adjutant General Frederick Townsend contacted Phisterer and offered him the post of assistant adjutant general of the New York National Guard with the rank of colonel. Phisterer accepted and moved to Albany, for a time supplementing his Guard income by teaching military science at a local boy's academy. By the mid-1880s, his duties with the Adjutant General's Department began taking up all of his time. He served in various command and staff positions, was secretary of a commission that revised New York's military code, worked with the state's Bureau of Muster Rolls to accurately document the Civil War service of New York volunteers, and each summer was post adjutant of the New York Guard's training camp near Peekskill. Phisterer received the Medal of Honor for his Stones River exploits in 1894 (ironically, Phisterer was one of the few officers of 2/18th U.S. who did not receive a brevet for that battle) and five years later was breveted as a National Guard brigadier general. He became a brevet major general in 1905. In addition to writing a number of essays about the Regular Army, Phisterer authored the voluminous *New York in the War of the Rebellion, 1861–1865*, compiled the groundbreaking *Statistical Record of the Armies of the United States*, and also wrote a number of training manuals for National Guardsmen. The 73-year-old Phisterer was still on duty with the Guard when he died in 1909. Upon his death, New York Governor Charles Evans Hughes proclaimed: "The life of General Phisterer, during a long career of Public Service, has been characterized by loyalty to country and unswerving devotion to duty. Few officers have done so much as he to promote the efficiency of the state's military forces, and he is entitled to be called 'the father of the National Guard of this state.'" Between Townsend and Phisterer, the New York National Guard could not have asked for surer hands to prepare that institution for the challenges of the twentieth century. Phisterer was laid to rest in Greenlawn Cemetery, Columbus, Ohio.[43]

* *

The 19th Infantry Regiment

The 19th U.S. Infantry was not the place to be after the Civil War. It spent nine long years on Reconstruction duty in Louisiana and Arkansas before moving west in 1874. After seven years of garrison duty in Colorado, Kansas, and Indian Territory, in 1881 the regiment was posted on the Rio Grande in Texas. Trying to avoid periodic yellow fever outbreaks took up most of the 19th Infantry's time in the Lone Star State, so its members were grateful in 1890 when the regiment was finally brought back East. Life in the 19th Infantry became considerably more exciting at the turn of the century. The regiment participated in the expedition to Puerto Rico in 1898 and went on to earn seven battle streamers in the Philippine War. The 19th Infantry garrisoned Hawaii for thirty-eight years prior to

World War II and was assigned to the 24th Infantry Division in 1941. With the 24th, it fought in the Southwest Pacific and spearheaded General Douglas MacArthur's return to the Philippines in 1944. The 19th Infantry was one of the first units sent to Korea in 1950, earning many honors during that conflict. Today, two battalions of this regiment are part of the Infantry Training Brigade at Fort Benning.[44]

Similar to the passing of William Terrill, the death of Major Stephen D. Carpenter cut short the career of an up-and-coming regular officer. The citizens of Bangor, Maine, partially motivated by the patriotic fervor displayed in February 1863 at Carpenter's burial, on June 17, 1864, dedicated a monument in Mt. Hope Cemetery to the community's war dead. This obelisk monument was the first Civil War memorial in Maine and certainly among the first in the country. Major Carpenter's casket was moved to the monument plat, which became the site of additional war burials and the focal point for the region's remembrance services. As the war went on and additional war dead were buried at Mt. Hope, the monument plat became crowded with graves. Yearly remembrance ceremonies were conducted there after the war, and several of the gravesites suffered damage. At the request of the families involved, all but two of the soldiers buried around the monument were eventually moved elsewhere in the cemetery. So, in 1881, the remains of the 19th Infantry's major were once again moved, this time to a hillside that overlooks the grave of Hannibal Hamlin, Lincoln's first vice president. The inscription on the oft-buried regular's grave marker reads: "A Brave Soldier and a Patriot, He Sleeps Well."[45]

Captain Alfred Lacy Hough's Civil War field experiences with the 19th Infantry were confined to just a few months in the spring and summer of 1862, but the detailed letters he wrote to his wife throughout the war (which were published in 1957 as *Soldier in the West: The Civil War Letters of Alfred Lacey Hough*) are a rich commentary on many aspects of the sectional conflict. Hough continued in the regulars after the war. Although he advanced steadily in rank and was promoted to colonel of the 9th Infantry two years prior to his retirement in 1890, Hough's most significant postwar service was not serving as an officer of the line. He was detailed to George Thomas's personal staff just prior to the end of the Civil War, and in the late 1860s became the general's principal aide-de-camp. Hough was present at Thomas's bedside when the general died in 1870; for twenty years thereafter he was a close friend of Thomas's wife. Colonel Hough became one of the late general's staunchest defenders during the 1870s and 1880s, the era when Grant, Sherman, and others were embellishing their own records at Thomas's expense, and was a major contributor to *The Life of Major-General George H. Thomas*, Thomas B. Van Horne's 1882 biography of the general. Colonel Hough died in 1908.[46]

Arthur B. Carpenter also remained in the army after the war. He quickly determined that drab peacetime routines were not nearly as exciting as wartime service. "I would rather be in the Field bleeding and dying for my Country," Carpenter wrote in late 1865 while on recruiting duty in Erie, Pennsylvania. He was promoted to captain in January 1866, but a few more years of garrison duty was all he could take. From the tone of his postwar letters it is apparent that Carpenter's transition from wartime to peacetime was painful. "Camp life agrees with me better than any other," he wrote to his mother in 1866, more than a year after the war. "I sleep with my windows open, and wash myself all over in cold water every Sunday." Carpenter married and started a family in 1869; he resigned his commission in 1871, another victim of the 1869 army downsizing, and died twenty years later. The collection of his letters deposited at Yale University is one of the most extensive primary sources available pertaining to the Civil War regulars.[47]

* * *

III: The Commanders

The three officers who commanded the Regular Brigade for the majority of the unit's existence, Oliver Shepherd, John King, and John Edie, all remained in uniform after the war. Their postwar careers were quite different.

Edie's military service came to a bitter end in 1871. Following promotion to lieutenant colonel of the 8th U.S. Infantry, Edie spent 1865 at Hancock Barracks in Baltimore. In January 1866, he assumed command of the post at Harper's Ferry, West Virginia. Edie's troubles began three years later, when Congress cut twenty infantry regiments from the Regular Army's roles. This reduction in force structure triggered a corresponding reduction in the strength of the army officer corps. Deciding who would go was a painful process. The mechanism for doing so was included in the 1870 Army Appropriations Bill. A "List of Supernumeraries" was created, upon which were placed the names of all officers without a billet in the remaining twenty-five regiments. The bill further specified: "All vacancies now existing, or which may occur prior to the first day of January next, in the cavalry, artillery, or infantry, by reason of such transfer or from other causes, shall be filled in due proportion by the supernumerary officers, having reference to rank, seniority and fitness, as provided in existing law regulating promotions in the army. And if any supernumerary officers shall remain after the first day of January next, they shall be honorably mustered out of the service with one year's pay and allowances."[48]

As 1870 drew to a close there were twenty-five infantry regiments in the army and twenty-six infantry lieutenant colonels on the active list. The excess officer was John Edie. On December 15, 1870, Lieutenant Colonel Edie was relieved from duty with the 8th Infantry and his name was placed on the supernumerary list. His future in the army looked bleak. Edie's prospects brightened later that December as Colonel John D. Stevenson of the 25th Infantry Regiment requested discharge. Secretary of War William W. Belknap signed the order on December 31, with the discharge to take effect the following day. Having heard of the impending vacancy, Edie journeyed to the commanding general's office in Washington on New Year's Eve, 1870. After listening to Edie's case, General Sherman penned a quick note to Secretary Belknap:

HEADQUARTERS ARMY OF THE UNITED STATES
Washington, D.C.
Dec 31 1870

Genl. W.W. Belknap
  Sec. of War

Dear Sir,

Excuse my intruding on you at this moment.

Lt Col Edie is here. He is the only Lt Col left out. [This is] unfortunate for he has served continuously since 1861, and was with us at Atlanta & Jonesboro.

By accepting Stevenson's resignation & promoting a Lt Col we can retain Edie.

Are you willing?

W.T. SHERMAN
Genl[49]

A clerk hurried to the secretary's office and delivered the message. He returned a few minutes later with Belknap's reply:

Dear General,

I have accepted Stevenson's resignation this morning & have arranged as to the promotions thereby occurring. Col. Mack has the list & left here a few moments ago. As to Edie I have heard so much against him that I do not like to retain him. Carlin spoke to me about his conduct at Jonesboro, which was very unfavorable. However I leave the matter to you & the President. If any change is made see Mack & correct his list. But I cannot conceal my unfavorable opinion as to Edie.

Yours truly, WWB[50]

There is no record of whether or not Sherman concurred with the secretary's opinion. What is known is that George L. Andrews, lieutenant colonel of the 25th Regulars, was appointed colonel of the regiment in place of Stevenson. Levi C. Bootes, a major in the 20th Infantry, moved up to Andrews's vacated position as lieutenant colonel of the 25th. Edie was mustered out of service effective January 1, 1871.

Belknap's response must have hit Edie like a slap in the face. There had never been any question of "unfavorable" conduct at Jonesboro. William P. Carlin, the person who had whispered this notion in Belknap's ear, immediately after that battle went out of his way to complement the regulars. He wrote in his Jonesboro report that the Regular Brigade's attack "was made with great energy and gallantry." Edie had subsequently been awarded a brevet colonelcy for "gallant and meritorious service during the Atlanta Campaign & at the battle of Jonesboro Ga." Perhaps Carlin was just trying to do everything he could to secure a promotion for George Andrews (Carlin had served under one of Andrews's relatives in the 6th U.S. Infantry during the 1850s). Perhaps also Carlin, who had received wartime brevet promotions to major general in both the Regular Army and the volunteer service, now simply could not stand the thought of being outranked by one of his former brigade commanders. Carlin, a West Pointer from the Class of 1850, had reverted to his Regular Army rank of major at war's end. He was still a major in December 1870. It was no doubt irritating to Carlin that Edie, who had resigned from West Point after less than a year at the Academy and was then directly appointed as a major of the

15th Regulars in 1861, now had a chance to be the colonel of a Regular Army infantry regiment.[51]

Edie did not take this treatment lying down. As a resident of Pennsylvania, he contacted Simon Cameron, the former secretary of war who was then serving as a United States senator:

Washington D.C.
Jany 22nd 1871

Genl Simon Cameron

Dear Sir,

I have the honor to submit for your consideration the following as, in my judgement, the true view of the law as applicable to my case.

By the Act of 15th July/70 the President was authorized to make transfers of officers from the Cavalry, Artillery, and Infantry to the list of Supernumerary officers and all vacancies existing prior to the 1st January/71 were to be filled by assignments from the Supernumeraries, having due regard to "Seniority, Rank, and Fitness."

Before the 1st Jan'y 1871, Col. John D. Stevenson resigned, thus leaving a vacancy in the list of Colonels to be filled according to law by the next ranking officer on the list of Supernumeraries. I was that next ranking officer and hold that the moment the vacancy occurred I was by operation of law the Colonel of the 25th Inf'y, this office being vacated by the resignation of Col. Stevenson, and consequently my muster out on the 1st of Jan'y/71 was illegal and void.

I have already submitted to you my military record and do not desire to trouble you with it again.

If I have not greatly erred in my view of the Case, a great wrong has been done me. Why I know not, but I much fear that the President has been deceived by some one who either wanted my place for himself or some friend.

Very Respectfully
Your Obedient Servant
JOHN R. EDIE[52]

Unfortunately for Edie, the extent of Cameron's assistance was simply to forward this letter to Secretary of War Belknap. Cameron did take the time to attach a note: "Respectfully referred to the Secy of War with the hope that whatever can be done for Mr. Edie will be done." While Belknap had no intention of doing "whatever" he could for Edie, he could not completely ignore a request from the powerful Pennsylvania senator. Belknap turned the case over to the Justice Department for final disposition. On February 11, 1871, U.S. Attorney General Amos T. Akerman (whose resume included service as an officer in the Confederate army) issued his opinion:

> There can be no question that on the 1st day of January Lieutenant Colonel Edie was a supernumerary officer, and that if he then possessed the proper rank, seniority, and fitness, he would have had a valid claim to promotion to a vacancy which had occurred prior to that day. I do not think that he had any just claim to a vacancy which did not begin to exist until that day. Colonel Stevenson's resignation took effect on that day. The vacancy thereby created did not occur prior to that day, and does not belong to that class of vacancies which, under the law, were to be filled by the supernumerary officers. The vacancies which Congress intended that supernumeraries should fill were, not all vacancies which might occur before their discharge, but only such vacancies as should occur before the first day of January 1871.
>
> I am, therefore, of the opinion that Lieutenant Colonel Edie was not lawfully entitled to the place made vacant by the resignation of Colonel Stevenson, and that he was lawfully mustered out of service by the order of January 2, 1871.[53]

The law could have easily been interpreted otherwise, that Congress did indeed intend for supernumerary officers to fill "all vacancies which might occur before their discharge." For that to have happened, Edie would have needed vigorous assistance from Sherman, Belknap, or Cameron. Carlin's smear campaign ensured that such assistance was not forthcoming. John Edie's ten years of service in the Regular Army shed light upon his life's story. With his return to civilian pursuits, his endeavors retreat back into the shadows. He died on August 27, 1888.[54]

* * *

For John H. "Iron Bull" King, there was no hesitation in deciding to remain in the army after the war—his military service totaled twenty-eight years by 1865 and soldiering was in his blood. While King had a very successful career both during the war and afterward, details about his life are unfortunately few. Any personal papers he may have left behind are yet to be discovered. Even his personnel file in the National Archives contains little useful information about his service. There can be no doubt, though, that John King was a respected officer and revered commander. Scattered references about him are unanimous in their praise. In the years following the war, King received the brevet of major general in both the Regular Army and the volunteers for his Civil War service.[55]

While commanding the Military District of Augusta, Georgia, in the summer of 1865, King was promoted to colonel of the 9th U.S. Infantry. The new colonel ended his Reconstruction responsibilities and returned to the frontier duty the Civil War had interrupted. He served his remaining years of active duty in the West, being stationed in California, Wyoming, and Nebraska. While commanding the post at Fort Omaha in 1877, King and his 9th Regiment were dispatched to Chicago to assist civil authorities in suppressing the widespread labor violence of that year's railroad strikes. King commanded a force of twenty-one companies of regulars in the Windy City, troops that performed yeomen service in ending the violence. William Bisbee, then a captain in the 22nd Infantry, served as King's adjutant during the Chicago operations. Commander and adjutant were billeted in the bridal suite of the Palmer House Hotel, where Bisbee remembered that their rough frontier uniforms and equipment stood in stark contrast "against the beautiful saffron draperies of the room."[56]

After nearly seventeen years in command of the 9th Infantry, King retired in 1882. He lived briefly in his hometown of Detroit before settling down in the nation's capitol. Pneumonia struck him down on April 27, 1888, and he was laid to rest in Arlington National Cemetery. A constellation of generals attended the military funeral, as well as most of Michigan's congressional delegation. Tributes for John King quickly followed, one of which was written by William T. Sherman:

> The period of his service was his whole manhood, covering the most important epoch of American history, and very few men of today realize what they owe of the growth in power, physical resources, cultivation, and refinement [of America] to the little Regular Army commanded by such men as John H. King. When in 1861 this whole country became convulsed by civil war, and when so many of his comrades abandoned their colors, he stood fast, firm in the faith and did a man's whole share. ...It would take a volume to do justice to the subject, and as much of his service was directly under my command, I do a simple but grateful duty in adding this small tribute to his memory.[57]

Six years after John King relinquished command of the 9th Infantry, the men of that regiment still recalled their former commander fondly. A few months after King passed away, the soldiers of his old regiment published a tribute to their late colonel in the *Army and Navy Journal*: "Time is said to blunt the sense of gratitude, but while memory shall last the nobility of his character will be treasured, and he will be revered as one who, in the possession of virtues that go to make up the Officer and Gentleman, had but few peers in the Army–old or new. NINTH INF.."[58]

* * *

Oliver L. Shepherd did not have any such tributes penned in his honor. While Shepherd may have taken pride in making both the 15th and 18th Regiments two of the Regular Army's finest, he was nothing but disappointed about his military record as the Civil War ended. Shepherd had been one of the army's rising stars prior to the rebellion. Between service in the Seminole War, numerous Mexican campaigns, and battles with the Navajos, he was one of the most combat-experienced officers of the antebellum army. In 1861 Shepherd was one of a small group of proven field-grade Regular Army officers upon whom the nation would look for military leadership.

Unlike so many of his peers, rank and recognition eluded Shepherd throughout the Civil War. He never held a high-ranking volunteer commission and had no powerful political allies. Having cast his lot with the regulars in the Western Theater throughout the conflict, Shepherd shared in the regulars' overall anonymity. He ended the war a colonel, and had not a single brevet promotion to his credit for Civil War service. Shepherd's lack of brevets was a common source of discontent among the veterans of the Regular Brigade, for very few of them received any brevets during the war. Those who did, such as Frank Guenther, were granted the honor only after intense lobbying efforts from multiple general officers. John King was as frustrated as anyone in the Regular Brigade. He took a big step toward correcting this lack of brevets by sending a list of deserving officers to the War Department just before the brigade was officially disbanded:

Headquarters, Regular Brigade
Army of the Cumberland

Lookout Mountain Tennessee
July 4th 1865

Genl L. Thomas
War Department,
Washington

Inasmuch as very many Officers of the Regular Army serving in the army of the Potomac, with Major Genl Sherman, and with various other commanders, have received one or more brevets during the progress of the late rebellion, as a simple act of justice to the meritorious Officers of the "Regular Brigade" Army of the Cumberland, I have the honor respectfully to request that the following named officers who are now or who have formerly been serving with this Brigade, may be recommended for Brevets in the Army of the United States.

JOHN H. KING
Brevet Maj Gen'l
Commd'g[59]

King's list included the names of fifty-eight officers. It was naturally weighted heavily in favor those who had served in the Regular Brigade during King's command tenure, the two-year period from mid-1863 through the summer of 1865. He was somewhat conservative in his requests, suggesting a single brevet for an officer and then listing the major battles in which the officer participated, such as: "Captain Thomas J. Norton, to be a Major by Brevet for the battle of Missionary Ridge and the Atlanta Campaign, to date from September 1st 1864." Lieutenant General Grant approved the list and sent it to the Secretary of War on November 3, 1865. The final version of the list that emerged from the United States Senate in early 1866 differed from King's original request, for the Senate had approved brevets for only the last battle in which an officer participated. When the smoke cleared, twenty-two regulars received brevets for the Atlanta Campaign, eight each received the honor for Stones River, Chickamauga, and Missionary Ridge, a single brevet was awarded for Shiloh, and three more were for generic service during the war. While the recipients appreciated the brevets, receiving them so long after the fact watered down their meaning considerably. Many of the officers had already been promoted in full to the brevet rank they were awarded.[60]

An interesting event occurred four days after General Grant approved King's brevet requests. Oliver Shepherd's long-lost request for Stones River brevets, written shortly after that battle, was retrieved from wherever it had been gathering dust in the War Department and was stamped "Received AGO [Adjutant General's Office] Nov 7 65." A clerk placed the list on the desk of Colonel Ely S. Parker, Grant's military secretary. Shepherd's list was undated; Parker probably did not realize that almost three years had passed since it was compiled, and thought it was just another postwar list of brevet requests for the Regular Brigade, similar to the King list. Since the latter list contained more names, covered more than just a single battle, and most importantly was already on its way to the Senate, Parker hurriedly dismissed Shepherd's list in a short note: "Gen. King's list of July 4 1865 for the Regular Infantry, Army of the Cumberland, is deemed the best."[61]

The first round of the Regular Brigade's struggle to receive Civil War brevets ended with only eight officers being honored for Stones River.[62] Oliver Shepherd was not one of them. John King had not included Shepherd's name on the 1865 brevet list, perhaps feeling that it was not appropriate for a subordinate to recommend a commander for an award. But if nothing else, Shepherd was an ambitious man when it came to his own record and the Regular Brigade's role in the winter battle near Murfreesboro. He organized another campaign to have the Regular Brigade's Stones River service receive just recognition. The effort began in early 1866, when a board of general officers convened in St. Louis to review the Civil War record of thousands of officers and confer brevets where appropriate. A letter from one of Shepherd's former 18th Infantry subordinates energized the colonel into action. The man who penned the correspondence had a desire for high rank and postwar military glory that even Shepherd could not match:

Cleveland, Ohio February 10th, 1866

My dear Colonel,

Feeling that you still entertain an interest for the 18th Infantry which has never ceased to acknowledge its great indebtedness to you for all that it is in discipline and efficiency, I have taken the liberty of addressing you in behalf of the officers of the 2nd Battalion of that Regiment who fought under you at "Stone River" and with you did there such good service. Though the services of the "Regular Brigade" on that day have been acknowledged by all inteligent officers connected with that army, and though it has received the highest praise from its gallant Division Commander, the only one of the army of Generals who at that time had the boldness to manifest any interest in us or to express a commendation of our services, no recognition has ever been made of those services by the Government[.] While Regular officers in the Eastern army have received two and even three brevets for services which though "gallant and meritorious" could not have been more so, than those rendered by the "Regulars" at "Stone River." Most of us have received brevets for "Atlanta" which while duly appreciated do not afford one tithe of the satisfaction which a Brevet for "Stone River" would confer. Stone River is the hardest and most eventful battle in the history of our Regiment, and the services of the Regiment there were probably of more value, than the balance of its services during the war, and the recognition of them by the Government would be correspondingly appreciated. We have been hoping that during the distribution of rewards for services of far less importance than we maintain ours to have been, that we would not be forgotten, but the "Regulars" of the west have received but little consideration from the Government. Had you remained in command we probably would have received full justice, for you were ever untiring in your labors for our interests. It is thought by the officers that the present is an excellent opportunity to prefer our claims. General Rousseau being in Congress, and a warm friend of yours and ours, besides being our Division Commander at the battle.

We are well aware that you are thoroughly acquainted with everything pertaining to the Regiment of which you were the parent and feel confident that you will be glad to do anything that will promote the interests of those with whom you were so long associated in so many hardships and dangers.

We have thought of you often since you left us, and never without regret that you were still not our Commander. Hoping that I may have the pleasure of hearing from you, I remain with highest esteem,

Yours very truly,

WILLIAM J. FETTERMAN[63]

Shepherd forwarded Fetterman's letter to Congressman Rousseau and sent a letter to General Sherman, who was a member of the St. Louis board, asking him "to urge our classmate Genl Thomas, to remember to do justice to the officers of the Regular Brigade in his [Army of the] Cumberland, which saved the important battle of Stone River Dec. 31, 1862."[64] He also contacted George Thomas directly:

Fort Adams, R.I.
March 12, 1866.

Major Genl Geo H. Thomas,
U.S. Army.

General:

Observing from the Army & Navy Journal, that you are detailed as a member of the Board to convene at St. Louis, to investigate the Subject of Brevet nominations and to make recommendations therefore, I take the liberty of enclosing a copy of a letter from Bvt. Major Fetterman, 18th Inf., where [is stated] the claims of Officers of the Regular Brigade under your Command at Stone River Dec 31, 1862.

He states in this letter that the Service of the Brigade equaled in Merit in that battle, all the balance of its service subsequently.

I was informed in March 1863, unofficially, by an officer in the Adjutant General's Office, that the Brevet of Brigadier, was to be conferred upon me for commanding that Brigade on so important an occasion, in which case I should have been too happy to have returned to the Army of the Cumberland, where further Service and distinction was hoped for.

My name however, was lost in the Swarm from the Army of the Potomac at that time.

I wish to see justice done to the gallant officers who survived the heroic dead at Murfreesboro, whose memory seems to desire some such recognition.

Your own observations will enable you to judge the merits of these officers.

Congratulating you upon your achievements, I have the honor to remain very truly your friend & Lieut.,

O.L. SHEPHERD
Col, 15th Inf..[65]

The St. Louis board completed its work in the early summer of 1866. General Thomas and his peers sent their recommendations to the War Department, where Secretary Stanton forwarded them to the president. On July 20, President Andrew Johnson sent the brevet recommendations to the U.S. Senate for approval. The recommendations were referred to the Committee on Military and Militia Affairs on July 26 and were approved the next day. The senators had quickly approved the awards, but it would be many months before the War Department printed and mailed the requisite certificates to all the recipients. As the year went by, Shepherd began to worry that his service had been overlooked once again. While traveling home on furlough to visit his family in New York City during December 1866, Shepherd shared a railcar with Ambrose Burnside, the former commander of the Army of the Potomac and recently elected Governor of Rhode Island. The two had become acquainted during Shepherd's assignment at Fort Adams. After listening to the colonel's concerns, Burnside sent a letter to the commanding general:

New York City
December 28th 1866

General U.S. Grant

My Dear General,

I would like to bring to your attention the name of an Officer whose faithful Service in the Army, not only during the Rebellion but in the Mexican War, when he distinguished himself and received flattering testimonials from his Commanding Officers, deserves recognition. I refer to Col O.L. Shepherd of the 15th Regular Infantry & now stationed at Macon Geo.

His case was brought before me incidentally while traveling with him in the cars, and it seems to me to be one of deserved merit, but has not been recognized by the Government.

Col Shepherd served with inferior rank in the war with Mexico, and afterwards on the frontier, being at the breaking out of the Rebellion in Texas, from which place he brought away a large force of Regular troops, against the designs of the Rebel Authorities then collecting their forces in that state. From the fall of 1861...up to the spring of 1863, his service was arduous, faithful and untiring; serving in the field and through the heaviest battles...motivated as I believe by a pure loyalty and an ardent love for the work he was doing.

At the Board of Generals, convened at St. Louis to recommend Brevets, the name of Col. S. was ommited and he failed to receive the rewards so deservedly merited by long and gallant service.

I bring his case before you hoping that some action may be taken to secure for him a Brevet to which, his gallantry and faithfulness so justly entitle him.

Very Truly Yours,
A.S. BURNSIDE[66]

Grant endorsed Burnside's letter with a note stating: "Approved for Brevet Brigadier General for gallant and meritorious services during the war, to date March 13 1865."

In early 1867, while Shepherd's brigadier brevet made its way from the War Department to the Senate, the St. Louis brevet board recommendations were finally being received in the field. Shepherd's effort was successful. The Senate awarded brevet promotions to forty-seven additional officers of the Regular Brigade for service at Stones River, including its commander. Shepherd had been a lieutenant colonel during the battle and received a brevet colonelcy, to rank from December 31, 1862, "for gallant and meritorious services at the battle of Murfreesboro Tennessee." But Shepherd had received full promotion to colonel on January 21, 1863, and thus considered this brevet to be a quite inadequate reward for his service. He returned the brevet certificate to the War Department, accompanying it with a lengthy letter about his service from commissioning in 1840 through Stones River in 1863. He then came to the heart of the matter:

> As a feeble acknowledgment for this service, the Brevet of Colonel is conferred, dating only twenty days before commissioned in full as Colonel, the latter [being awarded prior] to the rendition of the Official Reports of the Battle to the Department. I beg therefore respectfully to refer the honor of this Brevet for date at the Corinth Campaign. Regarding my compulsive absence from the field, from April 17th 1863, I have very respectfully to state that after the terrific contest at Murfreesboro, in which the Regular Brigade lost nearly half its number, it was by dint of hard work and resort to every proper expedient increased to nearly 2400 men undergoing instruction, drill, and discipline.
>
> Suddenly to the surprise of all, it was ordered that I should be relieved, by my junior, then Major R.S. Granger. ...The absence of rank being the cause [for relief]...and no other cause could be imagined, for being relieved, and as the enclosed Brevet confers no additional rank but simply antedates, only 20 days, the rank held at that time, I am constrained to return it as due to my proper self respect and to the memory of the brave officers and soldiers whom I had the honor to command and with whom to stand. Prizing highly Brevet Commissions, as evidence of appreciation by the Government, I hope that the Brevet returned, may be conferred for Corinth where it was properly deserved, and that the General Commanding may recommend a higher brevet as more befitting the gallantry and important service rendered at Murfreesboro, as detailed in the Reports of Generals Rousseau and Thomas.[67]

General Grant agreed with Shepherd's arguments. He attached an endorsement to Shepherd's letter: "Respectfully forwarded to the Secretary of War with the recommendation that Col. Shepherd be breveted Brig Gen'l for the battle of Stone River." Secretary of War Stanton hurriedly scribbled on the application "Colonelcy for Corinth Miss / Brig Genl for Stone River." The effective dates for these brevets were added in someone else's handwriting, probably that of a clerk in the Adjutant General's Office. For Corinth, the date entered was May 1, 1862; for Stones River, March 13, 1865. The Stones River date, incorrect for the battle, was the date the St. Louis Board had designated for brevets reflecting service for the entire war. It was also the date with which Grant had endorsed Burnside's letter about Shepherd two months before. By mid-1867 the president had submitted Shepherd's name to the Senate for a brigadier's brevet no less than three times: two for service during the war and once for Stones River. The effective date on all three requests was March 13, 1865. The Stones River brevet generalship finally emerged from the Senate on March 2, 1867, but with the March 1865 date. While pleased with the brevet, Shepherd again wrote the War Department, this time requesting to have the effective date changed to correspond with the actual date of the battle, and suggesting that perhaps the brevet of major general was appropriate for service throughout the war. Grant by then was tired of dealing with the 15th Infantry's persistent colonel. The commanding general's reply to this latest request consisted of three words: "Application not approved."[68]

Having lost the last round of the battle of the brevets, Shepherd spent the remainder of his career as colonel of the 15th Regulars and a brevet brigadier. He served in Reconstruction assignments for three years, culminating with an appointment as commanding general of the Reconstruction Sub-District of Alabama. With that state's re-admittance to the Union in the summer of 1868, Shepherd resumed much more enjoyable duties. Like John King, Shepherd spent his last years of active duty in the American West. From August 1868 until he retired in 1870, Shepherd commanded the 15th Infantry from various posts in New Mexico and Texas, the lands he had explored with the 3rd Infantry prior to the war.[69] Although the colonel resented the treatment his Civil War record had received, commanding a regiment in the familiar deserts of the southwest had rejuvenated much of the old soldier's spirit:

July 18, 1870

Bvt Major Genl E.D. Townsend
Adjt Genl U.S. Army
Washington, D.C.

General:

    I have the honor respectfully to request that I may be placed on the Retired List...for thirty years of faithful service.

    I desire also respectfully to state that I feel impelled to make this application owing to approaching infirmities, too apparent to pass unheeded, arising from long & frequent exposures, in the line of duty, which require more guard & attention than the duties of my official position. These, super added to domestic considerations, induce me thus, to break off the pleasure I have always naturally felt in the performance of the duties appertaining to my Commission as an officer of the Govt.

    Permit me, General, to say besides, for official record, that I should deem it a duty to hold myself in readiness, while life & health shall last, for recall to active service, in time of War or other great emergency–such readiness being held as an obligation not calculable, because of having received my education at the United States Military Academy.

I have the honor to
remain very respectfully your obdt Svnt,

O.L. SHEPHERD
Col 15th Inf. B.B. Genl 70

Oliver Shepherd retired in December 1870 and took up residence in Newport, Rhode Island. He had not left his military duties completely behind, for he was still responsible for the money that soldiers of the Regular Brigade had donated during the war to erect a monument on the Stones River battlefield. In 1863, Shepherd had invested the sum in government bonds, where it was to remain drawing interest until enough cash had accumulated to construct the memorial. He kept members of his former command appraised of the fund's status in the years immediately following the war. In June 1868, Shepherd wrote to representatives of the Regular Brigade's regiments and Battery H, suggesting that they all correspond "for the purpose of determining upon the erection of a suitable monument over the remains of the brave soldiers of the Regular Brigade...in the battle of Stone River." Shepherd had visited the former battlefield the previous

September: "I found that the National Cemetery comprised the identical ground [in which the regulars had been buried], and each soldier had a neat head and foot board marking his grave. ...The graves lie at the junction of the Sill and Gareshé Avenues, adjacent to the Centre Avenue, surrounding the mound on which the Flag Staff stands. Lieut. Simonds [James Simons, 18th U.S.] lies at the apex of the plat, where it would be proper to have the monument erected." Coordinating the efforts of five military organizations scattered across the nation proved difficult, and the project lost its driving force when Shepherd retired. Shepherd meanwhile entered into a number of lucrative business ventures, primarily Pennsylvania coal mining and New York City real estate. Just a few years after hanging up his uniform, his net worth exceeded $120,000.[71]

Veterans of the brigade in the early 1870s occasionally asked Shepherd what had become of the monument fund, but he became more and more evasive on the subject as the years went by. This state of affairs continued until 1875, when Samuel B. Lawrence took it upon himself to force the issue. Lawrence, who had served in the 16th U.S. during the war, was then a wealthy merchant in New York City. During late October 1875 Lawrence organized a meeting in New York City for officer veterans of the Regular Brigade to discuss what should be done with the fund. Lawrence told the group that he was involved with raising money for a monument to the late George Thomas and thought that perhaps Shepherd would agree to donate the Regular Brigade's money to the Thomas fund. Others disagreed. Captain Francis L. Guenther and Major R.E.A. Crofton in particular insisted that the Regular Brigade's money be used for its original purpose. Crofton drafted a letter to Shepherd. All present at the meeting signed the correspondence; it was then mailed to other veterans of the brigade to obtain additional signatures, a process that took most of the next year to complete. Finally, in October 1876, Frank Guenther mailed the chain letter to Oliver Shepherd, with a request that he send his response to Samuel Lawrence in New York:

> New York,
> November 1st, 1875

Col. O.L. Shepherd,
  U.S. Army
  Key St, Newport, R.I.

Colonel:

The undersigned members of the Regular Brigade, Army of the Cumberland, are desirous of having the fund created by the subscriptions of the Officers and men of that organization for the purpose of erecting a monument to those who were killed at the battle of Stone River, applied to its destined purpose. With this object in view, we request you to inform us of the amount now in your possession, how invested, and if immediately available.

We have decided to appoint three of our members [as] a committee to receive and receipt for the money, and to proceed with the necessary measures for the erection of the Monument, which, in our opinion, has been too long delayed.

The Gentlemen we have chosen for this purpose are:

Captain F.L. Guenther, 5th Artillery
Sam'l B. Lawrence, late Capt. 16th Infantry
Henry Keteltas, late Capt. 15th Infantry

> Very Respectfully
> Your Obedient Servants,
>
> R.E.A. CROFTON
> Major, 17th Infantry, USA
> HENRY BELKNAP
> HENRY KETELTAS
> SAMUEL B. LAWRENCE
> H. DOUGLASS
> Major, 11th Infantry, USA
> JOSEPH D. PROCTOR
> JOHN H. KING
> Col. 9th Infantry, USA
> ARTHUR W. ALLYN
> Capt. 16th Infantry, USA
> N.C. KINNEY
> F.L. GUENTHER
> Capt. 5th Artillery, USA
> R.L. MORRIS
> Capt. 18th Infantry, USA
> E. HAIGHT, JR.
> Late Capt. 16th U.S. Infantry[72]

Shepherd replied to Lawrence on November 2, 1876: "the total amount contributed was $1903.00, and to this there has been interest accruing. The precise amount of interest I cannot, just at this time, accurately state. ...All of which I hold myself responsible for, and will transfer to the Committee." Lawrence asked Samuel R.

Honey to personally represent the committee's interests with Shepherd. A Newport attorney, Honey had served as adjutant of 1/15th U.S. during 1863–1864 and knew his former commander well. Honey visited Shepherd shortly after the chain letter was delivered. Shepherd repeated his response to Honey: he did not know the exact amount of the fund, but as soon as he did, he would turn it over. Honey mentioned that since the fund probably would not cover the cost of a proper monument, it might be more realistic to have a special Regular Brigade tablet added to the planned Regular Army monument at West Point. Shepherd would have none of that, for the colonel fully agreed with the officers who had met the previous year in New York City. The Regular Brigade's money was not to be donated to the Thomas fund, to West Point, or to anywhere else. The dead of the Regular Brigade deserved their own Stones River monument just as much as the brigade's officers deserved the Stones River brevets for which Shepherd had fought so hard. Shepherd was determined to see this project through to the end he had proposed in April 1863. All he needed was time to transfer the fund to the Lawrence Committee. At least that is what Shepherd told Samuel Honey in October 1876.[73]

Shepherd became more evasive in the coming months. He made several appointments to see Lawrence in New York City, but always canceled them at the last moment. Further conversations with Honey revealed that the monument fund was no longer invested in bonds. Shepherd had gradually transferred the fund to real estate as his business endeavors expanded during the late 1860s and early 1870s. He withdrew $166 of interest in 1866 and another $500 in 1871, using the money to purchase a 182-acre farm in Pennsylvania that contained a developing coal mine and was adjacent to a railroad. In March 1869, Shepherd used the fund's principle as collateral against a loan to purchase some property in New York City. The ups and downs of the Gilded Age economy were hard to predict. In May 1871, Shepherd's creditors called in the loan, causing Shepherd to cash the bonds. He was not overly concerned about the monument fund at that time. Shepherd planned to sell some of his property in New York City whenever the money was actually needed, hopefully turning a handsome profit for the monument fund in the process. Unfortunately for the colonel, this course of action proved impossible. A depression known as the Panic of 1873 hit the nation and kept the economy in the doldrums for most of that decade.

Buyers for any type of real estate, particularly in New York City, became extremely hard to find. Shepherd's net worth plummeted, but he did not mention these woes to Honey.[74]

Shepherd wrote Lawrence on January 7, 1877, and told him the fund would be transferred no later than the end of March. The deadline came and went. Shepherd then set off on a different tack: according to the April 1863 circular that laid out the ground rules for the fund, a board of trustees consisting of a representative from each regiment and Battery H was to control the monument fund, and the unit representatives who had signed the circular (Reuben Mussey, William Fetterman, Francis Guenther, Horace Jewett, Joseph Proctor, and Edgar Kellogg) in fact constituted such a board. Samuel Lawrence and his compatriots were therefore not authorized to have anything to do with this money. Shepherd wrote to Lawrence, Honey, and even General-in-Chief William T. Sherman and explained that only a board duly appointed by the units could receive the fund. Although the surviving signatories of the 1863 circular denied they had ever been responsible for overseeing the fund's investment, Shepherd's argument had some merit. The units took most of 1877 to comply with the legal niceties:

Col. O.L. Shepherd, U.S. Army (Retired)
Newport,
Rhode Island.

Colonel:

The undersigned Officers of Battery "H" 5th Artillery and the 15th, 16th, 18th, and 19th Infantry, accept the positions of Trustees of the Fund created by the subscriptions of the Officers and men of the Regular Brigade, Army of the Cumberland, in the years 1863 and 1864, "for the purpose of erecting a monument to those members of the Regular Brigade who were killed at the Battle of Stone River, Tennessee, or died in consequence of wound there received."

In a letter to the General of the Army under date of June 11, 1877, you state that it is your purpose "to write to the original trustees, and to the Colonels of each regiment having no trustee, to ascertain a unanimous determination in respect to the fund and have it in readiness to turn over accordingly.

As such trustees, *original*, and since appointed, we request and demand, that the entire amount of said fund, principle and accrued interest, be immediately deposited with the Union Trust Company of New York City, subject to the joint order of the trustees, and request that the trustees may at once be notified to the fact.

Very Respectfully,
Your Obedient Servants,

Fort Brooke, Tampa, Fla. July 3rd, 1877	F.L. GUENTHER Capt 5th Arty.
Chattanooga, Tenn July 11th, 1877	E.R. KELLOGG Capt 18th Inf..
Camp Supply, I.T. September 26th, 1877	W.J. LYSTER Capt. 19th Inf.
Fort Wingate, N.M. October 13th, 1877	HORACE JEWETT Capt. 15th Infantry
Fort Sill, Indian Territory October 25th, 1877	ARTHUR W. ALLYN Captain 16th Infantry Trustee by appointment for the 16th Inf.. U.S.A.[75]

It would have been more useful for Shepherd had he thought of the board of trustees issue when first approached about the monument fund. By late 1877, his reasoning was thought to be just another delaying tactic, which it was. Shepherd was frantically trying to scrape together the money, meeting failure at every turn. He had plenty of property on the market, but there were no buyers to be had. He had been awarded $4,400 as part of a class-action suit against the city of New York in 1876 (one of Shepherd's buildings had been damaged when the city paved 10th Avenue), but on appeal, the settlement had been slashed to $1,500 and even that amount was tied up in red tape with no end in sight. The purchase of stock in a Boston company that had patented a process to plate metal with nickel should have yielded hefty dividends long before, but had not. If the colonel would have explained all this to Lawrence and the others in 1876, he probably would have found a sympathetic ear somewhere, but Shepherd's pride prohibited the airing of his personal financial problems. All that Lawrence, Honey, and the board of trustees knew was that Shepherd was tight-lipped and requested delay after delay. In December 1877, the trustees' patience ran out and they referred the case to Major General Winfield Scott Hancock, commanding general of the Military Division of the Atlantic and the Department of the East in New York City. Hancock in turn sent the facts to the commanding general of the army. Sherman sent his endorsement on the case back to Hancock on January 10, 1878:

> Respectfully returned to General W.S. Hancock...who is requested to notify Col. O.L. Shepherd by letter that General Sherman, his personal friend, is embarrassed by a charge against his old classmate of what he construes to be a breach of a Sacred Trust, which, in his opinion, amounts to conduct unbecoming an Officer and Gentleman, that he must within three days of the receipt of notice deposit the money held by him in trust in the repository named, subject to the order of those who represent the Trust, else he must be tried by a General Court Martial. Unless Col Shepherd complies with this most reasonable request, Gen'l Hancock will, as Department Commander, order his arrest, and trial by a General Court Martial on the charges preferred by any of the officers interested.[76]

Sherman later extended the deadline from three to thirty days at Shepherd's request. In the end, the extension did not matter, for in terms of having assets easily liquefiable into cash, Shepherd was broke. The Shepherd court-martial convened on February 26, 1878, at Hancock's headquarters, the Houston Street Army Building in Manhattan. Included among the twelve jury members were a number of officers who had played prominent roles in the Civil War, including Colonel Henry J. Hunt, chief of artillery in the Army of the Potomac, and Lieutenant Colonel Romeyn B. Ayres, who in 1863 succeeded George Sykes in command of the Regular Division. Colonel William F. Barry, Sherman's chief of artillery during 1864–1865, was president of the court. The charges against Shepherd consisted of four counts of the amorphous "conduct unbecoming an officer and gentleman," all relating to Shepherd's promising to hand over the monument fund and then failing to do so.[77]

Shepherd hired Elihu Root as his defense counsel, an up-and-coming New York City corporate lawyer who would become at the turn of the century one of the most influential secretaries of war in American history, and later serve as secretary of state and as a Republican elder statesman during the first quarter of the twentieth century, during which time he received the Nobel Peace Prize.[78] Root met his match during this trial in the form of Major G. Norman Lieber, a Civil War veteran of the 11th U.S. Infantry who had transferred to the Judge Advocate General's corps in 1867. As the army prosecutor, Lieber built up a solid case of dishonesty, evasion, and outright embezzlement on the part of the defendant. A dejected Shepherd sat by as former subordinates Samuel Lawrence, Samuel Honey, Henry Keteltas, and Frank Guenther all took the stand as witnesses for the prosecution. "It has been 14 years since the fund entrusted to Col. Shepherd was created for the purpose of erecting a monument to the fallen heroes of the battle of Stone River," Lieber stated in resting his case, "and I would ask what became of that fund, and upon whom should the blame rest for its misappropriation, if not on the accused? I also call the attention of the court to the sacredness with which such a fund should have been guarded, and impress the fact upon the court that money received in trust should under no circumstances be appropriated for any other purpose than that for which it was intended."[79]

Root conducted a spirited defense on Shepherd's behalf. He called on nine property brokers and financial experts to explain Shepherd's financial status and the depressed condition of the New York City real estate market. The final witness Root called was the defendant himself, but court-martial regulations of that era prohibited a defendant from testifying. Major Lieber mildly chastised Root for even suggesting such a dangerous precedent, although the judge advocate acknowledged that his counterpart was not well versed in military law.[80] All Shepherd could do was submit a written, unsworn statement. In this communiqué, Shepherd admitted that he was responsible for the money, but insisted that he had received the money "subject to no restrictions or directives as to the manner of its investment," and that "I did not use a dollar of this money. I invested it as I invested my own." Shepherd concluded with an appeal to his honor, which after all was the issue that had been called into question by the charges of conduct unbecoming:

> I have not evaded the payment of this money. Since I was called upon to account for it, I have made every effort within my power, and tried every expedient I could devise to procure it for payment. I have been defeated in my efforts by a state of affairs such as no one could foresee, such as no one has seen for forty years. ...I have hoped for success in one after another of these efforts...[but] have been frustrated by failure or delay.
>
> Perhaps, if I had been a younger man, a stronger man, a man skilled in business and with business connections or a man active in society, and with many friends, I should have succeeded. But I have passed a life of extreme exposure and hardship. During all but four

of the thirty years—from 1840 to my retirement in 1870—I was in active service in the field, during actual war or on the frontier.

I am old. I am enfeebled in health, and I fear in mind, by disease and distress. I have been broken in spirit by recent bereavement in my home, and I have been driven almost to insanity by the failure of my hopes and the disgrace of this accusation.

I have done all that I could. I have offered all that I had. I now offer again to convey all my property and my pay accounts to the trustees of this fund in trust to dispose of as they may see fit, for the purpose of obtaining the amount.

I am not permitted to testify to my statements under oath, as a witness, but for their truth and for the purity of and honor of my motives in all my acts, here called in question, I appeal to the record of my many years of honorable service and unstained reputation.[81]

In his own concluding statement, Root argued that "there is nothing reprehensible in Colonel Shepherd's action in relation to the fund, and that since he has never denied receiving it, never refused to surrender it to those duly authorized to receive it, and is ready and willing to hand it over as soon as he can realize the amount from his property, the court is bound to acquit him."[82]

Root failed to sway the jury. After eleven days of testimony and deliberation, Colonel Barry and his peers rendered their verdict on March 8, 1878. Shepherd was found guilty on three counts of conduct unbecoming, with the fourth specification being changed to "Conduct to the prejudice of good order and military discipline," of which the verdict was also guilty (a curious finding given that Shepherd was no longer serving in the army). Shepherd returned to Rhode Island and appealed the conviction through the secretary of war to the president. On April 6, President Rutherford B. Hayes approved the sentence: "Colonel Oliver L. Shepherd shall be confined within the limits of the post at Fort Adams, Newport, R.I. for one year, and as long thereafter, if needs be, until the said Colonel O.L. Shepherd, U.S. Army, retired, shall have paid to such depository as the Department Commander shall designate subject to the order of the duly authorized Trustees, the original amount of the Stone River Battle Monument Fund, viz: $1,903., together with interest thereon from June 1st 1864, to date of payment, said interest to be compounded at 6 per cent per annum currency."[83]

Shepherd was placed under guard at Fort Adams that day, a prisoner in the post he had once commanded. He was confined for one year, serving the time at Fort Adams and also at Fort Wood in New York City. For a period of three years following his conviction, he made steady deposits at the Union Trust Company of Manhattan to re-establish the monument fund. On February 15, 1881, he made the final deposit and the fund was repaid in full, a total of $3,758. General Sherman was pleased that Shepherd had repaid the debt: "Personally and officially I am deeply gratified to learn that the Sacred fund entrusted to Colonel O.L. Shepherd by his comrades of the Battle of Stone River Tennessee, has been made good by him. ... And so far as I am concerned wish that all officers of the Army to know that his good name is restored to him after the painful doubts & suspicions caused by his temporary misfortunes."[84]

Shepherd spent his remaining years living at the home of his eldest son, a physician, on Lexington Avenue in New York City. Although dampened in sprit by the unfortunate incidents of his Civil War years, he remained active in business affairs and was a familiar face at gatherings of the Aztec Club of 1847, a national organization of military and naval officers who had served in the Mexican War. Shepherd attended Aztec Club annual meetings each year from 1873 to 1886, with the exception of 1879. Age and infirmities restricted his movements during the late 1880s. He died of congestive heart failure on April 15, 1894.

Oliver Shepherd would have been pleased to know that he was buried with full military honors. A detachment of regulars from the 15th U.S. Infantry escorted the flag-draped casket from the late general's residence to St. John's Cemetery in Yonkers. Numerous members of the Aztec Club attended the funeral, as did Major General James B. Mulligan, a Civil War veteran of the 19th U.S., Confederate Major General Thomas Jordan, a West Point classmate of Shepherd's, and Major General Fitz-John Porter, the original colonel of the 15th Infantry whose own court-martial in 1862 had been an important link in the chain of events that led to Shepherd's relief from command of the Regular Brigade. Also in attendance was a crusty Old Army Regular, a retired sergeant known only as Franz, who had served with Shepherd in the 3rd Infantry during the Mexican War, at Fort Defiance, and through the long escape from Texas in 1861.[85]

* * *

The saga of the monument fund and the Shepherd court-martial had one positive effect, for it brought veterans of the Regular

Brigade closer together and convinced them that perhaps a more formal association was needed to look out for their corporate interests. Like many Civil War veterans, they formed a fraternal society to commemorate their service. They formed the "Association of Survivors, Regular Brigade, Army of the Cumberland" in 1883. The association held annual reunions until the early twentieth century, after which time the membership roles gradually dwindled as the old regulars passed away.

The Regular Brigade Association of Survivors held its 1895 meeting at Crawfish Springs, Georgia, on September 18–20. The gathering coincided with the dedication of the nearby Chickamauga and Chattanooga National Military Park. Of great interest to the aging regulars in attendance were five new monuments erected to commemorate the actions of the Regular Brigade in that titanic struggle. In the woods at the site of the Jay's Mill fighting, they found a solitary monument for Battery H, 5th U.S. Artillery, near the location where the guns were overrun on the first day of the battle. The other four monuments, regimental markers for the 15th, 16th, 18th, and 19th U.S. Infantry, were placed near the site of the Kelly Field fighting.

In the years leading up to the dedication of the park, the War Department stipulated that the design and inscription of all Chickamauga monuments would be forwarded to Washington via the Park Commission for approval. These guidelines were aimed at the state commissions responsible for construction and placement of monuments for volunteer units. For monuments pertaining to Regular Army units, the War Department took care of the design and detailed a committee of regular officers to determine where on the battlefield the regular monuments should be placed. Captain Joshua Fessenden of the 5th Artillery, the only officer of Battery H to survive the battle alive without being captured, visited the park in the summer of 1892. He informed Major Sanford C. Kellogg, the Park Commission's secretary, that he thought the woods west of Jay's Mill where the battery's guns had been overrun and then recaptured on the first day of the battle would be the most appropriate spot for a memorial to Lieutenant Howard Burnham's command. Fessenden also attempted to locate Battery H's actual guns for inclusion in the memorial, but was informed that the pieces had been melted down years before.

Other officers conducted a more extensive survey of the regulars' actions at Chickamauga the next year. In early May 1893, retired Brigadier General Absalom Baird, Colonel John W. Forsyth of the 7th Cavalry (adjutant of the Regular Brigade at Chickamauga), Colonel R.E.A. Crofton of the 15th Infantry, and Captain James H. Gageby of the 3rd Infantry all met in northern Georgia and spent a few days crisscrossing the former battlefield, spending most of their time determining the location of the Battery H fight near Jay's Mill. With the assistance of some former members of Van Derveer's brigade, they pinpointed the location. The four officers decided to place the regular infantry memorials at the site of the Regular Brigade's stand at Kelly Field.[86]

When the veterans inspected the memorials for the first time in 1895, they wished the War Department had also consulted the Regular Brigade Association of Survivors. The Association's members were satisfied with the location of the Battery H memorial (although one has to wonder why the two cannon that flank the Battery H monument today point westward, toward the Federal positions on the Lafayette Road), but they thought the monument for the 18th Infantry should have been positioned at least 100 yards further to the northeast from where it currently rests, and that the other Kelly Field regular monuments were sited much too close together. Other than the spacing issue, the monument positions for the 15th, 16th, and 19th regulars "seemed to be more correct" than that of the 18th Infantry. Today, these weathered stone sentinels still guard the left of the Kelly Field line as part of the magnificent collection of Federal monuments arrayed on Chickamauga's Battle Line Road.[87]

One of the contingents of regular veterans that made its way to Georgia that autumn went via a special train from Columbus, Ohio. The journey began on September 16, where one by one the old regulars greeted each other at the Union Depot. The train, consisting of four Wagner sleepers, two day coaches, and a baggage car, pulled out of the station that night. "It was decorated with flags and streamers," one of the veterans later wrote, "announcing to all that the survivors of the Regular Brigade and their friends were on board. A royal train full of loyal people." Additional members of the association boarded as the train passed through Cincinnati and Nashville. About thirty miles south of Nashville the cars slowed and gradually came to a stop beside a low, grassy knoll studded with headstones: the Stones River National Cemetery. The passengers made their way off the train and walked to the center of the cemetery, some of them spotting familiar names on headstones along the way. They gathered around the only monument gracing the area, an impressive stone column topped with a soaring bronze eagle. Prayers, speeches, and songs followed, after which a laurel wreath was laid at the base of the monument. The regulars gathered for a photo, took a final stroll past the ranks of their fallen comrades, and then continued the rail journey to Chickamauga.[88]

The monument the veterans rallied around that day had been unveiled during the association's inaugural year, on May 12, 1883. Much as Oliver Shepherd had desired, the veterans placed the Regular Brigade's Stones River monument in the cemetery at the spot where Battery H's guns had stood and to which the battalions of the Regular Brigade had rallied after their harrowing experience in the cedars. The monument's inscription reads:

In memory
of the Officers and Enlisted Men of the
15th, 16th, 18th, & 19th U.S. Infantry and
Battery H, 5th U.S. Artillery, who
were killed or died of wounds
Received at
The Battle of Stone River
Tennessee,
December 31st 1862 to January 3rd 1863
Erected
by
Their Comrades
of the
Regular Brigade
Army of
The Cumberland

The Stones River National Battlefield is small and subdued compared with its larger cousins, America's National Military Parks. A few square miles of forest and field tucked away in the rapidly urbanizing landscape between Nashville and Murfreesboro, the area was not set aside for preservation until 1927. Stones River thus missed the turn-of-the-century wave of monument building that transformed other Civil War sites into the gardens of stone so familiar today. Of the hundreds of units on both sides that fought on this hallowed ground northwest of Murfreesboro, veterans of only one unit returned to middle Tennessee after the war to leave behind a monument commemorating their services. The Regular Brigade monument stands alone as the only veteran-sponsored, postwar memorial standing watch along the banks of Stones River, a fitting tribute to the brigade's solitary stand a short distance away in a dark cedar forest.

APPENDICES

APPENDIX A: Regimental Strength and Battle Casualties

The number of men a unit took into action was considerably less than the unit's present for duty strength. Commanders reported only those soldiers actually present in the battalion line; band members, cooks, teamsters, and other unit members who were present for duty, but did not directly participate, were not included. Officer strengths listed below include battalion adjutants (who were present at the front, assisting their commander in leading the unit), but not brigade staff officers or battalion quartermasters (unless there is evidence indicating that a quartermaster officer was present in the line of battle).

The casualty figures are not 100% accurate. Many soldiers who were initially listed as missing in action or captured eventually returned to their units (note that 1/19th Infantry reported twenty-six soldiers missing at the Battle of Jonesboro, but only six missing for the overall Atlanta Campaign). If reports were written immediately after the battle, some men listed as wounded would later die of their wounds. With these caveats in mind, the casualty figures a commander listed in his report convey an accurate picture of the number of men absent from ranks as a battle ended.

Table A-1: Shiloh, April 7, 1862

	Taken into Action			Casualties			
	Officers	Men	Total	Killed	Wounded	Missing	Total
1/15th U.S.	19	318	337	4	59	0	63 (19%)
1/16th U.S.	13	276	289	6	49	0	54 (19%)
1/19th U.S.	11	200*	11	5	32	0	37 (18%)
Total	43	794	837	15	140	0	155 (18%)

*The enlisted strength for 1/19th U.S. at Shiloh is an estimated figure. Major Carpenter's report does not state the exact number of troops the battalion took into action. Since the average in-action strength of the companies in the other two battalions was slightly less than forty men each, 1/19th's five companies probably totaled about 200 troops.

Table A-2: Stones River, December 31, 1862—January 2, 1863

	Taken into Action			Casualties			
	Officers	Men	Total	Killed	Wounded	Missing	Total
1/15th U.S.	15	304	319	12	77	17	106 (33%)
1/16th U.S.	14	293	307	16	154	16	186 (61%)
1/18th U.S.	18	272	290	29	121	2	152 (52%)
2/18th U.S.	16	298	314	31	103	5	139 (44%)
1/19th U.S.	10	198	208	6	55	7	68 (33%)
H/5th U.S.	3	123	126	0	5	0	5 (4%)
Total	76	1488	1564	94	515	47	656 (42%)

Table A-3: Chickamauga, September 19—20, 1863

	Taken into Action			Casualties			
	Officers	Men	Total	Killed	Wounded	Missing	Total
1/15th U.S.	13	262	275	9	49	102	160 (58%)
1/16th U.S.	16	289	305	3	19	174	196 (65%)
1/18th U.S.	14	278	292	19	71	68	158 (54%)
2/18th U.S.	12	274	286	14	81	50	145 (51%)
1/19th U.S.	14	190	204	3	17	116	136 (67%)
H/5th U.S.	3	127	130	13	18	13	44 (34%)
Total	72	142	1492	61	255	523	839 (56%)

Table A-4: Missionary Ridge, November 25, 1863

	Taken into Action			Casualties			
	Officers	Men	Total	Killed	Wounded	Missing	Total
1/15th U.S.	7	90	97	1	5	0	6 (6%)
2/15th U.S.	7	135	142	3	6	1	10 (7%)
1/16th U.S.	8	106	114	1	9	0	10 (9%)
1/18th U.S.	10	176	186	1	15	0	16 (9%)
2/18th U.S.	5	173	178	0	13	0	13 (7%)
1/19th U.S.	6	82	88	0	3	1	4 (5%)
Total	43	762	805	6	51	2	59 (7%)

Table A-5: Jonesboro, September 1, 1864*

	Taken into Action			Casualties			
	Officers	Men	Total	Killed	Wounded	Missing	Total
1/15th U.S.	4	136	140	4	11	2	17 (12%)
2/15th U.S.	2	124	126	5	20	2	27 (21%)
16th U.S.	9	250	259	2	31	0	33 (13%)
18th U.S.	8	261	269	10	33	8	51 (19%)

	Taken into Action			Casualties			
	Officers	Men	Total	Killed	Wounded	Missing	Total
1/19th U.S.	5	118	123+	4	9	26	39 (32%)
Total	28	889	917	25	104	38	167 (18%)

*Of the numerous battles that occurred during the Atlanta Campaign, accurate strength and casualty figures are available only for the Battle of Jonesboro.
+Strength does not include Lt. Joseph J. Wagoner, four companies, and ninety-one recruits that did not participate in the assault.

Table A-6: The Atlanta Campaign, Regimental Present for Duty Strength at the Start of the Campaign, and Overall Casualties

	Present for Duty, May 6, 1864			Casualties			
	Officers	Men	Total	Killed	Wounded	Missing	Total
1/15th U.S.	8	376	384	39	103	2	144
2/15th U.S.	10	307	317	15	94	8	117
1/16th U.S.	8	245	253				
				16	94	10	120*
2/16th U.S.	5	257	262				
1/18th U.S.	13	257	270	17	86	5	108
2/18th U.S.	10	373	383	21	90	12	123
1/19th U.S.	11	266	277	14	56	6	76
Total	65	2081	2146	122	523	43	688

*Total for both 16th Infantry battalions

APPENDIX B: Orders of Battle

The following lists detail battalion organization and leadership for most of the regulars' major battles. If a company does not have an officer listed, there were no officers present for duty at that time. The names of sergeants serving as company commanders are stated whenever possible, although such persons can rarely be positively identified. Due to the sparse data available for the Atlanta Campaign, only its first and last major battles (Resaca and Jonesboro) are listed.
Abbreviations:
 KIA = killed in action
 DOW = died of wounds
 WIA = wounded in action
 C = captured
 *= awarded brevet

Shiloh: April 7, 1862
McCook's 2nd Division, Army of the Ohio

5th Brigade	Colonel Edward N. Kirk
6th Brigade	Colonel William H. Gibson

4th Brigade

Commander	Brigadier General Lovell H. Rousseau
Adjutant	Lieutenant D. Armstrong
Quartermaster	Captain W.M. Carpenter
Aides-de-Camp	Lieutenant Rousseau, 5th Kentucky Infantry
	Lieutenant John D. Wickliffe, 2nd Kentucky Cavalry

1st Ohio Infantry	Colonel Benjamin F. Smith
5th Kentucky Infantry	Colonel Harvey M. Buckley
6th Indiana Infantry	Colonel Thomas T. Crittenden
Battery H, 5th U.S. Artillery	Captain William R. Terrill

Regular Infantry Battalions

Commander	Major John. H. King, 15th U.S. Infantry

1st Battalion, 15th U.S. Infantry

Commander	Captain Peter T. Swaine*
Adjutant	Lieutenant Frederick D. Ogilby
Quartermaster	Lieutenant Clarence R. Bailey
Sergeant Major	Sergeant Major Gustavus E. Teubnes
Company A	Lieutenant Horace Jewett
Company B	Captain John V. Haughey
Company C	Captain William W. Wise,*
	Lieutenant Edward A. Curtenius
Company D	Captain Jacob B. Bell,
	Lieutenant James Y. Semple
Company E	Captain Henry Keteltas* (WIA),
	Lieutenant Charles A. Wikoff* (WIA),
	Lieutenant George K. Sanderson*
Company F	Captain John C. Peterson (WIA),
	Lieutenant Henry C. Gapen
Company G	Captain Joseph S. York,
	Lieutenant Solomon E. Woodward
Company H	Captain James Curtis* (WIA),
	Lieutenant William B. Occleston,*
	Lieutenant Silas W. Pettit

1st Battalion, 16th U.S. Infantry

Commander	Captain Edwin F. Townsend*

Adjutant	Lieutenant Louis M. Hosea
Quartermaster	Lieutenant William H. Ingerton*
Sergeant Major	Sergeant Major Edgar R. Kellogg
Company A	Captain R.E.A. Crofton,*
	Lieutenant Homer H. Clark
Company B	Lieutenant Edward Haight,
	Lieutenant William H. Arnold
Company C	Captain William H. Acker* (KIA)
Company D	Captain Patrick T. Keyes (DOW),
	Lieutenant John Power
Company E	Lieutenant Edward McConnell,
	Lieutenant William M. Bruse
Company F	Captain R. Peabody Barry
Company G	Lieutenant Edward L. Mitchell* (KIA)

1st Battalion, 19th U.S. Infantry

Commander	Major Stephen D. Carpenter*
Adjutant	Lieutenant Louis T. Snyder
Quartermaster	Lieutenant Charles Berg
Sergeant Major	Sergeant Major Charles F. Miller
Company A	Lieutenant William J. Lyster* (WIA),
	Lieutenant William R. Lowe
Company B	Captain Reuben D. Mussey,
	Lieutenant Joseph J. Wagoner
Company C	Captain Thomas C. Williams*
Company D	Lieutenant Albert H. Andrews,*
	Lieutenant Samuel S. Bigger
Company E	Captain Francis Fessenden (WIA),
	Lieutenant Jacob D. Jones

Stones River: 31 December 1862–3 January 1863

Rousseau's 1st Division, Thomas's Center Wing, Army of the Cumberland

1st Brigade	Colonel Benjamin F. Scribner
2nd Brigade	Colonel John Beatty
3rd Brigade	Colonel John C. Starkweather

Regular Brigade

Commander	Lieutenant Colonel Oliver L. Shepherd,*
	18th Infantry
Adjutant	Lieutenant Robert Sutherland,*
	18th Infantry
Quartermaster	Captain Nathaniel C. Kinney,*
	18th Infantry
Commissary	Lieutenant Anson Mills,* 18th Infantry
	(also commanded A/3/18th)

Surgeon	Assistant Surgeon Webster Lindsey, 18th Infantry
Sergeant Major	Commissary Sergeant John U. Gill, 18th Infantry

1st Battalion, 15th U.S. Infantry
Commander	Major John H. King (WIA)
Adjutant	Lieutenant Frederick D. Ogilby*
Quartermaster	Lieutenant Clarence M. Bailey (C)
Company A	Lieutenant Horace Jewett,* Lieutenant William G. Galloway
Company B	Captain Jesse Fulmer*
Company C	Captain William W. Wise* (DOW), Lieutenant Robert P. King
Company D	Captain J. Bowmen Bell* (KIA), Lieutenant James W. Semple*
Company E	Captain Henry Keteltas,* Lieutenant Charles A. Wikoff, Lieutenant Roman H. Gray
Company F	
Company G	Captain Joseph S. York* (KIA), Lieutenant Solomon E. Woodward*
Company H	Lieutenant William B. Occleston* (WIA)

1st Battalion, 16th U.S. Infantry
Commander	Major Adam J. Slemmer* (WIA/C)
Adjutant	Lieutenant John Power* (WIA)
Quartermaster	Lieutenant Jacob Kline
Sergeant Major	Commissary Sergeant James M. Howe (WIA)
Company A	Captain R.E.A. Crofton
Company B	Lieutenant William H. Bartholomew,* Lieutenant William W. Arnold
Company C	Lieutenant William D. Wedemeyer
Company D	Captain John C. King (KIA)
Company E	Lieutenant Edward McConnell*
Company F	Captain R. Peabody Barry* (WIA/C), Lieutenant Edgar R. Kellogg*
Company G	Lieutenant Arthur W. Allen*
Company H	Captain Newton L. Dykeman* (WIA), Lieutenant Samuel E. St. Onge*
Company B/2/16th	Captain James Biddle

1st Battalion, 18th U.S. Infantry
Commander	Major James N. Caldwell*

Adjutant	Lieutenant Richard L. Morris*
Quartermaster	Lieutenant Daniel W. Benham*
Sergeant Major	Sergeant Major Reuben F. Little
Company A	Captain Henry Douglass* (WIA),
	Lieutenant Nathaniel C. Kinney,
	Lieutenant Gilbert S. Carpenter* (WIA)
Company B	Captain William L. Thurston,
	Lieutenant Ebenezer D. Harding
Company C	Captain Charles E. Kneass* (KIA),
	Lieutenant Joseph L. Proctor*
Company D	Captain David L. Wood (WIA)
Company E	Lieutenant Thomas L. Brand,*
	Lieutenant Merrill N. Hutchinson
Company F	
Company G	Captain Robert B. Hull* (WIA),
	Lieutenant John J. Adiar* (WIA)
Company H	Lieutenant Samuel J. Dick
Company A/3/18th	Lieutenant Anson Mills
Company D/3/18th	Captain William H.H. Taylor,
	Lieutenant Joseph McConnell* (DOW)

2nd Battalion, 18th U.S. Infantry

Commander	Major Frederick Townsend*
Adjutant	Lieutenant Frederick Phisterer
Quartermaster	Lieutenant William P. McClery*
Sergeant Major	Sergeant Major John F. Lind
Company A	Captain William J. Fetterman*
Company B	Captain Charles E. Denison* (DOW),
	Lieutenant William H. Bisbee,*
	Lieutenant John F. Hitchcock* (KIA)
Company C	Captain Ansel B. Denton
Company D	Lieutenant Morgan L. Ogden* (WIA),
	Lieutenant William W. Arnold*
Company E	Captain Ai B. Thompson* (WIA)
Company F	Lieutenant James Simons* (DOW)
Company B/3/18th	Captain Henry Belknap
Company C/3/18th	Lieutenant Herman G. Radcliff
Company E/3/18th	Captain Henry Haymond*
Company F/3/18th	Captain Henry R. Mizner,*
	Lieutenant Henry B. Freeman*

1st Battalion, 19th U.S. Infantry

Commander	Major Stephen D. Carpenter* (KIA)
Adjutant	Lieutenant Louis T. Snyder
	(also commanded Company C)

Quartermaster	Lieutenant Howard E. Stansbury
Sergeant Major	Sergeant Major John W. Snarely
Company A	Lieutenant William R. Lowe
Company B	Lieutenant Joseph J. Wagoner
Company C	Lieutenant Louis T. Snyder
Company D	Lieutenant Albert H. Andrews*
Company E	Lieutenant Jacob D. Jones,*
	Lieutenant Arthur B. Carpenter
Company F	Captain James B. Mulligan,
	Lieutenant Alfred Curtis

Battery H, 5th U.S. Artillery

Commander	Lieutenant Francis L. Guenther*
Section Leader	Lieutenant Israel Ludlow
Section Leader	Lieutenant Joshua A. Fessenden*

Chickamauga: 19–20 September 1863

Baird's 1st Division, Thomas's XIV Corps, Army of the Cumberland

1st Brigade	Colonel Benjamin F. Scribner
3rd Brigade	Colonel John C. Starkweather

Regular Brigade

Commander	Brigadier General John H. King*
Adjutant	Captain John W. Forsyth,* 18th Infantry
Quartermaster	Lieutenant Joseph J. Wagoner, 19th Infantry
Commissary	Lieutenant Samuel S. Culbertson, 19th Infantry
Aide-de-camp	Lieutenant William J. Lyster,* 19th Infantry
Inspector general	Lieutenant Henry G. Litchfield,* 18th Infantry
Provost marshal	Captain James B. Mulligan,* 19th Infantry
Surgeon	Assistant Surgeon Edward J. Darken
Sergeant Major	Sergeant Major John U. Gill, 18th Infantry

1st Battalion, 15th U.S. Infantry

Commander	Captain Albert B. Dod
Adjutant	Lieutenant Samuel R. Honey
Quartermaster	Lieutenant Solomon E. Woodward
Sergeant Major	Sergeant Major James R. Bruce (WIA)
Company A	Lieutenant William G. Galloway* (C)
Company C	Lieutenant William H. Heilman*
Company E	Captain Henry Keteltas,*
	Lieutenant Charles A. Wikoff,*
	Lieutenant Roman H. Gray* (C)

Company F	Lieutenant James P. Brown* (C)
Company G	Lieutenant Edward M. Timony (C),
	Lieutenant John Williams* (WIA)
Company H	Captain David M. Meredith* (WIA),
	Lieutenant Theodore Kendall* (C)
Company E/2/15th	Lieutenant Samuel S. Holbrook* (C)

1st Battalion, 16th U.S. Infantry

Commander	Major Sydney Coolidge* (KIA)
Adjutant	Lieutenant Homer H. Clark* (DOW)
Quartermaster	Lieutenant Samuel E. St. Onge
Company A	Captain R.E.A. Crofton*,
	Lieutenant Walter Clifford* (C)
Company B	Captain Melville A. Cochran* (C),
	Lieutenant Martin Mahan (C)
Company D	Lieutenant William J. Stewart (C),
	Lieutenant William Mills (C)
Company F	Captain Alexander H. Stanton (C)
Company H	Lieutenant John K. Shiffler,
	Lieutenant William F. Goodwin* (WIA)
Company B/2/16th	Lieutenant Patrick W. Houlihan* (C)
Company C/2/16th	Lieutenant William H. Smyth* (C),
	Lieutenant John T. Mackey (C)
Company D/2/16th	Captain John Christopher* (C),
	Lieutenant Thomas J. Durnin* (C)

1st Battalion, 18th U.S. Infantry

Commander	Captain George W. Smith*
Detachment Adjutant	Captain James P. Wilson Neill* (WIA)
Battalion Adjutant	Lieutenant Henry B. Freeman* (C)
Quartermaster	Lieutenant Daniel W. Benham
Sergeant Major	Sergeant Major Isaac D'Isay (C)
Company B	Lieutenant Ebenezer D. Harding
Company D	Lieutenant John J. Adiar (WIA)
Company E	Lieutenant Thomas L. Brand (WIA),
	Lieutenant Reuben F. Little
Company F	Lieutenant John Lane* (DOW)
Company G	Lieutenant Alfred Townsend,*
	Lieutenant Frank T. Bennett* (C)
Company H	Captain Anson Mills*
Company G/3/18th	Captain William H.H. Taylor
Company H/3/18th	Lieutenant James Powell,*
	Lieutenant Edgar N. Wilcox*

2nd Battalion, 18th U.S. Infantry

Commander	Captain Henry Haymond
Adjutant	Lieutenant John F. Lind
Quartermaster	Lieutenant William W. Arnold
Company A	Lieutenant Robert Sutherland,
	Lieutenant Charles Whitacre
Company B	Lieutenant Thaddeus L. Kirtland
Company C	Lieutenant Rufus C. Gates (C)
Company D	Lieutenant Charles L. Truman* (KIA)
Company E	Lieutenant Merrill N. Hutchinson* (WIA)
Company F	Lieutenant Lucius F. Brown* (DOW)
Company G	Lieutenant Henry C. Pohlman (C),
	Lieutenant James S. Ostrander
Company H	Captain Tenador Ten Eyck (WIA/C)

1st Battalion, 19th U.S. Infantry

Commander	Major Samuel K. Dawson* (WIA)
Adjutant	Lieutenant Robert Ayres (WIA)
Quartermaster	Lieutenant Robert W. Barnard
Company A	Captain Verling K. Hart* (C),
	Lieutenant James H. Gageby (C)
Company B	Captain George S. Pierce (C),
	Lieutenant Walter O. Lattimore
Company C+	Captain Thomas C. Williams,*
	Lieutenant Douglas Edwards
Company E	Lieutenant Manuel C. Causten (C),
	Lieutenant Charles F. Miller* (DOW)
Company F	Lieutenant Thomas H.Y. Bickham (C)
Company G	Captain Edward L. Smith* (C)
Company H	Lieutenant Alfred Curtis,
	Lieutenant Arthur B. Carpenter
Company A/2/19th	Captain Thomas Cummings* (WIA/C),
	Lieutenant Michael B. Fogarty* (KIA)

+Division provost guard

Battery H, 5th U.S. Artillery

Commander	Lieutenant Howard M. Burnham (KIA)
Section Leader	Lieutenant Israel Ludlow (WIA/C)
Section Leader	Lieutenant Joshua A. Fessenden* (WIA)

Missionary Ridge: November 25, 1863
Johnson's 1st Division, Palmer's XIV Corps, Army of the Cumberland

1st Brigade	Brigadier General William P. Carlin
3rd Brigade	Colonel John C. Starkweather
2nd Brigade	

Commander	Colonel William L. Stoughton, 11th Michigan
Adjutant	Captain John W. Forsyth, 18th Infantry
Quartermaster	Lieutenant Joseph J. Wagoner, 19th Infantry
Aide-de-Camp	Lieutenant William J. Lyster, 19th Infantry
Inspector general	Lieutenant Henry G. Litchfield, 18th Infantry
Provost marshal	Captain James B. Mulligan, 19th Infantry
11th Michigan Infantry	Major Benjamin Bennet (KIA)
19th Illinois Infantry	Lieutenant Colonel Alexander W. Raffen
69th Ohio Infantry	Colonel Marshall F. Moore
Battery H, 5th U.S. Artillery+	Captain Francis L. Guenther

+detached

Demi-Brigade of Regulars

Commander	Major John R. Edie,* 15th Infantry

1st Battalion, 15th U.S. Infantry

Commander	Captain Henry Keteltas
Adjutant	Lieutenant Samuel R. Honey
Quartermaster	Lieutenant Solomon E. Woodward
Company A	
Company C	Captain George M. Brayton
Company E	Lieutenant Charles A. Wikoff
Company F	Lieutenant Henry C. Gapen
Company G	Lieutenant John Williams
Company H	Lieutenant Joseph C. Forbes

2nd Battalion, 15th U.S. Infantry

Commander	Captain William S. McManus*
Adjutant	Lieutenant Orson C. Knapp*
Quartermaster	Lieutenant Irwin W. Potter
Company A	Lieutenant Mason Jackson
Company B	
Company C	Captain Thomas C. Norton
Company D	Lieutenant Richard W. Derickson, Lieutenant Samuel L. Burness
Company E	Lieutenant Robert Harrison

Consolidated Battalion, 16th and 19th U.S. Infantry

Commander	Captain R.E.A. Crofton*
Adjutant, 16th U.S.	Lieutenant Charles W. Hotsenpillar
Adjutant, 19th U.S.	Lieutenant Robert Ayres*

Quartermaster	Lieutenant Samuel E. St. Onge
Company B/1/16th	Lieutenant Hugh A. Thacker
Company D/1/16th	Captain Charles F. Trowbridge
Company F/1/16th	Lieutenant Peter J. Cönzler (KIA)
Company H/1/16th	Lieutenant John K. Schiffler
Company B/2/16th	Captain William J. Slidell,*
	Lieutenant Felix H. Torbett
Company A/1/19th	Captain Henry S. Welton,
	Lieutenant Samuel S. Culbertson
Company C/1/19th+	Captain Thomas C. Williams,
	Lieutenant Douglas Edwards
Company E/1/19th	Captain James Mooney,
	Lieutenant Alfred Curtis
Company A/2/19th	Lieutenant Arthur B. Carpenter

+Division provost guard

1st Battalion, 18th U.S. Infantry

Commander	Captain George W. Smith
Adjutant	Lieutenant Reuben F. Little
Quartermaster	Lieutenant Daniel W. Benham
Sergeant Major	Sergeant Major A.C. Barrowes
Company B	Captain Andrew S. Burt,
	Lieutenant Ebenezer D. Harding*
Company D	Lieutenant John U. Gill
Company E	
Company F	Lieutenant Alfred Townsend
Company G	Captain Robert B. Hull*
Company H	Captain Anson Mills
Company G/3/18th	
Company H/3/18th	Lieutenant James Powell*

2nd Battalion, 18th U.S. Infantry

Commander	Captain Henry Haymond
Adjutant	Lieutenant John F. Lind
Quartermaster	Lieutenant Wilbur F. Arnold
Sergeant Major	Sergeant Major Edwin Beach
Company A	Lieutenant Frederick Phisterer
Company B	Lieutenant Thaddeus S. Kirtland
Company C	
Company D	Captain John H. Knight
Company E	
Company F	
Company G	
Company H	

Resaca, May 14–15, 1864

Johnson's 1st Division, Palmer's XIV Corps, Army of the Cumberland

1st Brigade	Brigadier General William P. Carlin
3rd Brigade	Colonel Benjamin F. Scribner
2nd Brigade	
Commander	Brigadier General John H. King
Adjutant	Lieutenant William J. Lyster,* 19th Infantry
Quartermaster	Lieutenant Joseph J. Wagoner, 19th Infantry
Commissary	Captain John R. Morledge, Commissary Service
Inspector general	Lieutenant Henry G. Litchfield,* 18th Infantry
Provost marshal	Captain James B. Mulligan,* 19th Infantry
Surgeon	Surgeon Lewis Slusser
11th Michigan Infantry	Colonel William L. Stoughton
69th Ohio Infantry	Colonel Marshall F. Moore

Demi-Brigade of Regulars

Commander	Major John R. Edie, 15th Infantry

1st Battalion, 15th U.S. Infantry

Commander	Captain Albert B. Dod
Adjutant	Lieutenant Samuel R. Honey
Quartermaster	Lieutenant Solomon E. Woodward
Sergeant Major	Sergeant Major James R. Bruce
Company A	
Company C	
Company E	Captain John C. Peterson, Lieutenant Henry C. Gapen
Company F	
Company G	Lieutenant John Williams
Company H	Captain James Curtis*
Company A/3/15th	
Company B/3/15th	Captain Horace Jewett*

2nd Battalion, 15th U.S. Infantry

Commander	Captain William C. McManus
Adjutant	Lieutenant Orson C. Knapp
Quartermaster	Lieutenant Irwin W. Potter
Sergeant Major	Sergeant Major Martin L. Brandt
Company A	Lieutenant Mason Jackson*
Company B	

Company C	Captain Thomas C. Norton*
Company D	Lieutenant Richard W. Derickson,
	Lieutenant Samuel L. Burness
Company E	Lieutenant Robert Harrison
Company F	Lieutenant Joseph C. Forbes

1st Battalion, 16th U.S. Infantry

Commander	Captain Alexander H. Stanton
Adjutant	Lieutenant Charles W. Hotsenpillar
Quartermaster	Lieutenant Samuel E. St. Onge
Company A	Lieutenant Jacob Kline
Company B	Lieutenant Charles H. Lewis
Company D*	Captain Charles F. Trowbridge
Company F	Lieutenant Edgar R. Kellogg
Company H	

*Division provost guard

2nd Battalion, 16th U.S. Infantry

Commander	Captain R. Peabody Barry
Company A	Captain Solomon S. Robinson,
	Lieutenant Lyman S. Strickland
Company B	Captain James Biddle,
	Lieutenant Felix H. Torbett
Company C	Captain William H. Prescott,
	Lieutenant William Mills*
Company D	Lieutenant Edward McConnell

1st Battalion, 18th U.S. Infantry

Commander	Captain George W. Smith
Adjutant	Lieutenant John U. Gill
Quartermaster	Lieutenant Daniel W. Benham
Sergeant Major	Sergeant Major A.C. Barrowes
Company B	Lieutenant Morgan L. Ogden
Company D	Captain Richard L. Morris
Company E	Lieutenant Alfred Townsend
Company F	Captain Andrew N. Burt*
Company G	Captain Robert B. Hull
Company H	Captain Anson Mills
Company G/3/18th	Captain Philip R. Forney
Company H/3/18th	Lieutenant James Powell

2nd Battalion, 18th U.S. Infantry

Commander	Captain Henry Haymond*
Adjutant	Lieutenant Frederick Phisterer*
Quartermaster	Lieutenant Frederick H. Brown
	(also commanded Company G)

Sergeant Major	Sergeant Major Christopher Peterson
Company A	
Company B	
Company C	Captain Ansel B. Denton
Company D	Lieutenant Horace Brown
Company E	Lieutenant Orrin E. Davis
Company F	Lieutenant James S. Ostrander,
	Lieutenant John I. Adair* (WIA)
Company G	Lieutenant Frederick H. Brown
Company H	Lieutenant Edgar N. Wilcox

1st Battalion, 19th U.S. Infantry

Commander	Captain James Mooney
Adjutant	Lieutenant Douglas Edwards
	(also commanded Company C)
Quartermaster	Lieutenant Walter O. Lattimore
Company A	
Company B	
Company C	Lieutenant Douglas Edwards
Company D	Lieutenant Egbert Phelps
Company E	Captain Robert W. Barnard
Company F	Lieutenant Alfred Curtis*
Company G	Lieutenant Samuel S. Culbertson
Company H	
Company A/2/19th	Lieutenant Arthur B. Carpenter

Jonesboro, September 1, 1864

Carlin's 1st Division, Davis's XIV Corps, Army of the Cumberland

1st Brigade	Colonel M.C. Taylor
3rd Brigade	Colonel Marshall F. Moore

Regular Brigade

Commander	Major John R. Edie,* 15th Infantry
Adjutant	Captain William J. Fetterman,*
	18th Infantry
Quartermaster	Lieutenant Daniel W. Benham,* 18th
	Infantry
Provost Marshal	Captain Anson Mills, 18th Infantry
Inspector General	Lieutenant Charles A.M. Estes,* 16th
	Infantry

1st Battalion, 15th U.S. Infantry

Commander	Captain Horace Jewett*
Adjutant	Lieutenant Samuel R. Honey*
Quartermaster	Lieutenant Solomon E. Woodward*
Company C	

Company F	
Company G	Lieutenant John Williams*
Company H	
Company A/3/15th	Sergeant Lovejoy
Company B/3/15th	Lieutenant Robert Harrison*
Company C/3/15th	Sergeant Carson

2nd Battalion, 15th U.S. Infantry

Commander	Captain William S. McManus
Adjutant	Lieutenant Orson C. Knapp*
Quartermaster	Lieutenant Irwin W. Potter*
Sergeant Major	Sergeant Major Brandt (WIA)
Company A	Sergeant Samuel Shane
Company B	Sergeant Edward Cummings (KIA)
Company C	Sergeant Philip Game (WIA)
Company D	
Company E	
Company F	Sergeant George Haller

Field Detachment, 16th U.S. Infantry

Commander	Captain R. Peabody Barry
Adjutant	Lieutenant Charles W. Hotsenpillar*
Quartermaster	Lieutenant Samuel E. St. Onge*
Company A/1	
Company B/1	
Company D/1+	Captain Charles F. Trowbridge*
Company F/1	Lieutenant Edgar R. Kellogg* (WIA)
Company H/1	
Company A/2	Captain Solomon S. Robinson,*
	Lieutenant Lyman S. Strickland*
Company B/2	Captain James Biddle,*
	Lieutenant Felix H. Torbett*
Company C/2	
Company D/2	Lieutenant Edward McConnell*

+Division provost guard

Field Detachment, 18th U.S. Infantry

Commander	Captain Lyman M. Kellogg* (WIA)
Adjutant	Lieutenant William H. Bisbee*
Quartermaster	Lieutenant Frederick H. Brown*
Sergeant Major	Sergeant Major Andrew Durfey
1st Company	Captain Robert B. Hull*
2nd Company	Lieutenant James S. Ostrander
3rd Company	1st Sergeant William W. Bell (WIA)
4th Company	Lieutenant James Powell*

5th Company	Lieutenant Reuben F. Little*
6th Company	1st Sergeant William Gordon
7th Company	Lieutenant Orrin E. Davis
8th Company	Lieutenant Thomas B. Burrowes*

1st Battalion, 19th U.S. Infantry

Commander	Captain James Mooney
Adjutant	Lieutenant Douglas Edwards
	(also commanded Company C)
Quartermaster	Lieutenant Joseph J. Wagoner*
Company A	
Company B	
Company C	Lieutenant Douglas Edwards*
Company D	Lieutenant George W. Johnson (WIA)
Company E	
Company F	
Company G	Lieutenant Samuel S. Culbertson
Company H	
Company A/2/19th	Lieutenant Arthur B. Carpenter*

APPENDIX C: Unpublished Reports

Four official reports from the Army of the Cumberland's regulars were not published in either the War Department's *War of the Rebellion: The Official Records of the Union and Confederate Armies* or Broadfoot Publishing's *Supplement to the Official Records of the Union and Confederate Armies.*

* * *

Nashville Tenn.
January 12th 1863

Lieut. Sutherland 18th Infty
A.A.A.G. Regular Brigade
3 Division

Sir:

I have the honor to report that on the morning of Dec 31s 1863, having placed my command ready for action, I entered the Cedar wood on the right, following the 15th Infantry. As soon as in position, the rebels were seen on the right, endeavoring to obtain a position to the right and rear. The 15th having retreated to the right and rear, it became necessary that my command should fall back, as we were fired on from the right, left, and front. I withdrew from the wood in as good order as possible, and at the edge of the road found, a battery and its support placed in our rear, holding the enemy in check on the right. I retreated across the road to the railroad, where the remainder of the Brigade was found. Having replenished our ammunition, I was again ordered to support the Battery on the right following its movements. Once more we approached the woods and when within a hundred yards, I was ordered to throw my battalion immediately in front of the Battery and on Major Carpenter's left. This was done, and the line advanced to the edge of the wood. Firing commenced on the right, and soon became general. Fearing we might be firing on our line in front, I gave the order Cease Firing. The first line soon came in on the left, and the enemy appeared in force in front, and began firing with great rapidity. Soon I found myself severely wounded in the left leg, just below the knee, and was compelled to face to the rear, to be taken care of.

The Officers and men of my command behaved with great coolness and personal courage. I cannot praise them too highly. Lieut. John Power, Adjutant of the Battalion, and Capt. R.E. Crofton, Acting Field Officer, rendered valuable and Effective service, and I present their names especially to your notice.

Out of fourteen Officers present, seven were wounded. Out of two hundred ninety five (295) men in ranks bearing arms in the morning, but Sixty five (65) reformed after this engagement.

> I am Sir very respectfully
> Your obt. Sevt.
>
> A.J. SLEMMER
> Major 16th Infantry[89]

* * *

> Hd. Qrs. 2d Batt. 15th Infy
> Chattanooga, Tenn.,
> December 1st 1863

Major John R. Edie, 15th Inf..
Comm'd'g demi Brig.

Major:-

I have the honor to submit the following report of the part taken in the last weeks' engagements with the enemy, by the 2d Batt., 15th U.S. Infy., 2d Brigade, 1st Div., 14 A.C.

On Wednesday, Nov. 25th, the Battlin being then seventy-two hours on picket duty, I received orders to call in the picket and join the Brigade, which I did at ten o'clock that morning, finding the Brigade with its right resting on the Rossville Road. At two o'clock, we moved with Brigade, in line of battle. The 1st Batt having been deployed as skirmishers, the right of the first line of the Brig. rested in the right of the 2d Batt.

Thus formed, we crossed the plane of three-quarters of a mile in width, separating us from the ridge, under a direct and a cross fire of the enemy's artillery, reaching the first line of the enemy's works and they being driven from behind them and up the slope of the ridge, we continued on to their secind line where they were again driven.

Here we halted, under cover, and waited for all our men to come up, the formation of the ground together with the obstructions thrown up by the enemy, making it impossible for a good line to be observed. Th enemy still holding possession of the ridge, the order was given to cross and charge upon them. The Batt. crossed, with the rest of the line, taking possession of the ridge in our front and driving the enemy down the eastern slope of the ridge. Wednesday night we encamped upon the ridge, and the next morning followed in pursuit of the enemy towards Graysville, reaching that place at half-past eleven, Thursday night, and went into camp, having assisted at 9 P.M., a short distance this side of Graysville in the capture of Furgesens' (rebel) Battery. Lt. Harrison, having been sent out with a company of skirmishers, discovered the presence of the Battery, at the same time capturing one of Gen. Braggs' couriers. Friday morning at half past six, the pursuit continued to Ringgold, Georgia, a distance of five miles from Graysville. Here Gen. Hooker had already engaged the enemy. The Brigade being formed in two lines, the 2d Batt. in the front line and on the left of the 1st Batt., advanced and took up a position on the left of the first Brigade, but with the exception of a few skirmishers thrown out, did not take any part in the engagement. At Ringgold we remained encamped until Monday morning, twelve o'clock, when the Batt. returned, with the Brigade, to Chattanooga reaching here at half past six, the same evening, having marched the distance of eighteen miles that day.

The loss sustained was upon Mission Ridge, and is as follow:

Killed:
    Private Matznich, Co. "A",
    Private Symington, Co. "B"
    and Corporal Carr, Co. "D"
Total loss in killed, - 3

Wounded:
Private Livermene, co. "A", severely in left arm;
Private Winchester, Co. "B", severely in left arm;
Private McGuire, Co. "C", slightly in arm;
Private Kimmey McHale, Co., "D",
and Private Peasley Co. E in Thumb.
Total wounded, - 6
Missing:
Sgt. H. Lyon, Co. "A",

In conclusion, I take pleasure in saying that both officers and men without an exception, behaved well.

I have the honor to be, Major, very respectfully, your obt servt.

W. McMANUS
Capt. 15th Infy.
Com'd'g 2d Batt.[90]

* * *

Head Quarters 2d Batt 15th U.S. Inf..
Chattanooga, Tennessee
December 3rd 1863

Capt Jas W Forsyth
AAAG 2d Bgd 1st Div
14 A.C.

Captain.

Having been assigned the command of that portion of this Brigade composed of the 15th 16th 18th & 19th U.S. Infantry during the operations of the past week, I have the honor to report, for the information of the Commandant of the Brigade, that about midday of Wednesday the 25th ult., after serving on picket duty from the previous Sunday morning, we were ordered into line of battle with the balance of the Brigade, with directions to take post on the right of Maj Gen Sheridan, division, and conform to his movements.

The order was promptly obeyed and the forces I have named moved forward, in accordance with instructions, til they encountered the enemy, protected by rifle pits, at the western base of Missionary Ridge. Those of the enemy, in our immediate front, were soon driven up the Hill to their second line and were hotly pursued by our advancing force.

The foe was driven from their second line, with the same promptness, that dislodged them from their pits at the foot of the ridge. Here we stopped a short time, the ascent being so abrupt as to have fatigued the men. As soon as they had rested, another advance was made, and the enemy was driven from the summit of the ridge, leaving our forces in undisputed possession of the battlefield.

It was near sun down when we reached the summit, and after throwing out the necessary picket, the command "bivouacked" for the night.

In the morning we started in pursuit of the retreating foe, and followed them all of Thursday, capturing (3) three pieces of artillery with three caissons and some horses and a large number of prisoners.

We stopped for the night at Graysville and on the morning of Friday moved on to Ringgold Ga. where we were again put into line of battle, but did not engage the enemy—that work having been effectually performed by another portion of the Army.

We remained at Ringgold until the 29th ult, when pursuant to orders we returned to our camp at this place.

It affords me great gratification to be able to say that the troops of my command, behaved with great gallantry in the action of the 25th ult, and throughout the entire week's operations their conduct merits the highest praise. Officers and men without exception strove diligently to perform their whole duty, and they succeeded. It would perhaps be invidious to make special references where all behaved gallantly, but duty requires me to thank Captains Keteltas and McManus, com'dg 1st and 2d Batt's 15th Inf.., Capt Crofton com'dg 16th and 19th Inf. and Capts. Smith and Haymond com'dg 1st and 2d Batt 18th Inf. for their energy, promptness and determined courage in the engagements.

2d Lieut. O.C. Knapp 15th Inf. Adjut 2d Batt has my warmest thanks for his valuable service in communicating orders to the different Battalion commanders.

> I have the honor to be Captain
> Very Respectfully
> Your Most Obdt Servt,
>
> JOHN R. EDIE
> Major 15th Inf.[91]

* * *

> Head Qrs. 1st Batt. 15th Infy
> Graysville, Ga. March 27, 1864

Capt. Forsyth
  A.A. Genl.
  2nd Brig. 1st Div.
  14th A.C.

Sir:-

In compliance with circular of this date, I have the honor to report that the battalion under my command marched from Chattanooga February 22nd camping at Ringgold. February 23rd following upon skirmishers of the 19th Illinois, it advanced with main column of the Brigade to within three fourths of a mile fo the town of Tunnel Hill, returning, under orders, three miles back to neighbourhood of the "Stone Church," and, strengthened by temporary consolidation with a battalion of the 19th Regulars, under Captain Mooney, occupying ridge at right of the road during the night. On the morning of the 24th slight skirmishing took place between the command, as consolidated, and a few advancing cavalry of the enemy—compelling the hasty retreat of the latter. Following upon our own cavalry, the battalion still united with the 19th moved forward after the above named skirmish, taking again the direction of Tunnel Hill. At a point a mile or more this side the town, it was ordered to advance upon a ridge upon the left of the road, to drive out a force of the rebel cavalry discovered along the crest. The rebels disappeared as my skirmishers advanced. No shots were fired on either side. Throwing out then a more extended line of skirmishers, I advanced my command, under an order of General commanding Brigade. In the road running into Tunnel Hill from the northerly side. Under the disposition for attack of Tunnel Hill proper. Then occupied by the enemy in greater or less force. My battalion advanced upon right of the first line of regulars—all the battalions of which line comprising in addition to my own, battalions of the 19th, 16th, and 18th were for the line placed under my direction. Suspending his fire against cavalry upon our right, the enemy limbered up with our advance and again retreating, we gained the hill without impediment on his part. Upon the evening of the 25th, my battalion, consolidated with the 2nd battalion of hte 18th under Captain Haymond, occupied as reserve to skirmishers, a steep hill at left of the rail to Dalton by Kinyan's Gap, being one of the series of hills, or ridges, known collectively as "Buzzards Roost." The morning of the 26th opened with lively skirmishing, which continued with greater or less severity during the day. The enemy's sharpshooters being able to reach at nearly every point, the hills held by both the pickets or skirmish line and the reserve. One man—name not reported to me—as killed out of the battalion of the 18th on my left. In my own battalion casualties none. Good service was done by twenty men of the 1st Battalion under an officer posted subsequently to my arrival. A the foot of the hill, to the right, others of my command were thrown out as sharpshooters on a low knoll to the right and front, aiding effectually to clear the enemy from guns posted on an opposite eminence, and to drive back stray parties along the railroad or elsewhere.

On being withdrawn on the night of the 26th my battalion marched with main column of Brigade, camping at stone church. 27th marched to Tyners station—subsequently being ordered to this point.

The conduct of officers and men of my battalion during the whole expedition was entirely satisfactory to myself, and creditable to them.

> Very Respectfully
> Your obdt. servt.
> MAJOR ALBERT TRACY
> 15th U.S. Infny.
> Comdg. 1st Batt.[92]

APPENDIX D: Colonels of Regiments

Officers who received commissions in the western regulars provided senior leadership for a number of volunteer regiments during the Civil War and went on to lead regular regiments into the next century.

Table D: Regular Officers Who Served As Regimental Commanders

Name	Regular Commission in Civil War	Colonel of Regiment
Barnard, Robert W.	Lt., 19th U.S., 1861	10th U.S.C.T., 1864-1866
Bidell, James	Capt., 15th U.S., 1861	6th Indiana Cavalry, 1862-1865
		9th U.S. Cavalry, 1891-1896
Bisbee, William H.	Lt., 18th U.S., 1861	13th U.S. Infantry, 1899-1901
Bomford, James V.	Lt. Col., 16th U.S., 1862	8th U.S. Infantry, 1864-1874
Burt, Andrew S.	Lt., 18th U.S., 1861	25th U.S. Infantry, 1892-1902
Carpenter, Gilbert S.	Lt., 18th U.S., 1862	18th U.S. Infantry, 1899
Chambers, Alexander	Capt., 18th U.S., 1861	16th Iowa Infantry, 1862-1863
		17th U.S. Infantry, 1886-1888
Cochran, Mellville A.	Capt., 16th U.S., 1861	6th U.S. Infantry, 1890-1898
Crofton, R.E.A.	Capt., 16th U.S., 1861	15th U.S. Infantry, 1886-1897
Dawson, Samuel K.	Maj., 19th U.S., 1861	19th U.S. Infantry, 1866-1869
Douglass, Henry	Capt., 18th U.S., 1861	10th U.S. Infantry, 1885-1891
Ewers, Ezra P.	Lt., 19th U.S., 1863	10th U.S. Infantry, 1899-1901
Fessenden, Francis	Capt., 19th U.S., 1861	25th Maine Infantry, 1862-1863
		30th Maine Infantry, 1864
Forsyth, James W.	Lt., 18th U.S., 1861	7th U.S. Cavalry, 1886-1894
Freeman, Henry B.	Lt., 18th U.S., 1861	24th U.S. Infantry, 1898-1901
Guenther, Francis L.	Lt., 5th U.S. Artillery, 1861	4th U.S. Artillery, 1896-1901
Harker, Charles G.	Capt., 15th U.S., 1861	65th Ohio Infantry, 1861-1864

Name	Regular Commission in Civil War	Colonel of Regiment
Hays, Alexander	Capt., 16th U.S., 1861	63rd Pennsylvania Inf.., 1861
Hough, Alfred L.	Capt., 19th U.S., 1861	9th U.S. Infantry, 1888-1890
Jewett, Horace	Lt., 15th U.S., 1861	21st U.S. Infantry, 1891-1897
Kelly, Patrick	Capt., 16th U.S., 1861	88th New York Infantry, 1862-1864
Kellogg, Edgar R.	Lt., 16th U.S., 1862	6th U.S. Infantry, 1898-1899
King, Edward A.	Lt. Col., 19th U.S., 1861	68th Indiana Infantry, 1863 6th U.S. Infantry, 1863
King, John H.	Maj., 15th U.S., 1861	9th U.S. Infantry, 1865-1882
Kline, Jacob	Lt., 16th U.S., 1861	21st U.S. Infantry, 1897-1903
Lyster, William J.	Lt., 19th U.S., 1861	9th U.S. Infantry, 1896-1897
Mizner, Henry R.	Capt., 18th U.S., 1861	14th Michigan Infantry, 1863-1864 17th U.S. Infantry, 1888-1891
Mills, Anson	Lt., 18th U.S., 1861	3rd U.S. Cavalry, 1892-1897
Mussey, Reuben D.	Capt., 19th U.S. 1861	100th U.S.C.T., 1864-1865
Potter, Joseph H.	Maj., 19th U.S., 1863	12th New Hampshire Infantry, 1862-1865
Ritter, John F.	Lt., 15th U.S., 1861	1st Missouri Cavalry, 1862-1864
Sanderson, John P.	Lt. Col., 15th U.S., 1861	13th U.S. Infantry, 1863-1864
Shepherd, Oliver L.	Lt. Col., 18th U.S., 1861	15th U.S. Infantry, 1863-1870
Slidell, William J.	Lt., 16th U.S., 1861	144th New York Infantry, 1864
Swaine, Peter T.	Capt., 15th U.S., 1861	99th Ohio Infantry, 1862-1864 22nd U.S. Infantry, 1884-1895
Tillson, John	Capt., 19th U.S., 1861	10th Illinois Infantry, 1862-1865
Townsend, Edwin F.	Capt., 16th U.S., 1861	12th U.S. Infantry, 1886-1895
Townsend, Frederick	Maj., 18th U.S., 1861	3rd New York Infantry, 1861
Wickoff, Charles A.	Lt., 15th U.S., 1861	22nd U.S. Infantry, 1897-1898
Willard, George L.	Maj., 19th U.S., 1861	125th New York Infantry, 1862-1863
Wilson, Lewis	Capt., 19th U.S., 1861	2nd Ohio Infantry, 1861

NOTES

Abbreviations

AGO   Adjutant General's Office.
C-C NMP   Chickamauga-Chattanooga National Military Park, Ft. Oglethorpe, Georgia.
GO   General Order (followed by order number, issuing headquarters, and date or series).
OR   *The War of the Rebellion: Official Records of the Union and Confederate Armies.*
NA MF   National Archives Microfilm Publication (followed by series and roll numbers).
NA RG   National Archives Record Group (followed by record group and entry or folder numbers).
SO   Special Order (followed by order number, issuing headquarters, and date or series).
SFO   Special Field Order (followed by order number, issuing headquarters, and date or series).
SRNB   Stones River National Battlefield, Murfreesboro, Tennessee.
USAMHI   United States Army Military History Institute, Carlisle Barracks, Pennsylvania.

Introduction

1 Charles W. Larned, *History of the Battle Monument at West Point* (West Point: n.p., 1898), pp. 3, 198.

2 Thomas E. Greiss, ed., *The West Point Military History Series: The American Civil War* (Wayne, New Jersey: Avery Publishing Group, 1987), pp. 19-21.

3 James B. Ronan II, "North's Unsung Regulars," *America's Civil War*, July 1993, p. 42; Frederick Phisterer, *Statistical Record of the Armies of the United States* (New York: Charles Scribner's Sons, 1883), pp. 10-11, 22-23. The exact number of Regular Army soldiers who served during the Civil War is difficult to determine. By actual count, 64,130 names appear on the Regular Army's Register of Enlistments for the Civil War (NA MF M233/26-29; I have defined wartime enlistments as those occurring between April 1, 1861, and March 31, 1865). To that number must be added the approximately 16,000 regular soldiers on duty as the war began. Re-enlistments, approximately 5,500, are embedded in the enlistment numbers. Deducting them yields a total of 74,630 Civil War regulars.

4 Artillery regiments were administrative entities and did not serve in the field; regular artillery batteries were parceled out throughout the Union Army. The Army of the Potomac's Reserve Cavalry Brigade, formed in February 1863, consisted of the 1st, 2nd, 5th, and 6th U.S. Cavalry Regiments (the 3rd Cavalry served in the Southwest and with the Army of the Tennessee, while the 4th Cavalry was assigned to the Army of the Cumberland). The operations of this brigade of regular mounted troops, commanded at

times by such prominent Union cavalry leaders as Brigadier General John Buford, Brigadier General Wesley Merritt, and Colonel Charles Russell Lowell, awaits examination. The best coverage of regular horsemen currently available, particularly their operations in 1861 prior to the formation of volunteer cavalry regiments in the Union Army, is Edward G. Longacre's *Lincoln's Cavalrymen: A History of the Mounted Forces of the Army of the Potomac* (Mechanicsburg, Pennsylvania: Stackpole Books, 2000).

5   Bruce Catton, *Reflections on the Civil War* (New York: Doubleday & Co. Inc., 1981), p. 175.

6   Frederick Phisterer, *The Regular Army of the United States: Read Before George S. Dawson Post, No. 63, Department of New York, Grand Army of the Republic, Albany, N.Y., April 13th, 1893* (Albany, New York: S.H. Wentworth, 1893), p. 16; Phisterer, *Statistical Record*, pp. 83-212.

7   William F. Fox, *Regimental Losses in the American Civil War, 1861-1865* (Albany, New York: Albany Publishing Co., 1889), pp. 520-521.

8   George T. Ness, Jr., *The Regular Army on the Eve of the U.S. Civil War* (Baltimore: The Toomey Press, 1990); Durwood Ball, *Army Regulars on the Western Frontier, 1848-1861* (Norman: University of Oklahoma Press, 2001).

9   Augustus Meyers, *Ten Years in the Ranks, U.S. Army* (New York: The Sterling Press, 1914); Michael N. Ingrisano, Jr., *An Artilleryman's War: Gus Dey and the 2nd United States Artillery* (Shippensburg, Pennsylvania: White Mane Publishing Company, Inc, 1998); Sidney Morris Davis, *Common Soldier, Uncommon War: Life as a Cavalryman in the Civil War* (Bethesda, Maryland: John H. Davis, Jr., 1993).

10   There were other regular infantry units that served in the Western Theater in addition to the 15th, 16th, 18th, and 19th Regiments. The 13th U.S. served in the Army of the Tennessee, while elements of the 1st U.S. were assigned to the Army of the Mississippi and various garrisons. Additional small detachments of regulars served in the Southwest. The operations of these units are beyond the scope of this narrative.

11   Ronan, "North's Unsung Regulars," pp. 44; Louis M. Hosea, "The Regular Brigade of the Army of the Cumberland," in *Sketches of War History 1861-1865: Papers read before the Military Order of the Loyal Legion of the United States, Ohio Commandery,* vol. 5 (Cincinnati: Monfort & Company, 1908), pp. 328-329.

12   James Kirby Martin and Mark Edward Lender, *A Respectable Army: The Military Origins of the Republic, 1763-1789* (Arlington Heights, Illinois: Harlan Davidson, Inc., 1982), pp. 6-28; Frederick D, Williams, ed., *The Wild Life of the Army: Civil War Letters of James A. Garfield* (East Lansing: Michigan State University Press, 1964), p. 125.

13   Bell I. Wiley, *The Life of Billy Yank: The Common Soldier of the Union* (Indianapolis: Bobbs-Merrill, 1952), pp. 324-325; Archer Jones, *Civil War Command and Strategy: The Process of Victory and Defeat* (New York: The Free Press, 1992), p. 5.

14   Mark W. Johnson, "Holding the Left of the Line: The Brigade of United States Regulars at Chickamauga." *Civil War Regiments: A Journal of the American Civil War* 7, no. 1 (2000): 33-74.

Prologue

1   Richard W. Johnson, *A Soldier's Reminiscences in Peace and War* (Philadelphia: J.R. Lippencott, 1886), pp. 148-149 (this officer is no relation to the author).

2   U.S. War Department, *The War of the Rebellion: Official Records of the Union and Confederate Armies,* 128 vols. (Washington: Government Printing Office, 1880-1901),

series I, vol. 1, p. 355; series III, vol. 1, pp. 24-25 (hereinafter cited as *OR*, all references are to series I unless otherwise noted).

3   Russell K. Brown, "An Old Woman with a Broomstick: General David E. Twiggs and the U.S. Surrender in Texas, 1861," *Military Affairs* 48 (April 1984), p. 59; Johnson, *A Soldier's Reminiscences*, p. 134; George T. Ness, Jr., *The Regular Army on the Eve of the U.S. Civil War* (Baltimore: The Toomey Press, 1990), p. 219; *OR*, vol. 1, pp. 502-503.

4   Johnson, *A Soldier's Reminiscences*, pp. 149-150; Thomas T. Smith, *The Old Army in Texas: A Research Guide to the U.S. Army in Nineteenth-Century Texas* (Austin: Texas State Historical Association, 2000), pp. 70, 102-103. Fort Lancaster, located on a tributary of the Pecos River in West Texas, was established in 1855 by Captain Stephen D. Carpenter of the 1st Infantry. Carpenter named the post for Lieutenant Job Lancaster, a fellow 1840 West Pointer and officer of the 1st Infantry, who was struck by lightening and killed in July 1841 during the 2nd Seminole War.

5   Johnson, *A Soldier's Reminiscences*, pp. 150-151; William H. Bell, *Ante Bellum; or, Before the War, A Paper Read before The Military Order of the Loyal Legion of the United States, Commandery of the State of Ohio* (Cincinnati: Peter G. Thompson, 1883), p. 18; "The Second Regiment of Cavalry From Texas," *The New York Times*, 28 April 1861, p. 3; Smith, *The Old Army in Texas*, p. 68. The 3d Infantry is the army's senior regiment due to a complicated reorganization of the nation's military forces in the aftermath of the War of 1812. The wartime establishment of forty-eight regular infantry regiments was reduced to eight in 1815. The 1st Regiment, having been established in 1784 and thus the oldest U.S. Army infantry regiment, was consolidated with the 5th, 17th, 19th, and 28th Regiments and the new unit was designated the 3d Infantry. Other, less senior regiments were consolidated to form the new 1st and 2nd Regiments.

6   USMA Association of Graduates, *Annual Reunion, 1894* (West Point, 1894), pp. 91-92; Francis B. Heitman, *Historical Register and Dictionary of the United States Army*, 2 vols. (Washington: Government Printing Office, 1903), vol. 1, p. 880 (all references are to volume 1 unless otherwise noted); William T. Sherman, *Sherman's Civil War: Selected Correspondence of William T. Sherman, 1860-1865*, edited by Brooks D. Sampson and Jean V. Berlin (Chapel Hill: University of North Carolina Press, 1999), p. 101.

7   Brevet promotions were honorary rank bestowed upon an officer for heroism in wartime. As the United States during the Civil War had no military medals prior to the Medal of Honor's establishment in 1863 (and no others until the early twentieth century), a brevet was the standard reward for gallantry in action.

8   Shepherd to Seward, 5 June 1861, NA MF M619/59; Francis F. McKinney, *Education in Violence: The Life of George H. Thomas and the History of the Army of the Cumberland* (Chicago: Americana House, 1991), p. 45; L.R. Bailey, *The Navajo Reconnaissance: A Military Exploration of the Navajo Country in 1859* (Los Angeles: Westernlore Press, 1964), pp. 59-66; Frank McNitt, *The Navajo Wars* (Albuquerque: University of New Mexico Press, 1972) p. 302; "D" [William Dickinson], "Reminiscences of Fort Defiance, 1860," *Journal of the Military Service Institution of the United States* 4 (1883), pp. 90-92; *Annual Report of the Secretary of War, 1860* (Washington, 1861), pp. 52-56; *OR*, series III, vol. 1, p. 24.

9   Smith, *The Old Army in Texas*, pp. 18, 59, 102-103; Ness, *The Regular Army*, pp. 166, 293 n. 60. Five of the six officers Shepherd identified were members of Colonel William W. Loring's Regiment of Mounted Riflemen, including Loring himself (who became a Confederate major general), Captain Andrew Jackson Lindsay (later a colonel

of Mississippi cavalry), Captain John G. Walker (also a future Confederate major general), and Captain Dabney H. Maury (another Confederate major general). Shepherd also suspected Lieutenant Lucius L. Rich of the 5th Infantry, who became a colonel of Missouri infantry. The only officer whose loyalties Shepherd misread was North Carolinian Alexander McRae, a lieutenant of the Mounted Rifles, who died in a Federal uniform at the Battle of Valverde, New Mexico, on February 21, 1862.

    10 *OR*, vol. 1, pp. 601-602; Brown, "An Old Woman and a Broomstick," pp. 59-60; Bell, *Ante Bellum*, pp. 6-7, 11-12; Heitman, *Historical Register*, p. 901. For a detailed account of the 3rd Infantry's 1861 experiences in Texas, see Timothy J. Reese, *Sykes' Regular Infantry Division, 1861-1864: A History of Regular United States Infantry Operations in the Civil War's Eastern Theater* (Jefferson, North Carolina: McFarland, 1990), pp. 16-28. The 2nd Cavalry's operations in and exodus from Texas are covered in James R. Arnold's *Jeff Davis's Own: Cavalry, Commanches, and the Battle for the Texas Frontier* (New York: John Wiley & Sons, Inc., 2000), one of the few modern studies of an antebellum Regular Army regiment.

    11 *OR*, vol. 1, pp. 573-574, 623; Frank Moore, ed., *The Rebellion Record; a Diary of American Events*, 11 vols. (New York: G.P. Putnam, 1861-1868), vol. 1, p. 119; Reese, *Sykes' Regular Infantry Division*, p. 22; Ness, *The Regular Army*, p. 223; Johnson, *A Soldier's Reminiscences*, p. 150.

    12 Shepherd to Thomas, 27 April 1861, NA MF M619/55; Bell, *Ante Bellum*, pp. 24-25; "Arrival of the Empire City with Troops From Texas," *New York Times*, 26 April 1861, p. 8; Freeman Cleaves, *Rock of Chickamauga: The Life of General George H. Thomas* (Norman: University of Oklahoma Press, 1948), pp. 62-63; McKinney, *Education in Violence*, p. 82. Field officers of the 2nd Cavalry who joined the Confederate army were Colonel Albert Sidney Johnston, Lieutenant Colonel Robert E. Lee, and Major Earl Van Dorn. Heitman, *Historical Register*, p. 71.

    13 Heitman, *Historical Register*, p. 284; *Bangor (Maine) Daily Whig and Courier*, 12 February 1863, p. 1; Smith, *The Old Army in Texas*, p. 61; *OR*, vol. 1, p. 542.

    14 *OR*, vol. 1, p. 543.

    15 "Military and Naval Movements. The Coatzacoalcos Troops," *New York Times*, 13 April 1861, p. 8; *New York Times*, 12 April 1861, p. 4.

    16 "John Haskell King," *The National Cyclopedia of American Biography*, vol. 30, p. 47; William B. Skelton, *An American Profession of Arms: The Army Officer Corps, 1784-1861* (Lawrence: University Press of Kansas, 1992), pp. 132-144; Heitman, *Historical Register*, p. 599; Johnson, *A Soldier's Reminiscences*, pp. 79, 240; McKinney, *Education in Violence*, pp. 88-89; Association of Survivors, Regular Brigade, Fourteenth Corps, Army of the Cumberland, *Proceedings of Reunions Held At Pittsburgh PA., Sept. 11-12, 1894, Crawfish Springs, GA., Sept 18-19, 1895, St. Paul, Minn., Sept. 1-2 1896, Columbus, Ohio, Sept. 22-23, 1897*, (Columbus, Ohio: John L. Trauger, 1898), p. 10; Cleaves, *Rock of Chickamauga*, p. 66.

    17 Brown, "An Old Woman and a Broomstick," p. 60; McKinney, *Education in Violence*, pp. 95-106; Reese, *Sykes' Regular Infantry Division*, pp. 39-40; *OR*, vol. 1, pp. 589, 597.

Chapter 1

    1 Anson Mills, *My Story* (Washington: Byron S. Adams, 1918), pp. 47-53, 61-62.

    2 Association of Survivors, Regular Brigade, *Proceedings of Reunions*, pp. 44-45. Signers of the letter included ten future general officers, three men who would earn Medals of Honor, and five cadets who ended up in Confederate uniforms.

3   Mills to Thomas, 22 June 1861, Mills personnel file, NA RG 94; Mills, *My Story*, pp. 78-79, 391.

4   Shepherd to Thomas, 25 June 1861, NA MF M619/56; Roy P. Basler, ed., *The Collected Works of Abraham Lincoln*, 8 vols. (New Brunswick, NJ: Rutgers University Press, 1953), vol. 4, p. 409.

5   OR vol. 2, pp. 670-671, 691-697; Reese, *Sykes' Regular Infantry Division*, pp. 35-42.

6   Henry B. Carrington, "Ohio Military Service in 1861 Resulting in Supplemental Service in the Regular Army," Ohio Civil War Memoranda of Official Data, Archives/Library Division, Ohio Historical Society, Columbus, p. 18; Shepherd to the adjutant general, 4 May 1872, Shepherd personnel file, NA RG 94; SO 179, War Department, AGO, series 1861.

7   Marvin A. Kreidberg and Merton G. Henry, *History of Military Mobilization in the United States Army, 1776-1945* (Washington: Department of the Army, 1955), pp. 61-82, 89-92; William A. Ganoe, *The History of the United States Army* (New York: D. Appleton, 1924), p. 250; OR, series III, vol. 1, pp. 23-26.

8   Emory Upton, *The Military Policy of the United States* (Washington, 1903), pp. 233-244. In addition to Franklin and McDowell, Army Adjutant General Lorenzo Thomas was also officially a member of the committee. He was so busy with his normal duties that he did not offer much input and simply rubber stamped the recommendations of the two junior officers.

9   The 3rd U.S. Cavalry Regiment was soon redesignated as the 6th Cavalry, a result of the army's six mounted regiments (1st & 2nd Dragoons, the Mounted Riflemen, and 1st, 2nd, & 3rd Cavalry) all being organized as cavalry regiments in August 1861. OR, series 3, vol. 1, pp. 398-399.

10   Ness, *The Regular Army*, pp. 37-46; GO 16, War Department, AGO, series 1861; Heitman, *Historical Register*, vol. 2, pp. 598-601; OR, series III, vol. 1, p. 304; Jones, *Civil War Command and Strategy*, p. 264; John R. Elting, *Swords Around the Throne: Napoleon's Grand Armée* (New York: The Free Press, 1988), pp. 211-216.

11   Upton, *Military Policy*, pp. 228-229. The concerns that prevented all Union infantry regiments from being organized in the multi-battalion format evidently did not apply to cavalry regiments. During August 1861 the Old Army's five mounted regiments were converted into the same 12-company, 3-battalion format authorized for the new 3rd (soon to be 6th) U.S. Cavalry, and most volunteer cavalry regiments were also organized with multiple battalions. Longacre, *Lincoln's Cavalrymen*, p. 16.

12   OR, series III, vol. 1, pp. 372-373.

13   Ibid., pp. 304, 374; Heitman, *Historical Register*, vol. 2, p. 601; Phisterer, *Statistical Record*, p. 62.

14   Henry B. Carrington, "Indiana in the Civil War. Major General H.W. Halleck's Statements confronted by Actual Facts," Ohio Civil War Memoranda of Official Data, Archives/Library Division, Ohio Historical Society, Columbus, p. 12.

15   OR, series III, vol. 1, p. 305; Edward M. Coffman, *The Old Army: A Portrait of the American Army in Peacetime, 1784-1898* (New York: Oxford University Press, Inc., 1986), p. 60. The new Regular regiments in 1855 were the 9th and 10th Infantry and the 1st and 2nd Cavalry.

16   Katherine McKeen, "Henry Beebee Carrington: A Soldier's Tale" (doctoral dissertation, State University of New York at Stony Brook, 1998), pp. 17, 33, 46, 48, 57, 66; Lucius Brown, "Henry B. Carrington," Letters: Appendix 2, p. 1, Brown Family Correspondence, 1844-1868, Manuscripts and Archives Division, New York Public Library. Carrington has been the subject of much writing over the years but has not

received a full-length biography. The most thorough examination of his life is Ms. McKeen's dissertation, although even this source barely mentions Carrington's role in organizing the 18th U.S. Infantry—which was perhaps Carrington's most significant military accomplishment.

17 Brown, "Henry B. Carrington," p. 1.

18 McKeen, "Henry Beebee Carrington," pp. 66-67.

19 Ibid., pp. 75-76; Henry B. Carrington, *Ohio Militia and the West Virginia Campaign of 1861* (Boston: R.H. Blodgett & Co., 1904), pp. 10-13.

20 McKeen, "Henry Beebee Carrington," pp. 76-77; Carrington, "Ohio Military Service," pp. 4, 5.

21 Quoted in Carrington, "Ohio Military Service," p. 5.

22 Roger D. Hunt and Jack R. Brown, *Brevet Brigadier Generals in Blue* (Frederick, Maryland: Olde Soldier Books, 1998), p. 623; Association of Survivors, Regular Brigade, *Proceedings of Reunions*, pp. 18-19; "Frederick Townsend," *The National Cyclopaedia of American Biography*, vol. 4, pp. 458-459; OR 2, p. 86; Carrington, "Ohio Military Service," p. 19.

23 Lucius Brown, "The Band of the 18th," Letters: Appendix 3, pp. 1-2, Brown Family Correspondence, 1844-1868, Manuscripts and Archives Division, New York Public Library.

24 Carrington, "Ohio Military Service," pp. 16-17.

25 Kellogg to McLille, 25 July 1861, collection of Dennis Keesee, Westerville, Ohio.

26 Earl J. Coates and Dean S. Thomas, *An Introduction to Civil War Small Arms* (Gettysburg, Pennsylvania: Thomas Publications, 1980), pp. 86, 88; Arthur B. Carpenter to parents, 22 December 1861, Arthur B. Carpenter Papers, Special Collections, Yale University, New Haven, Connecticut; Steedman to Denig, 21 November 1862, NA RG 393/5756.

27 Carrington, "Ohio Military Service," pp. 15-16.

28 GO 33, War Department, AGO, series 1861; Douglass to Carter, 17 May 1866, and Kennedy to the president, 25 October 1870, Douglass personnel file, NA RG 94; Heitman, *Historical Register*, pp. 367, 802, 888; James Barnet, ed., *The Martyrs and Heroes of Illinois in the Great Rebellion*, (Chicago: Press of J. Barnett, 1866), p. 17; William H. Bisbee, *Through Four American Wars* (Boston: Meador Publishing, 1931), p. 105.

29 Heitman, Historical Register, pp. 589, 928. Kellogg to Denison, 4 July 1861, Correspondence to the Governor and Adjutant General, 1861-1866, Series 147-1:33, Archives/Library Division, Ohio Historical Society, Columbus. During the May 1861 expansion appointments, Captain Henry S. Burton of the 3rd Artillery was initially assigned as a major in the 18th Infantry, but before those orders were published he received a majority in his own regiment. Burton remained with the Regular artillery throughout the war. The third major's slot in the 18th Infantry remained vacant until Stokes was appointed in September.

30 Mills, *My Story*, p. 79; Association of Survivors, Regular Brigade, *Proceedings of Reunions*, p. 7; Carrington, "Ohio Military Service," pp. 15, 23-25.

31 Carrington to Thomas, 4 November 1861, NA RG 391/1616 Paddy Griffith,. *Battle Tactics of the Civil War* (New Haven, Connecticut: Yale University Press, 1987), p. 87.

32 Quoted in Carrington, "Ohio Military Service," p. 28.

33 OR, series III, vol. 1, pp. 704-705; Armin Rappaport, "The Replacement System during the Civil War," in *Military Analysis of the Civil War* (Millwood, New York: KTO

Press, 1977), p. 123; David W. Smith, letter to wife, 8 October 1862, Special Collections, the Filson Historical Society, Louisville, Kentucky.

34   U.S. Army Register of Enlistments, NA MF M233/26-29; Bisbee, *Through Four American Wars*, p. 10.

35   Ella Lonn, *Foreigners in the Union Army and Navy* (Baton Rouge: Louisiana State University Press, 1951) pp. 84-85; Jacob Van Zwaluwenburg, typewritten memoir, Schoff Civil War Collection, William L. Clements Library, University of Michigan, Ann Arbor, p. 21 (hereinafter cited as "Van Zwaluwenburg memoir"); Mark W. Johnson, "'Where are the Regulars?' An Analysis of Regular Army Recruiting and Enlistees, 1861-1865" (History 609Q, State University of New York at Albany, May 2003), p. 21.

36   Carrington, *Ohio Militia and the West Virginia Campaign*, p. 15; OR, series III, vol. 1, p. 406; Robert Kennedy, "Army Life and Experiences of Robert Kennedy, 1861-1865," Civil War Miscellaneous Collection, USAMHI, p. 1.

37   Newspaper clippings, Frederick Phisterer papers, University of Wyoming American Heritage Center, Laramie; Allen Johnson and Dumas Malone, eds., *Dictionary of American Biography*, 22 vols. (New York: Charles Scribner's Sons, 1928-1944), vol. 17, p. 552; Karl G. Larew, "Frederick Phisterer: The Immigrant as Civil War Hero and Historian," paper presented at the 1984 Duquesne History Forum, pp. 5-6.

38   Frederick Phisterer, "My Days in the Army," Larew-Phisterer Family Papers, USAMHI, pp. 45-46; Phisterer to Hayes, 8 January 1881, NA MF M1064/115.

39   Carrington to Shepherd, 28 October 1861, NA RG 391/1616.

40   Unit abbreviations indicate company/battalion/regiment; this example means "Company C, 2nd Battalion, 18th U.S. Infantry."

41   Charles H. Cabaniss, "The Eighteenth Regiment of Infantry," Journal of the Military Service Institution of the United States 12 (1891), p. 1111; Heitman, Historical Register, p. 978; Amos Fleagle to family, 10 October 1861, Fleagle Family Letters, Civil War Miscellaneous Collection, USAMHI.

42   U.S. Army Register of Enlistments, April-December 1861, NA MF M233/27 & 28.

43   SO 285, War Department, AGO, series 1861.

44   SO 270, War Department, AGO, series 1861; Timothy D. Johnson, *Winfield Scott: The Quest for Military Glory* (Lawrence: University Press of Kansas, 1998), p. 233.

45   Ezra J. Warner, *Generals in Blue* (Baton Rouge: Louisiana State University Press, 1964), pp. 340-341, 377-378, 450-451; August 1861 return of the 16th Infantry, NA MF M665/173.

46   Heitman, *Historical Register*, pp. 325, 425; William Sheehan and Stephen James O'Meara, "Phillip Sidney Coolidge: Harvard's Romantic Explorer of the Skies," *Sky & Telescope* (April 1998), pp. 72, 74. Coolidge was named for the famous Elizabethan poet and soldier Sir Phillip Sidney (1554-1586), but preferred to use Sidney as his first name.

47   Lawrence to Stewart, 6 and 9 October 1861, NA RG 391/1548; Coolidge to Meigs, 27 September 1861, NA RG 391/1548.

48   Coolidge to Thomas, 20 September 1861, NA RG 391/1548; September and October 1861 returns of the 16th Infantry, NA MF M665/173.

49   Smyth to Thomas, 10 February 1862, NA MF 619/137.

50   Van Zwaluwenburg memoir, pp. 1, 4, 18. Regulations required recruits to be at least five feet, three inches tall. Some Regular recruiters rigidly adhered to this regulation in 1861, yet another factor working against Regular recruiting. Reese, *Sykes' Regular Infantry Division*, p. 55.

51 Coolidge to Meigs, 2 October 1861, NA RG 391/1548.

52 Heitman, *Historical Register*, pp. 339, 563, 967; November 1861 return of the 16th Infantry, NA MF M665/173.

53 Kellogg to Carter, 9 April 1866, Kellogg personnel file, NA RG 94; Edgar Romeyn Kellogg, "Recollections of Civil War Service with the Sixteenth United States Infantry," Civil War Miscellaneous Collection, USAMHI, pp. 1-2; "Military record of Captain E.R. Kellogg, 18th U.S. Infantry, Brevet Major U.S. Army," undated, Kellogg personnel file, NA RG 94.

54 Heitmen, *Historical Register*, p. 978; Carrington, "Ohio Military Service," pp. 24-25.

55 Carrington to Crosman, 19 January 1862, NA RG 391/1616; Chambers to Thomas, 29 May 1865, NA RG 391/1843. Camp colors were small flags (18 square inches) carried on the flanks of a regiment to help the commander determine where his line ended.

56 John Y. Simon, "Lincoln, Grant, and Kentucky in 1861," in Kent Masterson Brown, ed., *The Civil War in Kentucky: Battle for the Bluegrass State* (Mason City, Iowa: Savas Publishing Company, 2000), pp. 10-12.

57 McKinney, *Education in Violence*, p. 107; OR 4, p. 257; William T. Sherman, *Memoirs of General William T. Sherman* (New York: D. Appleton & Co., 1875), p. 216; Simon, "Lincoln, Grant, and Kentucky in 1861," pp. 6-8.

58 Carrington, "Ohio Military Service," p. 21; OR 4, p. 264.

59 King to Thomas, 11 July 1861, NA MF M619/33.

60 H.R. Brinkerhoff, "The Fifteenth Regiment of Infantry," *Journal of the Military Service Institution of the United States* 13 (1892), p. 1257.

61 Warner, *Generals in Blue*, p. 379; A. Howard Meneely, *The War Department in 1861: A Study in Mobilization and Administration* (New York: Columbia University Press, 1928), pp. 67, 108; Heitman, *Historical Register*, p. 859; Frank L. Klement, *Dark Lanterns: Secret Political Societies, Conspiracies, and Treason Trials in the Civil War* (Baton Rouge: Louisiana State University Press, 1984), pp. 75-90; November 1861 return of Newport Barracks, Kentucky, NA MF M617/846.

62 Heitman, *Historical Register*, pp. 397, 886; July 1861 post return of Newport Barracks, NA MF M617/846.

63 GO 33, War Department, AGO, series 1861; William H. Powell and Edward Shippen, *Officers of the Army and Navy (Regular) who served in the Civil War* (Philadelphia: L.R. Hamersly, 1892), p. 294.

64 Brinkerhoff, "The Fifteenth Regiment of Infantry," p. 1259.

65 Powell and Shippen, *Officers of the Army and Navy (Regular)*, p. 22; Ness, *The Regular Army*, p. 75; Heitman, *Historical Register*, pp. 180, 938; "A Brief Record of the War Services of Colonel Peter T. Swaine, 22nd U.S. Infantry," Swaine personnel file, NA RG 94; August and September 1861 returns of the 15th Infantry, NA MF M617/846; Brinkerhoff, "The Fifteenth Regiment of Infantry," p. 1265.

66 OR 4, pp. 264, 278; Powell and Shippen, *Officers of the Army and Navy (Regular)*, pp. 22, 413; Brinkerhoff, "The Fifteenth Regiment of Infantry," p. 1259; William Sumner Dodge, *History of the Old Second Division, Army of the Cumberland Commanders: McCook, Sill and Johnson* (Chicago: Church and Goodman, 1864), p. 69.

67 November 1861 return of the 19th Infantry, NA MF M665/202; Heitman, *Historical Register*, p. 599.

68 Alfred Lacey Hough, *Soldier in the West: The Civil War Letters of Alfred Lacey Hough*, edited by Robert G. Athearn (Philadelphia: University of Pennsylvania Press, 1957), pp. 25-26, 33-34; Heitman, *Historical Register*, p. 544.

69 OR 2, pp. 618-619, 627; Hough, *Soldier in the West*, p. 38.

70 Hough, *Soldier in the West*, pp. 51-52. Hough's name was in fact not present on War Department General Order 33, Series 1861, the document that doled out commissions in the New Army regiments. There were a number of vacancies in the 19th Infantry by late June, including the slot allotted to Captain James B. McPherson, who continued to serve in the Army's Corps of Engineers, and also the captaincy of Samuel H. Reynolds. This officer had chosen to wear gray and was by then commanding the 31st Virginia Infantry.

71 Ibid., pp. 52-53.

72 GO 7, Headquarters 19th U.S. Infantry, 10 August 1861, NA RG 391/1658.

73 Warner, *Generals in Blue*, pp. 67-68; C.C. Hewitt, "The Nineteenth Regiment of Infantry," *Journal of the Military Service Institution of the United States* 12 (1891), p. 835; Heitman, *Historical Register*, pp. 284, 599, 874, 1038; GO 33 and SO 283, War Department, AGO, series 1861.

74 Reuben to Barrett, 26 July 1861, Reuben D. Mussey Letters, Abraham Lincoln Collection, Regenstein Library, University of Chicago.

75 Hough, *Soldier in the West*, p. 54. Wilson had previously served as colonel of the 2nd Ohio Volunteers.

76 Thomas R. Bright, "Yankees in Arms: The Civil War as a Personal Experience," *Civil War History* 19 (1973), pp. 197-199.

77 Carpenter letters, 29 September 1861.

78 Ibid., 9 October 1861.

79 Ibid., 27 October 1861.

80 Eli Tarbell diary, entry for 10 October 1861, Civil War Miscellaneous Collection, USAMHI. In November 1861, Captain Lewis Wilson assumed command of Company D and Captain Thomas C. Williams was slotted at the commander of Company C.

81 OR 4, p. 299; Sherman, *Memoirs*, pp. 216-217, 232; Dodge, *History of the Old Second Division*, p. 69; Carrington, "Ohio Military Service," pp. 20-21, 34.

82 Brown, "Henry B. Carrington," p. 4.

83 Carrington to the adjutant general, 24 November 1861, NA RG 391/1616.

84 Carrington, "Ohio Military Service," pp. 35-36; Carrington to the adjutant general and Carrington to Shepherd, 27 November 1861, NA RG 391/1616.

85 Kellogg, "Recollections of Civil War Service," pp. 2-3; Luke Lyman to parents, 8 December 1861, Lyman Family Letters, 18th U.S. Infantry file, C-C NMP; Van Zwaluwenburg memoir, p. 19.

86 December 1861 return of the 16th Infantry, NA MF M665/173.

87 Coolidge to Thomas, 25 December 1861, NA RG 391/1548.

Chapter 2

1 Wiley Sword, *Shiloh: Bloody April* (New York: William Morrow, 1974), p. 3; James M. McPherson, *Battle Cry of Freedom: The Civil War Era* (New York: Oxford University Press, 1988), p. 392; Steven E. Woodworth, *Jefferson Davis and His Generals: The Failure of Confederate Command in the West* (Lawrence: University Press of Kansas, 1990), p. 55; Charles P. Roland, "The Confederate Defense of Kentucky," in Kent Masterson Brown, ed., *The Civil War in Kentucky*: Battle for the Bluegrass State (Mason City, Iowa: Savas Publishing Company, 2000), p. 28; OR 4, p. 531.

2 Carrington, "Ohio Military Service," p. 38.

3 Henry B. Freeman, "Early Experiences in Campaigning," H.B. Freeman Manuscripts, Wyoming Division of Cultural Resources, State Archives, Cheyenne, p. 1.

4   Enlistment documents, Freeman personnel file, NA RG 94; Henry B. Freeman, "Eighteenth U.S. Infantry From Camp Thomas, O., to Murfreesboro and the Regular Brigade at Stone River," in *Glimpses of the Nation's Struggle: Papers read Before the Military Order of the Loyal Legion of the United States, Minnesota Commandery*, vol. 3 (New York: D.D. Merrill, 1893), pp. 106–107.

5   Carrington, "Ohio Military Service," p. 39.

6   McPherson, *Battle Cry of Freedom*, pp. 304–305; McKinney, *Education in Violence*, pp. 97–103; 122–123; OR 7, p. 479.

7   Federal brigades, divisions, and corps used numerical titles as their official designations, but for clarity in this narrative they will often be referred to by the surname of their commanding officer, with the unit in small case: Shepherd's brigade, Rousseau's division, Thomas's corps. In contrast, Confederate units used the commanding officer's surname as their official designation. Therefore, this narrative refers to Confederate units by commander's name, with the unit capitalized: Stewart's Brigade, Cheatham's Division, Hardee's Corps.

8   Brinkerhoff, "The Fifteenth Regiment of Infantry," p. 1259; Dodge, *History of the Old Second Division*, p. 65.

9   Michael Heubner, "The Regulars," *Civil War Times Illustrated* (June 2000), p. 32; OR 51, pt. 1, pp. 369–370, pt. 5, p. 589; Sherman, *Memoirs*, p. 196; Ronan, "North's Unsung Regulars," pp. 46–47; A. Howard Meneely, *The War Department in 1861: A Study in Mobilization and Administration* (New York: Columbia University Press, 1928), pp. 175–176.

10   Upton, *The Military Policy of the United States*, p. 235; Huebner, "The Regulars," p. 31; OR, series III, vol. 1, pp. 138.

11   Heubner, "The Regulars," p. 32; OR, series III, vol. 1, p. 374.

12   Quoted in the *Harrisburg (Pennsylvania) Semi-Weekly Dispatch*, 15 November 1861, p. 2.

13   OR, series III, vol. 2, p. 238.

14   OR, series III, vol. 1, pp. 278, 704. In the Secretary of War's Annual Report for 1861, Simon Cameron advocated the cadre plan: "I submit for reflection the question whether the distinction between regulars and volunteers which now exists should be permitted to continue. The efficiency of the Army, it appears to me, might be greatly increased by a consolidation of the two during the continuance of the war." This statement may have been more of an attempt to end regular vs. volunteer infighting (by doing away with the regulars as a separate component) and to increase War Department efficiency (which the ineffective Cameron had done little to improve) than it was a bonafide attempt to establish systematic training for state regiments. In their postwar memoirs, both Grant and McClellan also came out in favor of the cadre plan. Many Northern leaders after the war believed that if regular officers had been authorized simultaneous appointments in April 1861, rather than July, the Union Army would have emerged victorious in its first major battle instead of being defeated at Bull Run. Such notions fail to take into consideration that a new volunteer regiment's primary tasks in the spring of 1861 were recruitment, mustering, and initial organization, not training. Regular mustering officers were already assisting in these tasks, and additional regular cadre would not have made much of a difference.

15   Heitman, *Historical Register*, p. 259; Stephen D. Engle, "Don Carlos Buell: Military Philosophy and Command Problems in the West," *Civil War History* 42 (1995), pp. 93–95; OR 16, pt. 1, p. 24; Thomas C. Buell, *The Warrior Generals* (New York: Crown Publishers, Inc., 1997), p. 153; McKinney, *Education in Violence*, p. 117; Major John C. White, "A Review of the Services of the Regular Army During the Civil War:

Part III, The Artillery," *Journal of the Military Service Institution of the United States* 46 (1910), p. 278.

16 Gerald J. Prokopowicz, *All for the Regiment: The Army of the Ohio, 1861–1862* (Chapel Hill: University of North Carolina Press, 2001), pp. 38–39; OR 7, pp. 460–461, 467–468; Phisterer, *Statistical Record*, p. 62.

17 Heitman, *Historical Register*, p. 638; OR, series III, vol. 1, p. 23; Constantine Grebner, *We Were the Ninth: A History of the Ninth Regiment, Ohio Volunteer Infantry, April 17, 1861, to June 7, 1864*, edited and translated by Frederic Trautmann (Kent, Ohio: Kent State University Press, 1987), pp. 15–17, 23; U.S. War Department, *Regulations for the Uniform and Dress of the Army of the United States, 1861* (Washington: George W. Bowman, 1861), pp. 2, 5. Robert L. McCook was one of the famed "Fighting McCooks," an Ohio family that produced fourteen Federal officers during the Civil War.

18 Carrington to Thomas, 11 December 1861, NA RG 391/1616.

19 Carrington to Shepherd, 29 November 1861, and Carrington to Haymond, 1 December 1861, NA RG 391/1616; GO 7, Headquarters 1st & 2nd Battalions 18th U.S. Infantry, 16 December 1861, NA RG 391/1650; OR 7, p. 479; Dee Brown, *The Fetterman Massacre* (Lincoln: University of Nebraska Press, 1962), p. 16. Katherine McKeen suggests that Secretary Chase never intended for Carrington to serve in the field, given the colonel's respiratory problems. McKeen, "Henry Beebee Carrington," pp. 77–78.

20 Freeman, "18th U.S. Infantry," pp. 109–110.

21 Bisbee, *Through Four American Wars*, p. 108; Shepherd to assistant quartermaster, 12 January 1862, NA RG 391/1650; GO 11, Headquarters 1st & 2nd Battalions 18th U.S. Infantry, 19 December 1861, NA RG 391/1650.

22 OR 52, pt. 1, p. 191; Herman Hattaway and Archer Jones, *How the North Won: A Military History of the Civil War* (Chicago: University of Illinois Press, 1983), pp. 61–62; McKinney, *Education in Violence*, pp. 109–124; Stephen D. Engle, *Don Carlos Buell: Most Promising of All* (Chapel Hill: University of North Carolina Press, 1999), p. 123.

23 OR 7, p. 79; Ron Nicholas, "Mill Springs: The First Battle for Kentucky," *The Civil War in Kentucky*, pp. 53–57; Grebner, *We Were the Ninth*, pp. 82–83.

24 OR 7, p. 925; Kennedy, "Army Life and Experiences," p. 1; Phisterer, "My Days in the Army," p. 46; Freeman, "18th U.S. Infantry," pp. 110–111.

25 Bisbee, *Through Four American Wars*, p. 109.

26 Thomas to Shepherd, 16 January 1862, NA RG 94/159, Subseries I, George H. Thomas Papers, Box 7: Letters Sent and Received, 1861–1863.

27 OR 7, pp. 79–82, 94; Nicholas, "Mill Springs," pp. 68–72; McCook is quoted in Merrill J. Mattes, *Indians, Infants, and Infantry: Andrew and Elizabeth Burt on the Frontier* (Lincoln: University of Nebraska Press, 1960), p. 11; McKinney, *Education in Violence*, pp. 127–131; Kennedy, "Army Life and Experiences," p. 2; Hattaway and Jones, *How the North Won*, p. 63.

28 Carrington to Shepherd, 22 February 1862, NA RG 391/1616; Cabaniss, "The Eighteenth Regiment of Infantry," p. 1112; George W. Cullum, *Biographical Register of the Officers and Graduates of the United States Military Academy* (West Point, 1890), p. 610; Theophilius F. Rodenbough and William L. Haskin, *The Army of the United States: Historical Sketches of Staff and Line with Portraits of Generals-in-Chief* (reprint: University Microfilms, 1966), pp. 407–408.

29 GOs 16 (5 February 1862) and 17 (8 February 1862), Headquarters Detachment 18th U.S. Infantry, NA RG 391/1650; OR 7, pp. 83, 426; Freeman, "18th U.S.

Infantry," p. 114; Cabaniss, "The Eighteenth Regiment of Infantry," p. 1112; Grebner, *We Were the Ninth*, p. 92; Benjamin Franklin Cooling, *Forts Henry and Donelson: The Key to the Confederate Heartland* (Knoxville: University of Tennessee Press, 1987), p. 229; Frederick W. Keil, *Thirty-fifth Ohio, a Narrative of Service from August 1861 to 1864* (Fort Wayne, Indiana: Acher, Housh, 1894), p. 60. Grant's command at this time was actually the Army of the District of West Tennessee. It was not until October 1862 that this force officially received the more familiar title Army of the Tennessee.

30 Heitman, *Historical Register*, p. 938; Cabaniss, "The Eighteenth Regiment of Infantry," p. 1112.

31 Warner, *Generals in Blue*, p. 413; Dodge, *History of the Old Second Division*, pp. 288–299; Joseph G. Dawson, "General Lovell H. Rousseau and Louisiana Reconstruction," *Louisiana History* 20 (1979), pp. 373–374; *Memoir of Lieut. Edward Lewis Mitchell, who Fell at the Battle of Shiloh, Aged Twenty-two Years* (New York: Metropolitan Fair for the U.S. Sanitary Commission, 1864), p. 37.

32 Dodge, *History of the Old Second Division*, pp. 89–92, 116; Van Zwaluwenburg memoir, p. 20.

33 Warner, *Generals in Blue*, p. 496; Heitman, *Historical Register*, p. 951; SO 233, War Department, AGO, series 1861.

34 Mohr to brother, 30 October 1861, James F. Mohr letters, Special Collections, the Filson Historical Society, Louisville, Kentucky.

35 Mohr letters, 9 November 1861.

36 Terrill to Fry, 8 February 1862, Guenther personnel file, NA RG 94.

37 *Memoir of Lieut. Edward Lewis Mitchell*, p. 27.

38 January and February 1862 returns of the 16th Infantry, NA MF M665/173; Hewitt, "The Nineteenth Regiment of Infantry," pp. 835–836.

39 Carpenter to Thomas, 25 January 1862, NA MF M619/82.

40 Hosea, "Regular Brigade," pp. 329–330.

41 Brinkerhoff, "The Fifteenth Regiment of Infantry," p. 1259; Reuben Delavan Mussey, 21 February 1862 letter, Abraham Lincoln Collection, Joseph L. Regenstein Library, University of Chicago. 21 February 1862.

42 Tarbell diary, 19 February 1862.

43 Carpenter letters, 24 March 1862.

44 Peter Fitzpatrick to wife, 9 September 1862, 5th U.S. Artillery file, SRNB.

45 Ibid.

46 OR 10, pt. 1, pp. 8–9, 22–24; pt. 2, p. 79; Jay A. Jorgensen, "Scouting for Ulysses S. Grant: The 5th Ohio Cavalry in the Shiloh Campaign," *Civil War Regiments: A Journal of the American Civil War* 4, no. 1 (1994), pp. 51–55; Jones, *Civil War Command and Strategy*, pp. 48–49; Engle, *Don Carlos Buell*, p. 205.

47 *Memoir of Lieut. Edward Lewis Mitchell*, pp. 28–29; Dodge, *History of the Old Second Division*, p. 165. General Wood assumed command of the Army of the Ohio's 6th Division on February 11, 1862.

48 Fitzpatrick letters, 9 September 1862, SRNB; Sword, *Shiloh*, pp. 44–45; Tarbell diary, 25 and 29 March 1862; Dodge, *History of the Old Second Division*, p. 173.

49 George K. Sanderson to father, 22 April 1862, John P. Sanderson Papers, Archives/Library Division, Ohio Historical Society, Columbus; W.W. Worthington, "Shiloh," in Richard B. Harwell, ed., *The Union Reader* (New York: Longmans, Green, and Co., 1958), p. 112.

50 Kellogg, "Recollections of Civil War Service," p. 5; Worthington, "Shiloh," p. 112; Dodge, *History of the Old Second Division*, p. 174; Worthington, "Shiloh," p. 113.

51 Jacob Van Zwaluwenburg, handwritten journal, Schoff Civil War Collection, William L. Clements Library, University of Michigan, Ann Arbor, p. 18.

52 Sanderson letter; *OR* 10, pt. 1, p. 302; Tarbell Diary, 6 April 1862.

Chapter 3

1 Sword, *Shiloh*, pp. 141–368; Worthington, "Shiloh," p. 115. Despite Shiloh's importance to the war in the West, modern historians have paid little attention to it. Prior to Larry J. Daniel's *Shiloh: The Battle That Changed the Civil War* (1997), this battle had been the subject of only two book-length studies: Sword's *Shiloh: Bloody April* (1974) and McDonough's *Shiloh: In Hell Before Night* (1977). None of these works discuss the fighting on April 7 at great length. The experiences of Rousseau's brigade as it advanced along the Corinth Road through Duncan, Review, and Woolf Fields on the battle's second day have never been examined in detail.

2 Sword, *Shiloh*, p. 371; C.C. Briant, *History of the Sixth Regiment Indiana Volunteer Infantry* (Indianapolis: W.B. Burford, 1891), p. 102.

3 Hosea, "The Regular Brigade," p. 331.

4 Sword, *Shiloh*, pp. 374–376; Van Zwaluwenburg memoir, p. 23; Briant, *History of the Sixth Regiment*, p. 102.

5 John A Cockerill, "A Boy at Shiloh," in *Sketches of War History 1861–1865: Papers read before the Military Order of the Loyal Legion of the United States, Ohio Commandery*, vol. 6 (Cincinnati: Monfort & Company, 1908), p. 30.

6 Hosea, "The Regular Brigade," p. 331.

7 Sword, *Shiloh*, p. 371; *Memoir of Lieut. Edward Lewis Mitchell*, p. 39 Van Zwaluwenburg journal, p. 19; Hosea, "The Regular Brigade," p. 332.

8 Sanderson letter; Worthington, "Shiloh," p. 116.

9 *OR* 10, pt. 1, p. 307; Hosea, "The Regular Brigade," p. 332; Van Zwaluwenburg memoir, p. 23.

10 Larry J. Daniel, *Shiloh: The Battle That Changed the Civil War* (New York: Simon & Schuster, 1997), p. 245.

11 *OR* 10, pt. 1, p. 293; Sword, *Shiloh*, pp. 380, 383–384.

12 *OR* 10, pt. 1, p. 307; Worthington, "Shiloh," p. 116.

13 Carpenter letters, 13 April 1862.

14 *OR* 10, pt. 1, pp. 305–306, 310.

15 Louis M. Hosea, "The Second Day at Shiloh," in *Sketches of War History 1861–1865: Papers read before the Military Order of the Loyal Legion of the U.S., Ohio Commandery*, vol. 5 (Cincinnati: The Robert Clarke Company, 1903), pp. 198–199.

16 *OR* 10, pt. 1, p. 308–309; Worthington, "Shiloh," p. 118; April 1862 return of the 15th Infantry, NA MF M665/164.

17 Sword, *Shiloh*, pp. 377–378, 386.

18 Hosea, "The Regular Brigade," p. 332; Van Zwaluwenburg journal, p. 20.

19 The New Army regiments in the Army of the Potomac's Regular Division did not enter combat until later in 1862 during the Peninsular Campaign. Reese, *Sykes' Regular Infantry Division*, pp. 76–101.

20 Worthington, "Shiloh," p. 118; Hosea, "The Regular Brigade," p. 332; Hosea, "The Second Day at Shiloh," p. 199; Larry Daniel claims Rousseau's skirmish line consisted of three companies of Regulars, one of which "collapsed in panic" during Russell's attack. Although McCook states that he ordered "two companies from each regiment of General Rousseau's brigade forward as skirmishers," Rousseau reported that King was ordered "to send out a company of skirmishers" and mentions only Captain Haughey's

company. There is no evidence of panic among the regular skirmishers in any eyewitness account of the fighting. Daniel, *Shiloh*, p. 277; *OR* 10, pt. 1, pp. 303, 308.

21 *OR* 10, pt. 1, p. 312; Worthington, "Shiloh," pp. 118–119.

22 Hosea, "The Second Day at Shiloh," p. 200.

23 *OR* 10, pt. 1, pp. 308, 617.

24 Ibid., pp. 617–618; Carpenter letters, 13 April 1862.

25 *OR* 10, pt. 1, pp. 308–309; Sword, *Shiloh*, p. 396.

26 *Memoir of Lieut. Edward Lewis Mitchell*, pp. 39–40.

27 *OR* 10, pt. 1, p. 309.

28 *Memoir of Lieut. Edward Lewis Mitchell*, p. 40.

29 Sanderson letter; Bisbee, *Through Four American Wars*, p. 241.

30 Kellogg, "Recollections of Civil War Service," p. 10; Van Zwaluwenburg journal, p. 21.

31 Worthington, "Shiloh," p. 120; *OR* 10, pt. 1, p. 313; Sanderson letter; Sword, *Shiloh*, pp. 396–399.

32 *OR* 10, pt. 1, p. 437.

33 Ibid., pp. 294, 321; Ebenezer Hannaford, *The Story of A Regiment: a History of the Campaigns, and Associations in the Field, of the Sixth Regiment Ohio Volunteer Infantry* (Cincinnati: n.p., 1868), p. 574.

34 *OR* 10, pt. 1, pp. 321–322, 551–552; Fitzpatrick letters, 9 September 1862; Daniel, *Shiloh*, pp. 272–274.

35 Quoted in Gary L. Ecelbarger, ed., "Shiloh," *Civil War: The Magazine of the Civil War Society*, April 1995, p. 68.

36 *OR* 10, pt. 1, p. 322; Mohr letters, 10 April 1862.

37 Hannaford, *The Story of A Regiment*, pp. 267–269; *OR* 10, pt. 1, p. 323.

38 *OR* 10, pt. 1, p. 325; Fitzpatrick letters, 9 September 1862.

39 Mohr letters, 12 May 1862; Sword, *Shiloh*, p. 394.

40 Sanderson letter, *OR* 10, pt. 1, pp. 374, 436–437.

41 Worthington, "Shiloh," p. 119; Sanderson letter; *OR* 10, pt. 1, p. 437. The 15th U.S. may not have acted alone in the capture of Stanford's Battery. Alexander McCook states that "Colonel Buckley's Fifth Kentucky Volunteers charged and captured" two guns during the day. This statement may refer to the action against Stanford, although it may pertain to actions of Buckley's regiment after the Kentuckians were detached from Rousseau's command. There is no 5th Kentucky Shiloh report in the *Official Records*, so the accuracy of the division commander's statement is difficult to determine. Lovell Rousseau states only that "my brigade [captured] several cannon." Wiley Sword believes the capture was a joint effort of the 15th U.S. and some of Boyle's troops of Crittenden's division and Larry Daniel makes a similar assertion. Some of Crittenden's troops may have come upon the cannon after Rousseau's brigade departed the Review Field area, but they probably did not participate in the initial capture. There can be little doubt that the 15th Infantry, on the right of Rousseau's line, overran Stanford's position. Among the reports of the regulars, only Captain Swaine of the 15th U.S. mentions the capture of enemy cannon. Also, both Lieutenant Sanderson and Private Worthington prominently mention the capture in letters they wrote immediately after the battle. If any element of Crittenden's division participated in the capture jointly with the 15th U.S., before reaching Stanford's position Crittenden's troops would have had to maneuver through the left-hand units of Rousseau's line (the 15th Michigan, 1st Ohio, 19th U.S., and 16th U.S.). *OR* 10, pt. 1, pp. 303, 310, 312; Sword, *Shiloh*, pp. 399–400; Daniel, *Shiloh*, p. 284.

42   OR 10, pt. 1, pp. 120, 251, 309, 314; 437; Hosea, "The Second Day at Shiloh," p. 202; Sword, *Shiloh*, p. 407–409.

43   OR 10, pt. 1, pp. 120, 303; Sword, *Shiloh*, p. 410.

44   Hosea, "The Regular Brigade," p. 334; Worthington, "Shiloh," p. 120; Hosea, "The Second Day at Shiloh," p. 204; Van Zwaluwenburg journal, p. 18.

45   OR 10, pt. 1, pp. 303, 317–318; Sword, *Shiloh,* p. 409; Peter Cozzens, *No Better Place to Die: The Battle of Stones River*, (Chicago: University of Illinois Press, 1990), p. 83; Hosea, "The Regular Brigade," p. 334; Hosea, "The Second Day at Shiloh," p. 205.

46   Worthington, "Shiloh," p. 121; OR 10, pt. 1, p. 304, 309.

47   Ibid., pp. 304, 311; Daniel, *Shiloh*, p. 287.

48   Ulysses S. Grant, *Personal Memoirs of U.S. Grant*, 2 vols. (New York: Charles L. Webster, 1885), vol. 1, p. 161; Sword, *Shiloh*, pp. 410–411, 417; OR 10, pt. 1, pp. 221, 304, 309, 311; Brinkerhoff, "The Fifteenth Regiment of Infantry," p. 1261.

49   Sword, *Shiloh*, p. 411; OR 10, pt. 1, p. 252; Rosecrans to War Department, 15 February 1863, King personnel file, NA RG 94; Hosea, "The Second Day at Shiloh," p. 207; C.C. Briant, *History of the Sixth Regiment* (Indianapolis: W.B. Burford, 1891), p. 109.

50   Hosea, "The Second Day at Shiloh," p. 208; OR 10, pt. 1, p. 310.

51   Kellogg, "Recollections of Civil War Service," p. 11.

52   Van Zwaluwenburg memoir, p. 21. A hogshead was a large barrel, capacity 52.5 imperial gallons.

53   Ibid., p. 22; Carpenter letters, 13 April 1862; OR 10, pt. 1, p. 307.

54   Worthington, "Shiloh," p. 121; *Memoir of Lieut. Edward Lewis Mitchell*, pp. 40–41.

55   Jones, *Civil War Command and Strategy*, pp. 56–58; George Mason, "Shiloh," in *Military Essays and Recollections: Papers Read Before the Commandery of the State of Illinois, Military Order of the Loyal Legion of the United States*, vol. 1 (Chicago: A.C. McClurg and Company, 1891), p. 102; Carpenter letters, 13 April 1862.

Chapter 4

1   Hough, *Soldier In the West*, pp. 57–59.

2   Ibid., p. 59.

3   OR 10, pt. 2, p. 83; pt. 1, p. 660; James Lee McDonough, *War in Kentucky: From Shiloh to Perryville* (Knoxville: University of Tennessee Press, 1994), pp. 30–31.

4   Hough, *Soldier In the West*, pp. 61, 64.

5   OR 10, pt. 1, p. 677; Carpenter letters, 19 April 1862.

6   McKinney, *Education in Violence*, p. 136; April 1862 return of the 18th Infantry, NA MF M665/191.

7   Court of Inquiry Pertaining to Disciplinary Measures in the 18th U.S. Infantry, June 1862, NA RG 153/ii985 (hereinafter cited as "18th Infantry Court of Inquiry"), testimony of Colonel Robert McCook.

8   Doctor Thomas P. Lowry, The Index Project, Inc., to author, 28 August 2000; Lyman letters, C-C NMP, 29 January 1864; Isaac B. Jones, letter to cousin, 10 July 1862, collection of Wiley Sword, Suwanee, Georgia.

9   John H. Knight, letter to wife, 20 June 1862, John Henry Knight Letters, Archives Division, State Historical Society of Wisconsin, Madison.

10   18th Infantry Court of Inquiry, testimonies of Lieutenant Anson Mills and Major Frederick Townsend.

11   GO 45, Headquarters Detachment 18th U.S. Infantry, 30 March 1862, NA RG 391/1652.

12 Joan W. Albertson, ed., *Letters Home to Minnesota: 2nd Minnesota Volunteers* (Spokane, Washington: P.D. Enterprises, 1992), letter 33.

13 18th Infantry Court of Inquiry, testimony of Lieutenant Anson Mills.

14 Shepherd to McCook, 26 March 1862, NA RG 391/1650.

15 Grebner, *We Were the Ninth*, pp. 11–13.

16 GO 40, Headquarters Detachment 18th U.S. Infantry, 26 March 1862, NA RG 391/1652.

17 18th Infantry Court of Inquiry, testimony of Assistant Surgeon Webster Lindsey.

18 Ibid., testimonies of Colonel Robert McCook, Asst. Surg. Webster Lindsey, and Captain Henry Douglass.

19 Ibid., exhibit A.

20 Shepherd to McCook, 28 March 1862, NA RG 391/1650.

21 The 8th Article of War: "Any officer or soldier who fails to suppress a mutiny shall suffer death."

22 Shepherd to Flint, 28 March 1862, NA RG 391/1650.

23 Keil, *Thirty-fifth Ohio*, p. 62. Cabannis, "The Eighteenth Regiment of Infantry," p. 1112; McKinney, *Education in Violence*, p. 137; Mills, *My Story*, p. 83.

24 Freeman, "Eighteenth U.S. Infantry," pp. 115–116.

25 Heitman, *Historical Register*, pp. 380–381; Dodge, *History of the Old Second Division*, p. 240; Powell and Shippen, *Officers of the Army and Navy (Regular)*, p. 127; Bisbee, *Through Four American Wars*, p. 113.

26 Bisbee, *Through Four American Wars*, p. 114.

27 Shepherd to Smith, 24 April 1862, NA RG 391/1650; Kennedy, "Army Life and Experiences," p. 2; May 1862 return of the 18th Infantry, NA MF M665/191; *OR* 10, pt. 1, p. 102; Bisbee, *Through Four American Wars*, p. 115.

28 *Harper's Weekly*, 31 May 1862, p. 343.

29 Knight letters, 11 July 1862.

30 Bisbee, *Through Four American Wars*, p. 115; McCook's words are quoted in a letter from Carrington to the Harper Brothers, 16 June 1862, NA RG 391/1616.

31 Carrington to Harper Brothers, 16 June 1862, NA RG 391/1616.

32 Keil, *Thirty-fifth Ohio*, p. 69.

33 *Cincinnati Daily Commercial*, 7 April 1862, p. 1.

34 18th Infantry Court of Inquiry, exhibit E; Thomas P. Lowry, *Tarnished Eagles: The Courts-Martial of Fifty Union Colonels and Lieutenant Colonels* (Mechanicsburg Pennsylvania: Stackpole Books, 1997), pp. 130–135.

35 Carrington to Shepherd, 14 April 1862, NA RG 391/1616.

36 Shepherd to Carrington, 2 June 1862, NA RG 391/650 (this letter was probably written near the end of April; the copy in the regimental letter book contains the notation, "The original of this letter was written some time ago but bad health and almost daily showers have delayed copying & mailing.")

37 Knight letters, 11 July 1862.

38 18th Infantry Court of Inquiry, exhibit D.

39 18th Infantry Court of Inquiry, exhibit J.

40 Edgerton to Stanton, 3 May 1862, NA MF M619/71.

41 Shepherd to Thomas, 20 May 1862, NA MF M619/71.

42 McKinney, *Education in Violence*, pp. 39–44.

43 Warner, *Generals in Blue*, pp. 440–441; Grebner, *We Were the Ninth*, p. 102.

44 *OR* 16, pt. 1, pp. 124–125; Heitman, *Historical Register*, p. 882; Grebner, *We Were the Ninth*, p. 102.

45 *OR* 2, p. 631.

46 Sherman to the adjutant general, 26 February 1867, Shepherd personnel file, NA RG 94.

47 47 OR 10, pt. 2, pp. 147, 148, 151, 478, 489–491; Robert F. Heflin, "The Siege of Corinth, " (master's thesis, Vanderbilt University, 1956), p. 79; Jones, *Civil War Command and Strategy*, p. 57.

48 OR 10, pt. 1, pp. 674, 804, 807–810; pt. 2, pp. 169–171, 177–178.

49 18th Infantry Court of Inquiry, testimonies of Lieutenant Anson Mills and Sergeant Jacob J. Wagmon, and exhibit L.

50 18th Infantry Court of Inquiry, testimony of Lieutenant Anson Mills.

51 OR 10, pt. 1, pp. 674, 839–840; pt. 2, pp. 184, 196, 200, 202.

52 Freeman, "Early Experiences in Campaigning," p. 7; Phisterer, "My Days in the Army," p. 48; Pierce to friends, May 1862, Lyman letters, 18th U.S. Infantry file, C-C NMP.

53 Shepherd to Thomas, 12 March 1866, Shepherd personnel file, NA RG 94; Hattaway and Jones, *How the North Won*, p. 182; Heflin, "The Siege of Corinth," p. 100; May 1862 return of the 18th Infantry, NA MF M665/191; Freeman, "Early Experiences in Campaigning," p. 7.

54 Freeman, "Early Experiences in Campaigning," p. 8.

55 May 1862 return of the 18th Infantry, NA MF M665/191; Sherman to the Adjutant General, 26 February 1867, Shepherd personnel file, NA RG 94; Freeman, "Early Experiences in Campaigning," pp. 7–8; OR 10, pt. 1, p. 739.

56 Sherman to the adjutant general, 26 February 1867, Shepherd personnel file, NA RG 94; OR 10, pt. 1, p. 844.

57 Freeman, "Early Experiences in Campaigning," pp. 10–11.

58 Ibid., pp. 9–11.

59 Fleagle letters, 26 May 1862.

60 Knight letters, 11 July 1862.

61 Shepherd to Burt, 25 May 1862, NA RG 391/1650.

62 Barnet, *The Martyrs and Heroes of Illinois*, p. 12.

63 Edgar N. Wilcox, journal-diary, entries for 29 December 1861, 10–13 January 1862, Wiley Sword Collection, USAMHI; John Robertson, *Michigan in the War* (Lansing: W.S. George and Co., 1882), pp. 331, 494–495.

64 Shepherd to Denig, 8 June 1862, NA RG 391/1650; Carrington to Kelton, 9 June 1862, NA RG 391/1616; Cabaniss, "The Eighteenth Regiment of Infantry," p. 1113; GO 83, Headquarters Detachment 18th U.S. Infantry, 1 July 1862, NA RG 391/1652.

65 Knight letters, 29 May 1862; OR, series II, vol. 3, p. 605.

66 Carrington, "Ohio Military Service," p. 44.

67 Ibid., p. 45.

68 Ibid., p. 46.

69 Knight letters, 29 May 1862.

70 Dodge, *History of the Old Second Division*, p. 222; Hough, *Soldier of the West*, p. 61; Carpenter letters, 18 May 1862.

71 OR 10, pt. 762–763; Heflin, "The Siege of Corinth," pp. 275–276, 280.

72 OR 10, pt 1, pp. 675–679, 775; pt. 2, p. 214; Dodge, *History of the Old Second Division*, pp. 223–224.

73 OR 10, pt. 1, pp. 679; Carpenter letters, 2 June 1862.

74 Hough, *Soldier In the West*, pp. 67–71.

75 Carpenter letters, 2 June 1862; OR 10, pt. 1, pp. 678–679.

76 Hattaway and Jones, *How the North Won*, p. 187; Heflin, "The Siege of Corinth," pp. 279–285; Hosea, "The Regular Brigade," p. 336; *OR* 10, pt. 1, p. 680; Van Zwaluwenburg journal, p. 23; Carpenter letters, 2 June 1862.

77 Kennedy, "Army Life and Experiences," p. 3.

78 Hough, *Soldier In the West*, p. 68; Jones, *Civil War Command and Strategy*, pp. 57–58.

Chapter 5

1 *OR* 10, pt. 2, pp. 255, 288; 52, pt. 1, p. 255.

2 Hattaway and Jones, *How the North Won*, pp. 205-206.

3 McDonough, *War in Kentucky*, pp. 36-42.

4 SFO 106, Head Quarters Dept. of the Mississippi, 15 June 1862, NA RG 153/ii985; Warner, *Generals in Blue*, pp. 454, 507; Heitman, *Historical Register*, pp. 385, 806; *OR* 10, pt. 2, pp. 248, 262.

5 18th Infantry Court of Inquiry, testimony of Colonel Robert L. McCook.

6 Ibid., testimony of Corporal J.T. McCoy.

7 Grebner, *We Were The Ninth*, pp. 256-257, n. 2, 4.

8 18th Infantry Court of Inquiry, testimony of Lieutenant Gustav Tafel.

9 Ibid., testimony of Asst. Surg. Webster Lindsey.

10 It would have been interesting for the historical record to hear testimony from Captain Wood, but he had been stricken with typhoid and was not able to appear before the court. Henry Tank was also not available to testify. The tormented private deserted on May 20 during the advance on Corinth, never to be seen again.

11 18th Infantry Court of Inquiry, testimony of Major Frederick Townsend.

12 Ibid., findings of the court.

13 *OR* 16, pt. 2, pp. 54, 61, 68-69, 169.

14 GO 74, Headquarters Detachment 18th U.S. Infantry, 25 June 1862, NA RG 391/1652; Frederick Phisterer, "Record of Events of the Second Battalion 18th Regt. of Infantry U.S. Army 1862," NA MF M665/191, entry for June 1862; Engle, *Don Carlos Buell*, pp. 260, 262.

15 GO 76, Headquarters Detachment 18th U.S. Infantry, 28 June 1862, NA RG 391/1652.

16 Isaac B. Jones letters, 10 July 1862; Kennedy, "Army Life and Experiences," p. 3; Phisterer, "My Days in the Army," p. 49.

17 Mills, *My Story*, p. 84.

18 Isaac B. Jones letters, 10 July 1862.

19 Knight letters, 3 June 1862.

20 Warner, *Generals in Blue*, p. 484; *OR* 10, pt. 1, pp. 668, 670; Knight letters, 5 June 1862.

21 Knight letters, 23 June 1863.

22 Ibid., 20 June 1862; Court martial of Private Frank Kelley, 18th Infantry, NA RG 153/mm105.

23 Knight letters, 27, 28, 29 June, and 2 July 1862.

24 May and June 1862 returns of the 15th Infantry, NA MF M665/164; May 1862 return of the 16th Infantry, NA MF M665/173.

25 "Major James H. Gageby, 12th Infantry, U.S.A.," collection of Jack Gageby, Simi Valley, California.

26 May 1862 return of the 19th Infantry, NA MF M665/202; Hewitt, "The Nineteenth Regiment of Infantry," p. 836.

27 July 1862 return of the 19th Infantry, NA MF M665/202; Gageby to parents, 6 August 1862, collection of Jack Gageby, Simi Valley, California.

28 September 1862 return of the 19th Infantry, NA MF M665/202; Carpenter to Thomas, 8 November 1862, NA MF M619/86; Hewitt, "The Nineteenth Regiment of Infantry," p. 837; Reese, *Sykes' Regular Infantry Division*, p. 406.

29 Rappaport, "The Replacement System during the Civil War," p. 123.

30 GO 154, War Department, AGO, series 1862.

31 Walworth to Rosecrans, 21 January 1863, NA RG 391/1558.

32 W.H.H. Terrell, *Indiana in The War of The Rebellion: Report of the Adjutant General*, vol. 1 (Indianapolis: Indiana Historical Society, 1960), p. 95.

33 Reprinted in Terrell, *Indiana in The War of The Rebellion*, vol. 1, p. 95. When Carrington stated that the bounties are the same, he was referring to Federal bounties paid to all Union soldiers, not the local bounties paid only to state volunteers.

34 *OR*, series III, vol. 2, p. 653; Terrell, *Indiana in The War of The Rebellion*, p. 93; GO 162, War Department, AGO, series 1862; Wilcox journal-diary, 22 December 1862.

35 Hough, *Soldier in the West*, pp. 85-86.

36 *OR*, series III, vol. 3, p. 1110; Regular Army Register of Enlistments, October 1862-February 1863, NA MF M233/27and 28; Phisterer, *Statistical Record*, p. 62. Total numbers for the transfer plan were determined through a systematic sampling of 2,583 Entries in the Register of Enlistments for the Civil War era. The sample netted 283 volunteers who transferred to the Regular Army under the auspices of the 1862-1863 transfer plan. By applying the percentages of volunteer transfers in the sample to the total number of entries in the Register of Enlistments for the months when the transfer program was in effect, it can be estimated that about 7,500 volunteers transferred to the Regular Army under this program. For the 270 transferrees for whom a regular regiment could be determined, only 46 (17 percent) joined infantry regiments. For a detailed examination of this systematic sample, see Johnson, "'Where are the Regulars?' An Analysis of Regular Army Recruiting and Enlistees, 1861-1865."

37 *OR* 16, pt. 1, p. 705.

38 Carpenter letters, 18 June 1862.

39 Dodge, *History of the Old Second Division*, pp. 279-280; Prokopowicz, *All for the Regiment*, pp. 122-123; Tarbell diary, 4 July 1862; Carpenter letters, 5 July 1862; Fitzpatrick letters, 4 July 1862.

40 Van Zwaluwenburg memoir, p. 26; Van Zwaluwenburg journal, p. 23.

41 *OR* 16, pt. 2, p. 203.

42 Carpenter letters, 10 August 1862.

43 Engle, *Don Carlos Buell*, p. 260; *OR* 16, pt. 1, p. 604; Hough, *Soldier in the West*, pp. 77, 81.

44 Dodge, *History of the Old Second Division*, p. 282; McDonough, *War in Kentucky*, pp. 45-53; Tarbell diary, 5-10, 14 July 1862; *OR* 16, pt. 1, pp. 248, 325-27, 603-608; pt. 2, pp. 38-39.

45 Kellogg, "Recollections of Civil War Service," pp. 15, 18; July 1862 return of the 16th Infantry, NA MF M665/173; Heitman, *Historical Register*, p. 229; *OR* 16, pt. 2, p. 659; Carpenter letters, 21 July 1862.

46 Tarbell diary, 25, 26, 28 July 1862.

47 Kellogg, "Reminiscences of Civil War Service," pp. 16-17.

48 Ibid., pp. 17-18.

49 Tarbell diary, 13 and 19 August 1862; Carpenter letters, 19 August 1862.

50 Fleagle letters, 20 July 1862; Knight letters, 6 July 1862.

51 Knight letters, 7 August 1862.

52 Ibid.

53 GO 113, Headquarters Detachment 18th U.S. Infantry, 1 August 1862, NA RG 391/1652.

54 *OR* 16, pt. 2, p. 223; Knight letters, 7 August 1862.

55 Knight letters, 7 August 1862; Warner, *Generals in Blue*, p. 297; *OR* 16, pt. 1, pp. 35-36; pt. 2, p. 227. Although Robert McCook's date of rank as a brigadier was 21 March 1862, the rank was not actually conferred until the latter half of June.

56 *OR* 16, pt. 1, pp. 839-841; Grebner, *We Were the Ninth*, pp. 106-107; Merrill J. Mattes, *Indians, Infants, & Infantry: Andrew and Elizabeth Burt on the Frontier* (Lincoln: University of Nebraska Press, 1988), p. 13; McDonough, *War in Kentucky*, pp. 95-96; Kenneth W. Noe, *Perryville: This Grand Havoc of Battle* (Lexington: University Press of Kentucky, 2001), pp. 45-46; Knight letters, 7 August 1862. After the sacking of Athens, Alabama, the previous month by Federal troops from Colonel John B. Turchin's brigade, Confederate guerillas in northeast Alabama were thirsty for revenge. The killing of Robert McCook was thought to be in retaliation for a looting spree by Turchin's men on May 2, which Turchin had encouraged after some of his men claimed they had been fired on by Athenian civilians. This tit-for-tat cycle of violence clearly indicated that the "soft war" policies advocated by Buell and others were making little headway in fostering reconciliation between North and South.

57 Knight letters, 7 August 1862; Fleagle letters, 24 August 1862.

58 Shepherd to Fry, 8 August 1862, NA RG 391/1650.

59 Shepherd to Steedman and Shepherd to Fry, 17 August 1862, NA RG 391/1650.

60 Robert P. King, letter to mother, 23 August 1862, Civil War Miscellaneous Files, USAMHI; Carpenter letters, 5 October 1862.

61 Knight letters, 28 August 1862.

62 King letter, 23 August 1862.

63 McDonough, *War in Kentucky*, pp. 27-29; Hattaway and Jones, *How the North Won*, pp. 217-219; Woodworth, *Jefferson Davis and His Generals*, p. 139; *OR* 16, pt.1, p. 698; pt. 2, p. 493; Phisterer, "Record of Events, 1862," entry for September.

64 James Biddle, diary entries for 14, 16 July; 1, 16, 23, 24 August; 14 September 1862, Burton Historical Collection, Detroit Public Library; July and August 1862 returns of the 16th Infantry, NA MF M665/173.

65 Earl J. Hess, *Banners to the Breeze: The Kentucky Campaign, Corinth, and Stones River* (Lincoln: University of Nebraska Press, 2000), pp. 30-46.

66 Wright is quoted in Carrington, "Ohio Military Service," p. 50.

67 Peterson to Wilcox, 8 September 1862, Wilcox letters, Civil War Miscellaneous Collection, USAMHI.

68 Swick to sister, 7 November 1862, collection of Dennis Keesee, Westerville, Ohio.

69 Bogart to mother, 19 November 1862, collection of Dennis Keesee, Westerville, Ohio.

70 *OR* 16, pt. 2, pp. 815, 816, 817-818; Kenneth E. Noe, *Perryville: This Grand Havoc of Battle* (Lexington: The University Press of Kentucky, 2001), pp. 66, 68-69.

71 OR 16, pt. 1, pp. 961-967; Kent Masterson Brown, "Munfordville: The Campaign and Battle Along Kentucky's Strategic Axis," *The Civil War in Kentucky*, pp. 148-166; Phisterer, "Record of Events, 1862," NA MF M665/191.

72 Woodworth, *Jefferson Davis and His Generals*, p. 147; McDonough, *War in Kentucky*, pp. 188-189; Hattaway and Jones, *How the North Won*, pp. 254-255.

73 Smith letters, 2 October 1862; Biddle diary, 14, 25 September 1862; Carpenter letters, 5 October 1862.

74 Knight letters, 26 September 1862.

75 Ibid., 28 September 1862.

76 Dodge, *History of the Old Second Division*, pp. 331-332; Tarbell diary, 27 September 1862.

77 Curt Anders, *Henry Halleck's War: A Fresh Look at Lincoln's Controversial General-in-Chief* (Carmel, Indiana: Guild Press of Indiana, 1999), pp. 286-291; OR 16, pt. 2, pp. 554-555.

78 Fleagle letters, 29 September 1862; Smith letters, October 1862; Carpenter letters, 5 October 1862; Mussey letters, 30 September 1862.

79 Knight letters, 5 September 1862.

80 OR 16, pt. 2, pp. 558-559; Prokopowicz, *All for the Regiment*, pp. 152-153, 157. Buell had originally selected General Nelson to command III Corps, but Nelson was murdered during an altercation with Brigadier General Jefferson C. Davis on September 29.

81 Wright to the president, 29 October 1891, Swaine personnel file, NA RG 94; OR 16, pt. 1, pp. 1034-1035; pt.2, p. 987; Thomas B. Van Horne, *The History of the Army of the Cumberland: Its Organizations, Campaigns, and Battles*, 2 vols. (Cincinnati: The Robert Clark Company, 1875), vol. 1, p. 184; Dodge, *History of the Old Second Division*, p. 336; McDonough, *War in Kentucky*, pp. 206-208, 225; Kellogg, "Recollections of Civil War Service," p. 18; Warner, *Generals in Blue*, p. 497; Heitman, *Historical Register*, pp. 951, 482; September 1862 return of the 5th Artillery, NA MF M727/33; Phisterer, "Record of Events, 1862," NA MF M665/191. President Lincoln nominated Gilbert as a brigadier general in response to Wright's scheming, but the Senate failed to act on the nomination and it expired in March 1863. Captain Gilbert was promoted to major in the 19th Infantry effective July 2, 1863. He never served with the 19th U.S. in the field during the Civil War.

82 Noe, *Perryville*, p. 187.

83 Terrill to the War Department, 27 September 1862, Guenther personnel file, NA RG 94.

84 Endorsements attached to Terrill 27 September 1862 correspondence, Guenther personnel file, NA RG 94; White, "A Review of the Services of the Regular Army During the Civil War, Part III: The Artillery, p. 277; J.C. Tidball, "The Artillery Service in the War of the Rebellion," *Journal of the Military Service Institution of the United States*, 14 (1893), p. 333.

85 OR 19, pt. 1, pp. 525-530; Reese, *Sykes' Regular Infantry Division*, pp. 131, 206.

86 Shepherd to Fry, 28 September 1862, NA RG 391/1627.

87 GO 153, Headquarters Detachment 18th U.S. Infantry, 30 September 1862, NA RG 391/1650.

88 Knight letters, 1 and 2 October 1862.

89 Kellogg, "Recollections of Civil War Service," pp. 20-21; Engle, *Don Carlos Buell*, p. 295; Carpenter letters, 5 October 1862; Tarbell diary, 1 October 1862; Biddle diary, 1 October 1862.

90 Dodge, *History of the Old Second Division*, p. 345; McDonough, *War in Kentucky*, p. 345.

91 Tarbell diary, 1 October 1862; Dodge, *History of the Old Second Division*, p. 345.

92 Kellogg, "Recollections of Civil War Service," p. 22.

93 McDonough, *War in Kentucky*, p. 200.

94 OR 16, pt. 2, pp. 925-926; Dodge, *History of the Old Second Division*, p. 353.

95 Kellogg, "Recollections of Civil War Service," pp. 23-24.

96 OR 16, pt. 1, pp. 1134-1136; Dodge, *History of the Old Second Division*, pp. 353-357, 364; Tarbell diary, 9 October 1862.

97 OR 16, pt. 1, pp. 1025, 1091-1092, 1109-1110.

98 Ibid., pp. 1026-1027, 1040-1041, 1010-1011; Kenneth W. Noe, "'Grand Havoc': The Climactic Battle of Perryville," *The Civil War in Kentucky*, pp. 183-200.

99 OR 16, pt. 1, pp. 655-656, 1025, 1072-1073, 1075, 1078, 1079-1080; Hess, *Banners to the Breeze*, pp. 102-104; McDonough, *War in Kentucky*, pp. 284-287.

100 OR 16, pt. 1, pp. 137, 1161.

101 Isaac B. Jones letters, 4 December 1862.

102 Fleagle letters, 13 October 1862; Kennedy, "Army Life and Experiences," p. 4.

103 Noe, "'Grand Havoc': The Climactic Battle of Perryville," pp. 202-203.

104 Woodworth, *Jefferson Davis and His Generals*, pp. 158-162.

105 Mussey letters, 16 October 1862.

106 Peter Cozzens, *No Better Place to Die: The Battle of Stones River* (Chicago: University of Illinois Press, 1990), pp. 1-14, 29; Warner, *Generals in Blue*, p. 52; Van Horne, *History of the Army of the Cumberland*, 1, pp. 207, 287. The Army of the Ohio's new designation was effective 24 October 1862. It was again redesignated, as the Army of the Cumberland, in January 1863. The name Army of the Cumberland was unofficially used prior to January 1863 and for clarity I will hereinafter refer to this army as the Army of the Cumberland.

Chapter 6

1 OR 16, pt. 2, pp. 640; 653-655; Dodge, *History of the Old Second Division*, p. 368.

2 November 1862 return of the 18th Infantry, NA MF M665/191; GO 18, Headquarters Department of the Cumberland, 18 November 1862, NA RG 394/1558.

3 Townsend to Ducat, 15 November 1862, NA RG 391/1651.

4 Carpenter to Thomas, 16 December 1862, NA MF M619/71.

5 Ibid.

6 OR 16, pt. 1, p. 844; pt. 2, pp. 340-341; 20, pt. 1, pp. 3, 40-41; pt. 2, pp. 9 15, 27, 41, 43, 93, 103; McDonough, *War in Kentucky*, p. 57; Woodworth, *Jefferson Davis and His Generals*, p. 169; Lyman letters, 7 December 1862, C-C NMP; Fleagle letters, 11 December 1862.

7 Townsend to 3rd Brigade adjutant, 27 and 28 November 1862, 1 December 1862, NA RG 391/1651.

8 Townsend to Denig, 29 November 1862, and Townsend to Adams, 1 December 1862, NA RG 391/1651.

9 Mills, *My Story*, pp. 87-89.

10 GO 172, Headquarters Detachment 18th U.S. Infantry, 10 December 1862, NA RG 391/1651.

11 OR 52, pt. 1, pp. 314-315.

12 Carrington, "Ohio Military Service," p. 50; McKeen, "Henry Beebee Carrington," pp. 87-88.

13 *OR* 23, pt. 2, pp. 193-194. Carrington's date of rank as a brigadier was November 29, 1862, but the promotion was not actually conferred until March 1863.

14 *OR* 20, pt. 2, p. 222.

15 Shepherd to Seward, 5 June 1861, NA MF M619/59; McKean to Cameron, 17 September 1861, and King to Lincoln, 21 October 1861, NA MF M619/57.

16 Heitman, *Historical Register*, 2, pp. 596, 598; Thomas to Lincoln, 16 December 1862, and McCook to Stanton, 8 December 1862, Shepherd personnel file, NA RG 94.

17 Rosecrans discontinued the Army of the Ohio's cumbersome unit numbering method. Henceforth, each corps/wing in the Army of the Cumberland had a 1st, 2nd, and 3rd division, with each division consisting of a 1st, 2nd, and 3rd brigade. Rousseau's command became the Center's 1st Division on December 19.

18 *OR* 20, pt. 2, pp. 206, 285; Phillip Katcher and Rick Scollins, *Flags of the American Civil War 2: Union* (London: Osprey Publishing Ltd., 1993), p. 21; Robert P. King, letter to mother, 25 December 1862, author's collection; Carpenter letters, 28 December 1862.

19 Freeman, "Eighteenth U.S. Infantry," p. 126; Grebner, *We Were the Ninth*, p. 120.

20 4th Brigade Committee Resolutions, NA RG 391/1548.

21 Dodge, *History of the Old Second Division*, p. 382.

22 Ibid., appendix, p. 8; Phisterer, "Record of Events, 1862," NA MF M665/191; December 1861 return of the 5th Artillery, NA MF M727/33; Heitman, *Historical Register*, p. 418.

23 Tarbell diary, 23 December 1862; Smith letters, 25 December 1862; Carpenter letters, 28 December 1862; Carpenter to Thomas, 16 November 1862, NA MF M619/86.

24 King letters, 25 December 1862; Hosea, "The Regular Brigade," p. 338.

25 *OR* 17, pt. 2, p. 800; pt. 1, p. 189; Van Horne, *History of the Army of the Cumberland*, 1, pp. 217-218; Hattaway and Jones, *How the North Won*, p. 318; Woodworth, *Jefferson Davis and His Generals*, pp. 183, 187.

26 Freeman, "Eighteenth U.S. Infantry," pp. 126-127; King letters, 25 December 1862.

27 *OR* 20, pt. 1, p. 184.

28 Only about half of the Center took to the field at the start of the campaign due to requirements to garrison Nashville and other points. The main elements present were six brigades: three from Rousseau's division, two from Brigadier General James S. Negley's division, and a single brigade from Brigadier General Speed S. Fry's division. *OR* 20, pt. 1, pp. 371-372.

29 Freeman, "Early Experiences in Campaigning," p. 17.

30 Freeman, "Eighteenth U.S. Infantry," p. 127; Freeman, "Early Experiences in Campaigning," p. 21; Van Horne, *History of the Army of the Cumberland*, 1, p. 227.

31 Cedar groves were present throughout the Stones River battle area, but "the cedars" in this chapter refers to the forested area north of the Wilkinson Turnpike, between Stones River and Overall Creek.

32 Tarbell diary, 29-30 December 1862; *OR* 20, pt. 1, pp. 249, 372, 377; Frederick Phisterer, *The Regular Brigade of the Fourteenth Army Corps, the Army of the Cumberland, in the Battle of Stone River* (New York: n.p., 1883), p. 2.

33 *OR* 20, pt. 1, pp. 192, 449; Van Horne, *History of the Army of the Cumberland*, 1, pp. 228-229; Mills, *My Story*, p. 90.

34 Henry Haymond, letter to mother, 7 January 1863, collection of Jerry Rancourt, St. Petersburg, Florida; Lyman letters, 31 January and 9 February 1863, C-C NMP.

35 Kennedy, "Army Life and Experiences," p. 4.

36 Court-martial of Private John Mallory, 18th Infantry, NA RG 153/kk665.

37 OR 20, pt. 1, pp. 280-281, 348-349, 377; Van Horne, *History of the Army of the Cumberland*, 1, pp. 229-235; Cozzens, *No Better Place To Die*, pp. 116-122.

38 OR 20, pt. 1, pp. 255-256, 349-350.

39 Kennedy, "Army Life and Experiences," p. 4.

40 Reuben Jones, letter to sister, 9 January 1863, 19th U.S. file, Stones River National Battlefield, Murfreesboro, Tennessee.

41 OR 20, pt. 1, pp. 377-378; Lyman letters, 8 January 1863, C-C NMP.

42 Ibid., pp. 378, 382; Alfred Pirtle, "Stone River Sketches," in *Sketches of War History 1861-1865: Papers read before the Military Order of the Loyal Legion of the U.S., Ohio Commandery*, vol. 6 (Cincinnati: Monfort & Company, 1908), pp. 99-100. The knoll upon which the batteries were positioned is the site of the present-day Stones River National Cemetery.

43 John Beatty, *Memoirs of a Volunteer, 1861-1863* (New York: W.W. Norton Co., 1946), p. 153; OR 20, pt. 1, pp. 383, 394.

44 William P. Carlin, *The Memoirs of Brigadier General William Passmore Carlin, U.S.A.*, edited by Robert I. Girardi and Nathaniel C. Hughes (Lincoln: University of Nebraska Press, 1999), p. 80.

45 OR 20, pt. 1, pp. 399-400; William J. Carson, letter to parents, 7 January 1863, *Civil War Times Illustrated* Collection, USAMHI.

46 January 1863; Carson letter.

47 OR 20, pt. 1, pp. 401, 983; Cozzens, *No Better Place To Die*, pp. 134-136; Townsend to the secretary of war, 8 November 1894, Phisterer personnel file, NA RG 94.

48 W.F. Beyer and O.F. Keydel, eds, *Deeds of Valor: How America's Civil War Heroes Won The Congressional Medal of Honor* (Detroit: Perrien-Keydel Co., 1903), pp. 129-130; OR 20, pt. 1, p. 401; Kellogg, "Recollections of Civil War Service," p. 26; Townsend to the secretary of war, 8 November 1894, Phisterer personnel file, NA RG 94.

49 Carson letter.

50 Pirtle, "Stone River Sketches," p. 101.

51 Henry R. Mizner, "The Fourteenth Michigan Infantry, the battle of Murfreesboro, Tennessee; the battle of Jonesboro, Georgia, and incidents of Army life," Bentley Historical Library, University of Michigan, Ann Arbor, p. 2.

52 Pirtle, "Stone River Sketches," pp. 102-103.

53 Barnet, *The Martyrs and Heroes of Illinois*, p. 18; King letters, 8 January 1863.

54 Bisbee, *Through Four American Wars*, p. 125; Phisterer, *The Regular Brigade*, p. 7; Carson letter; OR 20, pt. 1, p. 394.

55 Van Horne, *History of the Army of the Cumberland*, 1, pp. 237-239; Haymond letter, 7 January 1863; OR 20, pt. 1, p. 528.

56 There are a number of versions of Thomas's instructions to Shepherd (Bisbee, *Through Four American Wars*, p. 125; Phisterer, *The Regular Brigade*, p. 9; Hosea, *Regular Brigade*, p. 340; Freeman, "Eighteenth U.S. Infantry," p. 128). Freeman's writing is the most colorful: "Colonel Shepherd, put your brigade in there, and for God's sake keep those devils back for twenty minutes." This version goes against George Thomas's well-documented ability to remain calm and collected in battle. The words I

have used are from Phisterer; he was a prolific writer in the postwar era and generally accurate. His version is most in keeping with Thomas's personality.

57 OR 20, pt. 1, p. 395; Carpenter letters, 8 January 1863.

58 Van Zwaluwenburg journal, p. 24.

59 Phisterer, *The Regular Brigade*, p. 9.

60 Bisbee, *Through Four American Wars*, p. 124; Kellogg, "Recollections of Civil War Service," p. 27.

61 20, pt. 1, p. 395; Phisterer, *The Regular Brigade*, p. 10; Phisterer, "My Days in the Army," p. 53; Lyman letters, 14 January 1863, C-C NMP; Reuben Jones letter.

62 Pirtle, "Stone River Sketches," p. 104; Phisterer, *The Regular Brigade*, p. 10; Lyman letters, 8 January 1863, C-C NMP.

63 Haymond letter, 7 January 1863, Rancourt collection.

64 OR 20, pt. 1, pp. 395, 403, 727; Fitzpatrick letters, 8 January 1863, SRNB.

65 Kellogg, "Recollections of Civil War Service," pp. 27-28. The Confederate officer that Private Hicks unhorsed was probably Colonel H.L.W. Bratton, commanding the 24th Tennessee of Stewart's Brigade. OR 20, pt. 1, pp. 658, 730.

66 Bisbee, *Through Four American Wars*, p. 124-125.

67 Van Zwaluwenburg journal, p. 25. Van Zwaluwenburg did not recall his company mate's name correctly, for there is not a Private Fuller listed among the 16th Infantry's casualties. The nearest match is Private Fernando Ferguson.

68 Phisterer, "My Days in the Army," pp. 53-54. The Regular Army's record for protecting its colors is indeed admirable, although the fact that so few New Army regular battalions had flags issued to them explains much of that accomplishment. Another caveat must be attached to the claim that the regulars never lost a flag in battle during the Civil War. Confederate Major General Patrick Cleburne's Stones River report states: "J.K. Leslie, a brave and intelligent private of Company C, of this regiment [5th Arkansas], captured a beautiful stand of colors belonging to one of the enemy's regiments of regulars." The 5th Arkansas did not fight anywhere near the Regular Brigade, so it is doubtful that the flag Leslie captured belonged to the regulars. Bragg included with his own report a list a captured Union flags. Entry six is "Silk Stars and Stripes; regiment not known; December 31, 1862; captured by Private J. K. Leslie, Company C, Fifth Arkansas, Liddell's brigade." Only the two 18th Infantry battalions of the Regular Brigade carried national colors at Stones River, neither of which were captured. It is safe to say that Leslie's flag was not taken from the regulars. After the war, a number of Union flags the Confederates captured were turned over to the War Department. Around the turn of the century, the War Department's collection was transferred to the museum of the United States Military Academy at West Point. Among that collection is an infantry regimental standard. It is of regulation pattern and made of dark blue silk, indicating that it may have belonged to a regular infantry regiment. The part of the scroll on which the regimental number should be displayed is blank, making it impossible to precisely determine to which regiment it belonged. When the flag arrived at West Point, attached to it was a tattered note that stated, "Captured by Sgt. John F. Levin, 3d Confederate, at the Battle of Stone River." Entry seven on Bragg's captured flag list is "Regimental standard (regulars); regiment not known; December 31, 1862; captured by Sergt. John F. Levin, Company B, Third Confederate, Wood's brigade." Undoubtedly, this is the flag now at West Point. Major J.F. Cameron, commanding officer of the 3rd Confederate Infantry at Stones River, mentioned the flag's capture in his report: "The enemy's line was posted behind a fence. With the aid of 50 stragglers, I charged the fence, driving the enemy, capturing their colors and about 30 prisoners. The brigade then opened upon the retreating Abolitionists, killing great numbers." The action Cameron

describes took place in the afternoon; the timing and Cameron's mention of a fence does not mesh well with the time and terrain of the Regular Brigade's action in the cedars. The most likely explanation of the 3d Confederate's captured flag is that a volunteer regiment in the Army of the Cumberland had a color of the regulation pattern and lost it on December 31, 1862. *OR* 20, pt. 1, pp. 673, 848, 905; Letter, Michael J. McAfee (Curator of History, West Point Museum) to the author, 10 June 1997.

69 Leland W. Thornton, *When Gallantry Was Commonplace: The History of the Eleventh Michigan Volunteer Infantry, 1861-1864* (New York: Peter Lang Publishing, Inc., 1991),pp. 131-133; *OR* 20, pt. 1, p. 395; Cozzens, *No Better Place To Die*, pp. 155-156.

70 *OR* 20, pt. 1, p. 395; Hosea, "The Regular Brigade," p. 341.

71 Phisterer, *The Regular Brigade*, p. 16; Biddle diary, 31 December 1862; *OR* 20, pt. 1, p. 395; Kennedy, "Army Life and Experiences," p. 4; Haymond letter, 7 January 1863.

72 Lyman letters, 31 January 1863, C-C NMP.

73 Van Zwaluwenburg journal, p. 25.

74 Beyer and Keydel, *Deeds of Valor*, p. 127-128.

75 *OR* 20, pt. 1, pp. 380, 396; Carpenter letters, 8 January 1863. Prentice's Medal is on display at the Stones River National Battlefield.

76 Carson letter; Kellogg, "Recollections of Civil War Service," p. 32.

77 Douglass to the adjutant general, 14 April 1892, Freeman personnel file, NA RG 94; *OR* 20, pt. 1, pp. 399-402, 405-406, 730; Du Pont to Rice, 15 January 1895, Crofton personnel file, NA RG 94.

78 Slemmer to Regular Brigade adjutant, 12 January 1863, NA RG 391/1548; Phisterer, *The Regular Brigade*, p. 16; King letters, 6 and 8 January 1863; Smith letters, 22 January 1863.

79 Van Zwaluwenburg journal, pp. 25-26.

80 Kennedy, "Army Life and Experiences," p. 5.

81 Court-martial of Private John Mallory, 18th Infantry, NA RG 153/kk665.

82 A number of sources give statistics on the Regular Brigade's casualties during this engagement, all of which vary slightly (two reports are in the *Official Records*, at 20, pt. 1, pp. 210 and 398, another is in Phisterer's *Regular Brigade*, and additional numbers are listed in Fox's *Regimental Losses in the American Civil War*). The numbers I have given are derived from Oliver Shepherd's report on the battle (*OR* 20, pt. 1, p. 398), minus the strength and casualties of Battery H (which did not participate in the cedar fight) and the 50 casualties of the 15th Infantry that were identified as having occurred during the first clash in the cedars. Minor wounds such as Luke Lyman's were not deemed worthy of official notice in the Civil War, and it was later in the day before all the scattered regulars finally made it back to their units. Considerably fewer than 806 unscathed regular infantrymen rallied at the railroad tracks immediately after the fight. Relatively few were captured or missing, another indication of the brigade's overall discipline. Shepherd reported only forty-seven unaccounted for, most of those being from the 15th and 16th U.S., losses which probably occurred during the morning foray into the cedars.

83 Lyman letters, 8 January 1863, C-C NMP.

84 Kellogg, "Recollections of Civil War Service," p. 31; Kennedy, "Army Life and Experiences," p. 4; Cozzens, *No Better Place To Die*, p. 157.

85 This incident is described in the text accompanying the print *The Battle of Stone River or Murfreesboro'* sketched by A.E. Mathews, a participant in the battle with the

31st Ohio. The print is displayed at the visitor's center of the Stones River National Battlefield.

86　Phisterer, *Regular Brigade*, pp. 16-17; Bisbee, *Through Four American Wars*, pp. 125-126.

87　Freeman, "18th U.S. Infantry," p. 129; Phisterer, *The Regular Brigade*, pp. 13-14.

88　Quoted in David R. Logsdon, *Eyewitnesses at the Battle of Stones River* (Nashville, n.p., 1989), p. 49.

89　James L. McDonough, *Stones River—Bloody Winter in Tennessee* (Knoxville: University of Tennessee Press, 1980), p. 153.

90　Pirtle, "Stone River Sketches," pp. 104-107.

91　*OR* 20, pt. 1, pp. 726, 729.

92　Biddle diary, 31 December 1862; Mills, *My Story*, p. 91.

93　Carson letter; King letters, 8 January 1863.

94　Brinkerhoff, "The Fifteenth Regiment of Infantry," pp. 1264–1265.

95　*OR* 20, pt. 1, p. 396; Bisbee, *Through Four American Wars*, p. 127; Biddle diary, 1 January 1863.

96　Van Horne, *History of the Army of the Cumberland*, 1, pp. 248-250; *OR* 20, pt. 1, pp. 396, 399; Phisterer, *The Regular Brigade*, p. 14.

97　Robert P. King letters, 8 January 1863; Biddle diary, 3 January 1863.

98　Carpenter letters, 18 January 1863.

99　Bisbee, *Through Four American Wars*, p. 131; Phisterer, *The Regular Brigade*, p. 15; King letters, 8 January 1863; Haymond letter, 7 January 1863, Rancourt collection.

100　Biddle diary, 4 January 1863; King letters, 8 January 1863; Carpenter letters, 8 January 1863.

101　Hattaway and Jones, *How the North Won*, pp. 322-324; Mercy is quoted in Phisterer, *The Regular Brigade*, p. 24.; The *Philadelphia Press* is quoted in the King letters, 8 January 1863.

102　King letters, 8 January 1863.

103　McKinney, *Education in Violence*, p. ix; Buell, *The Warrior Generals*, p. 201; Hosea, "The Regular Brigade," p. 343; GO 1, Headquarters Detachment 18th U.S. Infantry, 16 April 1863, NA RG 391/1651; Haymond letter, 7 January 1863, Rancourt collection; Freeman, "18th U.S. Infantry," p. 129. Confusion about the brigade's initial and subsequent forays into the cedars obscured the regulars' role at Stones River for years. Many commanders experienced difficulty in writing accurate reports about the complicated series of events that occurred on the battle's first day. Rosecrans pays but a single sentence of tribute to Rousseau's division and mentions nothing of the regulars: "Rousseau's division, with a portion of Negley's and Sheridan's, met the advancing enemy and checked his movements." Given the extent to which Rosecrans doted on the regulars, this is a curious omission. He based his report on that of George Thomas and this is where the trail of confusion begins. While Thomas acknowledged the regulars' heavy losses, he never mentioned Shepherd's second, unsupported advance into the cedars: "From this last position [the line along the Turnpike] we were enabled to drive back the enemy, cover the formation of our troops, and secure the center on the high ground. In the execution of this last movement, the regular brigade…came under a most murderous fire…but, with the cooperation of Scribner's and Beatty's brigades and Guenther's and Loomis' batteries, gallantly held its ground against overwhelming odds." Thomas thus inadvertently confused the regulars' second fight in the cedars (when the "murderous fire" occurred) with the first (when the Regular Brigade entered the forest as part of a large, division-size maneuver). In *History of the Army of Cumberland*, author Thomas B. Van Horne relied on Thomas's report to formulate the book's description of the cedar fighting. Somehow, Van Horne managed to find even more supporting forces for the regulars: "The exultant enemy soon emerged from the cedar woods, but then fell under the musketry of Rousseau's division at short range. Colonel Shepherd's brigade of regulars quivered under the onset of the enemy...but this brigade, by the efficient support and co-operation of Scribner's and Colonel John Beatty's brigades, Loomis' and Guenther's batteries, and the pioneer brigade with Stokes' battery, withstood the attack." Van Horne's book remains the standard reference on the Army of the Cumberland's operations, despite the fact that it was first published in 1875. Subsequent accounts of Stones River relied on it heavily and thus perpetuated the confusion. It was not until 1990 that the Regular Brigade's second engagement in the cedars was placed in proper context, when Peter Cozzens did so in *No Better Place to Die*. OR 20, pt. 1, p. 193, 373; Van Horne, 1, p. 238; Cozzens, *No Better Place to Die*, pp. 155-156.

104 Carpenter letters, 8 January 1863.

105 *OR* 20, pt. 1, p. 397.

106 Ibid., p. 380.

107 Carpenter letters, 18 January 1863.

Chapter 7

1 Bisbee, *Through Four American Wars*, pp. 130-131.

2 The remains of other regular officers also now reside at Stones River National Cemetary. They were interred there after the war.

3 *Bangor Daily Whig and Courier*, 12 February 1863, p. 1.

4 Townsend to Madam Denison, 16 January 1863, NA RG 391/1843.

5 Fleagle letters, 20 March 1863. Amos Fleagle and David Bailey Flegeal (spelling of the surname varies) were second cousins in addition to being brothers-in-law. Three brothers of Amos Fleagle also served in the Union Army, Jacob, Josiah, and Uriah.. Private Uriah Fleagle of the 1st Maryland was killed at the Battle of Gettysburg on July 3, 1863. Amos's letters were donated to the Military History Institute by Colonel Foster Flegeal (U.S. Army, Retired), David Bailey Flegeal's grandson, in the 1970s (information courtesy of Mr. Frank H. Fleagle, son of Colonel Fleagle).

6 Kennedy, "Army Life and Experiences," p. 5.

7 Cabaniss, "The Eighteenth Regiment of Infantry," p. 648; February 1863 return of the 15th Infantry, NA MF M665/164; February 1863 return of the 16th Infantry, NA MF M665/173; February 1863 return of the 19th Infantry, NA MF M665/202; Van Horne, *History of the Army of the Cumberland*, 1, p. 287; Frederick H. Dyer, *A Compendium of the War of the Rebellion* (Des Moines, Iowa: The Dyer Publishing Company, 1908), pt. 1, pp. 443-444; Association of Survivors, Regular Brigade, *Proceedings of Reunions*, p. 19. Companies disbanded from the 18th U.S. were A, B, C, D, E, and F, 3rd Battalion, and A & C from the 1st Battalion. Other companies broken up were B and D of 1/15th, B and G of 1/16th, and D of 1/19th. GO 181, Headquarters Detachment 18th U.S. Infantry, 8 January 1863, NA RG 391/1651.

8 Biddle diary, undated entry following 5 January 1863; Carpenter letters, 10 February 1863.

9 Court-martial of Private John Mallory, 18th Infantry, NA RG 153/kk665.

10 Biddle diary, undated entry following 5 January 1863.

11 OR 20, pt. 1, p. 984; 23, pt. 1; Dyer, *Compendium*, pt. 2, p. 854; Carpenter letters, 3 March 1863; Tarbell diary, 2 March 1863; Association of Survivors, Regular Brigade, *Proceedings of Reunions*, p. 19; Van Zwaluwenburg journal, p. 28; Lyman letters, 6 March 1863, C-C NMP.

12 OR 23, pt. 2, pp. 67-68; William M. Lamers, *The Edge of Glory: A Biography of General William S. Rosecrans, U.S.A.* (New York: Harcourt, Brace & World, Inc., 1961), pp. 253-254.

13 Shepherd to Goddard, 13 January 1863, NA RG 391/1627.

14 Shepherd to Goddard, 9 April 1862, NA MF M619/182.

15 OR 23, pt. 2, p. 61; Frederick Phisterer, "Record of Events, of the Second Battalion, 18th Regt. of Infantry, U.S. Army. 1863," NA MF M665/192; Bogart letters, 25 March 1863.

16 OR 17, pt. 2, p. 146; 23, pt. 2, p. 65; 24, pt. 4, pp. 6, 30, 189, 415-416; 1862 annual return of the 16th Infantry, NA MF M665/173; March 1863 return of the 15th Infantry, NA MF M665/164.

17 Wilcox letters, 22 January 1863, USAMHI. H/2/18th U.S. was Captain Tenador Ten Eyck's company of regulars that was captured and paroled at Munfordville, Kentucky, during September 1862.

18 Quoted in Lucius Brown, "The 18th Infantry U.S.A.," Letters: Appendix 4, p. 5, Brown Family Correspondence, 1844-1868, Manuscripts and Archives Division, New York Public Library.

19 Wilcox letters, 30 April 1863, USAMHI.

20 Lucius F. Brown to Father & Sister, 15 and 17 March 1863, Brown Family Correspondence, Manuscripts and Archives Division, The New York Public Library, Astor, Lenox and Tilden Foundations.

21 October 1862 and March 1863 returns of the 16th Infantry, NA MF M665/173; Heitman, *Historical Register*, p. 325; Brown letters, 28 March and 21 April 1863.

22 OR, series III, vol. 1, p. 374; Regular Army Register of Enlistments for 1863, NA MF M233/27 and 28; August 1862 through May 1863 returns of the 15th Infantry, NA MF M665/164; Rappaport, "The Replacement System during the Civil War," p. 123; Hattaway and Jones, *How the North Won*, pp. 437-440; King letters, 23 August 1862.

23 Carpenter letters, 26 April 1863.

24 Kennedy, "Army Life and Experiences," p. 6.

25 Brown letters, 10 April 1863.

26 Tarbell diary, 21 February 1863.

27 Shepherd to Thomas, 26 January 1863, NA MF M619/211.

28 Smith to secretary of war, undated, Smith personnel file, NA RG 94; Thomas to Rosecrans, 14 November 1863, NA RG 94/159, George H. Thomas Papers, Box 18: Letters Sent, 1861-1862; Telegram, Steedman to Rosecrans, 21 November 1862, NA RG 391/1627.

29 Van Zwaluwenburg memoir, pp. 27-28; Heitman, *Historical Register*, p. 916.

30 Brown letters, 10 April 1863. The parenthesized word quoted here is as stated in the original.

31 Tarbell diary, 25 February and 5 April 1863.

32 Lyman letters, 15 May 1863, C-C NMP.

33 Tarbell diary, 19 March 1863; Carpenter letters, 23 March 1863.

34 Warner, *Generals in Blue*, p. 451.

35 Goddard to Flynt, 14 April 1863, NA RG 94/159, Subseries I: George H. Thomas Papers, Box 2: Letters Received, 1863.

36 Rosecrans to Thomas, 15 February 1863, NA MF 1064/11.

37 Rosecrans to Halleck, 27 February 1863, NA MF 1064/11; Shepherd to Thomas, undated, NA MF 1064/221; Rosecrans to the War Department, 15 February 1863, Crofton personnel file, NA RG 94; Rosecrans to the War Department, 15 February

1863, King personnel file, NA RG 94; King to Thomas, 11 February and 4 April 1863, NA MF M619/110; Heitman, *Historical Register*, p. 599.

38 Shepherd to Goddard, 13 February 1863, NA RG 391/1627.

39 Rosecrans to the War Department, 15 February 1863, Guenther personnel file, NA RG 94. The colors of the 30th Arkansas were captured by the 2nd Ohio of Scribner's brigade, a regiment that supported Battery H on December 31.

40 *OR* 6, p. 704; 23, pt. 1, p. 412; 30, pt.1, 236; Heitman, *Historical Register*, pp. 593; *Memorial of Lieutenant Howard M. Burnham, United States Army, Who Fell in the Battle of Chickamauga, Tenn., September 19th, 1863* (Springfield, Mass.: Samuel Bowles and Company, Printers, 1864), pp. 10-11, 15-16, 18, 35; June 1863 return of the 5th Artillery, NA MF M727/33.

41 Rosecrans to the War Department, 15 February 1863, Shepherd personnel file, NA RG 94. Rosecrans's reference to the Regular Brigade's Stones River losses is probably based on Rousseau's report on the battle, which stated only that "over one third" of the regulars were casualties.

42 Shepherd to Thomas, 12 March 1866, Shepherd personnel file, NA RG 94.

43 Court-Martial of Colonel (Retired) Oliver L. Shepherd, NA RG 153/qq546, exhibit 22.

44 Ibid., testimony of Samuel B. Lawrence.

45 Telegram, Rosecrans to Thomas, 9 April 1863, Shepherd personnel file, NA RG 94.

46 Heitman, *Historical Register*, pp. 496, 799; *OR*, series III, vol. 1, p. 704; Warner, *Generals in Blue*, pp. 182, 380; Dyer, *Compendium*, pt. 1, pp. 443-444. Porter's rank and good name were reestablished through an Act of Congress in 1886.

47 Shepherd to Thomas, 12 February 1867, Shepherd personnel file, NA RG 94.

48 Shepherd to Goddard, 11 April 1863, NA MF M619/213.

49 Ibid. It was irrelevant that Granger graduated from West Point in 1838, two years before Shepherd. In 1863 Shepherd was Granger's senior in Regular Army rank, which was all that mattered to Shepherd, but one-star volunteer rank entitled Granger to command of a brigade.

50 GO 186, Headquarters Detachment 18th U.S. Infantry, 14 April 1863, NA RG 391/1651.

51 GO 1, Headquarters Detachment 18th U.S. Infantry, 16 April 1863, NA RG 391/1651.

52 Shepherd to Thomas, 6 May 1863, NA MF M619/212.

53 Shepherd to Thomas, 13 May 1863 and 25 July 1863, NA MF M619/215; Shepherd to Thomas, 4 and 8 September 1863, NA MF M619/216; Shepherd to Thomas, 2 July 1863, NA MF M619/215; U.S. Army Register of Enlistments, NA MF M233/27 and 28.

54 SO 207, War Department, AGO, series 1863.

55 May and June 1863 returns of the 15th Infantry, NA MF M664/164; Heitman, *Historical Register*, p. 536.

56 Hough, *Soldier of the West*, pp. 90-91.

57 Ibid., p. 91; Phisterer, "My Days in the Army," p. 56; April 1863 return of the 5th Artillery, NA MF M727/33; Phisterer, "Record of Events, 1863," NA MF M665/192; Mussey letters, 30 August 1863; Biddle diary, undated entry following 16 March 1863; Association of Survivors, Regular Brigade, *Proceedings of Reunions*, p. 19.

58 Heitman, *Historical Register*, pp. 310, 314, 591, 614, 635, 684, 864; Phisterer, "Record of Events, 1863," NA MF M665/192. The two company commanders from the Regular Brigade who commanded the same units at both Stones River and Chickamauga

were Captain Henry Keteltas (E/1/15th U.S.) and Captain R.E.A. Crofton (A/1/16th U.S.). They also commanded these same companies at Shiloh, during which battle Keteltas was wounded.

59 OR 23, pt. 1, pp. 268-269.

60 Michael J. Barringer, "Diary Kept By Michael James Barringer, Private of Company D 2nd Batt. 18th U.S.I. From the 12th day of March/63 to the 15th day of July, 1865," collection of James Ogden, Ft. Oglethorpe, Georgia, entry for 25 April 1863; OR 23, pt. 1, p. 416.

61 Carpenter letters, 26 April 1863.

62 Kennedy, "Army Life and Experiences," p. 6.

63 "Proceedings of U.S. Army Courts-Martial and Military Commissions of Union Soldiers Executed by U.S. Military Authorities, 1861-66," NA MF M1523/1, court-martial of Private David Blaser, 4th Indiana Battery; Ella Lonn, *Desertion During the Civil War* (Gloucester, Massachusetts: American Historical Association, 1928), p. 169; Kennedy, "Army Life and Experiences," p. 6.

64 Van Zwaluwenburg journal, pp. 28-29; Kennedy, "Army Life and Experiences," p. 6; Tarbell diary, 20 June 1863; Brown letters, 20 June 1863.

65 Dyer, *Compendium*, pt. 1, p. 444; Hough, *Soldier of the West*, p. 96; Association of Survivors, Regular Brigade, *Proceedings of Reunions*, pp. 19, 58. Granger briefly served in the Army of the Cumberland's Reserve Corps before returning permanently to staff duty and rear area commands. Van Horne, *History of the Army of the Cumberland*, 1, p. 299; Warner, *Generals in Blue*, p. 182.

66 King to Goddard, 27 May 1863, NA MF M619/182.

67 King to Goddard, 28 May 1863, NA MF M619/182.

68 Heitman, *Historical Register*, p. 106; May-October 1863 returns of the 15th Infantry, NA MF M665/164.

69 Shepherd to Thomas, 21 May 1863, NA MF M1064/56.

70 Swick letters, 1 June 1863; OR 23, pt. 1, pp. 403-404; Jones, *Civil War Command and Strategy*, pp. 164-166.

71 Steven E. Woodworth, *Six Armies in Tennessee: The Chickamauga and Chattanooga Campaigns* (Lincoln: University of Nebraska Press, 1998), pp. 5-6; Michael R. Bradley, *Tullahoma: The 1863 Campaign for the Control of Middle Tennessee* (Shippensburg, Pennsylvania: Burd Street Press, 2000), pp. 33-36.

72 OR 23, pt. 1, p. 405; Lamers, *The Edge of Glory*, p. 278; Bradley, *Tullahoma*, p. 53.

73 OR 23, pt. 1, p. 430.

74 OR 6, p. 704; 23, pt. 1, p. 412; Bisbee, *Through Four American Wars*, p. 134.

75 OR 23, pt. 1, p. 434, 455; Margaret L. Stuntz, "Lightning Strike at the Gap," *America's Civil War*, July 1997, pp. 52-53; Woodworth, *Six Armies in Tennessee*, pp. 21-22; Peter Cozzens, *This Terrible Sound: The Battle of Chickamauga* (Chicago: University of Illinois Press, 1992), p. 18.

76 OR 23, pt. 1, p. 435, 451; Woodworth, *Six Armies in Tennessee*, pp. 28-30.

77 Bisbee, *Through Four American Wars*, p. 134; OR 23, pt. 1, p. 604; Carpenter letters, 30 June 1863.

78 OR 23, pt. 1, pp. 440-441; Bisbee, *Through Four American Wars*, pp. 134-135; Barnet, *The Martyrs and Heroes of Illinois*, p. 13.

79 Kellogg, "Recollections of Civil War Service," p. 34; Hough, *Soldier in the West*, p. 100; the report from the *New York Herald* is quoted in Barnet, *The Martyrs and Heroes of Illinois*, p. 13.

80 OR 23, pt. 1, p. 604-605; Hosea, "The Regular Brigade," p. 358.

81 OR 23, pt. 1, p. 431, 436, 440-441; Kellogg, "Recollections of Civil War Service," p. 34; Carpenter letters, 30 June 1863.

82 OR 23, pt. 1, pp. 431, 436; Tarbell diary, 28 June 1863.

83 Lyman letters, 4 July 1863, C-C NMP.

84 Brown letters, 15 August 1863.

85 Bisbee, *Through Four American Wars*, pp. 135-136. Bisbee's memory failed him on the timing of Captain Thompson's death. The captain had passed away the previous month, not week.

86 OR 23, pt. 2, pp. 559-560; Hough, *Soldier in the West*, p. 105.

87 Lamers, *The Edge of Glory*, pp. 253-254; Dyer, *Compendium*, pt. 1, p. 443; Heitman, *Historical Register*, p. 361; Brown letters, 28 July 1863; Hough, *Soldier in the West*, p. 84.

88 Brown letters, 26 July 1863; Gageby letters, 7 August 1863; Carpenter letters, 9 August 1863.

89 Carpenter letters, 16 August 1863.

90 Brown letters, 15 August 1863.

91 Woodworth, *Six Armies in Tennessee*, p. 63-65.

Chapter 8

1 Wilcox journal-diary, 11 August 1863.

2 Ibid., 16, 19, 20, 21, and 22 August 1863

3 Carpenter letters, 2 September 1863.

4 OR 30, pt. 3, p. 218.

5 *Memorial of Lieutenant Howard M. Burnham*, p. 23.

6 John A. Baird, Jr., "'For Gallant and Meritorious Service,' Major General Absalom Baird," *Civil War Times Illustrated*, June 1976, pp. 4-9.

7 OR 30, pt. 1, pp. 51-52, 312; pt. 3, pp. 132, 218, 231, 819; John C. White, "A Review of the Services of the Regular Army during the War of the Rebellion," *Journal of the Military Service Institution of the United States*, 49 (1911), p. 400; Brown letters, 6 and 10 September 1863; Carpenter letters, 2 September 1863; Dyer, *Compendium*, pt. 1, p. 443; August 1863 return of the 16th Infantry, NA MF M665/173; Kellogg, "Recollections of Civil War Service," p. 35.

8 Van Horne, *History of the Army of the Cumberland*, 1, pp. 314-325; OR 30, pt. 1, pp 53-54.

9 Haymond to the adjutant general, 15 September 1863, NA RG 391/1843; Brown letters, 15 September 1863.

10   Brown letters, 15 September 1863.

11 OR 30, pt. 1, pp. 54-55; pt. 2, p. 31; Van Horne, *History of the Army of the Cumberland*, 1, pp. 329-330.

12 Wilcox journal-diary, 18 September 1863; OR 30, pt. 1, pp. 55, 248-249.

13 Ibid., 19 September 1863.

14 Woodworth, *Six Armies in Tennessee*, pp. 84-85; Cozzens, *This Terrible Sound*, p. 123.

15 OR 30, pt. 1, p. 309; Wilcox journal-diary, 19 September 1863; Henry B. Freeman, "At the Battle of Chickamauga," Henry B. Freeman Manuscripts, Wyoming Division of Cultural Resources, Wyoming State Archives, Cheyenne, pp. 1-2.

16 Heitman, *Historical Register*, p. 177; Johnson, *A Soldier's Reminiscences in Peace and War*, p. 262; Carpenter letters, 4 October 1863.

17 Conversation between the author and James Ogden, C-C NMP staff historian, April 1993; OR 30, pt. 1, pp. 124-125, 249-250, 275; pt. 2, p. 524.

18 OR 30, pt. 1, pp. 309, 318, 319, 322; Van Horne, *History of the Army of the Cumberland*, 1, p. 334; Freeman, "At the Battle of Chickamauga," p. 2.

19 Van Zwaluwenburg journal, p. 30.

20 OR 30, pt. 1, p. 275-276, 297; Freeman, "At the Battle of Chickamauga," p. 4.

21 OR 30, pt. 1, p. 324; Van Zwaluwenburg memoir, p. 30; Henry Haymond, letter to father, 24-25 September 1863, 18th U.S. Infantry file, C-C NMP; Roderick H. Burnham, *Genealogical Records of Thomas Burnham, the Emigrant, who was among the Early Settlers at Hartford, Connecticut, U.S. America, and His Descendants* (Hartford: The Case, Lockwood & Brainard Co. Print, 1884), pp. 246-247.

22 Powell and Shippen, *Officers of the Army and Navy (Regular)*, p. 250; Van Zwaluwenburg journal, pp. 30-31; Carpenter letters, 29 September 1863. Two sergeants of Battery H were killed in action at Chickamauga, David C. Bickel and James T. Sinclair. It is unfortunately impossible to determine which of the two performed this act of extreme heroism.

23 Association of Survivors, Regular Brigade, *Proceedings of Reunions*, p. 121; OR 30, pt. 1, p. 317; pt. 2, pp. 258, 261.

24 Oscar P. Heath, "The Battle of Chickamauga as I saw it," 4th U.S. Artillery file, C-C NMP, p. 6; OR 30, pt. 1, pp. 428, 433-434. Author Peter Cozzens asserts that the Regular Brigade's retreat through Van Derveer's brigade included many acts of cowardice on the part of the regulars, such as shouting to the volunteers "to save themselves and retreat" and an 18th Infantry color bearer abandoning his flag in front of the 2nd Minnesota's lines. Cozzens's analysis is based on the postwar writings of two 2nd Minnesota officers (Lieutenant Colonel Judson Bishop and Captain Jeremiah C. Donahower), members of a regiment that had played a leading role in the March 1862 riot at Spring Hill and thus had no love lost for the 18th Infantry. The residue of Van Derveer and Shepherd's contempt for each other may have also influenced Bishop and Donahower's writings. The color bearers of the 18th Infantry battalions, Sergeants Roland Evans and Paul Fisher, were noted for the steadfastness under fire. For one of them to abandon his colors in this situation—at the end of a retreat and out of immediate danger—would have been completely out of character. While the retreat of the regulars was undoubtedly disorganized, Cozzens's sources were written by veterans with an axe to grind when it comes to their comments about the regulars. Cozzens, *This Terrible Sound*, p. 147.

25 Freeman, "At the Battle of Chickamauga," p. 4; OR 30, pt. 1, pp. 309, 314, 324, 1068; *Memorial of Lieutenant Howard M. Burnham*, pp. 26, 33.

26 Carpenter letters, 14 February 1863.

27 Freeman, "At the Battle of Chickamauga," p. 5; OR 30, pt. 1, p. 250; pt. 2, pp. 153-154.

28 Henry B. Freeman, "Lieutenant Henry B. Freeman's Report on his Capture," NA RG 391/1629; Freeman, "At the Battle of Chickamauga," pp. 6-7.

29 Van Horne, *History of the Army of the Cumberland*, 1, p. 340; Cozzens, *This Terrible Sound*, p. 294.

30 Van Zwaluwenburg journal, p. 31; Carpenter letters, 29 September 1863; Mills, *My Story*, p. 92.

31 Freeman, "Lieutenant Henry B. Freeman's Report on his Capture," NA RG 391/1629.

32 OR 30, pt. 1, pp. 51, 251, 277, 401-402, 540, 714.

33 Ibid., p. 310; Michael James Barringer diary, 20 September 1863, Collection of James H. Ogden, Fort Oglethorpe, Georgia; Carpenter letters, 29 September 1863. Peter Cozzens in *This Terrible Sound* claims that during the night of September 19-20 both

Baird and Thomas were worried about the Federal left flank being manned by the "badly demoralized Regulars of King's brigade." If Baird actually thought the regulars were demoralized it is hard to believe he would have placed King's troops in the division's most critical position. Baird reported after the battle "the performance of General King's command upon Saturday morning [September 19] was particularly brilliant." As for Thomas, Francis F. McKinney in *Education in Violence* maintains that the corps commander had the utmost confidence in King's troops on September 20: "Thomas's confidence in the regulars had been unaltered since [1861]. He put them where the enemy pressure would be the greatest." McKinney's writing echoes that of Jacob van Zwaluwenburg. The 16th Infantrymen states in his reminiscences that "the regular brigade was placed on the left where the great attack was expected." Thomas's decision to give the Regular Brigade the critical mission of holding the Reed's Bridge Road throughout the afternoon of September 19, without any support, is a fair indication that he did not hesitate to place heavy burdens on the regulars throughout the battle. Note that Thomas gave King's brigade the Reed's Bridge Road mission *after* the regulars had been routed at Jay's Mill. On the morning of September 20, Thomas was concerned only with the position of the unit holding the left of the line at Kelly Field, not with that unit's composition. Cozzens, *This Terrible Sound*, p. 297; OR 30, pt. 1, p. 280; McKinney, *Education in Violence*, p. 492, n. 11; Van Zwaluwenburg memoir, p. 30.

34 OR 30, pt. 1, pp. 277, 367-368, 556; Tarbell diary, 20 September 1863; Van Horne, *History of the Army of the Cumberland*, 1, p. 343; McKinney, *Education in Violence*, pp. 239-240.

35 OR 30, pt. 1, pp. 58, 251, 310, 367-368, 555; Carpenter letters, 29 September 1863.

36 Cozzens, *This Terrible Sound*, p. 309; Van Horne, *History of the Army of the Cumberland*, 1, pp. 345-346; Woodworth, *Jefferson Davis and His Generals*, pp. 235-236; OR 30, pt. 1, p. 319; pt. 2, pp. 203-204; Wilcox to Lottie, 22 September 1863, collection of Cal Packard, Mansfield, Ohio.

37 OR 30, pt. 1, pp. 402, 429-430; pt. 2, pp. 154-155, 363.

38 Ibid., pt. 1, pp. 309, 319; pt. 2, pp. 198-199, 233, 237; Van Horne, *History of the Army of the Cumberland*, 1, p. 345.

39 Beyer and Keidel, *Deeds of Valor*, p. 203; Association of Survivors, Regular Brigade, *Proceedings of Reunions*, pp. 120-121; OR 30, pt. 1, p. 317.

40 Carpenter letters, 29 September 1863; OR 30, pt. 1, pp. 309, 319; pt. 2, p. 233; Cozzens, *This Terrible Sound*, pp. 329-334; Wilcox letters, 22 September 1863, USAMHI.

41 Cozzens, *This Terrible Sound*, pp. 362-367; Woodworth, *Six Armies in Tennessee*, pp. 113-116; Buell, *The Warrior Generals*, pp. 265-266; Glenn Tucker, *Chickamauga: Bloody Battle in the West* (Indianapolis: Bobbs-Merrill, 1961), pp. 255-259.

42 I am indebted to James Ogden, C-C NMP staff historian, for enlightening me on this line of reasoning.

43 Van Horne, *History of the Army of the Cumberland*, 1, pp. 346-348; McKinney, *Education in Violence*, pp. 257-258.

44 OR 30, pt. 2, pp. 34, 142-143, 241, 245-246,

45 OR 30, pt. 1, pp. 311, 316, 319-320, 321; pt. 2, pp. 245-246; Barringer diary, 20 September 1863.

46 OR 30, pt. 2, pp. 253, 259-260.

47 OR 30, pt. 1, p. 316; pt. 2, p. 259.

48 Haymond letter, 24-25 September 1863, C-C NMP.

49 *OR* 30, pt. 1, p. 316; Court-martial of Lieutenant Edgar N. Wilcox, 18th Infantry, NA RG 153/ll1049.

50 *OR* 30, pt. 1, pp. 442-443; *Indiana at Chickamauga, 1863-1900. A Report of the Indiana Commissioners, Chickamauga National Military Park* (Indianapolis: Sentinel Printing Company, 1900), pp. 199-200.

51 *OR* 30, pt. 2, pp. 34, 79-80, 84; Cozzens, *This Terrible Sound*, pp. 488-490. Dana M. Mangham, "Cox's Wildcats: The 2nd Georgia Battalion Sharpshooters at Chickamauga and Chattanooga," *Civil War Regiments: A Journal of the American Civil War* 7, no. 1 (2000), pp. 115-116; McKinney, *Education in Violence*, p. 245; Haymond letter, 24-25 September 1863, C-C NMP.

52 *OR* 30, pt. 1, pp. 317-318; pt. 2, p. 85; 10, pt. 1, p. 313; June 1863 return of the 15th Infantry, NA MF M665/164.

53 Kennedy, "Army Life and Experiences," p. 8.

54 Van Horne, *History of the Army of the Cumberland*, 1, p. 355; McKinney, *Education in Violence*, pp. 254-255; *OR* 30, pt. 1, pp. 61, 140, 253, 279, 288.

55 *OR* 30, pt. 1, pp. 279, 310, 715; Van Horne, *History of the Army of the Cumberland*, 1, pp. 355-356; Brinkerhoff, "The Fifteenth Regiment of Infantry," p. 1266.

56 *OR* 30, pt. 1, p. 320; pt. 2, pp. 120, 178-179; Hosea, "The Regular Brigade," p. 352; Van Zwaluwenburg journal, p. 31; Du Pont to Rice, 15 January 1985, Crofton personnel file, NA RG 94; Haymond letter, 24-25 September 1863, C-C NMP.

57 Tenador Ten Eyck, "Report of Captain Tenador Ten Eyck on his capture and captivity," NA RG 391/1629. It is difficult to precisely determine which Federal brigade remained fighting at Kelly Field the longest, but the Regular Brigade's case is particularly strong. Thomas's orders were to fall back beginning with the most southerly units at Kelly Field, instructions that were generally complied with. Barnes's brigade was to the Regular Brigade's left (north/northwest) when the final Confederate assault began and, like King's brigade, received orders to retire from division commander Baird. It appears from reports that Barnes's regiments retired in relatively good order and without losing an inordinate of men captured, so it is reasonable to assume that Barnes's brigade retired while the regulars were still on the field. Other observers in King's brigade echoed Sergeant Major D'Isay's statement that he noticed troops "on the right and left of our Brigade falling back."

58 Rufus C. Gates, "Lieutenant Rufus C. Gates's Report on his capture," NA RG 391/1629.

59 Isaac D'Isay, "Lieutenant Isaac D'Isay's Report on his capture," NA RG 391/1629.

60 Kennedy, "Army Life and Experiences," p. 8.

61 *OR* 30, pt. 2, p. 177; Gates, "Lieutenant Rufus C. Gates's Report on his capture;" Court-martial of Lieutenant Edgar N. Wilcox, 18th Infantry, NA RG 153/ll1049; Kennedy, "Army Life and Experiences," p. 8; Reese, *Sykes' Regular Infantry Division*, p. 163.

62 Court-martial of Lieutenant Edgar Wilcox, 18th Infantry, NA RG 153/ll1049; Carpenter letters, 29 September and 4 October 1863.

63 *OR* 30, pt. 1, pp. 253-254, 312, 611; Wilcox journal-diary, 21 September 1863. Rosecrans was quick to point out after the battle that Rousseau's resumption of command was in no way a negative comment on Baird's performance: "On the return of Major-General Rousseau from an important mission for the benefit of this army, he resumed the command of his division. Brigadier General A. Baird being thus relieved of this division, the general commanding tenders to him his thanks for the prudence and

ability which he displayed while in command, for the unflinching courage and ability with which he carried his troops into action on the 19th and maintained his position during the terrific fight of the 20th in the glorious battle of the Chickamauga." *OR* 30, pt. 1, p. 281.

64 Phisterer, "Record of Events, 1863," NA MF M665/192; Van Horne, *History of the Army of the Cumberland*, 1, pp. 356, 363; *OR* 30, pt. 1, p. 279; McKinney, *Education in Violence*, p. 267; Wilcox journal-diary, 21 September 1863.

65 Freeman to Carpenter, 17 November 1863, Luther Freeman Collection, University of Wyoming American Heritage Center, Laramie; McKinney, *Education in Violence*, p. 261; *OR* 30, pt. 1, p. 312; Gageby letters, 14 November 1863. Lieutenant Gageby participated in the famous mass tunnel escape from Libby Prison on February 9, 1864, although according to Gageby, "we were not permitted to work in the tunnel, on account of the prejudice of some of the Volunteer Officers, we were charged with preventing the discovery of the tunnel while it was being constructed" (sparring between regulars and volunteers apparently extended even to prisoners of war). Other regulars who escaped through the tunnel included Lieutenant Frank Bennett (18th U.S.), Lieutenant Walter Clifford (16th U.S.), Captain Thomas Cummings (19th U.S.), Lieutenant Henry Freeman (18th U.S.), and Captain Edmund Smith (19th U.S.). All were recaptured within a week. Gageby was released from captivity through a prisoner exchange on March 1, 1865. He served in the Regular Army after the war, rising to the rank of major in the 12th Infantry. He died unexpectedly at his home in Johnstown, Pennsylvania, in 1896 while still on active duty. Military Order of the Loyal Legion of the United States, Commandery of the State of Nebraska, "In Memoriam James Harrison Gageby," Circular No. 8, Series of 1897.

66 Cozzens, *This Terrible Sound*, pp. 520-521, 534; Wilcox letters, 22 September 1863, USAMHI.

67 Baird to the president, 1 November 1891, Swaine personnel file, NA RG 94.

68 Rufus C. Gates, "Lieutenant Rufus C. Gates's Report on his capture," NA RG 391/1629.

Chapter 9

1 Ed Wilcox to Cousin Ria, 14 October 1863, Lucius F. Brown Letters, Manuscripts and Archives Division, New York Public Library; *OR* 30, pt. 3, p. 911.

2 Carpenter letters, 29 September 1863.

3 *Memorial of Lieutenant Howard M. Burnham*, p. 31. A number of Howard Burnham's personal effects, including his epaulets, riding spurs, and commission certificate, are on display at the Longmeadow Historical Society in Longmeadow, Massachusetts.

4 Van Horne, *History of the Army of the Cumberland*, 1, p. 386; Tarbell diary, 25 September 1863.

5 Carpenter letters, 29 September 1863; Van Zwaluwenburg journal, p. 32.

6 Carpenter letters, 10 October 1863.

7 September and October 1863 returns of the 15th Infantry, NA MF M665/164; Brinkerhoff, "The Fifteenth Regiment of Infantry," p. 1267; *OR* 30, pt. 2, p. 723; pt. 3, p. 871; Van Horne, *History of the Army of the Cumberland*, 1, p. 388.

8 Edie to Lowrie, 1 November 1863, and Edie to Goddard, 20 November 1863, NA RG 391/1747.

9 Edie to Goddard, 20 November 1863, NA RG 391/1747.

10 King to Thomas, 15 October 1863, NA MF M619/182; *OR* 30, pt. 3, p. 820; Carpenter letters, 4 October 1863.

11 King to Thomas, 29 December 1863, NA MF M619/183.

12 Mattes, *Indians, Infants, and Infantry*, p. 13; Heitman, *Historical Register*, pp. 314, 411, 456; Association of Survivors, Regular Brigade, *Proceedings of Reunions*, pp. 109-111.

13 Guenther to Thomas, 11 September 1863, Guenther personnel file, NA RG 94.

14 Bogart letters, 28 September 1863; Thornton, *When Gallantry Was Commonplace*, pp. 192-193; OR 30, pt. 3, pp. 209-213; Wiley Sword, *Mountains Touched By Fire: Chattanooga Besieged, 1863* (New York: St. Martin's Press, 1995), p. 50; Cozzens, *This Terrible Sound*, p. 429. Of these three volunteer regiments, only the 11th Michigan and 19th Illinois fought at Horseshoe Ridge. The 69th Ohio had been placed on guard duty in the weeks leading up to Chickamauga. During the battle it was temporarily attached to Colonel Daniel McCook's brigade of the Reserve Corps. On September 19, it participated in the initial skirmishes near Jay's Mill.

15 McKinney, *Education in Violence*, pp. 276-277.

16 Haymond letter, 24-25 September 1863, C-C NMP.

17 OR 30, pt. 4, p. 479; 31, pt. 1, pp. 69, 211; Van Horne, *History of the Army of the Cumberland*, 1, pp. 394-395; Peter Cozzens, *The Shipwreck of Their Hopes: The Battles for Chattanooga* (Chicago: University of Illinois Press, 1994), p. 7; McKinney, *Education in Violence*, pp. 268-272; David Evans, *Sherman's Horsemen: Union Cavalry Operations in the Atlanta Campaign* (Indianapolis: University of Indiana Press, 1996), p. 34.

18 Quoted in Dodge, *History of the Old Second Division*, p. 313.

19 Wilcox journal-diary, 11 and 12 November 1863; Tarbell diary, 13 November 1863. In the 1864 Congressional elections, Rousseau won a Kentucky seat in the U.S. House of Representatives as an Unconditional Unionist. He served in Congress from March 1865 until July 1866, during which time he was a steadfast supporter of President Andrew Johnson. In February 1866, during a heated argument on Capitol Hill about the operations of the Freedman's Bureau in Kentucky, Iowa Representative Josiah B. Grinnell stated that Kentucky's laws hindered the Bureau's operations. He accused Rousseau of not doing enough to change the laws, stating: "I care not whether the gentleman [Rousseau] was four years in the war on the Union side or four years on the other side." Verbal sparring continued between Rousseau and Grinnell until early summer. On June 11, Grinnell escalated things considerably: "The gentleman [Rousseau] begins courting sympathy by sustaining the President of the United States. ...Now, sir, if he is a defender of the President of the United States, all I have to say is, God save the President from such an incoherent, brainless defender. ...His military record! Who has read it? In what volume of history is it found? Some time ago the gentleman asked some of us, 'What did you do in the rebellion but make speeches?' And he told us that he was in the field. ...But where was he in any great fight?" Rousseau's temper flared at these repeated slights. A few days afterward, Rousseau followed the Iowan out of the Capitol. Rousseau took his cane to Grinnell on the East Portico of the Capitol Building, striking about a half dozen blows, but doing no serious harm. After a hearing on the matter, a Select Committee on Breach of Privilege voted to expel Rousseau for the assault. He was forced to resign his seat and return to Kentucky, but his district overwhelming reelected him in 1866. He returned to Washington in December of that year and served four additional months in Congress prior to receiving an appointment from President Johnson as a Regular Army brigadier general. Johnson dispatched the general to Alaska, where Rousseau oversaw the territory's transfer from Russia to the United States. In July 1868, Rousseau took command of the Department of Louisiana, overseeing Reconstruction efforts in that state and Arkansas from his headquarters in New Orleans. Rousseau

proved to be one of the few generals who was genuinely liked and respected by the Southern populace during the Reconstruction era; following his premature death from appendicitis on January 7, 1869, the procession of his flag-draped coffin through New Orleans, escorted by four companies of the 1st U.S. Infantry, was thought to be one of the largest funerals ever held in the Crescent City. Rousseau is interred in Arlington National Cemetary. House of Representatives, 39th Congress, 1st Session, Report No. 90, 2 July 1866; Dawson, "General Lovell H. Rousseau," pp. 374-375, 390-391.

20 Dyer, *Compendium*, pt. 1, p. 443; *OR* 31, pt. 3, p. 554; Carpenter letters, 20 November 1863.

21 Johnson, *A Soldier's Reminiscences*, pp. 240-241.

22 Benjamin F. Scribner, *How Soldiers Were Made; or the War As I Saw It Under Buell, Rosecrans, Thomas, Grant, and Sherman* (Chicago: Donohue & Henneberry, 1887), pp. 252-254.

23 Haymond letter, 24-25 September 1863, C-C NMP; Van Zwaluwenburg journal, p. 32.

24 Benham to MacKay, 1 November 1863, author's collection; Bogart letters, 5 November 1863.

25 Court-martial of Private John Mallory, 18th Infantry, NA RG 153/kk665; October 1863 return of the 18th Infantry, NA MF M665/192.

26 Van Horne, *History of the Army of the Cumberland*, 1, pp. 396-400; Cozzens, *The Shipwreck of Their Hopes*, pp. 114-116; *OR* 31, pt. 2, p. 16; 39, pt. 2, p. 63.

27 Phisterer, "My Days in the Army," p. 57.

28 *OR* 31, pt. 2, pp. 24, 32-33, 94-95.

29 *OR* 31, pt. 2, pp. 64; Van Horne, *History of the Army of the Cumberland*, 1, pp. 422-423; Sword, *Mountains Touched By Fire*, pp. 189-201.

30 *OR* 31, pt. 2, pp. 94-95, 674. Sword, *Mountains Touched By Fire*, pp. 202-221.

31 Van Zwaluwenburg journal, p. 33; Van Zwaluwenburg memoir, p. 32.

32 *OR* 31, pt. 2, pp. 95-96, 459, 481-482, 489; Cozzens, *The Shipwreck of Their Hopes*, pp. 144, 160, 204, 246-247; Phisterer, "My Days in the Army," p. 57.

33 *OR* 31, pt. 2, pp. 459, 479; Phisterer, "My Days in the Army," p. 57.

34 Cozzens, *The Shipwreck of Their Hopes*, pp. 15, 251-252; James Henry Hanie, *The Nineteenth Illinois: A Memoir of a Regiment of Volunteer Infantry Famous in the Civil War of Fifty Years Ago for Its Drill, Bravery, and Distinguished Services* (Chicago: M.A. Donahue & Co., 1912), pp. 270-271; Michael A. Hughes, "The Battle of Missionary Ridge, November 25, 1863," *Civil War Regiments: A Journal of the American Civil War*, vol. 7, no. 1, p. 11.

35 *OR* 31, pt. 2, p. 480; J.N. Stanford, "The Charge Up Mission Ridge," *The National Tribune*, 27 May 1886; Lyman letters, 26 November 1863, C-C NMP.

36 Du Pont to Rice, 15 January 1895, Crofton personnel file, NA RG 94; *OR* 31, pt. 2, pp. 488-489; Lyman letters, 5 December 1863, C-C NMP.

37 Stanford, "The Charge Up Mission Ridge"; Knight letters, 25 November 1863. Having been on sick leave for rheumatism during the winter of 1862-1863, which was followed by a recruiting assignment, John Knight reported for duty at Chattanooga on November 22. The rheumatism in his hip was still a problem and he was one of the last regulars to reach the top of the ridge. He departed Chattanooga on December 10 with orders to appear before Brigadier General Adam Slemmer's medical examining board in Cincinnati. Slemmer pronounced Knight fit for limited duty only. The captain served out the remainder of the war as a provost marshal in Detroit and was honorably discharged from the Regular Army in 1870. Phisterer, "Record of Events, 1863," NA MF M665/191; Heitman, *Historical Register*, p. 606.

38 Phisterer, "My Days in the Army," p. 58; Van Zwaluwenburg journal, p. 34. The additional troops that Phisterer and Van Zwaluwenburg observed advancing toward Mission Ridge were probably from Starkweather's brigade, which had been previously held in reserve but joined in the assault about a half hour after the Army of the Cumberland began its advance.

39 Mills, *My Story*, pp. 93-94; OR 31, pt. 2, pp. 84, 489; Stanford, "The Charge Up Mission Ridge;" Sword, *Mountains Touched By Fire*, p. 322.

40 McManus to Edie, 1 December 1863, NA RG 94/159; OR 31, pt. 2, p. 480; Carlin, *Memoirs*, p. 119.

41 Carlin, *Memoirs*, p. 119; OR 31, pt. 2, p. 480.

42 OR 31, pt. 2, pp. 461, 480, 487, 489.

43 Reese, *Sykes' Regular Infantry Division*, p. 110; Lyman letters, 26 November 1863, C-C NMP. The comments of Sergeant Major Ross are quoted in Richard A. Baumgartner's *Echoes of Battle: The Struggle for Chattanooga* (Huntington, West Virginia: Blue Acorn Press, 1996), p. 119.

44 Bogart letters, 7 December 1863.

45 Powell and Shippen, *Officers of the Army and Navy (Regular)*, p. 430; Brinkerhoff, "The Fifteenth Regiment of Infantry," pp. 1267-1268.

46 Cleaves, *Rock of Chickamauga*, p. 50; Kellogg, "Recollections of Civil War Service," p. 37; Heitman, *Historical Register*, p. 589. Captain Sanford Kellogg has often been misidentified as a nephew of George Thomas, but Sanford, Edgar, and Lyman Kellogg were actually nephews of Thomas's mother-in-law, meaning the general was a cousin by marriage. Sanford, a volunteer officer, was an aide-de-camp to General Thomas from March 1863 through the end of the war. In 1866 Sanford received a Regular Army commission in the 18th U.S. Infantry, and for a time in the 1880s served as an aide to General Phillip Sheridan. Sanford Kellogg retired in 1898. A fourth Kellogg brother, Roland Case, served in the Civil War as an officer of the 118th New York Infantry.

47 Austin Murphy diary, entry for 2 January 1864, Archives, Vigo County Public Library, Terre Haute, Indiana.

48 Carpenter letters, 6 January 1864; Van Zwaluwenburg journal, p. 32.

49 Andrew Burt to father, 5 February 1863, in Papers of Elizabeth Burt, 1797-1917, Manuscripts Division, Library of Congress.

50 Carpenter letters, 30 January 1864.

51 Ibid., 13 February 1864.

52 Edie to Steedman, 16 March 1864, NA RG 391/1747.

53 Albert Castel, *Decision In The West: The Atlanta Campaign of 1864* (Lawrence: University Press of Kansas, 1992), pp. 9-12; Carpenter letters, 6 January 1864; OR 32, pt. 1, p. 16.

54 Phisterer to Caldwell, 22 December 1863, NA RG 391/1843.

55 Thomas to Forsyth, January 1864, NA RG 391/1788; Phisterer to Whipple, 15 February 1863, NA RG 391/1627; Lyman letters, 29 January 1864, C-C NMP; GOs 25, 66, 215, and 216, War Department, AGO, series 1864; Telegram, Tracy to Shepherd, 4 February 1864, NA MF M619/300.

56 Van Zwaluwenburg memoir, p. 33; OR, series III, vol. 4, p. 812; Tarbell diary, 9 February 1864.

57 OR 32, pt. 1, pp. 8-9, 419; 451; Heitman, *Historical Register*, p. 721; April 1863-February 1864 returns of the 19th Infantry, NA MF M665/202.

58 Not to be confused with an identically named piece of ground near Chattanooga.

27 *OR* 38, pt. 1, pp. 67, 148, 571; William A. Gilday, "Sherman Had Narrow Escape," *The National Tribune*, 10 September 1925, p. 1.

28 Shepherd to Thomas, 15 August 1862, NA MF M619/111.

29 Kellogg to Stanton, 22 December 1862, NA MF M619/111.

30 GO 106, War Department, AGO, series 1862; Shepherd to Thomas, 15 August 1862, and Thomas to Kellogg, 11 October 1862, NA MF M619/111.

31 Kellogg to Thomas, 16 August 1864, NA MF 1064/115; GO 205, War Department, AGO, series 1864; Bisbee, *Through Four American Wars*, pp. 155-156.

32 Carpenter letters, 29 June 1864.

33 Kellogg, "Recollections of Civil War Service," p. 46.

34 *OR* 38, pt. 1, p. 506-507; McMurry, *Atlanta 1864*, pp. 105-107. In *Battle Tactics of the Civil War*, author Paddy Griffith relates a story from the memoirs of a Georgia officer about the Battle of Kennesaw Mountain that allegedly involved Federal regulars. The Georgians conducted an innovative nighttime trench raid at Kennesaw, crawling up to the Union lines and "at a given signal dashed right over them and into a regiment of United States regulars. They were taken completely by surprise. Their colonel and a good many officers of the line and private soldiers were captured." While the Georgians's nocturnal raid may have taken place, the prisoners they captured were not U.S. regulars. None of the regular battalions in Stoughton's brigade, the only regular infantrymen at Kennesaw, reported losing more than ten troops during the entire battle, much less "a good many officers" in a single night. Griffith, *Battle Tactics of the Civil War*, p. 157; James C. Nisbet, *Four Years on the Firing Line* (Jackson, Tennessee: McCowat-Mercer, 1963), pp. 203-204. Quote is from Nisbet.

35 Van Horne, *History of the Army of the Cumberland*, 2, pp. 86-96; Carpenter letters, 7 July 1864.

36 Gilday, "Sherman Had Narrow Escape"; Biddle diary, 3 July 1864; John Robertson, ed., *Michigan in the War* (Lansing: W.S. George and Co., 1882), p. 321.

37 *OR* 38, pt. 1, pp. 561, 590; Thornton, *When Gallantry Was Commonplace*, pp. 228-229; Phisterer, "My Days in the Army," p. 63; Carpenter letters, 7 July 1864; Kellogg, "Recollections of Civil War Service," p. 46. Stoughton's wounding during the Atlanta Campaign effectively brought an end to his military service. After resigning his commission in August 1864, he returned to his law practice in Sturgis, Michigan. In September 1864, the adjutant general of Michigan appointed Stoughton commandant of a training camp at Jackson, Michigan, and tasked him with reorganizing a new iteration of the 11th Michigan Infantry. Due to Stoughton's continuing bad health, little was accomplished in that endeavor. After the war, he was breveted major general of U.S. Volunteers "for gallant and meritorious service during the war." Stoughton subsequently served as Michigan's attorney general (1867-1868), and in 1869 was elected to the United States Congress, where he served two terms. He spent his remaining years practicing law in St. Joseph County, Michigan. He died in 1888 and is buried in Oak Lawn Cemetery in Sturgis.

38 Scribner, *How Soldiers Were Made*, pp. 304-305; *OR* 38, pt. 1, pp. 561-562; Scaife, *The Campaign for Atlanta*, pp. 76-77; Biddle diary, 5 July 1864.

39 Carpenter letters, 12 July 1864.

40 July and August 1864 returns of the 15th Infantry, NA MF M665/164; July and August 1864 returns of the 16th Infantry, NA MF M665/173; July and August 1864 returns of the 18th Infantry, NA MF M665/192; July and August 1864 returns of the 19th Infantry, NA MF M665/202; Kellogg to Thomas, 16 August 1864, NA MF 1064/115.

41 Van Horne, *History of the Army of the Cumberland*, 2, p. 110; Castel, *Decision in the West*, pp. 348-349.

42 OR 38, pt. 1, pp. 561, 571; GO 10, Head Quarters Detcht. 18th U.S. Infantry, 11 August 1864, NA RG 391/1651.

43 OR 38, pt. 1, p. 524; Kellogg, "Recollections of Civil War Service," p. 47.

44 Biddle diary, 20 July 1864.

45 Johnson to War Department, 6 May 1873, Smith personnel file, NA RG 94.

46 OR 38, pt. 1, pp. 73-75; Van Horne, *History of the Army of the Cumberland*, 2, pp. 109-118.

47 OR 38, pt. 1, pp. 562, 572; Carpenter letters, 26 July 1864; Biddle diary, 30 July 1864; Bisbee, *Through Four American Wars*, pp. 153-154; Mills, *My Story*, p. 94; August 1864 return of the 15th Infantry, NA MF M665/164.

48 Carpenter letters, 4 August 1864; Scaife, *The Campaign for Atlanta*, pp. 103-109; McMurry, *Atlanta 1864*, pp. 156-157.

49 OR 38, pt. 1, pp. 525, 562; Biddle diary, 5 August 1864.

50 Castel, *Decision in the West*, pp. 452-460; Thornton, *When Gallantry Was Commonplace*, p. 203 Scaife, *The Campaign for Atlanta*, p. 124.

51 OR 38, pt. 1, pp. 562, 567, 572, 582; Scaife, *The Campaign for Atlanta*, p. 125.

52 Quoted in Thornton, *When Gallantry Was Commonplace*, p. 236.

53 OR 38, pt. 1, pp. 510, 572, 580, 582.

54 Ibid., p. 579.

55 Bisbee, *Through Four American Wars*, pp. 154-155.

56 Carpenter letters, 9 August 1864.

57 OR 38, pt. 1, pp. 563, 582; Thornton, *When Gallantry Was Commonplace*, p. 237; Sherman, *Memoirs*, p. 574.

58 OR 38, pt. 1, pp. 579-580.

59 GO 7, Head Quarters Detcht 18th U.S. Inf.., 8 August 1864, NA RG 39/1651.

60 Carpenter letters, 14 August 1864.

61 Biddle diary, 17 August 1864.

62 Warner, *Generals in Blue*, p. 254; OR 38, pt. 1, pp. 512, 525, 585; Dyer, *Compendium*, pt. 1, p. 443; GO 40, Headquarters, 1st Battalion, 15th Infantry, 22 August 1864, NA RG 391/1545; Thornton, *When Gallantry Was Commonplace*, pp. 238-248. Given the disdain Sherman generally felt for mounted troops, Johnson's appointment as chief of cavalry was not a favorable action. In retrospect, Johnson's promotion from captain to brigadier in 1861 was perhaps too great a leap in command responsibility. Having missed Shiloh due to illness, Johnson's first real test came in command of a cavalry division in pursuit of John Hunt Morgan's raiders during the summer of 1862. Johnson bungled the effort and ended up being captured near Gallatin. After his parole and exchange, he took command of a division of McCook's corps in time for Stones River, another test he failed miserably. Johnson learned from his mistakes and from Chickamauga onward performed well, but division command was about the limit of his abilities. After serving a short time on Sherman's staff in the autumn of 1864, Johnson closed out his Civil War field experience in command of a cavalry division during Hood's incursion into middle Tennessee. Johnson retired in 1867 due to infirmities from battle wounds, having received volunteer and regular brevets as a major general for his Civil War service. In the postwar era, he taught military science at both the University of Missouri and the University of Minnesota. He lived in Minnesota many years (his wife hailed from St. Paul) and in 1881 was the Democratic Party's nominee for governor. He was defeated in that contest, his only attempt at politics. Richard Johnson died in 1897 and was buried in St. Paul's Oakland Cemetery.

63 *OR* 38, pt. 1, pp. 559, 592-593; September 1864 return of the 18th Infantry, NA MF M665/164; Castel, *Decision in the West*, pp. 457-458; Biddle diary, 21 May and 24 August 1864.

64 Phisterer to Thomas, 15 August 1864, Phisterer personnel file, NA RG 94.

65 Townsend to Townsend, 3 September 1864, Phisterer personnel file, NA RG 94.

66 *OR* 29, pt. 2, pp. 169-170; Ronan, "North's Unsung Regulars," p. 48; Reese, *Sykes' Regular Infantry Division*, pp. 339-340.

67 Biddle diary, 26 August 1864.

68 William A. Gilday, "Capturing Jonesboro: The Regular Brigade Assaulted First and Held Ground Until Reinforcements Came," *The National Tribune*, 15 December 1915, p. 1.

69 *OR* 38, pt. 1, pp. 525-526.

70 Ibid., pp. 164-166; Scaife, *The Campaign for Atlanta*, pp. 131-133.

71 *OR* 38, pt. 1, pp. 513, 526, 559, 564.

72 Heitman, *Historical Register*, p. 839; Kellogg, "Recollections of Civil War Service," p. 48; *OR* 38, pt. 1, pp. 526, 576; Gilday, "Capturing Jonesboro."

73 Gilday, "Capturing Jonesboro."

74 *OR* 38, pt. 1, pp. 513, 526, 592; Carlin, *Memoirs*, p. 135.

75 Castel, *Decision in the West*, p. 515; *OR* 38, pt. 1, p. 526; Scaife, *The Campaign for Atlanta*, p. 133.

76 *OR* 38, pt. 1, p. 569, 592, 600, 642; Castel, *Decision in the West*, p. 516.

77 David Melville to brother, 19 April 1870, Harrisburg Civil War Round Table Collection, USAMHI; *OR* 38, pt. 1, p. 569; Carlin, *Memoirs*, p. 135.

78 *OR* 38, pt. 1, pp. 558-559, 585-586; Kellogg, "Recollections of Civil War Service," p. 49.

79 Kellogg to the adjutant general, 27 May 1898, Kellogg personnel file, NA RG 94; Kellogg, "Recollections of Civil War Service," pp. 49-50.

80 Gilday, "Capturing Jonesboro"; Kellogg, "Recollections of Civil War Service," p. 50.

81 *OR* 38, pt. 1, pp. 558-559; Carpenter letters, 4 September 1864; Gilday, "Capturing Jonesboro."

82 *OR* 38, pt. 1, pp. 527, 641-642, 751-752, 810; Griffith, *Battle Tactics of the Civil War*, pp. 62-67.

83 *OR* 38, pt. 1, p. 515, 655; Scaife, *The Campaign for Atlanta*, p. 133; Powell and Shippen, *Officers of the Army and Navy (Regular)*, p. 280; Castel, *Decision in the West*, p. 517; Henry R. Mizner, "Reminiscences," in *War Papers: Being Papers Read Before the Commandery of the State of Michigan, Military Order of the Loyal Legion of the United States*, vol. 2 (Detroit, 1898), p. 81; "Personal," *The National Tribune*, 16 September 1897; Mizner, "The Fourteenth Michigan Infantry," pp. 15, 27. Colonel Mizner sent Coolidge's sword to the late major's brother, a physician in Boston. He returned the spurs to Govan in 1897.

84 *OR* 38, pt. 1, p. 558; Van Horne, *History of the Army of the Cumberland*, 2, pp. 145-148; McMurry, *Atlanta 1864*, pp. 173-175.

85 Biddle diary, 1 September 1864; *OR* 38, pt. 1, p. 559; Thomas is quoted in Mizner, "The Fourteenth Michigan Infantry," p. 17.

86 Oswego (New York) *Daily Palladium*, 5 September 1864.

Chapter 11

1 Carpenter letters, 14 September 1864; Biddle diary, 8 and 11 September 1864; Bisbee, "Record of Events, 1864," NA MF M665/192.

2   Mills, *My Story*, p. 94.

3   July-September 1864 returns of the 19th Infantry, NA MF M665/202; Carpenter letters, 22 September 1864.

4   *OR* 38/1:564; Powell and Shippen, *Officers of the Army and Navy (Regular)*, p. 294. The total Atlanta casualties for the 15th and 18th Infantry Regiments in the *Official Records* are often overlooked because they are listed separately for each battalion. When the battalion casualties are added together for a regimental total, one arrives at a more accurate assessment of the regulars' Atlanta Campaign losses.

5   Jewett to Thomas, 20 September 1864, NA RG 391/1545.

6   Shepherd to Thomas, 18 October 1864, NA MF M619/309.

7   *OR* 39, pt. 1, pp. 504-505, 542-546.

8   McKinney, *Education in Violence*, p. 372; *OR* 39, pt. 1, p. 585; Carpenter letters, 22 September 1864; Biddle diary, 22 September 1864.

9   Biddle diary, 28-29 September 1864; Carpenter letters, 1 October 1864.

10 Melville letter.

11 *OR* 39, pt. 1, pp. 546-548.

12 Ibid., pp. 801-802.

13 Ibid., pp. 582-583.

14 Ibid., pp. 802-803.

15 McKinney, *Education in Violence*, pp. 412-427; Castel, *Decision in the West*, pp. 557-558.

16 Gay to Fetterman, October 1864, NA RG 391/1548.

17 Gay to Whipple, 23 October 1864, NA RG 391/1548; Gay to Fetterman, 10 and 13 November 1864, NA RG 391/1558. Ebenezer Gay was posted to Fort Ontario on recruiting duty in the spring of 1865. He was mustered out of the service in January 1871 and died in September of that year.

18 October 1864 return of the 19th Infantry, NA MF M665/202; Biddle diary, 12 October 1864.

19 Young to Thomas, 23 October 1864, NA RG 391/1545.

20 Swaine to Wright, 8 January 1865, Swaine personnel file, NA RG 94.

21 Bisbee, "Record of Events, 1864," NA MF M665/192; Heitman, *Historical Register*, p. 293.

22 *OR* 45, pt. 1, p. 946; Carpenter letters, 4 December 1864.

23 Bisbee, *Through Four American Wars*, pp. 156-157.

24 Sketch accompanying GO 20, Headquarters, 2nd Battalion, 18th U.S. Infantry, 11 October 1864, NA RG 391/1651; Bisbee, *Through Four American Wars*, p. 157.

25 Carpenter letters, 20 February 1865.

26 Elizabeth Reynolds Burt, "An Army Wife's Forty Years in the Service, 1862-1902," in Papers of Elizabeth Burt, 1797-1917, Manuscripts Division, Library of Congress, pp. 25-26.

27 Van Zwaluwenburg memoir, pp. 35-36. After receiving some schooling in Holland, Michigan, and Poughkeepsie, New York, Jacob Van Zwaluwenburg went on to a successful business career in Michigan and California.

28 Tarbell diary, 10, 12, 14, and 20 October 1864. Tarbell returned to Wilmore, Pennsylvania, and before the year was out married Anne J. Burk, "the Girl that waited for her Soldier Boy to come Home." He sailed the Great Lakes again before settling down in his hometown in Ashtabula County, Ohio, in 1900. Tarbell died in 1906.

29 Kennedy, "Army Life and Experiences," pp. 8, 16, 18-20. Shortly after the war, Kennedy settled down in Tarentum, Pennsylvania, where he worked as a school director

and road supervisor. He died suddenly on January 5, 1934, "due to the infirmities of old age," at the age of 92. *Tarentum News Dispatch*, 6 January 1934, p. 1.

30 *Richmond Enquirer*, 13 February 1864; Freeman, "Lieutenant Henry B. Freeman's Report on his Capture," NA RG 391/1629.

31 Freeman, "Lieutenant Henry B. Freeman's Report on his Capture;" "A Striking Coincidence," *Confederate Veteran*, vol. 27 (1919), p. 114.

32 *OR*, series III, vol. 4, p. 812; October 1864 return of the 15th Infantry, NA MF M665/164; GO 1, Headquarters Regular Brigade, 14 November 1864, NA RG 94/159, Subseries II, Box 28: John H. King Papers.

33 Carpenter letters, 4 and 27 December 1864.

34 Burt, "An Army Wife's Forty Years in the Service," pp. 27-29.

35 Ibid., pp. 30-31.

36 Carpenter letters, 27 December 1864; Don Troiani, *Don Troiani's Soldiers in America, 1754-1865* (Mechanicsburg, Pennsylvania: Stackpole Books, 1998), p. 201; Allyn to father, 12 January 1865, Letters to Timothy W. Allyn, Connecticut Historical Society, Hartford; Bisbee, *Through Four American Wars*, p. 157.

37 Mills, *My Story*, pp. 96-97.

38 *OR* 39, pt. 2, p. 415; 49, pt. 2, p. 569; 52, pt. 1, p. 723; Tracy to Fetterman, 23 March 1865, NA RG 391/1545.

39 Norton to Thomas, 11 January 1865, NA RG 391/1747.

40 SO 473, War Department, AGO, series 1864; Court-martial of Private Henry Black, 19th Infantry, NA RG 153/mm2490; Court-martial of Private Peter Stroup, 16th Infantry, NA RG 153/oo1182.

41 Lonn, *Desertion During the Civil War*, p. 219. The number given for Regular Army desertions in Lonn's study (21,158) includes both "United States Regulars and Volunteers," the volunteers being units such as the regiments of United States Sharpshooters. These specialized Federal volunteers units were even fewer in number than regular regiments and the regulars accounted for the vast majority of these desertions. The 1866 report of the army's Provost Marshal General (an extract of which was reprinted in Phisterer's *Statistical Record of the Armies of the United States*, p. 67) states that total Union army desertions numbered 199,045, of which the Regular Army was responsible for 16,365 or 8.2 percent. Whatever the exact figures, a regular soldier appears to have been two to three times more likely to desert than a volunteer.

42 The desertion statistics of the 15th and 19th regulars were obtained through a month-by-month examination of their official returns, NA MF M665/164 and M665/202. Statistics on desertion courts-martial are from Thomas P. Lowry to the author, 4 June 2000. Political geography was a problem for two of the Regular Brigade's regiments when it came to late-war desertions. With Ft. Wayne being located less than a mile from Canadian soil, it was relatively simple for a deserter from the 19th Infantry to arrange a crossing of the Detroit River. The 16th Infantry had a similar problem, for only the Niagara River separated Ft. Ontario from Canada.

43 GO 5, Head Quarters General Recruiting Service, 6 July 1864, copy in the collection of Mark Slover, Indianapolis, Indiana.

44 GO 38, Hd. Qrs. Det. 15th Infty, 28 March 1865, NA RG 391/1545.

45 Court-martial of Sergeant John H. Poland, 19th Infantry, NA RG 153/oo665; Circular dated 18 December 1865, Hd. Qrs. Det. 15th Infty, NA RG 391/1545.

46 Circular dated 5 January 1865, Hd. Qrs. Det. 15th Infty, NA RG 391/1545.

47 Carpenter letters, 15 January 1865.

48 GOs 3 (13 January 1865), 9 (5 February 1865), and 31 (13 March 1865), Hd. Qrs. Det. 15th Infty, NA RG 391/1545; Court-martial of Private John Sheehy, 19th U.S. Infantry, NA RG 153/oo1237.

49 GOs 8 (4 February 1865) and 16 (24 February 1865), Hd. Qrs. Det. 15th Infty, NA RG 391/1545.

50 Courts-martial of Corporal Michael McFalls and Private Patrick Corcoran, 15th Infantry, NA RG 153/oo1237; Thomas P. Lowry to author, 12 July 2000.

51 GOs 18 (26 February 1865), 37 (28 March 1865), and Circular dated 28 March 1865, Hd. Qrs. Det. 15th Infty, NA RG 391/1545.

52 Tracy to Honey, 22 April 1865, NA RG 391/1545.

53 Heitman, *Historical Register*, pp. 110, 1036; May and June 1865 returns of the 15th Infantry, NA MF M665/164.

54 Allyn letters, 16 April 1865.

55 Carpenter letters, 21 April 1865.

56 *OR* 49, pt. 2, pp. 803-804.

57 Chambers to Thomas, 17 May 1865, NA RG 391/1843.

58 McPherson, *Battle Cry of Freedom*, p. 853; Reese, *Sykes' Regular Infantry Division*, p. 342.

59 Allyn letters, 5 August 1865; Wilkins to Honey, 14 July 1865, NA RG 391/1545.

60 GO 56, Headquarters Military Division of the Tennessee, 18 August 1865, NA RG 94/165.

Epilogue

1 Larned, *History of the Battle Monument at West Point*, p. 86.

2 Quoted in Larned, *History of the Battle Monument at West Point*, pp. 4-5.

3 Wilson was adept at such undertakings. Prior to his superintendence at the Military Academy, he served four years as Superintendent of Public Works and Grounds in the nation's capitol. During 1885-1888, Wilson supervised the completion of the Washington Monument.

4 Quoted in Larned, *History of the Battle Monument at West Point*, pp. 31-32.

5 White, "A Review of the Services of the Regular Army During the Civil War," p. 207; Reese, *Sykes' Regular Infantry Division*, p. 364.

6 James M. McPherson, *For Cause and Comrades: Why Men Fought in the Civil War* (New York: Oxford University Press, 1997), pp. 13, 47, 120.

7 Association of Survivors of the Regular Brigade, 14th Corps, Army of the Cumberland, *Roster of Members and Proceedings of Eleventh Annual Reunion, Washington, D.C., September 19, 20, and 21, 1892. Twelfth Annual Reunion, Indianapolis, September 4, 5, and 6, 1893* (Columbus, Ohio: Press of Nitschke Brothers, 1894), p. 21.

8 The 18th Infantry's returns, which are models of completeness, indicate that more than 4,700 soldiers served in this regiment during the war. The 15th Infantry returns are not as complete, but a month-by-month study of the returns that are available for the period December 1861 through December 1864 reveals that 2,386 men enlisted in the 15th Regulars. Adding in an estimate for the remaining months of 1861 and 1865 (the months in which the heaviest recruitment actually took place), this regiment's total enlistments certainly exceeded 3,000. An estimated 58,612 first-term regular army soldiers enlisted during the Civil War (see note 3 of the introduction).

9 Quoted in Larned, *History of the Battle Monument at West Point*, pp. 96-97.

10 Heitman, *Historical Register*, vol. 2, pp. 606-609; Ness, *The Regular Army on the Eve of the Civil War*, p. 71.

11 John K. Mahon and Romana Danysh, *Army Lineage Series, Infantry, Part I: Regular Army* (Washington, DC: Office of the Chief of Military History, United States Army, 1972), pp. 32, 144, 369.

12 Ibid., pp. 224, 256, 296.

13 Janice E. McKenney, *Army Lineage Series: Air Defense Artillery* (Washington: U.S. Army Center of Military History, 1993), pp. 114-115.

14 Heitman, *Historical Register*, p. 482; U.S. War Department, *Correspondence Relating to the War With Spain, Including the Insurrection in the Philippine Islands and the China Relief Expedition, April 15, 1898, to July 20, 1902*, 2 vols. (Washington: Government Printing Office, 1902), 1, p. 520; Guenther to the adjutant general, 2 June 1898, Guenther personnel file, NA RG 94.

15 Mills to the president, 5 November 1901, McCook to Schoeph, 9 February 1901, and Wheeler to the president, 25 November 1901, Guenther personnel file, NA RG 94.

16 McCook to Root, 12 November 1901, Guenther personnel file, NA RG 94.

17 Root to McCook, 13 November 1901, Guenther personnel file, NA RG 94; Heitman, *Historical Register*, p. 482.

18 Robert C. McFarland, *The History of the 15th Regiment in World War II* (Society of the Third Infantry Division, 1990), pp. xiii-xiv, 11-12.

19 Swaine to Thomas, 18 December 1865, Swaine personnel file, NA RG 94; Heitman, *Historical Register*, p. 938; Association of Graduates, U.S.M.A., *Register of Graduates* (1990 edition), pp. 276, 307; William Swaine to the adjutant general, 9 May 1904, Swaine personnel file, NA RG 94.

20 Heitman, *Historical Register*, p. 1034; Bisbee, *Through Four American Wars*, p. 241; U.S. War Department, *Correspondence Relating to the War With Spain*, 1, p. 124; James Rankin Young and J. Hampton Moore, *Reminiscences and Thrilling Stories of the War by Returned Heroes, Containing Vivid Accounts of Personal Experiences by Officers and Men* (Washington: J.R. Jones, 1899), p. 171.

21 Barry's file in the National Archives contains no details on exactly why this soldier received the medal.

22 Heitman, *Historical Register*, p. 891; Warner, *Generals in Blue*, p. 451.

23 Heitman, *Historical Register*, p. 339; Coffman, *The Old Army*, pp. 281-282; Brinkerhoff, "The Fifteenth Regiment of Infantry," p. 1274.

24 Baird to secretary of war, 24 December 1894, Crofton personnel file, NA RG 94.

25 Heitman, *Historical Register*, pp. 20, 23, 339.

26 Forwood to the adjutant general, 10 June 1899, Kellogg personnel file, NA RG 94; SO 292, Headquarters of the Army, AGO, Series 1899; Kellogg, "Reminiscences of Civil War Service," p. 51. Additional details about Kellogg's post-Civil War career were gleaned from a newspaper obituary appended to the copy of his reminiscences on deposit at the U.S. Army Military History Institute.

27 Brown, *The Fetterman Massacre*, pp. 11-20, 25.

28 Ibid., p. 147.

29 John D. McDermott, "Price of Arrogance: The Short and Controversial Life of William Judd Fetterman," *Annals of Wyoming* 63 (1991), pp. 44-45.

30 Fetterman to Shepherd, 10 February 1866, and Shepherd to Thomas, 12 February 1867, Shepherd personnel file, NA RG 94; U.S. Congress, *Journal of the Executive Proceedings of the Senate of the United States of America*, 39th Cong., 2nd sess., 26-27 July 1866.

31 Brown, *The Fetterman Massacre*, pp. 221-222; Heitman, *Historical Register*, p. 950.

32 Brown letters, appendix 3, p. 6; Dee Brown, *The Fetterman Massacre*, p. 226; Heitman, *Historical Register*, p. 286; McKeen, "Henry Beebee Carrington," pp. 229, 233, 238, 291-322.

33 Mahon and Danysh, *Army Lineage Series, Infantry*, pp. 396-397. As a result of the 1866 and 1869 reorganizations, the 18th Infantry troops garrisoning Ft. Phil Kearny eventually became part of the 9th Infantry. The presence at the fort of so many officers who served in the Civil War with the 18th provides a link to this regiment also.

34 Heitman, *Historical Register*, p. 267; Mattes, *Indians, Infants, and Infantry*, preface, pp. vi, 255, 270-273.

35 Smith to Clark, 16 December 1865, Smith to Carter 16 April 1866, and Smith to Thomas, 21 April 1866, Smith personnel file, NA RG 94.

36 Smith to Townsend, 26 August 1867, and Smith to the president, 16 June 1873, Smith personnel file, NA RG 94; Heitman, *Historical Register*, p. 898; Association of Survivors, Regular Brigade, *Proceedings of Reunions*, p. 125.

37 Heitman, *Historical Register*, p. 220; "William Henry Bisbee," available online at [Internet] http://www.arlingtoncemetary.com/whbisbee.htm.

38 Ibid., p. 435; U.S. War Department, *Correspondence Relating to the War With Spain*, 2, p. 1199; 1890 Efficiency Report, Freeman personnel file, NA RG 94; Freeman to Corbin, 9 December 1898, Freeman personnel file, NA RG 94; Perry D. Jamieson, *Crossing the Deadly Ground: United States Army Tactics, 1865-1899* (Tuscaloosa: University of Alabama Press, 1994), p. 110; GO 16, Headquarters of the Army, AGO, series 1893; "Recent Deaths," *Army and Navy Journal*, 23 October 1915, p. 234; "Passing of General Freeman," *Douglas (Converse County, Wyoming) Budget*, 21 October 1915, p. 1; George A. Schneider, ed., *The Freeman Journal: The Infantry in the Sioux Campaign of 1876* (San Rafael, California: Presidio Press, 1977). Freeman's name is connected with at least one more battle. The USS *General H.B. Freeman* (AP-143) was commissioned as a General G.O. Squier-class troop transport in April 1945. In December 1950, the ship participated in the evacuation of the 3d Infantry Division from the Hungnam beachhead in North Korea. The 3d Division at that time consisted of the 15th and 7th Infantry Regiments, units that both have historic ties to the Regular Brigade of the Civil War.

39 Mills, *My Story*, pp. 110-115; Johnson and Dumas, "Anson Mills," *Dictionary of American Biography*; Heitman, *Historical Register*, p. 713; Albert A. Lethern, *The Development of the Mills Woven Cartridge Belt, 1877-1956* (London: The Mills Equipment Company, 1956), pp. 1-9.

40 *Annual Report of the Adjutant-General of the State of New York* (Albany: Weed, Parsons & Co., 1881), p. 12; The *Albany Times* is quoted in Association of Survivors of the Regular Brigade, *Roster of Members*, p. 16.

41 GO 51, Headquarters 18th U.S. Infantry, 29 July 1866, NA RG 391/1627.

42 Karl G. Larew, "Frederick Phisterer and the Indian Wars," *Journal of the West* 30 (October 1991), pp. 22-28; Phisterer to the adjutant general, 28 July 1870, NA MF 1064/115.

43 "Memorial of General Frederick Phisterer," Phisterer papers, University of Wyoming American Heritage Center, Laramie; Johnson and Dumas, "Frederick Phisterer," *Dictionary of American Biography*; Heitman, *Historical Register*, p. 789; Karl G. Larew, "Frederick Phisterer: Father of the New York National Guard," paper presented at the 1988 Siena College History Symposium, pp. 5-12.

44 Hewitt, "The Nineteenth Regiment of Infantry," pp. 839-842; Mahon and Danysh, *Army Lineage Series, Infantry*, pp. 413-415.

45 Email correspondence between Mark Slover and Bruce Moore, 23-29 August 1998.

46 Heitman, *Historical Register*, p. 544; Hough, *Soldier in the West*, pp. 27-29; McKinney, *Education in Violence*, p. 481, n. 1.

47 Carpenter letters, 5 June 1866; Bright, "Yankees in Arms," p. 209; Heitman, *Historical Register*, p. 283.

48 GO 92, Headquarters of the Army, AGO, series 1870.

49 Sherman to Belknap, 31 December 1870, Edie personnel file, NA RG 94.

50 Belknap to Sherman, 31 December 1870, Edie personnel file, NA RG 94.

51 Carlin, *Memoirs*, p. 25; Heitman, *Historical Register*, p. 166.

52 Edie to Cameron, 22 January 1871, Edie personnel file, NA RG 94.

53 Attorney general to Belknap, 11 February 1877, Edie personnel file, NA RG 94.

54 Heitman, *Historical Register*, p. 397.

55 Ibid., p. 599.

56 Bisbee, *Through Four American Wars*, pp. 201-202.

57 Quoted in "John Haskell King," *The National Cyclopedia of American Biography*, vol. 30, p. 47.

58 *Army and Navy Journal*, 9 June 1888, p. 9. John King's son, Charles Brady King of Detroit, became an inventor, engineer, and machinist. He started his own company in 1894, which primarily made brakes for railroad cars. Charles King built the first automobile ever seen on the streets of Detroit. A replica of this vehicle, first driven on March 6, 1896, is on display at the Detroit Historical Museum.

59 King to the adjutant general, 4 July 1865, NA MF 1064/166.

60 Grant to Stanton, 3 November 1865, NA MF 1064/166.

61 Shepherd to Thomas, undated, NA MF 1064/221. Although Shepherd's list is undated, Shepherd signed it with the title "Lieutenant Colonel, 18th Infantry," meaning the list was composed in early 1863 while he was still commanding the Regular Brigade.

62 The officers who received Stones River brevets from King's list were Captain Joseph S. York (15th), Lieutenant Frederick D. Ogilby (15th), Lieutenant William B. Occleston (15th), Lieutenant William H. Bartholomew (16th), Lieutenant John Power (16th), Captain Thomas C. Williams (19th), Lieutenant Albert H. Andrews (19th), and Lieutenant Jacob D. Jones (19th).

63 Fetterman to Shepherd, 10 February 1866, Shepherd personnel file, NA RG 94.

64 Shepherd to Sherman, 12 March 1866, Shepherd personnel file, NA RG 94.

65 Shepherd to Thomas, 12 March 1866, Shepherd personnel file, NA RG 94. Shepherd's "swarm" is probably a reference to the flood of brevet requests that hit the War Department after the Battle of Fredericksburg.

66 Burnside to Grant, 28 December 1866, Shepherd personnel file, NA RG 94.

67 Shepherd to Thomas, 12 February 1867, Shepherd personnel file, NA RG 94.

68 U.S. Congress, *Journal of the Executive Proceedings of the Senate of the United States of America*, 39th Cong., 2nd sess., 29 January and 2 March 1867; 40th Cong., 1st sess., 23 March 1867; Shepherd to Grant, 20 July 1867, Shepherd personnel file, NA RG 94.

69 Powell and Shippen, *Officers of the Union Army and Navy (Regular)*, p. 375.

70 Shepherd to Townsend, 18 July 1870, Shepherd personnel file, NA RG 94.

71 Court-Martial of Colonel (Retired) Oliver L. Shepherd, NA RG 153/qq546, exhibit 29; "The Shepherd Court-Martial," *The New York Times*, 3 March 1878, p. 12.

72 Court-Martial of Colonel (Retired) Oliver L. Shepherd, NA RG 153/qq546, exhibit 1.

73 Ibid., exhibit 4 and testimony of Samuel R. Honey.

74 Ibid., testimony of Philip W. Crater; "The Shepherd Court-Martial," *The New York Times*, 28 February 1878, p. 18.

75 Court-Martial of Colonel (Retired) Oliver L. Shepherd, NA RG 153/qq546, exhibit 18.

76 Ibid., exhibit 23.

77 SO 31, Headquarters Department of the East, series 1878. In current legal practice a retired officer can be tried by court-martial for offenses that occurred while the officer was in the service. Since all of Shepherd's offenses took place subsequent to his retirement, it is questionable whether the War Department had jurisdiction in this case. Since the Army did not have a retirement system prior to the Civil War, the legal status of military retirees was still ambiguous territory in the 1870s. Looking at the case with twenty first-century hindsight, it would have been more appropriate for Shepherd to have been tried in a civil court.

78 As far as can be determined, the Shepherd court-martial was Root's first extensive contact with the American military.

79 "The Shepherd Court-Martial," *The New York Times*, 7 March 1878, p. 2.

80 Lieber was himself an up-and-coming attorney. When Secretary of War Elihu Root took charge of the War Department in 1899, the Judge Advocate General of the Army was Brigadier General G. Norman Lieber.

81 Court-Martial of Colonel (Retired) Oliver L. Shepherd, NA RG 153/qq546, exhibit B. Shepherd's reference to "bereavement in my home" refers to the 1877 death of one of his children.

82 "The Shepherd Court-Martial," *The New York Times*, 7 March 1878, p. 2.

83 Court-Martial of Colonel (Retired) Oliver L. Shepherd, NA RG 153/qq546, findings of the court; "Court-Martial of Colonel Shepherd," *The New York Times*, 8 April 1878, p. 1.

84 Endorsement on letter from Hancock to the adjutant general, 28 February 1881, Shepherd personnel file, NA RG 94.

85 Richard H. Breithaupt, Jr., *Aztec Club of 1847: Military Society of the Mexican War Sesquicentennial History, 1847-1997* (Universal City, California: Walika Publishing Company, 1998), pp. 31-65; "Death of Gen. O. L. Shepherd," *The New York Times*, 17 April 1888, p. 6.

86 Charles E. Belknap, *History of the Michigan Organizations at Chickamauga Chattanooga and Missionary Ridge 1863* (Lansing, Michigan: Robert Smith Printing Co., 1899), pp. 22-23; Fessenden to Kellogg, 10 August 1892, 5th U.S. Artillery file, C-C NMP; Park commissioner to the secretary of war, 12 July 1893, 5th U.S. Artillery file, C-C NMP.

87 Association of Survivors, Regular Brigade, *Proceedings of Reunions*, pp. 1-6, 34-36.

88 Ibid., pp. 30-31.

89 NA RG 391/1548.

90 NA RG 94/159, Subseries I: George H. Thomas Papers, Box 2: Letters Received, 1863.

91 Ibid.

92 NA RG 391/1545.

BIBLIOGRAPHY

MANUSCRIPTS

Allyn, Arthur W. Letters. Civil War Manuscripts Collection. Library of the Connecticut Historical Society, Hartford.

Barringer, Michael James. Diary. Collection of James H. Ogden, Fort Oglethorpe, Georgia.

Benham, Daniel W. Letter. Author's collection.

Biddle, James. Diary. Burton Historical Collection, Detroit Public Library.

Bogart, Charles W. Letters. Collection of Dennis Keesee, Westerville, Ohio.

Brown, Lucius F. Letters. Brown Family Correspondence, 1844–1868. Manuscripts and Archives Division. New York Public Library.

Burt, Andrew S. Letter. 18th U.S. Infantry File. Chickamauga-Chattanooga National Military Park Library, Fort Oglethorpe, Georgia.

Burt, Andrew S. Letter. In Papers of Elizabeth Burt, 1797–1917. Manuscripts Division. Library of Congress, Washington.

Burt, Elizabeth Reynolds. Manuscript. Papers of Elizabeth Burt, 1797–1917. Manuscripts Division. Library of Congress, Washington.

Carpenter, Arthur B. Letters. Civil War Miscellaneous and Manuscripts Collection. Yale University, New Haven, Connecticut.

Carrington, Henry B. Manuscripts. Ohio Civil War Memoranda of Official Data. Archives/Library Division, Ohio Historical Society, Columbus.

Carson, William J. Letter. *Civil War Times Illustrated* Collection. United States Army Military History Institute, Carlisle Barracks, Pennsylvania.

Fessenden, Joshua L. Letter. 5th U.S. Artillery File. Chickamauga-Chattanooga National Military Park Library, Fort Oglethorpe, Georgia.

Fleagle, Amos. Letters. Civil War Miscellaneous Collection. United States Army Military History Institute, Carlisle Barracks, Pennsylvania.

Fitzpatrick, Peter. Letters. 5th U.S. Artillery File. Chickamauga-Chattanooga National Military Park Library, Fort Oglethorpe, Georgia.

Fitzpatrick, Peter. Letters. 5th U.S. Artillery File. Stones River National Battlefield, Murfreesboro, Tennessee.

Freeman, Henry B. Manuscripts. Wyoming Division of Cultural Resources, Wyoming State Archives, Cheyenne.

Freeman, Henry B. Letters. Luther Freeman Collection. University of Wyoming American Heritage Center, Laramie.

Gageby, James H. Letters and manuscript. Collection of Jack Gageby, Simi Valley, California.

Haymond, Henry. Letter. 18th U.S. Infantry File. Chickamauga-Chattanooga National Military Park Library, Fort Oglethorpe, Georgia.

Haymond, Henry. Letter. Collection of Jerry Rancourt, St. Petersburg, Florida.

Heath, Oscar P. Manuscript. 4th U.S. Artillery File. Chickamauga-Chattanooga National Military Park Library, Fort Oglethorpe, Georgia.

Jones, Isaac B. Letters. Collection of Wiley Sword, Suwanee, Georgia.

Jones, Reuben. Letter. 19th U.S. Infantry File. Stones River National Battlefield, Murfreesboro, Tennessee.

Kellogg, Edgar Romeyn. Manuscript. Civil War Miscellaneous Collection. United States Army Military History Institute, Carlisle Barracks, Pennsylvania.

Kellogg, Lyman M. Letter. Collection of Dennis Keesee, Westerville, Ohio.

Kennedy, Robert. Manuscript. Civil War Miscellaneous Collection. United States Army Military History Institute, Carlisle Barracks, Pennsylvania.

King, Robert P. Letters. Author's collection.

Knight, John H. Letters. Archives. Wisconsin Historical Society, Madison.

Lyman, Luke C. Letter. Collection of Wiley Sword, Suwanee, Georgia.

Lyman, Luke, Oliver, and Phillip. Letters. 18th U.S. Infantry File. Chickamauga-Chattanooga National Military Park Library, Fort Oglethorpe, Georgia.

Mellville, David. Letter. Harrisburg Civil War Roundtable Collection. United States Army Military History Institute, Carlisle Barracks, Pennsylvania.

Mizner, Henry R. Manuscript. Military Order of the Loyal Legion of the United States Collection. Bentley Historical Library, University of Michigan, Ann Arbor.

Mohr, James F. Letters. Special Collections. The Filson Historical Society, Louisville, Kentucky.

Murphy, Austin. Diary. Special Collections. Vigo County Public Library, Terra Haute, Indiana.

Mussey, Reuben Delavan. Letters. Abraham Lincoln Collection. Joseph L. Regenstein Library, University of Chicago.

Phisterer, Frederick. Manuscript. Larew-Phisterer Family Papers. United States Army Military History Institute, Carlisle Barracks, Pennsylvania.

Phisterer, Frederick. Manuscripts. University of Wyoming American Heritage Center, Laramie.

Riley, Albert G. Letter. 18th U.S. Infantry File. Chickamauga-Chattanooga National Military Park Library, Fort Oglethorpe, Georgia.

Sanderson, George K. Letter. John R. Sanderson Papers. Archives/Library Division, Ohio Historical Society, Columbus.

Smith, David W. Letters. Special Collections. The Filson Historical Society, Louisville, Kentucky.

Swick, Trine. Letters. Collection of Dennis Keesee, Westerville, Ohio.

Tarbell, Eli. Diary. Harrisburg Civil War Roundtable Collection. United States Army Military History Institute, Carlisle Barracks, Pennsylvania.

Van Zwaluwenburg, Jacob. Manuscripts. Schoff Civil War Collection. William L. Clements Library, University of Michigan, Ann Arbor.

Wilcox, Edgar N. Journal-Diary. Wiley Sword Collection. United States Army Military History Institute, Carlisle Barracks, Pennsylvania.

Wilcox, Edgar N. Letters. Civil War Miscellaneous Collection. United States Army Military History Institute, Carlisle Barracks, Pennsylvania.

Wilcox, Edgar N. Letter. Collection of Cal Packard, Mansfield, Ohio.

NATIONAL ARCHIVES MICROFILM PUBLICATIONS

M233: Register of Enlistments in the U.S. Army, 1798–1914.

M617, roll 846: Post Return of Newport Barracks, Kentucky, January 1858-December 1871.

M617, roll 1269: Post Return of Camp Thomas, Ohio, December 1861-November 1865.

M619: Letters Received by the Adjutant General's Office (Main Series), 1861–1870.

M665, roll 164: Monthly Return of the 15th U.S. Infantry Regiment, December 1861–December 1865.

M665, roll 173: Monthly Return of the 16th U.S. Infantry Regiment, July 1861–December 1864.

M665, roll 191: Monthly Return of the 18th U.S. Infantry Regiment, December 1861–December 1862.

M665, roll 192: Monthly Return of the 18th U.S. Infantry Regiment, January 1863–December 1864.

M665, roll 202: Monthly Return of the 19th U.S. Infantry Regiment, August 1861–December 1865.

M727, roll 33: Monthly Return of the 5th U.S. Artillery Regiment, August 1861–December 1871.

M828: Summaries Relating to the History of Various Regular Army Units, Date of Organization to 1902.

M1064: Letters Received by the Commission Branch of the Adjutant General's Office, 1863–1870.

M1523, roll 1: Proceedings of U.S. Army Courts-Martial and Military Commissions of Union Soldiers Executed by U.S. Military Authorities, 1861–1866.

NATIONAL ARCHIVES AND RECORDS ADMINISTRATION, ARCHIVES I

Record Group 94: Office of the Adjutant General.

Entry 159: Generals' Letters and Papers.

Subseries I: George H. Thomas papers.

Subseries II: Henry B. Carrington papers, John H. King papers, Adam J. Slemmer papers.

Personnel files of: William H. Bisbee, Robert E.A. Crofton, John R. Edie, William J. Fetterman, Henry B. Freeman, Francis L. Guenther, Henry Haymond, Edgar R. Kellogg, Lyman M. Kellogg, John H. King, Anson Mills, Frederick Phisterer, Oliver L. Shepherd, George W. Smith, Peter T. Swaine.

Record Group 153: Office of the Judge Advocate General.

Folder ii985: Court of Inquiry Pertaining to Disciplinary Measures in the 18th U.S. Infantry, June 1862.

Folder kk665: Court-Martial of Private John Mallory, 18th U.S. Infantry, January 1863.

Folder ll1049: Court-Martial of Lieutenant Edgar N. Wilcox, 18th U.S. Infantry, November 1863.

Folder ll1122: Court-Martial of Captain George M. Brayton, 15th U.S. Infantry, December 1863.

Folder ll1313: Court-Martial of Captain Henry Keteltas, 15th U.S. Infantry, January 1864.

Folder ll3215: Court-Martial of Sergeant Benjamin F. Trine, 15th U.S. Infantry, December 1864.

Folder mm105: Court-Martial of Private Frank Kelley, 18th U.S. Infantry, August 1862.

Folder mm2125: Court-Martial of Corporal Jacob B. Chestnut, 16th U.S. Infantry, March 1865.

Folder mm2238: Court-Martial of Captain Arthur W. Allyn, 16th U.S. Infantry, March 1865.

Folder mm2371: Court-Martial of Private William McGuire, 19th U.S. Infantry, April 1865.

Folder mm2432: Court-Martial of Private James Riley, 18th U.S. Infantry, June 1865.

Folder mm2767:Court-Martial of Private Baughman Jefferson, 18th U.S. Infantry, August 1865.

Folder mm2940:Court-Martial of Private Henry Black, 19th U.S. Infantry, May 1865.

Folder mm2964:Court-Martial of Corporal Warren R. Reid, 16th U.S. Infantry, February 1865.

Folder mm3387:Court-Martial of Captain Walter Lattimore, 19th U.S. Infantry, November 1865.

Folder nn1110: Court-Martial of Captain Henry Keteltas, 15th U.S. Infantry, February 1864.

Folder oo665: Court-Martial of Private Patrick Cullen, 15th U.S. Infantry, March 1865.

Folder oo665: Court-Martial of Sergeant John H. Poland, 19th U.S. Infantry, February 1865.

Folder oo761: Court-Martial of Private George Smith, 18th U.S. Infantry, December 1864.

Folder oo1182: Court-Martial of Private Peter Stroup, 16th U.S. Infantry, May 1865.

Folder oo1237:Court-Martial of Private Patrick Corcoran, 15th U.S. Infantry, May 1865.

Folder oo1237:Court-Martial of Private John Sheehy, 19th U.S. Infantry, May 1865.

Folder oo1237:Court-Martial of Corporal Michael McFalls, 15th U.S. Infantry, May 1865.

Folder oo1237:Court-Martial of Private Daniel Ricker, 16th U.S. Infantry, May 1865.

Folder qq546: Court-Martial of Colonel (Retired) Oliver L. Shepherd, April 1878.

Record Group 391: Records of U.S. Army Mobile Units, 1821–1916.

Entry 1531 (15th Inf..): Letters, orders, and reports.

Entry 1545 (15th Inf..): Letters sent, register of letters received, and orders and circulars issued by a detachment, 1864–1866.

Entry 1548 (16th Inf..): Letters sent, April 1861-March 1865.

Entry 1549 (16th Inf..): Letters received and endorsements sent, 1861–1864.

Entry 1616 (18th Inf..): Press copies of letters sent, 1861–1863.

Entry 1622 (18th Inf..): Press copies of special orders issued, 1861–1862.

Entry 1627 (18th Inf..): Miscellaneous records, 1861–1916.

Entry 1629 (18th Inf..): Journal of events and a regimental history.

Entry 1650 (18th Inf..): Letters sent by a detachment, general and special orders received from superior commands, and general and special orders issued, 1861–63.

Entry 1651 (18th Inf..): Letters sent by a detachment, 1862–1864.

Entry 1652 (18th Inf..): General orders, special orders, and circulars issued by a detachment, 1861–1862.

Entry 1658 (19th Inf..): General orders, special orders, and circulars issued.

Entry 1747 (24th Inf..): Letters sent, 1863–1866.

Entry 1788 (25th Inf..): General and special orders received by Company C, 1863–1867.

Entry 1843 (27th Inf..): Letters sent, 1862–1869.

Entry 1925 (33rd Inf..): Letters sent, 1864–1869.

Record Group 393: Records of U.S. Army Continental Commands, 1821–1920, Part II.

Entry 5756 (3rd Brigade, 1st Division, Army of the Ohio): Letters, special orders and circulars sent August 1862-October 1863.

Entry 5844 (1st Division, XIV Corps): Special orders issued, April 1863- January 1864.

ACADEMIC PAPERS

Heflin, Robert F. "The Siege of Corinth." Master's thesis, Vanderbilt University, 1956.

Larew, Karl G. "Frederick Phisterer: Father of the New York National Guard." Paper presented at the 1988 Siena College History Symposium.

Larew, Karl G. "Frederick Phisterer: The Immigrant as Civil War Hero and Historian." Paper presented at the 1984 Duquesne History Forum.

Johnson, Mark W. "The Brigade of Regulars: The Civil War Campaigns of the 15th, 16th, 18th, and 19th U.S. Infantry Regiments, Regular Army." Master's thesis, University of Wyoming, 1998.

Johnson, Mark W. "'Where are the Regulars?' An Analysis of Regular Army Recruiting and Enlistees, 1861–1865." History 609Q, State University of New York at Albany, May 2003.

McKeen, Catherine A. "Henry Beebee Carrington: A Soldier's Tale." Doctoral dissertation, State University of New York at Stony Brook, 1998.

NEWSPAPERS

Army and Navy Journal
Bangor Daily Whig and Courier
Cincinnati Daily Commercial
Cincinnati Volkblat
Douglas (Wyoming) Budget
Harrisburg (Pennsylvania) Semi-Weekly Dispatch
Harper's Weekly
National Tribune
New York Times
Ohio State Journal
Oswego (New York) Daily Palladium
Richmond Enquirer
Tarentum (Pennsylvania) News Dispatch

PUBLISHED WORKS

Albertson, Joan W., ed. *Letters Home to Minnesota: 2nd Minnesota Volunteers.* Spokane, Washington: P.D. Enterprises, 1992.

Anders, Curt. *Henry Halleck's War: A Fresh Look at Lincoln's Controversial General-in-Chief.* Carmel, Indiana: Guild Press of Indiana, Inc., 1999.

Annual Report of the Adjutant-General of the State of New York. Albany: Weed, Parsons & Co., 1881.

Arnold, James R. *Jeff Davis's Own: Cavalry, Comanches, and the Battle for the Texas Frontier.* New York: John Wiley & Sons, 2000.

Association of Graduates, United States Military Academy. *Annual Reunion, 1894.* West Point: n.p., 1894.

Association of Graduates, United States Military Academy. *Register of Graduates.* West Point: n.p., 1990.

Association of Survivors of the Regular Brigade, 14th Corps, Army of the Cumberland. *Roster of Members and Proceedings of Eleventh Annual Reunion, Washington, D.C., September 19, 20, and 21, 1892. Twelfth Annual Reunion, Indianapolis, September 4, 5, and 6, 1893.* Columbus, Ohio: Press of Nitschke Brothers, 1894.

Association of Survivors, Regular Brigade, Fourteenth Corps, Army of the Cumberland. *Proceedings of Reunions Held At Pittsburgh PA., Sept. 11–12, 1894, Crawfish Springs, GA., Sept 18–19, 1895, St. Paul, Minn., Sept. 1–2 1896, Columbus, Ohio, Sept. 22–23, 1897.* Columbus, Ohio: John L. Trauger, 1898.

Bailey, L.R., ed. *The Navajo Reconnaissance: A Military Exploration of the Navajo Country in 1859.* Los Angeles: Westernlore Press, 1964.

Bailey, Anne J. *The Chessboard of War: Sherman and Hood in the Autumn Campaigns of 1864.* Lincoln: University of Nebraska Press, 2000.

Baird, John A., Jr. "'For Gallant and Meritorious Service,' Major General Absalom Baird." *Civil War Times Illustrated,* June 1976, 4–9.

Ball, Durwood. *Army Regulars on the Western Frontier, 1848–1861.* Norman: University of Oklahoma Press, 2001.

Barnet, James, ed. *The Martyrs and Heroes of Illinois in the Great Rebellion.* Chicago: Press of J. Barnett, 1866.

Basler, Roy P., ed. *The Collected Works of Abraham Lincoln.* 8 vols. New Brunswick, New Jersey: Rutgers University Press, 1953.

Baumgartner, Richard A. *Echoes of Battle: The Struggle for Chattanooga.* Huntington, West Virginia: Blue Acorn Press, 1996.

Beatty, John. *Memoirs of a Volunteer, 1861–1863.* New York: W.W. Norton Co., 1946.

Belknap, Charles E. *History of the Michigan Organizations at Chickamauga Chattanooga and Missionary Ridge 1863.* Lansing, Michigan: Robert Smith Printing Co., 1899.

Bell, William H. *Ante Bellum; or, Before the War, A Paper Read before The Military Order of the Loyal Legion of the United States, Commandery of the State of Ohio.* Cincinnati: Peter G. Thompson, 1883.

Beyer, W.F. and Keydel, O.F., ed. *Deeds of Valor: How America's Civil War Heroes Won The Congressional Medal of Honor.* Detroit: Perrien-Keydel Co., 1903.

Bisbee, William Haymond. *Through Four American Wars: The Impressions and experiences of Brigadier General William Henry Bisbee.* Boston: Meador Publishing Co., 1931.

Bradley, Michael R. *Tullahoma: The 1863 Campaign for the Control of Middle Tennessee.* Shippensburg, Pennsylvania: Burd Street Press, 2000.

Breithaupt, Richard H., Jr. *Aztec Club of 1847: Military Society of the Mexican War Sesquicentennial History, 1847–1997.* Universal City, California: Walika Publishing Company, 1998.

Briant, C.C. *History of the Sixth Regiment Indiana Volunteer Infantry.* Indianapolis: W.B. Burford, 1891.

Bright, Thomas R. "Yankees in Arms: The Civil War as a Personal Experience." *Civil War History* 19 (September 1973): 197–218.

Brinkerhoff, H.R. "The Fifteenth Regiment of Infantry." *Journal of the Military Service Institution of the United States* 13 (1892): 1256–1274.

Brown, Dee. *The Fetterman Massacre.* New York: G.P. Putnam's Sons, 1962.

Brown, Kent Masterson. "Munfordville: The Battle and Campaign Along Kentucky's Strategic Axis." In *The Civil War in Kentucky: Battle for the Bluegrass State,* edited by Kent Masterson Brown. Mason City, Iowa: Savas Publishing Company, 2000.

Brown, Russell K. "An Old Woman with a Broomstick: General David E. Twiggs and the U.S. Surrender in Texas, 1861." *Military Affairs* 48 (April 1984): 57–61.

Buell, Thomas B. *The Warrior Generals: Combat Leadership in the Civil War.* New York: Crown Publishers, Inc., 1997.

Burnham, Roderick H. *Genealogical Records of Thomas Burnham, the Emigrant, who was among the Early Settlers at Hartford, Connecticut, U.S. America, and His Descendants.* Hartford: The Case, Lockwood & Brainard Co. Print, 1884.

Cabaniss, Charles R. "The Eighteenth Regiment of Infantry." *Journal of the Military Service Institution of the United States* 12 (1891): 1111–1124.

Carlin, William P. *The Memoirs of Brigadier General William Passmore Carlin, U.S.A.* Edited by Robert I. Girardi and Nathaniel C. Hughes. Lincoln: University of Nebraska Press, 1999.

Carrington, Henry B. *Ohio Militia and the West Virginia Campaign, 1861.* Boston: R.H. Blodgett & Co., 1904.

Castel, Albert. *Decision in the West: The Atlanta Campaign of 1864.* Lawrence: University Press of Kansas, 1992.

Catton, Bruce. *Reflections on the Civil War.* New York: Doubleday & Co. Inc., 1981.

Cleaves, Freeman. *Rock of Chickamauga: The Life of General George H. Thomas.* Norman: University of Oklahoma Press, 1948.

Coates, Earl J. and Thomas, Dean S. *An Introduction to Civil War Small Arms.* Gettysburg, Pennsylvania: Thomas Publications, 1980.

Cockerill, John A. "A Boy At Shiloh." In *Sketches of War History 1861–1865: Papers read before the Military Order of the Loyal Legion of the U.S., Ohio Commandery.* Vol. 6. Cincinnati: Monfort & Company, 1908.

Coffman, Edward M. *The Old Army: A Portrait of the American Army in Peacetime, 1784–1898.* New York: Oxford University Press, 1986.

Cooling, Benjamin Franklin. *Forts Henry and Donelson: The Key to the Confederate Heartland.* Knoxville: University of Tennessee Press, 1987.

Cozzens, Peter. *No Better Place to Die: The Battle of Stones River.* Chicago: University of Illinois Press, 1990.

Cozzens, Peter. *The Shipwreck of their Hopes: The Battles For Chattanooga.* Chicago: University of Illinois Press, 1994.

Cozzens, Peter. *This Terrible Sound: The Battle of Chickamauga.* Chicago: University of Illinois Press, 1992.

Cullum, George W. *Biographical Register of the Officers and Graduates of the United States Military Academy.* West Point: n.p., 1890.

Daniel, Larry J. *Shiloh: The Battle That Changed the Civil War.* New York: Simon & Schuster, 1997.

Davis, Sidney Morris. *Common Soldier, Uncommon War: Life as a Cavalryman in the Civil War.* Bethesda, Maryland: John H. Davis, Jr., 1993.

Dawson, Joseph G., III. "General Lovell H. Rousseau and Louisiana Reconstruction." *Louisiana History* 20 (1979): 373–391.

Dean, Jeffery. "The Forgotten 'Hell Hole': The Battle of Picket's Mill." In *The Campaign for Atlanta & Sherman's March to the Sea: Essays on the American Civil War in Georgia, 1864,* edited by Theodore P. Savas and David A. Woodbury. Campbell, California: Savas Woodbury Publishers, 1994.

Dickinson, William. "Reminiscences of Fort Defiance, 1860." *Journal of the Military Service Institution of the United States* 4 (1883): 90–92.

Dodge, William Sumner. *History of the Old Second Division, Army of the Cumberland. Commanders: McCook, Sill and Johnson.* Chicago: Church and Goodman, 1864.

Dyer, Frederick H. *A Compendium of the War of the Rebellion.* Des Moines, Iowa: The Dyer Publishing Company, 1908.

Ecelbarger, Gary L., ed. "Shiloh." *Civil War: The Magazine of the Civil War Society,* April 1995, 66–69.

Elting, John R. *Swords Around A Throne: Napoleon's Grande Armée.* New York: The Free Press, 1988.

Engle, Stephen D. "Don Carlos Buell: Military Philosophy and Command Problems in the West." *Civil War History* 42 (1995): 89–115.

Engle, Stephen D. *Don Carlos Buell: Most Promising of All.* Chapel Hill: University of North Carolina Press, 1999.

Evans, David. *Sherman's Horsemen: Union Cavalry Operations in the Atlanta Campaign.* Indianapolis: University of Indiana Press, 1996.

Freeman, Henry B. "Eighteenth U.S. Infantry From Camp Thomas, O., to Murfreesboro and the Regular Brigade at Stone River." In *Glimpses of the Nation's Struggle: Papers read Before the Military Order of the Loyal Legion of the U.S., Minnesota Commandery.* Vol. 3. New York: D.D. Merrill Company, 1893.

Fox, William F. *Regimental Losses in the American Civil War, 1861–1865.* Albany, New York: Albany Publishing Co., 1889.

Ganoe, William A. *The History of the United States Army.* New York: D. Appleton & Co., 1924.

Geary, James W. *We Need Men: The Union Draft in the Civil War.* Dekalb: Northern Illinois University Press, 1991.

Gilday, William A. "Capturing Jonesboro; The Regular Brigade Assaulted First and Held Ground Until Reinforcements Came." *The National Tribune,* December 15, 1915, 7.

Gilday, William A. "Sherman Had Narrow Escape; The 15th U.S. Happened to Be Right There–Otherwise Sherman Might Have Been Captured." *The National Tribune,* September 10, 1925, 6.

Grant, Ulysses S. *Personal Memoirs of U.S. Grant.* 2 vols. New York: Charles L. Webster, 1885.

Grebner, Constantine. *We Were the Ninth: A History of the Ninth Regiment, Ohio Volunteer Infantry.* Kent, Ohio: The Kent State University Press, 1987.

Griffith, Paddy. *Battle Tactics of the Civil War.* New Haven, Connecticut: Yale University Press, 1987.

Hanie, James Henry. *The Nineteenth Illinois: A Memoir of a Regiment of Volunteer Infantry Famous in the Civil War of Fifty Years Ago for Its Drill, Bravery, and Distinguished Services.* Chicago: M.A. Donahue & Co., 1912.

Hannaford, Ebenezer. *The Story of a Regiment: a History of the Campaigns, and Associations in the Field, of the Sixth Regiment Ohio Volunteer Infantry.* Cincinnati: By the Author, 1868.

Hattaway, Herman, and Jones, Archer. *How the North Won: A Military History of the Civil War.* Chicago: University of Illinois Press, 1983.

Heitman, Francis B. *Historical Register and Dictionary of the United States Army.* 2 vols. Washington: Government Printing Office, 1903.

Hess, Earl J. *Banners to the Breeze: The Kentucky Campaign, Corinth, and Stones River.* Lincoln: University of Nebraska Press, 2000.

Hewitt, C.C. "The Nineteenth Regiment of Infantry." *Journal of the Military Service Institution of the United States* 12 (1891): 835–843.

Hosea, Louis M. "The Regular Brigade of the Army of the Cumberland." In *Sketches of War History 1861–1865: Papers read before the Military Order of the Loyal Legion of the U.S., Ohio Commandery.* Vol. 5. Cincinnati: The Robert Clarke Company, 1903.

Hosea, Louis M. "The Second Day at Shiloh." In *Sketches of War History 1861–1865: Papers read before the Military Order of the Loyal Legion of the U.S., Ohio Commandery.* Vol. 6. Cincinnati: Monfort & Company, 1908.

Hough, Alfred Lacey. *Soldier in the West: The Civil War Letters of Alfred Lacey Hough.* Edited by Robert G. Athearn. Philadelphia: University of Pennsylvania Press, 1957.

Huebner, Michael. "The Regulars." *Civil War Times Illustrated*, June 2000, 24–34, 64, 66–67.

Hughes, Michael A. "The Battle of Missionary Ridge, November 25, 1863." *Civil War Regiments: A Journal of the American Civil War* 7, no. 1 (2000): 1–31.

Hunt, Roger D., and Brown, Jack R. *Brevet Brigadier Generals in Blue*. Frederick, Maryland: Olde Soldier Books, 1998.

Indiana at Chickamauga, 1863–1900. A Report of the Indiana Commissioners, Chickamauga National Military Park. Indianapolis: Sentinel Printing Company, 1900.

Ingrisano, Michael N., Jr. *An Artilleryman's War: Gus Dey and the 2nd United States Artillery*. Shippensburg, Pennsylvania: White Mane Publishing Company, Inc, 1998.

Jamieson, Perry D. *Crossing the Deadly Ground: United States Army Tactics, 1865–1899*. Tuscaloosa: The University of Alabama Press, 1994.

Johnson, Allen and Malone, Dumas, eds. *Dictionary of American Biography*. 22 vols. New York: Charles Scribner's Sons, 1928–1944.

Johnson, Mark W. "Holding the Left of the Line: The Brigade of United States Regulars at Chickamauga." *Civil War Regiments: A Journal of the American Civil War* 7, no. 1 (2000): 33–74.

Johnson, Richard W. *A Soldier's Reminiscences in Peace and War*. Philadelphia: Press of J.R. Lippencott Company, 1886.

Johnson, Timothy D. *Winfield Scott: The Quest for Military Glory*. Lawrence: University Press of Kansas, 1998.

Jones, Archer. *Civil War Command and Strategy: The Process of Victory and Defeat*. New York: The Free Press, 1992.

Jorgensen, Jay A. "Scouting for Ulysses S. Grant: The 5th Ohio Cavalry in the Shiloh Campaign." *Civil War Regiments: A Journal of the American Civil War* 4, no. 1 (1994): 44–77.

Katcher, Philip and Scollins, Rick. *Flags of the American Civil War 2: Union*. London: Osprey Publishing, Ltd., 1993.

Keil, Frederick W. *Thirty-fifth Ohio, a Narrative of Service from August 1861 to 1864*. Fort Wayne, Indiana: Archer, Housh, and Company, 1894.

Klement, Frank L. *Dark Lanterns: Secret Political Societies, Conspiracies, and Treason Trials in the Civil War*. Baton Rouge: Louisiana State University Press, 1984.

Kreidberg, Marvin A. and Henry, Merton G. *History of Military Mobilization in the United States Army, 1776–1945*. Washington: Department of the Army, 1955.

Lamers, William M. *The Edge of Glory: A Biography of General William S. Rosecrans, U.S.A.* New York: Harcourt, Brace & World, Inc., 1961.

Larew, Karl G. "Frederick Phisterer and the Indian Wars." *Journal of the West* 30 (October 1991): 22–28.

Larned, Charles W. *History of the Battle Monument at West Point*. West Point: n.p., 1898.

Lethern, Albert A. *The Development of the Mills Woven Cartridge Belt, 1877–1956*. London: The Mills Equipment Company, Limited, 1956.

Logsdon, David R. *Eyewitnesses at the Battle of Stones River*. Nashville: n.p., 1989.

Longacre, Edward G. *Lincoln's Cavalrymen: A History of the Mounted Forces of the Army of the Potomac, 1861–1865*. Mechanicsburg, Pennsylvania: Stackpole Books, 2000.

Lonn, Ella. *Desertion During the Civil War*. Gloucester, Massachusetts: American Historical Association, 1928.

Lonn, Ella. *Foreigners in the Union Army and Navy*. Baton Rouge: Louisiana State University Press, 1951.

Lowry, Thomas P. *Tarnished Eagles: The Courts-Martial of Fifty Union Colonels and Lieutenant Colonels*. Mechanicsburg, Pennsylvania: Stackpole Books, 1997.

Mahon, John K., and Danysh, Romana. *Army Lineage Series, Infantry, Part I: Regular Army*. Washington: Office of the Chief of Military History, United States Army, 1972.

Mangham, Dana M. "Cox's Wildcats: The 2nd Georgia Battalion Sharpshooters at Chickamauga and Chattanooga." *Civil War Regiments: A Journal of the American Civil War 7*, no. 1 (2000): 91–128.

Martin, James Kirby and Lender, Mark Edward. *A Respectable Army: The Military Origins of the Republic, 1763–1789*. Arlington Heights, Illinois: Harlan Davidson, Inc., 1982.

Mason, George. "Shiloh." In *Military Essays and Recollections: Papers Read Before the Commandery of the State of Illinois, Military Order of the Loyal Legion of the United States*. Vol. 1. Chicago: A.C. McClurg and Company, 1891.

Mattes, Merrill J. *Indians, Infants, & Infantry: Andrew and Elizabeth Burt on the Frontier*. Lincoln: University of Nebraska Press, 1988.

McDermott, John D. "Price of Arrogance: The Short and Controversial Life of William Judd Fetterman." *Annals of Wyoming 63* (Spring 1991): 42–53.

McDonough, James L. *Stones River–Bloody Winter in Tennessee*. Knoxville: University of Tennessee Press, 1980.

McDonough, James L. *War in Kentucky: From Shiloh to Perryville*. Knoxville: University of Tennessee Press, 1994.

McFarland, Robert C. *The History of the 15th Regiment in World War II*. Society of the Third Infantry Division, 1990.

McKenney, Janice E. *Army Lineage Series: Air Defense Artillery*. Washington: U.S. Army Center of Military History, 1993.

McKinney, Francis F. *Education in Violence: The Life of George H. Thomas and the History of the Army of the Cumberland*. Chicago: Americana House, Inc., 1991.

McMurray, Richard M. *Atlanta 1864: Last Chance for the Confederacy*. Lincoln: University of Nebraska Press, 2000.

McNitt, Frank. *The Navajo Wars*. Albuquerque: University of New Mexico Press, 1972.

McPherson, James M. *Battle Cry of Freedom: The Civil War Era*. New York: Oxford University Press, 1988.

McPherson, James M. *For Cause and Comrades: Why Men Fought in the Civil War*. New York: Oxford University Press, 1997.

Memoir of Lieut. Edward Lewis Mitchell, who Fell at the Battle of Shiloh, Aged Twenty-two Years. New York: Metropolitan Fair for the U.S. Sanitary Commission, 1864.

Memorial of Lieutenant Howard M. Burnham, United States Army, Who Fell in the Battle of Chickamauga, Tenn., September 19th, 1863. Springfield, Massachusetts: Samuel Bowles and Company, Printers, 1864.

Meneely, A. Howard. *The War Department in 1861: A Study in Mobilization and Administration*. New York: Columbia University Press, 1928.

Meyers, Augustus. *Ten Years in the Ranks, U.S. Army*. New York: The Sterling Press, 1914.

Mills, Anson. *My Story*. Washington: Byron S. Adams, 1918.

Mills, Anson. "The Organization and Administration of the United States Army." *Journal of the Military Service Institution of the United States 24* (1899):398–417.

Mizner, Henry R. "Reminiscences." In *War Papers: Being Papers Read Before the Commandery of the State of Michigan, Military Order of the Loyal Legion of the United States.* Vol. 2. Detroit: By the Commandery, 1898.

Moore, Frank, ed. *The Rebellion Record: A Diary of American Events.* 11 vols. New York: G.P. Putnam, 1861–68.

The National Cyclopedia of American Biography. 63 vols. New York: J.T. White, 1898–1984.

Ness, George T. Jr. *The Regular Army on the Eve of the U.S. Civil War.* Baltimore: The Toomey Press, 1990.

Nicholas, Ron. "Mills Springs: The First Battle for Kentucky." In *The Civil War in Kentucky: Battle for the Bluegrass State,* edited by Kent Masterson Brown. Mason City, Iowa: Savas Publishing Company, 2000.

Nisbet, James C. *Four Years on the Firing Line.* Jackson, Tennessee: McCowat-Mercer, 1963.

Noe, Kenneth W. *Perryville: This Grand Havoc of Battle.* Lexington: University Press of Kentucky, 2001.

Noe, Kenneth W. "'Grand Havoc': The Climactic Battle of Perryville." In *The Civil War in Kentucky: Battle for the Bluegrass State,* edited by Kent Masterson Brown. Mason City, Iowa: Savas Publishing Company, 2000.

Phisterer, Frederick. *The Regular Army of the United States: Read Before George S. Dawson Post, No. 63, Department of New York, Grand Army of the Republic, Albany, N.Y., April 13th, 1893.* Albany: S.H. Wentworth, 1893.

Phisterer, Frederick. *The Regular Brigade of the 14th Army Corps, Army of the Cumberland, in the Battle of Stone River.* New York: n.p., 1883.

Phisterer, Frederick. *Statistical Record of the Armies of the United States.* New York: Charles Scribner's Sons, 1883.

Pirtle, Alfred. "Stone River Sketches." In *Sketches of War History 1861–1865: Papers read before the Military Order of the Loyal Legion of the U.S., Ohio Commandery.* Vol. 6. Cincinnati: Monfort & Company, 1908.

Powell, William H., and Shippen, Edward. *Officers of the Army and Navy (Regular) who served in the Civil War.* Philadelphia: L.R. Hamersly & Co., 1892.

Prokopowicz, Gerald J. *All for the Regiment: The Army of the Ohio, 1861–1862.* Chapel Hill: University of North Carolina Press, 2001.

Rappaport, Armin. "The Replacement System during the Civil War." In *Military Analysis of the Civil War.* Millwood, New York: KTO Press, 1977.

Reese, Timothy J. *Sykes' Regular Infantry Division, 1861–1864: A History of Regular United States Infantry Operations in the Civil War's Eastern Theater.* Jefferson, North Carolina: McFarland & Co., Inc., 1990.

Robertson, John, ed. *Michigan in the War.* Lansing, Michigan: W.S. George and Co., 1882.

Roland, Charles P. "The Confederate Defense of Kentucky." In *The Civil War in Kentucky: Battle for the Bluegrass State,* edited by Kent Masterson Brown. Mason City, Iowa: Savas Publishing Company, 2000.

Rodenbough, Theophilius F. and Haskin, William L. *The Army of the United States: Historical Sketches of Staff and Line with Portraits of Generals-in-Chief* (reprint: University Microfilms, 1966).

Ronan, James B., II. "Catching 'Regular Hell' at Shiloh." *America's Civil War,* May 1996, 42–48.

Ronan, James B., II. "North's Unsung Regulars." *America's Civil War,* July 1993, 42–48.

Scaife, William R. *The Campaign for Atlanta*. Atlanta: n.p., 1993.

Scaife, William R. "Waltz Between the Rivers: An Overview of the Atlanta Campaign From the Oostanaula to the Etowah." In *The Campaign for Atlanta & Sherman's March to the Sea: Essays on the American Civil War in Georgia, 1864*, edited by Theodore P. Savas and David A. Woodbury. Campbell, California: Savas Woodbury Publishers, 1994.

Schneider, George A., ed. *The Freeman Journal: The Infantry in the Sioux Campaign of 1876*. San Rafael, CA: Presidio Press, 1977.

Scribner, Benjamin F. *How Soldiers Were Made; or The War As I Saw It Under Buell, Rosecrans, Thomas, Grant and Sherman*. Chicago: Donohue & Henneberry, 1887.

Sheehan, William, and O'Meara, Stephen James. "Phillip Sidney Coolidge: Harvard's Romantic Explorer of the Skies." *Sky & Telescope* (April 1998), 71–75.

Sherman, William T. *Memoirs of General William T. Sherman*. New York: D. Appleton & Co., 1875.

Sherman, William T. *Sherman's Civil War: Selected Correspondence of William T. Sherman, 1860–1865*. Edited by Brooks D. Sampson and Jean V. Berlin. Chapel Hill: University of North Carolina Press, 1999.

Simon, John Y. "Lincoln, Grant, and Kentucky in 1861." In *The Civil War in Kentucky: Battle for the Bluegrass State*, edited by Kent Masterson Brown. Mason City, Iowa: Savas Publishing Company, 2000.

Skelton, William B. *An American Profession of Arms: The Army Officer Corps, 1784–1861*. Lawrence: University Press of Kansas, 1992.

Smith, Thomas T. *The Old Army in Texas: A Research Guide to the U.S. Army in Nineteenth-Century Texas*. Austin: Texas State Historical Association, 2000.

Stanford, J.N. "The Charge Up Mission Ridge." *The National Tribune*, 27 May 1886.

"A Striking Coincidence." *Confederate Veteran* 27 (1919): 114.

Stuntz, Margaret L. "Lightning Strike at the Gap." *America's Civil War*, July 1997, 50–56.

Sword, Wiley. *Mountains Touched with Fire: Chattanooga Besieged, 1863*. New York: St. Martin's Press, 1995.

Sword, Wiley. *Shiloh: Bloody April*. New York: William Morrow & Co., 1974.

Terrell, W.H.H. *Indiana in The War of The Rebellion: Report of the Adjutant General*. Indianapolis: Indiana Historical Society, 1960.

Tidball, J.C. "The Artillery Service in the War of the Rebellion." *Journal of the Military Service Institution of the United States* 13 (1892): 876–902, 1085–1109, 14 (1893): 1–31, 307–339.

Thornton, Leland W. *When Gallantry Was Commonplace: The History of the Eleventh Michigan Volunteer Infantry, 1861–1864*. New York: Peter Lang Publishing, Inc., 1991.

Troiani, Don. *Don Troiani's Soldiers in America, 1754–1865*. Mechanicsburg, Pennsylvania: Stackpole Books, 1998.

Tucker, Glen. *Chickamauga: Bloody Battle in the West*. Indianapolis: Bobbs-Merrill, 1961.

Upton, Emory. *The Military Policy of the United States*. New York: The Greenwood Press, 1968.

U.S. Congress. *Journal of the Executive Proceedings of the Senate of the United States of America*. Multiple vols. Washington: Government Printing Office, 1828.

U.S. War Department. *Annual Report of the Secretary of War, 1860*. Washington: Government Printing Office, 1861.

U.S. War Department. *Correspondence Relating to the War With Spain, Including the Insurrection in the Philippine Islands and the China Relief Expedition, April 15, 1898, to July 20, 1902*. 2 vols. Washington: Government Printing Office, 1902.

U.S. War Department. *Regulations for the Uniform and Dress of the Army of the United States, 1861*. Washington: George W. Bowman, 1861.

U.S. War Department. *The War of the Rebellion: Official Records of the Union and Confederate Armies*. 128 Volumes. Washington: Government Printing Office, 1880–1901.

Van Horne, Thomas B. *History of the Army of the Cumberland, Its Organization, Campaigns, and Battles*. 2 vols. Cincinnati: The Robert Clarke Company, 1875.

Warner, Ezra J. *Generals in Blue: Lives of the Union Commanders*. Baton Rouge: Louisiana State University Press, 1964.

White, John C. "A Review of the Services of the Regular Army During the Civil War." *Journal of the Military Service Institution of the United States* 45 (1909): 207–230, 46 (1910): 277–301, 48 (1911): 76–85, 237–246, 400–410, 49 (1911): 90–103, 401–412, 50 (1912): 64–69, 248–256.

Wiley, Bell I. *The Life of Billy Yank: The Common Soldier of the Union*. Indianapolis: Bobbs-Merrill, 1952.

Williams, Frederick D., ed. *The Wild Life of the Army: Civil War Letters of James A. Garfield*. East Lansing: Michigan State University Press, 1964.

Woodworth, Steven E. *Jefferson Davis and His Generals: The Failure of Confederate Command in the West*. Lawrence: University Press of Kansas, 1990.

Woodworth, Steven E. *Six Armies in Tennessee: The Chickamauga and Chattanooga Campaigns*. Lincoln: University of Nebraska Press, 1998.

Worthington, W.W. "Shiloh." In *The Union Reader*, edited by Richard B. Harwell. New York: Longmans, Green & Co., 1958.

Young, James Rankin, and Moore, J. Hampton. *Reminiscences and Thrilling Stories of the War by Returned Heroes, Containing Vivid Accounts of Personal Experiences by Officers and Men*. Washington: J.R. Jones, 1899.

CREDITS

TEXT IMAGES

Membership Badge of the Regular Brigade Association of Survivors courtesy of Doug Roush.

Recruiting Poster, 16th U.S. Infantry, Philadelphia, May 1862. Collection of the New-York Historical Society, Civil War Treasures.

Sheet Music, "Fifteenth Infantry Quick Step." Author's Collection. Photo courtesy of Rick Tuchscerer.

Battle of Shiloh. Author's collection. Photo courtesy of Rick Tuchscerer.

Harper's Weekly illustration. The Eighth Missouri Volunteers Charging Over the Eighteenth Regulars at the Battle of Pea Ridge, Tennessee. Courtesy of the Lincoln Museum, Fort Wayne, Indiana.

Recruiting Poster, 15th U.S. Infantry, Philadelphia, Summer 1863. Collection of the New-York Historical Society, Civil War Treasures.

PHOTO INSERT

Battle Monument at West Point. Author's Collection.

Oliver Lathrop Shepherd. Roger D. Hunt Collection, USAMHI.

George Henry Thomas. Gil Barrett Collection, USAMHI.

Richard W. Johnson. Dr. Russell D. Steele Collection, USAMHI.

Henry Beebee Carrington. Ohio Historical Society.

John Haskell King. Dennis M. Keesee Collection.

Frederick Phisterer. American Heritage Center, University of Wyoming.

Edgar Romeyn Kellogg. National Archives.

Frederick Townsend. Howard Hunt Collection, USAMHI.

Adam Jacoby Slemmer. Dennis M. Keesee Collection.

John Phillip Sanderson. Roger D. Hunt Collection, USAMHI.

Edward Augustin King. Allen Cebula Collection, USAMHI.

Arthur Brigham Carpenter. Manuscripts and Archives, Yale University Library.

Henry Blanchard Freeman. American Heritage Center, University of Wyoming.

Lovell Harrison Rousseau. Dodge, *History of the Old Second Division.*

William Rufus Terrill. Brian Pohanka Collection, USAMHI.

Francis Luther Guenther. Regular Brigade Association of Survivors, *Proceedings of Reunions.*

The 15th Infantry Band. Dennis M. Keesee Collection.

Charles Augustus Wickoff. USAMHI.

Alfred Lacey Hough. Chris Nelson Collection, USAMHI.

Robert Erskine Anderson (R.E.A.) Crofton. USAMHI.

Edward Lewis Mitchell. Division of Military and Naval Affairs, New York State Adjutant General's Office, Albany, NY, and USAMHI.

James Harrison Gageby. USAMHI.

Henry Douglass. Dennis M. Keesee Collection.

John Henry Knight. Dennis M. Keesee Collection.

Amos Fleagle. Frank H. Fleagle Collection.

George Washington Smith. Regular Brigade Association of Survivors, *Proceedings of Reunions.*

James Voty Bomford. Civil War Library and Museum, MOLLUS, Philadelphia, PA, and USAMHI.

Howard Burnham. *Memorial of Lieutenant Howard M. Burnham.*

Phillip Sydney Coolidge. Gil Barrett Collection, USAMHI.

Henry Haymond. Dennis M. Keesee Collection.

Robert Ayres. Civil War Library and Museum, MOLLUS, Philadelphia, PA, and USAMHI.

Albert Baldwin Dod. Bureau of Archives and History, New Jersey State Library and USAMHI.

Isaac D'Isay. Dennis M. Keesee Collection.

Roland W. Evans. Dennis M. Keesee Collection.

William Henry Bisbee. Civil War Library and Museum, MOLLUS, Philadelphia, PA, and USAMHI.

John H. King. Regular Brigade Association of Survivors, *Proceedings of Reunions.* Photo courtesy of Rick Tuchscherer.

Andrew S. Burt. Dennis M. Keesee Collection.

Frederick Townsend. Civil War Library and Museum, MOLLUS, Philadelphia, PA, and USAMHI.

Oliver L. Shepherd. Regular Brigade Association of Survivors, *Proceedings of Reunions.* Photo courtesy of Rick Tuchscherer.

Frederick Phisterer. Photo courtesy of Kasha Larew.

The Regular Brigade's Association of Survivors at Stones River National Cemetery, September 17, 1895. Regular Brigade Association of Survivors, *Proceedings of Reunions.* Photo courtesy of Rick Tuchscherer.

INDEX

Italics indicate illustrations, photographs, and maps.